Adobe®
Photoshop® CS
STUDIO TECHNIQUES

Ben Willmore

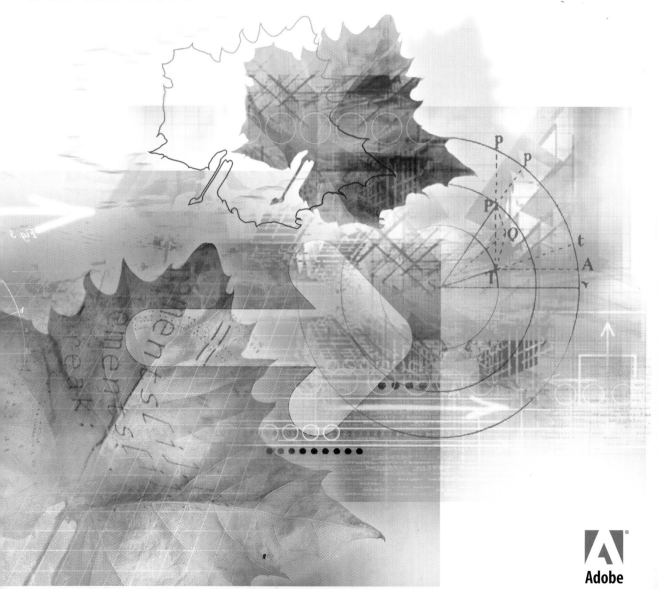

Adobe®

Adobe Photoshop CS Studio Techniques

Ben Willmore

Copyright © 2004 by Ben Willmore

This Adobe Press book is published by Peachpit Press. For information on Adobe Press books, contact:

Peachpit Press
1249 Eighth Street
Berkeley, CA 94710
(510) 524-2178
Fax: (510) 524-2221
http://www.peachpit.com

To report errors, please send a note to errata@peachpit.com
Peachpit Press is a division of Pearson Education

For the latest on Adobe Press books, go to http://www.adobe.com/adobepress

Executive Editor: Steve Weiss
Acquisitions Editor: Stacey Beheler
Development Editor: Susan Brown Zahn
Project Editor: Jake McFarland
Contributing Editors: Regina Cleveland, Mark Clarkson
Technical Editor: Tim Grey
Copy Editor: Toni Zuccarini Ackley
Compositor: Amy Hassos
Indexer: Cheryl Lenser
Cover Design: Aren Howell
Cover Illustration: Alicia Buelow

Notice of Rights

Notice of Liability

The information in this book is distributed on an "As Is" basis, without warranty. While every precaution has been taken in the preparation of the book, neither the authors nor Peachpit Press shall have any liability to any person or entity with respect to any loss or damage caused or alleged to be caused directly or indirectly by the instructions contained in this book or by the computer software and hardware products described in it.

Trademarks

Throughout this book trademarked names are used. Rather than put a trademark symbol in every occurrence of a trademarked name, we state we are using the names only in an editorial fashion and to the benefit of the trademark owner, with no intention of infringement of the trademark. Photoshop, Illustrator, GoLive, ImageReady, Acrobat, Streamline, and After Effects are all trademarks of Adobe Systems, Inc.

ISBN: 0-321-21352-1
LOC Number: 2003111675

9 8 7 6 5 4 3 2 1

Printed and bound in the United States of America

Contents

Part II Production Essentials

Part III Creative Explorations

About the Author

Ben Willmore is the founder of Digital Mastery, a Boulder, Colorado-based training and consulting firm that specializes in Photoshop. Ben has always been known to be a little nutty about all things technical, even as a child. Not long after he traded in his tricycle for training wheels, he started building cameras out of do-it-yourself kits. In 1981, at the tender age of 14, he made his official debut into computer nerd-dom when he attended CompuCamp. That's where he discovered his first two loves, computers and graphic design, and where he learned how to use a graphics tablet to produce art on an Apple][computer—three full years before the Macintosh said its first, "Hello."

Not surprisingly, he went on to become a graphic designer. In those days that meant knowing all about such primitive things as typesetting, keylining, and stat cameras. When the first tools of electronic publishing started showing up, Ben began his trend as an aggressive early adopter of new technologies. While most people in the business were holding back in a wait-and-see attitude, Ben was charging ahead and embracing the new tools like long-lost friends. His first serious push into the new arena was when he helped convert his college's daily newspaper from traditional techniques to electronic tools in the late 1980s.

Ben became known as someone who likes to push his tools to the limit, causing many printing companies and service bureaus to ask "How'd you do that?" His obsession with the nuts and bolts of electronic publishing turned him into an unwitting one-man customer support center for all his friends and coworkers. It was this, he discovered, that was his third love—helping others truly understand graphics software. And so he decided to go out on his own and teach his favorite program (Photoshop) full time.

In 1994 he created what has become the hugely successful seminar, Photoshop Mastery. Since then he has taught over 30,000 Photoshop users, and travels around the world presenting his seminars and speaking at publishing events such as Photoshop World. He writes a monthly column for *Photoshop User Magazine*. Ben can be reached at book@digitalmastery.com.

Mark Clarkson—self-described writer, artist, and dilettante—was a great help in reviewing and adding selected Photoshop CS updates and screenshots to five chapters of this edition of *Adobe Photoshop CS Studio Techniques*. Mark lives in Kansas. He is the author of *Photoshop Secrets of the Pros, The Photoshop Tennis Book, BattleBots: The Official Guide, Flash 5 Cartooning, The Guide to Cartooning with Macromedia Flash,* and *Windows Hothouse.* As Mark puts it, "I'm a book author, magazine writer, 3D animator, and Flash cartoonist. Yes, it's sad, but at 42 I still haven't decided what I want to do when I grow up." There's more about Mark at http://www.markclarkson.com.

Much Obliged!

Even though my name appears on the cover of this book, as with all collaborative efforts, this would not have been possible without the help of the following people:

Regina "GNR's" Cleveland, the Queen here at Digital Mastery, who (as usual) dedicated so many late night hours to this book that she has earned the title "Sleepless in Colorado." To her credit she only had one episode of crankiness during the sleepless weeks. She's recovered, but I'm always in the doghouse with her 10-year-old daughter, who thinks that Photoshop is part of the Evil Empire because it makes Mommy miss bedtime stories.

Steve Weiss (executive editor), for his persistence and diplomacy, and especially for always answering his cell phone, even when he's on vacation!

Stacey Beheler, for her efficiency, her quick responses, and for always being the first one to ask, "How can I help?"

Susan Brown Zahn and Tim Grey, two gifted hair-splitters, who toiled through the painstaking details and helped tighten things up.

Mark Clarkson, for coming through in a pinch, and for understanding the meaning of the word "deadline."

Chris Murphy for helping out with the color management chapter.

Kristine Evans, who has the uncanny ability to find just the right image at the right time, and who made it possible for me to get through this project without going completely insane.

Jay Nelson, who has helped me in more ways than I can imagine or remember. He's an amazing guy who always comes through in a pinch, and seems to be most happy whenever he's lending someone a hand.

Jerry Kennelly at Stockbyte and Stephanie Robey at PhotoSpin, whose generous contributions of stock imagery made it possible for us to include a bunch of great practice images on the CD at the back of the book.

Andy Katz, for keeping things lively with his maniacal laugh, and for his stunning imagery.

My brother Nik, who was always at the ready with as much constructive criticism as I could handle, when others would simply say "Oh, that's nice."

Scott Kelby, Jim Workman, Dave Moser, and the rest of the crazies at NAPP (National Association of Photoshop Professionals), who have made my life as a Photoshop hack more enjoyable than I thought possible.

To all the gifted artists and organizations who contributed images to this book. Your illuminating work transformed our bare pages into things of elegance, sparkle, and humor.

Howard Berman

Robert Bowen

Steve Bronstein

Alicia Buelow

Tom Nick Cocotos

Conner Huff

Gary Isaacs

Andy Katz

Lewis Kemper

Chris Klimek

Nick Koudis

Gregg Lauer

Bert Monroy

Michael Slack

Richard Tuschman

And finally, I thank all the people who have attended my seminars over the past 10 years. You've given me a limitless supply of inspiration and feedback and have allowed me to follow my passion for knowledge and understanding.

Foreword

Learning to use Adobe Photoshop is similar to learning to play an electric guitar—with a little instruction and a little practice, you can create some very pleasant art. Or, if you're really motivated, you can lock yourself in a closet with it for 12 years and emerge playing some amazing "licks." Most of us fall somewhere in between, and all of us have more to learn.

But the thing is, although few people are frightened by a guitar, many people find Photoshop intimidating. That's what is so great about Ben Willmore, the author of this book: He takes away your fear.

For the past several years, Ben has traveled across the United States, presenting his unique Photoshop seminar. Unique, because it focuses on real-world jobs done every day by Photoshop users, and unique because Ben explains concepts and techniques in a way that everyone in the room can understand. Ben's examples are based on his professional production experience, so everything he teaches helps you create images that successfully reproduce on paper or the web.

I attended his seminar and was especially impressed by his ability to avoid technical jargon and his uncanny knack for answering questions before they're asked. Ben is a rare teacher; even advanced users are satisfied, and rank beginners never feel lost. Like all great teachers, Ben uses metaphors, relating new ideas to concepts you're already comfortable with. In the pages of this book, you'll see Photoshop's most esoteric concepts clearly explained, while its major features are masterfully positioned into a framework of "How do I accomplish the task at hand?"

We each have different uses for Photoshop, and we each have different ways of learning. Fortunately for our increasingly overtaxed brains, less than half of Photoshop's features are used to accomplish most real-world tasks. And more fortunately for us, Ben Willmore has written this book.

Enjoy the time you share with Ben and Photoshop. I'm sure you'll find it a rare pleasure.

—Jay J. Nelson
Editor, *Design Tools Monthly*, www.design-tools.com

I

Introduction

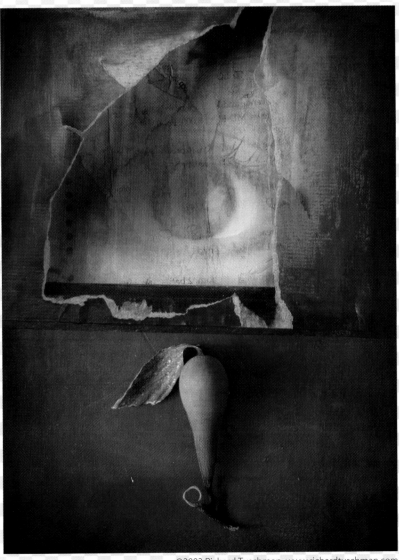

Introduction

Ben Willmore, Founder: Digital Mastery

My mission is to help you graduate from "I'm just going through the motions," to "At last, I really understand Photoshop."

Why This Book?

Well, I asked the same question when I set out on this project. I found myself at Barnes & Noble staring at a daunting abundance of Photoshop books, and I discovered that there were more special-effect "cookbooks" and technical tomes than I'd ever care to read. The problem was that none of the "cookbooks" gave enough detail to really let me feel like I understood the program (I just blindly followed the listed steps), and all of the technical books seemed to want to turn me into a slide rule–toting nerd (talking about terms like rasters, vectors, and bit-depth settings). That's when I decided that there was a void just begging to be filled. And that void is the primary reason that most people aren't truly comfortable with Photoshop. They either get the 1, 2, 3 steps (but no real understanding), or they get so many technical terms that it makes Photoshop impossible to grasp.

So how is this book different? My approach is to use the same language that you use in everyday life to explain everything from the simplest feature to the most advanced techniques. I acquired this approach as a result of teaching tens of thousands of people in hundreds of seminars and hands-on workshops. I'll still provide a fair share of step-by-step techniques, and we will delve into some rather advanced features, but through it all I'll use metaphors and stories that will make everything easy to understand and digest. Because often the difference between a confident Photoshop master and a struggling amateur is how much they truly understand the way Photoshop works behind the scenes.

With that in mind, my mission is to help you graduate from "I'm just going through the motions" to "At last, I *really* understand Photoshop." Once you've made that leap, you will experience an incredible ripple effect. Your efficiency will skyrocket. Your costs will go down. Your creative genius will come out of the closet like gangbusters, and your clients (or boss) will be thrilled. But what's most important to me is that through learning how to master Photoshop, you'll find the passion and energy that come from knowing you're really good at something.

Will I Understand It?

First and foremost, I hate technical mumbo jumbo! If words like raster, gamma, absolute colorimetric, bit-mapped, clipping paths, algorithms, dither, and anti-aliasing drive you crazy, you better believe that they drive me even crazier. I see no reason that those terms can't be done away with and replaced by plain English. I'll do what-ever it takes to communicate a concept to you, without rely-ing on 10-syllable words or terms that sound like they came from the inside of an engineer's head. And for those of you who have to deal with those technicians, you'll learn how to translate their techno-babble into English in my "Techno-Babble Decoder Ring" at the end of most chapters.

Does It Start at My Level?

In terms of skill level, this book is written in such a way that if you are generally comfortable with your computer, you should be able to fully comprehend the information, no matter how advanced the topic. I've made the assump-tion that you've either installed Photoshop or that you're using the *Photoshop User Guide* to figure out how to do that. (There's no reason to duplicate that kind of information here.) And if you're an advanced user, don't worry. Just be-cause this book is very understandable doesn't mean that we won't get into the real meat of Photoshop.

Mac or Windows?

From a functionality standpoint, Photoshop is pretty close to identical on Mac and Windows platforms. Anything you can do on one platform, you can do on the other. But those darn keyboards are different. You can put your worries aside, because *both* Mac and Windows keyboard commands are integrated right into the text. Because I'd get dizzy if I had to switch between the two for every screen shot, I just picked one platform and ran with it. And I just happened to choose Mac OS X.

What's on the CD?

To make it as easy as possible for you to follow along with my examples, I've provided a boatload of practice images for you to play with. You'll find these on the shiny disc that is hiding inside the back cover, in a folder called Practice Images. Stockbyte and PhotoSpin were kind enough to provide many of the images in this book and on the CD. If you like what you see, you can get more of their delicious imagery at their respective web sites, www.stockbye.com and www.photospin.com.

What About the Web Site?

It's really hard for me to call this book done and send it off to press because once I've finished writing, I feel like I'm struck mute until the next version of Photoshop ships. Well, I've found a way to keep the dialogue going. Every day that I play with Photoshop, I come up with new ideas, and rather than hold those ideas back, I thought it would be great to share them with you through a companion web site at www.digitalmastery.com. There's no password needed, and you'll find all this for free! Go ahead and visit the companion web site, where you will find hundreds of free tips, my magazine article archives, and a bunch of other resources.

If you'd like to get a regular dose of my tips and tricks, sign up for my free Extra-Strength Photoshop Tips by pointing your browser to www.digitalmastery.com/tips. I try to send out about two to three tips a month.

Then I'm sure you'll have a few questions while you read the book, so don't be afraid to send them my way at questions@digitalmastery.com. I read every one of them, but there aren't enough hours in the day to answer each person individually. So each week, I pick about a dozen readers' questions and answer them as part of my free Photoshop Questions Clinic. You can sign up for this service at www.digitalmastery.com/questions.

I also bet you'll end up with a few problem images where a simple question can't accurately describe the problem. Well, that's when you might want to consider sending it to me at problems@digitalmastery.com. (Please keep images under 200KB and include a description of the problem.) This is the emergency room for disaster images where I put on my surgical mask and tackle the image problems I feel will benefit my readers. The solutions come through future magazine articles and tutorials on my web site.

Finally, if you'd like to get beyond the pages of this book and the free resources of the companion site, be sure to check out my seminars, videos, and other products at www.digitalmastery.com.

Wassup with the "CS?"

If you are wondering why this version wasn't called Photoshop 8, you're not alone. Here's what happened. Adobe took a good long look at how people were using their publishing software and came to the conclusion that most folks were using more than one product to get the job done. For instance, if they were using Photoshop to prepare their images, they might also be using those images in a page layout program (like Adobe InDesign) or a web-authoring program (like Adobe GoLive). And so they came up with the concept of an "integrated design environment," which simply means that they've made it easier than ever to create something in one of the programs, and use it another one. They named this concept "CS," which stands for Creative Suite, and replaced the version numbers with the "CS" designation. The suite includes Photoshop, Illustrator, InDesign, Acrobat, and GoLive. There is a long list of specific benefits of this new integrated approach, which you can read about at www.adobe.com. The bottom line is that this version is not called Photoshop 8; instead, it is called Photoshop CS, so that is how it will be referred to in this book. If you feel sad about giving up Photoshop's number designation, you can still think of it as "8." I won't tell.

What Happened to the Web Section?

If you read previous versions of this book, you might notice that the section that used to cover web-specific features has disappeared. Adobe made some huge changes to Image-Ready (Photoshop's web companion program). The web section was going to dominate the book and, even then, I wasn't going to have the space to do it justice. So, I decided that instead of breezing over all the web features, I'd remove that section from the book because there are many books that cover the web features in-depth. This book is still very web friendly. It's just that there isn't a section that covers information that would only be useful to people who design web sites. Instead, I concentrate on techniques that will help everyone, regardless of whether their images will appear on the web, printed in a book, or output on their desktop printer. So, don't write the book off as not being for web people; instead, buy a web-specific book to supplement this one if you need to know about all the features that are designed specifically for the web.

Where Can I Find the New Stuff?

If you've owned a previous edition of this book or just want to jump right into the new features of Photoshop CS, this is the place to start. Instead of wading through the whole book, looking for what's new, I've compiled a mini guide to what's new and improved both in this revision to my book and in Photoshop CS in general.

Chapter 1 Tool and Palette Primer

Check out the enhanced File Browser (page 49) and Custom Keyboard Shortcuts (page 54).

Chapter 2 Selection Primer

The basic selection tools haven't changed in this version of Photoshop, but the Crop and Straighten Photos command is a welcome newcomer (page 72) and worth reading about, especially if you scan many photos at once.

Chapter 3 Layers Primer

The new Layer Comps (page 131) and Photo Filter Layers (page 123) are features worth reading about.

Chapter 4 Resolution Solutions

The concept behind resolution hasn't really changed with Photoshop CS, but for the film and video crowd, Adobe's latest brew offers support for nonsquare pixels (page 156), video document presets (page 158), and Automatic Action-Safe and Title-Safe Guides (page 158). For the rest of us, there are two new resampling methods: Bicubic Smoother and Bicubic Sharper (page 161), which give us improved options for reducing or enlarging our images.

Chapter 7 Understanding Curves

Curves itself hasn't changed in Photoshop CS, but the addition of the new Histogram palette (page 229) has the potential to completely change the way you think about adjusting images with Curves. The new Shadow/Highlight feature (page 236) is also covered in this chapter.

Chapter 10 Using Camera Raw

A brand new chapter! For the digital camera crowd, the Camera Raw feature is a substantial and welcome addition to Photoshop. If your camera can shoot in the RAW file format, do not pass GO; drop everything and read this chapter immediately (page 304)!

Chapter 11 Color Manipulation

In this chapter, we'll cover Photoshop CS's new Color Replacement tool (page 359), the Match Color command (page 356), and the Shadow/Highlight command (page 349). This is an entirely new chapter, so you'll find lots of new goodies within its pages.

Chapter 13 Advanced Masking

This brand new chapter offers new tricks and an in-depth approach to one of the all-time most common uses for Photoshop: isolating a complex object from its background.

Chapter 14 Sharpening

The sharpening controls have not changed in Photoshop CS; however, this chapter is brand new to this version of this book, so make sure to read it even if you've read a previous edition of this book. It's all about those very subtle details that can make the difference between a so-so image and one that pops off the page.

Chapter 16 Collage

This chapter includes coverage of Photoshop CS's new Photomerge feature (page 526). I also talk about clipping masks (page 493), and how to apply blending sliders to adjustment layers (page 508), among other things.

Chapter 17 Enhancement

Check out the new Hard Mix blending mode (page 568).

Chapter 18 Retouching

Photoshop CS hasn't introduced any new retouching tools, but I've made considerable changes to this chapter since the previous edition of this book. I think you'll find it a worthwhile read.

Chapter 19 Type and Background Effects

If you are one of those Adobe Illustrator-phobics who longs for that elegantly curved and swooping text but finds Illustrator way too scary, then you are in for a whopping treat. Photoshop CS has added the ability to place type on a path (page 656). Photoshop CS also features expanded support for the little bells and whistles of OpenType fonts (page 642).

Are You Ready to Get Started?

So, enough blabbing, let's get on with your personal Photoshop "transformation." I'll make it as easy on you as I possibly can, but just remember the words of my favorite character, Miracle Max, from the movie *The Princess Bride*: "You rush a miracle, man, you get rotten miracles."

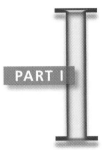

PART I

Working Foundations

1

Tool and Palette Primer

Courtesy of Michael Slack, www.slackart.com

Out of clutter, find simplicity.

—Albert Einstein

Tool and Palette Primer

Opening Photoshop for the first time and seeing all the tools and palettes competing for space on your screen can be a dizzying experience. You might find yourself thinking, "That's great, but they forgot to leave room in there for me to work!" Some of the more fortunate Photoshoppers get to have a second monitor, just to hold all their palettes. The rest of us make do and find ways to keep our screens neat and tidy. You'll discover that finding places to put your tools and palettes is almost as important as knowing how to use them. This chapter is all about effectively managing your workspace and getting acquainted with the oodles of gadgets and gizmos found in the tools and palettes.

Preparing Your Workspace

Before we get into functionality, we'll talk about how to control the prodigious profusion of palettes. But first, a word of advice: No matter how many times you feel like nuking a palette when it's in your way, no matter how many times your screen turns into a blinding jumble of annoying little boxes, just remember that you can organize the clutter into an elegant arrangement in just a few seconds.

Controlling Those Palettes

The first order of business is to get you enough space to work effectively with your images. We'll accomplish this by organizing the palettes so that they don't obstruct your view of your document. I don't think you'll like the default position of the palettes—that is, unless you use a 36-inch screen. The palettes take up too much valuable screen real estate (**Figure 1.1**).

Collapsing the Palettes

One way to maximize your workspace is to collapse the palettes when you're not using them and move them to the bottom of your screen. To collapse a palette, double-click any of the name tabs at the top of the palette. To reposition a palette, click the little bar at the top of the palette and then drag it toward the bottom of your screen. When you move a palette close to the bottom of the screen, it should snap into place (**Figure 1.2**).

NOTES

To force a palette to snap to the edge of your screen, press the Shift key as you reposition the palette.

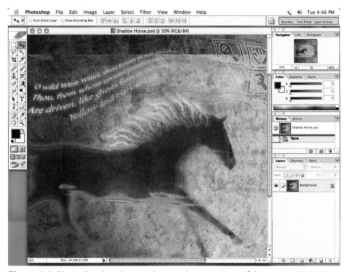

Figure 1.1 Photoshop's palettes take up a large portion of the screen. (©2003 Regina Cleveland)

Figure 1.2 Stowing palettes at the bottom of the screen.

NOTES

If you click on the Zoom tool and then turn on the Ignore Palettes button in the options bar, Photoshop will ignore your palettes, whether or not they're close to the right edge of your screen.

When you're repositioning your palettes, you need to make sure that you don't place any palettes too close to the right edge of your screen. This edge, affectionately known as palette alley, can cause you great pains when you zoom in on your images (**Figure 1.3**). Here's why: If you have a palette too close to the right edge of your screen and you press Command-+ (Mac) or Alt-Ctrl-+ (Windows), Photoshop can't resize the document window to the width of your screen. Instead, it leaves palette alley open and doesn't allow the document window to intrude into this space. This means your efforts to reposition the palettes in order to save space were futile.

If you need access to any of these palettes, double-click the palette's name tab, and the palette will instantly pop open (**Figure 1.4**). When you're done using the palette, just double-click its name tab to collapse it again.

If you turn off the Save Palette Locations check box in the File > Preferences > General dialog box, each time you launch Photoshop, the palettes will be at their default locations.

Regrouping the Palettes

Another way to maximize your screen real estate is to change the way your palettes are grouped. For example, if your most frequently used palettes are the Color and

Figure 1.3 Palette alley stays clear whenever a palette is close to the right edge of your screen.

History palettes, you can put them in one group so that you have one palette open at any given time instead of two. To regroup the palettes, drag the name tab of the palette you want to move (in this case, Color) on top of the palette grouping you want to move the palette into (in this case, History). You can then remove any palettes you don't want in this grouping by dragging the name tab of that palette onto an open area of the screen (**Figure 1.5**).

NOTES

If you really mess things up and your screen gets to looking like an M.C. Escher print, you can easily set all the palettes back to their default locations. To do this, choose Window > Workspace > Reset Palette Locations.

Figure 1.4 To collapse or expand a palette, double-click the name tab.

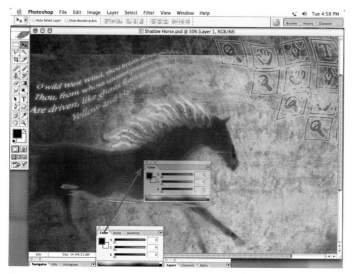

Figure 1.5 To separate a palette from a grouping, drag the name tab to an open area of your screen.

NOTES

You can also move a palette into the palette well by choosing Dock to Palette Well from the side menu of the palette.

The Palette Well

If you look in the options bar at the top of your screen, you should notice a dark gray area on the far right, which is known as the palette well. That's a special spot where you can drag the name of a few palettes to store them until they're needed. Then, when you'd like to have access to one of those palettes, just click on the name of the palette, and it will drop down from the palette well (**Figure 1.6**). After you're done using a palette, just click anywhere outside of the palette and it should collapse itself back into the palette well.

Figure 1.6 To temporarily expand a palette, click on the name of a palette in the palette well.

Stacking Palettes

You can stack palettes one on top of another, and if you move the top palette (by dragging the bar at the top of the palette), the palettes that are stacked will move together. To stack two palettes, drag the name tab of one palette to the middle of another palette and then drag down until you see a black rectangle appear across the bottom of the palette you are dragging onto. You can drag to the top or bottom edge of a palette, depending on how you'd like the palettes to be stacked. I like to stack the Character and

Paragraph palettes together so I can keep all the type settings in one convenient area (**Figure 1.7**). After you have two palettes stacked together, you can drag other palettes into the grouping so that the top palette might be a group of three and the bottom a single palette.

If, after moving and regrouping your palettes, you find that a palette appears to be missing, don't panic. You can always find it in the Window menu. This menu lists all the palettes that are available (**Figure 1.8**).

Workspace Presets

You might find that different palette layouts work better for different tasks. For instance, when retouching an image, you might find that you like to have the Brushes palette extend all the way down the right side of your screen and have most of the other palettes hidden away. Later, when you start to paint, you might prefer to have the Color, Swatches, and Brushes palettes along the right side of your screen. Well, that's when you'll want to save a workspace preset that will remember exactly where all your palettes were at the time you saved the preset. To save a preset, choose Window > Workspace > Save Workspace,

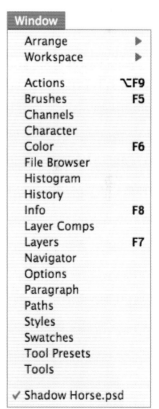

Figure 1.8 The window menu.

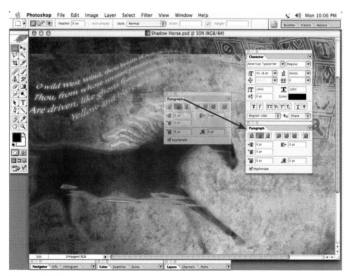

Figure 1.7 You can stack two palettes by dragging the name of one palette to the top or bottom of another.

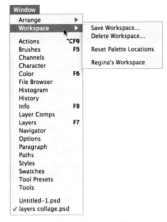

Figure 1.9 The Window > Workspace menu.

and give it a memorable name. Then to switch between different saved workspaces, just choose the name of the workspace you desire from the bottom of the Window > Workspace menu (**Figure 1.9**). This feature is great for people who have to share a computer with others because each user can have a different arrangement of palettes saved as a workspace, so different users can quickly swap between those workspaces.

Working with Screen Modes

Even with the palettes conveniently stowed at the bottom of your screen, your image still doesn't use all of the screen space available. You can use the three Screen Mode icons at the bottom of the Tools palette to easily solve this problem.

Standard Screen Mode

The first icon, Standard Screen Mode, is the default mode (**Figure 1.10**). You're probably used to working with this one. In this mode, the name of your document is at the top of the document window, and the scrollbars are on the side and bottom of that window.

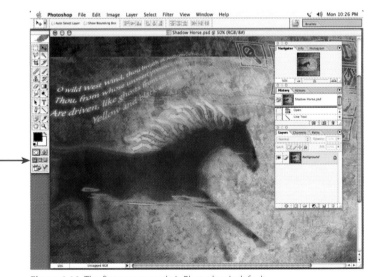

Figure 1.10 The first screen mode is Photoshop's default.

Full Screen Mode with Menu Bar

The second icon, Full Screen Mode with Menu Bar, lets the image flow all the way across your screen and slip right under the palettes (**Figure 1.11**). If you click this icon, the scrollbars will disappear, so you'll have to use the Hand tool to navigate around your document. But that's OK, because you can hold down the spacebar at any time to temporarily use the Hand tool. If you zoom out of a document so that it doesn't take up the entire screen, Photoshop will fill the area around the image with gray.

When using Full Screen mode, you can press Shift-F to toggle the menu bar on and off.

To temporarily use the Zoom tool—that is, to use the Zoom tool without deselecting the active tool—hold down Command-spacebar (Mac) or Ctrl-spacebar (Windows). Add the Option key (Mac) or Alt key (Windows) to this keyboard shortcut if you'd like to zoom out on your image.

If a gray surround isn't your taste, just change the foreground color and then grab the Paint Bucket tool and Shift-click in the gray area to change it. Not too many people know this trick, so you can use it to mess with your coworker's minds. Just set the color to an irritating shade, such as flourescent green.

Figure 1.11 The second screen mode allows you to use the entire screen.

In previous versions of Photoshop, your image was always centered on your screen when working in any of the full screen modes. In Photoshop CS, you can drag with the Hand tool to move your image within the gray or black surround that you get when viewing your image in the full screen modes.

Full Screen Mode

The third screen mode icon, Full Screen Mode, is my favorite. In this mode, Photoshop turns off even the menu bar! Now your image can take over the entire screen (**Figure 1.12**). You can still use many of the menu commands, as long as you know their keyboard equivalents. If you zoom

If pressing the Tab key doesn't toggle the visibility of your palettes, then press Return or Enter on your keyboard and try again. If you happen to be working on a number in the options bar, then instead of toggling the visibility of your palettes, the Tab key cycles through the different entry fields in the options bar. Pressing Return or Enter causes Photoshop to no longer focus on the numbers that appear in the options bar.

out while in this mode, Photoshop will fill the area around your image with black. (I don't know how to change that one.) I use this mode whenever I show images to clients. If you don't let them know you're in Photoshop, they might think you are in a cheap little slide-show program, and won't ask you to make changes on the spot. However, you won't be able to fool anyone if all those palettes are still on your screen. Just press Tab and they'll all disappear (**Figure 1.13**). Don't worry: You can get them back just as quickly by pressing Tab again.

Figure 1.12 The third screen mode uses the full screen and removes the menu bar.

Figure 1.13 Press Tab to hide or show the palettes.

Screen Mode Shortcuts

I use the different screen modes every single day, but it's not very often that I actually click those three little toolbox icons. Instead, I use keyboard commands. Just press the F key on your keyboard to cycle through the different screen modes. You can even press F twice and then press the Tab key while an image is opening; that way, when it's done loading, Photoshop will switch to the third screen mode and rid your screen of all the palettes!

Now that you have your screen under control, we can start to explore some of the tools and palettes.

A Quick Tour of the Tools

More than 40 tools are available in the Tools palette. Describing all of them in detail would take up a huge chunk of this chapter (which you probably don't have the patience for), so for now we'll take a look at the ones that you absolutely can't live without. Don't worry about missing out on anything—as you work your way through the book, you'll get acquainted with the rest of the tools. In the meantime, I'll introduce you to some tool names so that when I mention one, you'll know what to look for (**Figures 1.14** and **1.15**).

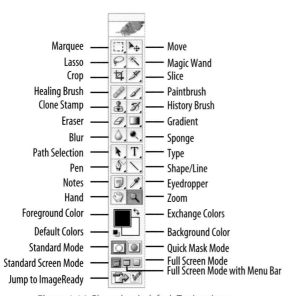

Figure 1.14 Photoshop's default Tools palette.

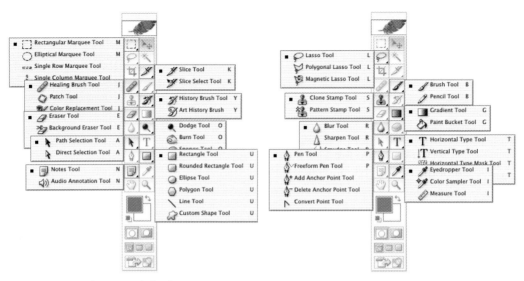

Figure 1.15 Photoshop's arsenal of tools.

The Options Bar

Most of the tools have settings associated with them. To access these settings, take a peek at the options bar that extends across the top of your screen.

You'll be able to change the various settings more quickly if you know exactly how to navigate the options bar. For example, each of the painting and retouching tools has a percentage setting near the right side of the bar. There are quite a few ways to change this number. One is to highlight the number and then type a new one. You can also click the number and then use the up arrow and down arrow keys on your keyboard. (Hold down the Shift key to change the number by increments of 10.) You can also click the arrow to the right of the number and drag across the slider that appears. And now in Photoshop CS, you can click on the name of the setting you'd like to change (like Opacity) and then drag your mouse to the right or left to change the setting. All of these options will work with any numeric entry in a palette (not just the options bar), but there is a special method for changing the percentage setting for your painting tools. If none of the text fields in the options bar is active for editing, you can just type a number (not in a field, just type). If you type 1, you'll end up with 10%, 23 will give you 23%, 0 will give you 100%, and so forth.

If there's more than one setting that lets you enter a number, press Return or Enter to highlight the first one, then Tab your way through the others. Once a number is highlighted, you can change it by pressing the up arrow and down arrow keys or by typing a new number.

If you've completely screwed up the settings that appear in the options bar, don't despair. You can Control-click (Mac) or right-click (Windows) on the Tool icon that appears on the far left of the options bar and choose Reset Tool to reset everything back to its default settings.

Navigating Your Document

Most of us struggle with monitors that are not large enough to view an entire document (except, of course, the more privileged Photoshoppers who have monitors that are practically as large as drive-in movie screens). To deal with this ever-present limitation, you must train yourself to be a quick and nimble navigator. Photoshop offers you a huge array of choices, and, as usual, you'll need to weed through them to find your favorite method. In this section, we'll cover the palettes and tools you need to maximize the speed with which you get around your document.

The Navigator Palette

If you do a lot of detail work where you need to zoom in on your image as if you're wearing glasses as thick as Coke bottles, you should love the Navigator palette (**Figure 1.16**). The Navigator palette floats above your document and allows you to quickly move around and zoom in and out of your image. A little red box indicates which area of the image you're currently viewing. By dragging this box around the miniature image of your document that appears in the Navigator palette, you can change which area you're viewing in the main image window. You can also just click outside the red box and the box will center itself on your cursor.

There are a number of ways to zoom in on your document by using this palette. Use the Mountain icons to zoom in or out at preset increments (50%, 66.67%, 100%, 200%, and so on), or grab the slider between them to zoom to any level. You can change the number in the lower-left corner

Figure 1.16 The Navigator palette.

If you don't like the color of the little red box, or if there's so much red in your image that the box becomes difficult to see, you can change the box color by choosing Palette Options from the side menu of the palette.

of the palette to zoom to an exact percentage. However, my favorite method is to drag across the image while holding down the Command key (Macintosh) or the Ctrl key (Windows), to zoom into a specific area.

Hand Tool

The Hand tool is definitely the most basic tool in Photoshop. By clicking and dragging with the Hand tool, you can scroll around the image. This tool is—excuse the pun—handy for scrolling around images that are too large to fit on your screen and for moving without the scrollbars. Because this tool is used so often, Adobe created a special way to get to it. While working with most of Photoshop's tools, if you press the spacebar, you will temporarily activate the Hand tool. When you release the spacebar, you'll be back to the tool you were using previously.

Zoom Tool

Whenever you click on your image by using the Zoom tool, you zoom in on the image to a preset level (just like the Mountain icons in the Navigator palette). I almost never use the tool in this way because it takes too long to get where I want to be. Instead, I usually click and drag across the area I want to enlarge, and Photoshop immediately zooms me into that specific area.

In addition to zooming in, you also have options for quickly zooming out. Double-click the Hand tool icon in the Tools palette to fit the entire image on-screen. You can also double-click the Zoom tool icon in the Tools palette to view your image at 100% magnification. (This will show you how large your image will appear when viewed in a web browser or in any program designed for multimedia. It is not an indication of how large it will be when printed.) Option-clicking (Macintosh) or Alt-clicking (Windows) with the Zoom tool zooms you out at preset levels. Clicking on Photoshop CS's Zoom Out icon in the options bar (**Figure 1.17**) will allow you to zoom out without having to hold a key on your keyboard. When the Zoom Out icon is chosen, holding down Option (Mac) or Alt (Windows) will cause you to zoom in on the image.

Figure 1.17 Photoshop's Zoom In and Zoom Out icons.

View Menu

If you're going to be doing a bunch of detail work in which you need to zoom in really close on your image, you might want to create two views of the same document (**Figures 1.18** and **1.19**). That way, you can have one of the views at 100% magnification to give you an overall view of your image, and you can set the second one to 500% magnification, for instance, to see all the fine details. To create a second view, choose Window > Arrange > New Window. This will create a second window that looks like a separate document, but it's really just another view of the same document. You can make your edits in either window, and both of them will show you the result of your manipulations.

Figure 1.18 100% magnification. (© 2003 PhotoSpin, www.photospin.com)

Figure 1.19 500% magnification.

From the View menu, you can also select from the Zoom In, Zoom Out, Fit On Screen, and Actual Pixels options. As you'll probably notice, each of these actions can also be accomplished by using the Zoom and Hand tools. The reason they're also listed under the View menu is to allow you to quickly use them with keyboard commands. Here are the View menu options:

▶ **Zoom In/Zoom Out:** Same as clicking with the Zoom tool. Uses the easy-to-remember keyboard shortcut Command-+ (Mac) or Ctrl-+ (Windows) to zoom in and Command-– (Mac) or Ctrl-– (Windows) to zoom out. Those are plus signs and minus signs, in case that's not completely clear.

NOTES

When zooming in or out on your image via keyboard shortcuts, you can hold Option (Mac) or Alt (Windows) to control whether the window that contains your image will change size with your image. On a Mac, holding Option will cause the window that contains your image to remain the same size as you zoom in or out of your image. In Windows, holding Alt will do the opposite, causing the window to change size as you zoom. If you want to reverse the default behavior of these keyboard commands, then choose Photoshop > Preferences > General, and change the Zoom Resizes Windows setting.

NOTES

The Print Size option rarely reflects how large your image will print. It assumes that your screen is using pixels that are .014 inches square (or 72 ppi). When the Mac was released back in 1984, it had a built-in screen that used pixels of that size. Now, there are so many kinds of monitors that there is no standard. If you really want to see how large an image will print, choose View > Show Rulers. You can set the ruler measurement system (inches, points, picas) by choosing Edit > Preferences > Units & Rulers (or double-click on the ruler). The keyboard command to show the rulers is Command-R (Mac) or Ctrl-R (Windows); to hide the rulers, press the same shortcut again. Then choose View > Print Size and hold a real ruler up to your screen to see how far off it is from reality.

▶ **Fit On Screen:** Same as double-clicking the Hand tool. Uses the shortcut Command-0 (Mac) or Ctrl-0 (Windows). That's a zero, not the letter O.

▶ **Actual Pixels:** Same as double-clicking the Zoom tool. Uses the shortcut Option-Command-0 (Mac) or Alt-Ctrl-0 (Windows). Again, that's a zero, not the letter O.

▶ **Print Size:** Allows you to preview how large or small your image will appear when it's printed.

Just when you thought there couldn't possibly be any more ways to zoom in and out of your document, Adobe threw in just one more method for good measure. You can change the percentage that appears in the lower-left corner of your document window (Mac), or at the bottom of the main Photoshop window when the status bar is visible (Windows); just drag across it and enter a new percentage.

There are indeed many ways to zoom around in Photoshop. Now all you have to do is test out all the options, decide which one you prefer, and ignore the rest.

Picking Colors

My father's Webster's dictionary—a 1940 model that's over half a foot thick—devoted four entire pages to describing one word: *color*. These pages are filled with lush descriptions of hue, tint, shade, saturation, vividness, brilliance, and much, much more. It's no wonder that choosing colors can be such a formidable task. Do you want Cobalt Blue or Persian Blue? Nile Green or Emerald? Carmine or Vermilion? Fortunately, Photoshop has done an excellent job of providing the tools you need to find the colors you want. Of course, each tool has advantages and disadvantages. You just have to play around with them and decide which one you prefer.

Foreground and Background Colors

The two square overlapping boxes that appear toward the bottom of your Tools palette are the foreground and background colors (**Figure 1.20**). The top box is the foreground color; it determines which color will be used when you use any of the painting tools. To change the foreground color, click it once. (This will bring up a standard

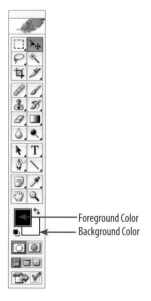

Foreground Color
Background Color

Figure 1.20 Foreground and background colors.

Color Picker.) The bottom box is the background color; it's used when you're erasing the background image or when you increase the size of your document by using Image > Canvas Size. When you use the Gradient tool with default settings, your gradient will start with the foreground color and end with the background color. You can swap the foreground and background colors by clicking the small curved arrows next to them in the Tools palette (or pressing the X key on your keyboard). You can also reset the colors to their default settings (black/white) by clicking the small squares in the lower-left corner of that same area. (Pressing D does the same thing.)

Color Picker Dialog Box

The Color Picker dialog box is available in many areas of Photoshop. The easiest way to get to it is to click your foreground or background color. There are many choices in this dialog box because there are many different ways to define a color. In this section, we'll cover all the various ways you can choose a color. I'll start off by showing you how to preview the color you're selecting.

Previewing a Color

While you're choosing a color, you can glance at the two color swatches to the right of the vertical gradient to compare the color you've chosen (the top swatch) to the color you had previously (the bottom swatch).

Be sure to watch for the out-of-gamut warning, which is indicated by a small triangle that appears next to these color swatches (**Figure 1.21**). This triangle warns you that the color you have chosen is not reproducible in CMYK mode, which means that it cannot be printed without shifting to a slightly different color. Fortunately, Photoshop provides you with a preview of what the color would have to shift to in order to be printable. You can find this preview in the small color swatch that appears directly below the triangle icon, and you can select this printable color by clicking the color swatch. Or, you can have Photoshop show you what all the colors would look like when printed by choosing View > Proof Colors while the Color Picker dialog box is open. That will change the look of every color that appears in the picker, but you will still have to click that little triangle symbol, because that's just a preview—it doesn't actually change the colors you're choosing.

NOTES

CMYK colors are meant to be printed (which involves ink), whereas RGB colors (which involve light) are meant for multimedia. Due to impurities in CMYK inks, you can't accurately reproduce every color you see on your screen.

The Proof Colors command is accurate only when you have the proper settings specified in the View > Proof Setup menu. The default setting indicates what your image will look like when converted to CMYK mode.

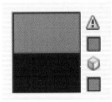

Figure 1.21 The warning triangle indicates a color that is not reproducible in CMYK mode. The cube symbol indicates that a color is not a web-safe color and might appear dithered in a web browser.

Choosing Web-Safe Colors

There is a set of special colors, known as web-safe colors, that are used for large areas of solid color on a web site. By using a web-safe color, you will prevent those areas from becoming dithered when viewed on a low-end computer (that is, simulated by using a pattern of two solid colors; for example, adding a pattern of red dots to a yellow area to create orange). So, if you are choosing a color that will be used in a large area on a web page, look for the Color Cube symbol (**Figure 1.21**). Web-safe colors are also known as colors that are within the color cube—that's why Adobe used a cube symbol for this feature. When you click the cube symbol, the color you have chosen will shift a little to become a web-safe color.

Selecting with the Color Field

Usually, the simplest method for choosing a color is to eyeball it. In the Color Picker dialog box, you can click in the vertical gradient to select the general color you want to use. Then click and drag around the large square area at the left to choose a shade of that color.

Selecting by Hue, Saturation, and Brightness

You can also change what appears in the vertical gradient by clicking any of the radio buttons on the right side of the dialog box (**Figures 1.22** to **1.24**). In this dialog box, H = Hue, S = Saturation, and B = Brightness. You can use the numbers at the right of the dialog box to describe the color you've chosen. (This can be a big help when you're describing a color to someone on the phone.) So, if you know the exact color you need, just type its exact numbers into that area.

> **WARNING**
>
> If your method for picking white is to drag to the upper-left corner of the color field, be sure to drag beyond the edge of the square; otherwise, you might not end up with a true white. Instead, you'll get a muddy-looking white or a light shade of gray.

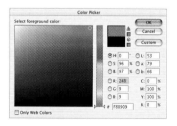

Figure 1.22 Hue.

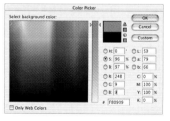

Figure 1.23 Saturation.

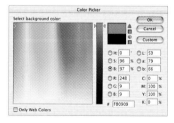

Figure 1.24 Brightness.

Selecting Custom Colors

If you want to pick your colors from a swatch book (PAN-TONE, TruMatch, and so on), click the Custom button. This will bring up the Custom Color Picker (**Figure 1.25**). Choose the swatch book you want to use from the pop-up menu at the top of the dialog box, then scroll through the list to find the color you desire. You can also type in numbers to select a specific color (I know, there isn't the usual text field to enter them in, but just start typing), but make sure you type really fast. I'm not sure why it works this way, but this part of Photoshop gets impatient with slow typists. For example, if you slowly type the number 356, Photoshop might jump to a color number starting with 3 and then go to one that starts with 5. This is sort of annoying, but it shouldn't pose a problem as long as you type the number quickly. (You can purchase swatch books at an art supply store.)

Color Palette

You can think of the Color palette as a simplified version of the Color Picker dialog box. Just as with the Color Picker, you can pick colors by typing in numbers. However, you first need to choose the type of numbers you want to use from the side menu (**Figure 1.26**).

There's one special option that's not available in the Color Picker dialog box and can only be used in the Color palette. Web Color Sliders will allow you to choose colors that are made from red, green, and blue light, but it will also force the sliders to snap to the tick marks that appear along the slider bars. Those tick marks indicate web-safe colors, and they make this choice especially useful for creating web graphics (**Figure 1.27**). You can turn on the Only Web Colors check box in the Color Picker dialog box if you'd like to make sure that you only select web-safe colors.

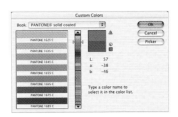

Figure 1.25 The Custom Color Picker.

Although the Custom Color Picker is great for users printing with CMYK inks, it's not so hot for those using true spot colors (metallic, fluorescent, and other colors that cannot be reproduced using CMYK inks). If you're going to be using true spot colors, see Chapter 12, "Channels."

Figure 1.26 Choosing the slider type from the palette's menu.

NOTES

The Copy Color As HTML choice in the side menu of the Color palette will allow you to paste the currently chosen color into an HTML editor. The HTML code that is used to create a web page uses a special method called *hexadecimal* to define colors, and that's what is copied when you choose this option.

You can change the gradient bar at the bottom of the Color palette by clicking it while holding down the Shift key. This will cycle between the settings available from the side menu. You can also Control-click (Mac) or right-click (Windows) on the gradient bar to access the same settings that are available from the side menu.

You can also pick colors by clicking the color bar at the bottom of the palette. (Use Option-click on the Macintosh or Alt-click in Windows to change your background color.) You can change the appearance of the color bar by choosing a color-range option near the bottom of the side menu of the palette (**Figure 1.28**). Here are the options:

▶ **RGB Spectrum:** Displays all the colors that are usable in RGB mode. Use this setting for multimedia and the web.

▶ **CMYK Spectrum:** Shows all the colors that are usable in CMYK mode. Use this setting for images that will be reproduced on a printing press.

▶ **Grayscale Ramp:** Shows shades of gray from black to white. Use this setting any time you need shades of gray that do not contain a hint of color (also known as neutral grays).

▶ **Current Colors:** Displays a gradient using your foreground and background colors.

▶ **Make Ramp Web Safe:** Shows only the colors that are web-safe from the previous choices.

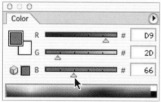

Figure 1.27 When you choose Web Color Sliders, the sliders will snap to the tick marks on the slider bars that indicate where web-safe colors are located.

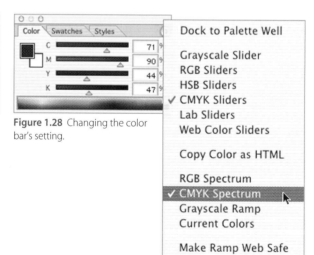

Figure 1.28 Changing the color bar's setting.

Eyedropper Tool

In addition to using the Color Picker and Color palette to select colors, you can use the Eyedropper tool. One advantage to the Eyedropper is that you can grab colors from any open Photoshop file. After selecting the Eyedropper, you can click any part of your image and bingo!—you've got a new foreground color. You can also Option-click (Mac) or Alt-click (Windows) to change your background color. You don't have to click within the document you're currently editing; you can click any open image.

You can also change the Sample Size setting in the options bar to choose how it looks at, or samples, the area you click (**Figures 1.29** to **1.32**). Here are your options:

With Photoshop's Eyedropper tool, you can click within a document and then drag to any area of your screen to choose a color. That means you can pick up a color from the menu bar, or any other area of your screen—not just from within Photoshop, but anything you can see on your monitor. I use this all the time to pick colors from my web browser.

▶ **Point Sample:** Picks up the exact color of the pixel you click.

▶ **3 by 3 Average:** Averages the area around your cursor using an area that's three pixels wide and three pixels tall.

▶ **5 by 5 Average:** Works the same was as 3 -by -3 Average, but with a larger area.

In many cases, you'll find it helpful to use one of the Average settings. They prevent you from accidentally picking up an odd-colored speck in the area from which you're grabbing, thereby ensuring that you don't select a color that isn't representative of the area you're choosing.

Figure 1.29 The Sample Size option determines the area the Eyedropper tool will average when you're choosing a color.

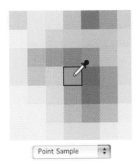

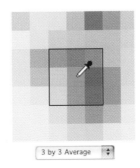

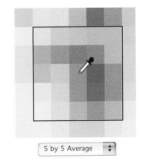

Figure 1.30 Point Sample.

Figure 1.31 3 by 3 Average.

Figure 1.32 5 by 5 Average.

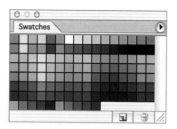

Figure 1.33 The Swatches palette using Small Thumbnail view.

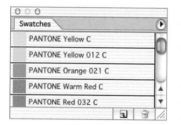

Figure 1.34 The Swatches palette using Small List view.

Swatches Palette

The Swatches palette is designed to store colors that you can use again and again. You can choose how you'd like to view the swatches by choosing either Small Thumbnail (**Figure 1.33**) or Small List (**Figure 1.34**) from the side menu of the Swatches palette. To paint with one of the colors stored in the Swatches palette, move your cursor over a swatch and click the mouse button. Your foreground color will change to the color you clicked. To change your background color, hold Command (Mac) or Ctrl (Windows) while clicking any swatch.

To store your current foreground color in this palette, just click in the open space below the swatches. Photoshop will prompt you to name the color and then will add that color to the bottom of the palette. If there is no open space, resize the palette by dragging its lower-right corner. You can also click the New Swatch icon (it looks like a sheet of paper with the corner turned up) at the bottom of the Swatches palette. That will add a new swatch without asking for a name. (Hold Option on the Macintosh or Alt in Windows to be prompted for a name.)

You can also remove a color from the Swatches palette by Option-clicking (Mac) or Alt-clicking (Windows) on the swatch. To reset the swatches to their default settings, choose Reset Swatches from the side menu of the palette.

If you'd like to change the order of the swatches, choose Edit > Preset Manager. Then choose Swatches from the pop-up menu at the top of the dialog box and click and drag to move the swatches around.

Figure 1.35 The dialog box for saving swatches.

After you've stored the colors you want, you can choose Save Swatches from the Swatches palette's side menu. This will bring up a standard Save dialog box to allow you to assign a name to your personal set of swatches (**Figure 1.35**). After saving a set of swatches, you can reload them by choosing Replace Swatches from the side menu.

Photoshop comes with a bunch of preset swatch files you can load into the Swatches palette. These files are stored in the Color Swatches folder in your Presets folder, which resides in your Photoshop application folder. If you save your swatches file into this folder, it will show up along with other preset swatch files at the bottom of the side menu in the Swatches palette (**Figure 1.36**). When you choose one of those presets, Photoshop will prompt you with a dialog box that has three options (**Figure 1.37**). Append will add the swatches you are loading to the bottom of the swatches that are already there; OK will replace the current swatches with what you are loading; and Cancel will abort loading the swatches. If you'd like to avoid this dialog box altogether, you can hold the Option key (Mac) or Alt key (Windows) when you choose one of the presets from the side menu, and Photoshop will replace the swatches automatically.

Info Palette

Although you can't actually choose a color by using the Info palette, you'll find it helpful for measuring the colors that already reside in your document. The top part of the Info palette measures the color that appears below your cursor.

You can change the measurement method used by the Info palette by clicking the tiny Eyedropper icons within the palette (**Figure 1.38**). RGB is usually used for multimedia purposes; CMYK for publishing. Total Ink adds the C, M, Y, and K numbers to indicate how much ink coverage will be used to reproduce the area under your cursor.

Most images opened in Photoshop contain 256 shades of gray, or 256 shades each of red, green, and blue (also known as 8 bits per channel). Photoshop CS features abundant support for 16-bit images, which can contain up to 32,768 shades of gray, or shades of red, green, and blue. If you're working on a 16-bit file (Image > Mode > 16 Bits/Channel), then you can see 16-bit numbers (0–32,768) instead of the standard 8-bit numbers (0–255) in the Info palette. (Do this by choosing Palette Options from the side menu of the Info palette and turning on the Show 16-bit Values check box.) I don't find this to be all that useful, but you're welcome to try it if you're a bona-fide numbers geek.

Figure 1.36 Preset swatch files are listed at the bottom of the menu.

Figure 1.37 The Replace Swatches dialog box.

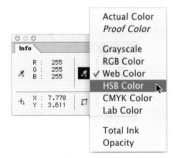

Figure 1.38 Changing how the Info palette measures color.

Figure 1.39 Color samples and Info palette readouts. (©2003 Stockbyte, www.stockbyte.com)

Figure 1.40 Info palette readouts while an adjustment dialog box is in use.

You can set up the Info palette to keep track of different areas of your image, so you can see what's happening when you make adjustments. You can do this by clicking your image using the Color Sampler tool (hidden under the Eyedropper tool). This will deposit a little crosshair on the area you click, and will also add another readout to the Info palette (**Figure 1.39**). You can add up to four of these "samples" to your image. Then when you are adjusting the image using any of the choices under the Image > Adjustments menu, the Info palette readouts will change into two readouts for each Color Sampler (**Figure 1.40**). The left number indicates what the color was before the adjustment; the right number indicates what the color will be after the adjustment. You can even add a color sample to your image while an adjustment dialog box is active by holding the Shift key and clicking on the image. (The Color Sampler tool does not need to be active to do this).

To remove a sample, hold the Option key (Mac) or Alt key (Windows), and click on the sample, or just drag it off the screen. Or, if you'd like to remove all the color samples, click the Clear button in the options bar. (It's available only when the Color Sampler tool is active.) Occasionally you may want to hide the sample points when you're working on your image; you can do this by choosing Color Samples from the side menu of the Info palette. We'll use these samples when you read about color correction in Chapter 9, "Color Correction."

Basic Editing Tools

You'll find, just as you've seen with the majority of Photoshop's features, that there's more than meets the eye with the editing tools. For now, we'll cover their most obvious applications, but as you make your way through the rest of the book, keep in mind that these deceivingly simple tools can perform some remarkable tricks. For example, the painting and gradient tools can be used for more than just painting and adding color—they can also be used for making intricate selections, compositing photos, and creating cool fadeouts. You can use them to create an infinite number of dazzling effects.

Painting

In Photoshop, you have two choices for painting: the Paintbrush (Brush) tool or the Pencil tool. The only difference between the two is that the Paintbrush always delivers a soft-edged stroke—even a hard-edged brush used with the Brush tool produces a slightly blended edge—whereas the Pencil tool produces a truly crisp edge (**Figures 1.41** and **1.42**).

All painting tools use the current foreground color when you're painting on the image, so before you begin painting, make sure the active foreground color is the one you want.

To quickly change the Opacity setting of a painting tool, use the number keys on your keyboard (1 = 10%, 3 = 30%, 65 = 65%, and so on).

Figure 1.41 Paint stroke created with the Paintbrush tool.

Figure 1.42 Paint stroke created with the Pencil tool.

You can change the softness of the Paintbrush tool by choosing different brushes from the Brushes palette. When the Pencil tool is active, all brushes will have a hard edge.

Opacity

If you lower the Opacity setting of the Paintbrush tool, you can paint across the image without worrying about overlapping your paint strokes (**Figure 1.43**). As long as you don't release the mouse button, the areas that you paint over multiple times won't get a second coat of paint.

If you're not familiar with the concept of opaque versus transparent, take a look at **Figures 1.44** and **1.45**.

Figure 1.43 A continuous stroke using the Paintbrush tool.

Figure 1.44 Opaque (left) versus transparent (right). (©2003 Stockbyte, www.stockbyte.com)

Figure 1.45 Varying opacity. (©2003 Stockbyte, www.stockbyte.com)

Flow

The Flow setting determines how much of the opacity you've specified will show up on your first paint stroke. When the Flow setting is set to 20%, you'll get 20% of the opacity you've specified in the options bar each time you paint across an area (**Figure 1.46**). Each time you pass over the same area with that setting, you'll build up another coat of 20% of the opacity you've chosen. No matter how many times you paint across an area, you will not be able to achieve an opacity higher than what's specified in the options bar, unless you release the mouse button. If you set the Flow setting to 100%, then it will effectively turn off this feature, so that you'll get the full opacity that you've requested each time you paint. The Pencil tool doesn't use the Flow setting, and therefore will deliver the desired opacity setting in a single pass.

Figure 1.46 Paint stroke using the Flow setting.

Now let's take a look at the options available to you when using the painting tools.

Blending Mode

The Mode pop-up menu in the options bar is known as the Blending Mode menu. We'll be covering all the options under this menu in Chapter 17, "Enhancement," so right now I'll just explain a few basic uses (**Figures 1.47** to **1.49**). If you would like to change the basic color of an object, you can set the blending mode to Hue. If you're using a soft-edged brush, you can set the blending mode to Dissolve to force the edges of your brush to dissolve out. That's all for now; we'll explore the rest of this menu in Chapter 17.

Figure 1.47 Normal. (©2003 Stock-byte, www.stockbyte.com)

Figure 1.48 Hue.

Figure 1.49 Dissolve.

Eraser Tool

If you use the Eraser tool while you're working on a background image (we'll talk about the background in Chapter 3, "Layers Primer"), it acts like one of the normal painting tools—except that it paints with the background color instead of the foreground color. It even lets you choose which type of painting tool it should mimic by allowing you to select an option from the pop-up menu in the options bar (**Figure 1.51**).

However, when you use the Eraser tool on a nonbackground layer, it really erases the area. If you lower the Opacity setting, it makes an area appear partially transparent. Bear in mind that the same does not apply to the background image. You cannot "erase" the background.

Brush Presets Palette

Let's look at how Photoshop deals with brushes in general, and then we'll start to explore how to create your own custom brushes. When a painting or retouching tool is active, you'll see the currently active brush shown in the options bar. If you click on that preview, the Brush Presets drop-down palette will appear (**Figure 1.52**). All of the painting and retouching tools available in the Tools palette use the Brush Presets palette to determine their brush size. Each individual tool remembers the last brush size you used with it, and will return to that same size the next time you select the tool. In other words, the brush size you choose doesn't stay consistent when you switch among the tools.

You can change the active brush by clicking once on any brush that's available in the Brush Presets palette.

> **NOTES**
>
> To draw straight lines, Shift-click in multiple areas of your image; Photoshop will connect the dots (Figure 1.50). You can also hold down the Shift key when painting to constrain the angle to a 45-degree increment.

Figure 1.50 Shift-click to create straight lines.

Figure 1.51 Choosing Eraser tool behavior.

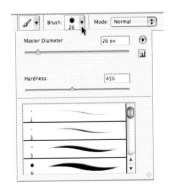

Figure 1.52 The Brush Presets palette.

(Double-clicking will choose a brush and then hide the Brush Presets palette.) Each brush has a number below it, which indicates how many pixels wide the brush is.

For even more fun, keep an eye on the brush in the options bar and then press the < or > key on your keyboard (without holding Shift). You can use these keys to cycle through all the brushes shown in the Brush Presets palette.

Brushes Palette

There are two versions of Photoshop's Brushes palette, each found in a different location in Photoshop. The one we've been talking about so far is the Brush Presets palette. When using that version (the "lite" edition), all you can do is switch between premade brushes. If you'd rather change the characteristics of a brush, then you'll need to abandon that palette and work with the full Brushes palette by choosing Window > Brushes (**Figure 1.53**). In this version of the palette (the "I'll take that with everything" edition), you can still access the Brush Presets by clicking on the words *brush presets* in the upper left of the palette. But you can do a heck of a lot more if you click on the choices that appear across the left side of the palette. When you do that, be sure to click on the *words* that describe the feature you'd like to change, not the check boxes. Clicking on the check boxes just lets you turn a feature on or off, and you won't see the options for that feature within the palette. To do that, you must click on the *name*, not the check box. By clicking on each of those choices, you'll find that there are well over 30 settings that you can apply to a brush. When I first saw them, it felt like I was going to need to go back to college to learn how to use everything. But then I looked a little closer and noticed that the settings aren't that hard to deal with, and that if you combine a bunch of the features, you can create some pretty awesome brush effects.

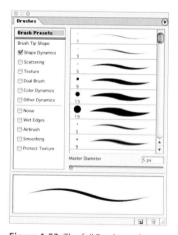

Figure 1.53 The full Brushes palette.

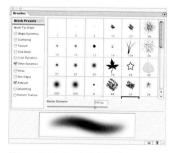

Figure 1.54 The left side of these brush presets are all round brushes; the right side are all sampled brushes.

There's one thing you'll need to think about before you start experimenting with all of Photoshop's brush settings. There are two types of brushes you can work with: round brushes and sampled brushes. A round brush is just what you'd expect…it's round. It's the way most brushes were created in previous versions of Photoshop. The second type of brush you can use is one that's based on a picture (known as a sampled brush) (**Figure 1.54**).

In order to work with a round brush, you must first select a round brush from the Brush Presets. To work with a sampled brush, either choose a nonround brush from the presets or select an area that you'd like to convert into a brush from the active document and then choose Edit > Define Brush. Once you've chosen the type of brush you'd like to work with, you're ready to start experimenting with all the brush settings.

Brush Tip Shape

When you click on the Brush Tip Shape in the upper left of the palette, the central portion of the palette will update to show you the settings that determine the overall look of your brush. A paint stroke is made from multiple paint daubs; that is, Photoshop fills the shape of your brush with the current foreground color, moves over a distance, and then fills that shape again (**Figure 1.55**). The Brush Tip Shape settings determine what the paint daubs will look like and how much space there will be between them.

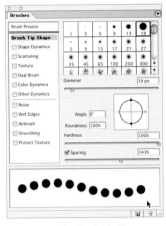

Figure 1.55 The Brush Tip Shape options.

▶ **Diameter:** Determines the size of the brush (**Figure 1.56**). You can use a setting between 1 and 2,500 pixels. The Use Sample Size button will appear anytime you're using a sampled brush that has been made larger or smaller than its original size. When you click the Use Sample Size button, Photoshop will reset the Diameter setting to the original size of the sampled brush, thereby delivering the highest quality. When you reduce the size of a sampled brush, it won't degrade the quality of the image much at all. Increasing the size of a sampled brush will cause the brush shape to have a less crisp appearance (**Figure 1.57**).

Figure 1.56 Diameter from top to bottom: 100 pixels, 50 pixels, 20 pixels.

Figure 1.57 Left: Sampled brush at actual size. Right: Sampled brush scaled to be much larger than sampled size.

33

NOTES

Instead of entering values for the Angle and Roundness settings, you can modify the diagram on the middle-right side of the dialog box. Drag one of the two small circles to change the Roundness setting; drag the tip of the arrow to change the Angle setting.

Lower the Spacing setting when using large, hard-edged brushes to prevent rough edges.

▶ **Hardness:** Determines how quickly the edge fades out. Default brushes are either 100% soft or 0% soft (**Figure 1.58**). This option is only available with round brushes.

▶ **Roundness:** Compresses a brush in one dimension. When using round brushes, changes to the Roundness setting will result in an oval-shaped brush (**Figure 1.59**). When working with a sampled brush, this setting will compress the brush vertically (**Figure 1.60**).

▶ **Angle:** Rotates oval and sampled brushes, but has no effect on round ones (**Figure 1.61**).

▶ **Spacing:** Determines the distance between the paint daubs that make up a brush stroke (**Figure 1.62**). Turning Spacing off will cause Photoshop to adjust the Spacing setting based on how fast you move the mouse while painting (**Figure 1.63**).

Figure 1.58 Hardness from top to bottom: 100, 50, 20.

Figure 1.59 Roundness from top to bottom: 100, 50, 20.

Figure 1.60 Roundness from top to bottom: 100, 50, 20.

Figure 1.61 Angle from top to bottom: 0, 45, 90.

Figure 1.62 Spacing settings from top to bottom: 25%, 75%, 120%.

Figure 1.63 Turning spacing off varies the Spacing setting based on the speed at which you paint.

The rest of the choices that are available on the left side of the Brushes palette allow you to change how the brush tip shape is applied to your image. You'll find that three basic concepts are used over and over with the brush options. Let's first take a look at these three concepts, so you won't have to listen to me repeat myself when we get to the actual settings involved. Jitter settings will allow a particular option (like size or opacity) to vary across a paint stroke (**Figure 1.64**). The higher the Jitter setting, the more the setting will vary. You will also find a setting called Minimum, which determines the range the Jitter setting can use to vary a setting (**Figure 1.65**). If the Minimum option is set to 10%, then the Jitter control will be able to vary a setting between the amount specified in the Brush Tip Shape panel or options bar and the amount you specified in the Minimum setting. (10% means 10% of the setting that's specified in the Brush Tip Shape panel or options bar.) The third setting you'll find is called Control, and it determines when Photoshop should vary a setting using Jitter. When it's set to Off, the Jitter command will apply all the time. Fade will cause the variance to slowly fade out in a particular number of brush applications. If you set Fade to 20, then Photoshop will start with whatever setting is specified in the Brush Tip Shape area or options bar, and then lower the setting over the next 20 paint daubs, where it will end up with the amount specified in the Minimum setting (**Figure 1.66**). Setting the Control pop-up menu to any of the bottom three choices (Pen Pressure, Pen Tilt, and Stylus Wheel) will cause the variance to be determined by the input of a graphics tablet.

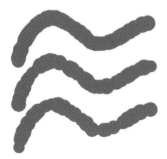

Figure 1.64 Jitter settings from top to bottom: 20, 50, 100.

Figure 1.65 Minimum settings from top to bottom: 1, 30, 75.

Figure 1.66 Fade settings from top to bottom: 20, 75, 130.

Shape Dynamics

These settings will change the shape of the brush you have chosen. In essence, they allow you to vary the same settings that you specified in the Brush Tip Shape section of the Brushes palette (**Figures 1.67** to **1.69**).

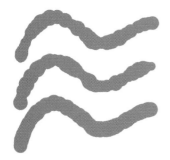

Figure 1.67 Size Jitter settings from top to bottom: 100, 50, 20. The higher the setting, the more variation in the blobs.

Figure 1.68 Angle Jitter settings from top to bottom: 100, 50, 20. The higher the setting, the more variation in the angle of the leaves.

Figure 1.69 Roundness Jitter settings from top to bottom: 100, 50, 20. This rotates the leaves on an axis parallel to the brush stroke.

Scattering

The Scatter setting will cause Photoshop to vary the position of the paint daubs that make up a stroke (**Figure 1.70**). The Count setting allows you to vary how many paint daubs are applied within the spacing interval that you specified in the Brush Tip Shape area of the Brushes palette (**Figure 1.71**).

Figure 1.70 Scatter settings from top to bottom: 20, 100, 200.

Figure 1.71 Count settings from top to bottom: 1, 3, 7.

Texture

The texture settings allow you to vary the opacity of your brush based on a texture that you specify (**Figure 1.72**). The Depth Jitter setting allows Photoshop to apply the texture in varying amounts. The Texture Each Tip setting must be turned on in order to use the Depth Jitter setting (**Figure 1.73**). If you find that the texture isn't changing the look of your brush, then experiment with the Mode pop-up menu until you get the result you are looking for.

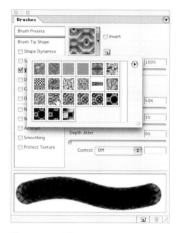

Figure 1.72 The texture settings.

Figure 1.73 Depth Jitter settings from top to bottom: 100, 50, 20.

Dual Brush

This option allows you to create a brush stroke that's made with two brushes at once. Paint will show up only where the two brush shapes would overlap each other (**Figure 1.74**). This is a nice way to create sponge effects. You simply choose a normal, round brush in the Brush Tip Shape area of the Brushes palette, and then choose a textured brush in the Dual Brush area. If you find that the brushes aren't combining the way you'd like them to, then experiment with the Mode pop-up menu and Spacing setting until you get the results you desire.

Figure 1.74 Three examples of dual brushes.

Color Dynamics

These settings allow you to vary the color of your brush across the brush stroke. The Foreground/Background setting allows Photoshop to vary the brush color between the two colors being used as foreground and background colors (**Figure 1.75**). The Hue setting allows Photoshop to change the basic color of the brush to random colors. The higher the setting, the more it will deviate from your foreground color (**Figure 1.76**). The Saturation setting varies the vividness of the color that you are painting with (**Figure 1.77**). The Brightness setting allows Photoshop to randomly darken the color you are painting with (**Figure 1.78**). The Purity setting lets you change the saturation of the color you are painting with. A setting of zero makes no change; negative settings lower the saturation and positive settings increase it (**Figure 1.79**).

Figure 1.75 Foreground/Background using red and blue settings from top to bottom: 100, 50, 20.

Figure 1.76 Hue settings from top to bottom: 100, 50, 20.

Figure 1.77 Saturation settings from top to bottom: 100, 50, 20.

Figure 1.78 Brightness settings from top to bottom: 100, 50, 20.

Figure 1.79 Purity settings from top to bottom: +50, 0, −50.

Other Dynamics

The Opacity and Flow settings allow you to vary the settings that appear in the options bar for the painting tool that is currently in use (**Figures 1.80** and **1.81**). When you use these controls, Photoshop will vary the Opacity and Flow settings across a brush stroke, but will never exceed the settings specified in the options bar.

Figure 1.82 A brush stroke with Noise applied.

Figure 1.83 The effect of the Wet Edges setting.

Figure 1.80 Opacity settings from top to bottom: 100, 50, 20.

Figure 1.81 Flow settings from top to bottom: 100, 50, 20.

Figure 1.83 The effect of the Wet Edges setting.

The Rest of the Brush Settings

Now let's look at the settings that are found at the bottom of the left side of the Brushes palette. The Noise setting will add a noisy look to soft-edged brushes (**Figure 1.82**). The Wet Edges setting will cause the center of your brush to become 60% opaque, and will apply more and more paint as it gets toward the edge of your brush (**Figure 1.83**). The Airbrush setting just toggles the Airbrush icon that appears in the options bar on or off. It works in concert with the Opacity and Flow settings found in the options bar. The Opacity setting always determines the maximum amount that you'll be able to see through your brush stroke. The Flow setting determines how quickly you will end up with the opacity that you specified. When Flow is set to 100%, you will achieve the opacity amount specified in the options bar on each paint stroke. Lower flow settings cause Photoshop to apply a lower opacity while you paint, but will allow you to overlap your brush strokes to build up to the Opacity setting that's specified in the options bar. The Airbrush setting comes into play when the Flow setting is below 100%. It causes paint to build up when you stop moving your cursor, just as it would if you held a can of spray paint in one position (**Figure 1.84**).

Figure 1.84 The Airbrush option causes more paint to apply wherever you pause when painting.

NOTES

Preset brushes are located in the Brushes folder within the Presets folder in your Photoshop program folder. If you want your own brushes to show up in the Brushes drop-down palette, you'll need to store them in the same location.

Saving Brushes

Once you have changed the settings of a brush, you have in essence created a new brush that is no longer related to the original one that you chose in the Brushes palette. But the changed brush won't show up in the Brushes palette unless you resave it by choosing New Brush from the side menu of the Brushes palette. Once you have created a collection of brushes you like, you can choose Save Brushes from the side menu of the palette to save the currently loaded brushes into a file. If you ever need to get back to a saved set of brushes, choose Replace Brushes from the same menu. You can also choose Reset Brushes to get the brushes back to the default settings.

Preset Brushes

Photoshop comes with a variety of preset brushes. You can load these sets by choosing either Replace Brushes or a specific name that appears at the bottom of the Brushes palette side menu (**Figures 1.85** to **1.88**).

Figure 1.85 The side menu of the Brushes drop-down palette.

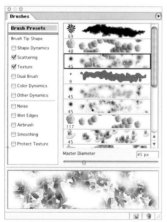

Figure 1.86 Special Effect brushes.

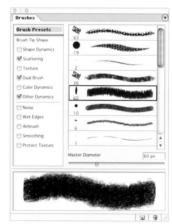

Figure 1.87 Dry Media brushes.

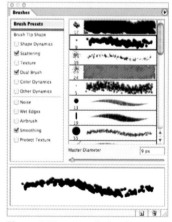

Figure 1.88 Wet Media brushes.

Paint Bucket Tool

Use the Paint Bucket tool to fill areas with the foreground color. Each time you click on the image, Photoshop will fill areas that contain colors similar to the one you clicked. You can specify how sensitive the tool should be by changing its Tolerance setting (**Figures 1.89** to **1.91**). Higher Tolerance settings will fill a wider range of colors.

Figure 1.89 The Paint Bucket options bar.

Figure 1.90 Tolerance: 32.

Figure 1.91 Tolerance: 75.

Shape Tools

The Shape tools are great for creating simple geometric shapes (**Figure 1.92**). These tools are much more powerful than what you'd expect at first glance. We'll look at the basics here, and then expand on them in later chapters.

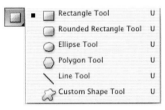

Figure 1.92 Press and hold one of the Shape tools to see a full list of the tools available.

Before you dive into the Shape tools, you need to think about what kind of result you want to achieve, because you have three ways of using these tools, each of which will lead you to a different outcome. You'll find the trio of choices in the far left of the options bar (**Figure 1.93**). The first (leftmost) choice will create a special layer. It's known as a Shape layer, and it has some very special qualities:

Figure 1.93 These three icons determine how the shape will be applied.

▶ It will have crisp edges when printed on a PostScript printer (even if the pixels that make up the image are large enough to cause the rest of the image to appear jagged).

▶ You can scale it (up or down) without degrading its quality. This makes it ideal for creating button bars on web sites where the client might decide to add more text to a button, which would require a larger button.

▶ You can add to or take away from it using the other Shape tools.

▶ It can be filled with a solid color, gradient, pattern, or adjustment.

Vector Masks were known as Layer Clipping Paths in previous versions of Photoshop.

The second choice in the options bar will deliver a path that will show up in the Paths palette. This can be useful when creating a Vector Mask, as we'll discuss in Chapter 16, "Collage." The third choice in the options bar will fill an area on the currently active layer using the current foreground color. I mainly use the Shape layer option (leftmost icon) because it seems to give me the most flexibility.

Once you've decided what type of result you want, you can click and drag across an image to create a shape. If you'd like to have a little more control over the end result, you can click on the small triangle that appears to the right of the Shape tools in the options bar. That will present you with options that are specific to the particular shape you are creating.

When using the Shape layer option, you can quickly create interesting effects by choosing a style from the drop-down menu (small triangle) next to the Layer Style preview image in the options bar. A layer style is a collection of settings that can radically transform the look of a layer by adding dimension, shadows, and other effects to the layer. You can also apply a layer style to any layer (it doesn't have to be one that was created using a Shape tool) by opening the Styles palette and clicking on one of the styles listed (**Figure 1.94**). We'll talk more about layer styles in Chapter 19, "Type and Background Effects."

Measure Tool

The Measure tool allows you to measure the distance between two points or the angle of any area of the image, which can be helpful when you want to rotate or resize objects precisely. As you drag with the Measure tool, the options bar at the top of your screen indicates the angle (A) and length (D, for Distance) of the line you're creating (**Figure 1.95**). The measurement system being used is the same as whatever your rulers are set to. After creating a line, you can click directly on the line and drag it to different positions. You can also click and drag one end of the line to change the angle or distance.

If you want to resize an image so that it fits perfectly between two objects, you can measure the distance between them with this tool and then choose Image > Image Size to scale the image to that exact width. Or, if you have a crooked image that you'd like to straighten, drag across an area that should be horizontal or vertical with the Measure tool and then choose Image > Rotate Canvas > Arbitrary and click OK. Photoshop will automatically enter the proper angle setting based on the measurement line that you drew.

Figure 1.94 The Layer Styles palette.

Figure 1.95 The Info palette indicates the angle of the Measure tool. (©2003 Stockbyte, www.stockbyte.com)

NOTES

To rotate a layer to a specific angle, first use the Measure tool to specify the angle you'd like to use, and then choose Edit > Transform > Rotate. Photoshop enters the angle of the line you drew into the options bar and rotates the active layer that amount.

You can also use the Measure tool to determine the angle between two straight lines. If you Option-drag (Mac) or Alt-drag (Windows) the end of the line, you can pull out a second line and move it to any angle you desire. Now the angle (A) number in the Info palette displays the angle between those two lines.

Gradient Tool

At first, you might not see any reasons to get excited about using the Gradient tool. However, after we cover layers (Chapter 3), channels (Chapter 12), and collage techniques (Chapter 16, "Collage"), you should find that the Gradient tool is not only worth getting excited about, but also downright indispensable. I want to make sure you know how to edit and apply gradients before we get to those chapters, so let's give it a shot.

First let's look at how to apply gradients to an image. To apply a gradient, simply click and drag across an image using the Gradient tool. You'll get different results depending on which type of gradient you've chosen in the options bar (**Figure 1.96**).

WARNING

Unless you select an area before applying a gradient, the gradient will fill the entire image.

NOTES

You can press Enter to show or hide the preset gradients without accessing the options bar.

Figure 1.96 The Gradient options bar.

Here's an explanation of the gradient settings:

▶ **Linear:** Applies the gradient across the length of the line you make (**Figures 1.97** to **1.99**). If the line does not extend all the way across the image, Photoshop fills the rest of the image with solid colors (the colors you started and ended the gradient with).

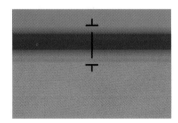

Figure 1.97 Linear gradient.

Figure 1.98 This book was created by transforming a PDF file so that it appears to be 3D. (Cover image courtesy Alicia Buelow)

Figure 1.99 Adding a linear gradient to the cover of the book effectively added subtle lighting to the cover.

▶ **Radial:** Creates a gradient that starts in the center of a circle and radiates to the outer edge (**Figures 1.100** to **1.102**). The point where you first click determines the center of the circle; where you let go of the mouse button determines the outer edge of the circle. All areas outside this circle will be filled with a solid color (the color that the gradient ends with).

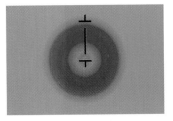

Figure 1.100 Radial gradient.

Figure 1.101 This brushed metal text appears rather flat and lifeless.

Figure 1.102 After adding a radial gradient, the text looks more interesting.

▶ **Angle:** Sweeps around a circle like a radar screen (**Figures 1.103** to **1.105**). Your first click determines the center of the sweep, and then you drag to determine the starting angle.

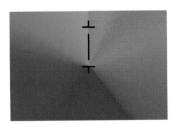

Figure 1.103 Angle gradient.

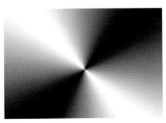

Figure 1.104 This angle gradient will be the base for an interesting trick.

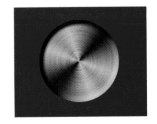

Figure 1.105 By adding texture and layer styles, the simple angle gradient was transformed into a drill hole in metal.

▶ **Reflected:** Creates an effect similar to applying a linear gradient twice, back to back (**Figures 1.106** to **1.107**).

Figure 1.106 Reflected gradient.

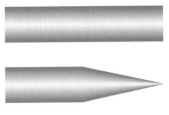

Figure 1.107 Top: A reflected gradient using metallic colors. Bottom: The end of the gradient was transformed to turn it into the tip of a pin.

▶ **Diamond:** Similar to a radial gradient except that it radiates out from the center of a square (**Figure 1.108**).

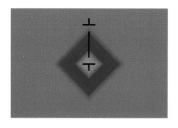

Figure 1.108 Diamond gradient.

Gradient Colors

You can choose from different preset color combinations by clicking on the small triangle that appears next to the gradient preview in the options bar (**Figure 1.109**). You can also reverse the direction of the gradient by turning on the Reverse check box in the options bar. Then, if you have a gradient that usually starts with blue and ends with red, it would instead start with red and end with blue (**Figures 1.110** and **1.111**). Some of the preset gradients will contain transparent areas. To disable transparency in a gradient, turn off the Transparency check box.

Figure 1.109 The Linear Gradient options bar.

Figure 1.110 Reverse "off."

Figure 1.111 Reverse "on."

Figure 1.112 Dither "off."

Dithered Gradients

When you print an image that contains a gradient, you'll sometimes notice banding across the gradient (also known as stair-stepping or posterization). To minimize this, be sure to turn on the Dither check box in the options bar. This will add noise to the gradient in an attempt to prevent banding. You won't be able to see the effect of the Dither check box on-screen; it just makes the gradient look better when it's printed (**Figures 1.112** and **1.113**). If you find that you still see banding when you print the gradient, you can add some additional noise by choosing Filter > Noise > Add Noise. (Use a setting of 3 or less for most images.)

Figure 1.113 Dither "on."

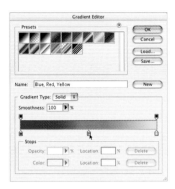

Figure 1.114 Click just below the gradient preview to add colors to the gradient.

Custom Gradients

The Gradient drop-down menu might not always contain the exact type of gradient you need. When that's the case, click directly on the gradient preview in the options bar to create your own custom gradient. The Gradient Editor dialog box that appears has so many options that it can sometimes feel overwhelming, but if you take it one step at a time, you shouldn't run into any problems (**Figure 1.114**).

The list at the top of the dialog box shows you all the gradients that usually appear in the options bar. Click any one of them, and you'll be able to preview it at the bottom of the dialog box. Once you have chosen the gradient you want to edit, you can modify it by changing the gradient bar (or you can click New to make a copy and proceed from there). To add colors (up to a maximum of 32), click just below any part of the bar. This adds a color swatch to the bar and changes the colors that appear in the gradient.

You have three choices of what to put into your new color swatches. You'll find these choices on the drop-down menu to the right of the color swatch at the bottom left of the dialog box. The Foreground and Background choices don't just grab your foreground or background colors at the time you create the gradient, as you might expect. Instead, they look at the foreground and background colors when you apply the gradient. Therefore, each time you apply the gradient, you can get a different result by changing the foreground and background colors. If you don't want the gradient to contain your foreground or background colors, then choose User Color from the same menu and click on the color swatch to access the Color Picker.

After you have added a swatch of color to the gradient bar, you can reposition it by dragging it from left to right, or by changing the number in the Location box below. I like to click the Location number and then use the up arrow and down arrow keys on my keyboard to slide the color swatch around. A little diamond shape, known as the midpoint, will appear between each of the color swatches; it indicates where the two colors will be mixed equally.

Transparent Gradients

You can also make areas of a gradient partially transparent by clicking just above the gradient preview. In this area, you cannot change the color of a gradient; you can only make the gradient more or less transparent. You can add and move the transparency swatches just as you would the color swatches below. Transparent areas are represented by the checkerboard pattern (**Figure 1.115**).

Notes Tool

When you use the Notes tool (which looks a bit like a Post-it Note), you can click and drag on your image to create a text box in which you can then type a note (**Figure 1.116**). Once you're done typing, you can close the note by clicking the tiny box in its upper-left corner (Mac) or in its upper-right corner (Windows), and all you'll see is a tiny icon that indicates there is a note in that spot. Then, when you want to read the note, just double-click on that icon and the note will expand. Each note can have a different color and author, which you specify in the options bar. If you find the notes to be distracting, then you are welcome to choose View > Show > Annotations to hide the notes.

Hidden under the Notes tool is another tool that allows you to record audio annotations. You'll have to have the proper hardware (such as a microphone) to get this feature to work. With the audio annotation, you simply click on your image, and a Record dialog box will appear (**Figure 1.117**). Click the Start button and then start talking. Once you're done, click the Stop button and you're all set. Now anytime someone double-clicks that audio annotation, he will hear your notes. That's pretty slick, but be careful, because audio annotations can really increase the file size of an image.

If you no longer need to keep the annotations you've created and you'd like to reduce your file size, you can click the Clear All button in the options bar. (The Annotations tool must be active for this button to be available.)

You can remove a color swatch or a transparency swatch by simply dragging it away from the gradient bar.

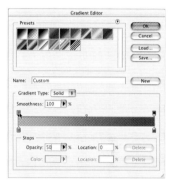

Figure 1.115 Editing the transparency of a gradient.

Figure 1.116 A text annotation. (© 2003 Stockbyte, www.stockbyte.com)

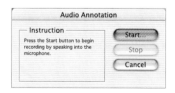

Figure 1.117 The Audio Annotation Record dialog box.

PDF Annotations

What's really special about annotations is that you can save them (along with the image, of course) in a PDF file. You can give that file to anyone; that person can read the annotations and see the image without having to use Photoshop. All he needs is a free program called Adobe Reader (available at www.adobe.com). Or, if he has the full version of Acrobat, he can add his own annotations to the PDF file. Then you can import them into the original Photoshop file by choosing File > Import > Annotations. This allows you to save an image in a universal file format, send it out for review to as many people as you like, and get back comments that you can reimport into the original high-resolution Photoshop file. It's a great way to communicate with clients.

Tool Presets

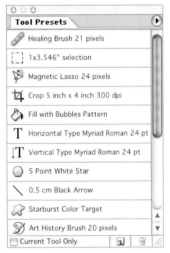

Figure 1.118 The Tool Presets palette.

Figure 1.119 The Include Color check box.

Tool presets allow you to store and retrieve your favorite tool settings. You can access the presets in two ways: Click on the Tool icon that appears on the left side of the options bar, or choose Window > Tool Presets (**Figure 1.118**). To save a preset, click on the new Preset icon at the bottom of the Tool Presets palette. (It looks like a piece of paper with the corner turned down.) You'll also find the same icon in the upper-right area of the drop-down palette that you can access from the options bar. When you save a preset, Photoshop remembers all the settings that were specified in the options bar and the Brushes palette (if you're using a painting or retouching tool). If you check the Include Color check box (**Figure 1.119**), it will even remember your foreground and background colors. Once you've saved a preset, you can get back to those settings at any time by clicking on the name of the preset from the Tool Presets palette.

There are two ways of working with the Tool Presets palette. The first is to use it as a replacement for Photoshop's main Tools palette. After all, when you click on a preset, Photoshop will switch to the referenced tool and load up the setting you saved, so you could completely replace the main Tools palette with the presets. The only problem with that is that it can get rather crowded once you have four or five settings saved for each tool. I prefer to select tools using the normal Tools palette, and then to streamline the tool in the Tool Presets palette, I choose Show Current Tool Presets so that I see only presets that relate to the tool I have active. I also usually close the palette and access it by clicking on the Tool icon that appears at the left end of the options bar. That way I reduce my screen clutter and can still quickly access the presets with a click or two of my mouse.

File Browser

Photoshop's File Browser is a great way to open and organize your images. With it, you'll be able to view thumbnail size previews of your images, sort and rotate them, and apply a variety of automated features. I no longer choose Image > Open to access the files on my hard drive. Instead, I choose File > Browse, or type Shift-Command-O (Mac) or Shift-Ctrl-O (Windows) to access the File Browser (or click on the new File Browser icon on the far right of the options bar). As if Photoshop 7's File Browser wasn't good enough, Adobe went ahead and redesigned it for Photoshop CS (**Figure 1.120**). The new File Browser has its own menu bar built right into the top of the dialog box and is organized into four panes, three across the left side and one on the right. The left side is divided into tabbed "palettes" that act much like the normal palettes in Photoshop. You can drag the name of a tab onto another palette grouping to include that palette in the group. You can double-click on a tab to collapse that area so it takes up minimal space, and you can drag the dividing bar between palettes to control how much space one area takes up as compared to the others.

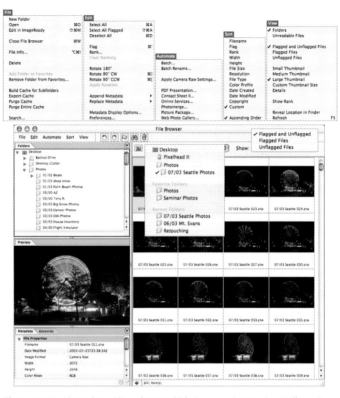

Figure 1.120 Photoshop CS's redesigned File Browser. (©2003 Ben Willmore)

Navigating Your Hard Drive

There are many ways to navigate your hard drive. In the File Browser's default configuration, the Folders pane will appear in the upper left of the browser window. That's where you can navigate your drive by clicking on arrows next to each folder to view its contents. If you've navigated to a folder that you'll want to access quite often, then choose Add Folder to Favorites from the File menu at the top of the File Browser window. Then, when you need to access that folder, expand the Favorite Folders area at the bottom of the folder list and click on the folder you added. You can also navigate your hard drive using the thumbnail preview area on the right side of the File Browser. Double-click on folders within the thumbnail view to open them, and click the Up One Level icon (it looks like a folder with an up arrow on it) to move one level closer to your desktop. The menu next to the Up One Level icon indicates which folder you are currently viewing. Clicking on that menu will present you with a list of recently accessed folders as well as any favorites you added. You can also find files by choosing Search from the File menu at the top of the File Browser window (or click the Binoculars icon at the top of the browser window). That will allow you to search based on filename, date modified, keywords, and many other criteria (**Figure 1.121**). One thing that's nice about Photoshop's search capability is that it allows you to view the results even if they happen to be located in multiple folders. If you end up viewing another folder after performing a search, you can get back to the search results by choosing Search Results at the bottom of the folder list.

Once you've navigated to the proper folder on your hard drive, you'll be presented with thumbnail images of the contents of that folder on the right side of the browser window. Double-click on any image that appears in the right side of the File Browser to open it within Photoshop. (Hold Option on a Mac or Alt in Windows to close the File Browser while opening an image.) You can Command-click (Mac) or Ctrl-click (Windows) to select multiple files, or Shift-click to select a range of files. If an image is sideways, then click one of the curved arrow icons at the top of the browser window to let Photoshop know that you'd like to rotate the actual image when it's opened in Photoshop. If you find an image that you simply don't need anymore, then click on it and then press Delete (Mac) or Backspace (Windows) to delete the file from your hard drive. You can even move a file on your hard drive by dragging it to one of the folder icons that appears in the upper left. If you'd rather make a duplicate, then hold Option (Mac) or Alt (Windows) to drag a copy.

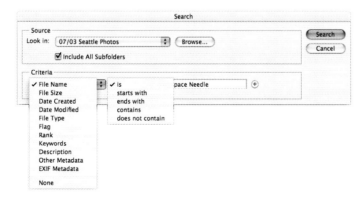

Figure 1.121 The File Browser's Search dialog box.

Figure 1.122 The File Browser Preferences dialog box.

Figure 1.123 The File Browser set up to display large preview images.

Alternative Thumbnail Sizes

Once you've got Photoshop pointed to the proper location on your hard drive, it will present you with thumbnail images for the files in that folder on the right side of the browser. (Click the tiny left/right arrow icon at the bottom of the window to hide the left panes of the browser.) You can control the size of the thumbnails by changing the settings that appear in the View menu at the top of the File Browser window. Smaller thumbnails will allow you to see more images at once, while larger thumbnails will allow you to see more detail in each thumbnail image. If you'd like to have direct control over the size of the thumbnails, choose Preferences from the Edit menu of the File Browser and specify the size you desire in the Custom Thumbnail Size field (**Figure 1.122**). To view your images with the thumbnail size you've specified, choose Custom Thumbnail Size from the View menu in the File Browser. Photoshop automatically creates thumbnail images that are 1,024×768 pixels, so as long as your custom thumbnail setting is lower than 1,024, they should look great. Anything above 1,024 might look a little soft because Photoshop will scale the thumbnail it created (1,024×768) to that size instead of looking at the original image to create the custom-sized thumbnail image.

If you prefer to view your images as large as possible (to see which ones are in sharp focus), then try this: Once you've navigated to the folder of images you'd like to view, double-click on both the Folders and the Metadata tabs to collapse those panes and make room for the preview pane. Next, drag the bar that separates the preview area from the thumbnails until the preview area dominates your screen and the thumbnails take up a very narrow area on the right side of your screen. Now choose Small Thumbnail from the View menu in the browser window and then click on the top thumbnail to make it active (**Figure 1.123**). Then use the down arrow key on your keyboard to cycle through the images in that folder.

If you like viewing your images with those huge previews, then choose Window > Workspace > Save Workspace. Once you're done looking at the huge preview images, choose

Reset Palette Locations from the same menu so that the File Browser uses its default configuration the next time you open it. Then anytime you'd like to get back to that huge preview setup, choose it from the Window > Workspace menu.

Sorting the Thumbnails

You can control the sorting order of the thumbnails by choosing from the options in the Sort menu at the top of the browser window. I really like that you can sort the files by file size and resolution. That makes it easy to find the images that can be used at a large size very quickly. At some point you'll want to sort your images in a way that has nothing to do with the choices that are found under the Sort menu. When that's the case, hold down the Command key (Mac) or Ctrl key (Windows) and click on the images you'd like to sort. To view just those images, click the Flag icon at the top of the browser window and then choose Flagged Files from the Show pop-up menu at the top of the browser window. Then, to sort the images, just click and drag each image into the position you'd like it to appear in. (You can always drag the thumbnails, not just when viewing flagged files.) After you've done that, Photoshop will indicate that your images are in a custom sort order in the Sort menu. One really nice aspect of being able to drag to create a custom sort order is that all of the features found under the Automate menu will respect the sort order you've created. If you end up using one of the standard sort choices in the future, you can always get back to the order you put the images into by choosing Custom from the Sort menu.

Renaming Files

You can quickly rename a file by clicking on its name and typing a new one. You can even press Tab to go to the next file in the list and rename it as well. That makes it very easy to rename an entire folder of images. If you'd like to do that even faster, then make sure you don't have any files highlighted in the browser and choose Batch Rename from the Automate menu at the top of the browser window (**Figure 1.124**). This is where you can have Photoshop

Figure 1.124 The Batch Rename dialog box.

automatically rename an entire folder's worth of images. This is great for when you get images off a digital camera where you get odd filenames like 09864-01.JPG. Just use Batch Rename and specify the naming convention you'd like to use by changing the pop-up menus that appear in the Batch Rename dialog box. I usually set the first field to something like "Ben's Vacation," set the second field to 3 Digit Serial Number, and then set the third field to "extension." That way, all the images end up being named "Ben's Vacation 00X.jpg," where the X is a unique number for each image.

Editing Keyboard Shortcuts

Have you ever been annoyed to find that Command-I (Mac) and Ctrl-I (Windows) inverts your image instead of bringing up the Image Size dialog box? Or that you have to press Option-Command-P (Mac) or Alt-Ctrl-P (Windows) to bring up the Print with Preview dialog box when Command-P (Mac) or Ctrl-P (Windows) seems much more logical? Well, in Photoshop CS, you have the ability to edit the keyboard shortcuts you use to access tools and menus in Photoshop.

Figure 1.125 The Keyboard Shortcuts dialog box.

Start by choosing Keyboard Shortcuts from the Edit menu to access the Keyboard Shortcuts editor (**Figure 1.125**). Now choose the type of keyboard shortcut you'd like to add or edit from the Shortcuts For pop-up menu. Photoshop will display a list of commands with editable keyboard shortcuts. Just click on the arrow next to the menu you'd like to work with to see the individual commands. Once you've located the command you want (you might have to scroll quite a bit to find it), just click on its name and then type the key combination you'd like to assign to that command. Every keyboard command must involve the Command key on the Mac or Ctrl key in Windows and a single letter, number, or symbol. The only exception is the F keys on the top of your keyboard, which can be used all by themselves. You can add any combination of Shift, Option, or Control (Mac) or Shift and Alt (Windows) to the keyboard shortcuts as well (although the Control key can't be used with F keys on the Mac). If the keyboard command you attempt to assign is already used by another command, Photoshop will warn you and ask if you'd like to undo or accept the change. If you choose to accept the change, then Photoshop will bring you to the command that was previously assigned that keyboard shortcut so you can assign it a new command, or leave it without one. Once you've changed all the keyboard shortcuts that you desire, click the Save Set icon (it looks like a floppy disk and is directly to the right of the Set pop-up menu) and give your newly assigned keyboard shortcuts a name (like "Ben's Favorites"). Finally, click the OK button to start using your reassigned keyboard shortcuts.

If you ever have to use someone else's computer and you find that person has edited all your favorite keyboard shortcuts, then you have two methods for regaining your sanity. First, you could choose Edit > Keyboard Shortcuts and choose Photoshop Defaults for the Set pop-up menu. If Photoshop prompts you to save the unsaved shortcuts, then click the Save button and give those settings a name so you can quickly get back to them when you're done using that computer. Or, if you'd rather use your own custom keyboard shortcuts, then go back to your machine, choose Edit > Keyboard Shortcuts, click the Save Set icon (it's the middle of the three icons that appear to the right of the Set pop-up menu), and save your keyboard shortcuts on your desktop. Now copy the resulting file to a floppy disc or CD and bring it to the machine you'd like to work on. Copy the file to the Photoshop > Presets > Keyboard Shortcuts folder, which should make it show up in the Set pop-up menu in the Edit > Keyboard Shortcuts dialog box.

The Logic Behind the Keyboard Commands

Did you notice that Adobe limits the keyboard shortcuts you can assign to different commands? That's because there is a general logic to what different keys on your keyboard do within Photoshop. The Command key (Mac) or Ctrl key (Windows) does one of two things. If you press it all by itself, then it will access the Move tool for however long that key is held. If you press it along with another key, then it will replace a menu command. The only exceptions you'll find are ones that involve an F key, which can also replace a menu command (like Shift-F5 to access the Edit > Fill dialog box in Photoshop CS). Now let's look at what the other modifier keys do in Photoshop so you won't be surprised by the keyboard shortcuts that you run across as your progress through this book.

The Shift key either constrains things or lets you work on more of something, depending on when you hold it down. For instance, if you grab the Paintbrush tool and hold Shift while you paint, Photoshop will constrain your movement to either horizontal or vertical. If you have multiple images open, then clicking on the Full Screen Mode icons near the bottom of your tool palette will affect only the topmost image. When that's the case, typing Command-W (Mac) or Ctrl-W (Windows) to close the topmost image will show you that the underlying images are not in Full Screen mode. To affect all the open images, hold the Shift key when you click on the Full Screen Mode icons, and all the images that are currently open will appear in Full Screen mode.

The Option key (Mac) or Alt key (Windows) changes the behavior of something. If a button can perform two functions, then you'll most likely have to hold Option or Alt to get to the second choice. For example, when you're in the Paintbrush tool, you can hold Option to temporarily access the Eyedropper tool, which will allow you to click on your image to choose a color to paint with. Or, if you make an adjustment with any of the choices found under the Edit > Adjustments menu, you can hold Option or Alt to change the Cancel button into a Reset button, which will allow you to get back to the default settings of that dialog box.

The Control key on a Mac isn't used very often. It's usually used with the mouse button to Control-click on something in Photoshop. That's the same as pressing the right mouse button in Windows, and it usually presents you with a menu full of choices that relate to the tool that you're currently using. For instance, Control-clicking (Mac) or right-clicking (Windows) on your image while the Paintbrush tool is active will open the Brush Presets palette as a temporary menu on your screen.

We've only explored a few examples of when these modifier keys are useful. I'll introduce you to additional uses for those keys as we progress through this book. The vast majority of the time, the keys I mentioned will conform to the logic we just went over. The only problem is that some icons, tools, and buttons can perform more than one function, so Adobe might have already used the key you're thinking of to do something else. For instance, when you click the New Layer icon (it looks like a sheet of paper with the corner turned over) at the bottom of the Layers palette, you will create a new empty layer. (We'll talk about layers in Chapter 3.) If you add Option (Mac) or Alt (Windows), then you'll be prompted to name the layer when you create it. If you hold Command (Mac) or Ctrl (Windows), it will create the layer below the one that is active. Not only that, but with so many chefs stirring the pot over there at Adobe, there were bound to be some who deviated from the standard logic. For instance, typing Command-W (Mac) or Ctrl-W (Windows) closes the frontmost image. You'd think that adding Shift to that would work on all of the images (like it does when working with the screen modes), but it doesn't. You have to instead hold down the Option key (Mac) or Alt key (Windows) to close all the open documents.

Closing Thoughts

If you've made it through this entire chapter, you've just passed through Photoshop's welcoming committee of tools and palettes. By now your screen should look neat and tidy and you should be able to zoom in and out and scroll around your image with ease. You should also have a nodding acquaintance with a good number of the tools and palettes—at least you should be familiar enough with them to know which ones you want to get more friendly with later.

Don't panic if some of this still seems like a blur. It will all begin to take shape once you spend some more time with the program. After a few intense Photoshop sessions, the things you learned in this chapter will become second nature to you. If any of the tools are completely new to you,

you should probably play around with them before you move on to the next chapter.

But for now, let's get into the first installment of Ben's Techno-babble Decoder Ring. And just for the fun of it, I'll throw in some keyboard commands that can really speed up your work.

Ben's Techno-Babble Decoder Ring

Anti-aliasing: Smoothing the edge of an otherwise hard-edged object by adding partially transparent pixels. These pixels help to blend the edge of the object into the surrounding image, making it harder to see the edge of the pixels and therefore avoiding a jaggy edge.

CMYK: A model for reproducing RGB colors using cyan, magenta, yellow, and black inks. (Black is abbreviated "K" for Key.) Any time you print an image, you will be using CMYK inks. Ideally, cyan ink would absorb only red light, magenta ink would absorb only green light, and yellow ink would absorb only blue light; you could therefore reproduce an RGB image by absorbing the light falling on a sheet of paper instead of creating the light directly. But due to impurities in these inks, CMYK inks (also known as process color) cannot reproduce all the colors that can be created using RGB light.

Dither: A way to simulate color by using a pattern of two solid colors (for example, adding a pattern of red dots to a yellow area to create orange). This term also refers to adding a pattern of noise to a sharp transition to make the edge less noticeable.

HSB: A method of manipulating RGB or CMYK colors by separating the color into components of hue, saturation, and brightness. Hue is the pure form of the color. (Red is the pure form of pink, maroon, and candy-apple red.) Saturation is the intensity or vibrancy of the color. (Pink is a not very saturated red; candy-apple red is a very saturated red.) Brightness is how bright or dark a color appears. (Pink is a bright, just not vibrant, tint of red; maroon is a dark shade of red.) So, when talking about the hue of a color, you are not describing how bright and vibrant (saturated) the color appears. When talking about saturation of a color, you do not reveal its basic color (hue), or how bright or dark it appears (brightness). When talking about the brightness of a color, you are not describing the basic color (hue) or how vibrant it appears (saturation).

Lab: A scientific method of describing colors by separating them into three components called Lightness, A, and B. The Lightness component describes how bright or dark a color appears. The "A" component describes colors ranging from red to green. The "B" component describes colors ranging from blue to yellow. Lab color is the internal color model used in Photoshop for converting between different color modes (such as RGB to CMYK).

Noise: A pattern of dots that resembles the static that appears on some televisions when no station is tuned in. This pattern is often used to break up crisp transitions between two colors by replacing a straight-line transition with one that has more of a random edge.

Posterization: The process of breaking up a smooth transition into visible steps of solid color. This is often called stair-stepping, or banding, when referring to a gradient.

RGB: A model for creating color using red, green, and blue light. You are able to see color because your eyes contain cones in their retinas that are sensitive to red, green, and blue. Scanners capture information by measuring how much RGB light is reflected off the original image. Computer monitors display information by shining RGB light into your eyes. All the colors you have ever seen with your eyes have been made from a combination of red, green, and blue light. It really is an RGB world out there.

Vector: Images can be raster, vector, or a combination of the two. Raster images are made out of a grid of pixels, which makes them inherently jaggy when viewed up close and causes them to appear blurry or jaggy when enlarged. Vector images, on the other hand, are made out of smooth curves and straight lines (known as paths) that can be scaled to any size without degrading the quality of the image. The most common program used for creating vector images is Adobe Illustrator.

Keyboard Shortcuts

Function	Macintosh	Windows
Zoom in	Command-+ (plus sign)	Ctrl-+
Zoom out	Command-– (minus sign)	Ctrl-–
Fit on Screen	Command-0	Ctrl-0
Temporarily use Zoom tool	Command-spacebar	Ctrl-spacebar
Zoom out by clicking	Option-Command-spacebar	Alt-Ctrl-spacebar
Show/Hide palettes	Tab	Tab
Cycle through screen modes	F	F
Hide/Show menu bar when in full screen mode	Shift-F	Shift-F
Temporarily use Hand tool	Spacebar	Spacebar
Show/Hide rulers	Command-R	Ctrl-R
Select previous brush	, (comma)	, (comma)
Select next brush	. (period)	. (period)
Select first brush	Shift-, (<)	Shift-, (<)
Select last brush	Shift-. (>)	Shift-. (>)
Increase brush size	]	]
Decrease brush size	[	[
Make brush edge softer	Shift-[	Shift-[
Make brush edge harder	Shift-]	Shift-]
Hand tool	H	H
Paintbrush tool	B	B
Eraser tool	E	E
Airbrush option	Option-Shift-P	Alt-Shift-P
Change opacity of tool	number keys	number keys
Change flow of tool	Shift-number keys	Shift-number keys
Change blending mode of tool	Shift-plus or minus	Shift-plus or minus
Reset foreground/background colors	D	D
Exchange foreground/background colors	X	X

Courtesy of Michael Slack, www.slackart.com

Courtesy of Michael Slack, www.slackart.com

2
Selection Primer

Courtesy of Tom Nick Cocotos, www.cocotos.com

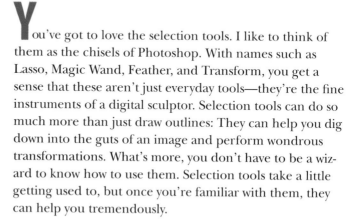

*I choose a block of marble and chop off whatever
I don't need.*

—François-Auguste Rodin, when asked how he
managed to make his remarkable statues

Selection Primer

You've got to love the selection tools. I like to think of them as the chisels of Photoshop. With names such as Lasso, Magic Wand, Feather, and Transform, you get a sense that these aren't just everyday tools—they're the fine instruments of a digital sculptor. Selection tools can do so much more than just draw outlines: They can help you dig down into the guts of an image and perform wondrous transformations. What's more, you don't have to be a wizard to know how to use them. Selection tools take a little getting used to, but once you're familiar with them, they can help you tremendously.

Whatever you do, don't skip this chapter, because the selection tools are central to your success in Photoshop. They allow you to isolate areas of your image and define precisely where a filter, painting tool, or adjustment will change the image. Also, selections are not specific to a particular layer (we'll talk about layers in Chapter 3, "Layers Primer"). Instead, they're attached to the entire document. That means you can freely switch among the different layers without losing a selection. After you've mastered the basics, you'll be ready to jump into more advanced selections in Chapter 12, "Channels."

What Is a Selection?

When you want to edit a portion of your image, you must first select the area with which you want to work. People who paint cars for a living make "selections" very much like the ones used in Photoshop. If you've ever seen a car being painted, you know that painters carefully place masking tape and paper over the areas they don't want to paint (such as the windows, tires, door handles, and so on). That way, they can freely spray-paint the entire car, knowing that the taped areas are protected from "overspray." At its most basic level, a selection in Photoshop works much the same way. Actually, it works much better, because with one selection, you have a choice—you can paint the car and leave the masked areas untouched, or you can paint the masked areas and leave the car untouched.

When you select an area by using one of Photoshop's selection tools (Marquee, Lasso, Magic Wand, and so on), the border of the selection looks a lot like marching ants. Once you've made a selection, you can move, copy, paint, or apply numerous special effects to the selected area (**Figures 2.1** and **2.2**).

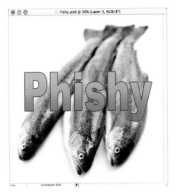

Figure 2.1 When no selection is present, you can edit the entire image. (©2003 Stockbyte, www.stockbyte.com)

Figure 2.2 When a selection is present, you can change only the selected area.

Figure 2.3 Normal selections have hard edges. (©2003 Stockbyte, www.stockbyte.com)

There are two types of selections in Photoshop: a normal selection and a feathered selection (**Figures 2.3** and **2.4**). A normal selection has a hard edge; that is, when you paint or apply a filter to an image, you can easily see where the effect stops and starts. On the other hand, feathered selections slowly fade out at their edges. This allows filters to seamlessly blend into an image without producing noticeable edges. An accurate selection makes all the difference when you're enhancing an image in Photoshop. To see just how important it can be, take a look at **Figures 2.5 to 2.7**.

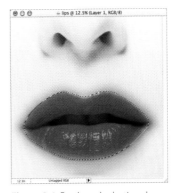

Figure 2.4 Feathered selections have soft edges.

65

Figure 2.5 The original image. (©2003 PhotoSpin, www.photospin.com)

Figure 2.6 An unprofessional selection.

Figure 2.7 A professional selection.

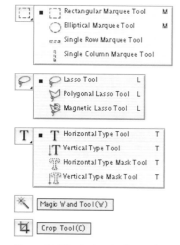

Figure 2.8 The basic selection tools.

NOTES

If you press any combination of the Option (Mac) or Alt (Windows) and Shift keys before you begin a selection, they might not perform as you expect, because these keys are also used to manipulate existing selections.

Basic Selection Tools

The Marquee, Lasso, Magic Wand, and Type Mask tools (**Figure 2.8**) are the essential ingredients in your selection toolkit, and they're the ones you'll be using the most in your everyday work. It's a good indication that you've come to master these tools when you find yourself trying to use them in other software programs where they don't exist. When using other programs, I sometimes find myself muttering, "Why can't I just lasso this thing?"

The Marquee tool is the most basic of all the selection tools, and we'll cover it first. However, don't let this tool's simplicity fool you—it can perform a surprising number of tasks, so there's quite a bit to learn about it. If you hold your mouse button down while your cursor is over the Marquee tool icon, you'll get a variety of choices in a pop-up menu. We'll cover these choices one at a time, and I'll throw in some tricks along the way.

Rectangular Marquee Tool

The Rectangular Marquee tool is the first choice listed in the Marquee pop-up menu. It can select only rectangular shapes. With it, you create a rectangle by clicking and dragging across your document. The first click creates one corner, and the point at which you release the mouse button denotes the opposite corner (**Figure 2.9**). To start in the center and drag to an outer edge, instead of going corner to corner, press Option (Macintosh) or Alt (Windows) after you have started to drag (**Figure 2.10**). If you want to create a square, just hold down the Shift key after you start to drag. You can even combine the Option (Mac) or Alt (Windows) and Shift keys to create a square selection by dragging from the center to an outer edge.

Figure 2.9 A corner-to-corner selection. (©2003 Stockbyte, www.stockbyte.com)

Figure 2.10 A center-to-edge selection.

Figure 2.11 Original selection is misaligned. (©2003 Stockbyte, www.stockbyte.com)

If you hold down the spacebar and drag around your screen while you're making a selection with the Marquee tool (but don't release the mouse button), you'll move the selection instead of changing its shape. This can be a real lifesaver. If you botch up the start of a selection, this enables you to reposition it without having to start over. After you have moved the selection into the correct position, just let go of the spacebar to continue editing the selection. After you've finished making the selection, you no longer need to hold the spacebar to move it. To move a selection after it's created, select the Marquee tool and then click and drag from within the selection outline (**Figures 2.11 and 2.12**).

Elliptical Marquee Tool

The second choice under the Marquee pop-up menu is the Elliptical Marquee tool. This tool works in the same way as the rectangular version, except it creates an ellipse (**Figure 2.13**). And it's a little bit trickier to define its size because you have to work from the "corner" of the ellipse, which doesn't really exist. (What were they thinking when they came up with this idea?) Actually, I find it much easier to choose View > Show Rulers and then drag out a few guides (you can get them by dragging from the rulers) and let the "corners" snap to them. Either that, or hold the spacebar

Figure 2.12 Use the spacebar to reposition a selection while creating it.

NOTES

To discard the areas that appear outside a rectangular selection border, choose Image > Crop.

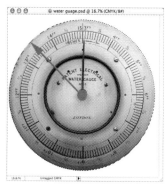

Figure 2.13 The Elliptical Marquee tool in action (from center to edge). (©2003 Stockbyte, www.stockbyte.com)

to reposition the selection before you release the mouse button, just as I mentioned with the Rectangular Marquee tool.

Now let's look at the choices in the Marquee options bar (**Figure 2.14**). When you click on any of the Marquee tools, their options will automatically be available in the options bar at the top of your screen. The following list describes the options you'll find in this palette:

Figure 2.14 The Marquee options bar.

▶ **Feather:** Allows you to fade out the edge between selected and unselected areas. I usually leave this option turned off, because I might forget that a Feather setting had been typed in previously. This one little setting might mess up an otherwise great selection. Instead, I find it much easier to make a selection and then press Option-Command-D on the Mac or Alt-Ctrl-D in Windows (or just choose Select > Feather).

▶ **Anti-aliased:** Determines whether a one-pixel-wide border on the edge of a selection will blend with the image surrounding it. This provides nice, smooth transitions, and helps prevent areas from looking jagged. I recommend that you leave this check box on at all times, unless, of course, you have a great need for jaggies (sometimes they're preferred for multimedia applications).

▶ **Style menu:** Controls the shape and size of the next selection made. When the Style pop-up menu is set to Normal, your selections are not restricted in size or shape (other than their having to be rectangles or ellipses). After changing this menu to Fixed Aspect Ratio, you'll be confronted with Width and Height settings (**Figure 2.15**). By changing the numbers in these areas, you can constrain the shape of the next selection to the ratio between the Width and Height settings. For example, if you change Width to 2 and leave Height at 1, your selections will always be twice as wide as they are tall. This can be useful when you need to find out how much of an image needs to be cropped when printing it as an 8 by 10, for example.

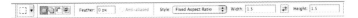

Figure 2.15 The Fixed Aspect Ratio option.

I use the Fixed Size option (**Figure 2.16**) much more often than the Fixed Aspect Ratio option. Fixed Size lets you type in an exact width and height; that way, anytime you click using either the Rectangular or Elliptical Marquee tool, you'll get a selection exactly that size. What's more, if you didn't get it in exactly the right spot, you can just drag the selection around the screen before releasing the mouse button. For instance, Macintosh OS 9 desktop icons are always 32 pixels wide and 32 pixels tall, so I use these numbers when selecting something I want to use as an icon. When entering a Width or Height setting, you can specify a measurement system by adding a few letters after the number you enter; otherwise Photoshop will default to the measurement system used for the rulers.

Figure 2.16 The Fixed Size option.

Single Row and Single Column Marquee Tools

The third and fourth choices under the Marquee tool pop-up menu are the Single Row and Single Column Marquee tools. These tools are limited in that they select only a one-pixel-tall row or one-pixel-wide column. To be honest, I rarely use them (maybe once or twice a year). However, they have gotten me out of few tight spots, such as when I had to clean up a few stray pixels from in between palettes when taking screen shots for this book.

Crop Tool

Two spaces below the Marquee tool, you'll find the Crop tool. Although the Crop tool doesn't produce a selection, it does allow you to isolate a certain area of your image. Using this tool, you can crop an image, as well as resize and rotate it at the same time (**Figures 2.17** and **2.18**).

When you click and drag over an image with the Crop tool selected, a dashed rectangle appears. When the Shield Cropped Area check box is turned on, the area outside the

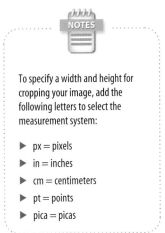

NOTES

To specify a width and height for cropping your image, add the following letters to select the measurement system:

▶ px = pixels
▶ in = inches
▶ cm = centimeters
▶ pt = points
▶ pica = picas

If the cropping rectangle extends beyond the edge of your screen, the extended areas will be filled with the current background color (if you have a background image) or will be transparent (filled with a checkerboard pattern) if you don't have a background image.

To match the size of another open document, click that document to make it active for editing and then click the Front Image button in the options bar. This will enter the Width, Height, and Resolution settings of that document into the options bar. Now you can use the Crop tool on any open document, and the result will match the size of the original document. When you're rotating the cropping rectangle, the Info palette will indicate the exact angle you're using.

If you don't want to resize the image when you crop it, click the Clear button in the options bar to clear out the Width, Height, and Resolution fields before you create a cropping rectangle.

Figure 2.17 The original image. (©2003 Stockbyte, www.stockbyte.com)

Figure 2.18 The original image cropped and rotated.

cropping rectangle will be covered with the color indicated in the options bar and might appear to be partially transparent, depending on the Opacity setting (**Figure 2.19**). You can drag any one of the hollow squares on the edge of the rectangle to change its size. Also, you can hold down the Shift key while dragging a corner to maintain the width-to-height proportions of the rectangle. Anything beyond the edge of the rectangle is discarded when the image is cropped (if you haven't turned on the Hide option).

To rotate the image, you can move your cursor just beyond one of the corner points and drag (look for an icon that looks like a curve with arrows on each end). You can also drag the crosshair in the center of the rectangle to change the point from which the rectangle will be rotated. Press Esc to cancel, or press Return or Enter (or double-click within the cropping rectangle) to complete the cropping. If you're working on a layer (instead of the background) and the Delete option is chosen in the options bar, then all information that appears outside the cropping rectangle will be discarded. If the Hide option is chosen, then the area outside the cropping rectangle will not be discarded, but will instead remain as image data that extends beyond the bounds of the visible image. This option is very useful when you are creating animations in ImageReady and you'd like part of the image to start outside the image area.

Occasionally, you'll need to crop and resize an image at the same time. Maybe you need three images to be the exact same size, or perhaps you need your image to be a specific width. You can do this by specifying the exact Width, Height, and Resolution settings you desire before you create a cropping rectangle. Once you've created a cropping rectangle on your image, you'll notice that different options appear in the options bar (**Figure 2.20**). By typing in both a Width and a Height setting, you constrain the shape of the rectangle that you draw. I occasionally leave one of these values empty so that I can still create any rectangular shape.

Figure 2.19 The cropping rectangle. (©2003 Stockbyte, www.stockbyte.com)

Figure 2.20 The options bar after a cropping rectangle is added to the image.

When the Perspective choice in the options bar is turned on (it becomes available once you've created a cropping rectangle), you will be able to move each corner of the cropping rectangle independently. This allows you to align the four corners with lines that would be level in real life but may appear in perspective in a photograph (**Figure 2.21**). Once you have all four corners in place, you can press Return or Enter to crop the image and correct the perspective of the image in one step (**Figure 2.22**).

Figure 2.21 Getting the corners to line up with level lines. (©2003 PhotoSpin, www.photospin.com)

Figure 2.22 Result of applying a perspective crop.

location to establish the perspective of the image, move the side handles—or Option-drag (Mac)/Alt-drag (Windows) the corner handles—until the area you'd like to keep is within the cropping rectangle, and then press Enter (**Figures 2.23** and **2.24**).

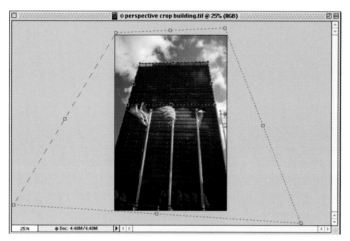

Figure 2.23 Establishing perspective and extending the cropping rectangle.

Figure 2.24 Result of correcting perspective.

Crop and Straighten

Even with all of Photoshop's nifty selection, transformation and crop tools, the task of scanning in bunches of photographs has, up until now, required an annoying amount of rotation, cropping, copying, and pasting. Each photo in the scan had to be individually selected, then cropped or copied and pasted to a new document. Despite your best efforts, the photos are rarely perfectly aligned; at least a few usually cant off to one side or the other a few degrees, requiring further rotation and cropping (**Figure 2.25**).

But Photoshop's new Crop and Straighten Photos does most of that work for you, identifying the individual photographs within the scan, rotating them into perfect horizontal and vertical alignment, and then copying them into new documents. It leaves the original document untouched.

The Crop and Straighten Photos command doesn't do as well with very low resolution scans; scan in photos at 150dpi or more for the best results. You can always scale down the images later.

Figure 2.25 Breaking a scan of multiple photos into individual images used to require a lot of cropping and straightening by hand. (©2003 Mark Clarkson)

To use the command, place a handful of photos on your scanner and arrange them so that none of the images overlap, there is a good amount of space between each image, and none of them are pressed up against the edges of the scanner glass. The more space you leave between each image, the better of a chance there is for Photoshop to successfully crop and straighten each image. Once you've scanned them into Photoshop, make sure the layer containing the scan is active and then choose File > Automate > Crop and Straighten Photos. Without further notice, Photoshop will start chugging away at your document, creating one file for each image. It will also attempt to straighten each image (**Figure 2.26**). Crop and Straighten Photos does a pretty good job, but it can get confused. I find that it's always good to double-check its work because a few images might need to be fine-tuned by hand.

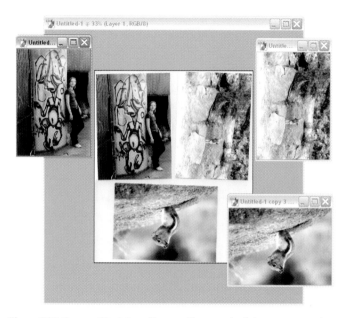

Figure 2.26 Crop and Straighten Photos will automatically locate, crop, and straighten multiple photos from a single scan. (©2003 Mark Clarkson)

If Crop and Straighten Photos insists on breaking one of your photos in two or, conversely, treating two photos as one, you may have to give it a little help. Use the Marquee tool to draw a selection around the problem photo. Now, hold down the Option key (Mac) or the Alt key (Windows) when you choose the command. Holding down this key tells Photoshop that there is only one photo within the selection, making it easier for the program to locate the borders. Even if you have to select some photos one at a time, the Crop and Straighten Photos command still saves you the work of rotating and cropping the photo, and then copying it to a new document.

Lasso Tool

The Lasso tool is the most versatile of the basic selection tools. By holding down the mouse button, you can use the Lasso to trace around the edge of an irregularly shaped object (**Figure 2.27**). When you release the button, the area will be selected. Be sure to create a closed shape by finishing the selection exactly where you started it; otherwise, Photoshop will complete the selection for you by adding a straight line between the beginning and end of the selection.

Sometimes you'll need to add a few straight segments in the middle of a freeform shape. You can do this by holding down Option (Mac) or Alt (Windows) and then releasing the mouse button (but not the Option or Alt key). Now, each time you click your mouse, Photoshop will connect the clicks with straight lines (**Figure 2.28**). To go back to creating a freeform shape, just start dragging and then release the Option key (Mac) or Alt key (Windows).

NOTES

You can zoom in on your document to get a more precise view by typing Command-+ (Mac) or Ctrl-+ (Windows). You don't even have to let go of the mouse button—just press this key combination as you're dragging.

I suggest you zoom in on your image to make sure you're creating an accurate selection. If you can't see the entire image, you can hold the spacebar to access the Hand tool. You can do this without ever releasing the mouse button, which means you can alternate between scrolling and selecting until you've got the whole object.

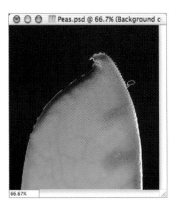

Figure 2.27 The Lasso tool in action. (©2003 Stockbyte, www.stockbyte.com)

Figure 2.28 Using the Option or Alt key while clicking to create straight-line segments. (©2003 Stockbyte, www.stockbyte.com)

Polygonal Lasso Tool

You can use the Polygonal Lasso tool whenever you need to make a selection that consists mainly of straight lines. Using this tool, you just click multiple areas of the image, and Photoshop connects the dots for you (**Figure 2.29**). If you need to create a freeform selection, hold down Option (Mac) or Alt (Windows) and drag. To finish a selection, you can either click where the selection began or double-click anywhere, which will create a straight line between where you double-clicked and where the selection started.

Magnetic Lasso Tool

Whereas the Lasso and Polygonal Lasso tools are relatively straightforward, the Magnetic Lasso tool has a bunch of neat tricks up its sleeve. This tool can be a huge timesaver in that it allows you to trace around the edge of an object without having to be overly precise. You don't have to

Figure 2.29 The Polygonal Lasso tool in action. (©2003 Stockbyte, www.stockbyte.com)

break a sweat making all of those tiny, painstaking move-ments with your mouse. Instead, you can make big sloppy selections, and the Magnetic Lasso will do the fine-tuning for you. What's more, if it doesn't do a great job in certain areas, you can hold down Option (Mac) or Alt (Windows) to use the freeform Lasso tool. However, before using the Magnetic Lasso tool, you'll want to change its settings in the options bar (**Figures 2.30** to **2.32**). Let's take a look at these settings:

Figure 2.30 The Magnetic Lasso options bar.

Figure 2.31 A Magnetic Lasso selection with a Frequency setting of 5. (©2003 Stockbyte, www.stockbyte.com)

Figure 2.32 A Frequency setting of 99.

Edge Contrast

I think this setting is the most important of the bunch. It determines how much contrast there must be between the object and the background for Photoshop to select the object. If the object you're attempting to select has well-defined edges, you should use a high setting (**Figure 2.33**). You can also use a large Lasso tool width. On the other hand, if the edges are not well defined, you should use a low setting and try to be very precise when dragging (**Figure 2.34**).

If the Magnetic Lasso tool is not behaving itself, you can temporarily switch to the freeform Lasso tool by holding down Option (Mac) or Alt (Windows) as you drag. You can also periodically click to manually add anchor points to the selection edge. If you want to use the Polygonal Lasso tool, hold down Option (Mac) or Alt (Windows) and click in multiple areas of the image (instead of dragging). If you don't like the shape of the selection, you can press the Delete key to remove the last anchor point. (Pressing Delete multiple times deletes multiple points.) Once you have a satisfactory shape, finish the selection by pressing Return or Enter or by double-clicking. Remember, if you don't create a closed shape, Photoshop will finish it for you with a straight-line segment.

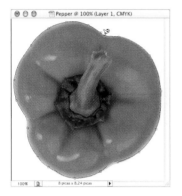

Figure 2.33 High edge contrast (20%). (©2003 Stockbyte, www.stockbyte.com)

Figure 2.34 Low edge contrast (7%).

If you really get used to the features available with the Magnetic Lasso tool, you'll be able to create most of your basic selections with this tool alone. This will take some time, and you'll sometimes have to supplement its use by holding down Option (Mac) or Alt (Windows) to access the other Lasso tools for areas the magnetic one has trouble selecting. And if it ever gets completely out of hand, you can always press the Escape key to abort your selection and then start from scratch again.

Magic Wand Tool

The Magic Wand tool is great for selecting solid (or almost solid) colored areas, because it selects areas based on color—or shades of gray in grayscale mode—as shown in **Figure 2.35**. This is helpful when you want to change the color of an area or remove a simple background.

Figure 2.35 A simple click of the Magic Wand tool can select a solid area of color with ease. (©2003 Stockbyte, www.stockbyte.com)

To quickly change the Tolerance setting, press Enter and then type the desired number and press Enter again. I know it sounds weird, but try it—it works.

You'll probably find it easier to understand how this works if you start by thinking about grayscale images, because they're less complex than color images. Grayscale images can contain up to 256 shades of gray. When you click one of these shades with the Magic Wand tool, it will select any shades that are within the Tolerance specified in the options bar. For instance, if you click shade 128 (Photoshop numbers the shades from 0 to 255) and the Tolerance is set to 10, you'll get a selection of shades that are 10 shades darker and 10 shades brighter than the one you clicked (**Figures 2.36** to **2.38**). When the Contiguous check box is turned on, the only shades that will be selected are those within an area that touches the spot you clicked—Photoshop can't jump across areas that are not within the tolerance.

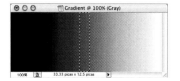

Figure 2.36 Tolerance: 10.

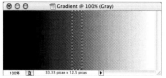

Figure 2.37 Tolerance: 20.

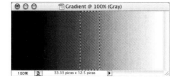

Figure 2.38 Tolerance: 30.

Just in case you're not comfortable thinking in the 0-to-255 numbering system and would rather think about percentages, I've included a conversion table (**Table 2.1**). Otherwise, you can make this conversion by multiplying any percentage by 2.55 (1% in the 0-to-255 numbering system). Remember, the Magic Wand tool will select twice as much as the number you type in.

Color images are a little more complex. They're made from three components: red, green, and blue (that is, when you're working in RGB mode). The Magic Wand tool will analyze all the components (known as channels) in your file to determine which areas to select. For example, if you click a color made up of the components 32 red, 120 green, 212 blue (these numbers can be found in the Info palette) and you use a Tolerance setting of 10, Photoshop will look for colors between 22 and 42 in the red channel, 110 and 130 in the green channel, and 202 and 222 in the blue channel. The only colors selected are ones that fall within all three ranges. Doesn't that sound complicated?

TABLE **2.1** Percentage Conversions

PERCENTAGE	TOLERANCE SETTING
0%	0
10%	26
20%	51
30%	77
40%	102
50%	128
60%	153
70%	179
80%	204
90%	230
100%	255

Well, I have to confess, I don't usually think about the numbers, because they're something of a pain. Instead, I just experiment with the setting until I get a good result. Now, doesn't that sound a lot easier than dealing with all those numbers? If you really want to understand all about the color channels, take a look at Chapter 12, "Channels."

Type Tool

You can use Photoshop's Type tool to create a selection by choosing the Type Mask tool, which is hanging out with the normal Type tool in the Tool palette (**Figure 2.39**). When you use that tool, Photoshop will show you a preview of the selection (with a red overlay on the image, as shown in **Figure 2.40**) while you are editing the text, and then it will deliver a selection when you press Enter. I'll cover the options of this tool in Chapter 19, "Type and Background Effects."

Figure 2.40 The selection will be previewed using a red overlay on the nonselected areas.

Figure 2.39 The options for the Type Mask tool.

Refining a Selection

Selecting complex objects in Photoshop usually requires multiple selection tools. To combine these selection tools, you'll need to either use a few controls in the options bar (**Figure 2.41**) or learn a few keyboard commands that will allow you to add, subtract, or intersect a selection.

Figure 2.41 These four choices in the options bar allow you to create, add, subtract, or intersect a selection.

Adding to a Selection

To add to an existing selection, either click on the second icon on the far left of the options bar (it looks like two little boxes overlapping each other) or hold down the Shift key when you start making the new selection. You must press the key before you start the selection; you can release it as soon as you've clicked the mouse button (**Figures 2.42 to 2.44**). If you press it too late, the original selection will be lost. Let's say, for example, you would like to select multiple round objects. One way would be to use the Elliptical Marquee tool multiple times while holding down the Shift key. But you might find it easier to use the choice available in the options bar because then you don't have to remember to keep any keys held down.

Figure 2.42 The original selection. (©2003 Stockbyte, www.stockbyte.com)

Figure 2.43 Adding to the selection.

Figure 2.44 The end result.

Removing Part of a Selection

To remove areas from an existing selection, either click on the third icon on the far left of the options bar (it looks like one little box stacked on top of another) or hold down Option (Mac) or Alt (Windows) when you begin making the selection. If, for example, you want to create a half circle, you could start with an Elliptical Marquee tool selection and then switch over to the Rectangular Marquee tool and drag while holding down Option (Mac) or Alt (Windows) to remove half of the circle (**Figures 2.45 to 2.47**).

Figure 2.45 The original selection. (©2003 PhotoDisc)

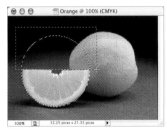

Figure 2.46 Subtracting a second selection.

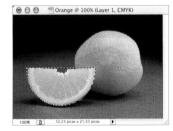

Figure 2.47 The end result.

Clicking while holding down the Option (Mac) or Alt (Windows) key is particularly helpful when you're using the Magic Wand tool to remove areas of a selection (**Figures 2.48** and **2.49**). With each click of the Magic Wand tool, you can use a different Tolerance setting.

Figure 2.48 The original selection.

Figure 2.49 Option-clicking (Mac) or Alt-clicking (Windows) with the Magic Wand tool.

Intersecting a Selection

To end up with only the overlapped portions of two selections, click on the fourth icon on the far left of the options bar (it looks like two squares intersecting, with the overlap area colored in), or hold down Shift-Option (Mac) or Shift-Alt (Windows) while editing an existing selection. Sometimes I use the Magic Wand tool to select the background of an image and then choose Select > Inverse to get the object (or objects) of the selected image (**Figure 2.50**). However, when there are multiple objects in the image, as there are in **Figures 2.51** and **2.52**, I often have to restrict the selection to a specific area by dragging with the Lasso tool while holding down Shift-Option (Mac) or Shift-Alt (Windows).

Figure 2.50 Applying the Magic Wand tool to the background and then choosing Select > Inverse. (©2003 Stockbyte, www.stockbyte.com)

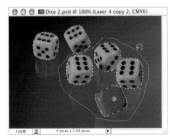

Figure 2.51 Dragging with the Lasso tool while holding down Shift-Option (Mac) or Shift-Alt (Windows).

Figure 2.52 The end result.

The Select Menu

The Select menu offers you many choices that supplement the basic selection tools. Learning these features is well worth your time because they'll help you save heaps of it in your everyday work. We'll look at these features in the same order they appear in the menu; then, later in this chapter, I'll show you how to replace many of these commands with an alternative that allows you to think visually instead of numerically.

Select All

Select > All selects the entire document. This can be useful when you need to trim off any part of an image that extends beyond the edge of the document (**Figure 2.53**). You can crop out those areas by choosing Select > All and then Image > Crop (**Figure 2.54**). Also, if you need to copy an entire image, you'll need to select everything, because without a selection, the Copy command will be grayed out.

Deselect/Reselect

If you're done using a selection and would like to work on the entire image, choose Select > Deselect. If you don't have a selection, you can work on the entire image. Now, if you need to use the last active selection (and there isn't a selection on your screen), you can choose Select > Reselect. This is great when you need to use the same selection over and over again. I use these two commands all the time. However, I usually opt for the keyboard commands: Command-D (Mac) or Ctrl-D (Windows) for Deselect, and Shift-Command-D (Mac) or Shift-Ctrl-D (Windows) for Reselect.

Inverse

As you might expect, the Inverse command selects the exact opposite of what you originally selected. If, for example, you have the background of an image selected, after choosing Select > Inverse, you'll have the subject of the image selected instead (**Figures 2.55** and **2.56**). I use this command constantly, especially with the Magic Wand tool. Sometimes it's just easier to select the areas that you

Figure 2.53 An example of areas that extend beyond the document's bounds (these areas are not usually visible). (©2003 Stockbyte, www.stockbyte.com)

Figure 2.54 When cropping the image, the information that used to extend beyond the document's bounds is discarded.

don't want and then choose Select > Inverse to select what you really want to isolate. Sound backward? It is, but it works great.

Figure 2.55 A Magic Wand tool selection. (©2003 Stockbyte, www.stockbyte.com)

Figure 2.56 The selection after using the Select > Inverse command.

Color Range

You can think of the Select > Color Range command as the Magic Wand tool on steroids. With Color Range, you can click multiple areas and then change the Fuzziness setting (how's that for a technical term?) to increase or reduce the range of colors that will be selected (**Figures 2.57** and **2.58**).

Figure 2.57 The original image. (©2003 Stockbyte, www.stockbyte.com)

Figure 2.58 The same image in the Color Range dialog box after clicking on multiple areas within her blouse.

As you click and play with the Fuzziness control, you'll see a preview of the selection in the middle of the Color Range dialog box. Areas that appear white are the areas that will be selected. The Selection and Image radio buttons allow you to switch between the selection preview and the main image. (I never actually use these two controls because I find it easier to switch to the image view at any time by just holding down Command on the Mac or Ctrl in Windows.) You can also see a preview of the selection within the main image window by changing the Selection Preview pop-up menu to Grayscale, Black Matte, White Matte, or Quick Mask (**Figures 2.59** to **2.61**).

Figure 2.59 Choosing Grayscale will display the same preview that appears in the Color Range dialog box.

Figure 2.60 Choosing Black Matte or White Matte will fill the unselected areas with black or white.

Figure 2.61 Choosing Quick Mask uses the settings in the Quick Mask dialog box to create a preview of the image.

The Eyedropper tool on the right side of the dialog box allows you to add and subtract colors from the selection. Using the Eyedropper with the plus symbol next to it is really helpful, because it allows you to click the image multiple times. With each click, you tell Photoshop which colors you want it to search for. A low Fuzziness setting with many clicks usually produces the best results (**Figures 2.62** and **2.63**).

The selections you get from the Color Range command are not ordinary selections, in that they usually contain areas that are not completely selected. For instance, if you're trying to select the red areas in an image and there happens to be a flesh tone in the same image, the fleshy areas will most likely become partially selected. If you then adjust the image, the red will be completely adjusted, and the flesh tones will shift only a little bit.

If a selection is already present when you choose Select > Color Range, the command will analyze the colors only within the selected area. This means you can run the command multiple times to isolate smaller and smaller areas. If you want to have the Color Range command added to the current selection, be sure to hold down the Shift key when choosing Select > Color Range.

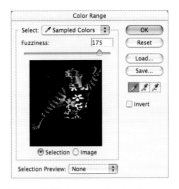

Figure 2.62 An example of a single click with a high Fuzziness setting.

Feather

Unlike the Feather option in the selection tools, this version affects only the selection that's currently active; it has no effect on future selections. You can't reduce the amount of feathering with this command once it's applied. Therefore, if you apply it once with a setting of 10 and then try it again on the same selection using a setting of 5, it will simply increase the amount again. It's just like blurring an image—each time you blur the image, it becomes more and more blurry.

Figure 2.63 An example of five clicks with a low Fuzziness setting.

I prefer using this command instead of entering Feather settings directly into the tool's options bar (where they affect all "new" selections). If you enter these values directly, you might not remember that the setting is turned on days later, when you spend hours trying to select an intricate object. By leaving the tools set at 0, you can quickly press Option-Command-D (Mac) or Alt-Ctrl-D (Windows) to bring up the Feather dialog box and enter a number to feather the selection. Because this affects only the current selection, it can't mess up any future ones (**Figures 2.64** and **2.65**).

Figure 2.64 A coin pasted with a normal selection. (©2003 PhotoSpin, www.photospin.com)

Figure 2.65 A coin copied using a feathered selection and then pasted into this document.

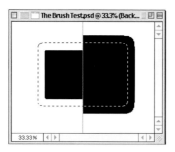

Figure 2.66 The left half of this split image shows where the selection would start to fade out and blend with the underlying image. The right half shows where the selection would stop affecting the image. Notice that the marching ants show up halfway between those two areas.

The problem with the Feather command is that there is no way to tell if a selection is feathered by just looking at the marching ants. Not only that, but most people think the marching ants indicate where the edge of a selection is, and that's simply not the case with a feathered selection. If you take a look at **Figure 2.66**, you'll find that the marching ants actually indicate where a feathered selection is halfway faded out.

Modify

The features in this little menu have helped get me out of many sticky situations. At first glance, it might not be obvious why you would ever use these commands, but I guarantee they'll come in very handy as you continue through the book. Here's a list of the commands found under the Select > Modify menu, as well as descriptions of what they do:

▶ **Border:** Selects a border of pixels centered on the current selection. If you use a setting of 10, the selection will be 5 pixels inside the selection and 5 pixels outside the selection. You can use this to remove pesky halos that appear when you copy an object from a light background and paste it onto a darker background (**Figures 2.67** and **2.68**).

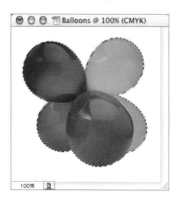

Figure 2.67 The original selection. (©2003 Stockbyte, www.stockbyte.com)

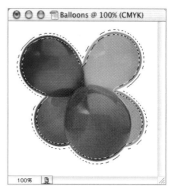

Figure 2.68 A 10-pixel border.

▶ **Smooth:** Attempts to round off any sharp corners in a selection (**Figure 2.69**). This can be especially useful when you want to create a rounded-corner rectangle. It can also produce an interesting effect after you've used the Type Mask tool (**Figures 2.70** and **2.71**).

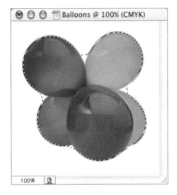

Figure 2.69 Smooth 16 pixels.

Figure 2.70 The original selection.

Figure 2.71 After applying a Smooth setting of 6.

▶ **Expand:** Enlarges the current selection while attempting to maintain its shape (**Figure 2.72**). This command works well with smooth, freeform selections, but it's not my first choice for straight-edged selections because it usually slices off the corners.

▶ **Contract:** Reduces the size of the current selection while attempting to maintain its shape (**Figure 2.73**). The highest setting available is 16. If you need to use a higher setting, just use the command more than once.

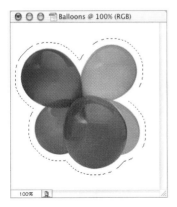

Figure 2.72 Expand 12 pixels.

Figure 2.73 Contract 12 pixels.

Figure 2.74 The original selection. (©2003 PhotoSpin, www.photospin.com)

Figure 2.75 The selection after Select > Grow is used.

Grow

The Select > Grow command will search for colors that are similar to an area that has already been selected (**Figures 2.74** and **2.75**). In effect, it will spread your selection in every direction—but only into areas that are similar in color. It cannot jump across areas that are not similar to the ones selected. The Grow command uses the Tolerance setting that's specified in the Magic Wand options bar to determine the range of colors for which it will look.

Similar

The Select > Similar command works just like the Grow command except that it looks over the entire document for similar colors (**Figures 2.76** and **2.77**). Unlike the Grow command, the colors that Similar selects don't have to touch the previous selection. This can be very useful when you've selected one object out of a group of same-colored objects. For example, if you have a herd of gray elephants standing in front of a lush green jungle, you can select the first elephant and then use Select > Similar to get the rest of the herd (provided, of course, that they're all a similar shade of gray). The same works for a field of flowers, and so on.

Figure 2.76 The original selection.

Figure 2.77 The selection after Select > Similar is used.

Transform Selection

After making a selection, you can scale, rotate, or distort it by choosing Select > Transform Selection. This command places handles around the image. By pulling on the handles and using a series of keyboard commands, you can distort the selection as much as you like. Let's take a look at the neat stuff you can do with Transform Selection:

▶ **Scale:** To scale a selection, pull on any of the handles. Pulling on a corner handle will change both the width and height at the same time. (Hold the Shift key to retain the proportions of the original selection.) Pulling on the side handles will change either the width of the selection or its height, but not both. This can be a great help when working with elliptical selections because it lets you pull on the edges of the selection instead of its so-called corners (**Figures 2.78** and **2.79**).

Figure 2.78 The original selection. (©2003 Stockbyte, www.stockbyte.com)

Figure 2.79 After choosing Select > Transform to scale the selection.

▶ **Rotate:** To rotate the image, move your cursor a little bit beyond one of the corner points; the cursor should change into an arc with arrows on each end. You can control where the center point of the rotation will be by moving the crosshair that appears in the center of the selection (**Figures 2.80** to **2.82**).

▶ **Distort:** To distort the shape of the selection, hold down the Command (Mac) or Ctrl (Windows) key and then drag one of the corner points. Using this technique, you can pull each corner independently (**Figures 2.83** to **2.85**).

Figure 2.80 The original selection. (©2003 Stockbyte, www.stockbyte.com)

Figure 2.81 Rotating and scaling the selection.

Figure 2.82 The end result.

Figure 2.83 The original selection. (©2003 Stockbyte, www.stockbyte.com)

Figure 2.84 Dragging a corner while holding down Command (Mac) or Ctrl (Windows).

Figure 2.85 The selection after all four corners have been dragged.

▶ You can also distort a selection so that it resembles the shape of a road vanishing into the distance. You do this by dragging one of the corners while holding down Shift-Option-Command on the Mac or Shift-Alt-Ctrl in Windows (**Figures 2.86** to **2.88**).

Figure 2.86 The original selection. (©2003 Stockbyte, www.stockbyte.com)

Figure 2.87 Dragging a corner while holding down Shift-Option-Command (Mac) or Shift-Alt-Ctrl (Windows).

Figure 2.88 The end result.

▶ To move two diagonal corners at the same time, hold down Option-Command on the Mac or Alt-Ctrl in Windows while dragging one of the corner handles (**Figures 2.89** and **2.90**).

▶ Finalize your distortions by pressing Enter (or by double-clicking inside the selection). Cancel them by pressing Esc.

NOTES

If you forget the keyboard commands that are required to distort a selection, you can instead choose Select > Transform Selection and then Control-click (Mac) or right-click (Windows) to choose the type of distortion you want to perform (**Figure 2.91**).

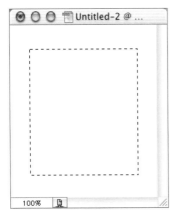

Figure 2.89 The original selection.

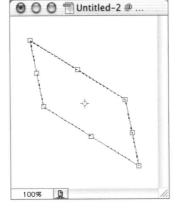

Figure 2.90 Dragging a corner handle while holding down Option-Command (Mac) or Alt-Ctrl (Windows).

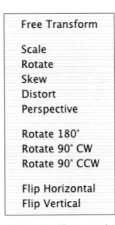

Free Transform

Scale
Rotate
Skew
Distort
Perspective

Rotate 180°
Rotate 90° CW
Rotate 90° CCW

Flip Horizontal
Flip Vertical

Figure 2.91 The menu that appears as a result of Control-clicking (Mac) or right-clicking (Windows) while you're transforming a selection.

Load Selection and Save Selection

If you've spent hours perfecting a selection and think you might need to use it again in the future, you can apply the Select > Save Selection command (**Figure 2.92**). This stores the selection as an alpha channel (you can think of channels as stored selections). Don't worry, you don't need to know anything about channels to use these commands—all you have to do is supply a name for the selection. If you want to find out more about channels, you can check out Chapter 12.

These saved selections remain in your document until you manually remove them using the Channels palette (see Chapter 12 to find out how to delete a channel). They won't be saved on your hard drive until you actually save the entire file. Only the Photoshop (.psd), Photoshop PDF (.pdf), and TIFF (.tif) file formats support multiple saved selections.

When you want to retrieve the saved selection, choose Select > Load Selection and pick the name of the selection from the Channel pop-up menu (**Figure 2.93**). When you use this command, it's just like re-creating the selection with the original selection tool you used, only a whole lot faster.

Figure 2.92 The Save Selection dialog box.

Figure 2.93 The Load Selection dialog box.

Quick Mask Mode

Remember when we were talking about the marching ants and how they can't accurately show you what a feathered selection looks like? Well, Quick Mask mode can show you what a feathered selection really looks like and can also help create basic selections. The quick-mask icon is located directly below the foreground and background colors in your Tools palette (**Figure 2.94**). When the left icon is turned on, you are in Standard mode, which means you create selections using the normal selection tools, and they will show up as the familiar marching ants. The right icon enables Quick Mask mode, and that's where selections will show up as a translucent color overlay.

To see how it works, first make a selection using the Marquee tool, and then turn on Quick Mask mode by clicking on the right icon under the foreground and background colors (or just type **Q** to do the same thing). In Quick Mask mode, the selected area should look normal and all the nonselected areas should be covered with a translucent color (**Figures 2.95** and **2.96**).

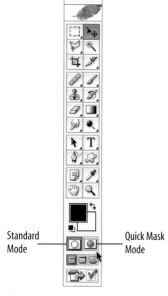

Standard Mode — Quick Mask Mode

Figure 2.94 The quick-mask icons.

Figure 2.95 A selection shown in Standard mode. (©2003 Stockbyte, www.stockbyte.com)

Figure 2.96 The same selection shown in Quick Mask mode.

Now that you're in Quick Mask mode, you no longer need to use selection tools to modify a selection. Instead, you use standard painting tools and paint with black to take away from the selection, or white to add to it. When you're done modifying the selection, switch back to Standard mode and you'll be back to marching ants (**Figures 2.97** and **2.98**).

Figure 2.97 A selection modified in Quick Mask mode.

Figure 2.98 End result after switching back to Standard mode.

Now let's see what feathered selections look like in Quick Mask mode. Make another selection using the Marquee tool. Next, choose Select > Feather with a setting of 10, and then switch to Quick Mask mode and take a look (**Figures 2.99** and **2.100**). Feathered selections appear with blurry edges in Quick Mask mode. This happens because partially transparent areas (that is, ones that are more transparent than the rest of the mask) indicate areas that are partially selected (50% transparent means 50% selected).

The confusing part about this process is that when you look at the marching ants that appear after you switch back to Standard mode, they only show you where the selection is at least 50% selected. That isn't a very accurate picture of what it really looks like (**Figure 2.101**). But in Quick Mask mode, you can see exactly what is happening on the image's edge. So, if you want to create a feathered selection in Quick Mask mode, just choose a soft-edged brush to paint with. Or, if you already have a shape defined, choose Filter > Blur > Gaussian Blur, which will give you the same result of feathering but will show you a visual preview of the edge.

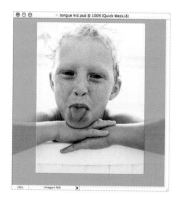

Figure 2.99 Normal. (©2003 Stockbyte www.stockbyte.com)

Figure 2.100 Feathered.

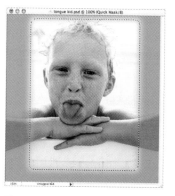

Figure 2.101 The marching ants show up where an area is at least 50% selected.

Shades of Gray

Try this out. Turn on Quick Mask mode—you don't need a selection to begin with. Type **D** to reset the foreground color to black, and then Option-Delete (Mac) or Alt-Backspace (Windows) to fill the Quick Mask. Now paint within the Quick Mask with 20% gray (you can use the Color Picker palette to choose grays). Then turn off Quick Mask mode and paint in the selected area with bright red. Now choose Select > Deselect, lower the opacity of the painting tool to 80%, and paint with bright red. Your reds should look exactly the same. That's how Photoshop makes a selection fade out—by simply lowering the opacity of the tool you are using. This can sometimes be confusing, though, because the marching ants show up only where an image is at least 50% selected. So, try this one on for size. Turn on Quick Mask mode and paint with 49% gray, and then paint in another area with 51% gray. Then go back to Standard mode and paint across the area. Only the areas that are at least 50% gray show up as marching ants, but the other areas are still selected, even though the marching ants don't show up in those areas (**Figure 2.102**). Now turn on Quick Mask mode, reset the foreground color by typing **D**, type Option-Delete (Mac) or Alt-Backspace (Windows) to fill the Quick Mask, and then paint with 55% gray. Now go back to Standard mode, and you'll get a warning message (**Figure 2.103**).

We really haven't done anything fancy yet, so let's try something fun. To start with, you have to remember that when you work in Quick Mask mode, Photoshop treats the selection as if it is a grayscale image that you can paint on. That means you can use any tool that is available when working on grayscale images. So select an area using the Marquee tool, turn on Quick Mask mode, choose Filter > Distort > Ripple, and mess with the settings until you've created something that looks a little kooky (**Figure 2.104**). Finally, go back to Standard mode and see what you've got. You can create infinite varieties of fascinating selections with this simple technique.

You can also convert a logo or sketch into a selection using Quick Mask mode. All you need to do is copy the image, turn on Quick Mask mode, choose Edit > Paste, and then choose Image > Adjustments > Invert (**Figure 2.105**). If the logo was in color, then you might end up with shades of gray (which will look like shades of red in Quick Mask mode). In that case, you'll need to choose Image > Adjustments > Levels and pull in the upper-right and upper-left sliders until the image is pure black and pure white. Once everything looks right, turn off Quick Mask mode and you'll have your selection.

Figure 2.102 When painting in Quick Mask mode, only the areas that contain less than 50% gray will be visible when the selection is viewed as marching ants.

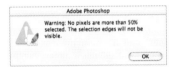

Figure 2.103 When you paint with shades brighter than 50% gray, a warning will appear when you go back to Standard mode.

Figure 2.104 Applying the Ripple filter in Quick Mask mode. (©2003 Stockbyte, www.stockbyte.com)

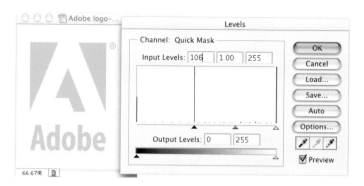

Figure 2.105 Adjusting a logo using the Levels dialog box.

Now let's figure out how to "unfeather" a selection using Quick Mask mode (**Figure 2.106**). Remember, a feathered edge looks like a blurry edge in Quick Mask mode. All you have to do to remove that blurry look is to then choose Image > Adjustments > Threshold. This will give the mask a very crisp, and therefore unfeathered, edge.

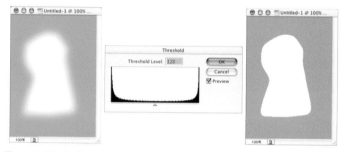

Figure 2.106 Unfeathering a selection using Threshold. Left: Original image. Center: Threshold setting used. Right: Result of applying Threshold.

Selections in Quick Mask Mode

You can even use a selection to isolate a particular area of the Quick Mask (**Figure 2.107**). A selection in Quick Mask mode can help you create a selection that is only feathered on one side. To accomplish this, turn on Quick Mask mode, type **D** to reset the foreground color, and then type Option-Delete (Mac) or Alt-Backspace (Windows) to fill the Quick Mask. Next, choose the Marquee tool and select an area. Now use the Gradient tool set to Black, White (the third choice from the left in the gradient presets drop-down menu) and create a gradient within the selected area. Once you're done, switch off Quick Mask mode. Now, to see exactly how this selection will affect the image, choose Image > Adjustments > Levels and attempt to lighten that area by dragging the lower-left slider.

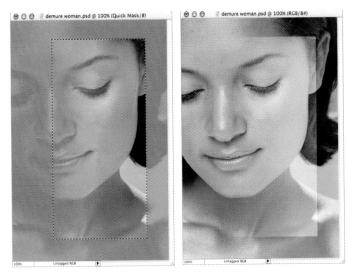

Figure 2.107 Using a selection in Quick Mask mode to restrict which areas can be edited. (Original image ©2003 Stockbye, www.stockbyte.com)

Color

Photoshop also allows you to switch where the color shows up. You can specify whether you want the selected or unselected areas to show up. To change this setting, double-click on the quick-mask icon and change the Color Indicates setting (**Figures 2.108** and **2.109**). Photoshop uses the term *Masked Areas* to describe areas that are not selected.

You can change the color that is overlaid on your image by clicking the color swatch in the Quick Mask Options dialog box. The Opacity setting determines how much you will be able to see through the Quick Mask.

Figure 2.108 Changing the Color Indicates setting changes where the color overlay appears.

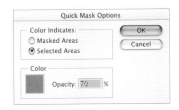

Figure 2.109 Quick Mask Options settings used.

Closing Thoughts

After a few practice rounds with the various tools we covered in this chapter, you should be selecting like a pro. We'll go over more advanced methods of creating selections in Chapter 13, "Advanced Masking." Until then, it really is worth your while to build up your selection skills because you will be using them every day in Photoshop. And now it's time for another dose of Ben's Techno-babble Decoder Ring.

Ben's Techno-Babble Decoder Ring

Big data: Any area of a layer that extends outside the physical dimensions of the document.

Cropping: The process of reducing the dimensions of an image by removing unneeded space from the edge of the document. Also used to remove big data.

Feather: The process of converting a hard-edged selection into one that blends into the underlying image as you move closer to its edge.

Marching ants: Term used to describe the edge of a selection. Used because the edges appear as very small moving specks (similar to ants).

Marquee: Like the rectangular marquees (signs) used at movie theaters to display the movies that are currently showing. In Photoshop, the Marquee tool is used to create rectangular (or elliptical) selections, and the resulting marching ants even resemble the flashing lights that used to be found surrounding movie marquees.

Keyboard Shortcuts

Function	Macintosh	Windows
Select All	Command-A	Ctrl-A
Deselect	Command-D	Ctrl-D
Reselect	Shift-Command-D	Shift-Ctrl-D
Select Inverse	Shift-Command-I	Shift-Ctrl-I
Feather	Option-Command-D	Alt-Ctrl-D
Marquee tool	M	M
Lasso tool	L	L
Magic Wand tool	W	W
Fill selection	Shift-Delete	Shift-Backspace
Fill with Foreground	Option-Delete	Alt-Backspace
Fill with Background	Command-Delete	Ctrl-Backspace

Courtesy of Tom Nick Cocotos, www.cocotos.com

Courtesy of Tom Nick Cocotos, www.cocotos.com

3

Layers Primer

Courtesy of Michael Slack, www.slackart.com

The first rule to tinkering is to save all the parts.

— Paul Ehrlich

Layers Primer

Our capacity to take things for granted seems to have no bounds. How often do you sit back and think, "Wow, life has really changed since the days when Smith Corona ruled and an Apple was just something you ate for lunch"? Probably seldom. However, if you think about it, you'll realize that colossal changes have taken place. We attained a unique kind of digital freedom when we evolved from the primordial ooze of manual typewriters, stat cameras, and typesetters. For graphic artists, this change has been nothing short of revolutionary.

In its own way, Photoshop's introduction of the Layers palette has had an equally profound impact on the graphic arts community. Before the Layers palette, we were forced to be very precise and final in our thoughts, because having to redo the work was incredibly time-consuming. The Layers palette released us from the shackles of single-layer images and gave us the chance to really let loose and explore our creative ideas.

How Do Layers Work?

At first glance, layers might seem complex, but the idea behind them is rather simple. You isolate different parts of your image onto independent layers (**Figure 3.1**). These layers act as if they are separate documents stacked one on top of the other. By putting each image on its own layer, you can freely change your document's look and layout without committing to the changes. If you paint, apply a filter, or make an adjustment, it affects only the layer on which you're working. If you get into a snarl over a particularly troublesome layer, you can throw it away and start over. The rest of your document will remain untouched.

Figure 3.1 Layers isolate different parts of the image. (©2003 Regina Cleveland)

You can make the layers relate to each other in interesting ways, such as by poking holes in them to reveal an underlying image. I'll show you some great techniques using this concept in Chapter 17, "Enhancement."

But first, you need to pick up on the basics—the foundations—of layers. If you've used layers for a while, you might find some of this chapter a bit too basic. On the other hand, you might find some juicy new tidbits.

Meeting the Layers

Before we jump in and start creating a bunch of layers, you should get familiar with their place of residence: the Layers palette (**Figure 3.2**). You're going to be spending a lot of time with this palette, so take a moment now to get on friendly terms with it. It's not terribly complicated, and after you've used it a few times, you should know it like the back of your hand.

As you make your way through this chapter, you'll learn about the Layers palette and the fundamental tasks associated with it. Also, I'll throw in a few layer styles just for the heck of it. Now, assuming that you've done your part and introduced yourself to the Layers palette, let's get on with the business of creating and manipulating layers in Photoshop.

Creating Layers

Photoshop will automatically create the majority of the layers you'll need. A new layer is added anytime you copy and paste an image or drag a layer between documents (we'll talk about this later in the chapter). If you're starting from scratch, however, you can click the New-Layer icon at the bottom of the Layers palette to create a new, empty layer.

If you hold the Command key (Mac) or Ctrl key (Windows) when clicking the New-Layer icon, the new layer will appear below the active layer instead of on top of it. The only time that won't work is when the background is active…. Photoshop can't add a new layer below the background.

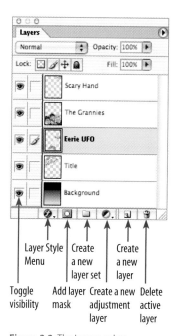

Figure 3.2 The Layers palette.

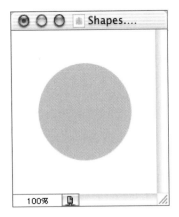

Figure 3.3 A new layer.

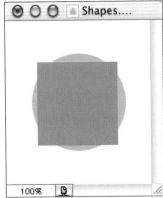

Figure 3.4 The second layer.

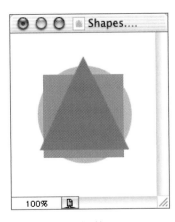

Figure 3.5 The third layer.

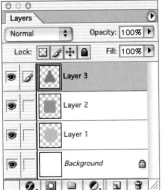

Figure 3.6 The Layers palette view.

Give it a try: Create a new document, and then use the Layers palette to create a new layer. Pick a bright color to paint with and then use one of the shape tools (using the rightmost setting of the three available in the upper left of the options bar) to draw a big circle (**Figure 3.3**). Now create another layer, and draw a square on it, using a different color (**Figure 3.4**). Finally, create a third layer, and draw a triangle on it (**Figure 3.5**). You can use this simple document you've just created to try out the concepts in the following sections that describe the features of the Layers palette (**Figure 3.6**).

Active Layer

You can edit only one layer at a time. Remember, Photoshop thinks of the layers as if they were separate documents. The layer you're currently working on is highlighted in the Layers palette. You should also see a little paintbrush icon next to it—that's just another indication that the layer is active for editing. To change the active layer, just click the name of another layer. Only one layer can be active at a time.

To quickly change which layer is active, Command-click (Mac) or Ctrl-click (Windows) on your image while the Move tool is active. That will cause the topmost layer that contains information under your cursor to become active. If you use this shortcut, be aware that you are just temporarily toggling the Auto Select Layers check box in the options bar. I prefer to leave that check box turned off; otherwise, every time I click with the Move tool a different layer might become active. I'd much rather just hold Command or Ctrl and click those times when I need to switch which layer is active.

Stacking Order

You can change the stacking order of the layers by dragging the name of one layer above or below the name of another layer in the Layers palette. The topmost layers can often obstruct your view of the underlying images. You can change this by reordering the layers by dragging them up or down in the Layers palette so that small images are near the top of the stack and the larger ones are near the bottom (**Figures 3.7** to **3.10**).

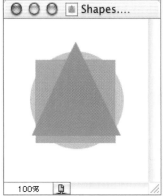

Figure 3.7 The original image.

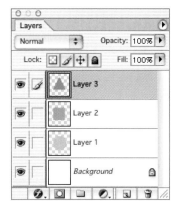

Figure 3.8 The original Layers palette.

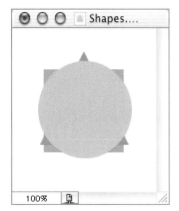

Figure 3.9 The changed stacking order.

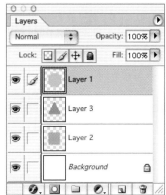

Figure 3.10 The revised Layers palette.

To quickly turn off all the eyeballs in the Layers palette and view only the layer you're interested in, simply Option-click (Mac) or Alt-click (Windows) one of the Eyeball icons. Option- or Alt-clicking a second time will bring those same layers back into view. If you'd rather make all the layers visible, then Control-click (Mac) or right-click (Windows) on the Eyeball icon and choose Show/Hide All Other Layers.

Background Image

Photoshop will not permit you to drag a layer below the background, because it doesn't think of the background as a layer. If you liken the layers to the individual pages in a pad of tracing paper, you could think of the pad's cardboard backing as the background layer. The background is always opaque and cannot be moved. In some circumstances, though, you might want to delete the background. For example, when you output images to videotape, they can't be overlaid onto video if the background layer is present.

However, most of the time, keeping the background or not is just a personal preference. You don't have to have a background in your document. If you want to convert the background into a normal layer, just change its name (the background image must be named "Background"; otherwise, it becomes a normal layer). To change the name of a layer, double-click the layer's name in the Layers palette and then type a new name.

The Eyeballs: What They See Is What You Get

The eyeballs in the Layers palette aren't just cute; they determine which layers will be visible in your document as well as which ones will print. The eyeballs turn on and off in a toggle effect when you click them: Now you see them, now you don't.

You can change the checkerboard's appearance by choosing Edit > Preferences > Transparency & Gamut. You can even change it to solid white by changing the Grid Size setting to None.

If you turn off all the eyeballs in the Layers palette, Photoshop will fill your screen with a checkerboard. This checkerboard indicates that there's nothing visible in the document. (If Photoshop filled your screen with white instead, you might assume that there was a layer visible that was filled with white.) You can think of the checkerboard as the areas of the document that are transparent. When you view a single layer, the checkerboard indicates the transparent areas of that layer. As you turn on the other layers in the document, the checkerboard is replaced with the information contained on those layers. When multiple layers are visible, the checkerboard indicates where the underlying image will not be obstructed by the elements on the visible layers (**Figures 3.11** to **3.14**).

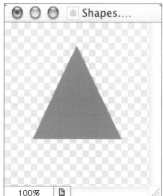

Figure 3.11 The checkerboard indicates a transparent area.

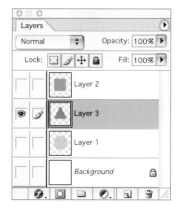

Figure 3.12 The Layers palette view.

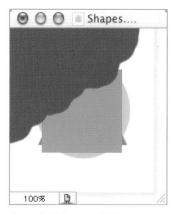

Figure 3.13 As more layers become visible, the transparent areas become smaller.

Opacity

The Opacity setting at the top of the Layers palette controls the opacity of the active layer. When this setting is lowered, the entire layer becomes partially transparent (transparent is the exact opposite of opaque). If you want to lower the opacity in a specific area instead of the entire layer, you can lower the opacity of the Eraser tool and then brush across the area of the layer you want to become more transparent—that is, unless the background is active. If you use the Eraser tool on the background, it will simply paint with your background color instead of truly deleting areas (remember, the background is always opaque).

Try this: Open the document you created earlier in this chapter. Create a new layer, and then use any painting tool to brush across the layer. Now, lower the Opacity setting in the Layers palette to 70% (**Figures 3.15** to **3.17**).

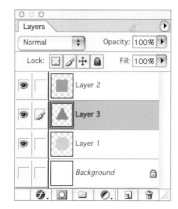

Figure 3.14 The Layers palette view.

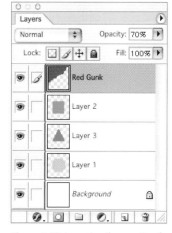

Figure 3.17 Lowering the opacity of a layer affects the entire layer.

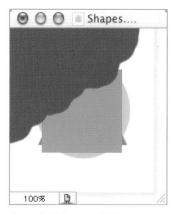

Figure 3.15 Layer at 100% opacity.

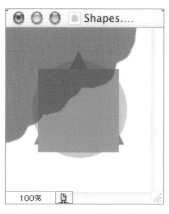

Figure 3.16 Layer at 70% opacity.

To quickly change the opacity of a layer, switch to the Move tool (typing V will switch you to the Move tool), and then use the number keys on your keyboard (1 = 10%, 3 = 30%, 56 = 56%, and so on).

You can figure out the exact opacity of an area by Option-clicking (Mac) or Alt-clicking (Windows) a layer's Eyeball icon and then opening the Info palette. Click the eyedropper in the Info palette, and choose Opacity; you'll get a separate readout that indicates how opaque the area is below your cursor.

Now let's compare this effect with what happens when you lower the Opacity setting of the Paintbrush tool. Create another new layer; however, this time leave the layer's Opacity setting at 100%. Now choose the Paintbrush tool, change the tool's Opacity setting to 70% (in the options bar), and then brush across the layer (just don't overlap the paint you created earlier). The paint should look exactly the same as the paint that appears in the other layer (**Figures 3.18** and **3.19**).

Figure 3.18 The Paintbrush options view.

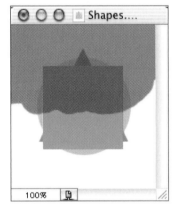

Figure 3.19 Painting with a 70% Opacity setting.

Finally, create one more new layer, and paint across it with the tool's Opacity setting at 100%. Now, brush across an area with the Eraser tool using an Opacity setting of 30% (**Figures 3.20** and **3.21**).

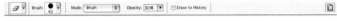

Figure 3.20 The Eraser options view.

You'll be using the Move tool a lot. Because of this, Adobe has provided a quick way to temporarily switch to the Move tool: Just hold down Command (Mac) or Ctrl (Windows). As long as that key is held down, you're using the Move tool (even though it isn't highlighted in the Tools palette).

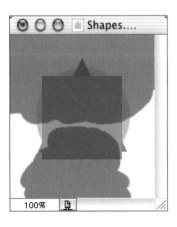

Figure 3.21 Using the Eraser tool with a low Opacity setting will also make areas of a layer transparent.

All of these options do the same thing to your image. You just have to think a bit: Do you want to apply the Opacity setting to the entire layer? If so, use the Layers palette's Opacity setting. Do you want to apply the Opacity setting to only part of the layer? If so, use the Opacity setting in the tool's options bar. Do you want to change the opacity of an area you've already painted across? If so, use the Eraser tool with an Opacity setting.

Photoshop always (well, almost always) offers you more than one way of doing things. It reminds me of my favorite hardware store, McGuckins. It's the kind of place that takes your breath away—it has everything! If you just want a screwdriver, you'll probably find an entire aisle full of screwdrivers, each one designed for a specific use. Photoshop has the same approach; you just have to play around with it to figure out which tool best suits your needs.

Moving Layers

If you want to move everything that's on a particular layer, first make that layer active by clicking its name; then use the Move tool to drag it around the screen (**Figure 3.22**). If you drag the layer onto another document window, Photoshop will copy the layer into that document. If you want to move just a small area of the layer, you can make a selection and then drag from within the selected area using the Move tool.

You can also use the arrow keys on your keyboard (when the Move tool is active) to nudge a layer one pixel at a time. Holding Shift while using the arrow keys will nudge the active layer 10 pixels at a time.

Trimming the Fat

If you use the Move tool to reposition a layer, and a portion of the layer starts to extend beyond the edge of your document, Photoshop will remember the information beyond the edge (**Figure 3.23**). Therefore, if you move the layer away from the edge, Photoshop is able to bring back the information that was not visible. You can save a lot of memory by getting Photoshop to clip off all the information

NOTES

If you've made a portion of a layer partially transparent with the Eraser or Paint tool set to a low opacity, you can attempt to bring a layer back to 100% opacity by duplicating it multiple times. Keep in mind that it might take quite a few duplicates to get the layer back to full opacity. Once the image is completely opaque, just merge all the duplicate layers together. I'll show you how to merge layers later in this chapter.

When I need to precisely position a layer, I usually lower the Opacity setting just enough so I can see the underlying layers. You can do this quickly by using the number keys on your keyboard (0 to 9) when using the Move tool. After positioning the layer, just press 0 to bring the layer back to 100% opacity.

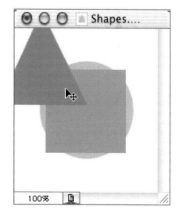

Figure 3.22 Using the Move tool to reposition a layer.

Use the "trim the fat" technique only if you're absolutely sure you won't need the information beyond the edge of the document, because you cannot get it back once you've cropped it (that is, without resorting to the History palette).

The default setting in the Crop tool is to delete the areas that extend beyond the edge of your image. You can prevent it from deleting those areas by clicking the Hide setting in the Crop tool options bar (it will be available only in files that contain layers). That will cause Photoshop to reduce the size of the image based on the cropping rectangle you specify, but it will retain the information that extends beyond the edge of the image. This setting can be useful when you're creating an animation in Adobe ImageReady and you'd like an object to start off-screen.

beyond the edge of the document (**Figure 3.24**). Here's a little trick for trimming off that fat. Just choose Select > All and then choose Image > Crop—no more wasted memory.

Figure 3.23 The original image. (multiple images ©2003 PhotoSpin, www.photospin.com)

Figure 3.24 After the image is cropped.

It also wastes memory when you leave extra white space around the edge of your image (**Figure 3.25**). Because the paper you print on is white to begin with, that extra white space just makes your file size larger, and has no effect on how the image will look when it's printed. You can choose Image > Trim to have Photoshop remove any unnecessary white space (**Figure 3.26**). Just adjust the Based On setting so that it will find white information in your image (depending on which corner of your image contains white), and then specify which edge of the document you'd like to trim away—I usually leave all four of the Trim Away check boxes turned on (**Figure 3.27**).

Figure 3.25 The white space around this image wastes space on your hard drive.

Figure 3.26 After applying the Trim command, the extra white space is gone.

Figure 3.27 The Trim settings used on Figure 3.25.

So far we've talked about how to make your images smaller to save memory and hard drive space, but now let's do the opposite with Photoshop's Image > Reveal All command. When you choose that command, Photoshop will enlarge your document to include any information that extends beyond the bounds of your document (**Figures 3.28** and **3.29**). That means that all the layers that you've moved beyond the edge of your document will become visible once again.

Copying Between Documents

When you use the Move tool, you can do more than just drag a layer around the document on which you're working. You can also drag a layer on top of another document (**Figure 3.30**). This copies the entire layer into the second document. The copied layer will be positioned directly above the active layer. This is similar to copying and pasting, but it takes up a lot less memory because Photoshop doesn't store the image on the clipboard. You can achieve the same result by dragging the name of a layer from the Layers palette onto another document window.

Figure 3.28 Many of the layers in this document extend beyond the document's bounds.

Figure 3.29 After applying the Reveal All command, the elements that used to extend beyond the document's bounds are now completely visible.

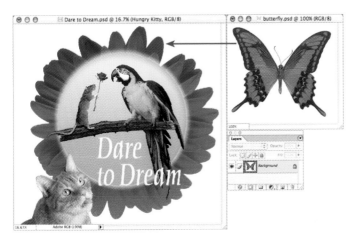

Figure 3.30 To copy between documents, use the Move tool to drag from the image window, or drag the name of the layer in the Layers palette.

NOTES

When dragging between documents, Photoshop will position the layer based on where your cursor was when you clicked the image and where you released the mouse button in the second document. To center the image, hold down the Shift key when dragging to another document.

When you drag layers between documents, occasionally an image will appear as if it has not only been copied, but also scaled at the same time. That's not what's really happening. Instead, you're viewing the two images at different magnifications (**Figure 3.31**). Look at the tops of the documents; if the percentages do not match, the image size will appear to change when you drag the image between the documents. If you view both images with the same magnification, this won't happen. It doesn't change how large the image is; it simply gives you a preview of how large it will look. It's just like putting your hand under a magnifying glass: Your hand looks larger, but when you pull your hand out, it looks normal again.

Figure 3.31 Images viewed at different magnifications.

Duplicating Layers

If you have a picture of Elvis, and you want to make Elvis twins, just drag the name of the layer onto the New-Layer icon at the bottom of the Layers palette. This icon has two purposes: It will duplicate a layer if you drag one on top of it, or it will create a new empty layer if you just click it. You can also type Command-J (Mac) or Ctrl-J (Windows) to duplicate the currently active layer. Just make sure you don't have a selection active; otherwise, this command will copy only the area that is selected instead of the whole layer.

Deleting Layers

If you've created a document that looks a little cluttered, you can delete a layer by dragging its name onto the Trash icon at the bottom of the Layers palette. Or, if you have a long distance to drag to get your layer in the trash, try Option-clicking (Mac) or Alt-clicking (Windows) the Trash icon instead (the Option or Alt key prevents a warning dialog box from appearing). However, this icon does not work like the trash on a Mac or the recycle bin in Windows. Once you put something in it, you can't get it back (that is, without resorting to the History palette).

Leapin' Layers! More Tools and Toys

Photoshop packs a large array of layer-manipulation controls. These controls allow you to go way beyond just creating, duplicating, and deleting layers. You'll be able to distort, adjust, and add wild effects after you wade through all these options.

Transforming Layers

To rotate, scale, or distort a layer, choose one of the options in the Edit > Transform menu; then pull the handles to distort the image. This will distort the current layer as well as any layers linked to it (**Figures 3.32** and **3.33**). When you like the way your image looks, press the Enter key to commit to the change (press Esc to abort). If you want to know more about the transformation controls, see Chapter 2, "Selection Primer."

Linking Layers

If you need to move or transform more than one layer at a time, just click to the left of one of the preview thumbnails in the Layers palette. When you do, a link (chain) symbol will appear (**Figure 3.34**). This indicates that the active layer is now linked to all the layers that have the link symbol next to them. When you use the Move tool or choose Edit > Transform, the current layer and all the layers linked to it will change. This feature doesn't allow you to do anything other than move or transform layers (for example, you can't apply a filter to multiple layers).

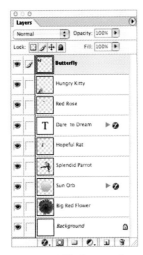

Figure 3.32 The Layers palette view.

Figure 3.33 Transforming a layer.

Figure 3.34 The Chain icon indicates linked layers.

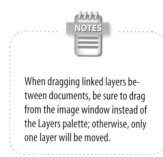

When dragging linked layers between documents, be sure to drag from the image window instead of the Layers palette; otherwise, only one layer will be moved.

If you hold Shift-Command (Mac), or Shift-Ctrl (Windows) and click on your image when the Move tool is active, you'll link the layer that appears under your cursor to the currently active layer.

To quickly unlink a bunch of layers, hold the Option key (Mac) or Alt key (Windows) and click the Paintbrush icon that appears to the left of the currently active layer.

When layers are linked, you can choose one of the options from the Layer > Align Linked menu or the Move tool options bar to change their position relative to each other. For example, you can align the top edges of the linked layers, or you can center them horizontally.

Locking Up

The icons at the top of the Layers palette allow you to lock the transparency, image, and position of an individual layer (**Figure 3.35**). Once a layer has been locked, changes that can be performed on that layer are limited.

Figure 3.35 The Lock icons.

Lock Transparency

The Lock Transparency icon (which looks like a checkerboard) at the top of the Layers palette gets in my way most often (because I forget it's turned on). Lock Transparency prevents you from changing the transparency of areas. Each layer has its own Lock Transparency setting. Therefore, if you turn on the Lock Transparency icon for one layer and then switch to another layer, the Layers palette will display the setting for the second layer, which might be different from the first one.

Try using the Eraser tool when Lock Transparency is turned on—it will mess with your mind! Because the Eraser tool usually makes areas transparent (by completely deleting them), it will start painting instead when Lock Transparency is turned on. It will fill with the current background color any areas you drag over. However, if you paint across an area that's transparent, it doesn't change the image at all (because the transparent areas are being preserved). You can see how it can get in your way if you forget you turned it on.

Try this: Open a photo, and delete areas around it using the Eraser tool. To accomplish this, you'll have to change the name of the background first (you can't poke a hole in the background, but you can on a layer); then make sure Lock Transparency is turned off. Otherwise, you can't make areas transparent. Now use the Eraser tool to remove the areas that surround the subject of the photo, and then choose Filter > Blur > Gaussian Blur and use a really high setting. You'll notice that the edge of the image fades out and blends with the transparent areas surrounding it (**Figure 3.36**). Now, choose Edit > Undo and try doing the same thing with the Lock Transparency option turned on (**Figure 3.37**). Notice that the edge cannot fade out because Photoshop will not change the transparency with this option turned on.

Figure 3.36 Lock Transparency is off.

Here is another example: Create a new layer, and scribble across it with any painting tool, making sure the Lock Transparency option is turned off. Next, drag across the image with the Gradient tool. The gradient should fill the entire screen (**Figure 3.38**). Now, choose Edit > Undo, and try doing the same thing with the Lock Transparency option turned on (**Figure 3.39**). Because Photoshop can't change the transparency of the layer, it cannot fill the transparent areas, and therefore is limited to changing the areas that are opaque to begin with.

Figure 3.37 Lock Transparency is on.

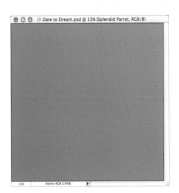

Figure 3.38 Lock Transparency is off.

Figure 3.39 Lock Transparency is on.

NOTES

The Lock Image icon might prevent you from directly modifying the pixels that make up a layer, but it does not completely prevent you from changing the appearance of that layer. You can still add an adjustment layer directly above the layer in question to change its general appearance.

When you're trying to use any of the techniques in this book, be sure to keep an eye on that little Lock Transparency icon. If it's turned on when you don't want it to be, it might ruin the entire effect you're trying to achieve. Therefore, unless I specifically tell you to turn it on, you should assume that it should be left off (that's the default setting). If I ever tell you to turn it on, I'll let you know when to turn it back off again so that you don't get messed up when trying to reproduce a technique from this book. Now, turn off that pesky (but useful) setting, and let's continue exploring Photoshop.

Lock Image

The Lock Image icon (which looks like a paintbrush) at the top of the Layers palette prevents you from changing the pixels that make up a layer. That means you won't be able to paint, erase, apply an adjustment or filter, or do anything else that would change the look of that layer (although you can still move or transform the layer). Just as with Lock Transparency, each layer has its own Lock Image setting. I use this feature after I've finished color-correcting and retouching a layer so I don't accidentally change it later on.

Lock Position

The Lock Position icon (which looks like the Move tool) at the top of the Layers palette prevents you from moving the active layer. I select this feature to prevent someone else from accidentally moving an element that I've taken great care to position correctly.

You can press the forward slash key "/" at any time to toggle the last lock you changed on or off.

Lock All

The Lock All icon (which looks like a padlock) at the top of the Layers palette locks the transparency, image, and position of the current layer.

Layer Styles

A bunch of really neat options are available under the Layer > Layer Style menu (**Figure 3.40**). You'll find the same options under the Layer Style pop-up menu at the bottom of the Layers palette (it's the leftmost icon). To experiment with these options, first create a new, empty layer, and paint on it with any of the painting tools. Then apply one of the effects found in the Layer > Layer Style menu: Drop Shadow, Inner Shadow, Inner Glow, Outer Glow, Bevel and Emboss, and so on (**Figures 3.41** to **3.43**). You can use the default settings for now. After applying an effect, use the Eraser tool to remove some of the paint on that layer. Did you notice that the layer effect updates to reflect the changes you make to the layer? Layer Styles create in one simple step the same results that would usually require multiple layers and a lot of memory.

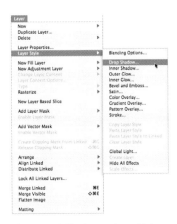

Figure 3.40 The Layer > Layer Style menu.

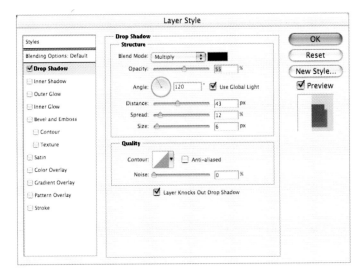

Figure 3.41 The Layer Style dialog box with the Drop Shadow panel.

Figure 3.42 The original image.

Figure 3.43 Drop Shadow style was applied to the text layer.

119

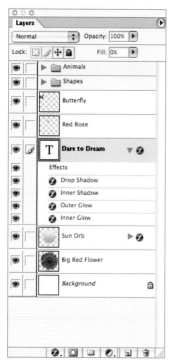

Figure 3.44 Click on the triangle that appears next to the "f" symbol to see a list of the Layer Styles that are applied to that layer.

Once you have at least one Layer Style applied to a layer, you'll see a black circle with a small "f" inside it in the Layers palette. That's the only indication that a layer has a Layer Style attached to it. You can click on the triangle that appears next to that symbol to see a list of the Layer Styles that are applied to that layer (**Figure 3.44**). If you drag one of the Layer Styles from that list and release your mouse button when it's just below another layer, you'll copy that Layer Style to the layer directly below. Dragging the word "Effects" will copy all of the Layer Styles that are attached to that layer. If you'd like to remove one of the Layer Styles, just click on its name in the list and drag it to the Trash icon at the bottom of the Layers palette.

You can even lower the Fill setting at the top of Photoshop's Layers palette to reduce the opacity of the layer contents (or hold Shift and type a number while the Move tool is active) while keeping the Layer Style at full strength (**Figure 3.45**). Not only that, you can choose Layer > Layer Style > Create Layer to have Photoshop create the layers that would usually be needed to create the effect. For example, you might want to choose Create Layer when you're going to give your file to someone who is using an older version of Photoshop. Let's take a look at what different layer styles do to your image (**Figures 3.46** to **3.49**).

Figure 3.45 A result of lowering the Fill opacity to 0.

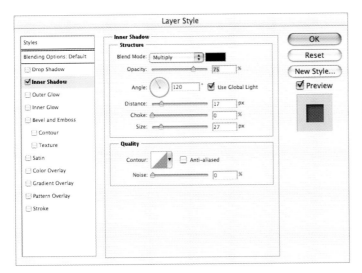

Figure 3.46 The Layer Style dialog box with the Inner Shadow panel.

Figure 3.47 Inner Shadow style is applied to the text layer.

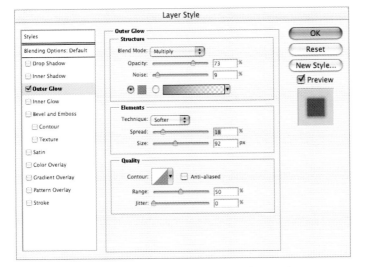

Figure 3.48 The Layer Style dialog box with the Outer Glow panel.

Figure 3.49 Outer Glow style is applied to the text layer.

Adjustment Layers

When you choose an option available in the Image > Adjustments menu, it affects only the layer that's currently active. (Remember, Photoshop treats each layer as if it were a separate document.) However, there's a special type of layer that will allow you to apply these adjustments to multiple layers. This is known as an adjustment layer.

To create an adjustment layer, choose Layer > New Adjustment Layer, or choose the type of adjustment you'd like from the Adjustment Layer pop-up menu at the bottom of the Layers palette (it looks like a circle filled with half black and half white). After you choose which type of adjustment you want to use (I'll discuss most of the adjustment settings in Part II of this book, "Production Essentials"), the changes will modify all the layers that are underneath the adjustment layer. You can move the adjustment layer up or down in the layers stack to affect more or fewer layers.

These changes are not permanent; at any time you can simply turn off the Eyeball icon on the adjustment layer and the image will return to normal. You can also lessen the effect of the adjustment layer by lowering its Opacity setting. To change the adjustment settings, simply double-click the Adjustment Layer icon on the left side of the adjustment layer (**Figures 3.50** to **3.54**).

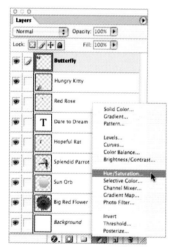

Figure 3.50 The Adjustment Layer pop-up menu.

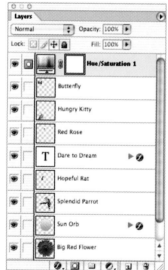

Figure 3.51 The Hue/Saturation adjustment layer at the top of the Layers palette.

Figure 3.52 Hue/Saturation affects all layers.

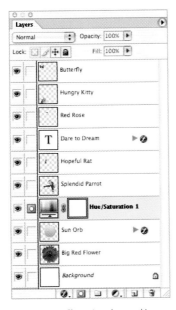

Figure 3.53 Changing the stacking order of the Hue/Saturation adjustment layer.

Figure 3.54 The adjustment layer applies to all layers below it but not to the layers above it.

Applying Photo Filter Adjustments

Now that you have an idea of how adjustment layers work, let's experiment with one special type of adjustment so you can get started applying adjustment layers to your images. Photoshop CS contains a new type of adjustment known as a Photo Filter. A Photo Filter adjustment layer will allow you to quickly shift the overall color in your image. It has an effect that is much like placing a colored filter in front of a camera lens or putting on colored sunglasses. All you have to do is open an image and choose Photo Filter from the Adjustment Layer pop-up menu at the bottom of the Layers palette. When the Photo Filter dialog box appears (**Figure 3.55**), either choose a preset color from the Filter pop-up menu or click on the color swatch to choose your own custom color. Once you've chosen the color you desire, adjust the Density slider to control how radically the filter will affect the image (**Figures 3.56** to **3.58**). If you find that your image is getting very dark as you increase the Density setting, then I bet the Preserve Luminosity check box is turned off. When that check box is turned

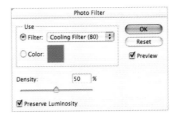

Figure 3.55 The Photo Filter dialog box.

off, adding a Photo Filter adjustment will darken your image, just as colored sunglasses allow less light to enter your eye. Turning on the Preserve Luminosity check box will prevent Photoshop from changing the brightness of your image, but will still allow you to shift its colors. I leave the Preserve Luminosity check box on for the vast majority of images that I adjust. I'd much rather make a separate adjustment layer (Levels, Curves, or any other type) if I want to change the brightness of the image.

Figure 3.56 The original image. (©2003 Ben Willmore)

Figure 3.57 Result of applying a blue Photo Filter with a Density of 20%.

Figure 3.58 Result of applying a blue Photo Filter with a Density of 50%.

Figure 3.59 This image was taken at sunrise, and therefore has a strong orange colorcast. (©2003 Ben Willmore)

You'll learn a lot more about manipulating the colors in your images when you get to Chapter 11, "Color Manipulation," but before you get to that point, let me clue you in on a basic concept of color manipulation. When you use a Photo Filter layer, you'll be pushing all the colors in your image toward one side of the color wheel. If your image has an obvious colorcast, then all of the colors within the image will be shifted to one side of the color wheel (**Figures 3.59** and **3.60**). When that's the case, you can often remove the colorcast by applying a Photo Filter that uses the color that's found directly across the color wheel from the color that is contaminating your image (blue in this case) (**Figures 3.61** and **3.62**).

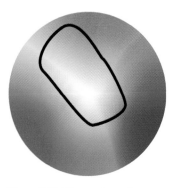

Figure 3.60 When an image has an orange colorcast, all of the colors within the image will be shifted toward the orange side of the color wheel.

Fill Layers

The options in the Layer > New Fill Layer menu allow you to add solid color, gradient, and pattern content to a layer. This is especially useful when combined with Vector Mask, as described in Chapter 16, "Collage." If you don't want a fill layer to fill your entire document, then make a selection before creating one, which will create a layer mask. After a fill layer has been created, you can reset your foreground and background colors to black/white by pressing D. Then you can use the Eraser tool to hide the area and the Paintbrush tool to make areas visible again.

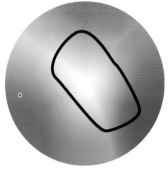

When using a Layer Mask, you can also stick with the Paintbrush tool and simply paint with black to hide areas and paint with white to make them visible again.

Figure 3.61 After applying a blue Photo Filter adjustment layer, the colorcast is gone.

Figure 3.62 Applying a blue Photo Filter adjustment layer shifted the colors away from the orange side of the color wheel, bringing them closer to the blue side.

Solid Color Layer

Choosing Layer > New Fill Layer > Solid Color will bring up a dialog box that asks you to name the layer you're creating. Once you click OK, it will open the color picker, where you can specify the color that will be used for the solid color layer. After you've created one of these layers, you can double-click the leftmost thumbnail of the layer in the Layers palette to edit the color.

Gradient Layer

Choosing Layer > New Fill Layer > Gradient will bring up a dialog box that asks you to name the layer; this will create a new layer that contains a gradient (**Figure 3.63**). The gradient is always editable by double-clicking the leftmost thumbnail in the Layers palette. If the Align with Layer check box is turned on, then the start and end points of the gradient are determined by the contents of the layer instead of the document's overall size.

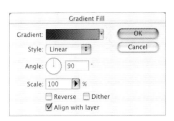

Figure 3.63 The Gradient Fill dialog box.

Pattern Layer

Choosing Layer > New Fill Layer > Pattern allows you to create a new layer that contains a repeating pattern (**Figure 3.64**). I like to use this type of layer to add a brushed-aluminum look to a background. Then, if I ever decide to change the pattern, it's as simple as double-clicking the thumbnail in the Layers palette and choosing New Pattern from the drop-down menu.

Figure 3.64 The Pattern Fill dialog box.

The Blending Mode Menu

The Blending Mode menu at the top left of the Layers palette is immensely useful. It allows the information on one layer to blend with the underlying image in interesting and useful ways. Using this menu, you can quickly change the color of objects, colorize grayscale images, add reflections to metallic objects, and much more. This is an advanced feature, so you'll have to wait until you get to Chapter 13, "Advanced Masking," to find out more about it.

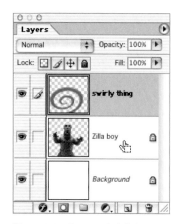

Figure 3.65 Command-click (Mac) or Ctrl-click (Windows) a layer to select all the objects on that layer.

Automatic Selections

To select everything on a particular layer, just Command-click (Mac) or Ctrl-click (Windows) the name of the layer. If the layer fills the entire screen, then it will select all because this trick looks for transparent areas. You can hold down the Shift key to add to a selection that already exists, or use the Option key (Mac) or Alt key (Windows) to take away from the current selection (**Figures 3.65** to **3.68**).

Figure 3.66 The result of Command-clicking (Mac) or Ctrl-clicking (Windows).

Figure 3.67 Refining the selection with the Lasso tool, while holding down Option (Mac) or Alt (Windows) to take away from the selection.

Figure 3.68 The result of copying the selected area of Godzilla and pasting it on a layer above the swirl (look at his head and chest).

Via Copy

The Layers menu offers you a wide variety of options for copying, merging, and manipulating layers. Let's look at one of these choices. If you select an area of your image and then choose Layer > New > Layer Via Copy, the area you've selected will be copied from the layer you were working on and moved to a brand-new layer in the same position (**Figure 3.69**). This is particularly handy when you want to move just a portion of a layer so that you can place it on top of another layer.

Use All Layers

When you're editing on a layer, some of the editing tools might not work the way you expect them to. This happens because most of the tools act as if each layer is a separate document—they ignore all layers except the active one; that is, unless the tool has the Use All Layers check box (labeled All Layers in the Paintbucket tool) turned on in the options bar of the tool you're using. This check box allows the tools to act as if all the layers have been combined into one layer (**Figures 3.70** to **3.72**).

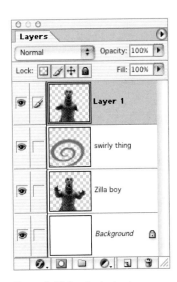

Figure 3.69 Result of using Layer > New > Layer Via Copy and moving the new layer over the swirly layer.

Figure 3.70 Using the Paint Bucket tool to add color with the All Layers option turned off.

Figure 3.71 Using the Paint Bucket tool with All Layers turned on.

Figure 3.72 The All Layers check box in the Paint Bucket options bar.

Shortcuts

You'll be doing a lot of switching between layers, and this can get a bit tedious. Therefore, I'll show you some quick shortcuts. First, you can Command-click (Mac) or Ctrl-click (Windows) anywhere in the image window when using the Move tool to activate the layer directly below your cursor. Then you can find out which layer you're working on by glancing at the Layers palette.

You won't always need the layer below your cursor, so instead of Command-clicking (Mac) or Ctrl-clicking (Windows), try Control-clicking (Mac) or right-clicking (Windows). This will bring up a menu of all the layers that contain pixels directly below your cursor; you just choose the name of the layer you want to work on and Photoshop will switch to that layer.

Remember that you can get to the Move tool temporarily at any time by holding down the Command key (Mac) or Ctrl key (Windows). Therefore, if you hold down Command and Control (Mac) or Ctrl and right-click (Windows) at the same time, no matter what tool you are using, Photoshop will present you with the pop-up menu.

Layer Sets

Have you ever had one of those mega-complicated images with dozens of layers? If so, you are probably familiar with the agony of having to fumble through an endless sea of layers, hoping you won't drown before you find the right one. If this describes you, you'll be ecstatic to know you can group a bunch of layers into a set. A set looks like a folder in the Layers palette. You can view all the layers in the set or just the set name.

To create a set, click the Layer Set icon at the bottom of the Layers palette (it looks like a folder). A folder appears in the list of layers. You can move any number of layers into the set by dragging and dropping them onto the folder you just created. The set will have a small arrow just to its left that allows you to collapse the set down to its name or expand the set to show you all the layers it contains. In Photoshop CS, you can even drag one folder onto another

NOTES

You can also create a layer set by linking multiple layers and then choosing New Set From Linked from the side menu of the Layers palette.

to create a hierarchy of up to five levels of folders (**Figures 3.73** and **3.74**). This can greatly simplify the Layers palette, making a document of 100-plus layers look as if it's made of only 5 layers.

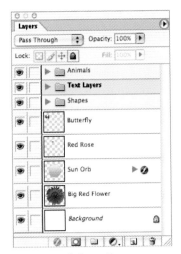

Figure 3.73 Collapsed layer sets.

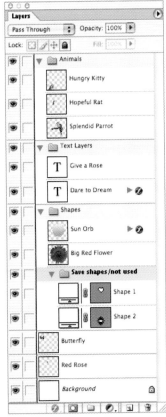

Figure 3.74 Expanded layer sets.

NOTES

To get rid of a set without throwing away the layers that are inside it, click on the set to make it active, and then click on the Trash icon at the bottom of the Layers palette and choose Set Only when prompted.

Option-clicking (Mac) or Alt-clicking (Windows) on the arrow next to a layer set will expand or collapse all the sets and Layer Style lists within that set. Adding the Command key (Mac) or Ctrl key (Windows) will expand or collapse all the sets in the entire document.

Layer sets can also be useful when you want to reorganize the layers in your image. If one of the layers within a set is active, then using the Move tool will affect only that layer (unless it's linked to other layers). If the layer set is active, then using the Move tool will move all the layers within that set. You can also move multiple layers up or down in the layers stack by first putting them into a set, and then dragging the name of the set up or down in the layers stack.

No Thumbnail Mode

If, after organizing your image into layer sets, you still find that the Layers palette is a mess, then you might want to simplify the way Photoshop displays layers. If you choose Palette Options from the side menu of the Layers palette, you'll find the option that allows you to turn off the layer thumbnails. Once you've done that, you should find that the list of layers takes up a lot less space, but you still have the full functionality of all of Photoshop's features (**Figures 3.75** and **3.76**). This also speeds up the screen redraw of the Layers palette.

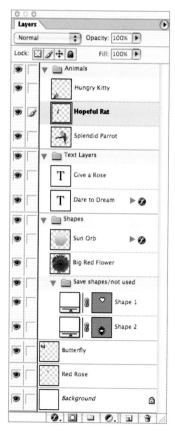

Figure 3.75 The Layers palette using the default thumbnail size.

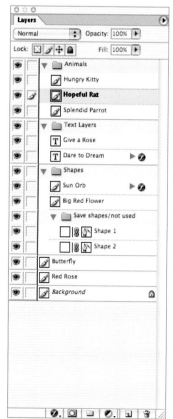

Figure 3.76 The Layers palette after setting the Thumbnails setting to None.

Color Coding

If you work within a large group of Photoshop users, it can be useful to assign colors to layers to indicate their current status. Maybe some text needs to be proofed, maybe the client approved a certain part of the image, or perhaps an area needs to be sent off for color correction. All you have to do is Control-click (Mac) or right-click (Windows) on the name of a layer and choose Layer Properties. That will bring up a dialog box where you can color code a layer or layer set (**Figures 3.77** and **3.78**).

Figure 3.77 The Layer Properties dialog box.

Layer Comps

Adobe introduced the concept of layer comps in Photoshop CS. A layer comp is a record of the position, visibility, and general appearance (opacity, blending mode, and Layer Styles) of all the layers in the active document. By saving multiple layer comps, you can quickly switch between different layouts of the same document. This feature can be very useful when you need to create multiple versions of the same document.

Let's say you're going to create the cover for a brochure, and you'd like to show your client multiple options. In one you place their company logo in the lower-left corner of the page and put the headline near the middle (**Figure 3.79**). In another variation, you place the logo centered at the top with the headline directly above it (**Figure 3.80**). If you save both versions as layer comps, then you'll be able to save them both in the same file without having any duplicate layers, and quickly switch between the layouts when the client comes to visit.

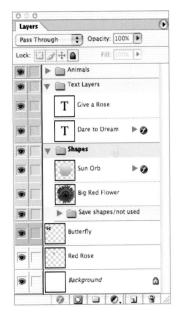

Figure 3.78 Each layer can be color coded using one of seven colors.

Figure 3.79 The initial version of the image to be saved as a layer comp.

Figure 3.80 The second version of the image to be saved as a layer comp.

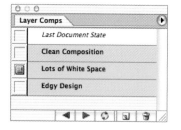

Figure 3.81 The Layer Comps palette.

Figure 3.82 The New Layer Comp dialog box.

To save the current state of your document as a layer comp, choose Window > Layer Comps (**Figure 3.81**) and click the New Layer Comp icon at the bottom of the palette. When you do that, Photoshop will prompt you for a name and other information (**Figure 3.82**). I suggest that when you're first starting to use layer comps that you always turn on all three check boxes; otherwise, the layer comp you save might not reflect the current state of your document. You can also include a note with the layer comp so you can remember why you created each comp. After you've created a few layer comps, you can cycle through them. To do this, you first have to select the comps you'd like to view. You can do this by either Shift-clicking on two comps and Photoshop will select all the comps between the two, or you can Command-click (Mac) or Ctrl-click (Win) to add individual comps to the selection. When the comps are selected, clicking the arrow icons will cycle through only those comps that are selected.

You can make changes to the layer comps after you save them. Start by clicking to the left of the comp that you'd like to modify to make it visible. Then change the position, opacity, visibility, or Layer Styles of any or all of the layers in your document. To update the layer comp so that it reflects the current state of your document, click the Update Layer Comp icon at the bottom of the palette (it looks like two curved arrows).

Once you have all the layer comps you desire, you can save your document in the Photoshop or TIFF file format, and the comps will be saved within the file so they show up each time you open the image. If you'd like to save the look of each comp as a separate document, then choose File > Scripts > Layer Comps to Files (**Figure 3.83**). You can also save the comps as a multi-page PDF file or as a Web Photo Gallery from the same menu.

Figure 3.83 The Layer Comps To Files dialog box.

Remember, layer comps are limited to keeping track of the position, visibility, and general settings attached to a layer. That means that if you paint on a layer, rotate it, or scale it up or down, the changes will be reflected in all of the layer comps that are saved in that document. To get around that limitation, you'll need to duplicate a layer and hide the original version of the layer before you make that kind of change, so the next comp you save will show the scaled, rotated, or otherwise modified layer instead of the original. That way, one of the comps will show the original layer and the second one will show an alternative version of that layer that is really a modified duplicate.

To create a layer comp using the same options that were used for the last layer comp, hold the Option key (Mac) or Alt key (Windows) when you click on the New Layer Comp icon.

Photoshop will place a yellow triangle next to a layer comp if you've made a change that invalidates a layer comp. When that triangle appears it means that the document has changed in a way that will cause the layer comp to not reflect the state the document was in when the comp was created. That will happen when you delete layers, merge layers, or change the color mode of the image. Just click the triangle icon to turn off the warning.

Merging Layers

When you create a complicated image that contains dozens of layers, your project can start hogging memory, which in turn makes it difficult to manage all the layers. Every time you create a new layer and add something to it, Photoshop gobbles up more memory. Photoshop not only has to think about what's on that layer, but also has to remember what's below the layer (even if that information is completely covered by the information on the layers above).

Whenever possible, I try to simplify my image by merging layers. This combines the layers into a single layer, and thus saves memory (because Photoshop no longer has to remember the parts of those layers that were previously being covered). The side menu on the Layers palette and the Layer menu itself give you several ways to do this:

Once you've merged two layers, it's awfully hard to get them apart—the only way to do so is to use the History palette. However, even with the History palette, you might lose all the changes you've made since you merged the layers.

▶ **Merge Down:** Merges the active layer into the layer directly below it.

▶ **Merge Visible:** Merges all the layers that are currently visible in the main image window.

▶ **Merge Linked:** Merges all the layers that have the link symbol next to them, along with the active layer.

▶ **Merge Layer Set:** Merges all the layers that are within the active layer set.

▶ **Flatten Image:** Merges all visible layers into the background, discards hidden layers, and fills empty areas with white.

When I'm creating a complex image, I often end up with a bunch of layers that don't really contribute to the result I was looking for. Maybe they were some experimental layers that I thought I might use later or some extras that I decided made the image look too busy. If that's the case, then I usually turn off the Eyeball icons for each of those layers and then choose the Delete Hidden Layers command from the side menu of the Layers palette. Or, if there are a few hidden layers that I want to keep, I can still link all the disposable layers and then use the new Delete Linked command from the same menu.

If you want to know how much extra memory the layers take up as you're modifying your image, choose Document Sizes from the menu that appears at the bottom center of the document for Macintosh users (**Figure 3.84**) or at the bottom of the main Photoshop window for Windows users. If you're a Windows user and the status bar isn't visible, select Window > Status Bar from the menu. The number on the left should stay relatively constant (unless you scale or crop the image); it indicates how much memory your image would use if all the layers were merged together. The number on the right indicates how much memory the image is using with all the layers included. This number changes as you add and modify your layers. Keep an eye on it so that you can see how memory-intensive the different layers are.

Figure 3.84 Memory usage indicator.

The number on the right might get huge if you're using a lot of layers; however, keep in mind that you'll know exactly how large the image will be when you flatten the layers by glancing at the left number.

Done Playing Around?

You've spent hours toiling away on your image, and now you're ready to save your file so it can go on to its next stop (which might be a printing company or one of your clients, or perhaps it's going to be posted to the web). Then again, maybe it's not going anywhere—you just want to rest your eyes, take a break, and work on it later. Wherever the image ends up, you need to make sure to save it in a format you can work with in Photoshop (complete with layers, paths, channels, and so on). Then you can save it in another format that's appropriate for its destination.

It would be wonderful if all software programs could work with the same format, but alas, they can't. Therefore, it's worth your while to get familiar with the various file formats available in Photoshop.

Saving Layered Files

If you're not too familiar with file formats, you might wonder why there are so many options in the Save dialog box. It's like anything else with Photoshop—you just have to think about the end use. If you're going to use the file in Photoshop and keep the layers, you'll want to save it in the Photoshop file format (also known as PSD). Photoshop, TIFF, and PDF are the only formats that recognize layers.

I mainly use the Photoshop format, because Photoshop 5.5 cannot extract the layers from a TIFF or PDF file. Unfortunately, most other programs cannot open files saved in the Photoshop file format, so it's a good habit to save the original image in Photoshop's native PSD format and then make a copy of the image without layers and save it in another format—JPEG or TIFF, for example.

Most formats other than Photoshop's native PSD format and the TIFF format (EPS, JPEG, and so on) can't handle multiple layers, so you'll have to merge all the layers into the background of your image. You can do this quickly by choosing Flatten Image from the side menu of the Layers palette. Flatten Image combines all your layers, and any areas that were transparent are filled with white. The transparent areas are filled in because the other file formats don't know what to do with them. I usually save two versions of my files—one in the Photoshop file format (so I can get back to the layers) and one in TIFF or EPS format (to use in my page-layout program) or GIF or JPEG format (for the web).

When you save a layered image in a file format that doesn't support layers (like JPEG), the image will automatically be flattened.

Closing Thoughts

Layers play such a huge role in Photoshop that to deny yourself any crucial information about them is asking for trouble. With every new release, Adobe likes to pack more and more functions into the Layers palette. So as time goes on, understanding them will become even more crucial. This is definitely a chapter you should feel comfortable with before you move on to the more advanced areas of Photoshop.

Ben's Techno-Babble Decoder Ring

Lock Transparency: A function in Photoshop that "freezes" the transparency of a layer. While Lock Transparency is in effect, you cannot increase or decrease how transparent an area will appear.

Opacity: A setting that determines how opaque (the opposite of transparent) the information on a layer will appear. An Opacity setting of 100% will not allow you to see the underlying image. A setting below 100% will allow the underlying image to partially show through the current layer.

Keyboard Shortcuts

Function	Macintosh	Windows
Show/Hide Layers Palette	F7	F7
New Layer	Shift-Command-N	Shift-Ctrl-N
New Layer Via Copy	Command-J	Ctrl-J
New Layer Via Cut	Shift-Command-J	Shift-Ctrl-J
Toggle Lock Transparency	/	/
Make Top Layer Active	Shift-Option-]	Shift-Alt-]
Make Next Layer Active	Option-[	Alt-[
Make Previous Layer Active	Option-]	Alt-]
Make Bottom Layer Active	Shift-Option-[	Shift-Alt-[
Move Layer Up	Command-]	Ctrl-]
Move Layer Down	Command-[	Ctrl-[
Merge Down	Command-E	Ctrl-E
Merge Visible	Shift-Command-E	Shift-Ctrl-E

©2003 Bert Monroy, www.bertmonroy.com

©2003 Bert Monroy, www.bertmonroy.com

PART II

Production Essentials

4

Resolution Solutions

The difference between failure and success is doing a thing nearly right and doing it exactly right.

—Edward C. Simmons

Resolution Solutions

Resolution is one of those concepts that have a huge impact on the quality of your images, yet most people don't understand it. Part of the reason is that the term *resolution* can relate to so many things (monitors, printers, scanners, digital cameras, images, and more), and with each device it might mean something slightly different. To add to the confusion there are numerous terms used to describe the resolution for each of the different devices (ppi, dpi, lpi, megapixels, and so on). But the subject is by no means beyond the grasp of someone who is committed enough to read through this chapter a few times. The rewards are smaller file sizes, higher-quality images, and significantly less frustration. Let's start off with the general concept of resolution.

Understanding Pixel Size

Every photograph you ever see in Photoshop is made out of a grid of different-colored squares that are known as pixels. So, imagine that you printed a photograph and then zoomed in on it with a microscope. Once you start to see the individual pixels, you can start to think about how large they are. If you slid a ruler under that microscope, you could measure the size of an individual pixel (**Figure 4.1**). Resolution is simply a measurement of how large a pixel is when it's printed. Maybe you end up with pixels that are 0.0769 inches in size. The only problem is that that's not a very friendly number, because most people don't like dealing with decimals. So, instead, why don't we look at more than one pixel and simply measure how many of them fit in 1 inch? In that case we'd end up with 13 pixels per inch, or ppi (**Figure 4.2**). The smaller the pixels are, the more of them you can fit into an inch, so higher ppi settings mean smaller pixels (**Figure 4.3**). Resolution simply means how large a pixel is when you print it, and it's usually measured in pixels per inch.

NEW IN CS

The concept behind resolution hasn't really changed with Adobe Photoshop CS, but for the film and video crowd, Adobe's latest brew offers support for nonsquare pixels, video document presets, and Automatic Action-Safe and Title-Safe Guides. For the rest of us, there are two new resampling methods—Bicubic Smoother and Bicubic Sharper—that give us improved options for enlarging or reducing our images.

NOTES

Notice that I said "every photograph," not every image. Some features in Photoshop are not made out of pixels. Those include paths, shape layers, and type layers, which print out with crisp edges regardless of the resolution setting of the document.

Figure 4.1 This pixel measures 0.0769 inches.

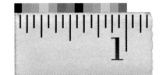

Figure 4.2 Here, 13 pixels fit in 1 inch.

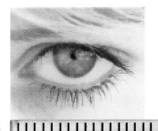

Figure 4.3 From left to right: 30 ppi, 100 ppi, 200 ppi. (©2003 Stockbyte, www.stockbyte.com)

Let's see how that applies to an image. Imagine you have an image that's 4 by 6 inches, and you wanted to fit 300 pixels in each inch. With that information and a little simple math, you can figure out the total number of pixels there would be in the width and height of the image. If you add up how many inches you and multiply that by 300, then you could say you have 1,200 by 1,800 at 300ppi (**Figure 4.4**). With that information, you could also go the other direction and figure out how many inches wide and tall the image is. Just take the width in pixels and divide it by how many pixels you'll be printing in each inch (1,200/300 = 4). So 1,200 by 1,800 at 300ppi is also 4 by 6 inches at 300ppi. Either way, you would be describing the same image. That's exactly what Photoshop does when you choose Image > Image Size (**Figure 4.5**). At the top of the dialog box, Photoshop shows you the total number of pixels you have in the width and height of your image. At the bottom, it shows you how large those pixels will be when you go to print your image. That's usually the same number you typed into your scanner when you scanned the image, or, if you created the image from scratch, Photoshop would have asked you for the resolution setting you wanted to use. For Photoshop to figure out the width in inches, all it does is take the total width in pixels and divide that by how many pixels you'll be printing in each inch.

Figure 4.4 Adding up the pixel count. (original image ©2003 Andy Katz)

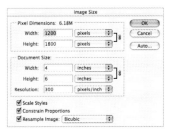

Figure 4.5 The Image Size dialog box.

Figure 4.6 Dye-sub output.

Figure 4.7 Inkjet output.

Figure 4.8 Laser printer output.

Printing

Now let's see how resolution applies to printing. You can use many kinds of printers—an inkjet, a dye sub, a laser printer, or a commercial printing press. The problem is that most of those printing devices can't reproduce exactly what you see on your screen. Instead, the device simulates what you see onscreen using four solid colors. Look at **Figures 4.6**, **4.7**, and **4.8**. The first one shows how a dye-sub printer would reproduce an image, the second how an inkjet printer would reproduce it, and the third how a laser printer or printing press would output the same image. When you compare them, you'll notice that the dye sub gives the most detail and the laser printer gives the least. Wouldn't it make sense that you will need more info in your scan if it is going to be printed on a dye-sub printer instead of a laser printer or inkjet? Let's look at the different types of printers we can choose from and see how each one reproduces an image differently and why the image needs to have a different resolution.

Resolution and Line Art

When you have a pure black and pure white image, that's known as line art. With that type of image, you'll end up needing to use a special setting that you wouldn't normally use for photographic images. With any type of printer, find out the resolution of the printer and type the exact same number into your scanner when you scan the image. For instance, my laser printer is 600dpi, so when I scan a line art image for this printer, I use a scanning resolution of 600. That way the pixels that make up the image will be the same size as the dots that the printer will use to print it. If you're not sure what the resolution of your printer is, look in the manual for the printer or look in an ad or catalog that features that model and it will usually be listed.

Resolution and Grayscale or Color Images

When your image contains more than just solid black and solid white pixels, then the resolution of your image shouldn't be a 1:1 relationship to the resolution of your printer. For instance, you can have up to 256 shades of gray in a normal grayscale image. But when you print that grayscale image, most printers are limited to using dots of solid black ink. Different printer types use different methods for simulating shades of gray out of those solid black dots. It's the same with color images in that your printer is limited to using solid dots of cyan, magenta, yellow, and black ink to simulate the millions of colors you might have in a full color image. Let's take a look at how the different types of output devices reproduce your images and the resolution requirements for each device.

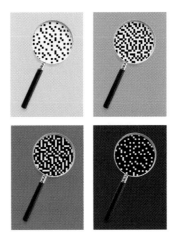

Figure 4.9 Inkjets use tiny dots to simulate shades of gray.

Inkjet

Let's see how an inkjet printer would simulate shades of gray (**Figure 4.9**). Most inkjets use fixed-size dots and just pack them closer and closer together to create darker shades of gray. As long as those dots are so small that your eyes can't focus on them, your eye can't tell the difference between those solid black dots and the original photograph. When you print a full-color photograph, it's just a bit different. The ink cartridge in most inkjet printers has four colors of ink (some have two shades of cyan, two of magenta, and two of black, for a total of seven). That means that it has to reproduce your color images using only solid cyan, magenta, yellow, and black dots. Just look at **Figure 4.10** and you'll see what I mean. It's the same concept as creating shades of gray, only it's doing it with four colors of ink instead of just one.

Figure 4.10 Color images are made from four solid inks. (original image ©2003 PhotoSpin, www.photospin.com)

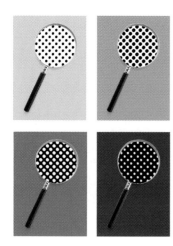

Figure 4.11 Simulating shades of gray using a halftone.

Figure 4.12 Five circles fit in an inch.

You'll get very high-quality results on most inkjet printers if you use images with resolution settings between 240 and 360ppi. Anything over 360 is just overkill. I doubt you'd notice the difference between a 360ppi image and one with a higher resolution even if you use a magnifying glass to compare them. If you have an older inkjet that has a printer resolution of 720 or below, or if you work with textured papers, then use 240ppi images. But if you have one of the newest models that is higher resolution and you print on very smooth glossy paper, then you should consider using resolutions closer to 360ppi. It's really a personal choice because not everyone has perfectly sharp images, and everyone has different quality standards. Do a few tests with different image resolutions to figure out the lowest setting that gives you acceptable results. The lower the resolution of your image, the smaller the file size will be and the faster it will print.

Laser Printer/Printing Press

A laser printer uses a different method than an inkjet printer to simulate shades of gray. Most laser printers are not attempting to deliver the photorealistic quality you can achieve on an inkjet printer. That's mainly because they use opaque toner instead of transparent ink. Because that's the case, they are more likely to be used as the starting point for an image that will eventually be reproduced on a printing press. If you ever look really closely at a grayscale photo in a newspaper, you might notice that it's made out of tiny black circles on a grid (**Figure 4.11**). That's known as a halftone, and it's used because commercial printing presses that are used to print newspapers, brochures, and magazines can't reproduce those incredibly tiny dots that result in near-photographic quality. When you print an image on a laser printer, there's a setting involved that determines how large those circles are. If we were to hold a ruler up to the image and count how many circles fit in an inch (in this case, they are on a grid that's rotated to 45 degrees), you might end up with five (**Figure 4.12**). So, you'd think that would be called 5 circles per inch, right? But it's not. That's because we don't always use a grid of circles. Printers can also use squares, diamonds, ovals, and other shapes (**Figure 4.13**). So we simply call this setting lines per inch, or lpi, really meaning how many lines (of whatever shape is being used) will fit in 1 inch. Once they get small enough that your eye can't focus on them anymore, then you get to the point where your eye can't tell the difference between those little black circles and a real grayscale photograph (**Figure 4.14**).

With a color image, the same thing happens. The only difference is that we use four colors of ink—cyan, magenta, yellow, and black (**Figure 4.15**). When the moment arrives that you finally click on the Print button (using Adobe Photoshop, Adobe InDesign, QuarkXPress, or the like), the program you're printing from needs a very important piece of information about how you want the printed version of your image to look: lines per inch (lpi). If you don't provide it, the program will use its own default setting, and that could be disastrous. You specify the lpi setting to use when printing by choosing File > Print with Preview, turning on the Show More Options check box, and clicking the Screen button.

Figure 4.13 Different printers can output different shapes on a grid.

Figure 4.15 Full-color photo created from four solid colors of ink. (original image ©2003 PhotoSpin, www.photospin.com)

Figure 4.14 Dots small enough that your eye can't focus on them.

So what does all this have to do with resolution? To find out, let's look at the most common lpi settings used for different printing processes. Keep in mind that the cruder the printing process (such as a high-speed newspaper press printing on cheap paper), the harder it is to reproduce tiny dots, and the more precise the process (such as a slow-speed, sheet-fed printing press with high-quality paper), the better it can reproduce those tiny dots. So it's the printing process (newspaper versus magazine, and so on) you'll be using that usually dictates which setting is necessary, rather than the printer type (laser, thermal wax, and so on). **Table 4.1** shows the most common settings used. It also doesn't matter what the resolution of your printer is. Here's how the lpi setting you use when printing your image relates to resolution.

TABLE 4.1 Common LPI Settings

LPI	GENERAL USE
85	Newspaper advertisements
100	Newspaper editorial section
133	Magazines and brochures
150	High-end magazines and high-quality brochures
175	Annual reports and high-end brochures
53	300dpi laser printers
106	600dpi laser printers
212	1,200dpi laser printers

To determine the best resolution for your image, multiply the desired lpi setting by 1.5 if you want to see a lot of detail, or multiply it by 2 if you would rather have the image look smoother. For example, a portrait used in a newspaper ad would be something that should look smooth; otherwise, you'll exaggerate the detail in the face, which usually makes people look older. Because newspapers usually use an lpi setting of 85 and I want things to look smooth, I'll multiply 85 by 2 and end up with 170, which is the resolution setting I should use when scanning the image. If I use anything higher than that, I'll end up with more information (detail) than I need, which might cause me to do a bunch of retouching onscreen (unnecessary because my printer simply isn't capable of reproducing that much detail). If I use a setting lower than that, the pixels might end up being so large that you can see them (giving you the jaggy look).

There is one special instance when you'll want to use higher settings than what I've mentioned here. That would be when your image contains high-contrast lines. Examples would be guitar strings or a sailboat mast. If you're ever going to notice jaggies, it will be in these high-contrast lines. So, to ensure that the pixels are small enough, you'll want to bump up the resolution setting to at least 2.5 times the lpi setting that will be used to print the image (**Figures 4.16** and **4.17**).

You can use Photoshop's Image Size dialog box as a quick resolution calculator. With any image open, choose Image > Image Size and click on the Auto button. When you do, Photoshop will prompt you for the lpi setting that will be used when printing. Use the Good setting if you'd like to multiply the lpi by 1.5 to get crisp detail, or use the Best setting to multiply it by 2 and get a smooth result. The answer to the calculation will appear as the resolution setting once you click OK.

Dye-Sub Printers

Instead of using solid cyan, magenta, yellow, and black dots (like an inkjet or laser printer), dye-sub printers can really print shades of gray and shades of color without using solid dots. For this type of printer, you need to find out how small the pixels are that your printer is capable of printing. That's known as the resolution of your printer. The pixels that make up your image should be the exact same size (measured in ppi) as the resolution of the dye-sub printer (measured in dpi). So if you have a 314dpi dye-sub printer, the resolution of your images should be set to 314ppi. That will make the pixels in your image exactly the same size as the dots your printer uses to print them out with, so you will get the highest quality. You are welcome to use a lower setting than that, but if you do, you'll be sacrificing quality for the convenience of a smaller file size.

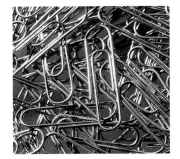

Figure 4.16 Scanned at standard resolution. Look closely at the top paperclip and you might notice a hint of jagginess on its edges. (©2003 Stockbyte, www.stockbyte.com)

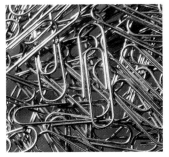

Figure 4.17 Scanned at optimal resolution for high-contrast lines. The top paperclip looks crisp and smooth with no jaggies.

35mm Slides

Slides are similar to multimedia in that the resolution setting attached to the image is ignored. That's because you're always printing to the same-size end result, and Photoshop will just scale your info up or down to fit that size. Like a dye-sub printer, slides can truly reproduce shades of gray and color instead of using only four solid colors. In this case, we need to have the same number of pixels that our output device will use to reproduce the image. If you ask someone who owns a slide recorder, they might tell you they have a 2K or 4K slide recorder. That's just like people saying they have a 300dpi or 600dpi laser printer; it's just that slide recorders are measured in K instead of dpi. K stands for 1,024. That means a 2K slide recorder can reproduce 2,048 pixels in the width of the slide (2 × 1,024 = 2,048) and a 4K recorder can handle 4,096 pixels (4 × 1,024 = 4,096). To find the proper scanning resolution, you need to figure out how many pixels your slide recorder can reproduce and then divide that by how wide your original image is in inches. So, if I have a 6-inch-wide original and I'll be printing it to a 4K slide recorder, then I'd want to divide 4,096 by 6, and I'd end up with a scanning resolution of 683. That's the exact setting needed to end up with the right amount of information for that kind of slide recorder—that is, if you want to get the absolute highest quality. You're welcome to use lower settings, but if you do, you simply won't be getting as much quality as what that slide recorder is capable of.

Multimedia/Internet

Figure 4.18 The Image Size dialog box.

Let's talk about how your web browser thinks about your images. It ignores the resolution setting. To show you what I mean, open Photoshop and choose Image > Image Size. Notice that the top describes how many pixels your image is made from and the bottom shows you how large the image will be when printed (**Figure 4.18**). But, if we switch to ImageReady, which is designed for web graphics, you will notice that it takes a different approach. Because web browsers ignore the resolution setting, ImageReady doesn't even list a resolution setting when you create a new document (**Figure 4.19**) or choose Image Size (**Figure 4.20**). Remember that a number called pixels per inch usually determines how large the pixels will be when they are printed. That's also why you'll never find the width or height of your image measured in inches in ImageReady. It has no idea how large the pixels are on your screen, so it has no idea how much space your image will take up on your screen. When Photoshop is only thinking about on-screen use, it ignores the ppi setting of the image. That's because Photoshop can't control how large the pixels are that make up your screen. Instead, you are in control of it. You can change it by adjusting your operating system's settings. In Mac OS X, choose Apple menu > System Preferences and then click on the Displays icon; in Mac OS 9, choose Apple menu > Control Panels > Monitors; or in Windows choose Start > Settings > Control Panel, then double-click Display and click on Settings. That's where you can determine how much information can fit on your screen. (Remember, you might be able to change this setting on your screen, but you won't be able to change it for all the people who will be visiting your web site. They will choose their settings, and you can't do anything about it.)

Figure 4.19 ImageReady's New Document dialog box.

Figure 4.20 ImageReady's Image Size dialog box.

The more information you display, the smaller the pixels become. For example, let's say we used a setting of 1,024 by 768. That means that we'll have 1,024 pixels in the width of the screen and 768 in the height, which means we'd need an image that's exactly 1,024 by 768 pixels to fill that screen. Let's figure out how we'd end up with that. Let's say the physical original that I'm going to put on my scanner is 6 inches wide. Really what we're trying to figure out is how many pixels the scanner should capture in each inch of the original to end up with 1,024 pixels total. It's just simple math. Take the number of pixels we need to end up with and divide that by how many inches wide the original is. In this case 1,024/6 = 171. So that's what I'd need to type into my scanner to end up with exactly 1,024 pixels total.

But what if you don't want to fill your entire screen? Instead, maybe you want the image to be about the same size as the original you put on your scanner. When that's the case, just use a generic setting of 85. There really isn't any ideal setting; this is just the average pixel size for most people's screens. Two numbers you'll hear quite often are 72 and 96. That's because the original Macintosh had a built-in screen that displayed exactly 72 pixels per inch. But once Apple stopped making Macs with a built-in screen, that was no longer true. On other monitors, the "generic" setting has always been 96ppi. My preference is simply an average of those two: 85ppi should give you something close to actual size onscreen.

To complicate matters, when you first open an image in Photoshop, it's not trying to show you how large the image will appear when printed or viewed in a web browser; instead, it's just zooming out until you can see the entire image. To see exactly how large your image will look in a web browser, you'll want to view it at 100% scale. To view it at 100% magnification, double-click on the Zoom tool, or choose View > Actual Pixels. If you find that that's too large, here's a simple technique I use for resizing things for the web: Start by viewing it at 100%, then choose Window > Navigator. Move the slider at the bottom of the palette to scale the image. If it can't make the image small enough, use the large and small mountain icons to go even further. Once you've got it at the size you need, note the percentage that appears in the lower left of the Navigator palette. That indicates exactly how much you need to scale your image to get it to appear that size in a web browser. Now, to actually scale the image, choose Image > Image Size, turn on the Resample Image check box, then change the Inches pop-up menu to Percent and enter the number you saw in the Navigator palette (**Figure 4.21**). When you click OK, you'll notice that the image gets much smaller. To see how large it will appear in a web browser, double-click on the Zoom tool and you should end up with exactly what you were looking for.

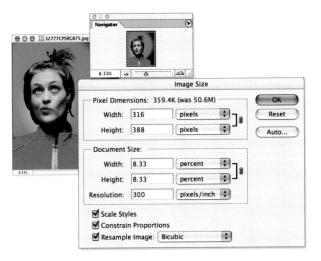

Figure 4.21 Entering the percentage from the Navigator palette. (original image ©2003 Stockbyte, www.stockbyte.com)

Digital Cameras

The resolution of a digital camera is not measured in pixels per inch; instead, it's measured in megapixels. A megapixel is simply 1 million pixels. To find out how many megapixels you need to create a particular image size, try the following: Choose File > New, set the resolution to what's needed for your type of output, and then set the width and height to what you desire. Once you've done that, click on the Resolution field and then change the Width and Height pop-up menus to Pixels. Then multiply the width by the height to find out the total number of pixels you need. Finally, divide the result by 1 million and you'll find out how many megapixels you need to end up with an image of that size. So, if you want to print 8-by-10-inch prints at 300ppi, then Photoshop would let you know that you need 2,400 by 3,000 pixels. Multiplying 2,400 by 3,000 lets you know that you need 7,200,000 pixels total, which is 7.2 megapixels. Now, when you're out shopping for a digital camera, you know exactly what type of camera you need.

When you open an image from a digital camera, you'll find that the resolution is almost always set to 72ppi. That's because the camera doesn't know how large you want to print your pixels, so it just plops in the default setting. I'll show you how I deal with that type of image once we get a chance to talk about something that's known as resampling.

Video

The pixels that make up all the images you ever open in Photoshop are perfectly square. In fact, the pixels that make up your whole screen (regardless of which program you're using) are square. That makes life pretty easy in Photoshop, but if your images are destined for video, it's another story.

When images are displayed on a video monitor (like your TV set or video camera), the image will appear to be squished (**Figure 4.22**). That happens because video hardware renders pixels as rectangles instead of squares. How squished your image will look depends on which video format is used—NTSC normal definition television, NTSC widescreen television, European PAL television, or high-definition television, for example. Each one of those formats produces a different amount of distortion by squishing or stretching your image horizontally.

Figure 4.22 The image on the right is how it would appear in Photoshop, whereas the image on the left is as it would appear in video. (©2003 Mark Clarkson)

The amount of distortion can be specified as the ratio between the height and width of the pixels as they get rendered to video. If the height of a pixel appears to be four times taller than it is wide, then that would be known as a 4:1 ratio. Photoshop simplifies that by calling it a factor of 4. All it's doing is describing how different the height of a pixel will be compared to its width, assuming the measurement for the width is always 1. The only problem with that is that sometimes you'll run into ratios like 4:3, meaning that if the width were divided up into three equal parts, then the height would equal four of those same-sized parts. To convert on odd ratio into a factor of 1, just divide the second number into the first number. In this example, 3 divided by 4 makes a factor of .75 (**Figure 4.23**). Pixels that are wider than they are tall will have a factor less than one. Pixels that are taller than they are wide will have a factor greater than one.

Unless you tell it otherwise, Photoshop will assume that your image will be displayed using square pixels. That means that if you draw a perfect square, Photoshop will create it out of an equal number of pixels in its width and height. On video, that "square" will become squished and look like a rectangle instead. If you want to get Photoshop to think of what your image will look like in video, you'll need to tell it the aspect ratio at which the pixels will be displayed. You can do that by choosing one of the choices under the Image > Pixel Aspect Ratio menu in Photoshop CS.

In a rectangular pixel document, Photoshop modifies the behavior and appearance of shapes, text, and brushes according to the pixel aspect ratio. For example, holding down Shift to draw a square object in a document set to a 2:1 Anamorphic ratio will produce a shape that is twice as many pixels tall as it is wide. By default, Photoshop turns on Pixel Aspect Ratio Correction when you create a document with nonsquare pixels, which will make that same square appear as it would in video. Pixel Aspect Ratio Correction distorts the image to make it appear normally proportioned within Photoshop, so that circles look round, squares look square, and so forth (**Figures 4.24** and **4.25**).

To create a custom pixel aspect ratio, choose Image > Pixel Aspect Ratio > Custom Pixel Aspect Ratio. The current image will be assigned the new pixel aspect ratio, and the new pixel aspect ratio will be added to the choices available in the future.

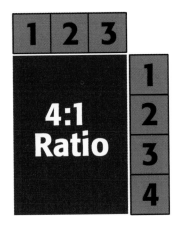

Figure 4.23 This image has a 4:3 ratio.

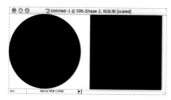

Figure 4.24 Image viewed with View > Pixel Aspect Ratio Correction turned on.

Figure 4.25 Image viewed with View > Pixel Aspect Ratio Correction turned off.

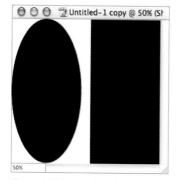

Figure 4.26 The most commonly used video formats appear in Photoshop's file presets.

The more common video frame settings are also available from the Preset drop-down menu when you create a new document (**Figure 4.26**). When you choose one of these presets, Photoshop will automatically create a set of guides in the new document. The area within the outer set of guides is called the Action Safe area—a TV set should display everything within this area, more or less. If an element absolutely, positively has to be visible on a TV screen, make sure it fits within the inner set of guides, called the Title Safe region.

It's possible to create multiple views of a single document by choosing Window > Arrange > New Window, and then choosing Pixel Aspect Ratio Correction to show one document as it will appear on a nonsquare device.

Resolution and File Size

Let's see how the resolution setting you scan with affects your file sizes. Let's say you have a 1-by-1-inch original. If you scan it at 200ppi, the file size will be 117KB (uncompressed). At 100 ppi, it would be 29KB, and at 50ppi, it would be only 7KB (**Figure 4.27**). In general, it's best to go with the lowest setting that will give you a good result. The settings mentioned earlier in this chapter are the optimal settings, which in general will be the settings that give you the absolute highest-quality result. If you decide to use anything lower than what I mentioned earlier, be sure to do a test to ensure that your image doesn't become pixilated when it's printed.

If you're not sure how the image will be reproduced, then scan for the most demanding type of output you think you'd ever use, because you can always change things later. Let's take a look at what your options are for post-scan resolution changes.

Resampling

If you'd like to change how large the pixels are that make up your image (the ppi setting), just choose Image > Image Size and turn on the Resample Image check box.

Any changes you make to the resolution setting will make the pixels larger or smaller, but the image will stay the same overall size (**Figure 4.28**). This is useful when you get an image that was scanned for a high-end purpose (such as a brochure) and you want to, for example, reuse it in a newspaper. So, it might start with a resolution of 300ppi, but you need it to be only 170ppi. By making that change, the file size would become less than half of what it was at the higher resolution.

NOTES

Pixel Aspect Ratio Correction stretches and squashes displayed pixels, so it doesn't give you the highest quality preview. To maximize image quality, toggle off this option by choosing View > Pixel Aspect Ratio Correction.

Figure 4.27 Top to bottom: 200ppi, 100ppi, 50ppi. (original image ©2003 Stockbyte, www.stockbyte.com)

Figure 4.28 Top to bottom: Resampled from 50ppi to 200ppi, resampled from 100ppi to 200ppi, scanned at 200ppi. (original image ©2003 Stockbyte, www.stockbyte.com)

When Resample Image is turned on, it's kind of like printing your image and then placing it on a scanner and scanning it. That would be fine, as long as you're not asking to get more info out of it, because there simply isn't any more in the image. It doesn't usually harm an image to reduce its resolution using resampling because you are asking for less information than what's in the original, but there is no advantage to increasing the resolution. So, when using resampling, you should be fine as long as the file size is going down because you're starting with more than what you needed. But if it's going up, then Photoshop doesn't really have enough info to do what you're asking for, which won't improve the quality of your image.

By watching the Pixel Dimensions area in the Image Size dialog box, you can tell if the changes you're making will cause Photoshop to discard pixels or add new ones. If the file size listed is smaller than the one shown to its right [128.2K (was 492.7K), for example], then Photoshop will need to discard information (pixels) to accomplish the change you've requested. If, on the other hand, the first number is larger than the second [513.0K (was 492.7K), for example], then Photoshop will have to create some new pixels in order to end up with the amount of information you've requested. To see how Photoshop thinks about adding pixels to your image, let's take a look at a very simple example: a 2-pixel–by–2-pixel checkerboard, with two each black and white pixels (**Figure 4.29**). If you enlarge this image to 200% so that it becomes 4 pixels by 4 pixels, the new image will contain four times as many pixels as the original. Photoshop must invent 12 new pixels to fill it out.

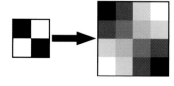

Figure 4.29 Left: The original 2-pixel-square image. Right: The result of enlarging the image to 4-pixels square.

The pop-up menu that appears to the right of the Resample Image check box determines how Photoshop will go about producing the number of pixels that make up your image. In previous versions of Photoshop, you had only three choices: Nearest Neighbor, Bilinear, and Bicubic. Out of those three choices, Bicubic would almost always produce the highest quality results. Some people would use tricks in an attempt to get higher quality results. One such trick was to scale an image up by 10% multiple times until you ended up with the size you desired. Tricks like that are no longer necessary, because Adobe added two new choices in Photoshop CS: Bicubic Smoother and Bicubic Sharper. Let's take a look at each choice individually. I'll mention which choices to use in different situations.

▶ **Nearest Neighbor:** This choice attempts to maintain the look of each pixel in the image by turning each pixel into a same-colored square. The results usually look as if you've simply zoomed in on the image in Photoshop. Unlike the other choices, it doesn't compare pixels to their neighbors (unless you scale your image up or down in increments less than 100%), so it is usually the fastest out of all the choices. This choice is good for enlarging screen shots (in increments of 100%) so that you can add higher resolution text or callouts to the image (**Figures 4.30** and **4.31**). It can also be useful when scaling down crisp-edged text and graphics. It's the only choice that attempts to maintain crisp edges when scaling an image up or down.

Figure 4.30 The original image with the area to be enlarged highlighted.

Figure 4.31 Enlarged 1200 percent using Nearest Neighbor.

▶ **Bilinear:** This choice analyzes each pixel in an image based on how it relates to the pixels that surround it. It only pays attention to the pixels directly above, below, and to the right and left of itself. That's 1/4 of the number of pixels that the Bicubic methods use, which makes this choice a bit faster than the other, but it does not produce high-quality results (**Figure 4.32**).

▶ **Bicubic:** As with all the bicubic choices, pixels are analyzed based on all eight pixels that surround them (including the diagonal neighbors that Bilinear ignores). Because Bicubic uses four times as much information as Bilinear, it will be slower, but it will almost always produce a higher quality result. Use this mode when you want to get similar results to what earlier versions of Photoshop would produce (**Figure 4.33**).

▶ **Bicubic Smoother:** This choice analyzes the same amount of information as the Bicubic choice, but uses slightly different math in an attempt to produce less abrupt transitions in your image. This choice is usually best when enlarging images (file size increasing) because it will produce a less jaggy-looking result compared to the other choices (**Figure 4.34**).

Figure 4.32 Enlarged 1200% using Bilinear.

Figure 4.33 Enlarged 1200% using Bicubic.

Figure 4.34 Enlarged 1200% using Bicubic Smoother.

▶ **Bicubic Sharper:** This choice is also similar to Bicubic, but it attempts to produce more abrupt transitions in your image, which will usually cause it to appear sharper than what you'd get with the other choices. This choice is usually the best when reducing images (file size decreasing) because it produces a less soft-looking result than the other choices (**Figure 4.35**).

That being said, as a rule of thumb, use Bicubic Sharper when you're making the image smaller, use Bicubic Smoother for making the image larger, and use Bicubic when you're not sure which choice to use (when using Actions for example).

If you turn Resample Image off, then you're going to keep the same amount of information and just change the size the pixels will be when they are printed. The entire image will shrink, but you don't lose any information; you just make the pixels smaller (**Figure 4.36**). This is what you need to do to images that come from a digital camera, because it doesn't degrade the image in any way. The resolution is almost always set at 72, but the overall width and height are quite large. For instance, on my digital camera, I get images that are 35 by 26 inches at 72ppi. With a resolution setting that low, the images always print out jaggy. But, if I go to the Image Size dialog box, turn Resample Image off, and change the resolution to 300, I end up with an 8.5-by-6.5-inch image, and it doesn't look jaggy when it's printed.

Another approach is to ignore the resolution setting when scanning and instead shoot for the correct file size. Let's see how that would work. You'd start off by using Photoshop's New dialog box as a file-size calculator. Simply enter the width and height you'd like to print your image at (let's say 12 by 14 inches) and enter the resolution setting required for the type of printing you'll be using (let's say 300ppi). With that information entered, set the Color

Figure 4.35 Enlarged 1200% using Bicubic Sharper.

Figure 4.36 Top to bottom: 200ppi, 100ppi, 50ppi. (original image ©2003 Stockbyte, www.stockbyte.com)

Figure 4.37 The New dialog box.

If you plan to scan in 16-bit mode, you'll need to create the document I just mentioned and choose Image > Mode > 16 Bits/Channel. Then, to find the file size you need to shoot for, choose Image > Image Size and look at what's listed at the top of the dialog box.

Mode pop-up menu to RGB and then note the image size listed on the right side of the New dialog box (**Figure 4.37**). In my example, Photoshop indicated that I'd need a 43.3MB file. Now let's say we're scanning a 35mm slide, which is a little less than 1.5 inches in size. Using the file-size trick, I don't have to figure out the proper resolution and scaling settings; instead, I'd just experiment with those settings until my scanner indicates that I'd end up with a 43.3MB file. Then, once I'm done scanning the image, I'd have to choose Image > Image Size, turn off the Resample Image check box, and enter the width I was looking for (12 inches, in my case). That will keep the same amount of information in the file but will make sure that the pixels are set to the proper size to get what I was looking for. I'd end up with a 12-by-14-inch image with a resolution of about 300ppi. Try it out; it sounds much more complicated than it really is.

If you send out for a high-end scan, the company that scans your image might not care what resolution you are looking for. They often only care about the file size. If that's the case, then use the New dialog box to calculate the file size that is needed for the output you desire, just as we did earlier.

Other Resolution Tricks

There are a lot of little tricks that I use when working with resolution. In this section I'll share the ones I use the most.

Scanning with Maximum Resolution

I often don't know how my images will be printed and am not sure what size I'll need at the time they are scanned. In that case, I look at the most demanding type of printing that I might use (the highest resolution I'd need) and also think of the largest size I'd ever need the image to be, and I'll scan for that. That way I'll have enough information no matter how I end up using the image. Once I know the final size and output type, then I'll simply choose Image > Image Size and enter the proper settings, which will cause Photoshop to reduce the file size so the image is optimized for that type of output.

Sharpening

When you sharpen an image, Photoshop will add tiny halos around the edges of objects. This makes it easier to see the detail that was already present in your image. I sharpen images only when they have been scaled to their final size and their resolution has been set to what's proper for the type of output that will be used. If you sharpen an image before scaling or resampling it, then the halos that make the detail easier to see will often get averaged into the rest of the image, resulting in a rather soft-looking image.

Res Versus PPI

If you use a use high-end scanner, you may not be able to find a setting called ppi in the scanner software. Instead, you'll be able to specify the resolution in small numbers such as res 4 or res 8. All that means is that the particular scanner is using the metric system. Here's how to quickly convert between pixels per inch and resolution. Choose Image > New and enter the Resolution setting you desire. Now, click on the Width field so Photoshop knows you're done entering the resolution, and then change the pop-up menu next to the Resolution setting to pixels/cm. Finally, move the decimal one place to the left and you'll know the res equivalent of the ppi setting you were looking for.

Print Size

The View > Print Size command is supposed to show you how large your image will be when it's printed, but it's usually not accurate because it assumes that 72 pixels fit on each inch of your screen. You can find out if that's true on your screen by creating a document that is exactly 72 pixels wide (the resolution, mode, and height don't matter), then double-clicking on the Zoom tool to view the image at 100% magnification. Once you've done that, just hold a real physical ruler up to your screen and measure how wide that document is. If it's not exactly an inch wide, then your screen does not display 72 pixels per inch, and therefore the Print Size command will not be accurate.

Figure 4.38 Matching onscreen with a physical ruler. (original image ©2003 Stockbyte, www.stockbyte.com)

Here's how to get an accurate print preview: Open your image, choose View > Rulers, and then choose Window > Navigator. Now hold a real ruler up to your screen and move the slider in the Navigator palette until the onscreen ruler matches the one you are holding in your hand. If the slider can't make things small enough, then experiment with the percentage setting that appears in the lower left of the Navigator palette. Once both rulers match, you're getting an accurate preview of how large your image will be when it's printed (**Figure 4.38**).

Closing Thoughts

With some practice and a bit of patience, you should be able to figure out the proper resolution for any job. The majority of people using Photoshop aren't comfortable with the concept of resolution, so don't feel bad if it takes a while before you feel like you know what you're doing.

Ben's Techno-Babble Decoder Ring

Dots per inch (dpi): Determines the size of the dots an output device will use when printing an image. A 300dpi laser printer uses black dots that are 1/300 of an inch. This term is often used incorrectly to describe the resolution of an image (which should be measured in pixels per inch).

Downsample: To reduce the number of pixels that make up the width and/or height of an image without changing its general appearance (no cropping or adding of white space).

Dye sub: Short for dye sublimation. A type of output device that produces a continuous-tone result by heating CMY dyes until they turn into a gas (without first becoming a liquid). The output of a dye-sub printer has a continuous-tone glossy look that resembles a photographic print.

Imagesetter: A type of high-end output device that is used to output images onto photographic paper or film. Imagesetters are capable of outputting only pure black and pure white dots. The minimum resolution of an imagesetter is 2,540dpi.

Inkjet: A type of output device that sprays CMYK inks onto special paper. Upon close inspection, the output of an inkjet printer typically appears "noisy" because the printer uses a dither pattern to simulate shades of gray.

Lines per inch (lpi): Determines the spacing of halftone dots and therefore their maximum size. The higher the lines-per-inch setting, the more apparent detail you can reproduce.

Pixels per inch (ppi): Determines how small the pixels in an image will be when printed. A setting of 150ppi means that pixels will be 1/150 of an inch when printed. The higher the setting, the smaller the pixels.

Samples per inch (spi): Determines the area a scanner will measure to determine the color of a single pixel. You can figure out the samples-per-inch setting that you need by multiplying the desired image resolution (ppi) by the amount the image will be scaled. Example: If the desired resolution is 300ppi and the image will be scaled 200%: $300 \times 200\% = 600$spi.

Thermal wax: A type of CMYK output device that bonds a waxy substance to a special type of paper. If you scratch the output of a thermal-wax printer with your fingernail, you will usually be able to scratch off some of the waxy substance.

Upsample: To increase the number of pixels that makes up the width and/or height of an image without changing its general appearance (no cropping or adding of white space).

©2003 Lewis Kemper, www.lewiskemper.com

5

Line Art Scanning

Only those who have the patience to do simple things perfectly will acquire the skill to do difficult things easily.

—Johann Schiller, German poet and playwright

Line Art Scanning

Not all scanners use the same names for their scanning modes. Line Art mode might be parading around under a different name, such as Text mode.

Scanning line art is a wonderful opportunity to learn how to do a relatively simple thing perfectly. Line art images consist of black lines on a white background. You see examples of line art every day in the text, logos, and signatures that are all around us. You'd think that scanning this type of image would be simple; after all, it's only pure black and white, right? Well, in order to really get control over your line art images, you'll need to go through a few hoops in Photoshop, but with a little effort, you can achieve stunning results.

Almost all scanners have a Line Art mode that gives you a pure black and pure white end result. However, don't be fooled by your scanner. Scanning in Line Art mode produces an image that doesn't contain anywhere near the amount of detail found in the original (**Figures 5.1** and **5.2**).

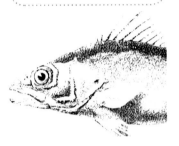

Figure 5.1 A "raw" line art scan.

If you scan an image in Line Art mode, it will open in Photoshop in Bitmap mode, which is Photoshop's mode for dealing with pure black and white images. That's practically useless, because Photoshop is not able to enhance images that are in Bitmap mode. (For example, you can't use most of the editing tools, rotate the image in precise increments, or apply filters.) This is why so many people end up with line art reproductions that have jagged edges, broken lines, and dense areas that are all clogged up.

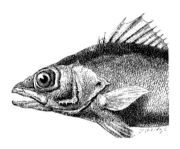

Figure 5.2 Line art scanned using the techniques in this chapter.

But that's not going to happen to you. You're going to ignore your scanner's advice and scan in Grayscale mode instead of Line Art mode. After the image is scanned in Grayscale mode, you can take full advantage of Photoshop's enhancement controls. With very little practice and a handful of tricks that you'll learn in this chapter, you'll be able to create beautiful line art reproductions as they were intended to be—with crisp edges and sharp detail.

When you're done producing your line art and are pleased with the result, you should convert your image into Bitmap mode. This will keep your file size small and prevent you from accidentally adding shades of gray to the image. After all, true line art contains only pure black and pure white, with no shades of gray. By converting your image to Bitmap mode in the end, you'll guarantee that it won't be contaminated with grays. Shades of gray are reproduced using a pattern of black circles, known as a halftone, which makes the lines of your image appear fuzzy (**Figure**s **5.3** and **5.4**).

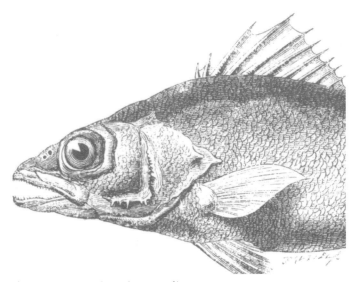

Figure 5.3 A Grayscale mode image of line art.

Figure 5.4 Magnified version of grayscale line art as reproduced on a laser printer.

Figure 5.5 Jaggy line art.

When scanning a line art image for onscreen display (for multimedia, the Web, and so on), the image will usually look better if you leave it in Grayscale mode. I know, I know, that really isn't true line art, but it will look better onscreen. Why? Because the pixels that make up your screen are quite large (between 72 and 96ppi), so it's easy to see the jagged edges of the pixels that make up your image. By including shades of gray, the edges of the image will fade out and have a smoother look. When scanning for onscreen use, use a resolution setting of 85.

Avoiding the Jaggies

The most common complaint I hear about line art is that it has jagged edges (**Figure 5.5**). This happens when the pixels in the image are so large that you can easily see them when the image is printed. Thankfully, avoiding the "jaggies" is the easiest part of dealing with line art.

Resolution Is the Key

Photoshop gives users the ability to try a lot of wild things with images. But the one thing all users have in common is the desire to get the highest quality possible. And when you're working with pure black-and-white line art, that means you'll want each pixel in your image to be the exact same size as the smallest dot your printer can reproduce.

The size of the pixels in your document is determined by the resolution setting of your file. This is measured in pixels per inch (ppi). The resolution of your printer dictates the smallest dot it can reproduce. This is measured in dots per inch (dpi). You'll want to find out the resolution of your printer and use that setting when scanning your image. This makes your pixels the same size as the smallest dot your printer can reproduce, thus giving you the best possible results.

Most people think higher settings produce better results, but that's not necessarily the case. If your end result is printed on a restaurant receipt printer, and you feed it an image with 300 pixels per inch, there's no way it can print dots that small. So it must distill the image and discard the extra information—and that's when your image will suffer. You're much better off using the correct resolution setting in the first place.

Printing companies and service bureaus have expensive output devices that offer resolutions of at least 2,540 dots per inch. I've found that files with resolutions above 1,200ppi don't seem to produce better detail; they just give you huge file sizes and therefore slow down your computer. **Figure**s **5.6** to **5.11** show the effect of resolution on file size and quality.

Figure 5.6 Resolution: 72ppi. File size: 22KB.

Figure 5.7 Resolution: 150ppi. File size: 23KB.

Figure 5.8 Resolution: 300ppi. File size: 31KB.

Figure 5.9 Resolution: 600ppi. File size: 48KB.

Figure 5.10 Resolution: 800ppi. File size: 61KB.

Figure 5.11 Resolution: 1,200ppi. File size: 93KB.

Photoshop Can Fake It

If your scanner is not capable of using a resolution setting as high as you need, you can have Photoshop increase the resolution of the image and add the extra information your scanner couldn't deliver. To do this, scan with the highest resolution setting available, and then choose Image > Image Size. Select the Resample Image check box, set the pop-up menu to Bicubic (that's the kind of math Photoshop will use to add information to your image), type the resolution of your printer in the Resolution field, and then click OK. Remember, your image must be in Grayscale mode; otherwise, this step will not improve image quality. This step is unique to line art images; if you were to increase the resolution of a photographic-quality image, the result would appear blurry. In the case of line art, the extra information will not harm the image, because we're going to convert it to a pure black-and-white bitmap, which is incapable of appearing blurry.

NOTES

Line art file sizes will vary depending on which file format is used. The preceding images were saved as TIFF files with LZW compression turned on. LZW compression is ideal for images that contain large areas of solid color. The 1,200ppi image above would have been 410KB if LZW compression had not been used.

Figure 5.12 Photoshop looks at the line you drew and automatically calculates the rotation amount needed and puts it in the dialog box.

NOTES

Straighten a scan while it's still in Grayscale mode. If your image is in Bitmap mode, it can be rotated only in 90-degree increments.

Whenever possible, avoid straightening scans in other software programs, such as your page-layout program. If scans are straightened in other programs, the screen redraw will take longer and printing time will increase. Also, the quality of the art will suffer, and you'll not have a true image preview.

When you scan grayscale images that have already been printed using a halftone screen, you'll often get an unwanted repetitive pattern. You might get a better result by scanning the preprinted image as line art (even though it's a grayscale photo). This method will try to capture the halftone look instead of converting the image into a grayscale file. Using the line art technique described in this chapter, you can scan grayscale images that were printed with a halftone screen of 85 lines per inch or below. If an image was printed with a halftone screen above 85 lines per inch, the image should be scanned as a normal grayscale image instead of using the line art technique.

Straightening the Image

If the image you've scanned needs to be straightened, you can use the Measure tool (it looks like a ruler and is grouped with the Eyedropper tool). Draw a line across an area that should be perfectly vertical or horizontal. If there's more than one area of the image that should be straightened, you can click the middle of the measurement line and drag it around your screen to make sure it matches all the affected areas. If you need to adjust the angle of the measurement line, just drag one of its ends.

When you're certain the line is at the proper angle, check to make sure the background color is set to white and then choose Image > Rotate Canvas > Arbitrary. Photoshop has a great feature that automatically calculates how much the image needs to be rotated based on the line you drew, so all you have to do is click OK (**Figure 5.12**). Once you're done, you can get rid of the measurement line by clicking the Clear button in the Options bar at the top of your screen.

Improving Definition

When you convert an image to Bitmap mode (which we'll do at the end of this chapter), any areas that are darker than 50% gray will become pure black. This usually causes detail in the darkest, most densely packed areas to clog up and become a black blob. You can prevent this from happening by sharpening the image. Sharpening will add more contrast to those densely packed areas and produce better detail. However, before you sharpen an image, you'll want to take a snapshot of the unsharpened image so you can use it later to enhance the result.

Taking a Snapshot

Choose New Snapshot from the side menu of the History palette to record what the image looks like before you sharpen it. Name the snapshot something like "Unsharp Version" so you can remember what it contains. The snapshot you create will appear near the top of the History palette (**Figure 5.13**). Click the column just to the left of the snapshot thumbnail icon to tell Photoshop to use this version of the image when using the History brush.

If you need to have a transparent background for the web, press Option-Command-~ (Mac) or Alt-Ctrl-~ (Windows) to select the background of the image. (You'll use the tilde key, which is located to the left of the number 1 key.) Next, choose Select > Inverse to select the line art. Then create a new layer, choose Edit > Fill and fill the layer with black, and finally drag the original layer to the trash at the bottom of the Layers palette.

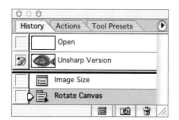

Figure 5.13 After creating a new snapshot, click to the left of the snapshot thumbnail image to set the History brush to that snapshot.

Sharpening the Image

Now that you've created a snapshot version of the image, it's safe to proceed with the sharpening process. Double-click the Zoom tool in the Tools palette to view the image at 100% magnification; otherwise, the onscreen preview of the sharpening filter will not be accurate. Choose Filter > Sharpen > Unsharp Mask, and set the amount to 500, the radius to 1.2, and the threshold to 2. This is usually a good starting point because it will make the detail in the dark areas more defined.

Now adjust the Radius setting until any tiny elements (which usually come in as light shades of gray) turn dark. You're really looking for a balance between good shadow detail and dark tiny elements. Radius settings between .5 and 5 usually produce the best results (**Figure 5.14**).

A Threshold setting of 0 will sharpen all shades in the image, including the lightest grays. High threshold settings will sharpen only the darker thick lines in the image. I usually keep the Threshold setting at 2, unless any paper texture starts to show up. If you notice that the paper texture is being exaggerated, increase the Threshold setting until the paper smoothes out again, and then readjust the Radius setting to maintain that shadow/tiny-detail balance I mentioned earlier.

NOTES

You can also click on the camera icon at the bottom of the History palette to create a snapshot. Hold the Option key (Mac) or Alt key (Windows) if you'd like to be prompted for a name.

The Unsharp Mask filter is used here because it's the only sharpening filter that gives you enough control over the end result. The other filters deliver a more generic result because there are no user-defined settings involved.

Converting to Line Art

When you print an image that contains shades of gray, your printer uses a halftone screen, which prevents your grayscale image from having crisp edges. In order for you to get nice, crisp edges, the image must contain only pure black and pure white—that's true line art. So, how do you get there?

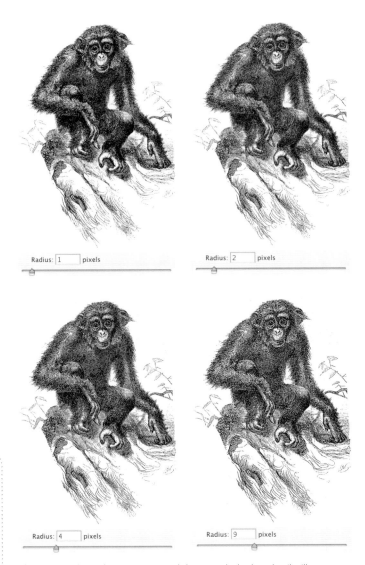

Radius: 1 pixels   Radius: 2 pixels

Radius: 4 pixels   Radius: 9 pixels

Figure 5.14 The Radius setting controls how much shadow detail will appear.

NOTES

There is no need to apply a Threshold layer if your end result will be used onscreen for the Internet or multimedia, but you might need to enhance the contrast of the image by choosing Image > Adjustments > Levels. Move the upper-left slider until the lines in your image become completely black, and then move the upper-left slider until the background is completely white. If you've done that, then you can stop right here and save your image in the GIF file format.

Adding a Threshold Adjustment Layer

You can use the Threshold command to rid the image of all shades of gray, leaving only pure black and pure white. By applying Threshold on an adjustment layer instead of directly to the image, you'll be able to easily make changes after the image is black and white. To achieve an accurate preview, you must view the image at 100% magnification. Double-click the Zoom tool in the Tools palette to quickly zoom to 100%. Create a new Threshold adjustment layer by choosing Layer > New Adjustment Layer > Threshold. Adjust the slider until the lines in the image have the desired thickness and detail. You can compare the black-and-white result to the grayscale version of the image by turning the Preview option off and on.

The Threshold level forces anything darker than the threshold number to black and anything lighter to white (**Figure**s **5.15** to **5.20**). Refer to the table in Chapter 6, "Optimizing Grayscale Images," to see what the threshold numbers mean.

Figures **5.21** to **5.23** show the quality improvement that is possible by scanning in Grayscale instead of Line Art mode. Even more detail could be brought out of **Figure 5.23** by using the enhancement techniques that were applied to **Figure 5.24**.

Figure 5.15 The lines appear to be breaking up.

Figure 5.17 This image shows good highlight detail without plugging up the shadow detail.

Figure 5.19 This image has no shadow detail and the lines are too thick.

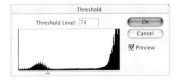

Figure 5.16 The Threshold setting is too low.

Figure 5.18 Proper Threshold setting.

Figure 5.20 The Threshold setting is too high.

Figure 5.21 Raw line art scan (same as scanning in Grayscale mode and using the default Threshold setting). File size: 448KB.

Figure 5.22 Raw grayscale scan (lines are not crisp, and the file size is very large). File size: 7.9MB.

Figure 5.23 Grayscale scan with sharpening and a proper Threshold setting (shows good shadow detail). File size: 584KB.

Refining Areas

To retain additional detail, you must enhance the grayscale image that's below the adjustment layer. To do so, click the name of the layer that contains the original image. There are many ways to enhance the image, including the following. (Refer to **Figure 5.24** for examples of these settings.)

You can change the current brush size at any time by pressing [or] (square brackets).

The Dodge tool with 100% exposure setting.

The History brush using Multiply blending mode.

The History brush using Screen blending mode at 45% opacity.

The History brush using Lighten blending mode.

Figure 5.24 Refining the image.

▶ **Increase shadow detail:** Brush across the image with the Sharpen tool to bring out detail in shadow areas.

▶ **Fix broken lines:** Brush across the image with the Burn tool (with the Range option set to Shadows) to clean up broken lines or to make lines thicker. If the Burn tool doesn't change the image enough, use the History brush with the Mode option set to Multiply or Darken to increase the line thickness. Lower the Opacity setting if the changes are too extreme.

▶ **Reduce line thickness:** Brush across the image with the Dodge tool (with the Range option set to Highlights or Midtones) to reduce the thickness of lines. If the Dodge tool doesn't change the image enough, use the History brush with the Mode option set to Screen or Lighten to make the lines thinner. Lower the Opacity setting if the changes are too extreme.

If the Dodge and Burn tools don't change the image enough, use the History brush with the Mode option set to Hard Light to make lines thinner. Lower the Opacity setting if the changes are too extreme.

▶ **Remove paper texture:** Choose either Despeckle or Median from the Filter > Noise menu (**Figures 5.25 to 5.27**).

Figure 5.25 Unrefined image.

Figure 5.26 Result of applying the Despeckle filter.

Figure 5.27 Result of applying the Median filter.

▶ **Control text thickness:** If you're scanning text at large point sizes, you can make the text thicker by choosing Filter > Other > Minimum, or make it thinner by choosing Filter > Other > Maximum. If the adjectives used in these menu options seem contrary to common sense, well, they are. Just remember to apply reverse logic when dealing with text thickness (**Figure 5.28**).

Figure 5.28 This image is split into thirds vertically. The middle is the original, the top is after applying Minimum, and the bottom is after applying Maximum.

Minimizing File Size

Nobody likes dealing with big, bloated files. They're greedy resource hogs that slow down your system and wreak havoc on your ability to work quickly and efficiently. Any extra white space around the image is a file-fattening waste because it's not necessary for printing the image. One way to simplify the image is to choose Flatten Image from the side menu of the Layers palette, and then use the Eraser tool to clean up any stray pixels in the white area surrounding the image. Finally, to discard any extra space, choose Image > Trim, turn on all the check boxes at the bottom, and then choose whichever top choice would make Photoshop find a white pixel (**Figure 5.29**).

Figure 5.29 The Trim command will discard any extra space in your image.

You have to perform the trimming step when the image is still in Grayscale mode because the Trim command does not work on images that are in Bitmap mode.

In Bitmap mode, the image can contain only pure black and pure white; therefore, the file size is much smaller than for a grayscale image. In fact, grayscale images are eight times as large as bitmap images.

Converting to Bitmap

Your image is now pure black and white, but the file itself is still in Grayscale mode. You can click the eyeball icon next to the adjustment layer to toggle it off and on and see that it's being applied to a grayscale image. The image must be converted to Bitmap mode to save disk space and to make sure that any final editing doesn't produce unwanted shades of gray. Convert the image from Grayscale to Bitmap by choosing Image > Mode > Bitmap. This brings up the Bitmap dialog box (**Figure 5.30**), which is where you can change the resolution of your image. If you followed the steps mentioned in the "Avoiding the Jaggies" section at the beginning of this chapter, then the resolution of your image should be just right. If that's the case, then make sure the input and output resolution numbers match, so Photoshop doesn't mess with the Resolution setting, and then click OK.

Figure 5.30 The Bitmap dialog box.

Figure 5.31 The EPS Options dialog box.

If you resize an image that's already in Bitmap mode, the individual pixels in the image become large black squares. To maintain good quality, convert the image to Grayscale mode and then use the Gaussian Blur filter with a setting just high enough to introduce shades of gray (**Figure 5.32**). Now you can use the techniques listed in this chapter to enhance the image and convert it back to Bitmap mode.

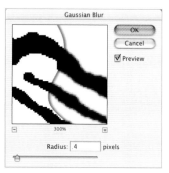

Figure 5.32 The Gaussian Blur dialog box.

Choosing a File Format

If your image is destined to be printed, then you'll want to use the EPS or TIFF file format. The EPS file format allows you to specify whether the white areas should be solid or transparent (**Figure 5.31**).

Line art images that are destined for the web should be saved in the GIF file format.

Closing Thoughts

Lately I've been noticing that a lot of the line art out there is inferior to what I used to see only a few years ago. Check it out for yourself! Pick up any magazine (even the high-end ones sometimes have this problem) and look through it for line art images. If your experience is anything like mine, you'll probably see some really mediocre stuff—edges are jagged, lines are broken up, and patterns look clogged. My theory is that people stopped sending out for line art scans and started performing them in-house.

That's fine, but only if you're not sacrificing quality for convenience. After reading this chapter, I hope you'll agree with me that you can have both. As long as you know how to get a good scan that captures the right amount of detail, and then know how to enhance the scanned image in Photoshop, there's no reason why you can't end up with exquisite line art.

And as a side note, I want you to know that just because you can achieve high-quality results using these techniques doesn't mean you will want to use them for every line art scan. I occasionally have to scan dozens of images for a single project. In that case, I might decide that speed is more important than quality and just scan in Line Art mode to begin with. But if I'm scanning my own signature, a high-quality etching, or a logo I'll be using over and over again, then I will definitely spend the extra time to get a high-quality result.

Ben's Techno-Babble Decoder Ring

Bitmap: A confusing term, because Photoshop uses it in an unusual way. Technically, "bitmap" means a grid of pixels. That means that any image you ever see in Photoshop that contains pixels is technically a bitmap image. That's why the native format for transporting pixel-based images on the Windows platform is called a BMP file. That stands for Windows Bitmap. Adobe has decided to reserve the term to describe images that contain only pure black and pure white (no grays or color). The reason can be attributed to Apple. The Macintosh was one of the first personal computers that was designed to deal with pixel-based images, and in its first incarnation it contained a black-and-white screen (no grays). "Bitmap" got associated with any pixel-based image on that first Mac model, and that's how the dual meaning came about.

Line art: Any artwork that consists of pure black lines on a pure white background. Line art images always contain extremely crisp edges and no shades of gray or color.

Resample: The process of changing the total number of pixels in an image without cropping or adding empty space.

Threshold: An adjustment that converts all shades of gray to pure black or pure white. Any shades of gray brighter than the threshold value will become white, and any shades darker than the threshold value will become black.

6

Optimizing Grayscale Images

Courtesy of Tom Nick Cocotos, www.cocotos.com

If you go through life convinced that your way is always best, all the new ideas in the world will pass you by.

—Akio Morita, founder of Sony

Optimizing Grayscale Images

When inexperienced users first try to adjust a grayscale image, they usually look for something familiar and easy, and the Brightness/Contrast dialog box is frequently where they end up (**Figure 6.1**). With a mere flick of the mouse, they can dramatically change their image. Big results, little effort. At first glance, the Brightness/Contrast dialog box seems to hold great promise. But does it really do the job?

If you were to compare images adjusted with Brightness/Contrast with the images you see in high-end magazines and brochures, you'd notice that the quality of the Brightness/Contrast images is inferior (**Figures 6.2** and **6.3**). Why? Because the Brightness/Contrast dialog box adjusts the entire image an equal amount. So, if you decide to increase the overall brightness of an image until an area that was 10% gray becomes white, then areas that are black will also be changed the same amount and become 90% gray. Using controls like these, it is extremely hard to achieve professional quality. When you correct one problem, you usually introduce another.

Figure 6.1 The Brightness/Contrast dialog box.

Figure 6.2 Image optimized using Brightness/Contrast. (©2003 Andy Katz)

Figure 6.3 Image professionally optimized.

Common adjustment complaints include

▶ Images appearing flat (lacking contrast)

▶ Images printing overly dark

▶ Blown-out detail in the highlights (bright white areas in the middle of people's foreheads)

▶ Lack of detail in the shadows

All of these problems—and others—can be solved in one dialog box.

Levels Is the Solution

The Levels dialog box (choose Image > Adjustments > Levels) is the cure for most common complaints about grayscale image quality (**Figure 6.4**). It offers you far more control and feedback than Brightness/Contrast. Instead of having only two sliders to adjust, Levels offers you five, as well as a bar chart that indicates exactly what is happening to the image. And unlike the sliders in Brightness/Contrast, the Levels sliders don't change the entire image in equal amounts.

NOTES

To reset sliders to their default positions, hold down Option (Mac) or Alt (Windows) and click on the Cancel button, which has temporarily become the Reset button. Or, you can type Option-Command-. (that's a period) on the Mac.

If you have a color original that will be reproduced as a grayscale image, be sure to scan the original as color and then convert it to grayscale in Photoshop. Also, be sure to check out Chapter 11, "Color Manipulation," where you'll learn how to produce a higher-quality grayscale conversion.

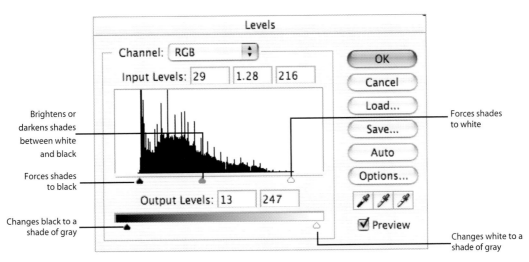

Figure 6.4 Understanding the Levels sliders.

NOTES

The height of the bars in a histogram suggest, visually, how much space the shades take up in an image. The height doesn't indicate an exact number of pixels; instead, it measures how much space the shade takes up—how much it's used compared with the other shades in the image. It's as if everyone in a room stood up and you compared how tall each person was without using a ruler. You wouldn't know exactly how tall anyone was, but you'd have an idea of how tall each person was compared with the others (**Figure 6.5**).

It might take several pages to describe all the controls in the Levels dialog box, but once you know how to use them, it will take you less than a minute to optimize an image. Just remember to apply all of the controls in Levels, because each builds on the last. You can liken the steps in Levels to the ingredients in crème brulée—leave one out and you might end up with pudding instead of perfection.

The Histogram Is Your Guide

You can use the bar chart (also known as a histogram) at the top of the Levels dialog box to determine whether the adjustments you're making are going to harm the image or improve it. The histogram indicates which shades of gray your image uses and how much space those shades take up—that is, how much they are used in the image. If you find a gap in the histogram, you can look at the gradient directly below it to see which shade of gray is missing from your image.

By looking directly below the first bar that appears on the left end of the histogram, you can determine the darkest shade of gray in the image. If there were anything darker than that, then there would have to be some bars above those shades in the histogram. By looking directly below the last bar that appears on the right end of the histogram, you can determine the brightest shade of gray in the image. So if you look at **Figure 6.6**, you might notice the image contains no pure blacks or pure whites. The darkest shade of gray is about 95%, and the brightest shade is about 6%.

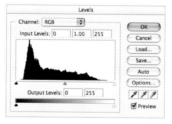

Figure 6.5 This histogram indicates that the shades between around 90% and 75% gray take up a lot of space (tall bars), and the shades between around 5% and 15% take up little space (short bars).

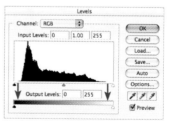

Figure 6.6 Look at the gradient bar directly below the ends of the histogram to determine the brightest and darkest shades present in the image.

There is no ideal when it comes to a histogram; it's simply a reflection of which shades of gray are most prevalent in your image (**Figure 6.7**). Tall bars indicate a shade of gray that takes up a lot of space in the image, and short bars indicate a shade that isn't very prevalent in the image. A histogram that extends all the way across the space available and does not have tall spikes on either end indicates an image that has the full range of shades available, and is usually a sign of a good scan or a well-adjusted image.

Figure 6.7 Each image will have its own unique histogram.

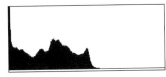

©2003 PhotoSpin, www.photospin.com   ©2003 PhotoSpin, www.photospin.com   ©2003 PhotoSpin, www.photospin.com

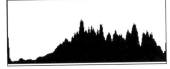

©2003 PhotoSpin, www.photospin.com   ©2003 PhotoSpin, www.photospin.com   ©2003 PhotoSpin, www.photospin.com

Evaluating and Adjusting Contrast

The brightest and darkest areas of your computer monitor are nowhere near as bright or dark as the objects you'll find in the real world. The difference is even more extreme when you look at the brightest and darkest areas of a printed brochure—the paper is actually pretty dull, and the ink isn't all that dark. Because of this, you'll need to use the full range of shades from black to white in order to make your photos look as close to reality as possible.

By adjusting the upper-right and upper-left sliders in the Levels dialog box, you can dramatically improve the contrast of an image and make it appear more lifelike. When you move the upper-left slider in the Levels dialog box, you force the shade of gray directly below it and any shade darker than it (see the gradient) to black. So moving that slider until it touches the first bar on the histogram forces the darkest shade of gray in the image to black, which should give you nice dark shadows.

When you move the upper-right slider, you will force the shade that appears directly below the slider and any shade brighter than it to white. So, similar to dark colors, moving the right slider until it touches the last bar on the histogram forces the brightest shade of gray to white, which should give you nice white highlights.

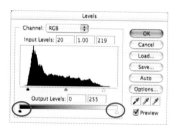

Figure 6.8 The shades that are beyond the upper-right and upper-left triangles will become pure black and pure white.

By adjusting both sliders, your image will be using the full range of shades available to a grayscale image (**Figure 6.8**). If you move the sliders past the beginning and end of the histogram, you will get even more contrast, but you risk losing important detail in the process.

Hidden Features to the Rescue

To achieve maximum contrast without sacrificing detail, Adobe created a hidden feature in the Levels dialog box. It's known as Threshold mode because it acts like the Threshold dialog box that we used in Chapter 5, "Line Art Scanning." This feature allows you to see exactly which areas are becoming black or white, and it's the key to ensuring that you don't sacrifice detail. To get to the hidden feature, hold down the Option key (Mac) or Alt key (Windows) when you move the upper-right or upper-left sliders in the Levels dialog box.

When you move the upper-left slider with Threshold mode turned on, your image should turn white until the slider touches the first bar on the histogram; then small black areas should start to appear. These are the areas that will become pure black. With most images, you'll want to make sure you don't force a large concentrated area to black, so move the slider until only small areas appear. You also want to make sure the areas that are becoming black still contain detail. Detail will show up looking like noise (not the kind you hear—the kind you see on television when you don't have an antenna hooked up), so make sure those small areas also look noisy. You'll need to repeat this process with the upper-right slider to make sure you get optimal contrast (**Figures 6.9** to **6.18**).

Three things might cause an image to have large areas of black or white from the start:

1. Your scanner isn't capable of capturing good shadow detail.

2. The image simply didn't have any detail in the shadows to begin with.

3. The image has been adjusted without Photoshop's Threshold mode.

NOTES

If you're in the market for a new scanner, be sure to compare the D-max specifications for each scanner you are considering. Higher D-max specs indicate a scanner that is capable of capturing more shadow detail than a scanner with a lower D-max spec. It's often worth the extra money to get a scanner that can deliver good shadow detail.

Figure 6.9 Original. (©2003 Ben Willmore)

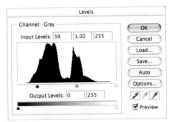

Figure 6.10 Upper-left slider adjusted way too far.

Figure 6.11 Large areas of the image are losing detail and becoming pure black.

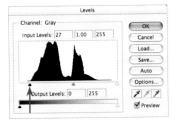

Figure 6.12 Upper-left slider adjusted correctly.

Figure 6.13 Small areas become black but still contain detail (noise).

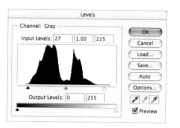

Figure 6.14 Upper-right slider adjusted too far.

Figure 6.15 Large areas are losing detail and become pure white.

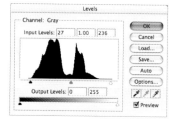

Figure 6.16 Upper-right slider adjusted correctly.

Figure 6.17 Small areas become white but still contain detail (noise).

Figure 6.18 Final result.

Figure 6.19 A Slinky.

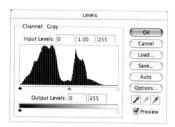

Figure 6.20 After adjusting the top two sliders, your image should use the full range of shades available.

The Histogram Gives You Feedback

Once you have applied an adjustment to your image, you can see an updated histogram by choosing Image > Adjustments > Levels again. You should notice that after adjusting the upper-right and upper-left sliders, the histogram will stretch all the way across the area available. It's just like stretching out a Slinky…you remember, "It walks down stairs, alone or in pairs" (**Figure 6.19**). As you pull on the ends of the Slinky, the loops stretch out and start to create gaps. The same thing happens to a histogram—because Photoshop can't add more bars to the histogram, it can only spread out the ones that were already there. And remember, gaps in the histogram mean that certain shades of gray are missing from the image. So the more you adjust an image using Levels, the more you increase the possibility that you'll lose some of the smooth transitions between bright and dark areas (**Figure 6.20**).

If you see large spikes on either end of the histogram (**Figure 6.21**), it's an indication that you've lost detail. That's because you forced quite a bit of space to white or black using Levels. But you'd know you did that, because you were using the hidden feature, right? Or maybe you couldn't control yourself, and were using that Brightness/Contrast dialog box, where you can't tell if you damage the image! You might also get spikes on the ends of the histogram if you scan an image with too high of a contrast setting, a brightness setting that is way too high or low, or if your scanner wasn't capable of capturing enough shadow detail (see information about D-max in the earlier Note).

NOTES

If you'd like to see a histogram that continuously changes to reflect any modifications you make to your image, then choose Window > Histogram. I'll tell you all about Photoshop CS's new Histogram palette in the next chapter of this book.

If you find evenly spaced spikes in the histogram of an unadjusted image, it usually indicates a noisy scan (**Figure 6.22**).

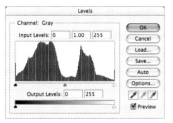

Figure 6.21 Spikes on the end of a histogram usually indicate lost detail.

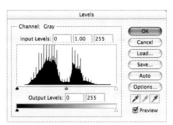

Figure 6.22 Noise.

Adjusting Brightness

After you have achieved good contrast, your image might look too bright or dark. The middle slider in the Levels dialog box can fix that. (Techies love to call this slider the Gamma setting, but we plain folks call it the midpoint.) If you move the middle slider to the left, the image will become brighter without messing up the dark areas of your image. Black areas will stay nice and black. Or you can move the middle slider to the right to darken the image without messing up the bright areas of the image. White areas will stay bright white (**Figure 6.23**). This is the one setting that is a personal choice. I can't tell you how bright or dark your image should be.

If you want to know what this adjustment is doing, just look directly below the middle slider; the shade of gray there will become 50% gray. Moving it to the left will brighten your image because you'll be shifting what used to be a

Spikes that show up after an image has been adjusted with Levels do not indicate noise. It's as if you took your trusty Slinky and tried to squish it down to a centimeter wide. Something would have to budge. The only way I can do it is to bend the Slinky into a V shape where the loops start piling up, one on top of the other. Otherwise, the loops just line up in a nice row and limit how much I can compress the Slinky. Well, the same thing happens with the histogram. Let's say you try to squish 20 bars into a space that is only 15 pixels wide on the histogram. Five of the bars have to disappear. They are going to just pile on top of the bars next to them and make those bars about twice as tall. When this happens, you get evenly spaced spikes across part of the histogram.

dark shade of gray to 50% gray. Moving the middle slider to the right will darken your image as you shift a bright shade to 50% gray. If you look at an updated histogram of the image, it will look like you stretched out a Slinky, then grabbed one side and pulled it to the middle (**Figure 6.24**). Some bars will get scrunched (is that a technical term?) together, while others get spread apart.

Setting Up Your Images for Final Output

If your images are going to be printed, especially with ink on paper, chances are that they will end up looking a lot darker than they did when you viewed them onscreen. This is known as dot gain. Fortunately, Photoshop allows you to compensate for it. You can tell Photoshop ahead of time how you intend to output your images, and it will adjust the onscreen appearance of your image to look as dark as it should be after it's printed.

To select or enter dot-gain settings, choose Edit > Color Settings (Photoshop > Color Settings in OS X). In the Working Spaces area, you'll use the Gray pop-up menu (**Figure 6.25**). You'll definitely want to ask your printing company about what settings to use; otherwise, you'll just be guessing and you might not like your end result. But just in case you're working at midnight or don't have time to ask your printing company, you can use the settings that appear in **Table 6.1**. Once you've specified the Dot Gain setting that is appropriate for your printing conditions, choose Image > Mode > Assign Profile, and select the Working Gray setting. That will set up Photoshop to properly preview what your image will look like under those printing conditions.

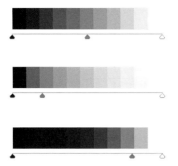

Figure 6.23 Effects of the middle slider.

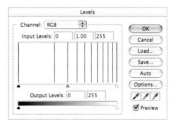

Figure 6.24 The adjustment shown on the left results in the histogram shown on the right.

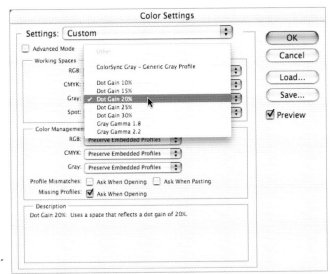

Figure 6.25 The Color Settings dialog box.

TABLE 6.1 Dot-Gain Settings	
Newspapers	34%
Magazines and brochures	24%
High-end brochures	22%

Preparing for a Printing Press

Take a close look at the black-and-white image in **Figure 6.26**, and imagine that you took that image to Kinko's and made a copy of it. Then you took the copy and copied it again at your local library. Then you took the library copy and ran it through the copy machine in your office. Then you held the version that had been copied three times next to the original. Would you expect them to look the same? Of course not. In fact, the tiny dots that are in the brightest part of the image would have begun to disappear and become pure white, because every time you make a copy, you lose some quality. Well, the same thing happens when you hand over your image to a printing company. When you give your printing company your original output, they will have to make three copies of it before it makes it to the end of the printing process. They start by converting the original into a piece of metal called a printing plate, to make the first copy. Then they put the plate on a big, round roller on the printing press and flood it with water and ink. The oily ink will stick to the plate only where your images and text should be; the water will make sure it doesn't stick to the other areas (using the idea that oil and water don't mix). Next to that roller is another one known

Figure 6.26 Copy this image three times and you'll lose detail in the brightest part of the image. (©2003 Ben Willmore)

Printing a grayscale image on a color inkjet printer will usually produce an image that has a colorcast. To avoid that problem, be sure to print grayscale images using only black ink. This can usually be accomplished in the print settings for your inkjet printer.

If the dot-gain setting you need isn't listed in the Working Spaces area, you'll need a custom setting. Turn on the Advanced Mode check box at the top of the dialog box, and then choose Custom Dot Gain from the Gray pop-up menu. To get a traditional dot-gain measurement (in which you measure only 50% gray), just add 50 to the dot gain setting you need, and enter the result in the 50% field.

If your image will be displayed only onscreen (and not printed), then change the Gray pop-up menu to the Gamma choice your monitor is set to. I'll show you how to set up your monitor in Chapter 8, "Color Management," but for now you should know that most Macs are set to 1.8 and most Windows machines are set to 2.2.

If your images are destined for multimedia output (such as web, video, or animation), then you can skip over the next few steps and go directly to Chapter 14, "Sharpening," to find out how to finish off your images.

as a blanket; it's just covered with rubber. The plate will come into contact with the blanket so the ink on the plate will transfer over to the blanket—that's your second copy. Finally, the blanket will transfer the ink onto a sheet of paper to create the last copy (**Figure 6.27**). Each time a copy is made, you lose some of the smallest dots in the image. Until you know how to compensate for this, you're likely to end up with pictures of people with big white spots in the middle of their foreheads.

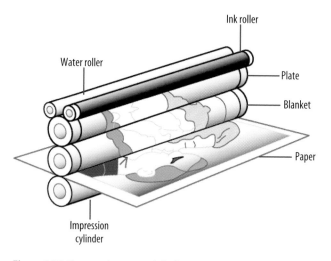

Figure 6.27 Three copies are made before your image turns into a printed page.

Before I show you how to compensate for the loss of detail in the bright areas of your image, let's look at what happens to the darkest areas, since we'll have to deal with them as well. When you print with ink on paper, the ink always gets absorbed into the paper and spreads out—just like when you spill coffee on your morning newspaper. This will cause the darkest areas of an image (97%, 98%, 99%) to become pure black. If you don't adjust for this, you will lose detail in the shadows of your image.

Most printing companies create a simple test strip that they print on the edge of your job, in the area that will be cropped after it's printed. This test strip contains shades of gray from 1% to about 5% to determine the lightest shade of gray that doesn't disappear on press and become pure white. Of course, the folks in the printing industry don't just use plain English to describe it; instead, they invented the term "minimum highlight dot reproducible on press." The test strip area also contains shades of gray from 99% to about 75% so they can see the darkest shade of gray that doesn't become pure black. For that one, they came up with the term "maximum shadow dot reproducible on press." If you ask your printing company, they can usually tell you exactly which settings to use. I know you don't always know who will print your images or don't have the time to ask, so I'll give you some generic numbers to use (**Tables 6.2** and **6.3**). But first, let's find out how we adjust for minimum highlight and maximum shadow dots.

Here's where you come in, and also where we get back to Levels. By moving the lower-right slider in the Levels dialog box, you will change white to the shade of gray the slider is pointing to. You want to move this slider until it points to the minimum highlight dot—that is, the lightest shade of gray that will not disappear and become white on-press.

You don't want to just eyeball this setting, so instead of just looking at the shades of gray, we'll use the Output Level numbers in the Levels dialog box. There is one problem with these numbers: They range from 0 to 255 instead of 0 to 100%! This is because you can have up to 256 shades of gray in a grayscale image, and Photoshop wants you to be able to control them all. When you're using this numbering system, think about light instead of ink. If you have no light (0), then it would be pitch black; if you have as much light as possible (255), you could call that white. So that you won't need a calculator, I'll give you a conversion table (**Table 6.4**).

TABLE 6.2 Common Minimum Highlight Settings

Newspapers	5%
Magazines and brochures	3%
High-end brochures	3%

TABLE 6.3 Common Maximum Shadow Settings

Newspapers	75%
Magazines and brochures	90%
High-end brochures	95%

NOTES

If you'd like to measure the minimum highlight and maximum shadow settings for an output device that you own, be sure to try the highlight/shadow test that's available on this book's companion web site at www.digitalmastery.com/test.

TABLE **6.4** Percentage Conversion Table

100%	0	66%	87	32%	174
99%	3	65%	90	31%	177
98%	5	64%	92	30%	179
97%	8	63%	95	29%	182
96%	10	62%	97	28%	184
95%	13	61%	100	27%	187
94%	15	60%	102	26%	189
93%	18	59%	105	25%	192
92%	20	58%	108	24%	195
91%	23	57%	110	23%	197
90%	26	56%	113	22%	200
89%	28	55%	115	21%	202
88%	31	54%	118	20%	205
87%	33	53%	120	19%	207
86%	36	52%	123	18%	210
85%	38	51%	125	17%	212
84%	41	50%	128	16%	215
83%	44	49%	131	15%	218
82%	46	48%	133	14%	220
81%	49	47%	136	13%	223
80%	51	46%	138	12%	225
79%	54	45%	141	11%	228
78%	56	44%	143	10%	230
77%	59	43%	146	9%	233
76%	61	42%	148	8%	236
75%	64	41%	151	7%	238
74%	67	40%	154	6%	241
73%	69	39%	156	5%	243
72%	72	38%	159	4%	246
71%	74	37%	161	3%	248
70%	77	36%	164	2%	251
69%	79	35%	166	1%	253
68%	82	34%	169	0%	255
67%	84	33%	172		

By moving the lower-left slider in the Levels dialog box, you will change black to the shade of gray the slider is pointing to (**Figure 6.28**). You want to move this slider until it points to the darkest shade of gray that will not plug up and become black (known as the maximum shadow dot).

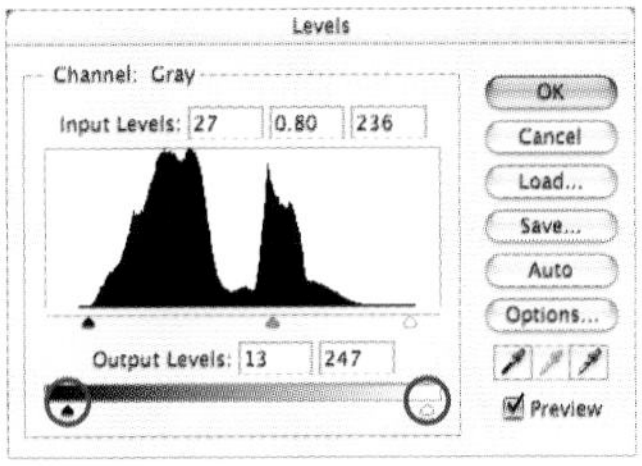

At first glance this stuff might seem complicated, but it is really quite simple. All you do is use the numbers from the tables or ask your printing company for settings. If you always print on the same kind of paper, you'll always use the same numbers.

Figure 6.28 The bottom sliders reduce image contrast to compensate for the limitations of the printing press.

A Quick Levels Recap

There are several steps to using Levels to adjust grayscale images, but as I've said, they're all quick and easy once you get used to them. Here's a brief recap of the role of each of the sliders in the Levels dialog box:

1. Move the upper-left slider until it touches the first bar on the histogram to force the darkest area of the image to black. Use the hidden Threshold feature—hold Option (Mac) or Alt (Windows)—to go as far as possible without damaging the image (**Figures 6.29** and **6.30**).

2. Move the upper-right slider until it touches the last bar on the histogram to force the brightest area of the image to white. Again, use the hidden feature to go as far as possible without damaging the image (**Figure 6.31**).

3. Move the middle slider until the brightness of the image looks appropriate (**Figure 6.32**).

4. Move the lower-left slider to make sure the shadows won't plug up and become pure black on the printing press. Use the tables I've provided for settings, or ask your printer for more precise ones (**Figure 6.33**).

5. Move the lower-right slider to make sure you don't lose detail in the highlights when the smallest dots in your image disappear on the printing press. Use the tables for settings, or ask your printer for more precise ones (**Figure 6.34**). I usually adjust all five sliders before clicking OK to apply them.

Figure 6.29 The original image.

Figure 6.30 Result of adjusting upper-left slider.

Figure 6.31 Result of adjusting upper-right slider.

Figure 6.32 Result of adjusting middle slider.

Figure 6.33 Result of adjusting lower-left slider.

Figure 6.34 Result of adjusting lower-right slider.

NOTES

If you own a 30-bit or higher scanner and your scanning software contains a histogram and has the same adjustment controls available, you can make adjustments within your scanning software. Most scanners can deliver a histogram without gaps because they can look back to the image and pick up extra shades of gray that would fill the gaps. These days, almost all scanners are 30-bit or higher. If your scanner is capable of delivering a 16-bit grayscale image to Photoshop, then the only adjustment you need to make during scanning is to make sure the highlights and shadows still have detail. If the histogram in your scanner has spikes at the ends, then lower the contrast setting and rescan until you don't get the spikes.

Postadjustment Analysis

Anytime you adjust an image, you run the risk of introducing some artifacts that might not be all that pleasant. So let's take a look at what can happen to your image after applying Levels. But don't worry—remember, in Photoshop there is usually at least one "fix" for every artifact.

Recognizing Posterization

When you look at an updated histogram, you might see wide gaps in the histogram—this indicates posterization (**Figure 6.35**). Posterization is when you should have a smooth transition between areas and instead you see a drastic jump between a bright and dark area. Some call this banding or stair-stepping. As long as the gaps in the histogram are smaller than three pixels wide, you probably won't notice it at all in the image.

Adjusting the image usually causes these gaps. As you adjust the image, the bars on the histogram spread out and gaps start to appear (remember that Slinky). The more extreme the adjustment you make, the wider the gaps. And if you see those huge gaps in the histogram, it'll probably mean that the posterization is noticeable enough that you'll want to fix it (it usually shows up in the dark areas of the image).

Eliminating Posterization

Here's a trick that can minimize the posterization. I should warn you that you have to apply this technique manually to each area that is posterized. Although it might take you a little bit of time, the results will be worth it.

To begin, select the Magic Wand tool, set the Tolerance to 0, and click on an area that looks posterized. Next, choose Select > Modify > Border, and use a setting of 2 for slight posterization or 4 for a moderate amount of posterization. Now apply Filter > Blur > Gaussian Blur until the area looks smooth (**Figures 6.36** and **6.37**). Repeat this process on all of the posterized areas until you're satisfied with the results. If you find that a large number of your images end up with post-scan posterization, then you might want to look into getting a scanner that's capable of delivering 16-bit images to Photoshop. A typical grayscale image will contain no more than 256 shades of gray, which is technically known as an 8-bit image. That's sufficient for most images, but extreme adjustments will cause posterization. One way to avoid posterization is to use a scanner that can produce images that contain thousands of shades of gray, which is technically known as a 16-bit image. Most scanners are capable of capturing more than 256 shades of gray from a photograph, but few are capable of actually delivering all those shades to Photoshop. So, the next time you shop for a scanner, be sure to ask if it is capable of delivering 16-bit images to Photoshop.

Closing Thoughts

Even though it's taken me a whole chapter to describe how to optimize your grayscale photos, keep in mind that the whole process takes about a minute once you're used to it. When you feel that you have mastered Levels, you will be ready to take on the ultimate adjustment tool—Curves. Curves is equipped to do the same basic corrections as

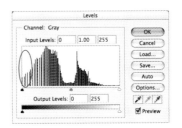

Figure 6.35 Gaps in a histogram indicate posterization.

To see an updated histogram after adjusting the image, you must first apply the adjustment, and then reopen the Levels dialog box. You can also choose Window > Histogram in Photoshop CS to see before and after histograms overlaid on each other.

I don't use this technique on every image, just on those that have extremely noticeable posterization.

Figure 6.36 Turn off the Preview check box to see the edges of the posterized area.

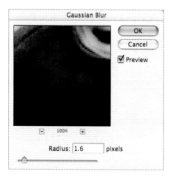

Figure 6.37 With the Preview check box turned on, increase the Radius setting until the posterized area appears smooth.

Levels, but can also do much, much more. In general, with grayscale images I always start out using Levels, and then move on to Curves to fix any problems that Levels can't handle; I also use Curves to work with color. It's like graduating from a Chevette to a Ferrari. The Ferrari takes more skill and coordination to master, but you get one hell of a ride. But that's another chapter.

Ben's Techno-Babble Decoder Ring

30-bit: Designates how many colors a scanner can capture (10 bits of red + 10 bits of green + 10 bits of blue = 30 bits total). So 10 bits per channel (RGB) is the same as 30 bits total. 10 bits = 2 to the tenth power, which equals 1,024. So a 30-bit scanner can capture 1.1 billion colors (1,024 × 1,024 × 1,024 = 1.1 billion), whereas a 24-bit scanner can capture only 16.7 million colors. When scanning in grayscale, a 24-bit scanner captures 256 grays and a 30-bit scanner captures 1,024 grays.

Maximum shadow dot: The largest halftone dot that will not combine with the surrounding halftone dots to become pure black. This is usually measured as a percentage, and reflects the highest percentage of ink that could be used without losing detail when printed. The type of paper usually determines what the maximum shadow dot setting will be.

Minimum highlight dot: The smallest halftone dot that is reproducible using a particular printing process. This is usually measured as a percentage, and reflects the lowest percentage of ink that will not lose detail when printed.

Keyboard Shortcuts

Function	Macintosh	Windows
Levels	Command-L	Ctrl-L
Auto Levels	Shift-Command-L	Shift-Ctrl-L
Reapply Previous Setting	Option-Command-L	Alt-Ctrl-L

©2003 Andy Katz

©2003 Andy Katz

Understanding Curves

Courtesy of Nick Koudis, www.koudis.com

Have patience. All things are difficult before they become easy.

—Saadi

Understanding Curves

NEW IN CS

Curves itself hasn't changed in Photoshop CS, but the addition of the new Histogram palette has the potential to completely change the way you think about adjusting images with Curves. The new Shadow/Highlight feature, useful when you need to make the detail in the shadow or highlights of an image easier to see, is also covered in this chapter.

If I were going to be dropped on a deserted island and could bring only one thing with me, I might choose a Swiss Army knife. With that knife, I could cut firewood, spear fish, and clean my teeth (remember the toothpick?). Much like a Swiss Army knife, Image > Adjustments > Curves can be used for just about anything. In fact, if I had to pick one adjustment tool to use all the time, it would definitely be Curves. By mastering the Curves dialog box, you have so much control over your images that you might wonder why you would ever need to use the Levels or Brightness/Contrast dialog box. Let's take a look at some of the things you can do with the Curves dialog box. You can

▶ Pull out far more detail than is possible to see with the Sharpening filters (**Figures 7.1** to **7.3**).

▶ Lighten or darken areas without making selections (**Figures 7.4** and **7.5**).

▶ Turn ordinary text into extraordinary text (**Figures 7.6** and **7.7**).

▶ Enhance color and contrast in seconds (**Figures 7.8** and **7.9**).

Figure 7.1 The original image. (©2003 Ben Willmore)

Figure 7.2 After applying the Unsharp Mask filter.

Figure 7.3 After a simple Curves adjustment.

Figure 7.4 The original image. (©2003 Ben Willmore)

Figure 7.5 After a simple Curves adjustment.

Figure 7.6 The original text effect.

Figure 7.7 After a simple Curves adjustment.

Figure 7.8 The original image. (©2003 PhotoSpin, www.photospin.com)

Figure 7.9 After a simple Curves adjustment.

None of these changes could be made by using Levels or Brightness/Contrast (that is, not without making complicated selections or losing control over the result). Now you can see why you'll want to master Curves!

Using Curves, you can perform all the adjustments available in the Levels, Brightness/Contrast, and Threshold dialog boxes, and much, much more. In fact, you can independently adjust each of the 256 shades of gray in your image (**Figure 7.10**).

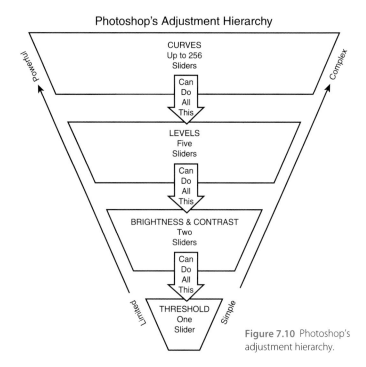

Figure 7.10 Photoshop's adjustment hierarchy.

With Power Comes Complexity

I find that the majority of Photoshop users never truly master (or even become comfortable with) Curves, just as some people never drive cars with manual transmissions. Perhaps the first time they tried to drive with a clutch, they drove up a really steep hill and encountered a stop sign at the top. Then, maybe a big garbage truck pulled up behind them within what seemed like an inch of their bumper.

If you've ever driven a car with a clutch, you know what I'm getting at. When you're not comfortable with something and are forced to use it in a challenging situation, the tendency is to give up. However, if you've spent enough time getting comfortable with a manual transmission, you don't even think about it when you're driving. Curves works the same way. If you just play around with it, you might get scared off, but if you hang in there, it becomes easier to use, and you'll find yourself doing some amazing things to your images. This chapter might seem long-winded, but the truth is that until you truly "get" Curves, you will be a prisoner of Photoshop's less powerful tools. So, fasten your seatbelt, adjust your rearview mirror, and settle in for the ride.

But First, a Test!

Before we delve into Curves, I want to test your present knowledge of the Curves dialog box. Don't worry, though, because the lower your score, the more you should enjoy this chapter.

Look at the curve shown in **Figure 7.11** and see if you can answer the following questions:

▶ Which shades will lose detail from this adjustment?

▶ Which shades will become brighter?

▶ What happened to 62% gray?

▶ What happened to the image's contrast?

If you truly understand the Curves dialog box, then you found these questions extremely easy to answer. However, if you hesitated before answering any of them or couldn't answer them at all, then this chapter was designed for you.

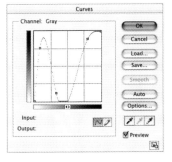

Figure 7.11 Can you figure out exactly what this curve will do to an image?

The Idea Behind Curves

Because the Curves dialog box allows you to adjust every shade of gray in an image independently of the others (256 in all), it works quite a bit differently from the other adjustment tools. To get a clearer picture of what Curves does, let's construct our own Curves dialog box from scratch, using something you're already familiar with: the plain old vanilla bar chart. You know what I'm talking about—those wretched bar charts that can't be avoided in magazines, brochures, television, and pretty much everywhere you look. Now we can finally put one to good use by using it to help us understand Curves.

What if you create a bar chart that indicates how much light your monitor uses to display each color in an image? This bar chart would be just like any other that you've seen, where taller bars mean more light and shorter bars mean less. You could show the shade of gray you are using below each bar, and then draw a line from the top of each bar over to the left so you could label how much light is being used for each shade. I think you'd end up with something that looks like **Figure 7.12**. Or you could just as easily change the chart to indicate how much ink your ink-jet printer would use to reproduce the image. Now that we're talking about ink, short bars would mean less ink, which would produce a light shade of gray, and tall bars would mean a lot of ink and would produce a dark shade of gray. To make the change, all we'd have to do is flip all the shades at the bottom of the graph so the dark ones are below the tall bars and the bright ones are below the short bars. The result would look like **Figure 7.13**, right?

All the techniques mentioned in this chapter apply equally to images prepared for web pages and those prepared for print. You might notice that I concentrate on ink settings throughout this chapter. I find that most users are more comfortable thinking about how ink would affect their image instead of light. Ink is the exact opposite of light, so Photoshop can easily translate what you're attempting to do, even if your image will be displayed using light.

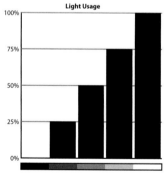

Figure 7.12 This bar chart indicates the amount of light used to display the shades of gray shown at the bottom.

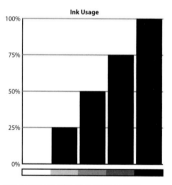

Figure 7.13 Flip the shades at the bottom, and you've got a graph that represents ink usage.

Okay, now that you've got the concept, let's expand on that to accommodate the real world. Our basic bar chart might work for a simple logo with just a few shades of gray (one bar representing each shade), but most of your images will contain many more than that. So, we just increase the number of bars (**Figure 7.14**), right? Well, sort of. The fact is, your image can contain up to 256 shades of gray. But if we jam 256 bars (one for each shade) into our chart, then they won't look like bars anymore; they'll just turn into a big mass (**Figure 7.15**). You can't see the individual bars because there isn't any space between them.

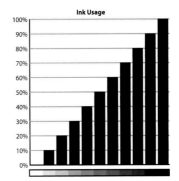

Figure 7.14 Add more bars for additional accuracy.

All the same, our images contain up to 256 shades of gray, so we really need that many bars in our chart. Now that they're all smashed together, we don't have room to label each bar, so why don't we just overlay a grid (**Figure 7.16**) and label that instead? If that grid isn't detailed enough for you, we could add a more detailed grid, such as the one shown in **Figure 7.17**.

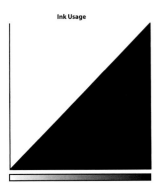

Figure 7.15 The 256 bars take up so much space that the chart no longer looks like a bar chart.

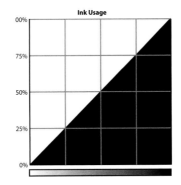

Figure 7.16 A grid can help you figure out how much ink is used.

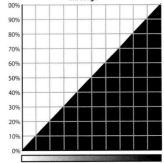

Figure 7.17 The more detailed grid allows you to be even more accurate.

If you've followed along and this makes sense to you, then you have grasped the principle behind Curves. We have just a bit more to go. Stick with me, and trust me—all these details are well worth slogging through because they'll help you get a much deeper understanding of Curves.

The sample chart we've created isn't really all that useful… yet. It's not telling you anything you can't find in the Info

NOTES

16-bit images in Photoshop can contain up to 32,767 shades of gray. When working with this type of image, Photoshop still presents you with a curve that represents only 256 shades of gray, even though it's accurately adjusting all the 32,767 shades that are in your image.

or Color palettes. For example, if you really want to know how much ink (or light) you'd use to reproduce a shade of gray, you could just open the Info palette by choosing Window > Info (**Figure 7.18**), and then move your pointer over the image; the Info palette would indicate how much ink would be used in that area. The Color palette (Window > Color) is set up similarly, and will tell you how much ink or light makes up a shade of gray (**Figure 7.19**). The main difference between the two methods is that the Info palette gives you information about your image—specifically, what's under the pointer. The Color palette isn't image-specific but gives you generic information about how much ink or light makes up a shade of gray.

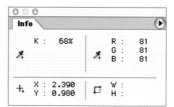

Figure 7.18 The Info palette indicates how much ink or light would be used to reproduce the color that is under the pointer.

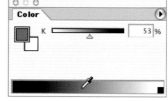

Figure 7.19 The Color palette indicates how much ink would be used to reproduce your current foreground color.

The Curves dialog box, meanwhile, is really just a simple bar chart—with a lot of bars that are very close together—that shows how much ink or light will be used in your image. The gradient at the bottom shows all the shades of gray you could possibly have, and the chart above shows how much ink or light will be used to create each shade. But the wonderful thing about the Curves dialog box is that it doesn't just sit there like a static bar chart that only gives you information. It's interactive—you can use it to change the amount of ink (or light) used to reproduce your image (**Figure 7.20**).

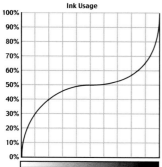

Figure 7.20 Changing the shape of the line in the Curves graph changes how much ink is used throughout the image.

Think of our Ink Usage bar graph: As the shades of gray get steadily darker, each shade uses slightly more ink, resulting in a straight diagonal line. But in the Curves graph, you can move points on the line. For example, you can flatten the line so that in your modified image, many shades of gray are represented by a single shade. Or you can make a dramatic change to the line, dragging a point up or down so that a shade changes to become much darker or lighter.

The Gradients Are Your Guide

Go ahead and pick any shade of gray from the gradient, and then look above it to figure out how much ink would be used to create it (**Figure 7.21**). You can use the grid to help you calculate the exact amount of ink used (about 23% in this case). But wouldn't you rather see what 23% looks like? Suppose we replace those percentage numbers with another gradient that shows how bright each area would be (**Figure 7.22**). Just to make sure you don't get the two gradients confused, read the next two sentences twice: The bottom gradient represents the shades of gray you are changing. The side gradient indicates how bright or dark a shade will become if you move the line to a certain height (**Figure 7.23**).

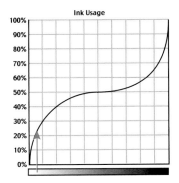

Figure 7.21 Use the grid to help determine how much ink is used in an area.

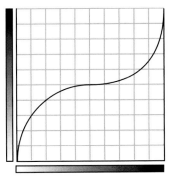

Figure 7.22 The gradient on the left indicates how dark an area will become if the curve is moved to a certain height.

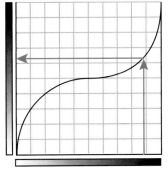

Figure 7.23 The bottom gradient scale is what you're changing. The left gradient scale is what you changed it to.

Congratulations. You've survived Ben's Bar Charts 101. Now you're ready to graduate from charts and take flight with the full-fledged Curves dialog box (**Figure 7.24**). Does it look familiar? It should. You might notice that the Curves dialog box is a bit smaller than the bar chart we were using. To get a larger grid, click the zoom icon in the lower right of the Curves dialog box. Each time you click this symbol, it toggles between a grid that's 171 pixels wide and one that's 256 pixels wide (**Figure 7.25**). I generally use the large grid because it shows all the grays you can have in your image, which makes it easier to be precise. In fact, if you use the small version, you can't control every shade of gray (your image contains 256 shades of gray, and the smaller grid is only 171 pixels wide). I use the 171-pixel version only when working on a small screen, because then the large version covers up too much of the image.

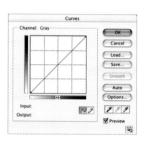

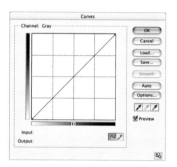

Figure 7.24 The grid in the small version of the Curves dialog box is only 171 pixels wide.

Figure 7.25 The grid in the large version of the Curves dialog box is 256 pixels wide.

Ben, Are We There Yet?

I know what you're thinking. "I wanna play with Curves, now!" Be calm, you're almost ready. There are just a couple of thoughts I need to plant in your brain first.

If you go back to when we first started to create the bar chart, you'll remember that we started measuring how much light our monitor was using to display things. Then we flip-flopped and measured how much ink we'd use for printing. The same thinking applies to the Curves dialog box. Remember how we accomplished that switch earlier in the chapter—didn't we just reverse the shades of gray at the bottom of the chart? Hold that thought, and look at the middle of the gradient at the bottom of the Curves dialog box. Clicking those arrows reverses the gradient, which toggles the chart's context between ink and light (**Figures 7.26** and **7.27**).

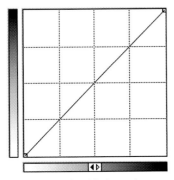 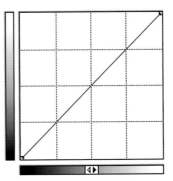

Figure 7.26 When black is at the top, you are using ink (remember, up means more).

Figure 7.27 When white is at the top, you are using light (again, up means more).

The *mode* of your image determines what you'll start with. Photoshop assumes that images that are in grayscale, CMYK, or Lab mode will be printed, and therefore it defaults to using the gradient that represents ink. Because your monitor displays everything using red, green, and blue light, images in RGB mode will cause Photoshop to use the gradient that represents light.

Photoshop doesn't care which system you use. It can easily translate between the two, because light is the exact opposite of ink. When you switch from one scale to the other, not only do the light and dark ends of the gradients get swapped, but also the curve flips upside down. Be sure to look out for which mode I use throughout the examples in this chapter; otherwise, you might end up getting the exact opposite result of what you see in this book! I'll stick to the default settings unless there's a good reason to change them, and when I do, I'll clue you in.

Remember, the side gradient indicates what you'll end up with if you move a point on the curve to a certain height. You can always glance at the side to find out how much light or ink you're using. Just remember that up means more of something, and that you can use either light or ink.

Next comes the grid. Remember how we ended up with one that is more detailed than the one we started with? Well, you can toggle between those two grids by Option-clicking (Mac) or Alt-clicking (Windows) anywhere within

You can press the Option (Mac) or Alt (Windows) key when choosing Image > Adjustments > Curves to apply the last settings used on an image.

the grid area. It's up to you which grid you use. It doesn't affect the result you'll get in Curves; it's just a personal preference (**Figure 7.28**).

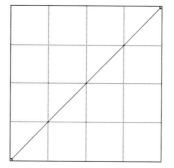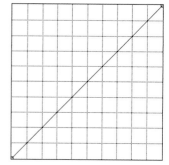

Figure 7.28 Option-click (Mac) or Alt-click (Windows) anywhere on the grid to toggle between a 25% increment grid (left) and a 10% increment grid (right).

Taking Curves for a Test Drive

Okay, start your engines. We're going to stop babbling and start driving! Go ahead—open an image, choose Image > Adjustments > Curves, and start messing with the curve. Just click anywhere on the curve to add a point, and then drag it around to change the shape of the curve. If you want to get rid of a point, drag it off the edge of the grid. You can also click a point and then use the arrow keys on your keyboard to nudge it around the grid. You can even add the Shift key to the arrow keys to nudge it in larger increments.

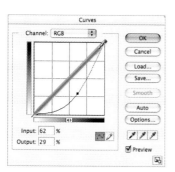

Figure 7.29 Use a pencil to represent the original line.

You should quickly find that it's pretty easy to screw up your image! That's because we haven't talked about specific types of adjustments yet. So, let's explore the final piece of the Curves puzzle. To understand what you're doing, you must compare the curve you're making to the original line. After all, how can you know how much of a change you've made unless you know where you started? I usually just grab a pencil and hold it up to the screen to represent the original line (**Figure 7.29**). Now let's see what we can do with all this.

Improving Dark Images

Try this: Open any grayscale image you think is too dark (I'll show you how to work with color in a minute), like the one shown in **Figure 7.30**. Next, choose Image > Adjustments > Curves, and add a point by clicking the middle of the line. Pull the line straight down, and see what happens to your image (**Figure 7.31**). Compare the curve with the gradient at the left of the Curves dialog box. The farther you move the curve down, the less ink you use and therefore the brighter the image becomes. If part of the curve bottoms out, the shade represented by that area becomes pure white because there will be no ink used when the image is printed.

Figure 7.30 Start with a dark grayscale image. (©2003 PhotoSpin, www.photospin.com)

Figure 7.31 Move the curve down to reduce how much ink is used.

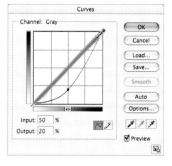

Figure 7.32 Comparing the curve with the gradients.

Any part of a curve that's below the original line indicates an area that is using less ink, which means that it has been brightened. Look at the gradient directly below those areas to determine which shades of the image were brightened (**Figure 7.32**). The farther the line is moved down from its original position, the brighter the image will become (**Figure 7.33**).

Previewing the Changes

You can compare the original and changed versions of the image by checking or unchecking the Preview check box. As long as the check box is unchecked, you'll see what the image looked like before the adjustment. When you click to check it, you'll see the changes you just made.

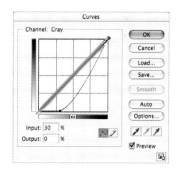

Figure 7.33 To figure out how much ink you've removed, look below where the line used to be.

Color Is Different

The concepts and adjustments we talk about with Curves apply equally to grayscale and color images. But when you

Figure 7.34 Choose Edit > Fade Curves to limit your changes to the brightness of your image.

Figure 7.35 When creating an adjustment layer, change the Mode menu selection to Luminosity.

work on a color image, you have to be more careful; otherwise, you might end up shifting the colors, rather than just the brightness, of your image. There are two ways to apply Curves to your image, and therefore two methods for limiting its effect on the brightness of a color image. First, you can apply Curves to the currently active layer by choosing Image > Adjustments > Curves. Immediately after applying Curves, you can choose Edit > Fade Curves and set the Mode pop-up menu to Luminosity (**Figure 7.34**). The Fade command will limit the last change you made (Curves, in our case) to changing only the brightness (luminosity is just another word for brightness) of the image—it will not be able to shift the colors or change how saturated they are.

Your other choice would be to apply Curves to more than one layer by choosing Layer > New Adjustment Layer > Curves. Then, when prompted (**Figure 7.35**), you would set the Mode pop-up menu to Luminosity. An adjustment layer will affect all the layers below it but none of the layers above it. It's also a nonpermanent change, because you can double-click on the adjustment-layer thumbnail in that layer to reopen the Curves dialog box and make changes. That means that any Curves techniques you use for adjusting grayscale images will work on color images if you use the Luminosity blending mode (**Figures 7.36** to **7.38**).

Figure 7.36 Original image. (©2003 Stockbyte, www.stockbyte.com)

Figure 7.37 After adjusting contrast with Curves, the color and saturation change.

Figure 7.38 Using the Luminosity blending mode prevents adjustments from shifting the colors in the image.

Color shifts aren't the only problems you'll encounter when adjusting color images with Curves. The mode your image is in might be having an adverse effect on the adjustment. RGB color images are made from three components (red, green, and blue). A bright green color might be made out of 0 red, 255 green, and 128 blue. When you first open the Curves dialog box, the pop-up menu at the top of the dialog box will be set to RGB, which will cause any points to affect the exact same R, G, and B values. Clicking on that green color in your image will display a circle at 165 on the curve, which will affect all the areas that contain 165 red, 165 blue, and 165 green. Equal amounts of R, G, and B create gray. So, simply clicking on the curve of a color image will usually cause the colors to shift in an unsatisfactory way, because the circle that appears when clicking on your image will not accurately target the area you clicked on. While working in RGB mode, all color areas will shift because their RGB mix will change as the Curves dialog box shifts the RGB values in equal amounts. Ideally it would affect only the exact mix of RGB that the color is made from, but it doesn't work that way in RGB mode. The solution to this problem is to convert your image to Lab mode by choosing Image > Mode > Lab Color. In Lab mode, your image is made from three components: Lightness, A, and B. When you adjust your image, the Curves dialog box will automatically set itself to work on the Lightness information, which will prevent your adjustment from shifting the color of your image and will also make it so that the circle will show up in the correct position to make accurate adjustments. Once you're done with your adjustment, I'd suggest that you convert the image back to RGB mode because many of Photoshop's features are not available in Lab mode. I don't use Lab mode for every color image; I reserve it for those images that are troublesome in RGB mode.

Increasing Contrast and Detail

So far, we've learned that moving the curve up or down will increase or decrease the amount of ink or light used to make the image. Now let's look at how changing the angle of the curve can help us. What if you had an image where

You can hold down Option (Mac) or Alt (Windows) to set options such as the Blending mode when you are creating an adjustment layer.

Figure 7.39 You can't see much detail in this image because the brightness is limited to 0%–25%. (©2003 Andy Katz)

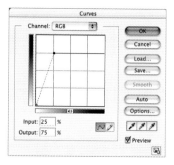

Figure 7.40 This curve adds more contrast, making it easier to see the detail in the whole image.

Figure 7.41 After making the curve steeper, it's easier to see the detail.

the brightest area was white and the darkest area was only 25% gray? Would it be easy to see the detail in the image? I don't think so (**Figure 7.39**).

Now think about how that image would change if we applied the curve shown in **Figure 7.40**. If you look closely at this curve, you'll notice that areas that are white in the original image wouldn't change at all and areas that used to be 25% gray would end up being around 75% gray. Wouldn't that make it much easier to see the detail in the whole image? In an overexposed image like this one, you have to make the curve steeper in the lighter part of the curve. (We already learned that in an underexposed image—refer to **Figure 7.30**—you have to make the dark part of the curve steeper to bring out the detail.) You always have to compare the curve with the original line to determine how much of a change you've made. If you make the curve just a little steeper than the original, then you'll add just a little contrast to that area. Anytime you add contrast, it becomes easier to see the detail in that area because the difference between the bright and dark parts becomes more pronounced (**Figure 7.41**). Remember to look at the gradient below to figure out which shades of gray you are changing.

Open any grayscale image, and choose Image > Adjustments > Curves. Move your pointer over the image, and then click and drag across the area where you want to exaggerate the detail. You'll notice that a circle appears in the Curves dialog box. Photoshop is simply looking at the bottom gradient to find the shade of gray under your pointer; it then puts a circle on the curve directly above that shade. This circle indicates the area of the curve that needs to be changed to affect the area you're dragging across. Add control points on either side of this area of the curve. Next, move the top point you just added up toward the top of the chart, and move the bottom point down toward the bottom of the chart. The area you dragged across should appear to have more detail (**Figures 7.42** to **7.44**).

Figure 7.42 Original image. (©2003 Andy Katz)

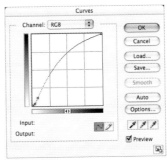

Figure 7.43 Find the range you'd like to change, and then make the curve steeper in that area.

Figure 7.44 After making the curve steeper.

You might also need to fix the rest of the curve to make sure that the contrast in those areas doesn't change radically. You can do this by adding another point and moving it so that the majority of the curve looks normal—that is, diagonal (**Figure 7.45**).

Figure 7.45 Fix the rest of the curve so you don't exaggerate the contrast in other areas.

Decreasing Contrast and Detail

Any part of the curve that's flatter (more horizontal) than the original line indicates an area where the contrast has been reduced (shades of gray become more similar). Look at the gradient directly below these areas to determine which shades of the image were changed. The flatter the line becomes, the less contrast you'll see in that area of the image. When you lower the amount of contrast in an image, it becomes harder to see detail. This can be useful if you want detail to be less visible. If the curve becomes completely horizontal in an area, you've lost all detail there (**Figures 7.46** to **7.48**). Remember, it's a bar chart—the same height means the same brightness.

NOTES

Clicking on a CMYK image will not display a circle. That's because black ink is used only in the darker areas of an image, which means that it would be ideal to adjust it separately from the other colors that make up a CMYK image.

Figure 7.46 Original image. (©2003 Andy Katz)

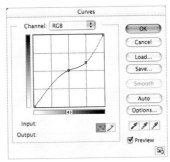

Figure 7.47 Curves used to reduce apparent detail in woodwork.

Figure 7.48 Result of applying Curves to reduce apparent detail.

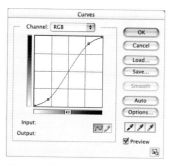

Figure 7.49 A classic S curve.

Let's Analyze a Classic Tip

Have you ever heard the tip, "Make an S curve"? Well, let's explore exactly what an S curve does (**Figure 7.49**).

Remember, to find out what a curve is doing to your image, you should compare the curve with the original line. Look at the areas of the curve that are steeper than the original line—in this case, the middle of the curve. The shades represented by these steeper areas will appear to have more detail. Whenever you pull detail out of one part of an image, you'll also lose detail in another part. Therefore, look at either end of the curve, at the areas of the curve that are flatter than the original line (more horizontal). These areas appear to have less detail. Thus, an S curve attempts to exaggerate detail in the middle grays of the image. However, it also gives you less detail in the highlights and shadows.

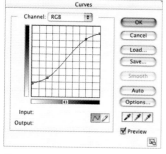

Figure 7.50 After this adjustment, the image won't contain any areas darker than 90% or brighter than 18%.

Checking Ink Ranges

Look at **Figure 7.50** and concentrate on the gradient at the left side of the Curves dialog box. This gradient indicates how dark an area will become if you move the curve to a particular height. Pick a shade of gray from that gradient (such as 90%); then look directly to the right of it to determine if you'll have any areas that shade of gray. Pick another shade and do the same thing. If the curve starts in the lower-left corner and ends in the upper-right corner, each one of the shades should be used somewhere in the image. However, there might be a few shades that are used in more than one area of the curve.

You can reset the Curves dialog box back to the default line by pressing and holding Option (Mac) or Alt (Windows) and then clicking the Reset button. The Cancel button turns into a Reset button when you hold down the proper key.

Inverting Your Image

Think of a stock-market chart that indicates what's happening to the market over a month's time. If you're like most investors, whenever the market's going up, you're happy. However, you're always carefully watching that chart to see if the market starts to dip. If it does, that's when you start to panic. You can think of curves in the same way. As long as the curve is rising, you're fine; however, if the curve starts to fall, you should expect unusual results. Look at **Figure 7.51**, and try to figure out what's happening in the area that's going downhill. The dark areas of the image (around 75%) became bright, and the bright areas (around 25%) became dark. That means you've inverted that part of the image. You'll usually want to minimize or avoid this situation unless you're going for a special effect (**Figures 7.52** and **7.53**).

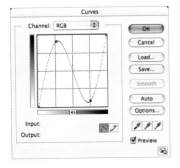

Figure 7.51 Areas between 25% and 75% have been inverted.

Figure 7.52 Original image. (©2003 PhotoSpin, www.photospin.com)

Figure 7.53 Result of applying the curve shown in Figure 7.51 and fading it using Luminosity mode.

Freeform Curves

To change the curve, you're not limited to adding and moving points. Another way to define a curve is to click the pencil icon at the bottom of the Curves dialog box and draw a freeform shape (**Figure 7.54**). However, the shape you draw has to resemble a line moving from left to right. Go ahead, just try to draw a circle. You can't do it. That's because the Curves dialog box is just like a bar chart, and you can't have two bars for a single shade. Just for giggles, draw a really wild-looking line across the grid area, and then look at your image. Drawing your own line with the Pencil tool is usually better for special effects than for simple image adjustments.

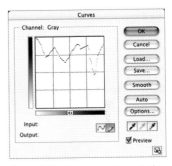

Figure 7.54 A curve created with the Pencil tool.

Let's take a quick look at some of the things you can do when working with a freeform curve:

▶ **Smoothing:** After creating a curve with the Pencil tool, you can click the Smooth button to smooth out the shape you drew (**Figure 7.55**). Go ahead and click it multiple times to keep smoothing the curve.

▶ **Converting to points:** To convert any line drawn with the Pencil tool into a normal curve, click the curve icon (**Figure 7.56**).

▶ **Drawing straight lines:** You can also draw straight lines with the Pencil tool (**Figure 7.57**). Just Shift-click across the graph area, and Photoshop will connect the dots to create a straight line.

▶ **Posterizing:** By drawing a stair-step shape with the Pencil tool, you can accomplish the same effect as if you had used the Posterize command (**Figure 7.58**).

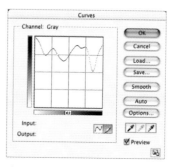

Figure 7.55 A freeform curve after Smooth is applied.

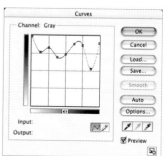

Figure 7.56 The result of converting a freeform curve into a normal curve.

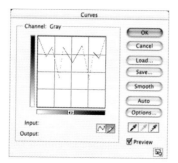

Figure 7.57 Straight lines drawn by Shift-clicking with the Pencil tool.

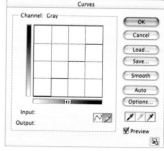

Figure 7.58 Drawing stair-steps is the same as choosing Image > Adjust > Posterize.

To try this out, open the image called chrome.jpg from the CD, and then play around with the Pencil tool in the Curves dialog box. Try making a huge M or W, and experiment with different shapes. You should be able to transform the 3D type into some cool-looking chrome text if you experiment long enough (**Figures 7.59 to 7.61**).

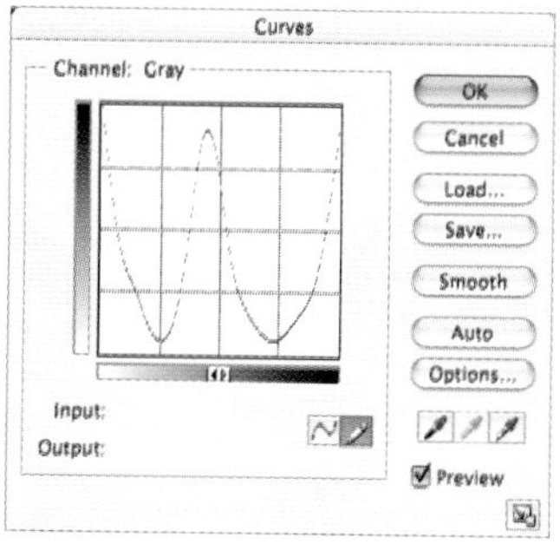

Figure 7.59 Freeform curve used to create chrome effect.

Figure 7.60 Image from the CD.

Figure 7.61 Result of applying the curve in Figure 7.59.

Input and Output Numbers

The Input and Output numbers at the bottom of the Curves dialog box allow you to be very precise when adjusting an image. Input is the shade of gray being changed; Output is what it will become. When the points on the curve appear as hollow squares, the Input and Output numbers relate to your pointer. The Input number tells you which shade of gray is directly below your pointer. The Output number tells you what the shade of gray (height of the bar chart) would be if you moved the curve to the height of your pointer.

Try it. First, click the curve icon (not the pencil), and then make sure that none of the points on the curve are solid. Do this by moving your pointer around until it looks like a white arrow, and then click the mouse. Now move your pointer around the grid area. You'll notice the Input and Output numbers changing. All they're doing is telling you which shades of gray are directly below and to the left of your pointer (**Figure 7.62**). If you trace over the shape of a curve, the Input and Output numbers will show you exactly what the curve is doing to all the shades of gray in your image.

Two Numbering Systems

Two different numbering systems can be used in the Curves dialog box. You can switch between the 0–100% system and the 0–255 numbering system (which we used in Levels) by switching between ink and light (remember the little arrows that appear in the middle of the bottom gradient). Go ahead and give it a try (**Figure 7.63**).

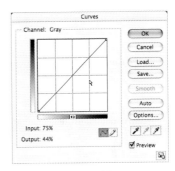

Figure 7.62 Input and Output numbers indicate the location of your pointer relative to the two gradients in the Curves dialog box.

Figure 7.63 Click the arrow symbol to switch numbering systems.

If you're working on an image that's in RGB mode, Photoshop assumes you're going to use the image on-screen instead of printing it. Therefore, when you open Curves, it uses Input and Output numbers ranging from 0 to 255. These numbers represent the amount of light your monitor will use to display the image onscreen (0 = no light, or black; 255 = maximum light, or white). Using this numbering system allows you to have control over each shade.

If you're working on an image that's in grayscale or CMYK mode, Photoshop assumes you'll be printing the image. Therefore, when you open Curves, it uses numbers ranging from 0% to 100%. These numbers represent the amount of ink used to reproduce each level of gray in the image (0% = no ink; 100% = solid ink).

When you click the arrows that switch between the two numbering systems, Photoshop also reverses the gradients at the bottom and left of the graph. It does this to keep the zero point of each numbering system in the lower-left corner of the graph, which effectively changes between light and ink. You don't have to remember or understand why this happens—it's just nice to know there's a reason behind it.

When you switch the numbering system, this also changes the gradient on the left side of the Curves dialog box. Therefore, if you're using the 0–255 numbering system, you have to move a curve up to brighten the image and down to darken it (the exact opposite of what you do in the 0–100% numbering system). I always look at the gradient on the left to remind me: If black is at the top (the 0–100% system), you're using ink, and moving a curve up will darken the image. If white is at the top of the gradient (the 0–255 system), you're using light, and moving a curve up will brighten the image.

Entering Numbers

After you've created a point, it will appear as a solid square. This represents the point that's currently being edited. The Input and Output numbers at the bottom of the dialog box indicate the change this point will make to an image. The Input number represents the shade of gray that's being changed. The Output number indicates what's happening to the shade of gray—the value that you're changing it to. As long as the point appears as a solid square, you can type numbers into the Input and Output fields to change the location of the point (**Figure 7.64**).

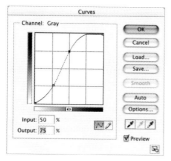

Figure 7.64 To alter the position of a point on the curve, just change one of the numbers.

Those numbers can be very useful. We'll end up depending on them once we get into the chapter on color correction (Chapter 9). But for now, let's see how they can be useful when attempting to change the brightness of an image. Remember that you can click on your image and a circle will appear in the Curves dialog box that indicates what part of the curve would affect the shade in that area? Well, you can also Command-click (Mac) or Ctrl-click (Windows) on your image and Photoshop will add a point where that circle would show up. So, what if you'd like two areas of your image to have the same brightness level? Command-click or Ctrl-click one of them to lock in its brightness level. Then, before you release the mouse button, glance at the numbers at the bottom of the Curves dialog box to see exactly how bright that area is. Command-click or Ctrl-click the second area, and change the Output number to match that of the first object (**Figure 7.65**). The bar chart will be the same height in both areas, which means that both areas will end up with the same brightness. But you have to be careful when doing this, because the bar chart will flatten out between those two points. When that happens, there won't be any detail in those shades, so other parts of your image might seem to disappear (**Figures 7.66** and **7.67**).

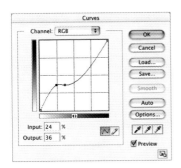

Figure 7.65 When two points are at the same height, those two areas will have the same brightness level.

Figure 7.66 Original image. (©2003 PhotoSpin, www.photospin.com)

Figure 7.67 Result of making the far and close buildings the same brightness levels.

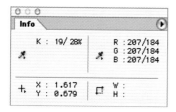

Figure 7.68 The left number is what you have before using Curves; the right number is what you get after using Curves.

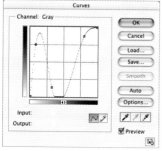

Figure 7.69 Can you figure out what this curve will do to an image?

The Info Palette

The Info palette can also show you how Curves affects your image (**Figure 7.68**). When you move your pointer over the image, the Info palette indicates what's happening to that area of the image. (If you want a more precise cursor, press the Caps Lock key to change your cursor from the default eyedropper to the crosshairs.) The left number in the Info palette tells you how dark the area is before using Curves. The right number tells you how dark it will be after Curves is applied.

A Quick Recap

Now, to verify that you're ready to move on, you should make sure you understand the general concepts. Take a look at the curve in **Figure 7.69** and see if you can answer the following questions:

▶   Which areas of the image will lose detail with this adjustment?

▶   Which areas of the image will become brighter?

▶   What happened to 62% gray?

▶   What happened to the image's contrast?

Just in case you couldn't answer all these questions, let's recap what we've covered:

▶   Flattening a curve will reduce contrast and make it more difficult to see detail.

▶   Making a curve steeper will increase contrast and make it easier to see detail.

▶   Up means darken in the 0–100% system.

▶   Down means darken in the 0–255 system.

▶   Up means brighten in the 0–255 system.

▶   Down means brighten in the 0–100% system.

The Histogram Palette

The new Histogram palette is a really useful addition to Photoshop and, used properly, can help you make sure that your adjustments don't get out of control and end up harming your images instead of improving them. So, now that you have an idea of how to think about Curves, let's figure out how to use the Histogram palette (**Figure 7.70**) to make sure we don't go too far with our adjustments.

Figure 7.70 The Histogram palette.

Actually, histograms aren't new to Photoshop CS, but in previous versions you could see one only while you were adjusting your image with Levels, or after you'd finished an adjustment (by choosing Image > Histogram). In Photoshop CS, you can see a histogram at any time, no matter which adjustment feature you've decided to use. To display the Histogram palette, choose Window > Histogram.

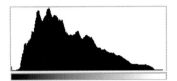

Figure 7.71 Imagine that there is a gradient below the histogram.

A histogram is a simple bar chart that shows you the range of brightness levels that your image is made out of and how prevalent each shade is compared to the others. When you look at the histogram, imagine that there's a gradient stretched across the bottom of the bar chart that has black on the left and white on the right (**Figure 7.71**). Then if you look above any shade of gray, you can see if that brightness level is present in your image. If there's a bar above the shade, then it's used somewhere in your image. If there's no bar, then that brightness level is nowhere to be found in your image. The height of the bar indicates how prevalent a particular brightness level is compared to the others that make up your image.

NOTES

The Histogram palette can be used in two different sizes—Compact or Expanded. I prefer to use the Expanded version because it is exactly 256 pixels wide and most images contain 256 shades of gray, which makes that version the most accurate histogram for your image. You can switch between the two different views on the side menu of the Histogram palette.

When you start to adjust an image, the Histogram palette will overlay a histogram that represents the current state of the image (black) with another histogram that represents what the image looked like before you started adjusting it (gray) (**Figure 7.72**).

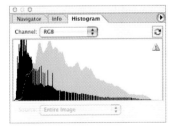

Figure 7.72 The gray histogram reflects the unadjusted image, whereas the black version reflects the adjusted image.

Figure 7.73 This image has a very limited brightness range. (©2003 Ben Willmore)

Figure 7.74 The histogram for the image in Figure 7.73.

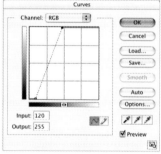

Figure 7.75 The Curves adjustment used to add contrast to the image.

Achieving Optimal Contrast

If the histogram doesn't extend all the way across the full width of the histogram area, then your image has a limited brightness range (**Figures 7.73** and **7.74**). When that's the case, you can usually move the upper-right and lower-left points on a curve toward the middle, which will widen the histogram (**Figures 7.75** and **7.76**). As you do, keep an eye on the histogram. Most images will look their best (**Figure 7.77**) when the histogram extends all the way across the area available, without producing any tall spikes on either end.

Figure 7.76 The histogram for the adjusted image.

Figure 7.77 The result of applying the curve shown in Figure 7.75.

Preventing Blown-Out Highlights and Plugged-Up Shadows

Because the height of the bars indicates how much space each shade takes up in your image, tall spikes on the ends of the histogram indicate that white or black takes up a considerable amount of space (**Figure 7.78**). That is usually an indication that you don't have any detail in the brightest or darkest areas of the image (**Figure 7.79**). If your image contains shiny areas that reflect light directly into the camera (like shiny metal or glass), then it's OK if those areas end up with no detail. But if that's not the case, then part of your curve must have topped or bottomed out. You should think about moving that area of the curve away from the top or bottom so you can get back the detail that was originally in that part of your image (**Figures 7.80** and **7.81**).

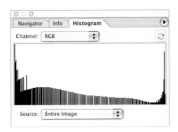

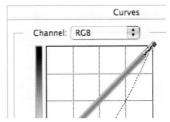

Figure 7.78 This histogram indicates that black and white take up a lot of space in the image.

Figure 7.79 This image does not contain detail in the highlights or shadow areas. (©2003 Andy Katz)

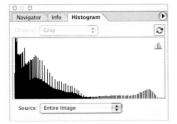

Figure 7.80 The histogram no longer has spikes on the ends after adjusting the curve to prevent topping or bottoming out.

Figure 7.81 The result of preventing the curve from bottoming or topping out.

Avoiding Posterization

If you notice the histogram developing gaps that sort of look like a comb (**Figure 7.82**), then you'll want to keep an eye on the brightness levels that are directly below that area of the histogram. Gaps in a histogram indicate that certain brightness levels are nowhere to be found in your image, which can indicate posterization (stair-stepped transitions where there would usually be a smooth transition—as in **Figure 7.83**). That usually happens when you make part of a curve rather steep. As long as the gaps are small (two to three pixels wide), then it's not likely that you'll notice it in your image. If they start getting a lot wider than that, you might want to inspect your image and think about making your curve less steep.

If you really want to see what I mean, then try this: Create a new grayscale document, click and drag across it with the Gradient tool, and then look at the Histogram palette. Then, choose Image > Adjustments > Posterize and experiment with different settings while you watch the histogram—the gaps don't have to be all that wide before you notice it (**Figure 7.84**).

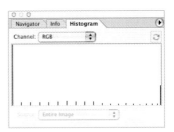

Figure 7.82 This comb-like histogram indicates possible posterization.

Figure 7.83 This stair-stepped area used to be smooth before a steep curve was applied to the image.

NOTES

If you notice slight posterization in your image, then you might want to apply a little bit of noise to it (Filter > Noise > Add Noise, Amount: 3, Gaussian), which should make it less noticeable. If that doesn't quite do the trick, then go back to the gray-scale chapter (Chapter 6, "Optimizing Grayscale Images") and check out the manual method for eliminating posterization.

You can force Photoshop to always use your full-size, 16-bit image to create its histograms by doing the following: Choose Photoshop > Preferences > Memory & Image Cache, set the Cache Levels to 1, click OK, and then quit and relaunch Photoshop. The only problem with this approach is that Photoshop might become rather sluggish when you adjust your image because it has to think of the full-size image when it updates the histogram.

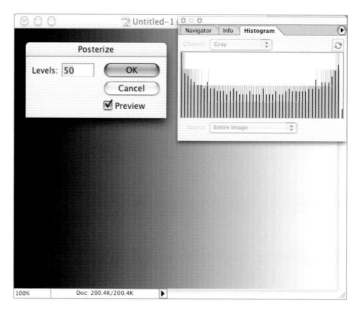

Figure 7.84 Posterize a grayscale image to get a sense of how wide the gaps have to be to see the posterization in your image.

You can minimize posterization by working with 16-bit images. Unlike standard 8-bit images that are made from 256 shades of gray (or 256 shades each of red, green, and blue), 16-bit images contain up to 32,767 shades of gray. You can obtain 16—bit images from RAW format digital camera files when opening them in the Camera Raw dialog box (see Chapter 10, "Camera Raw," for more details), or from some newer flatbed or film scanners. You can tell if you're working with a 16-bit file by looking at the title bar for the image. After the filename, you should see something like (RGB/16). That would indicate that you have a 16-bit RGB-mode image.

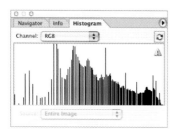

Figure 7.85 This histogram is indicating that the image might be posterized.

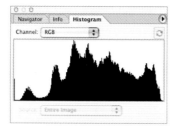

Figure 7.86 The uncached histogram is a more accurate view of your image.

The Histogram palette is usually thinking about an 8-bit cached image, just to make sure it updates quickly. A cached image is a smaller version of your image that has 8 bits of information. If you notice the comb look when adjusting a 16-bit image (**Figure 7.85**), then look for the warning triangle near the upper right of the histogram. That indicates that the histogram is being created from a lower resolution 8-bit image. Clicking the triangle will cause the histogram to be redrawn directly from the high resolution 16-bit file, which should eliminate the comb look and therefore indicate that your image isn't really posterized (**Figure 7.86**).

Sneaky Contrast Adjustments

Flattening a curve is usually harmful to an image because the detail in the area you are adjusting will be very difficult to see. You can often cheat, however, by analyzing the histogram to determine which areas of your image won't be harmed by flattening the curve. Because short lines in a histogram indicate shades that are not very prevalent in the image, those areas can often be flattened in a curve without noticeable degradation to the image. Flattening one part of the curve will allow you to make the rest of the curve steeper, which will increase the contrast of those areas and make the area appear to have more detail.

Here's how it works: While you're in the Curves dialog box, glance over at the Histogram palette and look for short, flat areas. When you find a flat area (not all images have them), choose Show Statistics from the side menu of the Histogram palette and then click and drag across that area in the Histogram palette, but don't release the mouse button (**Figure 7.87**). Now, look at the Level numbers that show up just below the histogram (if you don't see any numbers under the histogram, then choose Expanded View from the side menu of the Histogram palette). Next, release the mouse button and move your cursor around the Curves dialog box to see whether the numbers at the bottom are 0–100% or 0–255 numbers. If they are ranging from 0–100%, then click the arrows that appear in the center of the bottom gradient in the Curves dialog box to switch to the 0–255 numbering system. Now click in the middle of the curve and change the numbers that appear in the Input and Output fields at the bottom of the Curves dialog box to the first number you saw in the Histogram palette (**Figure 7.88**). Add a second point and do the same for the second number you saw in the Histogram palette. Finally, move the upper dot straight down and the lower dot straight up until the area between the two becomes almost horizontal (**Figure 7.89**). (Keep an eye on your image to see how flat you can get away with without screwing up the image.) That should increase the contrast across most of the image, while reducing contrast in those brightness

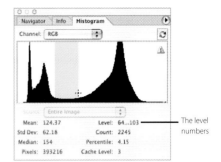

The level numbers

Figure 7.87 Drag across the extremely low areas of the histogram.

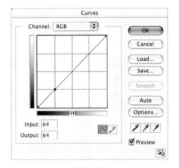

Figure 7.88 Add the first point and then enter the number from the Level area of the Histogram palette.

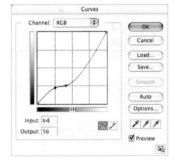

Figure 7.89 After adding the second point, move one point up and the other down to flatten part of the curve.

levels that are not very prevalent in the image (**Figures 7.90 and 7.91**).

Figure 7.90 The original image. (©2003 Ben Willmore)

Figure 7.91 Result of applying the curve shown in Figure 7.89.

Figure 7.92 The original image contains bright and dark areas that are not part of the actual photograph. (©2003 Ben Willmore)

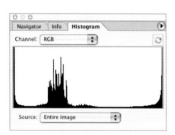

Figure 7.93 The histogram is looking at the entire image, including its border and background.

Concentrating on Important Areas

When you work with images that contain large areas of white/black (like ones with fancy borders—see **Figure 7.92**), the histogram can become less than useful because it will indicate that your image contains the full range of brightness levels (**Figure 7.93**) even though the image itself (minus the border) might be rather low contrast. That's when you might want to consider taking steps to limit what the histogram looks at when it analyzes your image. That way you can optimize the contrast of the important areas of the image without having to look at the spikes at the ends of the histogram that would reflect the large areas of black or white that are in the border area. I also use this technique when I want to radically enhance the contrast of an image while retaining detail only in the most important areas.

To limit what the histogram looks at, select the important areas of your image and then create an adjustment layer by choosing Layer > New Adjustment Layer > Curves. When a selection is active, the Histogram palette will analyze only the selected area (**Figure 7.94**), but the moment you create an adjustment layer, it will start thinking about the entire image again because the selection is converted into a layer mask. To get the histogram to think about only the area you had selected a moment ago, click OK in the Curves dialog box without adjusting the image. Now, look in the Layers palette (**Figure 7.95**) and Command-click (Mac) or Ctrl-click (Windows) on the layer mask that is on the adjustment layer you just created (it's the black and white rectangle near the right side). That will bring your selection back and limit the area of the image that the histogram looks at. Then, to adjust the image, double-click on the adjustment layer thumbnail that's just to the left of that layer mask and adjust away. When you use this technique, the adjustment will apply only to that same selected area (**Figure 7.96**). But don't worry, as long as you used an adjustment layer, you'll be able to force the adjustment to apply to the entire image. Once you've finished your adjustment, click OK in the Curves dialog box and then look in your Layers palette. The layer mask that is attached to the adjustment layer should contain some black. That's what's limiting which areas of the image your adjustments are applying to. All you have to do to get the adjustment to apply to the entire image is Select > Deselect, type **D** to reset your foreground color, and then type Option-Delete (Mac) or Alt-Backspace (Windows) to fill the layer mask that's attached to that layer with white. By doing that, you will have adjusted the whole image (**Figure 7.97**) while the histogram only looked at the selected area of the image— but in the end, the adjustment applies to the entire image.

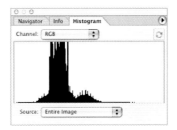

Figure 7.94 This histogram is looking only at the selected area of the image.

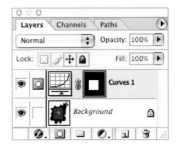

Figure 7.95 The Layers palette includes an adjustment layer with a layer mask that is partially filled with black.

Figure 7.96 The adjustment is affecting only the selected areas.

Figure 7.97 After filling the layer mask with white, the adjustment affects the entire image.

NOTES

When a mask is active, resetting your foreground and background colors will change your foreground color to white and your background color to black, which is the opposite of what you'd get if a mask wasn't active.

Just because I've decided to talk about the Histogram palette here in the Curves chapter, doesn't mean that I only use it when making that type of an adjustment. You can glance at the Histogram palette when performing any type of adjustment.

I don't adjust my images based solely on what the histogram is showing me. Instead, I adjust the image until I like its general appearance and then I look at the Histogram palette to look for signs that I might have gone too far. If I notice spikes on the ends, or a huge comb look, then I'll take a closer look at my image to determine if it's worth backing off from my adjustment. Who cares what the histogram looks like in the end—it's the visual look of your image that is most important. The histogram is just like that seatbelt warning light in your car—you're welcome to ignore it, but there's a reason it's on.

Shadow/Highlight

The new Image > Adjustments > Shadow/Highlight command (**Figure 7.98**) is a good alternative to Curves when working with images that need more pronounced shadow and/or highlight detail. In its simplest form, you just move the Shadows slider to brighten the darker areas of your image (**Figures 7.99** and **7.100**) and/or move the Highlights slider to darken the brighter areas of your image (**Figures 7.101** and **7.102**).

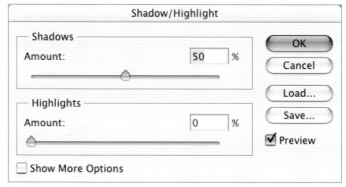

Figure 7.98 The simple version of the Shadow/Highlight dialog box.

Figure 7.99 Original image. (©2003 Andy Katz)

Figure 7.100 Result of moving the Shadows slider to the right.

Figure 7.101 Original image. (©2003 Andy Katz)

Figure 7.102 Result of moving the Highlights slider to the right.

If you really want to get control over the adjustment, you'll definitely want to turn on the Show More Options check box so you can see the full range of settings available (**Figure 7.103**). I suggest that you start by setting the Amount to 0%, the Tonal Width to 50%, and the Radius to 30px in both the Shadows and Highlights area. The Amount setting determines how radical a change you'll make to your image. Because you're starting with that setting at zero, these settings won't do a thing to your image—yet.

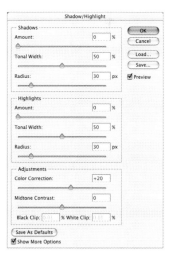

Figure 7.103 The expanded Shadow/Highlight dialog box.

Figure 7.104 Original image.

Figure 7.105 Tonal Width 0%.

Figure 7.106 Tonal Width 30%.

Figure 7.107 This image is divided into thirds—the left uses a Radius of 0px, the middle uses 50px, and the right uses 100px. (©2003 Ben Willmore)

If you want to pull out some detail in the dark areas of your image, move the Amount slider in the Shadows area toward the right while you watch your image. Keep moving it until the dark areas of your image become the desired brightness. Now start messing with the Tonal Width setting. That will control the brightness range in your image. Extremely low settings will limit the adjustment to the darkest areas of your image; higher settings will allow the adjustment to creep into the brighter areas of your image (**Figures 7.104** through **7.106**). The Shadow/Highlight command adjusts areas based on the brightness level of the surrounding image. So, once you've defined the brightness range you'd like to work with (via the Tonal Width slider), you'll need to experiment with the Radius slider. That setting determines how much of the surrounding image you want Photoshop to look at when determining how to blend the changes you're making into the surrounding image. Just slide it around until the changes to the dark areas of the image look appropriate considering their surroundings. Moving it toward the right will cause the area you're adjusting to blend into the surrounding image more, whereas moving it to the left will cause a more pronounced difference between the shadows and midtones of your image (**Figure 7.107**). Once you've finished your first round with the settings, you'll most likely want to go back to the Amount and Tonal Width settings to fine-tune the result.

The Highlights area works with the same concepts we just talked about, but it attempts to darken the brightest areas of your image to exaggerate the detail in that area.

When you brighten the shadows or darken the highlights, you'll often exaggerate any color that was lurking in those areas (**Figures 7.108** and **7.109**). If you find the color to be a little too distracting, try moving the Color Correction slider toward the left to make the areas you've adjusted less colorful (**Figure 7.110**). Or, on the other hand, if you'd like to make those areas even more colorful, then move the slider toward the right. The default setting is +20, which is a good starting point.

Figure 7.108 Original image.

Figure 7.109 After adjusting the image with Shadow/Highlight, the color in those areas is exaggerated.

Figure 7.110 Moving the Color Correction slider toward the left will reduce the amount of color that shows up in the brightest and darkest areas of the image.

Once you have the brightness and color looking good, you'll need to fine-tune the contrast in the areas of the image that you haven't changed. You can do that by moving the Midtone Contrast slider to the left (to lower contrast) or right (to increase contrast). There aren't any set rules for using these sliders. Your image is your guide (**Figures 7.111** through **7.113**).

Figure 7.113 Adjusted with Shadow/ Highlight, Midtone Contrast +40.

Figure 7.111 Original image. (©2003 Andy Katz)

Figure 7.112 Adjusted with Shadow/ Highlight, Midtone Contrast −40.

Darkening the highlights on some images can make them look rather dull, especially when working with something that contains bright shiny objects (**Figure 7.114**). In order for something to look truly shiny, the brightest areas of the image (usually direct reflections of light into the camera lens) need to be pure white. If it's not white, then you get dullsville (**Figure 7.115**). If you notice those bright reflections becoming darker when you adjust the Highlights setting, then you'll need to mess with the White Clip setting that's found at the bottom of the Shadow/Highlight dialog box. With it set to zero, Photoshop is capable of darkening all the bright areas of the image. As you raise that setting, Photoshop will force a narrow range of the brightest shades in your image to pure white. The higher the setting, the wider the range of shades that Shadow/Highlight will end up forcing to white. Just watch your image and increase the White Clip setting until those shiny reflections look nice and bright (**Figure 7.116**).

The Shadow/Highlight command cannot be used as an adjustment layer because it is too complex an adjustment. Adjustment layers are limited to things that can take any input (any shade of gray or color) and know what to do with it without having to know what the rest of the image looks like. Because Shadow/Highlight compares the area you're adjusting to its surroundings, it's not simple enough to be implemented as an adjustment layer.

If you're having trouble seeing exactly what an adjustment is doing to your image, you should experiment with an extremely simple image until you get the hang of it. Try it on a new grayscale image that you've applied a gradient to.

Figure 7.114 The original image. (©2003 Stockbyte, www.stockbyte.com)

Figure 7.115 After darkening the highlights, the image looks a little dull.

Figure 7.116 Increasing the White Clip setting produces a higher-contrast image.

The Black Clip setting forces the darkest areas of your image to black to make sure that they won't be lightened when you move the Shadows Amount setting. That can be useful if you want high-contrast shadow areas or if you have text or other line art that wouldn't look right if they were lightened.

I'm amazed at how many images can benefit from a quick visit to the Shadow/Highlight dialog box. I use it so often that I've defined a keyboard shortcut to it. If you'd like to figure out how to do the same, be sure to check out the section on editing Keyboard Shortcuts in Chapter 1, "Tool and Palette Primer."

Closing Thoughts

My hope is that after you've read this chapter you'll have come to the conclusion that the Curves feature really isn't such a brain twister. And if you come out of it thinking of ways you might use Curves in the future, even better. The Curves dialog box is one of a handful of Photoshop features that separate the experts from everyone else. But there's no reason why you can't propel yourself into the expert category. Once you get comfortable with Curves (Okay, it might take a while), you'll be able to do so much more than you can do with any other dialog box. And don't forget to take some time to work with the Histogram palette (and don't just use it with Curves) as well as the new Shadow/Highlight feature. They can give you that extra bit of versatility and control that can make a big difference with your next adjustment. So hang in there and stick with it. The initial learning curve might be somewhat daunting, but the fringe benefits are dynamite.

Ben's Techno-Babble Decoder Ring

Contrast: The range between the brightest and darkest areas of an image (or a portion of the image).

Histogram: A bar chart that indicates which brightness levels are present in the image and how prevalent each shade is within the image.

S curve: A generic curve used to exaggerate the detail in the midtones of an image by suppressing the detail in the highlights and the shadows.

Keyboard Shortcuts

Function	Macintosh	Windows
Curves	Command-M	Ctrl-M
Move point up 1	Up arrow	Up arrow
Move point down 1	Down arrow	Down arrow
Move point left 1	Left arrow	Left arrow
Move point right 1	Right arrow	Right arrow
Move point up 10	Shift-Up arrow	Shift-Up arrow
Move point down 10	Shift-Down arrow	Shift-Down arrow
Move point left 10	Shift-Left arrow	Shift-Left arrow
Move point right 10	Shift-Right arrow	Shift-Right arrow
Select next point	Command-Control-Tab	Ctrl-Tab
Select previous point	Shift-Command-Control-Tab	Shift-Ctrl-Tab
Deselect all points	Command-D	Ctrl-D

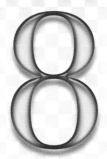

8

Color Management

Courtesy of Michael Slack, www.slackart.com

This would be so much easier if I weren't color-blind.
— Donkey from the movie *Shrek*

Color Management

This chapter should probably be named "Confessions of a Photoshop Expert," and it's the chapter that I wish I could have read myself a few years ago. My embarrassing secret? Until recently I've found color management to be so painstakingly cumbersome and time consuming that I found every reason to avoid it. That all changed with the introduction of Photoshop 6, and I'm now pleased to be able to help you successfully negotiate the rat maze of issues that are involved in getting your colors to behave themselves.

For years, I was frustrated because I'd scan an image and adjust it so it looked great onscreen; then I'd print it on my desktop color printer and it just never looked right. The colors were oversaturated, or the whole thing looked bluish. Then I'd work with it more until it was "acceptable" on both my screen and desktop printer, but when I sent it out to be printed in a brochure, it would look quite different. I just couldn't fathom why the colors were never consistent. That was back in prehistoric times when I was using Photoshop 3.

Later, when Photoshop 5 was released, there was a great deal of hype about its wonderful "new and improved" color-management features. It was supposed to make everything perfect. Your screen would match your desktop printer and you could have either one of them simulate a printing press. But when I tried to learn what was necessary to get everything set up, the experts just seemed to talk in a foreign language that I simply didn't understand. They loved to talk about gamut, profiles, delta E, colorimeters...and the terms just kept coming. They just didn't speak my language, and when I tried to implement everything they were telling me about, I got so frustrated that I just ended up turning off all those fancy features. I mean, I'm supposed to be a Photoshop expert and here I was turning off the one feature that was supposed to help me the most. I was even on a first-name basis with the people who write Photoshop and with many color-management "experts" around the country, and I couldn't get my head around it.

Every time Adobe released a new version of Photoshop, I'd throw myself back into the color-management labyrinth, driving my "expert" friends crazy as I tried to distill all the terms, technology, and techniques into something workable. But it was still too complicated for me to get it to really work comfortably in my situation. Along came Photoshop 5 and I went at it again. But, still, there were just too many details and far too many settings. I'd have to have a color-management expert on staff just to keep things running correctly. At last, Photoshop 6 came along, and that's when I felt things had matured to the point that I could get some traction with all this wizardry.

I finally realized that all those highfalutin terms were just the technical people strutting their stuff. It's not rocket science we're talking about, after all. The truth is that all this stuff can really work if you can just get over a bunch of terms and figure out how to deal with a few simple settings. And once it's all set up, you don't have to do that much to maintain everything. Not only that, but with things working properly, you can do some amazing things. You can get your screen to match your printer, get your desktop printer to simulate a printing press, and much more. So, now that I've bared my soul, let's jump in and see what all the fuss is about.

For me to truly understand anything in Photoshop, I usually have to simplify it to such an extent that it becomes almost obvious. So, let's start out from the beginning and slowly work our way into the more technical bits. I promise this will all make sense and will be easy for you to set up things for your situation. Stick with me, because once you've gotten this nailed, your Photoshop life will be infinitely easier. Here goes....

How Color Works

In figuring out color management, I read all about how our eyes work and that's when I learned that we could see only three colors of light—red, green, and blue. Everything we see is a combination of those colors. That's right, when you look at a rainbow, all your eyes see are red, green, and blue (**Figures 8.1 and 8.2**). When we see all three of those colors in a balanced amount (equal amounts

Figure 8.1 The color wheel.

Figure 8.2 The RGB components of the color wheel.

245

of red, green, and blue), we see white light. The more light there is, the brighter it is; the less light there is, the darker it is. We often call a low level of white light gray, so that's what I'll call a balanced amount of red, green, and blue. When they aren't balanced, we see color. Photoshop works the same way.

Go ahead and launch Photoshop, click on your foreground color, and pick any color you'd like. Now glance over at the RGB numbers that appear in the right side of that dialog box—they show you how that foreground color can be made out of a combination of red, green, and blue (**Figure 8.3**). That's also how your computer screen works (**Figure 8.4**). Each pixel that makes up your screen is made out of three tiny bars of color right next to each other—again RGB. A digital camera works on the same principle; it just measures how much RGB light travels through the lens. So, it really is an RGB world out there. But things change just a tiny bit when you print things.

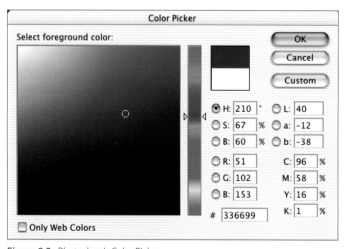

Figure 8.3 Photoshop's Color Picker.

Figure 8.4 A magnified view of your screen.

Remember that white light is made from a balanced amount of red, green, and blue light. So, for red ink to look red when you shine white light at a sheet of paper, it has to let only red light reflect off it and into your eyes;

otherwise, it wouldn't look red (**Figure 8.5**). That means that red ink absorbs green and blue in order to just let the red light bounce off the sheet of paper. So if that's the case, then blue ink must absorb everything but blue, and green light must absorb everything but green. So, when you combine any two of those inks (let's say red ink printed on top of green ink), all you'd get is black because the inks end up absorbing all three colors of light (**Figure 8.6**). That presents a problem that is easily solved. When we print, we don't need red, green, and blue inks; instead, we need three inks that control how much RGB bounces off a sheet of paper. We need one ink that controls how much red light enters our eye, another to control green light, and a third to control blue.

So, let's figure out what we need. Take a look at **Figure 8.7**. It represents three flashlights, one with a red filter, one with green, and one with blue. Now, check out the area where the blue and green flashlights overlap, but the red one does not; you should see cyan. That means that cyan ink simply absorbs red light, while allowing the other two colors of light to bounce off the sheet of paper. If you analyze **Figure 8.7** further, you might be able to figure out that magenta ink absorbs green light and yellow ink absorbs blue light. That's why the Info palette is arranged the way it is (**Figure 8.8**). One side looks at light and the other looks at ink. If you're wondering about the K in CMYK, it stands for key, which is really just a term used for black ink. It's used because a lot of people in the printing industry call cyan blue and they didn't want to confuse anyone by calling black B (and B is already used in RGB), so they came up with K instead to confuse the rest of us. Since black ink can't shift the color of anything, we'll talk about it later in this chapter. I know we haven't really gotten into color management yet, but this information is completely relevant to what we need to accomplish in this chapter. Now that we've got a basic idea of how color is reproduced, let's take a look at why your screen doesn't match your desktop printer and why your printer delivers a different result than your next-door neighbor's—in essence, why we need to bother with color management.

Figure 8.5 Red ink absorbs green and blue light.

Figure 8.6 Red and green ink create black.

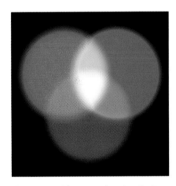

Figure 8.7 Three overlapping flashlight beams.

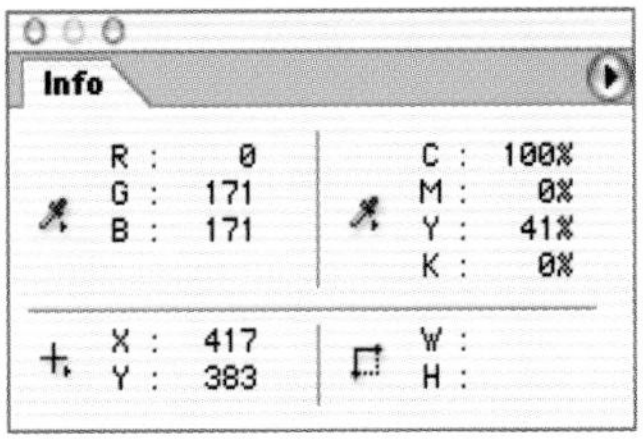

Figure 8.8 The Info palette.

The Problem with Color

Here are the problems we need to overcome: If you were to purchase a red felt-tip marker from three different manufacturers (maybe Crayola, Sharpie, and a generic brand), would you expect them to produce identical results? It's true that they are all red, but each one would, in fact, be a different shade of red. Maybe a Sharpie marker would produce a darker red and a Crayola a more vivid red. Not only that, but buying two red markers from the same company doesn't even guarantee consistent results; after all, they could be from different batches or one could be older than the other.

Well, the same thing goes for printing. Each printer will deliver a slightly different result when printing the same image because the inks are slightly different, so don't expect to send the same info to an Epson and a Canon printer and get the same results. The problems don't stop there.

Would you expect a Sony television set to look the same as a Panasonic? Just take a stroll through your local electronics superstore and look at all the TVs that are tuned to the same station. Even though they are being sent the exact same signal, they all look different. That's because they all use different shades of red, green, and blue. So why would you expect two different brands of monitors to look the same? They also use different shades of RGB.

Color Management to the Rescue

This is why color management is needed. It's designed to deal with all these variations among devices (monitors, scanners, printers, cameras, and so on). All we have to do is measure the exact color of red, green, and blue that your scanner and monitor use and also measure which shades of CMY that your printer uses (I'm ignoring the K in CMYK because black ink won't shift the color of things). Then Photoshop can use its wizardry to send different information to each device to compensate for its unique qualities in an attempt to get consistent results on all those devices.

There is one more issue to deal with before we figure out how to get all this stuff to work in our favor. Remember when I said that your eyes see white light when a balanced amount of red, green, and blue light enters your eye? Well, you don't end up with white when you use a balanced amount of RGB or CMY on your monitor, printer, or scanner. Remember that all your equipment uses slightly different shades of RGB or CMY (just like those felt-tip pens), which means that equal amounts of red, green, and blue would produce slightly different results on each device. So balanced RGB on one device might look a little greenish or bluish instead of looking gray. That can cause a lot of problems because many of Photoshop's features (such as color correction) make the assumption that equal amounts of R, G, and B produce no color at all.

The solution to that problem is to make your images out of idealized shades of red, green, and blue that have nothing to do with your monitor, scanner, or printer. We do that partially because the monitor you use to view your image isn't capable of accurately displaying what 100% cyan ink looks like and your printer isn't capable of reproducing the deepest blue that you can see on screen, so you don't want your images to have the same limitations as those devices. This special set of RGB colors is what all our images will be made from; then Photoshop will go to work to make sure it can print and display things correctly using the less-than-ideal colors of RGB or CMY used by our monitor and printers (**Figure 8.9**).

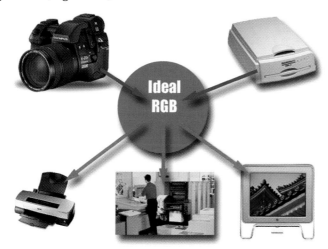

Figure 8.9 The overall concept of different RGBs being used.

Implementing Color Management

This is where things will become a little technical, but don't worry, I'll be here as your plain-English translator. First, let's see how all this relates to Photoshop's color-management features. When we measure the exact shade of RGB or CMY that a device uses, the end result will be an ICC profile. An ICC profile is just a small file that describes how something reproduces color. It's in a format that is approved by the International Color Consortium (ICC). That's the file you feed Photoshop so it can do the magic necessary to produce consistent color on each device. You'll end up with a profile for your monitor, your desktop printer, your scanner, and in rare cases your digital camera (the camera's white balance settings is often used as a substitute for having a custom camera profile), with each profile telling Photoshop which shades of RGB or CMY it uses to make color.

If you compare two printers and one has a more vivid set of CMY inks loaded, then that printer will be capable of reproducing a more vivid range of colors than the other one (just like different brands of markers). Each set of RGB colors (or CMY, for that matter) will reproduce color in a unique way. The range of colors you can reproduce on any given device is known as its gamut. That's not a completely foreign term; after all, haven't you heard someone say something like "it runs the gamut from low priced to high." Let's say that you can reproduce a nice deep blue on your inkjet, but you can't on your friend's inkjet (maybe it comes out as a more muted blue). That just means the particular color was in gamut on your printer but was out of gamut on your friend's printer. And, as you might already know, more exotic colors like fluorescent orange are out of gamut on just about any desktop printer.

There's just one more term with which I want you to get familiar. Remember that idealized version of RGB out of which we're going to create our images? The one where a balanced amount of RGB makes gray? Well, that's known as our RGB working space. A working space indicates what you'll make your images out of when you create a new document instead of opening an existing one.

So, now that we know some of the terms Photoshop will be throwing at us, we can get to the business of getting all this stuff set up properly. We'll figure out the details of picking that idealized version of RGB, measuring the shades of RGB and CMY that our devices use, and learn how to tell Photoshop how to deal with all that information.

Choosing an RGB Working Space

The first order of business is to pick that idealized version of RGB (known as your RGB working space) out of which we'll make our images. Picking a working space is just like picking which brand and type of film to use for a 35mm camera. If there was one best choice in that area, then that would be all that's available. A lot of people just grab Kodak 400-speed film, but there are legions of photographers who will happily debate the merits of each film type. It's the same with RGB working spaces. One might be better for your specific situation than another, but they will all work. Let's see what's available: To see your choices, choose Edit > Color Settings (Photoshop > Color Settings in Mac OS X) and click on the RGB pop-up menu (**Figure 8.10**). Here's my general take on this menu: With most of the choices, equal amounts of R, G, and B make gray. The main difference is in the range of colors that you can create (also known as gamut). Don't stress about it. It's just like film for a camera—they all take OK photos, but there might be one that's better for your specific needs. Here's how I think about each of the RGB Working Spaces you can choose from:

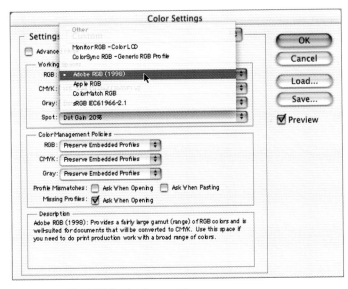

Figure 8.10 The RGB Working Space setting.

NOTES

Make sure the Color Management Policies pop-up menus are all set to Preserve Embedded Profiles; otherwise, you just might want Photoshop to warn you when opening an image or when pasting.

NOTES

If you turn off all three check boxes at the bottom of the Color Settings dialog box, then you'll want to look for a "#" or "*" in the title bar of your image once you open it. A "*" indicates an image with a profile that does not match your RGB working space, while a "#" indicates an image that is untagged (missing profile).

RGB Working Spaces

The RGB working spaces include the following:

▶ **Adobe RGB:** The best general choice for people who end up printing their images on desktop inkjet printers or send them to commercial printing presses.

▶ **Apple RGB:** A less-than-ideal choice because adjustments won't affect the image evenly from light to dark. Useful if you have old images that didn't use color management, which will be talked about later.

▶ **ColorMatch RGB:** Not a bad choice for images that will end up on a commercial printing press, but not quite as ideal as Adobe RGB for that purpose.

▶ **ProPhotoRGB:** Ideal for photographs that are scanned in 16-bit mode from color transparencies, because it offers a very wide range of colors. Can cause posterization in 8-bit images.

▶ **Monitor RGB:** Use when you'd like your images to look identical in both Photoshop and your Web browser. An alternative to sRGB, but it does not take into consideration what other people will see when viewing your web site.

▶ **sRGB:** Good for people who create Web graphics and would like to limit the colors used in their images to those that can be seen on an average user's screen. Less than ideal for anyone who will end up printing on a commercial printing press (but is okay for newsprint) or photographic process because it has such a limited range of colors available.

Figure 8.11 Turn on the Embed Color Profile check box to "tag" an image.

Now that we've gotten our RGB working space out of the way, let's make sure that our images will be friendly to others. We'll do that by including a profile of our working space with each image we create. That way when someone else opens it, their copy of Photoshop will know what colors of RGB the image was made from, so it can display it properly. When you save an image, make sure the Embed Color Profile check box is turned on (**Figure 8.11**). That will "tag" the image with an ICC profile.

If you don't tag your images, Photoshop will ask you to guess which colors of RGB the image was made from when you re-open the image (**Figure 8.12**). If you guess wrong, the image won't look like it's supposed to. I get a lot of untagged images, but I really don't like the way Photoshop makes you blindly choose a profile without seeing the consequences. If you get an untagged image, here's what I suggest you do: Just choose the Leave As Is option and then click OK. Then, immediately after opening it, choose Image > Mode > Assign Profile. Then try the top four choices listed under the profile pop-up menu (just make sure the Preview check box is on). Each time you change that setting, you should see your image change. Keep cycling through until you find one that makes your image look good. The person who sent you the image didn't include enough info for Photoshop to know what the colors should look like, so you're just guessing. And, no, it's not worth calling the person who sent it to you because they obviously don't know enough about color management to have it set up correctly, so you'll just end up confusing them by asking which setting to use.

Figure 8.12 The Missing Profile dialog box.

At this point in the chapter, I'm assuming that you haven't messed with any color-management settings except for the ones we've discussed. If you aren't seeing any mismatch warnings, then turn on the three check boxes that appear at the bottom of the Color Settings dialog box.

Profile Mismatch Warnings

Now, just because your image has a proper profile assigned to it doesn't mean that Photoshop will stop bugging you about all this color business. If you open an image and the profile that is assigned to it is not the same as what you used when creating new documents (known as your RGB Working Space), then Photoshop will warn you (**Figure 8.13**). Most of the time, you'll just want to choose the top option and click OK, which will tell Photoshop not do anything special with the image. But, if the embedded profile that's attached to the image is the name of a product (scanner, monitor, printer, and so on), then equal amounts of red, green and blue might not make a perfect gray. When that's the case, you should choose the Convert option if you plan on adjusting the image in Photoshop.

Figure 8.13 The Embedded Profile Mismatch dialog box.

Figure 8.14 The Paste Profile Mismatch dialog box.

Photoshop will also warn you if you copy and paste between two documents that have different profiles attached to them (**Figure 8.14**). When that happens, you'll almost always want to choose the Convert options since it's the only choice that will not shift the colors in your image. But, if you happen to have an image that contains web-safe colors (if you don't know what this is, then I can almost guarantee that you don't have them in your image) or scientific data (like information downloaded off of a weather satellite), then you might want to choose the bottom option.

The numbers that make up an image are usually more important than the actual look of the image when you have web- safe colors or scientific data and the bottom choice is the only option that will ensure that those numbers don't change.

I don't know about you, but I get sick of seeing all those color mismatch dialog boxes. There are so few times when it matters that the profile attached to an image is different than your RGB Working space that I like to take measures to minimize how much Photoshop warns me about things like that. I suggest that you turn off the three check boxes that show up at the bottom of the Color Settings dialog box (**Figure 8.15**). That will prevent Photoshop from warning you about missing or mismatched profiles altogether. But, after you've done that, you'll have to make sure you take the proper steps when you do run across an image that actually needs to use something other than the default settings.

From now on, when you open an image, take a quick look at the bottom edge of the document (Mac), or bottom edge of your screen (Windows). That's where you'll find a triangle that points to the right. Click on that triangle and choose Document Profile to find out what profile is attached to the image. If you ever see an image that says "Untagged RGB," it means that the image might not display properly. That's when you'll want to choose Image > Mode > Assign Profile and try the top four choices that appear until you find the one that makes your image look its best (**Figure 8.16**).

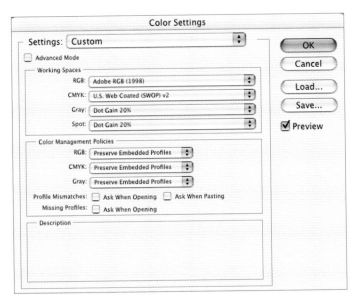

Figure 8.15 Turn off the three check boxes at the bottom of the Color Settings dialog box.

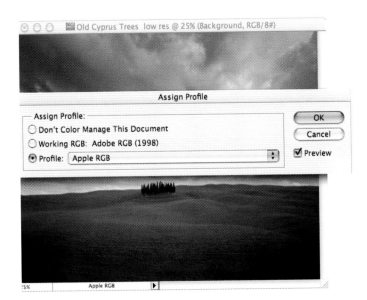

Figure 8.16 Assign Profile dialog box.

Figure 8.17 The Convert to Profile dialog box.

If, on the other hand, you see the name of a product (scanner, monitor, printer, and so on), then that means that equal amounts of red, green, and blue might not produce gray, which means color correction and other features might not work as they were designed to. That's when you'll want to choose Image > Mode > Convert to Profile (**Figure 8.17**). In the Convert to Profile dialog box, choose Working RGB from the Profile pop-up menu and leave all the others settings at their default settings (I'll mention what those other settings mean later in this chapter).

Device Profiles

Now that you have Photoshop set up for creating new images and opening pre-existing ones, let's get all your devices set up. Remember, a profile tells Photoshop what color of RGB or CMY your device uses. This is also where you're going to need to start thinking about how accurate you need things to be and therefore how much money you are willing to spend.

The more precise the profile, the more accurate your color will be. There are three ways to get a profile and they each come with their own level of cost and quality:

▶ **Canned profiles:** Just like canned spinach, it's nothing like the real thing, but better than going hungry. These profiles are usually free and are usually created at the factory and do not take into account the variations among products and the specifics of your situation (paper lot and ink batch for printer, and so on). They can often be found on the CD that came with the device or on the manufacturer's web site.

▶ **Visual adjustment:** Like 14-day-old carrots—better than frozen, but not by much. These profiles are created using low-cost or free software that depend on your eyes to be the measurement devices to create a profile. This method is mainly used for computer displays and usually involves much guesswork. Some people swear that they can get a good profile this way, while others swear exactly the opposite because they believe that profiles created with visual tools are terrible. Nobody can agree, so use them at your own risk—risk of bad colors, that is.

▶ **Custom profiles:** Like fresh-picked garden vegetables, nothing compares to it. These profiles are the most accurate and are completely customized to your specific situation. They are created using sophisticated measurement devices and will deliver the most accurate color matching between devices.

If you're on a budget, then you'll be working with one of the first two choices. But if you're really serious about color, then you'll want to look into the last option.

Creating a Monitor Profile

Let's start by making sure Photoshop knows how to display images correctly on your screen. We'll do that by measuring the exact colors of RGB that your monitor uses and also measuring how bright your monitor is. I wouldn't even think about using a canned profile for a monitor unless it's an LCD screen. Unlike standard CRT monitors, LCDs are much more consistent among batches and over time. It would be most ideal to use a hardware measurement device to profile your monitor, but since they cost money and each one comes with different software and most offer few options, I'll just show you how to profile your screen using your eyes and free software that comes with your machine. The method for creating visually measured profiles varies depending on which operating system you use. In Mac OS 9, choose Apple Menu > Control Panels > Monitors, click on the color icon, and then click the Calibrate button. In Mac OS X, choose System Preferences from the Apple Menu, click the displays icon, then click the Color tab, and finally click the Calibrate button. In Windows, choose Start > Settings > Control Panel and then double-click on the Adobe Gamma icon. No matter which operating system you are using, the setting will be very similar to what you see later. You'll get different choices depending on what type of monitor you have (LCDs have fewer settings). Let's take a look at what you might expect when creating a profile in Mac OS X. Not every option that you see here will be available when you try it—it depends on the type of monitor you own and how much information your monitor can share with the calibration software. Since you'll find similar settings in Adobe Gamma on Windows, this information should apply to everyone, regardless of what type of computer you have.

It's most ideal to perform this calibration while you are working under the same lighting conditions that you'll use throughout the day. So, make sure you don't have radically different lighting conditions between the time you calibrate and the time you want to use your monitor for critical color judgments. It's also a good idea to let your monitor warm up for at least a half hour before you proceed.

Using Apple's Calibration Utility

When the calibration utility starts up, you'll be presented with an Introduction screen. Checking the Expert Mode check box requires you to make more adjustments than the standard mode, so I suggest you turn it on because you'll end up with a more accurate profile (**Figure 8.18**).

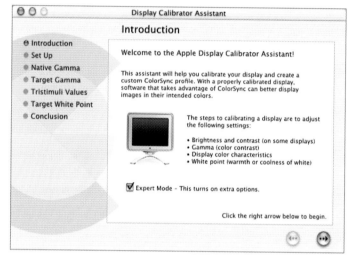

Figure 8.18 The Introduction screen.

The second screen (**Figure 8.19**) will ask you to adjust the brightness and contrast of your display so that it can use the full range of your monitor's capabilities. There's not much to say here, so let's continue to the next step.

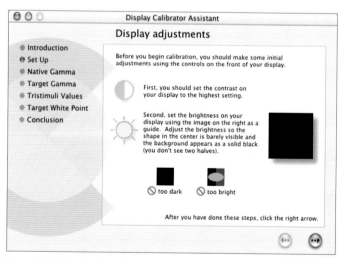

Figure 8.19 The Display Adjustments screen.

The third screen will ask you to adjust the gamma of your monitor. It's really just trying to figure out what it takes to get all three colors (red, green, and blue) at the same brightness level, which will make it possible to display a true gray when it's requested. The outside of the three squares are created from alternating stripes of solid black and whichever color you are adjusting. The general idea is to squint your eyes so those strips blur into a single tone and then move the slider until the middle portion of the square matches the edges in brightness (**Figure 8.20**). After you've done that, it will ask you what gamma setting you'd like to use (**Figure 8.21**). Gamma is a technical term that describes how bright your monitor will be. The standard setting for a Mac is 1.8, so go ahead and choose that (use 2.2 for Windows).

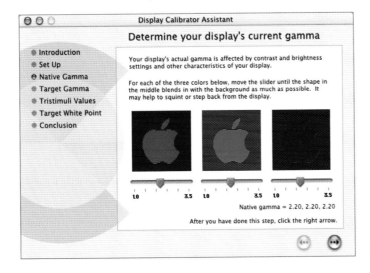

Figure 8.20 Current gamma setting.

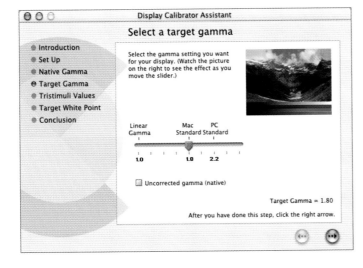

Figure 8.21 Target gamma setting.

The next screen is the challenging one (**Figure 8.22**). That's where you're supposed to indicate which shades of red, green, and blue are used by your specific display (known as phosphor colors). For most people, this will be a total guessing game because their specific brand of monitor is not likely to be listed, and even if it is, it will be a generic description of a similar monitor that isn't the same age as yours. Trinitron displays are rather popular and you can find out if you have one by looking very closely at your screen. See if you can find two very thin dark lines running horizontally across your screen. They will be about 1/3 and 2/3 of the way down your screen. If you can see them, then you have a Trinitron; if you don't, then it's anyone's guess which choice to use (although you might be able to find your phosphor colors listed in the specifications page of your monitor's manual). If your brand of display isn't listed and you don't find those two thin lines on your screen, then you're going to completely end up guessing—that's why I really would prefer to use a different method to create a profile.

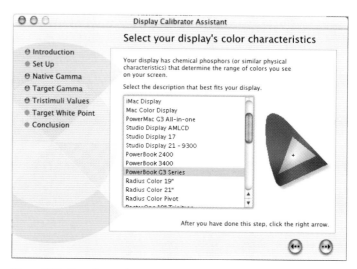

Figure 8.22   Phosphor setting.

After you're done fumbling around trying to find the name of your monitor from that list, you'll be asked to select a white point (**Figure 8.23**). That will determine what color you get when your screen is displaying the brightest white of which it is capable. I find that most of these settings darken your screen too much, so I'd use the No White Point Correction setting. It's more important that Photoshop knows the setting that you've chosen than to choose the one that makes the white look its best because Photoshop can compensate for whichever setting you decide to use. The last step is to give your newly created profile a name (**Figure 8.24**). I usually call it something like "Ben's display 10/15/2003" so I can remember how long it's been since I created it.

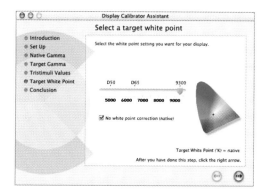

Figure 8.23   White point setting.

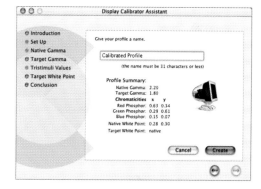

Figure 8.24   Saving the profile.

Once you've saved your profile, the Calibration utility will automatically save it in the proper location so that Photoshop uses the proper information. Your monitor profile doesn't get loaded into Photoshop; instead, your operating system gets the profile so it can use the same profile with all applications that are designed to deal with color management. Then when Photoshop needs to display your image properly, it talks to your computer's operating system to figure out which profile should be used. You can always check which profile is being used and make sure Photoshop is aware of it by checking the RGB Working

Space pop-up menu in the Color Settings dialog box (**Figure 8.25**). (It will be listed as the Monitor RGB setting.) Just be sure not to actually set your RGB Working Space to that setting because it's most ideal to have that setting be independent of your monitor or printer. The color and brightness of your screen changes over time, so you should create a new profile at least every three months.

Now, I don't know about you, but I didn't feel overly confident when I was creating that profile. After all, I had to guess at what colors of RGB my display uses, and it seemed to be overly easy to screw things up (such as choosing an unusual white point setting). Because of that, I don't suggest you rely on a visually measured profile if you do any serious color work in Photoshop. Instead, I'd invest in a color-measurement device that will do all the work for you and will deliver a much more accurate profile.

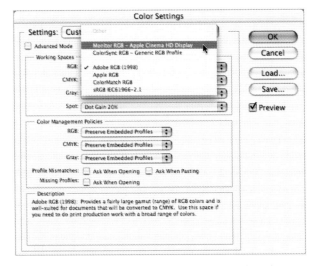

Figure 8.25 The RGB Working Space pop-up menu in the Color Settings dialog box.

Creating a Custom Profile

This is where you'll have to start shelling out some bucks if you want accurate color. I think it's well worth the money for anyone who is a true Photoshop professional. After all, you can easily end up paying just as much to fix a mistake that was made because of inaccurate color (such as reprinting a brochure). You'll need to purchase a colorimeter (**Figure 8.26**), which start at about $200, to get an accurate profile. You can purchase one from computer catalogs or web sites such as www.rodsandcones.com or www.profilecity.com. When you open the box, you'll find three things: the colorimeter, a manual, and a CD. So, plug the thing in (it usually connects via a USB port), pop the CD into your computer, and install the software. Then, when you run the software, it will ask you to put the colorimeter on the middle of your screen. Then it will flash a bunch of colors in front of it, and before you know it, you'll have a custom profile. In general, this hardware/software combo ends up measuring the exact shades of RGB that your specific display uses and it measures how consistent it is across the range from bright to dark.

Figure 8.26 A colorimeter.

If you're going to drop the cash needed to purchase a colorimeter, then you might as well profile your display once a week. After all, it takes only a few minutes, and you never know how much your display has changed over time.

Creating a Printer Profile

The next step is to create a printer profile so that we can get the printer to accurately simulate what you see on that newly profiled display of yours. When profiling a printer, you have three choices: a canned profile, a scanner-based profile, and a custom profile. Let's see what's needed to get those set up.

Most desktop color printers come with an ICC profile right on the CD that shipped with the unit. If you don't find it there, try visiting the manufacturer's web site. It will often be part of the driver software you can download. They don't always mention that it contains a profile on the web site, though. That's what happened to me with my old Epson Stylus Photo 2000P inkjet printer. I went to Epson's web site and didn't find any downloadable item that mentioned a profile, but when I downloaded the drivers for my printer, the profiles just happened to be part of the installation. This is what would be considered a canned profile because it was created using someone else's printer (same model though), using their batch of paper and ink. Canned profiles are usually perfectly acceptable for casual Photoshop users. You just have to be aware that they are specific to the ink and paper set used when the profile was made. That means that the profile might produce unsatisfactory results if you use a brand of paper or ink that is different from what the profile was designed for. Once you download that canned profile, you'll need to put it in a special place on your hard drive so that Photoshop knows where to find it. Here's where they belong:

▶ **Windows 2000:** WinNT/System/Spool/Drivers/Color

▶ **Windows NT:** WinNT/System32/Color

▶ **Windows XP:** Windows/System32/Spool/Drivers/Color

▶ **Windows 98:** Windows/System/Color

▶ **Mac OS 9:** System Folder/ColorSync Profiles

▶ **Mac OS X:** Users/CurrentUser/Library/ColorSync/Profiles

While you're playing around in that folder, you might as well throw away the profiles that are for devices that you'll never use (but only delete ones that you're absolutely sure you won't need; otherwise, you'll have to reinstall Photoshop to get them back). That way Photoshop's Profile pop-up menu (we'll talk about that in a little bit) won't be so cluttered with choices.

If you really want the most accurate color reproduction from your desktop color printer, you should think about having a custom profile made. Creating a profile isn't very difficult. All you do is purchase a color-measurement device and install the software. Then you get the reference image that comes with the software and measure the result using the measurement device (**Figure 8.27**). The only problem is that the measurement device can easily set you back $1,500 or more! That's fine if you work for a large company that has dozens of printers or if you are a commercial printing company, but it's out of reach for most other users. But that's OK, because there is a way to get the benefit of a custom profile without parting with the money for that spiffy measurement device. You can visit a web site such as www.profilecity.com, where they will create one for you. Here's how it works: You pay them just under $100 (don't quote me on that now) and they email you a reference image. Then, you print that image and snail mail it back to them. They use one of those expensive measurement devices to create a profile and then they email it to you. The only problem is that you really should have a profile for each ink and paper combination that you'll end up sending through your printer. That means one for the extra-glossy stuff that almost feels like plastic and works great for photos and another for the slightly shiny version you use for brochures and maybe a third for that dull cheap paper that you have loaded most of the time. As you can guess, the money can add up quite quickly. But that kind of money is pocket change if you work for a commercial printing company and you want to make sure that you can supply your customers with an accurate profile of a particular ink/paper/press combination.

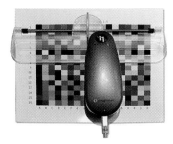

Figure 8.27 A $1,500 device used to create a printer profile.

There are two more alternatives, and they will cost about as much as two or three of those custom profiles. You can buy a special scanner designed specifically for creating printer profiles (but not as accurate as the device I mentioned previously), or for a little less money, you can use your own scanner and a piece of software called Monaco EZ Color 2. Let's take a quick look at how each of those choices work.

Figure 8.28 Color Vision's PrintFIX scanner.

Your first choice is Color Vision's PrintFIX. It's a small desktop scanner (**Figure 8.28**) that can be used to create printer profiles. It's pretty simple to use. After installing the hardware and software, you choose File > Automate > PrintFIX (**Figure 8.29**), and simply choose the model of printer you'd like to profile and click the OK button. That will open a special image (**Figure 8.30**) that you should print on the printer you'd like to profile.

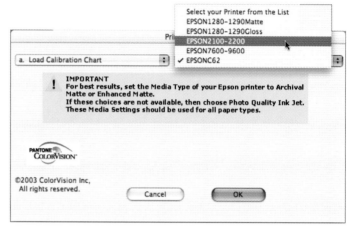

Figure 8.29 Choosing the name of the printer to be profiled.

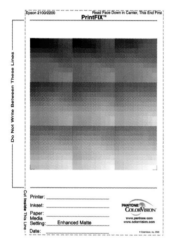

Figure 8.30 The PrintFIX target image that will be printed and then scanned.

Figure 8.31 The PrintFIX scanning dialog box.

The next step is to scan that printed image back into Photoshop. To access the scanner from Photoshop, choose File > Import > PrintFIX (**Figure 8.31**). That's where you specify the resolution of your printer and which type of image you're scanning (grayscale or color). But before you scan your printed image, you'll want to calibrate the scanner to ensure that you get an accurate scan. The PrintFIX scanner comes with a small sheet of paper that contains some black strips. All you have to do is insert that image into the slot on the PrintFIX scanner and then click the Calibrate button in the PrintFIX software. Then to actually scan your printed image, slip it into the little plastic sleeve that came with the printer, insert it into the slot on the scanner, and then click the Read button to start the scan. Once the scan is complete, you'll have the resulting image open in Photoshop.

To turn that scanned image into a profile for your printer, choose File > Automate > PrintFIX and choose Build Profile from the pop-up menu (**Figure 8.32**) and then click OK. The PrintFIX software will prompt you for a name for your profile (**Figure 8.33**) and will save it in the proper location so that Photoshop will be able to see it.

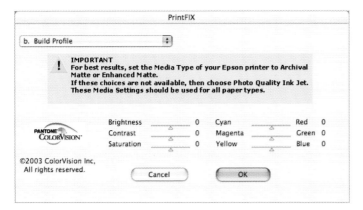

Figure 8.32 Building a profile in PrintFIX.

Figure 8.33 Once PrintFIX is done working on the image, it will prompt you to save the printer profile.

Once you have a profile made, you should print a few images to see just how accurately it reproduces your images. If you find that it's not 100% accurate, then choose File > Automate > PrintFIX once again and tweak the settings that appear at the bottom of the dialog box (Brightness, Contrast, and so on) and do another test print to see if you've improved your profile.

If you don't want to spend the money on the PrintFix solution, then you might want to consider purchasing a special piece of software (such as Monaco EZcolor 2) that will allow you to use your flatbed scanner as a measurement device to create a printer profile. Let's see how it works: You start by choosing what type of profile you'd like to create

(**Figure 8.34**). The software is capable of creating display, printer, and scanner profiles and can use a colorimeter for the display portion if you own one.

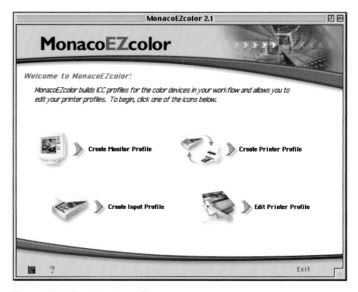

Figure 8.34 Choosing the profile type.

When you indicate that you'd like to create a printer profile, it will walk you through a series of steps that include printing a reference image (**Figure 8.35**). Then, once that print has dried, you grab a special image that was supplied in the box for the product and put both the special image and the image you just printed onto your scanner and scan them. Then you indicate where the edges of the images are (**Figure 8.36**) and the software measures all the colors based on what your scanner captured. The end result is a set of profiles—one for your scanner and one for your printer. That way, you can create as many profiles as you'd like and you don't have to pay $100 a pop for each one. I've found that these profiles are good enough for most Photoshop users, although it can be hit or miss depending on how good of a scanner you use.

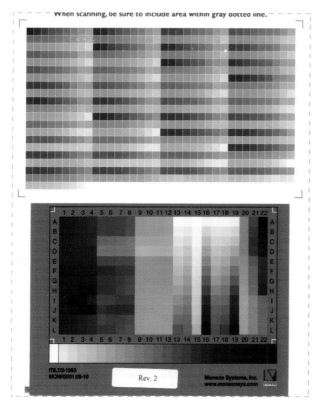

Figure 8.35 Printing a reference image.

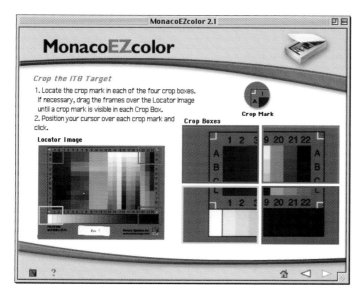

Figure 8.36 Defining the edges of the image.

Profiling a Printing Press

If you ever plan to reproduce your images on a commercial printing press, you'll have to convert your images to CMYK mode before you send them off. For Photoshop to correctly convert your image to CMYK mode, it will need a bunch of information about how the image will be reproduced (supplied by an ICC profile). When I'm creating an image that will be printed at a commercial printer, the first thing I do is call my sales rep and ask if he has an ICC profile for the press/paper combination that I'll be using. Most of the time he tells me that he doesn't. I don't blame him because commercial printers deal with hundreds of ink and paper combinations, so it would be very time consuming and expensive to profile each one. But sometimes I get lucky, and if so, I simply plop the profile in the proper folder, choose Edit > Color Settings (Photoshop > Color Settings in Mac OS X), and set the CMYK Working Space pop-up menu to that choice. Most of the time, though, I have to take a different approach.

Adobe was nice enough to include a bunch of profiles that can be used for different printing conditions. They show up in the CMYK Working Space pop-up menu that I mentioned previously. You just have to make sure you have a profile selected that accurately reflects the printing conditions that will be used to reproduce your image before you convert to CMYK mode. I'll attempt to translate their names and then show you how to get better results.

Here's the rundown on choosing a profile for many standard publication types:

NOTES

It turns out that the U.S. Sheetfed Uncoated and U.S. Web Uncoated profiles are identical. It's still a good idea to choose the one that is specific to your printing conditions, though; otherwise, people who open your files might assume that they are not set up properly.

▶ Use U.S. Sheetfed Coated for glossy brochures.

▶ Use U.S. Sheetfed Uncoated for dull-finish brochures.

▶ Use U.S. Web Coated (SWOP) for magazines.

▶ Use U.S. Web Uncoated for dull-finish publications.

The profiles that come with Photoshop are making huge assumptions about the paper and inks that you are using.

That means it's possible to get a much better result if you happen to have a custom profile created specifically for the paper and press on which you'll be printing. If you find that your printing company doesn't have a custom profile available and you aren't getting acceptable results from the profiles I mentioned previously, then you might want to bypass profiles altogether and set up the CMYK conversion the traditional way. You'll find information about that on my web site: www.digitalmastery.com/book.

Profiling Your Scanner

You don't have too many options when it comes to scanners. There aren't too many manufacturers that provide canned profiles (some high-end ones do), and you can't visually create a profile. But the good news is that you don't have to buy any expensive hardware to get the job done. All you need is a piece of software (such as Monaco EZcolor 2). The software will come with a reference image that's known as an IT8 target (**Figure 8.37**). All you have to do is scan the image and then feed it to the software and out pops an ICC profile for your scanner. You'll want to place it in the same location I mentioned when I was talking about printer profiles.

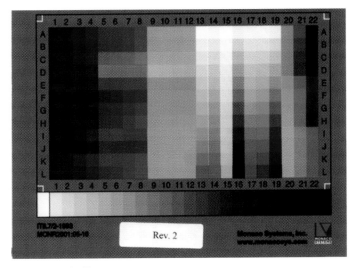

Figure 8.37 An IT8 target.

Color Management in Action

Now that we have everything set up and placed in the proper location, let's see what we can do with all this fancy stuff. Let's say you've used a colorimeter to profile your screen, and you used some software to create scanner and printer profiles (just don't forget to put those profiles in the proper location, as I mentioned previously). Now here comes the fun part.

Accurate Scans

Some scanners will automatically assign the proper profile to your images. You can find out if your scanner does this by clicking on the black arrow that appears at the bottom of a Photoshop document (Mac), or bottom of your screen (Windows) and choosing Document Profile. Then scan an image and see if your scanner's profile is listed at the bottom of the document window. If it is, then there is no reason to assign a profile because it already has the correct one assigned.

From now on, when you scan an image, you won't have to worry about all the color settings that are in your scanner. You just turn all that stuff off and let color management take over. You simply specify the resolution and scaling settings you'd like to use and then press the Scan button. Then, once the image is in Photoshop, choose Image > Mode > Assign Profile (**Figure 8.38**) and choose your scanner profile from the Profile pop-up menu. That's it! The profile supplies the information needed for Photoshop to know how your scanner captures color and therefore should produce an accurate scan (assuming your profile is accurate, that is).

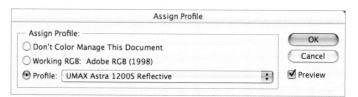

Figure 8.38 The Assign Profile dialog box.

Well, actually that's not quite it, after all. Remember when I talked about equal amounts of red, green, and blue creating gray and that that's not what you get when you use the less-than-ideal shades of RGB that your monitor, printer, and scanner use? Well, if you plan to manipulate your image, you'll most likely want to convert it into that idealized version of RGB that we call our RGB working space.

To do that, choose Image > Mode > Convert to Profile (**Figure 8.39**). When that dialog box pops up, you might get a little scared because it's full of overly techie terms, but don't worry about it. At the top it simply lists the profile you assigned after you scanned the image. Next, it asks you for the profile you'd like to convert it to. That's where you want to choose Working RGB, which should be the top choice (the name will also have something like "Adobe RGB" attached to it to remind you of what you chose when you set up that part of Photoshop). Leave the Engine setting at its default. There aren't too many reasons to change that one, and if you knew about the reasons, you'd be writing this book instead of reading it—you'd have to be that color savvy. Then experiment with the choices that appear under the Intent pop-up menu. Just look at your image and try the different choices to see which one gives you the best result. I'll talk about what those settings really mean later in this chapter.

Now, there is an important difference between assigning a profile and converting to a profile. They might sound similar but so does being pulled over for speeding versus being arrested for speed. With one, you'd just be out a few bucks, while with the other you just might end up in jail! Assigning a profile is informing Photoshop what colors of RGB the image is made out of. That will make the colors shift in your image as Photoshop uses the same amount of red, green, and blue, but uses different shades of color (like different brands of markers). Or you could think of it like substituting ingredients in a recipe without adjusting the amount that's used to compensate for the new ingredient. Converting to a profile means to simulate the current look of the image (trying not to change the overall look of the image), but to make it out of different shades of RGB than the original. That's like replacing an ingredient in a recipe and adjusting the amount you use to compensate for the difference between what the recipe called for and what you ended up substituting. Read over those last few sentences three times to make sure you really understand the difference because it can sound rather subtle, but it's not.

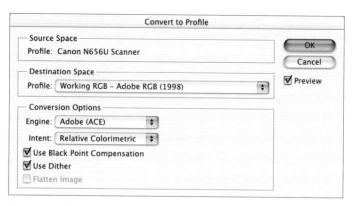

Figure 8.39   The Convert to Profile dialog box.

Simulating a Printing Press Onscreen

I often create images that will end up being reproduced on a commercial printing press. Sometimes it's for a brochure and other times it's for a magazine article, but whatever it is for, I want to see what the printed result will look like onscreen in Photoshop. To accomplish that, I usually choose View > Proof Setup > Working CMYK. That should do two things: It will go to the Color Settings dialog box to see what type of printing conditions will be used (we talked about that earlier in this chapter) and it turns on the View > Proof Colors setting. With Proof Colors turned on, Photoshop will attempt to simulate what your image will look like when it's printed on a commercial printing press. I use this setting anytime I'm making an adjustment to the saturation of the image because the range of colors that can be reproduced on a printing press (known as its gamut) is much smaller than what you can see onscreen. Deep blues and vivid colors can shift wildly. That happens because those colors simply can't be reproduced using the CMYK inks that are used in commercial printing. To stop this simulation, turn off the Proof Colors setting from the View menu.

Accurate Prints

Now that you have a profile for your printer ready, Photoshop can give you much more accurate prints, but you'll have to make sure everything is set up correctly to deliver what you want. Choose File > Print with Preview, turn on the Show More Options check box, and choose

Color Management from the pop-up menu. Photoshop will now prompt you to make some choices (**Figure 8.40**). Let's take a look at them one by one: First, under the Source Space heading, choose Document if you'd like the printer to simulate what you saw on your screen, or choose Proof Setup if you'd like your desktop printer to simulate what your image will look like when printed on a commercial printing press (or a different device if you have changed the View > Proof Setup settings).

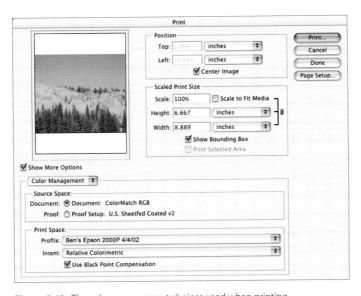

Figure 8.40 The color-management choices used when printing.

Second, for Photoshop to accurately simulate colors on your desktop printer, you have to feed it an ICC profile for that device. Do that by changing the Profile pop-up menu in the Print Space area of the Print with Preview dialog box. And finally, you can choose whether you'd like to simulate the paper color of a printing press. Choose Relative Colorimetric if you don't want to see the paper color or Absolute Colorimetric if you would like to simulate the paper stock (which might be a lot darker than the sheet of paper you have loaded into your desktop printer). I also recommend that you leave the Black Point Compensation check box turned on for most images. The only other thing you have to do is turn off any color-adjustment controls that your printer driver offers, since we're letting Photoshop do all the work instead (otherwise it will double compensate, which will make your image look terrible).

I suggest that you leave your image in RGB mode when printing to an ink jet printer. Even though the printer uses cyan, magenta, yellow, and black ink, Photoshop uses the same software that draws your screen image to send information to the printer. That software only handles RGB information, so there is no advantage to printing from CMYK. Postscript language printers can bypass that screen-drawing software and therefore can produce acceptable results from either RGB or CMYK mode.

Better CMYK Conversions

You'll want to convert your images to CMYK mode if they will be printed on a commercial printing press. The traditional way of doing that is to simply choose Image > Mode > CMYK. That's fine if you're in a hurry, but by doing that you are bypassing a bunch of settings that might make your image look better. Here's your alternative: Choose Image > Mode > Convert to Profile (**Figure 8.41**). It looks complicated, but it's not. The top just tells you the colors of RGB that your image is made from (that's known as your source space). Then, as long as you've set up the CMYK working space to what's right for your printing conditions, all you have to do is choose Working CMYK from the Destination Space pop-up menu. And now all that's left is to play with the Intent pop-up menu and those two check boxes to see which combination of settings will produce the best result. Earlier, I kind of glossed over what the Intent pop-up menu does, so let's take a look at the choices that are available. Most images will start off with many colors that are just too vivid to be reproduced in CMYK mode (known as colors that are out of gamut for you techie folks). When you convert to CMYK mode, Photoshop has to do something with those colors to get them into the range of what can be reproduced on a printing press. The choices in the Intent pop-up menu determine how Photoshop will deal with those out-of-gamut colors.

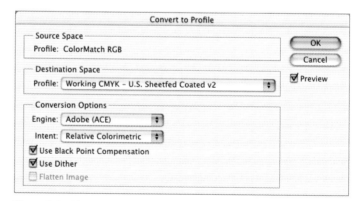

Figure 8. 41 The Convert to Profile dialog box.

Perceptual

With this option, Photoshop will alter not only those colors that are not printable, but also the ones that can be reproduced just to make sure the relationship between the colors remains consistent. That way you don't have to worry about one overly vivid color becoming the exact same shade of a less vivid color that's right next to it. The only problem with this feature is that it has no idea which colors are actually in your image, so it shifts colors around even if all the colors in your image are within the range of colors that can be reproduced in CMYK mode. That means that all of the colors in your image will become less saturated just to ensure that colors that can't be printed will get shifted to printable ones.

Saturation

This choice will take the most saturated colors in your image and make sure they end up as the most saturated colors that are possible in CMYK mode. That might sound nice, but it doesn't take into account the brightness, color, and saturation differences between colors. That means that it is free to shift the colors in your image as long as saturated colors remain saturated, even if they don't end up looking anything like the color at which they started. That limits its usefulness to solid-colored graphics such as bar charts and business graphics where the relationship between colors isn't important and you just want to maintain vivid colors no matter what.

Relative and Absolute Colorimetric

Both Relative and Absolute Colorimetric shift only those colors that are not reproducible in CMYK, leaving the rest of the colors largely unchanged. The main difference between the two is that Relative Colorimetric makes sure that white in the original image will end up as white in CMYK mode. That's not overly important unless you're using an RGB working space that creates a white that is darker than what you can create in CMYK mode. This feature is mainly used in the Print dialog box when printing an image to a desktop color printer that can reproduce a brighter white than a printing press. In that situation the difference between relative and absolute is the difference between simulating the "whiteness" of the paper that will be used on the printing press (such as newsprint) or not. If your image doesn't contain too many overly vivid colors, you might find that Relative Colorimetric might not be a bad choice.

When I'm converting an image to CMYK, I'm not consciously thinking about what all these choices mean; instead, I'm just trying each one and looking at my image to see which choice produces the most pleasing result. Each choice has both advantages and disadvantages, and the only way to find the best setting is to experiment.

Closing Thoughts

If you worked up a sweat reading this chapter and thought to yourself, "This is truly a cesspool of unending terms and settings, and I'm never going to get through it all," you're not alone. That's what I thought at first. But after going through the motions a few times, and perhaps reading this chapter again, you'll get more comfortable with the concepts here and find some sanity in the chaos. In a perfect world we wouldn't have to deal with all this, but the truth is that, from the viewpoint of your hardware, you're really asking for a gargantuan thing when you want your screen to match your printout. All your devices are different, and Photoshop really needs all this information to manage everything gracefully. But if you spend the time, effort, and money it takes to get everything working properly, you will be generously rewarded with very consistent color across all your devices. And your life will become a lot easier when you can trust your screen and know that your $200 inkjet printer is doing a darn good job of both simulating what you saw onscreen and what will appear on a printing press.

Ben's Techno-Babble Decoder Ring

Color management: A system used to achieve consistent color between scanner, monitor, and printer.

Gamut: The range of colors that are reproducible on a particular device.

ICC profile: A standard file format used to describe the unique characteristics of a scanner, monitor, or printer.

9
Color Correction

The camera, you know, will never capture you. Photography, in my experience, has the miraculous power of transferring wine into water.

—Oscar Wilde in *Lillie*

Color Correction

In the previous chapter, "Color Management," we learned how to make colors consistent among our various devices (monitor, scanner, printer, camera, and so on). In this chapter, we're dealing with color correction, which is an entirely separate matter. This chapter is all about controlling the colors in your image and getting rid of colorcasts that might be having an adverse effect on the final result.

After presenting hundreds of seminars, I've learned that the majority of people perform color correction by picking their favorite adjustment tool (Color Balance, Hue/Saturation, Curves, or the like) and then using a somewhat hit-or-miss technique. They blindly move a few sliders back and forth in the hope that their onscreen image will improve. If that doesn't work, they simply repeat the process with a different adjustment option. Those same people often turn to me asking for "advanced color-correction techniques" because they're frustrated and don't feel like they're really in control of the color in their images. If this describes the way you're adjusting your colors, you'll be pleasantly surprised when you learn about the science of professional color correction, where 95% of all guesswork is removed and where you know exactly which tool and what settings to use to achieve great color. First, let's look at a general concept that will help us to color correct an image. Then I'll walk you through the step-by-step technique I use to get good-looking color in Photoshop.

Use Gray to Fix Color?!?

For the time being I want you to wipe out any thoughts of color. And, no, I'm not crazy. This approach really works, so stick with me. Do you remember how to make gray in the idealized RGB mode that we talked about in the "Color Management" chapter? Equal amounts of red, green, and blue, right? With that in mind, let's open an image and see if we can find an area that should be gray. Then we can look in the Info palette to see if it really is gray in Photoshop—all without having to trust your monitor or your eyes! On the CD, open the image that's called make gray.jpg. The door on the right should be a shade of gray. If the RGB numbers in the Info palette aren't equal—no matter what it looks like on your monitor—it's not gray. If it's not gray, then it must be contaminated with color (**Figure 9.1**). But could that color be contaminating more than the gray area? Most likely. Then why not use the door as an area to measure what's wrong with the entire image so we have the information we need to fix it? Let's give it a try.

NOTES

Just because I mention RGB mode throughout this chapter doesn't mean that the techniques don't work just as well in CMYK mode. It's just that the initial concept I show you really needs to be performed in RGB mode. So, even though you'll end up dealing with RGB settings at the beginning, Photoshop can translate them into CMYK numbers once you start performing the steps listed under the "Professional Color Correction" section of this chapter. If you just look at the CMYK area of the color picker, you'll see what you'd end up with in CMYK mode.

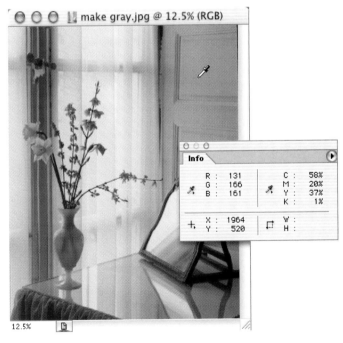

Figure 9.1 If the RGB numbers are not equal, then that area is not gray. (©2003 Andy Katz)

Using the example image, you'll see that the RGB numbers are not equal, telling us that there is indeed color lurking somewhere in that gray. How could those contaminating colors get in there? Here are a few potential culprits: indoor, artificial lighting (you know how "off" that can be); the temperature of the chemicals used to develop the film being too hot or too cool; inappropriate filters used in a photographic enlarger when your prints are being made; and aging bulbs in a scanner that might shift the colors during the scanning process. We're going to use the Curves dialog box to make our adjustment. But don't worry, you don't have to remember everything from Chapter 7, "Understanding Curves" to do this. For what we're trying to accomplish, here's what you need to know:

▶ Command- or Ctrl-clicking on your image will add a point.

▶ The Input number indicates what you are changing.

▶ The Output number determines what you'll end up with in the area you are changing.

And don't worry, even if you skipped the chapter on curves, you'll still be able to quickly color correct your images. At this stage, we're only going to manually adjust a curve. After that, I'll show you a much faster and easier method, so just stick with me knowing that it will end up being really easy.

Start by putting your cursor on the gray door. Now glance over at the Info palette and write down the RGB numbers (131R, 166G, and 161B in my case). To make that door area a real gray, we'll need to make those RGB numbers equal. But we don't want to change the brightness of the door. To make sure that doesn't happen, grab a calculator and add the three RGB numbers together to find out the total amount of light that is making up the door (131 + 166 + 161 = 458, for example). We don't want to change the brightness of the door, so we'll want to keep the total amount of light used the same as what we started with, but

NOTES

When performing RGB color correction, make sure that white appears at the top of the gradient that is on the left of the Curves dialog box; otherwise, the numbers will range from 0%–100% instead of 0–255. If black appears at the top of the gradient, click on the symbol in the center of the horizontal gradient at the bottom of the Curves dialog box. That will flip the gradients and use the numbering system needed for RGB color correction.

using equal amounts of red, green, and blue. To figure out the exact numbers to use, just divide the total brightness of the door (458 in my case) by three ($458 \div 3 = 152.6667$), and then round off the result so you don't have any decimals (153 in my case). Now that we know what we're starting with (from the Info palette) and what we want to end up with (from the calculator), we can adjust our image.

If you choose Image > Adjustments > Curves and then Command-click on your image while the menu at the top of the dialog box is set to RGB, you'll end up changing red, green, and blue in equal amounts, which would just change the brightness of the image (which is what we did in the curves chapter). But for our purposes, we want to work on the individual colors separately. To have Photoshop add a point to each of the red, green, and blue curves, hold Shift-Command (Mac) or Shift-Ctrl (Windows) and click on the gray door. If you want to see what happened, choose one of the colors that show up under the Channel pop-up menu at the top of the Curves dialog box. You should find a new point on each of those curves. The position of each one of those points is based on the numbers that showed up in the Info palette. All you need to do is switch between the red, green, and blue curves and change the output numbers for each one so that they match the numbers you came up with when you used a calculator to average the RGB numbers (153 in my case) in the Info palette (**Figure 9.2**). After you've done that, you can take a peek at your image to see what you've done (**Figure 9.3**). The door should be gray. If it's not, and you're quite sure you followed the steps correctly, your monitor is way out of whack and may need calibration (see Chapter 8, for details on how to do that).

Figure 9.3 When you're done, the area should be gray. The left numbers indicate what was originally in the image; the right numbers indicate the result of our adjustment.

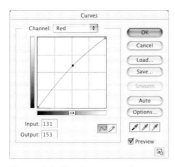

Figure 9.2 The Output number you enter for each curve will move the point to the correct position.

But now, look back at the three curves we applied to this image (**Figures 9.4** to **9.6**). We measured what was wrong with the image in the gray areas, but our adjustment changed the entire image. That's logical enough, because whatever is wrong with the gray areas is also affecting the rest of the image. But when you look at those curves, does it look like we really changed the full length of the curve? Almost—but not quite. We didn't change the brightest and darkest areas. So, we really haven't accomplished our color correction, and we won't until we've taken some more steps. But from this exercise, we saw that our concept of measuring and adjusting gray works. Now let's see how we can make this process faster and easier, and then we'll move on to adjusting the brightest and darkest areas.

It might feel quite low tech to be scribbling a bunch of numbers on a sheet of paper and using a calculator when we have a multi-thousand-dollar computer in front of us. The folks at Adobe realized that, and gave us a tool that will do 99% of the work for us, so let's see what they came up with. Choose File > Revert to return that door and flowers image back to its original state, and then choose Image > Adjustments > Curves. Click on the middle eyedropper in the lower right of the dialog box, and then move your cursor out onto the image and click on that gray door again. With a single click, it should change to gray. Photoshop is using the same concept we used when we wrote down the RGB numbers and averaged them; it's just doing it in a fraction of a second and there is no paper involved. In fact, those eyedroppers will help us even more if we adjust the full range of shades from the brightest to the darkest. Let's see how it works.

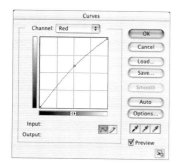

Figure 9.4 The red curve.

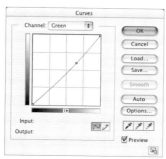

Figure 9.5 The green curve.

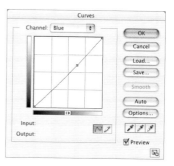

Figure 9.6 The blue curve.

Professional Color Correction

Okay, you can start thinking in color again. We will look at the process of professional color correction in three parts: balancing colors, adjusting skin tones, and adjusting saturation. You don't always have to perform all three parts, but the more you do, the better your result will be.

Balancing Your Colors

To eliminate any color casts that are in your image, you'll need to look for color contamination in the gray areas of your image, and then use that information to help correct the whole image. Three standard areas of your image will usually contain a shade of gray: the brightest area of the image, which is known as the highlight; the darkest area of the image, which is known as the shadow (on most photos, the highlight and shadow areas shouldn't contain color); and a gray object in the image.

Now that we know which areas need to be adjusted, let's go ahead and make the actual adjustment. Start by choosing Image > Adjustments > Curves. We'll be working with all three eyedroppers that show up in the lower right. All three adjust the area you click on so that it ends up with a balanced combination of red, green, and blue, which effectively removes any color contamination for that area. The only difference between the eyedroppers is that the one full of black makes things really, really dark, the eyedropper full of white makes things really bright, and the middle eyedropper doesn't change the brightness of an area. We'll use those to adjust the shadow, highlight, and gray areas, respectively. But we first have to set up things correctly.

Double-click on the rightmost eyedropper to bring up the Color Picker. This eyedropper will be used to adjust the brightest part of the image (the highlight). You don't want the highlight to become pure white because it would look too bright. You want to reserve pure white for those areas that shine light directly into the camera lens (like lightbulbs and shiny reflections). That means you want the highlight to be just a tad bit darker than white.

If you remember the chapter on grayscale images (Chapter 6, "Optimizing Grayscale Images"), I mentioned that the lightest percentage of ink you can use on a printing press is usually 3% (5% for some newspapers). That means we don't want to use less than 3% of any ink in the brightest part of our image; otherwise, we might lose critical detail. But we're adjusting our image in RGB mode, and when you do that, you'll be using a numbering system that ranges from 0 to 255, not 0% to 100%. So let's figure out how to create a minimum of 3% ink in RGB mode.

After double-clicking the rightmost eyedropper, set the saturation setting (S) to 0 and the brightness setting (B) to 100%, and click on the number next to the letter B (brightness). Use the down arrow key to change that setting until the magenta (M) and yellow (Y) readouts indicate at least 3%. Cyan (C) will be higher, but don't worry about that. At this point, the numbers will show you exactly what RGB values are needed to produce that much ink—in my case, 240R, 240G, 240B (**Figure 9.7**).

NOTES

Black ink is usually limited to the darkest areas of the CMYK printing process, so no black will show up when you're looking for 3% ink values.

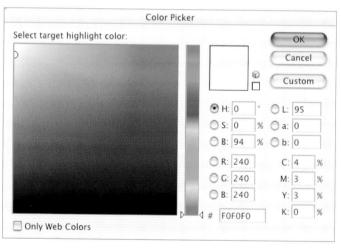

Figure 9.7 A good highlight value is 240R, 240G, 240B.

Now, on to the dark side. We're going to make the darkest area of your image pure black (0R, 0G, 0B) in order to use the full range your computer monitor is capable of displaying. Black wouldn't be a good choice if you are really outputting to a printing press (you'd lose a lot of detail), but we'll set it up so that Photoshop will adjust your image automatically if you have to convert to CMYK mode. That way we'll be guaranteed that no detail will be lost no matter what the output. So, double-click on the leftmost eyedropper and make sure it's set to black. When you click OK in the Curves dialog box, Photoshop will ask you if you would like to "Save the new target colors as the defaults?". I suggest that you click the Yes button so that Photoshop remembers those settings and uses them every time you use the eyedroppers to color correct your images.

Now that we have everything set up properly, let's start adjusting images. Open any image that needs to be color corrected, and then choose Layer > New Adjustment Layer > Curves. Click the black eyedropper and then click on the shadow area. When I mention the shadow, I don't mean a traditional shadow like the kind cast from an object; instead, I'm talking about the darkest area of an image. All images have a shadow area, but it can sometimes be hard to locate because there may be multiple candidates. (I'll show you how to find them before we're done with this chapter.)

Once you've done that, click on the white eyedropper and then click on the brightest part of the image. That is the brightest area that should still contain detail. You'll often find it in a white shirt collar or button, a Styrofoam cup, the whites of someone's eyes, or a sheet of paper. In **Figure 9.8**, the brightest white falls on a fold in the sheer curtain material.

Figure 9.8 The brightest white falls on a fold in the curtain.

Finally, click on the middle eyedropper and then click on any area that should be gray in the final image—not bluish gray or pinkish gray, but pure gray (also known as neutral gray). You might have to really hunt for a gray; it is not always obvious. It could be a sweatshirt, a white shirt, or the edge of a book. On the other hand, you might run across an image that has dozens of gray areas to choose from. In that case, try to pick one that is not overly bright or dark, because we are already adjusting the highlight and shadow of the image. The closer we get to a middle gray, the more effective your adjustment will be. If you have any doubt at all that the area you have chosen should be gray, just experiment by clicking on one area to see what happens; then press Command-Z (Mac) or Ctrl-Z (Windows) to undo the change, and then try another area. Repeat this process until you've found an area that really causes the image to improve, but don't try too hard—not every image contains a true gray. For example, you might not be able to find one in a photograph of a forest. If you can't find one, then (of course) don't adjust it.

Using Threshold to Locate Highlight and Shadow

If you hate having to guess at anything, here's how to find the highlight and shadow areas without guessing. Choose Image > Adjustments > Threshold and move the slider all the way to the right; then slowly move it toward the middle (**Figure 9.9**). The brightest area of the image will be the first area that shows up as white (you can use the up and down arrow keys to move the slider). You don't want to find the very brightest speck (that could be a scratch or a reflection on something shiny), so be sure to look for a general area at least five or six pixels in size (something that's easy enough to click on without having to be overly precise). Once you've found the correct area, you can hold down the Shift key and click on that part of your image to add a color sample to that area (**Figure 9.10**). (You have to hold Shift only if you're still in an adjustment dialog box like Threshold.) A color sampler is simply a visual reminder of where that area is.

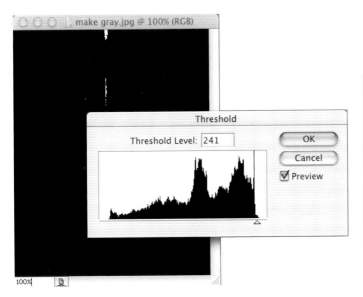

Figure 9.9 Use the Threshold command to find elusive highlights.

Figure 9.10 After using the Color Sampler tool, you should see a crosshair on the image.

Now let's use Threshold to find the darkest area of the image. This time, start with the slider all the way to the left, and then slowly move it toward the center. This will show you where the darkest area of the image is hiding. You don't want to find the darkest speck (that could be dust), so be sure to look for a general area at least five or six pixels in size. Once you've located the shadow, Shift-click on that area to place a sample point on top of it, and then click Cancel to get out of the Threshold dialog box. If you click OK instead of Cancel, your image will remain completely black and white. Now you should have two crosshairs on your image, one for the highlight and one for the shadow, as shown in **Figure 9.11**. When you use the eyedroppers in the Curves dialog box, you can press Caps Lock to turn your cursor into a crosshair, which will make it easy to tell when you're lined up with those color samplers. You can get rid of the color samplers by choosing the Color Sampler tool (it's hidden under the Eyedropper tool) and clicking the Clear button in the Options bar.

NOTES

You can use the up and down arrow keys to move the Threshold slider. That will allow you to concentrate on your image instead of having to concentrate on being precise with the mouse.

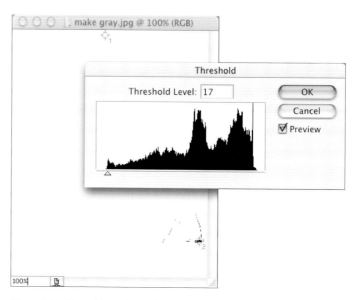

Figure 9.11 After adding a second sample point, you should see two crosshairs on your image.

Only use those eyedroppers that help to improve the look of your image. If one of them shifts the colors in an undesirable way, press Command-Z (Mac) or Ctrl-Z (Windows) to undo that step and either try another area or don't use that eyedropper. But just because a single eyedropper harms your image doesn't mean that the other two eyedroppers won't help it. You'll find that the white eyedropper doesn't help images that have desirable color casts. That's where you want the image to look warm or cool. Examples would be dinner by candlelight, a fireplace, and sunrise or sunset. And if you find that none of the eyedroppers seems to help, be sure to check out the techniques I mention in the "Color Manipulation" chapter.

Now let's explore two alternative methods for adjusting the highlight, shadow, and gray areas of an image.

Using a Grayscale to Correct Multiple Images

Here's an interesting trick I like to use when I know I'll be color correcting a large number of images that will be shot under the same lighting conditions, or when I photograph artwork. If you stop by a high-end camera store, you can ask for a grayscale (also known as a step wedge or a grayscale step wedge—**Figure 9.12**). Once you have one, you can place it in the scene where you are about to take a large number of photos (let's say for a yearbook or a product brochure) or when shooting any kind of art. Now, this is important—before you start shooting your actual scenes, you will want to take a photograph of the wedge under the exact same lighting conditions and exact same film type that you'll be using for the rest of the photos. That way you can use it as a reference that will pick up the color influence of the lighting and film.

Once the images are developed, scanned, and loaded into Photoshop, create a new Curves adjustment layer. Click on the white eyedropper and then click on the brightest gray rectangle on the grayscale. Next, click on the black eyedropper and then click on the darkest rectangle; and finally, click on the middle eyedropper and then click on the middle gray rectangle. That should remove any colorcast that was present in the image.

NOTES

The grayscale correction technique is appropriate only when you want to end up with an image that looks like it was shot under a white light source. It won't improve the look of images that contain desirable colorcasts like those shot under candlelight or during sunrise or sunset.

Figure 9.12 A grayscale from a high-end camera store.

You can apply that same adjustment to the other images by dragging the Curves adjustment layer from the grayscale image and dropping it onto another image that was photographed under the same lighting conditions. That way you can perform color correction with no guesswork and quickly apply the same adjustment to a large number of images.

You might find that this technique changes the contrast of your image too much. If that's the case, then either just use the middle eyedropper (skipping the other two) or use a Blending mode to control how the adjustment affects your image. If you applied your image directly (by choosing Image > Adjustments > Curves), then choose Edit > Fade Curves right after applying the adjustment and change the pop-up menu to Color. Or, if you used an adjustment layer, change the Blending mode menu that's found at the top of the Layers palette to Color. That will prevent the adjustment from changing the brightness or contrast of your image, but will still allow it to shift the colors.

Auto Color

Photoshop includes a great feature that attempts to automate the process of color correction: Auto Color (**Figure 9.13**). It uses the same general concepts we've been talking about in this chapter, and you'll find that it works well with a large variety of images. You can access Auto Color by creating a new Curves adjustment layer and then clicking on the Options button. The Shadows, Midtones, and Highlights settings use the same setting that we specified when we double-clicked on the eyedroppers in the Curves dialog box. The only difference is that Photoshop attempts to locate the highlight, shadow, and gray areas automatically. This dialog box is interactive—changes will immediately affect the image. I'd set the Shadows Clip value to 0.25% and the Highlights Clip value to 0.10%, and then choose the Find Dark & Light Colors option at the top of the dialog box so that Photoshop uses Threshold to find the bright/dark areas and applies the eyedroppers to them. Then turn on the Snap Neutral Midtones check box so it uses the middle eyedropper on areas that are close to being gray. I find that this automated feature works on a surprising number of images. But as with most automated features, you'll find that you have to take over and use the old eyedroppers technique whenever Auto Color fails to deliver a satisfactory result.

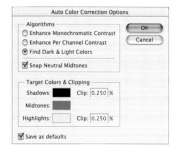

Figure 9.13 The Auto Color Correction Options dialog box.

If you find that the highlights in your image become blown out (no detail), you can click on the White Clip setting and press the down arrow key on your keyboard a few times until you see the detail return. You can do the same thing with the Black Clip setting to make sure you don't lose detail in the shadows of your image. I generally use the .10% setting that I mentioned earlier, and I only change it when I actually notice that I'm losing detail. If you're usually satisfied with the .10% values, then be sure to turn on the Save As Defaults check box so Photoshop will remember those settings. Then, you can quickly apply the new default settings to any image by choosing Image > Adjustments > Auto Color. And if you notice the contrast of the image changing too much, choose Edit > Fade Auto Color right after applying that command and set the pop-up menu to Color. That will prevent any brightness or contrast shifts.

Adjusting the highlight, shadow, and gray areas of an image can dramatically improve the quality of an image. But even with those adjustments, you occasionally need to fine-tune any skin tones that might be in the image.

Adjusting Skin Tones

You might be thinking that I'm going to give you some kind of magic formula for creating great skin tones (kind of like what I did with grays), but if I give you just one formula, then every skin tone in nature's vast diversity would look identical in your images! I'd much rather show you how to get a unique formula for each color of skin you might run across—Asian skin, olive skin, sun-burnt skin, fair skin, and all the different shades of black skin. Even better, we can do all that without trusting your monitor at all. (Of course, they will still look good on your screen, but unless you've calibrated your screen using a hardware device, then you shouldn't make critical decisions based on your screen image.)

Literally dozens of companies, such as Stockbyte, sell royalty-free stock photography. If you call these companies and ask for a catalog of images, they'll be more than happy to send you a really thick book chock-full of images (it will either be free or they might charge you for shipping and

Figure 9.14 Reference photo from a stock photo catalog. (©2003 Stockbyte, www.stockbyte.com)

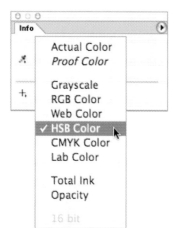

Figure 9.15 Change the sampler mode to HSB to determine the brightness of the area you are working on.

handling). At the back of that book will be a CD that contains tiny versions of those images, complete with the stock photo company's logo slapped in the middle of it so you'd never use it for a real project. But we don't care about that, because right now we're after something else—most of them contain a veritable treasure trove of flesh that you can transform into your own personal stockpile of skin tones. So, flip through one of those wonderful catalogs, pick the person who has the skin tone that best matches your needs, and then open the corresponding image from the CD at the back of the catalog. Next, use the Eyedropper tool and click on an area of the skin that is a medium brightness (**Figure 9.14**). Now click on your foreground color to see the RGB formula needed to create that exact color.

Now let's figure out how to use that information to improve your image that contains skin tones. Open the image you need to correct and use the Color Sampler tool to click on the area that contains the troublesome skin. Be sure to click in an area with medium brightness, similar to the level in the other (stock photo) image. That should give you an extra readout in the Info palette (readout #1 if you just opened a fresh image, or readout #4 if you still have the three we used earlier in this chapter).

Next, click on the eyedropper icon that shows up next to that new readout in the Info palette. Choose HSB from the menu (**Figure 9.15**), note the brightness (B) setting, and then set that menu back to RGB. Now, click on your foreground color to look at the color from the stock photo again. We want to use that basic color, but we don't want to change the brightness of our image much. To accomplish that, change the brightness (B) setting to what you saw in the photo you are attempting to color correct and then write down the RGB numbers that show up in the Color Picker (**Figure 9.16**). In just a moment, we're going to use those RGB numbers to tell Curves how to shift the skin color in the problem photo to match the skin color in the reference photo.

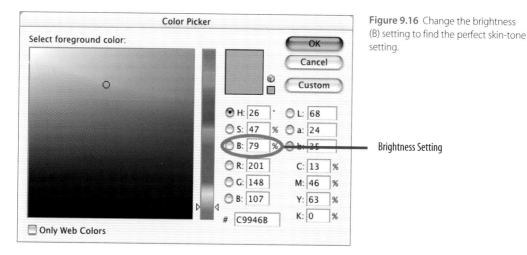

Figure 9.16 Change the brightness (B) setting to find the perfect skin-tone setting.

But first, it's time to isolate the skin tones in your problem image and then make your adjustment. I usually choose Select > Color Range to isolate the skin. If you've never used it before, then be sure to read about it in Chapter 2, "Selection Primer." Once you have a general selection of the skin (don't worry if it's not perfect), it's time to make the adjustment.

Remember earlier when we used an adjustment layer to change the highlight, shadow, and gray areas? That adjustment layer should still be in the Layers palette (unless you're working on a different file). Make sure that layer is active and then choose Layer > New Adjustment Layer > Curves; otherwise the new adjustment layer you're creating won't appear above the initial curves adjustment you applied. Then, to add a point to each of the red, green, and blue curves, hold Shift-Command (Mac), or Shift-Ctrl (Windows) and click on that same medium brightness area we sampled from earlier. Now, all you have to do is switch between the Red, Green, and Blue curves (use the menu at the top of the Curves dialog box) and type in the R, G, and B numbers you calculated and wrote down a few minutes ago (the ones you got from the Color Picker) in the Output of the Red, Green, and Blue curves. Once you've got the right numbers typed in, your skin tone should look much better (**Figure 9.17**).

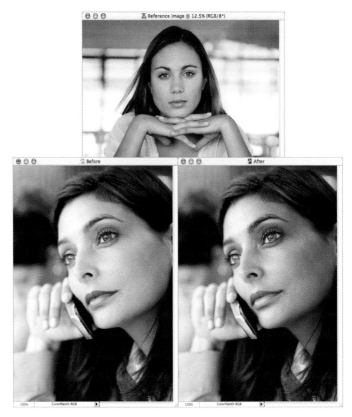

Figure 9.17 After adjusting for skin tones, the skin should look similar to the stock photo version. (original images ©2003 Stockbyte, www.stockbyte.com)

Now that you've performed the adjustment, you should take a look at your image to determine if the selection you made earlier accurately isolated the skin. If you need to fine-tune where the adjustment applies, you can go back and paint on the layer mask that is attached to the Curves adjustment layer to control which areas of the image are affected. If you're not familiar with layer masks, be sure to check out Chapter 13, "Advanced Masking," and Chapter 16, "Collage."

The more you get accustomed to using this technique, the less you'll have to rely on that catalog for reference photos.

You'll get used to knowing that the more red you pull out of your image, the more tan someone looks, and that the balance between green and blue determines the fairness of someone's skin.

If the skin-tone adjustment was a little too much for you to handle, then just start off by adjusting the highlight, shadow, and gray areas, and come back to this chapter after you've gotten comfortable with those. That might make it a little easier to understand and implement. The general concept is easy (and sneaky), but the execution isn't quite as simple as all that, because we have to make sure we don't mess up our earlier adjustments.

Refining the Result

Now that the colors have been optimized, let's explore some methods for improving the image even more. These steps are optional, but I usually end up performing them on the majority of images that I adjust.

Refinements to Brightness and Contrast Adjustments

The process we've gone through up until now was designed to correct the colors in the image. Now that the colors are better, you can also use all the ideas I showed you in the curves chapter to further enhance the brightness and contrast of the image. Just be careful not to shift the colors of the image. (You can prevent that by setting the blending mode of all future Curves adjustments to Luminosity, as was explained in the chapter on Curves.)

But adjusting color, contrast, and brightness still won't guarantee that your images are as vivid as they could be. Now let's figure out how to make the colors in your images really pop.

Optimizing Saturation

Once you've adjusted your colors, you can choose Layer > New Adjustment Layer > Hue/Saturation and increase the Saturation setting. Choose View > Gamut Warning to see how you're doing; if no gray appears over your image, then you can keep increasing the saturation until you start seeing small areas of gray (**Figure 9.18**). You've gone too far if you see large, concentrated gray blobs on your image. After you've adjusted the image, you can get rid of those gray areas by turning off the Gamut Warning. You can also choose View > Proof Colors if you'd like to see a preview of what the colors will look like when printed or converted to CMYK mode. That way you can adjust your image without having to worry about what will happen to the color when you print the image.

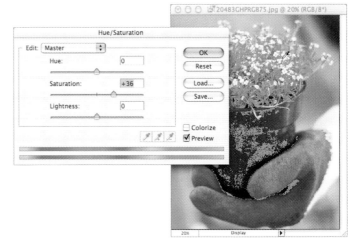

Figure 9.18 Keep increasing the saturation until a lot of gray shows up. (original image ©2003 Stockbyte)

Closing Thoughts

The techniques described in this chapter are the very same ones used by the high-paid color maestros who are responsible for all of those ever-so-perfect glossy magazine ads. It will take you a while to really get the hang of these techniques, but once you do, it should take you less than two minutes to correct most images.

Here's one last bit of advice: Make sure to always correct your images separately before blending them together. That way, you will be able to maintain the color integrity of each component of your big picture.

Ben's Techno-Babble Decoder Ring

Gamut: The range of colors that are reproducible on a particular device (monitor, printer, and so on).

Neutral gray: A pure gray that does not have any hint of color.

Specular highlight: An intense reflection that contains little or no detail. You'll find specular highlights in jewelry, metallic objects, and very shiny surfaces.

Keyboard Shortcuts

Function	Macintosh	Windows
Auto Color	Shift-Command-B	Shift-Ctrl-B
Curves	Command-M	Ctrl-M
Hue/Saturation	Command-U	Ctrl-U
Toggle Gamut Warning	Shift-Command-Y	Shift-Ctrl-Y
Toggle Proof Colors	Command-Y	Ctrl-Y

10

Using Camera Raw

There is a building. Inside this building there is a level where no elevator can go, and no stair can reach. This level is filled with doors. These doors lead to many places. Hidden places. But one door is special. One door leads to the source.

—The Keymaker, *The Matrix Reloaded*

Using Camera Raw

If you work with images from high-end digital cameras, then you might want to consider shooting in RAW file format (not all cameras offer RAW format). RAW files are different from JPEG or TIFF images in that they contain all the data that was captured from the camera with minimal processing.

Your digital camera has to do quite a bit of processing in order to turn the raw data from your camera into a JPEG or TIFF file (white balance, gamma, color profile, interpolation, sharpening, saturation, and other adjustments). You can think of a RAW file as the pure unadulterated data that came from the camera's sensor. Most programs can't open RAW images directly, but Photoshop CS can. (Actually, Camera Raw used to be a plug-in you could buy separately from Photoshop, but now Adobe has updated it and included it with Photoshop.) When you shoot RAW files, you don't have to worry about the white balance setting on your camera because you can specify that setting when opening the image in Photoshop.

WARNING

Some digital cameras (like the Canon 1D and 1Ds) save the raw camera data as part of a TIFF file. They save a 300×200 pixel preview of the image that can be read by any program that can handle a TIFF file. Inside that TIFF file, however, is the full resolution raw data from the camera, which is ignored by most programs that handle TIFF files. If you happen to have one of those cameras, then be very careful who you let work on your files. If someone opens one of those TIFF files in a program that isn't designed to deal with raw format images, then they will only see the 300×200 pixel preview image. They could then easily resave the file, which will completely overwrite the raw data that was originally in the file, leaving you with an image that contains only 300×200 pixels.

When you attempt to open a RAW format image in Photoshop, you will be presented with the Camera Raw dialog box (**Figure 10.1**). This is where you can adjust everything from the overall color of the image to the brightness and contrast, as well as control how much sharpening will be applied.

Figure 10.1 The Camera Raw dialog box. (©2003 Ben Willmore)

NOTES

Photoshop's RAW format isn't the same as Camera Raw format. The names sound almost identical, but Camera Raw files can only originate from a digital camera, and Photoshop cannot change the file at all. Camera Raw files are locked because they are designed to contain only the information that came from your digital camera; therefore, they cannot be directly modified after the photo is taken. Think of it like the files on a CD. You can open them, but you can't save back to the CD because it's locked. That doesn't limit at all what you can do to the images; it just means that you have to save the changes to your local hard drive instead of the CD. With Camera Raw files, it means that changes have to be saved in a different file format (like TIFF, Photoshop, or JPG). Photoshop's RAW file format, on the other hand, is mainly used to export images so they can be imported into unusual software that can't handle common file formats (it's something I doubt you'll ever have to use).

The Camera Raw Dialog Box

Let's start with a brief overview of the layout of the Camera Raw dialog box, and then we'll dive deeper and look at each specific setting.

In the upper left of the dialog box, you'll find the familiar Zoom and Hand tools, along with an Eyedropper tool that works much like the middle eyedropper that is found in both the Levels and Curves dialog box (we covered them in Chapter 9, "Color Correction"). We'll talk more about the Eyedropper tool when we start talking about the features that appear on the right side of the Camera Raw dialog box. When you're navigating your image, you should know the following keyboard shortcuts: Typing Command-Minus (Mac) or Ctrl-Minus (Windows) will zoom out from your image. Typing Command-Plus (Mac) or Ctrl-Plus (Windows) will zoom in on your image. Holding the spacebar will temporarily make the Hand tool active.

Across the bottom of the dialog box you'll find settings that don't change the general appearance of the image, but instead control its size and other attributes that tell Photoshop how to treat the image when it's opened. This is also where you can zoom in or out on your image, rotate it, and preview the changes you've made with all those sliders that show up on the right side of the dialog box.

In the upper right of the dialog box, you'll find a histogram that shows you how the sliders are affecting the overall tonality of the image. If you're not familiar with histograms, be sure to look back at Chapter 6, "Optimizing Grayscale Images," and Chapter 7, "Understanding Curves," for more information.

Below the histogram, you'll find a dazzling array of sliders organized into tabs of different categories (Adjust, Detail, Lens, and Calibrate), each with its own set of controls. This is where you can radically change the appearance of your image and optimize it before you open it in Photoshop.

Let's look at these settings one at a time. I'll describe them in the same order in which I usually adjust my own images.

The Adjust Tab

The Adjust tab should be your mandatory first stop in the Camera Raw dialog box. I use it for every image I ever open with Camera Raw (**Figure 10.2**); all the other settings under the other tabs can be considered optional. The Adjust tab is where we can change the overall color feeling of the image, adjust the brightness and contrast, and make sure we retain as much detail as possible. I like to start with the White Balance settings.

White Balance

This setting allows you to shift the overall color of your image, making it feel warm, cool, or neutral. There are three ways to set the white balance of your image: the pop-up menu, the sliders, or the Eyedropper tool.

The majority of the time, I end up using the White Balance pop-up menu because it's simple and easy. That's where you'll find presets for different types of lighting conditions (Daylight, Cloudy, Tungsten, Fluorescent). If you know which type of light an image was shot under, then choose that preset so Photoshop will correct for that particular light source. If you're not sure what the lighting conditions were when the image was shot, then just click through them and watch your image change until you find the one that makes the colors in your image look their best (**Figures 10.3** and **10.4**). Or, if you're in a big hurry, just set the menu to Auto and Photoshop will use the setting that it thinks is appropriate for the lighting conditions of your image. All this pop-up menu is doing is moving the Temperature and Tint sliders to preset positions. But before you start fiddling with those sliders, I'd recommend beginning with the pop-up menu because that will easily get you to a good starting point, which you can then fine-tune with the sliders.

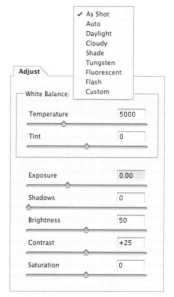

Figure 10.2 The settings found under the Adjust tab.

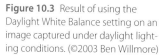

Figure 10.3 Result of using the Daylight White Balance setting on an image captured under daylight lighting conditions. (©2003 Ben Willmore)

Figure 10.4 Result of using the Tungsten White Balance setting on an image captured under daylight lighting conditions. (©2003 Ben Willmore)

Moving the Temperature slider toward the left will shift the colors in your image toward blue; sliding it to the right will shift them toward yellow. The Tint slider will shift the color in your image toward green or magenta. The combination of these two sliders will allow you to shift the image toward just about any color you can think of. For instance, if you move both the Temperature and Tint sliders toward the right, you'll be simultaneously shifting the image toward yellow and magenta. Those two colors combined produce red, so that's the color your image will shift toward. Moving them in the opposite direction would shift things toward both blue and green, which will send the colors toward cyan.

If you want your image to look completely neutral (not warm or cool feeling), you might consider using the Eyedropper tool that is located in the upper left of the Camera Raw dialog box. With that tool active, you can click on your image and Photoshop will figure out the proper Temperature and Tint settings that would be needed to remove all the color from the area you clicked on. All you have to do is find an area that shouldn't contain color and then click on it (**Figures 10.5** and **10.6**). Just look for anything that appears to be a shade of gray in the image. It could be someone's gray sweatshirt, a wall that's painted white, a button on someone's shirt, or anything else that shouldn't contain a trace of color. Then, if you feel the image is just too sterile looking, you're welcome to adjust the Temperature and Tint sliders to make the image a little warmer (toward yellow and magenta) or cooler (toward green and blue).

Depending on how much you've zoomed in, the Eyedropper will look at different numbers of pixels in your image. If you view your image at 100%, it will look at the exact pixel that is under your cursor when you click the mouse button. Viewing your image at 50% will make the Eyedropper look at a 2×2 pixel area of your image. I find that I like the results better when I'm viewing my image at 25% or 50%, because I don't have to worry about clicking on an odd-colored pixel that would get averaged into the colors that are surrounding it.

Figure 10.5 Image opened with random Temperature and Tint settings. (©2003 Ben Willmore)

Figure 10.6 Image opened by clicking with the Eyedropper tool on an area that should not contain color. (©2003 Ben Willmore)

There isn't always an ideal White Balance setting for each image. Your personal interpretation of what you'd like your image to look like will determine the setting you use. I often use these settings to manipulate the color of my images.

Let's say I took a photo under the midday sun, but I really wish I could have been at that location during sunrise or sunset so I would have ended up with a very warm-looking image. Well, all I have to do is experiment with the Temperature and Tint sliders, and I'll be able to manipulate the overall feeling of the image. It doesn't really matter which of the three methods you use (pop-up menu, sliders, or Eyedropper) because in the end, all of them are just manipulating the Temperature and Tint sliders to produce the end result you see.

Exposure Slider

The Exposure slider will control the brightness of the brightest area of your image. It's a lot like the upper-right slider in the Levels dialog box (we talked about that one back in Chapter 6). As you move the Exposure slider farther to the right, more areas of your image become pure white. Because of that, you have to be very careful; otherwise, you'll end up trashing the detail in the brightest part of your image. Go ahead, open a RAW image (if you don't have one, I put one on the CD for you in Chapter 10 in the Practice Images folder) and move the Exposure slider around. Be sure to move it all the way to the left and right to see how radical of a change you can make (**Figures 10.7** through **10.9**). It's not very often that I would adjust this slider by eye; I'd much prefer to use a hidden feature that will make it much easier to tell if I'm trashing too much detail.

Figure 10.7 Result of moving the Exposure slider all the way to the left. (©2003 Ben Willmore)

Figure 10.8 Result of leaving the Exposure slider at its default setting.

Figure 10.9 Result of moving the Exposure slider all the way to the right.

If you hold down the Option key (Mac) or Alt key (Windows) while you move the Exposure slider, Photoshop will change the way it displays your image (**Figure 10.10**). It will show you any areas that have the potential of losing detail (known as a clipping display). You don't have to worry about the areas that appear solid black because those areas should still have detail. But when an area shows up as solid white, then it has absolutely no detail and will end up solid white when the image is opened in Photoshop. If, on the other hand, you start seeing different colors showing up, that means that you're starting to get less detail in those areas, but you haven't blown them out to pure white quite yet. Rather, it means that you've maxed out one or more of the red, green, and blue colors that make up your image—max out all three and you'll end up with white.

Figure 10.10 If you hold the Option/Alt key when dragging the Exposure slider, you'll get a clipping display.

Figure 10.11 Hold Option/Alt and drag the Exposure slider until you see the first hints of white.

My approach to adjusting this slider is to move it toward the right (with Option/Alt held down) until I see the first hints of white showing up (**Figure 10.11**). Then I'll back off a tiny amount and think of that as the farthest I'd want to move it (**Figure 10.12**) (unless I have a photo of something that should have huge areas of pure white, like text on a white background). Then I'll look at the colored areas that are showing up, and if there are areas that contain critical detail, I'll continue to move the slider back toward

Figure 10.12 Back off on the Exposure setting until you don't see any white.

the left until I see only small areas of color. I don't mind having large areas of color if I want my image to look really saturated, because you have to max out at least one of the colors that make up your image (red, green, and blue) in order to get a truly saturated color. Once I've found the general range that I like, I'll let go of the Option/Alt key and see how this setting is affecting the brightest areas of my image, and then fine-tune it if necessary. The vast majority of the time I end up leaving it at the position that was just shy of seeing solid white when I had the Option/Alt key held down. The one exception to that rule is when your image contains direct reflections of light on a shiny object (such as water, glass, or metal). In that case, your image will usually look better if those bright reflections don't have any detail and are blown out to pure white.

If for some reason you decide not to use the clipping display (by holding Option or Alt while dragging the slider), then be sure to keep an eye on the histogram that appears at the top right of the Camera Raw dialog box (**Figure 10.13**). Detail is made out of a combination of red, green, and blue, and the height and color of the spikes on the end of the historgram will tell you how much detail is being lost. If you see a spike on the right end of the histogram, then you might be losing detail in the brightest area of your image. If the spike is white, then you're starting to get larger areas of solid white. If, on the other hand, the spike is a color (like red, green, or blue), then you haven't lost all the detail in your highlights, but you're starting to have less than what you started with.

Figure 10.13 If you're not using the clipping display, be sure to keep an eye on the histogram.

The Exposure setting is only used to control how bright the absolute brightest areas of your image should be. I don't suggest you try to control the overall brightness of your image with this slider. There are better ways to do that, which we'll get to in a few moments. Right now, let's think about the darker areas of your image.

Shadows Slider

The Shadows slider controls how dark the absolute darkest areas of your image will be. It's very similar to the upper-left slider in the Levels dialog box (which we talked about in Chapter 6). It works just like the Exposure slider in that you can hold Option or Alt to see which areas are becoming solid black (they will look black), which areas are starting to have less detail (colored areas), and which areas haven't lost any detail (they will look white). You can move the Shadows slider until you see the first hints of pure black showing up and then back off just slightly so you don't trash the detail anywhere (**Figure 10.14**).

If you decide not to use the clipping display feature when moving the Shadows slider, be sure to keep an eye on the histogram at the top of the dialog box. Again, acting just like the Exposure slider, but working with shadows instead of bright areas, a spike on the far left of the histogram is an indication that you might be losing detail in the shadows of your image. If the spike is white instead of a color, then you're starting to get some solid black areas in your image.

Figure 10.14 When moving the Shadows slider, try not to force any areas to black.

Brightness Slider

Now that we've determined how bright the brightest areas should be and how dark the darkest areas should be, it's time to adjust the brightness levels that fall between black and white.

The Brightness slider is very similar to the middle slider in the Levels dialog box because it attempts to adjust the overall brightness of your image without screwing up the brightest or darkest areas. Move the slider to the left if your image needs to be darker (**Figures 10.15** and **10.16**), or move it to the right to brighten the image (**Figure 10.17**). If you're planning to make radical changes in brightness, I recommend that you use curves (see Chapter 7) after you've opened the image in Photoshop. You'll simply have a lot more control over the process that way, but it won't hurt if you make a slight tweak using the Brightness slider.

Figure 10.15 Image opened using default Brightness setting of 50. (©2003 Ben Willmore)

Figure 10.16 Result of moving the Brightness slider all the way to the left to darken the image.

Figure 10.17 Result of moving the Brightness slider all the way to the right to brighten the image.

The clipping display is not available when moving the Brightness slider, so be sure to keep an eye on the histogram to see if you're losing detail in the highlights or shadows. Look for spikes developing on the ends of the histogram. If you see one on the left side, then either move the brightness slider toward the right to brighten the image or readjust the Shadows slider until the spike has been minimized—assuming you don't want to lose detail in the darkest areas of your image. If the spike is on the right end of the histogram, then either move the Brightness slider toward the left to darken the image or readjust the Exposure slider to see if you can reduce or eliminate the spike. Remember that white spikes mean no detail whatsoever (solid black or white), whereas colored spikes indicate that you're getting close to losing all detail in an area, but you still have a hint of detail left. My personal preference is to go back and readjust the Exposure or Shadows slider when I get a spike instead of backing off on the Brightness adjustment; otherwise, I might end up with an overly bright or dark image—it's only the brightest and darkest areas that would lose detail, so why not go back to the settings that specifically control those areas?

Contrast Slider

I consider the Contrast slider to be optional. Most of the time, I'd rather adjust the contrast of my images using curves because they provide much more control than I'd ever get by moving a generic Contrast slider. But, when I'm in a hurry, I often limit my adjustments to what's available in the Camera Raw dialog box. For instance, when I do a photo shoot, I often want to email my girlfriend just to show her a few of the shots I took. That's when I don't want to spend too much time adjusting individual images, so I'll settle for the generic Contrast adjustment instead of spending the time it would take to fine-tune it with curves (**Figures 10.18** through **10.20**).

NOTES

The main reason that the Contrast slider is available is so that you can quickly adjust your image when applying an action, and so you can include the entire adjustment as a single step in the action.

Figure 10.18 Image opened with –40 contrast setting. (©2003 Ben Willmore)

Figure 10.19 Image opened with default contrast setting of +25.

Figure 10.20 Image opened with +70 contrast setting.

The Contrast slider can also cause detail loss in the highlights and/or shadow areas of your image, but it's not as easy to screw up your image as it is with the Exposure, Shadows, and Brightness sliders. If you're really cranking up the contrast, you might want to glance at the histogram to see if you're blowing out the detail in the shadows or highlights (remember, spikes on the end equals clipping).

Saturation Slider

I think of the Saturation slider as optional. The truth is, you'll have much more control over your image if you adjust it in Photoshop with the Hue/Saturation dialog box. But, if you're in a hurry, or if you're recording an action that will be applied to a large number of similar images, then you might decide to use this slider instead of taking the time to do it as two steps. If you have more time, you can test the waters with this slider, and make the actual adjustments with the Hue/Saturation dialog box afterward (**Figures 10.21** through **10.23**).

Figure 10.21 Image opened with –50 Saturation setting. (©2003 Ben Willmore)

Figure 10.22 Image opened with 0 Saturation setting.

Figure 10.23 Image opened with +50 Saturation setting.

If you want a better idea of how the White Balance setting is affecting the colors of your image, you can temporarily pump up the saturation of your image with this slider. Then, once you like the overall color of the image, bring the Saturation slider back to zero, so you can instead adjust saturation in Photoshop.

Don't feel bad if you decide to use the Contrast or Saturation sliders. There's nothing wrong with them. You'll just have much more control if you use curves to adjust the contrast and Hue/Saturation to adjust the saturation. So, if you ever get frustrated with these two somewhat crude controls, be sure to check out Chapter 7, "Understanding Curves" and Chapter 11, "Color Manipulation."

Now let's move on and explore the settings found under the other tabs that appear on the right side of the Camera Raw dialog box. Those are the ones that I consider to be optional because not every image will benefit from those features, and you can often get more control if you use similar settings after your image is opened in Photoshop.

The Detail Tab

Digital cameras often produce images that look a bit soft and can often contain tiny specks of noise that can be distracting. The Detail tab is where you can deal with these problems, and hopefully produce a sharp and noise-free image. These settings make rather subtle changes to your image, so it's best to work with them when you're viewing your image at 100% magnification.

Sharpness

I must confess that I almost never use the Sharpness slider because I prefer to sharpen my image as the final step right before I print. It's ideal if you sharpen an image after it has been scaled down to its final size, and the Unsharp Mask filter gives you much more control because it has three sliders to control sharpening instead of just one. But whatever you do, don't ignore this setting because the default sharpness amount is 25, not 0.

But, again, if you're in a hurry, recording an action, or feeling just plain lazy, there are merits to the Sharpness slider. You might find that moving the slider doesn't appear to do anything to your image. That usually happens when you're zoomed out so you can see the entire image. Before you start to sharpen your image, double-click on the Zoom tool in the upper left of the Camera Raw dialog box. That will get you to 100% view, where you'll be able to see exactly what the Sharpness slider is doing to your image. When you're done, you can always double-click on the Hand tool to get back to the view that shows your entire image. I won't say much about sharpening here because there is an entire chapter (Chapter 14, "Sharpening") dedicated to the subject later in this book.

NOTES

If you plan to sharpen your images in Photoshop, then choose Preferences from the side menu that appears just above and to the right of the Detail tab and change the Apply Sharpening Settings to Pop-up Menu to Preview Images Only. When you do that, the Sharpness setting will apply only to the onscreen image preview, and no sharpening will be applied when you open the image in Photoshop.

Luminance Smoothing

Luminance Smoothing is designed to reduce the noise that shows up when you use high ISO settings with your digital camera (**Figure 10.24**). It won't deal with those colorful specks you see on occasion (that's what Color Noise Reduction is for), but it should be able to handle the dark specks that you get when you try to brighten up an image that was shot in low lighting conditions. All you need to do is zoom in to 100% view (double-click on the Zoom tool to get there), and then experiment with the slider until the noise is minimized (**Figure 10.25**). Just be sure to look at the fine detail in your image to make sure it hasn't removed important detail like freckles or skin texture.

Figure 10.24 Zooming in on this image reveals bright specks.

Figure 10.25 The specks are less obvious after adjusting the Luminance Smoothing setting.

Color Noise Reduction

The Color Noise Reduction slider will attempt to blend in any colorful specks that appear on your image (**Figure 10.26**) by making them look similar to the colors that surround them (**Figure 10.27**). These colorful specks are often the result of shooting with high ISO settings on your digital camera. Just like with Luminance Smoothing, you'll want to be at 100% view and move the slider just high enough to blend the multicolored specks into your image.

You have to be careful with the Luminance Smoothing and Color Noise Reduction sliders because they will both soften your image. Be sure to toggle the Preview check box at the bottom of your image off and on to make sure it's worth applying these settings. Sometimes it's better to have a noisy image that still has detail and sharpness than one with no noise that looks overly soft. Also, remember that you can always sharpen your image after you open it in Photoshop, which means that it doesn't have to remain as soft as it might appear after you apply smoothing and noise reduction.

Now that you know how to adjust your image and minimize noise, let's start to explore some of the more obscure features of Camera Raw. There are two more tabs that are available in Camera Raw, but you have to choose Advanced in the upper right of the dialog box for them to appear. Adobe divided the features in Camera Raw into basic and advanced just to keep clutter down and to try to minimize intimidating new users.

Figure 10.26 With the Color Noise Reduction setting at zero, you can see specks of many different colors.

Figure 10.27 After adjusting the Color Noise Reduction slider, the colorful specks blend into the surrounding colors.

Figure 10.28 The sliders found under the Lens tab are designed to compensate for problems related to the camera lens.

The Lens Tab

This is another collection of settings that are completely optional (**Figure 10.28**). I use them only when I notice specific problems with my images that have to do with the lens that I used to shoot them.

Some lenses—particularly wide-angle lenses—often have the problem of focusing different wavelengths of light at different points. When that happens, you can end up with a halo of color on the edge of objects that would usually be white or black (and to a lesser extent colored objects). I'm no expert on optics, but I've been told that this particular problem is called *chromatic aberration*. I just think of it as messed up color on the outer portions of images taken with wide-angle lenses, because that's where I've run into it. The higher the contrast between objects, the more obvious it will be.

If you notice a halo of red on one side of an object and cyan on the opposite side, try moving the Chromatic Aberration R/C (for Red/Cyan) slider back and forth to see if you can reduce the halos (**Figures 10.29** through **10.31**). If, on the other hand, you see blue and yellow halos, then adjust the Chromatic Aberration B/Y slider instead. You might need to adjust both of the sliders depending on exactly what colors you're seeing on the edges of objects. Because these sliders are performing a very simple operation—scaling the colors that make up your image—they can't always get rid of this type of problem.

Figure 10.29 Original image. (Courtesy of Tim Whitehouse)

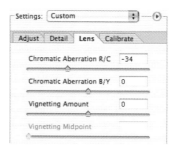

Figure 10.30 The Chromatic Aberration settings used to correct the image shown in Figure 10.29.

Figure 10.31 After adjusting the Chromatic Aberration settings, the color halos are no longer obvious.

The two Vignetting sliders are designed to compensate for light falloff on the edge of your image. *Vignetting* is a term the photography folks like to throw around that generally refers to lighter centers with darker edges. So, if you ever notice that the outer edges of your image are darker than the middle, then move the Vignetting Amount slider toward the right until the brightness of the edge looks more like the middle of your image. Once you've done that, you'll need to adjust the Vignetting Midpoint setting to control how far the brightening effect of the last slider encroaches on the center of your image. Just move it until the formerly dark edges blend into the rest of the image.

You can also use these sliders to add vignetting to your image (**Figures 10.32** and **10.33**), which will effectively darken the corners and edges of the image. Photographers often like that effect because it draws the viewer's attention toward the center of the image. I like to do that in combination with lowering the Saturation and Contrast sliders under the Adjust tab to simulate the look of an old faded photo (**Figure 10.34**).

Figure 10.32 Original image. (©2003 Ben Willmore)

Figure 10.33 Moving the Vignetting slider all the way to the left darkened the corners of the image.

Figure 10.34 Lowering the Contrast and Saturation settings helps the image look more like an old faded photo.

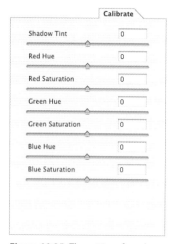

Figure 10.35 The settings found under the Calibrate tab allow you to change how Photoshop interprets the colors in your image.

The next section of Camera Raw is one that I would reserve for advanced users. So, if you're a Photoshop newbie, you might want to skip over this next section and pick things back up when I start talking about the workflow settings.

The Calibrate Tab

You have to choose Advanced at the top of the Camera Raw dialog box in order to access the Calibrate tab; this is the same place you found the Lens tab. The sliders under the Calibrate tab (**Figure 10.35**) allow you to change the way Photoshop interprets the color information that your camera delivers to Photoshop. You can use these settings to simulate different film types and to compensate for problems that come along with certain digital cameras.

You might find that certain models of digital cameras produce images that have an annoying colorcast in the darkest areas of your image (**Figure 10.36**). If you have one of those cameras, then just about every image you open will have a cast in the shadows of the image. The Shadow Tint slider will allow you to shift the color of the darkest areas of your image toward green or magenta (**Figure 10.37**).

Figure 10.36 Original image. (©2003 Ben Willmore)

Figure 10.37 Result of adjusting the Shadow Tint slider.

Finally, if you find that you're simply not happy with the color that you get from your digital camera, you might want to experiment with the Red, Green, and Blue Hue and Saturation sliders. These sliders can also be used to simulate different traditional film types (**Figures 10.38** and **10.39**). For instance, Fuji Velvia film delivers higher-contrast images with saturated colors, whereas Kodak Porta is fine-tuned to produce good-looking skin tones.

Figure 10.38 Original image.

Figure 10.39 Result of experimenting with the RGB settings.

The red, green, and blue sliders will not change areas that are neutral gray. The red sliders will mainly affect the appearance of reds in your image, and will affect yellow and magenta areas to a lesser extent. The green sliders will mainly affect the appearance of greens in your image, and will affect cyan and yellow areas to a lesser extent. The blue sliders will mainly affect the appearance of blues in your image, and will affect magenta and cyan areas to a lesser extent.

I'd suggest that you first choose Camera Default from the pop-up menu above the Calibrate tab before you start messing with the Calibrate settings. That way, you can make sure that the changes you see on your image are solely caused by the Calibrate settings. Just move the sliders around while you watch your image—you can easily replace experience with experimentation when adjusting

Figure 10.40 Choose Only Calibration from the pop-up menu at the top of the Save Settings Subset dialog box.

these sliders. Once you get your image to look the way you'd like it to, choose Save Settings Subset from the fly-out menu that appears just above and to the right of the Calibrate tab. Choose Only Calibration from the pop-up menu (**Figure 10.40**) in the Save Settings Subset dialog box, and then click the Save button. Now, the next time you work on an image that you'd like to have the same color qualities as the one you just adjusted, just choose the name of the preset you saved from the Settings pop-up menu. Or, if you'd like to use those settings on all the images you open from that specific camera, choose Set Camera Default from the same menu.

Now that we've made it through all the settings that appear under the tabs on the right side of the Camera Raw dialog box, we're ready to tackle the settings that appear at the bottom of the dialog box. These are the settings that don't affect the overall look of your image, but are still important because they ensure that Photoshop will receive the proper amount of information to make your images look great when they are printed.

Workflow Settings

Just below the preview image, you'll find settings that relate to the general way you choose to work in Photoshop (**Figure 10.41**). This is where we'll have to deal with some technical mumbo-jumbo that is necessary for Photoshop to reproduce the image properly. Hold on because we're about to jump into the world of bit depth, color spaces, and resolution. It will be a painful but necessary journey, so hold on to your seat...here we go.

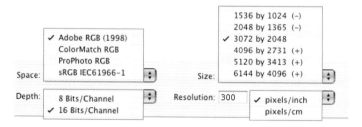

Figure 10.41 The Workflow settings are located below the image preview in Camera Raw.

The Space pop-up menu tells Photoshop the exact colors of RGB that your image is made from, and therefore the range of colors it can contain. I suggest that you set the Space pop-up menu to the same setting you chose for your RGB working space, which we talked about in Chapter 8, "Color Management" (most people use Adobe RGB).

How Many Bits Is That?

Next, you can decide between 8- and 16-bit color depths. Sixteen-bit images contain billions of colors instead of the standard 16 million colors that are possible in an 8-bit file. Sixteen-bit files are ideal when you plan to make radical changes to the brightness and/or contrast of an image after it's opened in Photoshop. But 16-bit files are also twice as big, so Photoshop will run slower, and the files you end up with will be larger than 8-bit files. If you'd like to save space on your hard drive, you can always choose Image > Mode > 8 Bits/Channel after you are done adjusting the image in Photoshop. By doing that, you'll take advantage of the additional color when you need it the most (during adjustment), but you'll end up with a smaller file in the end. I can't think of a single output device that can reproduce more than 8 bits of information, so there really is no advantage to keeping all those extra shades around after you're done adjusting your image.

Previous versions of Photoshop have limited support for 16-bit images, but that has changed in Photoshop CS. You can now use the vast majority of Photoshop's features on 16-bit images. The main exception is that some of the more complex filters will work only after you convert your image to 8-bit mode.

Size and Resolution

After you've decided if you want to jump on the 16-bit bandwagon, you'll need to specify the size and resolution of your image. The combination of these two settings will determine how large your image will be when it's printed or loaded into another program.

The default setting for the Size pop-up menu reflects the native resolution (often measured in megapixels) of the digital camera that was used to take the photo. For instance, a 5 megapixel camera will deliver an image that contains approximately 5 million pixels. If you multiply the two numbers that show up in the Size pop-up menu and then move the decimal place six digits to the left (to see how many millions it is), you can find out how many mega-pixels your camera is. My camera delivers a 3072×2048 image, which means that it's a 6.3 megapixel camera (3072×2048 = 6,291,456).

The Resolution setting determines how large those pixels will be when you print your image. The higher the resolu-tion, the more pixels will fit in an inch, and therefore the smaller they will be. If you were to divide the width of your image (in pixels from the Size menu) by the Resolution setting, you'd be able to find out how wide your image would be when it's printed.

My digital camera delivers a 3072×2048 image and the default resolution setting is 240, so with default settings, I'd end up with a 12.8×8.5 inch image. If I were to raise the resolution setting to 300 (which forces more pixels into each inch, making them smaller), then I'd end up with a 10.24×6.8 inch image instead. I really wish that Adobe would have provided that information so I don't have to do math in my head—after all, there's empty space available just to the right of those settings. That would make it much easier to figure out how to get a 5×7 ", 8×10 ", or other standard-size image, but instead you can use Table 10.1 to get an idea of what you'll end up with when using differ-ent combinations of Size and Resolution. If you're not sure which Resolution setting you should use, be sure to look over Chapter 4, "Resolution Solutions," which will describe how to pick an appropriate resolution setting.

TABLE 10.1 Common Resolution Settings and Corresponding Sizes in Inches

PIXELS	@72PPI	@128PPI	@150PPI	@170PPI	@200PPI	@225PPI	@240PPI	@266PPI	@300PPI
6144	85.3	48.0	41.0	36.1	30.7	27.3	25.6	23.1	20.5
5120	71.1	40.0	34.1	30.1	25.6	22.8	21.3	19.2	17.1
4096	56.9	32.0	27.3	24.1	20.5	18.2	17.1	15.4	13.7
3413	47.4	26.7	22.8	20.1	17.1	15.2	14.2	12.8	11.4
3072	42.7	24.0	20.5	18.1	15.4	13.7	12.8	11.5	10.2
2731	37.9	21.3	18.2	16.1	13.7	12.1	11.4	10.3	9.1
2048	28.4	16.0	13.7	12.0	10.2	9.1	8.5	7.7	6.8
1536	21.3	12.0	10.2	9.0	7.7	6.8	6.4	5.8	5.1
1365	19.0	10.7	9.1	8.0	6.8	6.1	5.7	5.1	4.6
1024	14.2	8.0	6.8	6.0	5.1	4.6	4.3	3.8	3.4

If you plan to make your image larger or smaller than what its native resolution can provide, you can select an appropriate setting in the Size pop-up menu (**Figure 10.42**). The choices that are available in the Size pop-up menu will be based on how much information your digital camera supplied to Photoshop. Settings with a plus sign (+) next to them will cause Photoshop to scale your image up, which will deliver a larger image, but Photoshop will have to use math (known as interpolation) to create the additional information needed, which might cause the image to look a little soft. You can always sharpen the image in Photoshop, or with the Sharpness slider under the Detail tab in Camera Raw, to compensate for the softness introduced by scaling the image up. Numbers with negative signs (-) next to them will cause Photoshop to scale your image down from its native size. Scaling down does not harm your image, so these settings are very safe to use. Scaling an image up using the Size pop-up menu in Camera Raw will produce a higher-quality result than what you'd get if you scaled the image up in Photoshop. If the exact size you need isn't listed in the Size pop-up menu,

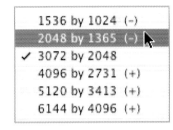

Figure 10.42 The Size pop-up menu in Camera Raw.

then choose the setting that is closest to what you desire and then use the Image > Image Size dialog box (**Figure 10.43**) in Photoshop to fine-tune the size.

Once you have adjusted the appearance of your image with the settings found under the tabs and specified the size and color depth, you're ready to click OK to open the image in Photoshop.

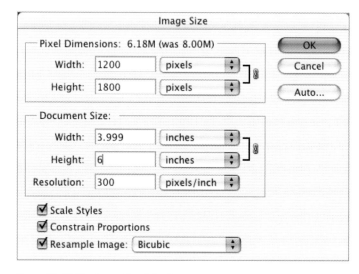

Figure 10.43 The Image Size dialog box.

Finishing Touches

When you open your image in Photoshop, the settings you used will be saved. The next time you open the same RAW format image, Photoshop will remember the settings you used (it remembers all the settings except the ones related to workflow). If you'd rather just save the settings you currently have in the Camera Raw dialog box so that Photoshop will use them the next time you open the image, then hold down the Option key (Mac) or Alt key (Windows) and click the Update button (the OK button changes to Update when Option/Alt is held down). When you do that, Photoshop assumes that you want to attach those settings to your image instead of actually opening it in Photoshop. Updating images can be useful if you plan to use them with Actions or the choices found under the Automate menu in the File Browser.

If you'd rather not use the Camera Raw dialog box when opening a RAW image in Photoshop's regular File Browser, then try holding the Shift key when you open the image. That will bypass the Camera Raw dialog box, but will still use the Camera Raw settings you used the last time you opened the image, or it will use the default settings if you've never opened the image before.

If you have a few images that were shot in similar lighting conditions, you might want to think about opening one of those images and then using the same settings on the subsequent images. You can do that by opening one image with the Camera Raw settings you want to use and then choosing Previous Conversion from the Apply Settings From pop-up menu in the Apply Camera Raw Settings dialog box on the other images. Or, if you have a bunch of images that you'd like to use those settings with, select them in the File Browser and then choose Apply Camera Raw Settings from the Automate menu of the File Browser (**Figure 10.44**). That will allow you to choose the name of the file you'd like to copy the Camera Raw settings from, or use any of the presets that you saved from the Camera Raw dialog box. Then, when you decide to open the files, you can hold Shift to bypass the Camera Raw dialog box altogether.

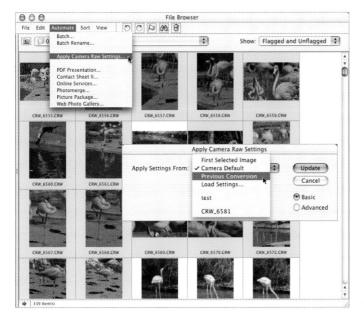

Figure 10.44 Choose Apply Camera Raw Settings from the Automate menu to apply settings to multiple files.

NOTES

You can turn on the Advanced radio button in the Apply Camera Raw Settings dialog box to have precise control over the settings that will be applied to your file. That's also a quick way to see what all the preset settings contain.

Finally, if you're a Camera Raw fanatic, you can choose Metadata Display Options from the side menu of the Metadata tab of the File Browser (**Figure 10.45**). That's where you can turn on the Camera Raw check box so you'll see all the Camera Raw settings that are attached to the file that is currently selected in the File Browser (**Figure 10.46**).

Figure 10.45 The Metadata Display Options dialog box.

Figure 10.46 Viewing the metadata in the File Browser.

Closing Thoughts

At first glance, the Camera Raw dialog box may look like an unruly beast, and it may have taken me a couple dozen pages to describe all the settings available when working with raw files, but you should know that it usually only takes me about a minute to adjust most images. Once you've gone through the settings a few times, it should be the same for you.

Ben's Techno-Babble Decoder Ring

Chromatic aberration: An effect that causes small halos of different colors on the edges of objects. This happens when a lens focuses different colors of light in different places on the image.

Luminance: Another word for brightness. When someone talks about the luminance of an image, they usually ignore all issues relating to color and just concentrate on what's happening to the brightness of the image.

RAW file format: A special file format that contains the raw data that was captured with a digital camera's sensor. This unadulterated information gives you the most versatility when opening an image in Photoshop. Unlike the other file formats available (like JPEG and TIFF), RAW files allow you to change important settings like White Balance at the time you open the image. JPEG and TIFF images have those settings locked into the image so they can't easily be changed after the photo is taken.

Vignetting: Darkening of the corners and edges of an image due to light falloff in the lens of the camera.

Keyboard Shortcuts

Function	Macintosh	Windows
Switch Tabs	Command-1, 2, 3, 4	Ctrl-1, 2, 3, 4
Rotate Clockwise	R	R
Rotate Counterclockwise	L	L
Toggle Preview	P	P
Bypass Camera Raw dialog box when opening from File Browser	Shift	Shift

©2003 Ben Willmore

11
Color Manipulation

Courtesy of Gregg Lauer, www.gregglauer.com

Oh yes. Dr. Brisbane felt that color had a great deal to do with the well being of the emotionally disturbed.

—Nurse Diesel, *High Anxiety* (1978)

Color Manipulation

In this chapter we'll cover Photoshop CS's new Color Replacement tool and the Match Color command. This is an entirely new chapter, so you'll find lots of new goodies within its pages.

If you've been going through this book in sequence, you've made it through Chapter 8, "Color Management" (where you learned how to get consistent color between devices), and Chapter 9, "Color Correction" (where you learned how to fix, balance, and adjust colors). By now you've certainly realized that the whole business of color is truly a whale of a subject. Although the other two chapters might be considered mandatory, especially for you pre-press and production folks, and perhaps less than thrilling, I'd like to think that the time devoted to those subjects was well spent, as if you were a piano tuner getting every key finely tuned. And now that you've got perfect pitch, you're ready to rev up your creative engine and start the music. We're going to learn to do things like change the color of a car, colorize a grayscale photo, make our skies bluer than blue, and basically enjoy ourselves while we use color to manipulate our visual reality.

Look at this chapter as a box chock-full of color manipulation tools and methods. There is no one surefire all-purpose tool, because, as expected, Photoshop has provided an abundance of ways to shift the colors in your image. Which tool and method you use will depend on what type of original image you have and what type of change you envision. This chapter is organized on a simple premise: I'll start with my personal favorites, and then progress into the less well-known methods that I don't use very often, but which, from time to time, can still be very effective.

Okay, I know I promised fun, but first you need basic knowledge about color because that is essential to understanding what's going on behind the scenes with Photoshop's color manipulation tools.

At the Core Is the Color Wheel

The vast majority of Photoshop's color controls are based on a classic color wheel (**Figure 11.1**). If you understand a few basic concepts about the color wheel, then you'll be ahead of the game when it comes to controlling color in Photoshop.

Hue = Basic Color

Take another look at **Figure 11.1** and you'll notice that only six basic colors are shown: cyan, blue, magenta, red, yellow, and green. That's because every color you could ever imagine is based on one of those colors or what you get in the transition between them. Take red, for example. Darken it and you get maroon, or make it less vivid and you'll have pink. But in the end both are just different versions of red.

The basic color that any color is based on is known as its hue. Photoshop describes these basic colors, or hues, using numbers that it gets by figuring out how many degrees the color is from red going clockwise around a color wheel. If you divide the color wheel into sixths and start with red at 0, then you'll find the other colors as follows: yellow at 60°, green at 120°, cyan at 180°, blue at 240°, and magenta at 300° (**Figure 11.2**). You don't have to remember any of those numbers, but it will be helpful to know that hue numbers in Photoshop are based on the color wheel. When you adjust the hue (using an adjustment like Hue/Saturation), you're effectively spinning the color wheel by moving each basic color in your image an equal amount (or angle) around the edge of the color wheel.

The other way you can shift the basic colors in your image is to push them toward one of the six primary colors that are found in the color wheel (using an adjustment like Color Balance). Red, green, and blue are the exact opposites of cyan, magenta, and yellow. Cyan ink's sole job in life is to absorb red light, magenta ink's job is to absorb green light, and yellow ink absorbs blue light. That's why you'll never find an adjustment that allows you to shift something toward cyan and red at the same time. They are

Figure 11.1 Most of Photoshop's color adjustment features are based on the color wheel.

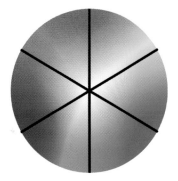

Figure 11.2 If you divide the color wheel into six equal parts, you'll find the primary colors that make up your image (RGB, CYM).

opposites, so moving toward red automatically takes you away from cyan. When you push your image toward one of the primary colors, all the colors within the image shift in that direction and become more similar, whereas shifting the hue by spinning the color wheel leaves colors as different as they used to be and moves each one an equal distance around the color wheel.

Saturation = How Colorful

If you move from the outer ring of a color wheel toward the center, you'll notice that the colors mellow out and become much less colorful. In fact, the shades in the absolute center of the color wheel contain no color at all (they're gray). Photoshop describes how colorful something is by using percentages, and calls it *saturation*. If something has no saturation at all (0%), then it has no color at all (no hint of any of the basic colors that show up around the outer edge of the color wheel), and therefore will only contain shades of gray. If, on the other hand, you have something that has 100% saturated colors, it will be as colorful as possible (just like the colors that appear on the outer rim of the color wheel).

Brightness/Lightness/Luminosity

The only things missing from our color wheel are the different brightness levels for all those colors. You could create a 3D color wheel in the shape of a cylinder with dark colors at its base and the brightest colors at the top (**Figure 11.3**). But because we'll probably never see anything that fancy in Photoshop, we'll just describe the brightness of a color using one of three words: brightness, lightness, and luminosity. Each of those words is just a slightly different way to describe how bright a color is, and as you become more traveled in Photoshop, you'll notice that Adobe can never seem to make up its mind on which one to use. So don't let all the terms confuse you, because they basically mean the same thing.

Every color you've ever seen in Photoshop can be described as a combination of hue, saturation, and brightness (HSB). You'll find me referring to that term every once

Figure 11.3 A three-dimensional color wheel would have dark colors at the bottom and bright colors at the top.

in a while. The adjustments we'll be doing will end up shifting the colors in our image based on that color wheel. Most of what we do will result in either moving a color around the wheel to change its hue or shifting it toward another color by pushing it to the opposite side of the wheel. Now that you have a general idea of how to think about a color wheel, let's jump in and see how we can mess with the colors in our images. So, crack your knuckles and push up your shirtsleeves, cause we're ready to start mousing around. We'll warm up with my favorite method for manipulating color.

The Hue/Saturation Dialog Box

Choose Hue/Saturation from the adjustment layer pop-up menu at the bottom of the Layers palette to get started. (The icon looks like a circle, half of which is filled with black.) That will create an adjustment layer, and send you into the Hue/Saturation dialog box (**Figure 11.4**). You can make three types of changes with this type of an adjustment—changes to Hue, Saturation, and Lightness.

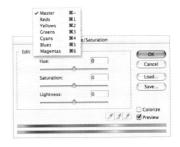

Figure 11.4 The Hue/Saturation dialog box.

If you look at the bottom of the Hue/Saturation dialog box, you'll see two strips of color, which show you all the possible hues you can use in Photoshop. Those color strips are really just a standard color wheel that's been straightened out. The color on the far left is the same as the one on the far right, so you could easily bend it into a circle to make a color wheel. The Hue slider will allow you to change the basic colors that make up your image. Go ahead and open any colorful image and move the Hue slider around to see what happens (**Figures 11.5** to **11.7**). The top strip of color indicates all the hues that you could possibly have in your image, whereas the bottom bar indicates what you've done to each of the hues. You can pick a color from the top strip and look straight down to the lower strip to figure out what Photoshop has done to it. For now, just remember that hue means basic color, and that the Hue slider will change the basic color of everything in your image. In a little while I'll show you how to get much more control over the specific colors in your image, but first we should look at the other two types of changes we can make with the Hue/Saturation dialog box.

Figure 11.5 The original image. (© 2003 PhotoSpin, www.photospin.com)

Figure 11.6 Moving the Hue slider will shift all the hues in your image.

Figure 11.7 The result of applying the adjustment shown in Figure 11.6.

Figure 11.8 This image is divided in half; the left side shows the original image, and the right side shows what happens when you move the Saturation slider all the way to the right. (©2003 PhotoSpin, www.photospin.com)

Using the same photo, move the Saturation slider all the way to the left; your image should become completely black and white. Move the slider all the way to the right and all the colors in your image should become ridiculously vivid (**Figure 11.8**). Most images can use a modest saturation boost; for now that's all I'll say on the subject, but I'll get back to it in a little while.

The last control is a bit more straightforward than the other two, but you'll have to be very careful when you adjust the Lightness slider. Go ahead and slide it all the way to the left and then all the way to the right to see what happens to your image. You should end up with a solid black image at one extreme and a solid white one at the other. That's a pretty generic adjustment, and can easily mess up your image (especially when applying it to the entire image). It's not quite as bad as using the Brightness and Contrast control (from the Image > Adjustment menu), which brightens or darkens every shade in your image an equal amount, but it's close. This slider will become much more useful once we figure out how to isolate a range of color to adjust.

Isolating a Range of Colors

When the Edit pop-up menu at the top of the Hue/ Saturation dialog box is set to Master, then any change you make will affect all the colors in your image. If you'd rather have your changes affect only certain colors, choose a color from that pop-up menu before adjusting your image. Watch what happens to those two color strips at the bottom of the dialog box as you switch between the choices that are available from the Edit pop-up menu (**Figure 11.9**). The tiny sliders that show up indicate the range of colors that you'll be changing. It will fully apply to the hues between the two vertical bars and then fade out as it nears the hues that appear above the triangular sliders. The problem is that the Edit pop-up menu lists only six generic colors, and the color you need to isolate could be in between one of those colors.

Figure 11.9 Choosing a color from the Edit pop-up menu causes sliders to show up between the two strips of color.

To get around that limitation, all you have to do is move your mouse over the image and click on the color you would like to change. The sliders will center on the color you click on. The sliders should now be in the right position to work with that color. Go ahead and try it. Create a Hue/Saturation adjustment layer (by selecting Hue/Saturation from the adjustment layer pop-up menu at the bottom of the Layers palette), choose a color from the Edit pop-up menu, and then click on a color in your image before moving any of the sliders in that dialog box.

If you really want to get precise control over the range of colors you're attempting to alter, then you'll need to mess with those tiny sliders that appeared after you chose a color from the Edit pop-up menu. I like to start by smashing them together into one mass, which will force Photoshop to work on the narrowest range of colors possible. So go ahead and do that, and then, to make sure it's focusing on the right color, click on the color within your image that you want to change (remember that this centers the sliders on the color you click on). At this point, you probably can't tell if it's going to change a wide enough range of colors, so you can move the Saturation slider all the way to the left just to see what changes in your image. That will make parts of the image become black and white (**Figure 11.10**). If it's not working on a wide enough range of colors, then hold down the Shift key and click on additional areas of the image (you can also click and drag across an area to get all the colors in an object). Shift-clicking will spread out

Figure 11.10 Clicking on the image and lowering the saturation setting will turn areas black and white. (©2003 Stockbyte, www.stockbyte.com)

If you find that the sliders are wrapping around the ends of those color strips (which usually happens when working on cyan and green objects), then you might want to "spin the color wheel." When that's the case, hold the Command key (Mac) or Ctrl key (Windows) and move your mouse over the color strips until your cursor looks like a hand. Then drag left or right until the sliders end up near the middle of the Hue/Saturation dialog box.

I've found that it's much easier to isolate a range of colors when working in RGB mode instead of CMYK mode. In CMYK, I'll often Shift-click on an area and the sliders won't move the correct distance to affect the color I just clicked on. But, if I simply choose Image > Mode > RGB, I'll have no problem isolating the colors. If I really need to end up with a CMYK image, I'll just choose Image > Mode > CMYK after adjusting the image. If you used an adjustment layer to make the change, then Photoshop will prompt you to flatten the image when you convert it to CMYK mode. It does that because it cannot make the same change while the image is in CMYK, so it wants to permanently apply the change before converting. Just click Flatten when it prompts you; otherwise, your image will revert back to what it looked like before you adjusted it.

the vertical sliders, causing Photoshop to work on a wider range of colors. If you accidentally click on a color that you don't want to shift, then hold Option (Mac) or Alt (Windows) and click on that area again to remove it from the range of colors that are being adjusted (it will narrow the gap between the two vertical sliders). With the Saturation slider all the way to the left, you will have all the areas you want to shift showing up as black and white (**Figure 11.11**). Now move the Saturation slider back to the middle and mess with all three main sliders (Hue, Saturation, and Lightness) until you get the change you're looking for (**Figure 11.12**).

Figure 11.11 Shift-click on additional colors until all the colors you'd like to shift become black and white.

Figure 11.12 Once you've isolated the range you'd like to change, then move all three adjustment sliders to get to the color you desire.

The eyedropper tools that show up near the lower right of the Hue/Saturation dialog box also control where the sliders appear. By default, the leftmost eyedropper will be active (as long as the Edit pop-up menu is set to a color, not Master). When you click on your image with that tool selected, you'll be centering the sliders on the color you clicked on. If you click on the plus eyedropper and then click on your image, it will spread out the vertical bar sliders to include the colors you click across (just like when we held Shift earlier). The minus eyedropper will narrow the width between the vertical sliders and therefore narrow the range of colors that are being affected (just like when we Option/Alt-clicked earlier). I usually don't mess with those icons at all, preferring to use the keyboard commands I mentioned.

If the area you're trying to change is in motion, out of focus, or blends into the surrounding colors (**Figure 11.13**), you'll need to deal with the transition between it and its surroundings. To make the adjustment fade into the surrounding colors, move one or both of the triangular sliders away from the vertical bars and watch your image until the change smoothly blends into what's around the object you were attempting to adjust (**Figure 11.14**).

Figure 11.15 This image could use a saturation boost. (©2003 Andy Katz)

Figure 11.13 You have to be careful working with colors that blend in with their surroundings. (©2003 Ben Willmore)

Figure 11.14 Moving the outer slider toward the color you need to blend into will fade the adjustment into those colors.

Now let's get to work and figure out specific uses for the Hue/Saturation dialog box.

Saturating Your World

Most images that come from a digital camera or flatbed scanner can benefit from a boost in saturation (**Figure 11.15**). For a general boost of color, I recommend making a Hue/Saturation adjustment layer and ratcheting up the Saturation slider until the colors in your image start to pop (**Figure 11.16**). When you do that, you'll probably notice that some colors become too vivid before others have reached their true potential. To avoid oversaturating, choose the color that's objectionable from the Edit pop-up menu, click on the color within your image to center the color isolation sliders, and then move the Saturation slider toward the left to mellow it out (**Figure 11.17**).

Figure 11.16 After saturating the image, the green areas are just too colorful.

Figure 11.17 After isolating the greens and lowering their saturation, the image looks great.

Enhancing Skies

If you've ever looked at a lot of photographs that contain blue skies, you might have noticed that many of those skies are actually closer to a light shade of cyan than a shade of true blue (**Figure 11.18**). If you like your skies to look as genuinely blue as possible, start by creating a Hue/Saturation adjustment layer, and choose Blues from the Edit pop-up menu. Click somewhere within the sky to center the sliders and then make the following adjustment: Move the Lightness slider toward the left to darken the sky; move the Saturation slider toward the right to make the sky more colorful; and then experiment with the Hue slider until you get the best shade of blue (**Figures 11.19** and **11.20**).

Figure 11.18 This cyanish sky could use a tweak. (@2003 PhotoSpin, www.photospin.com)

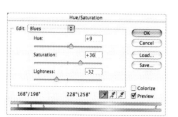

Figure 11.19 The Hue/Saturation adjustment used to produce Figure 11.20.

Figure 11.20 After adjusting the image with Hue/Saturation, the sky is true blue.

The only problem with this technique is that you might run into an image that contains blue areas that are not part of the sky (**Figures 11.21** and **11.22**). If those are areas that you don't want to shift, then you'll have to make changes after you're done creating the Hue/Saturation adjustment layer. If you look at an adjustment layer, you'll find that it contains a white rectangle just to the right of the adjustment layer icon for that layer. That rectangle is a layer mask, and it can be used to further limit the areas that your adjustment will apply to. All you have to do is grab the Paintbrush tool and paint with black at full opacity, and you'll prevent the adjustment from applying to the areas you paint over. As long as the Hue/Saturation adjustment layer is active in your Layer palette, then the paint you apply will affect where the adjustment applies. Painting with black will hide the adjustment; painting with white will bring it back. So, after enhancing a sky, you might want to grab a large, soft-edged brush and paint with black over any areas that you wish to preserve (**Figure 11.23**).

Figure 11.21 The original image. (©2003 PhotoSpin, www.photospin.com)

Figure 11.22 After adjusting the sky, areas of the foreground have shifted slightly.

Figure 11.23 Painting with black on the layer mask of the adjustment layer prevents the adjustment from applying to the bottom of the image.

Color to Grayscale

If you want to get much more control over your color-to-grayscale conversions, then you might want to think about using Hue/Saturation. A lot of people will suggest using the Channel Mixer or other techniques, but the problem with most approaches is that they force you to think like Photoshop instead of giving you an intuitive approach. To convert to black and white with Hue/Saturation, create an adjustment layer and then move the Saturation slider all the way to the left (**Figures 11.24** and **11.25**). Then, to control what happened to the colors in your image, turn the Preview check box off and then on again, and decide which color area needs to be tweaked (areas that used to be yellow might need to be brighter, for example). Next, make sure the Preview check box is turned on, pick the color that needs to be adjusted from the Edit pop-up menu, and then adjust the Lightness slider until it looks good (**Figure 11.26**). Repeat this process for any other colors that need tweaking until your image looks great (**Figure 11.27**). If you'd like to start with those same settings in the future, make sure to do all the adjustments as part of a single adjustment layer, and then click the Save button in the upper right of the Hue/Saturation dialog box and give that setting a name. Then the next time you want to apply those same settings to convert an image to grayscale, just add a Hue/Saturation adjustment layer, click the Load button, and point to the file you saved earlier.

Figure 11.24 Original image. (©2003 Stockbyte, www.stockbyte.com)

Figure 11.25 Result of lowering saturation.

Figure 11.26 Adjust individual colors to enhance the result.

Figure 11.27 After adjusting multiple colors, the image should start looking good.

I often like to create partially black and white images, where part of the image is in color and part is grayscale. To accomplish that, apply the technique we just talked about and then paint with black to prevent the adjustment from applying to the areas that you'd like to keep in color (**Figure 11.28**) (or make a selection before creating the adjustment layer to begin with). Also, if you'd rather not bring your image all the way to black and white, just don't move the Saturation slider all the way to the left, or lower the opacity of the adjustment layer once you're done (**Figure 11.29**). Or, if you'd rather just have certain objects turn black and white, you can use the techniques we talked about earlier (smash sliders together, Shift-click to spread them apart) to get the sliders to isolate a range of colors, and then move the Saturation slider all the way to the left to pull all the color out.

If you really want your image to end up with no color whatsoever, then you'll want to choose Image > Mode > Grayscale after you've removed the color using a Hue/ Saturation adjustment layer. (FYI: Grayscale mode images are one-third the file size of RGB color images.)

Figure 11.28 Painting on the adjustment layer's layer mask will limit which areas become black and white.

Figure 11.29 Lower the opacity of the adjustment layer to bring back a hint of color.

Colorizing Grayscale Photos

If you enjoy the look of hand-tinted photographs but don't want to deal with the chemicals and mess that are usually involved, then you might get excited enough about some of Photoshop's features to make you want to drop your brush and start colorizing your images with a mouse.

You can use a Hue/Saturation adjustment layer to add color to a black and white image. All you have to do is choose Image > Mode > RGB, select one of the areas you'd like to add color to, and create a Hue/Saturation adjustment layer. With this choice, you'll first need to turn on the Colorize check box, which should shift the selected area to a color similar to your foreground color (**Figure 11.30**). When the color has been applied, you can adjust the Hue setting to cycle through the full spectrum of colors. Once you've chosen the basic color, you can adjust the Saturation setting to control how vivid the color is, and change the Lightness setting to determine how dark the area should be (**Figure 11.31**).

Figure 11.30 When you first turn on the Colorize check box, the color you'll get is based on your foreground color. (©2003 Stockbyte, www.stockbyte.com)

Figure 11.31 You can fine-tune the color by adjusting the Hue, Saturation, and Lightness sliders.

Figure 11.32 As you apply color to more and more areas, you'll end up with a lot of adjustment layers.

With this select-and-adjust approach, you'll need to create a new adjustment layer for each color you'd like to use (**Figure 11.32**). After you've created an adjustment layer, you can fine-tune the result by painting with black or white while the adjustment layer is active. Painting with white will cause the adjustment to apply to a larger area of the image, whereas black will limit which areas get adjusted. If you find that the color is too intense, then simply paint with a shade of gray on the adjustment layer, which will cause the adjustment to apply in differing amounts. The darker the shade of gray, the less the adjustment will apply. You can also double-click on the thumbnail icon for the adjustment layer (to the left of the name of the layer) to modify the settings that are being applied.

What you want to watch out for with this type of adjustment is that there will usually be way too much color in the darkest and brightest areas of your image (**Figure 11.33**). To limit the amount of color applied to these areas, you'll need to use the blending sliders by choosing Layer > Layer Style > Blending Options while the adjustment layer is active. Then pull in the lower-left slider in the Blend If area until you notice all the color disappearing from the darkest areas of your image. You don't want to completely remove the color, so hold the Option key (Mac) or Alt key (Windows) and pull on the left edge of the slider that you just moved until you get a smooth transition in the shadow areas of your image. Then, before you click OK, move the right slider a short distance and then Option-drag (Mac) or Alt-drag (Windows) its right edge until the color blends into the brightest parts of the image. With a little experimentation, you'll be able to find the setting that looks best for your image (**Figures 11.34** and **11.35**).

The blending sliders are covered in much more detail in Chapter 16, "Collage."

Figure 11.33 There is too much color in the darkest areas of this image. (©2003 Stockbyte, www.stockbyte.com)

Figure 11.34 These are the blending slider settings used to create Figure 11.35.

Figure 11.35 After reducing the amount of color in the shadow areas, the image looks more realistic.

Digging a Little Deeper

If you ever need to go back to re-edit a Hue/Saturation adjustment layer that you created earlier, you'll need to be extra careful. You can double-click on the adjustment layer icon on the left side of the adjustment layer to change the adjustment. But, before you start to make changes, you'll

Figure 11.36 When returning to an adjustment layer, look at the color bars at the bottom and try to figure out which color you adjusted previously (yellow, in this case).

need to choose the same color you originally chose from the Edit pop-up menu; otherwise, any changes you make will affect the entire image because the Edit pop-up menu will be set to Master. If you can't remember which color you worked on previously, then glance at the color strips at the bottom of the dialog box to see if you can figure out which areas in the bottom strip are different than the top one (**Figure 11.36**). Then look at the top strip directly above that area to figure out which color to choose from the Edit pop-up menu. Once you choose the proper color from that pop-up menu, Photoshop will get you back to adjusting the specific color you isolated when you originally created the adjustment layer.

Moving the Saturation slider too far to the right can end up distorting the relationship between the colors in your image. As one color reaches its maximum saturation, it simply can't become more saturated, but the other colors in the image will continue to become more vivid as you move the Saturation slider farther toward the right. You can figure out the maximum saturation boost to give your image without distorting the relationship between the colors by paying attention to what happens in the Info Palette. Just choose Window > Info, and then click on the eyedropper icon in that palette and choose HSB. Then, when you're increasing the saturation of your image, move your cursor over the most saturated areas of your image and make sure to stop increasing the saturation once you see that the "S" (Saturation) number in the HSB part of the Info Palette reaches 100%. If you go any further than that, you'll be distorting the relationship between colors in your image.

Replacing Color

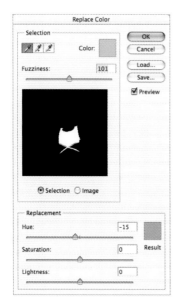

Figure 11.37 The Replace Color dialog box is a combination of the Color Range command and the Hue/Saturation dialog box.

If you like the general ideas we just worked with but didn't have complete success isolating areas based on hues, then you might want to try choosing Image > Adjustments > Replace Color (**Figure 11.37**). In essence, Replace Color combines the Select > Color Range command that we talked about back in Chapter 2, "Selection Primer," with the same color shifting controls that are found in the Hue/Saturation dialog box. The one advantage of using the Replace Color command is that instead of having to figure out the exact Hue/Saturation/Lightness settings necessary to get the result you're looking for, you can define the color you'd like to end up with by clicking the color swatch that shows up in the lower right of the dialog box. But unfortunately, Replace Color is not available as an adjustment layer, so I don't use it all that often. I prefer to use the Select > Color Range command and then create a Hue/Saturation adjustment layer because I find it gives me much more flexibility if I ever need to fine-tune things after the initial adjustment.

Both Hue/Saturation and Replace Color effectively rotate the color wheel to shift the colors in your image. Now let's take a look at how we can shift the general color of an image toward one of the primary colors (red, yellow, green, cyan, blue, magenta).

Variations

If you like simple and easy features, then you'll enjoy using the Image > Adjustments > Variations command (**Figure 11.38**). It starts off with your original image in the middle of a seven-image cluster. When you click one of the surrounding images, it will replace the one in the middle and repopulate the surrounding views with new alternatives (**Figure 11.39**). You can control how different the alternatives are from the center image by adjusting the Fine/Coarse slider in the upper right of the dialog box. This type of adjustment will concentrate on either the brightest areas of the image (known as Highlights), the middle brightness levels (known as the Midtones), or the dark areas of the image (known as the Shadows). You can adjust all three areas in one adjustment, but you'll have to choose them one at a time and make an adjustment before clicking OK. After you've made a change to the image, you'll be able to compare the original to your current selection by comparing the two images that appear in the upper left of the dialog box.

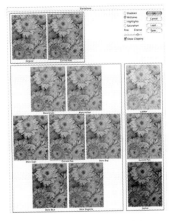

Figure 11.38 The Variations dialog box presents you with simple previews of multiple adjustments. (©2003 PhotoSpin, www.photospin.com)

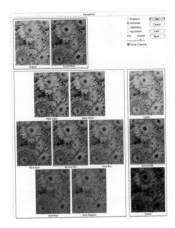

Figure 11.39 After you click on one of the choices, the surrounding views repopulate with new choices.

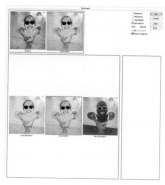

Figure 11.40 If you ever see very out of place colors, it's usually an indication that clipping has occurred, which is a sign that you might be losing detail in those areas. (©2003 Stockbyte, www.stockbyte.com)

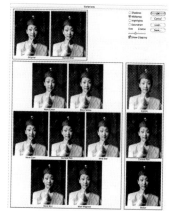

Figure 11.41 Adding color to a grayscale image is easy with Variations. (©2003 Stockbyte, www.stockbyte.com)

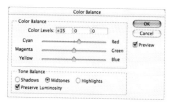

Figure 11.42 The Color Balance dialog box is a good alternative to Variations.

You can change the brightness and saturation of your image using Variations. However, I find that Levels and Curves are far superior for adjusting the brightness, and I prefer to use Hue/Saturation to adjust saturation because I can have much more control over which colors become saturated.

If you notice intense colors showing up in areas where they don't belong (**Figure 11.40**), that's most likely Photoshop stepping in to warn you that you might be losing detail in that area. If you'd rather not see those unusual colors, then turn off the Show Clipping check box near the upper right of the dialog box.

I mainly use Variations for very basic chores where I prefer a simple visual interface, the most common of which would be to tint a grayscale photo. All I have to do is change the mode of the image to RGB (Image > Mode > RGB) and then I can go to Variations and click away until I get the color tinting I desire (**Figure 11.41**).

Color Balance

Most of the time, I pass over Variations in favor of the Color Balance command (**Figure 11.42**) because it's available as an adjustment layer, which makes future changes much easier. Just like in Variations, the Color Balance dialog box allows you to shift the color of the Highlights, Midtones, or Shadows toward one of the primary colors; the only difference is that you'll have to look at the main screen to get a preview. Moving a slider to +15 or –15 is approximately the same as making one click in the Variations dialog box with the default setting on the Fine/Coarse slider. But because you're not forced to make adjustments in preset increments, I feel that it's much easier to be precise with this feature than with Variations.

Both Variations and Color Balance effectively shift the colors of your image toward one side of the color wheel. It's almost as if you start at the center of the color wheel and then shift toward one of the primary colors (**Figure 11.43**). All the colors in the image move toward that color, whereas

Hue/Saturation and Replace Color spin the color wheel, which shifts all the colors in unusual ways (not just toward one particular color). There are a bunch of other commands that allow you to shift toward cyan or red, magenta or green, and yellow or blue in a less obvious way. Let's take a look at a few of the adjustments that allow you to work with those primary colors.

Levels/Curves

Choosing Image > Adjustments > Curves will allow you to pick between red, green, and blue, or cyan, magenta, and yellow (depending on which mode your image is in) in the Channel pop-up menu (**Figure 11.44**). When you work on the Red channel, you'll be able to shift the overall color of your image toward either red or cyan by moving the curve up or down. If you work on the Green channel, you'll be able to shift toward green and magenta, and the Blue channel will allow you to shift toward blue and yellow.

I find that it's most effective if you Command-click (Mac) or Ctrl-click (Windows) on the area of the image you'd like to concentrate your adjustment on. That will add a point to the curve in the specific location needed to accurately focus on the area you clicked on. Once you've done that, you can use the up and down arrow keys to shift the colors toward one of the primary colors (which one will depend on the choice you made from the Channel pop-up menu) (**Figure 11.45**).

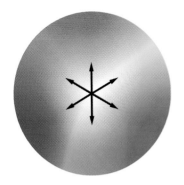

Figure 11.43 Color Balance pushes the colors in your image toward one of the primary colors.

Clicking on the arrows icon that appears in the middle of the bottom gradient in the Curves dialog box will reverse the effect of moving the curve up or down. For instance, if moving the curve up used to shift things toward blue, after clicking the arrows icon you'll need to move the curve down to shift things toward blue.

Command-clicking does not work in CMYK mode.

If the brightness of your image shifts too much when using the Channel Mixer, try changing the blending mode of the adjustment layer to Color at the top of the Layers palette.

Figure 11.44 Move the curve up or down to push the colors in your image toward or away from the color you choose in the Channel pop-up menu. (©2003 PhotoSpin, www.photospin.com)

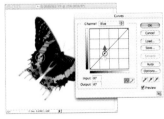

Figure 11.45 Command-click on your image to add a point to the curve, then use the up/down arrows to shift the color. (©2003 PhotoSpin, www.photospin.com)

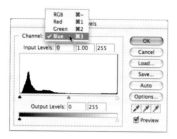

Figure 11.46 You can also use Levels to make adjustments similar to what we did with Curves.

Figure 11.47 The original image. (©2003 PhotoSpin, www.photospin.com)

Figure 11.48 Adjusting the image with Auto Color to shift it toward warm tones.

Figure 11.49 When prompted, be sure to click No; otherwise, you'll introduce a colorcast to every image you attempt to color correct with Auto Color.

You can make similar changes using the Image > Adjustments > Levels command. It also allows you to choose from the channels that make up your image (RGB or CMYK) (**Figure 11.46**). Moving any of the upper sliders toward the left will push the color of your image toward the color you have chosen from the Channel pop-up menu. Moving the sliders toward the right will shift the colors toward the opposite of that color. Moving the bottom sliders will do the opposite—moving them toward the right shifts things away from the color you've chosen in the Channels pop-up menu, and moving them left will send things toward that color.

Auto Color

I often get frustrated when attempting to make generic color shifts using Levels or Curves because the image can change in unexpected ways (due to the fact that you're not just controlling the highlight/midtones/shadows like many other adjustments). If I'm having trouble getting the overall look I was aiming for, then I'll end up clicking on the Options button in either Levels or Curves, which sends me into the Auto Color Correction Options dialog box. I like to set the Algorithms setting to Enhance Monochromatic Contrast so I don't get rid of color in the highlights or shadows of the image. Then, to shift the overall color of the image, I turn on the Snap Neutral Midtones check box and click on the color swatch that appears next to the word Midtones. It should start with gray, but if you shift that color toward another color, the general atmosphere of the photo should change as you introduce a colorcast (**Figures 11.47** and **11.48**). That's great for changing the overall feeling of a photo to make it appear more warm (toward red/orange) or cool (toward blue/cyan).

When you click OK in both the Auto Color dialog box and Levels itself, you'll be asked if you'd like to use the new target colors as the default (**Figure 11.49**). I'd click No unless you plan on shifting the overall look of a large number of photos. Otherwise, when you use Auto Color for color correction (as mentioned in Chapter 9), it will introduce colorcasts instead of getting rid of them.

I also like to use Auto Color when combining two images that differ in general color (**Figures 11.50** and **11.51**). If one image has what I like to call a desirable colorcast (fireplace, sunset, and candlelight are examples) and the other does not, then they will not look like they belong together (**Figure 11.52**). I want Photoshop to transfer the desirable colorcast to the second image by analyzing what's going on in the brightest and darkest areas of the image (because a colorcast will contaminate those areas that otherwise would not contain any color). To accomplish that, I'll place each image side by side so I can see both documents at the same time. Then, with the image that doesn't have a colorcast active, I'll choose Image > Adjustments > Curves, click on the Options button, and then set the Algorithms setting to Find Dark & Light Colors, and turn off the Snap Neutral Midtones check box (**Figure 11.53**). Now all we have to do is plug in the right colors in the Highlights and Shadows areas. Click on the Shadows color swatch to access the color picker, and then move your mouse over the image that contains the desirable colorcast and click on the darkest area of the image (**Figure 11.54**). Next, click on the Highlights color swatch to access the color picker once again, and this time click on the brightest area of the image that contains the desirable colorcast (**Figure 11.55**) (but avoid areas that are blown out to pure white) and then click OK. That should change the color of the active photo so that it will have a colorcast similar to the second image (**Figure 11.56**).

Figure 11.50 This image has a desirable colorcast. (©2003 Stockbyte, www.stockbyte.com)

Figure 11.51 This image is more neutral than the one in Figure 11.50. (©2003 Stockbyte, www.stockbyte.com)

Figure 11.52 When the two images are combined, they don't look like they belong together.

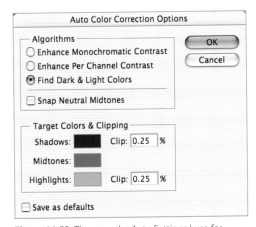

Figure 11.53 These are the Auto Settings I use for matching two images.

Figure 11.54 Click on the Shadows swatch and then click on the darkest part of the image that has the colorcast.

Figure 11.55 Click on the Highlights swatch and then click on the brightest area of the image.

Figure 11.56 After adjusting the color, the two images have similar color qualities.

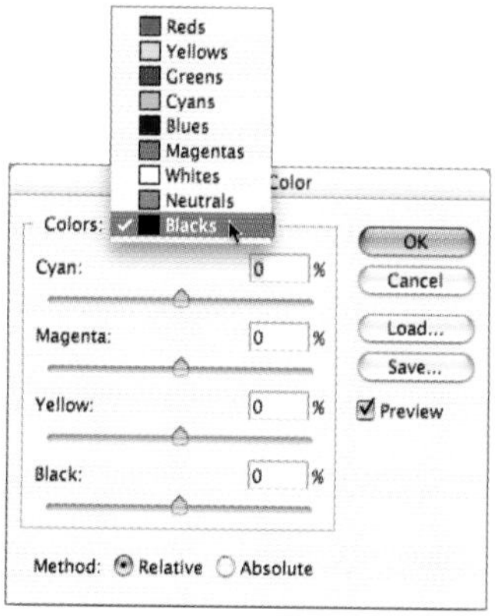

Figure 11.57 With Selective Color you can push certain colors toward any of the primary colors.

Selective Color

Auto Color isn't the only way to force colors into the brightest, darkest, and neutral gray areas of an image. If you choose Image > Adjustments > Selective Color, you can select which general colors you'd like to change from the Colors pop-up menu and then shift them toward a primary color (**Figure 11.57**). Moving the sliders toward the right will shift the selected color toward the color listed to the left of the slider. Moving the slider toward the left will shift it away from the color listed and toward its exact opposite. So, even though this dialog box only lists cyan, magenta, yellow, and black, you can still shift things toward red, green, and blue by moving the sliders toward the left. If the Relative radio button is turned on, then you'll change areas relative to what they started at. That means that if you have 50% cyan and you move the Cyan slider to 10%, you'll end up with 55% cyan because 10% of 50% is 5%. If, on the other hand, you use the Absolute setting, you'll simply add the exact amount that you dial in. That means that if you have 50% cyan and you move the Cyan slider to 10%, you'll end up with 60% cyan because it added the exact amount of cyan that you dialed in.

One nice aspect of Selective Color is that you can shift the color of the blacks in your image. All you have to do is choose Blacks from the Colors pop-up menu, move the Black slider toward the left to lighten the area, and then move whichever color sliders you'd like to use toward the right to push color into those areas (**Figures 11.58** to **11.59**). Or, if you're working in CMYK mode, you can make the black areas of your image richer by moving the Cyan slider toward the right. This adjustment is commonly used when creating large areas of black in an image that will be printed on a commercial printing press. I often like to have at least 40% cyan in those areas.

Figure 11.58 The original image. (© 2003 Stockbyte, www.stockbyte.com)

Figure 11.59 Using Selective Color you can shift the color of black areas.

You can also use Selective Color to brighten the highlights in your image by choosing Whites from the Colors menu and then moving the Cyan, Magenta, and Yellow sliders toward the left (**Figures 11.60** to **11.62**). This change can be useful for metallic objects where the brightest areas need to be pure white in order to make the object appear to be highly polished and therefore shiny.

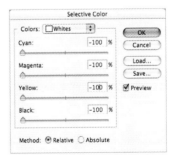

Figure 11.60 The original image. (©2003 Stockbyte, www.stockbyte.com)

Figure 11.61 After adjusting the Whites, the highlights are much brighter, making the object look more polished.

Figure 11.62 The Selective Color adjustment used to brighten the highlights.

Match Color

Match Color is an interesting new addition to Photoshop CS. It attempts to match the general color and contrast of two images. Let's start off with simple examples and then progress into more complex and unusual solutions.

Let's say you have two images, one of which has a very warm feeling and the other of which is rather neutral. But both images have somewhat similar content color and contrast (**Figures 11.63** and **11.64**). In order to match the general feeling of the two images, you need to first open both images, then click on the image you'd like to change and choose Image > Adjustments > Match Color (**Figure 11.65**). At the bottom of the Match Color dialog box, change the Source pop-up menu to the name of the image to which you'd like to match the color. If the image contains adjustment layers, then be sure to choose Merged from the Layer pop-up menu. That's all there is to it (**Figure 11.66**)!

Figure 11.63 This is the image that I'd like to match. (©2003 Andy Katz)

Figure 11.64 This is the image that needs adjusting. (©2003 Andy Katz)

Figure 11.65 The Match Color dialog box.

Figure 11.66 The result of matching the color between the two images.

If you find that the results are less than stellar, then you'll need to give Photoshop a little help to better match the images. Go back to the image you like and select an area that contains the most important information that defines the general look of the image (**Figure 11.67**). Then switch back to the photo you'd like to change and make a selection of the areas that define the general look of that image (**Figure 11.68**). When you get to the Match Color dialog box, turn on the two check boxes near the bottom so Photoshop refers to only the selected area of each image when attempting to match the color. You will probably also want to turn on the Ignore Selection When Applying Adjustment check box so that Photoshop can adjust the entire image while comparing the selected areas in the two images (**Figures 11.69** and **11.70**).

Figure 11.67 Select the area of the reference photo you want to match. (©2003 Stockbyte, www.stockbyte.com)

Figure 11.68 Select the area of the image you want to adjust that should look like the reference photo. (©2003 Stockbyte, www.stockbyte.com)

Figure 11.69 The result of matching two images without a selection.

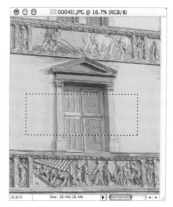

Figure 11.70 The result of matching two images using a selection.

After you've produced an acceptable match between the two images, you might want to adjust the Image Options to fine-tune the end result. The Luminance slider will change the brightness of the image, whereas the Color Intensity slider will control how saturated the colors are. If you don't want to precisely match the reference photo, but would like to instead head in that general direction, then try increasing the Fade setting. If you set the Fade setting to 100, you'll see the original unchanged image (plus any Luminance and Color Intensity adjustments). By lowering the Fade setting, you can start to push the image toward the look of the reference image. Just move the Fade slider around until you like the amount of change you are getting.

On occasion, you might need to adjust a multitude of images to match a single source image. When that's the case, set the Source menu to the name of the image you want to match, then click the Save Statistics button and name that preset. Now, at any time in the future, you can click the Load button to use the general feeling of that photo again even though Photoshop won't need to open the file itself. I have a bunch of these files saved—one for warm sunset-like images, another for cool water-like images, and yet another for high contrast, less colorful images. That way I can quickly get a certain effect without having to remember which photo I originally matched.

Figure 11.71 The original image has a blue cast. (©2003 Stockbyte, www.stockbyte.com)

Now the Match Color dialog box might be designed to match two photographs, but that doesn't mean that it's not useful on single images. Just set the Source pop-up menu to None and then mess with the Image Options settings. You might just find that you prefer the Color Intensity setting over the Saturation setting that is found in the Hue/Saturation dialog box.

If you have an image that has an obvious colorcast, like one taken underwater, for example (**Figure 11.71**), then you might want to try turning on the Neutralize check box. That will cause the Match Color dialog box to attempt to color correct the image. The results aren't always perfect, but it's often a good start for those images that have massive colorcasts (**Figure 11.72**).

Figure 11.72 After neutralizing the cast, the image looks less blue.

I also like to use the Match Color command to colorize grayscale photographs. I'll open a full-color reference photo, select an area (like an area of skin that contains both bright and dark areas) so Photoshop knows what I'd like to match to (**Figure 11.73**). Then, I'll switch to the grayscale photo, choose Image > Mode > RGB so that it's in a mode that can contain color. Now I make a very precise selection of the area I'd like to add color to (like all the skin in the image) and choose Image > Adjustments > Match Color. To make sure Photoshop thinks only about the selected areas, I'd turn on the two check boxes at the bottom of the dialog box and turn off the check box at the top. This often produces a result that is superior to what you'd get with other tools because instead of applying a generic color across the entire area, it will usually apply a slightly different color to the bright and dark areas of an object (**Figure 11.74**).

Figure 11.73 Make a selection on the reference photograph to indicate the color you'd like to match. (©2003 Stockbyte, www.stockbyte.com)

Figure 11.74 Convert the grayscale image to RGB mode, make a precise selection, and then match the color.

Color Replacement Tool

The Color Replacement tool allows you to quickly paint across an area and change its color. What's really nice about this tool is that you don't have to be overly precise with your painting because you're only going to affect the area you paint across. That's because Photoshop will replace only the colors that you mouse over with the cross-hair that shows up in the center of your brush cursor.

When you paint, Photoshop will use your foreground color to change what's in the active layer based on the choice you've made in the Mode pop-up menu in the options bar at the top of your screen (**Figure 11.75**):

Figure 11.75 The options bar determines how the Color Replacement tool will interact with your image.

Figure 11.76 I created this two-tone car (the original was red) with five clicks of the mouse button and a soft-edged brush. (©2003 PhotoSpin, www.photospin.com)

▶ **Hue:** Allows you to change the basic color of an area without changing the brightness (**Figure 11.76**). You also can't change how colorful an area is or introduce color into an area that didn't already have it. This choice is useful when you'd like to change the basic color of an object like a car where it wouldn't look appropriate to intensify or mellow out the original colors.

▶ **Saturation:** Allows you to make an area as colorful as your foreground color. Does not allow you to change the basic color or brightness of an area. I love to use this option to remove the color of certain areas of a photo. I love that I don't have to be all that careful when I'm painting because it uses the same technology as the Background Eraser. To force areas to black and white, just paint with black, white, or any shade of gray. Your foreground color doesn't contain any color, so the area you end up painting over will have all its color removed (**Figures 11.77** and **11.78**).

▶ **Color:** Allows you to change both the basic color and the saturation of the color, but will not allow you to change the brightness. In essence, it applies the color you are painting with to the brightness of the original image. This choice is useful when you need to push a lot of color into an area that didn't have much color to begin with. An example would be a dark brown field that should look green. Just paint with a relatively vivid version of green so the field becomes much more colorful than it was in the original image (**Figure 11.79**).

Figure 11.77 The original image. (©2003 Ben Willmore)

Figure 11.78 I removed the color from the background using Saturation mode and painting with black.

Figure 11.79 The left side of this image was changed by painting with green in Color mode. (©2003 Andy Katz)

▶ **Luminosity:** Allows you to change the brightness of an area to match the brightness of the color you are painting with. This mode will not allow you to shift the colors at all. I don't use this option very often, but it can be helpful if you need to fix red-eye. I just choose a very dark color that's almost black and then click in the center of the eye (**Figure 11.80**).

If you find that you're having trouble getting good results with this tool, you'll want to learn more about the setting that determines which areas are changed and which are ignored. This tool uses the same technology as the Background Eraser tool, which we'll cover in detail in Chapter 13, "Advanced Masking." So go check out that chapter and then come back and try these ideas again.

This tool applies your foreground color to the active layer, so you should know that you could change your foreground color by holding the Option key (Mac) or Alt key (Windows) and clicking on your image.

Figure 11.80 A single click on one of the eyes removed the red-eye problem. (©2003 Kristine Evans)

Channel Mixer

So far, most of the adjustments we've talked about have been relatively straightforward. You usually tell Photoshop what you want to change (midtones, highlights, and so on) and then tell it what you'd like to shift them toward. But the Channel Mixer is a different beast. It forces you to think about how Photoshop works behind the scenes. The Channel Mixer lets you literally mix the contents of the channels that show up in the Channels palette (Window > Channels).

When you choose Image > Adjustments > Channel Mixer, you can choose the channel you'd like to affect from the Output Channel pop-up menu. Then you can move the Source Channels sliders to brighten or darken the output channel (**Figure 11.81**). Because RGB mode creates your image out of red, green, and blue light, moving sliders toward the right will add more light and therefore brighten the output channel based on the contents of the channel whose slider you moved. Moving the slider in the opposite direction will reduce the amount of light being applied to the output channel. CMYK mode creates your image out of four colors of ink, so moving a slider toward the right will add additional ink to the output channel, thereby darkening it. Moving a slider to the left in CMYK mode will lessen the amount of ink in the output channel, effectively brightening it. This might sound complicated at first, but once you see a few examples, you should start to see the simplicity behind it.

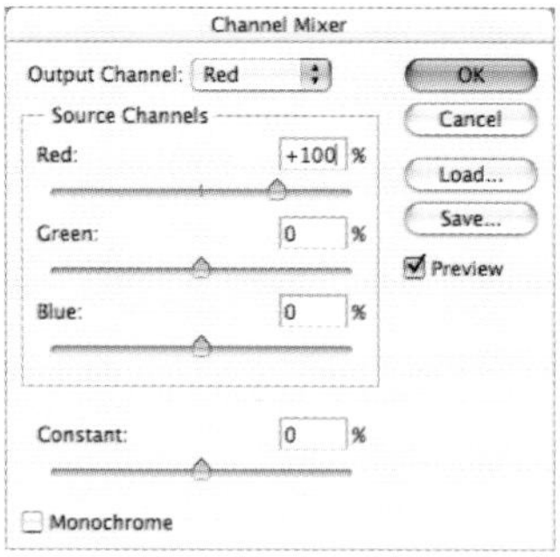

Figure 11.81 The Channel Mixer dialog box.

Let's say you have a CMYK mode image of a banana (**Figure 11.82**) and you'd like to reproduce it using only two colors of ink. That way you could save money and show off to your friends that you've really mastered Photoshop. Well, because most bananas are yellow, I think we'll end up using yellow ink for the banana, and then we'll use some black ink so we can get shadows that are darker than the yellow ink. I'd start by choosing Image > Adjustments >

Channel Mixer, and then I'd choose Cyan from the Output Channel pop-up menu and move the Cyan Source Channels slider all the way to the left to indicate that you don't want to use any of what was originally in the Cyan channel (**Figure 11.83**). Then choose Magenta from the Output pop-up menu and move the Magenta slider all the way to the left to clear out the Magenta channel (**Figure 11.84**). Now the image should be made out of just yellow and black ink, but it most likely looks quite light because there's not enough black ink to compensate for not using any cyan or magenta ink. To fix that, choose Black from the Output Channel pop-up menu, and then slide the Cyan and Magenta sliders toward the right until the brightness looks as close to the original as you can get (**Figure 11.85**). (Turn the Preview check box off and back on again to compare the original to the end result.) Once you have it as close as you can get to the look of the original, click OK and then drag the Cyan and Magenta channels to the trash at the bottom of the Channels palette. Finally, to get a more appropriate shade of yellow, double-click to the right of the name of the Yellow channel in the Channels palette so you can pick a new color and experiment until the image looks the best it can (**Figure 11.86**). If you'd like to know more about reproducing images using inks other than CMYK, then be sure to check out the Spot Color section in Chapter 12, "Channels."

Figure 11.82 The original banana image is in CMYK mode. (©2003 PhotoSpin, www.photospin.com)

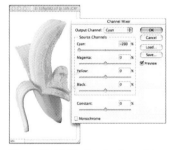

Figure 11.83 Moving the Cyan slider all the way to the left will remove all cyan from the image.

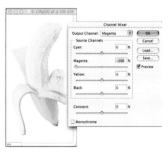

Figure 11.84 Moving the Magenta slider all the way to the left will remove all magenta from the image.

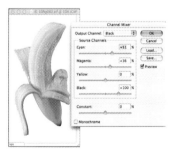

Figure 11.85 Adding what used to be in the Cyan and Magenta channels to the Black channel will compensate for using fewer inks.

Figure 11.86 The final image is made out of only two colors of ink!

Now that you've seen one example, let's use the Channel Mixer to convert a full-color image into a grayscale one. You might think that you could just choose Image > Mode > Grayscale and be done with it. Well, that's fine if you don't really care about the quality of the end result or if you're in a big hurry. But, if you want the highest-quality result, then you'll either want to use the technique I talked about in the Hue/Saturation section of this chapter or you'll want to experiment with the Channel Mixer. But before you get started, go open the Channels palette and click through all the channels to get an idea of what you'll be working with (**Figure 11.87**). You'll need to start with one of those channels as the base of your grayscale conversion, so make note of which one displays the best grayscale version of the image. Now, choose Image > Adjustments > Channel Mixer, and turn on the Monochrome check box at the bottom of the dialog box to remove all the color from your image. Then, to start with the channel you liked best, move the appropriate slider to the 100% position and move the other sliders to 0% (**Figure 11.88**). Now experiment with moving the other sliders to the right and left to see how they affect the image. As you move a slider toward the right, the image will get brighter, which will necessitate that you move another slider toward the left to compensate. By using different mixes of the channels, you'll get different grayscale results. There is no obvious formula for what will give you the best results; you'll just have to experiment until you like the detail, contrast, and brightness of the end result (**Figure 11.89**). A general rule of thumb is that getting the sliders to add up to 100% should deliver an image that is close to the same brightness as the original image. Once you like what you have, click OK and then choose Image > Mode > Grayscale.

Figure 11.87 Channels from left to right: red, green, blue. (©2003 Stockbyte, www.stockbyte.com)

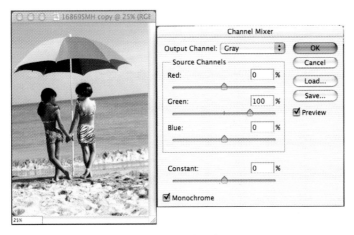

Figure 11.88 Dial in the channel that looked the best.

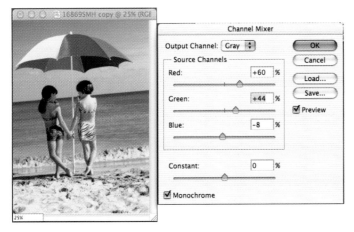

Figure 11.89 This is just one of many end results you could get with a few minutes of experimentation.

Gradient Map

The Image > Adjustments > Gradient Map (**Figure 11.90**) does a rather simple and unusual thing: It first converts an image to grayscale, and then replaces the shades of gray in the image with different colors that show up in a gradient. When you first get into the dialog box, it will default to a black and white gradient, which should just make your image look grayscale. Then, if you click on the down-pointing arrow to the right of the gradient preview, you'll be able to choose a preset gradient to replace the shades of gray that

Figure 11.90 The Gradient Map dialog box.

Figure 11.91 The original image. (©2003 Stockbyte, www.stockbyte.com)

were in the original image (**Figures 11.91** and **11.92**). If you'd prefer to bypass the preset gradients and create your own gradient, you can click in the middle of the gradient preview to access the gradient editor. If you'd like to know how to create your own gradients, be sure to read the information about the Gradient tool in Chapter 1, "Tool and Palette Primer."

The main problem with using the Gradient Map command is that you can easily end up with bright colors across the full range of the image, which will trash the contrast of your image (**Figure 11.93**). To prevent that, choose Layer > New Adjustment Layer > Gradient Map. When prompted, set the Mode pop-up menu to Color, and then click OK to get to the Gradient Map dialog box. Because the adjustment layer you just created is using the Color blending mode, it will be able to change only the colors in your image, and will not be able to mess with the brightness (**Figure 11.94**).

Figure 11.92 Applying a Gradient Map replaces the brightness levels in your image with different colors.

Figure 11.93 The contrast of the image has changed radically.

Figure 11.94 Using the Color blending mode prevents the Gradient Map from messing up the contrast of the image.

I often use the Gradient Map command to transform a backlit image into one that looks like it was taken at sunset (**Figures 11.95** and **11.96**). All you have to do is create a gradient that starts with black and slowly fades to orange and then yellow (**Figure 11.97**). If you want to turn the image into more of a silhouetted image, then just slide the black color swatch in the gradient editor toward the right until you no longer see much detail in the subject of the photo (**Figure 11.98**).

Figure 11.95 The original image. (©2003 Stockbyte, www.stockbyte.com)

Figure 11.96 The result of applying a black, orange, yellow gradient map.

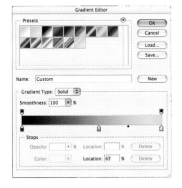

Figure 11.97 The three-color gradient used to create Figure 11.96.

Figure 11.98 The result of dragging the black slider toward the middle of the gradient.

Closing Thoughts

As you've seen in this chapter, a boggling multitude of techniques exist for manipulating the colors in your images. You don't have to know or remember how to use every single one of them—just pick out the ones you're most comfortable with and stick with them for a while. Then, once you feel confident with them, come on back and read this chapter again and add a few more techniques to your adjustment arsenal. To be honest, I mainly use Hue/Saturation, Auto Color, and the Color Replacement brush for most of my color manipulation tasks. But don't use those three just because I do; instead, try them all and find your own favorites.

Ben's Techno-Babble Decoder Ring

Channel: The components that an image are made out of. Most photographic images are composed of either red, green, and blue light, or cyan, magenta, yellow, and black ink. The Channels palette is where Photoshop keeps track of exactly how much of those primary colors are needed to create your full-color image.

Clipping: An indication of where an image is potentially losing detail by becoming too bright and thereby blowing out any detail.

Colorcast: An unwanted color that contaminates an image.

Hue: The pure form of a color without considering how dark or how vivid the color is. Maroon and pink are both based on a red hue.

Luminance: Another word for brightness. It describes how much light is used to create a color or shade of gray.

Monochrome: Something that contains no color and therefore contains only brightness levels; for example, a grayscale photo.

Neutralize: Unwanted colorcasts are easy to spot when you look at objects that should be gray. When a shade of gray is not bluish-gray or yellowish-gray and doesn't have a hint of any other color in it, it's known as being neutral gray. You can neutralize a colorcast by adjusting the entire image based on an area that should be gray. In essence, you measure how strong a colorcast is by measuring how much color is showing up in an area that should be gray and then use that information to remove the colorcast from the entire image. That will effectively neutralize it.

Saturation: How colorful a color is without considering the specific color or how dark it is.

Keyboard Shortcuts

FUNCTION	MACINTOSH	WINDOWS
Color Balance	Command-B	Ctrl-B
Curves	Command-M	Ctrl-M
Hue/Saturation	Command-U	Ctrl-U
Levels	Command-L	Ctrl-L
View Red channel	Command-1	Ctrl-1
View Green channel	Command-2	Ctrl-2
View Blue channel	Command-3	Ctrl-3
View all RGB channels	Command-~	Ctrl-~

12
Channels

Why take the escalator when I have a perfectly good canoe right here?

—Austin Powers in the movie Austin Powers, International Man of Mystery

Channels

If you just did a double take on the chapter quote and said, "huh, what?" then you reacted the same way that most people do the first time they hear about channels. To get to the root of all this confusion, you have to go back to when channels were first conceived and given their misbegotten name. The very name "channels" breeds confusion because it doesn't relate to anything in the real world, and so it doesn't mean anything to anybody. As a result, most people just give it a nickname. I've heard them called stencils, masks, friskets, rubyliths, and amberliths, to name a few. I don't know about you, but in the course of normal conversation (as opposed to Photoshop-speak), when I hear someone talk about channels, things like HBO, NBC, and CNN are the first ones that come to mind.

So, taking all of that into consideration, you might wonder what in blazes Adobe was thinking when they came up with that name? I can't answer that. But I can tell you that regardless of the hopeless misnomer, channels are absolutely essential to your work in Photoshop. Once you've mastered them, you will have one of Photoshop's most powerful tools at your beck and call.

Channels Are Worth the Pain!

To be fair, I have to tell you that a lot of people who try channels for the first time throw their hands in the air and give up. They convince themselves that they don't really need channels, and they learn how to patch things up in other ways. But I believe that if they really knew what they were missing, they'd take another crack at it.

Let's say you just met a secretary named Minnie. In her office there are two pieces of equipment: an old IBM Selectric typewriter and the best personal computer that money can buy. Whenever Minnie's boss gives her a memo to type, she immediately loads up the Selectric with a fresh piece of paper and starts rat-tatting away. "Minnie," you ask, "Why don't you use the computer for that?" Minnie just gives you a dirty look over her bifocals. So you try to reason with her: "But, Minnie, what if you make a mistake or the boss changes his mind? Wouldn't it be easier to have that memo stored in your computer?" Minnie lets out a long impatient sigh (the kind that only mothers can do justice to). Then she gives it to you straight: "Look, smarty-pants, maybe it would be easier, maybe it wouldn't, but whichever way you look at it, that thing is just too doggoned hard to learn." And with that, she swivels around, hunches over her beloved Selectric, and finishes her memo.

Of course, everybody knows that Minnie is crazy as a loon not to use the computer. And anyone who uses a computer knows that, yes, it might have been a little challenging at first, but once you learned it, how could you possibly live without it? That's exactly how it is with channels! Channels are so completely integrated into Photoshop that there's nothing you can do to your images without affecting the information that's stored in the Channels palette. And if they have that much influence on your images, wouldn't you want to know what they are all about? Of course you would.

Without channels, it would be impossible to save the shape of a selection so that you can get it back later. It would also be impossible to force a shadow to print with only black ink (which makes it look better). And you'd have terrible troubles working with metallic or fluorescent inks without the help of channels. So, let's take a headlong plunge into the not-so-mysterious world of channels. And for the purposes of this chapter, when we talk about them, we're going to be using just two terms: channels and masks.

Three Varieties of Channels

There are three varieties of channels: color channels, spot channels, and alpha channels (**Figure 12.1**). They all look about the same, but they perform completely different tasks. However, they do have some things in common: They have the same dimensions as the document that contains them; they can contain up to 256 shades of gray; and Photoshop treats them as if they were individual grayscale documents. Let's take a surface look at them; then we'll explore each one in depth.

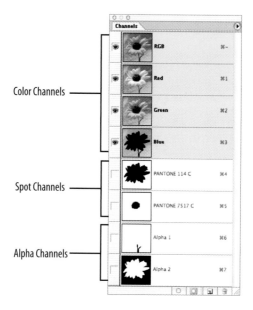

Figure 12.1 Channel types.

Color Channels

The topmost channels in the Channels palette are known as color channels because they keep track of all of the colors that will be printed and displayed. The names of these channels correspond to the mode your image is in (an RGB image will contain red, green, and blue channels; a CMYK image will contain cyan, magenta, yellow, and black channels). So when you paint, edit, or apply a filter to your image, you're really changing the information in the color channels.

Sample Use: You have an image taken by a digital camera. It's not just any image; it's your Granny blowing out candles on her 90th birthday. You know that pictures from digital cameras are notorious for looking "noisy," but this one takes the cake (so to speak). Your beloved Granny looks like her face is covered with blackheads. If you didn't know better, you'd probably just try to blur the image to get rid of the noise. But you do know better, because you've learned that if you did that, you'd end up removing the majority of the detail in the image. So instead, you switch over to color channels and start working on your image "under the hood." In just a few moments you've gotten rid of the noise and sharpened the overall image as well. Granny looks much better.

Spot Channels

Directly below the color channels are the spot channels. This type of channel is used in documents that will be printed using colors other than (or in addition to) cyan, magenta, yellow, and black. The name of a spot channel is usually the name of the ink that will be used (like PANTONE 185 CVC). Only documents that have been specifically set up for spot color work will contain this type of channel.

Sample Use: You're asked to create a "look" that resembles the cover of *Wired* magazine. You thumb through a few copies and notice that they go for the big eye-stopping colors: neon, fluorescent, metallic. You know—disco colors. You go to the standard Color Picker and choose a far-out shade of metallic purple not seen since the days of *Saturday Night Fever*. But you get flagged down by the CMYK Police: "Gamut Warning! Color Cannot Be Reproduced in CMYK, you idiot!" Nooo problem. Like a flash, you switch over to spot channels, where you confidently create your spaced-out color, knowing that you are also creating the necessary information needed by your printer to reproduce it accurately. Groovy.

Alpha Channels

Channels that appear at the bottom of the palette are called alpha channels. This is the real McCoy—the stuff people are usually talking about when they bring up channels, and the stuff they're most scared of. Alpha channels have user-defined names; or, if a name isn't supplied when a channel is created, Photoshop uses a generic name like

"Alpha 1." An alpha channel is a saved selection—it's that simple (well, almost that simple).

Sample Use: You just spent the good part of an hour making an eye-straining selection of every curl and wisp of hair on a model who's got a mane bigger than Tina Turner's. You're doing this because your client requested a redhead when you only had a blonde, but you're on to this guy and justifiably suspicious that in the end he'll probably want a brunette. So, as usual, you outsmart him and save that selection as an alpha channel, knowing that you will be prepared for anything, even zebra stripes if necessary. (Then you have the option of charging the client for all the time you saved, or not.)

Navigating the Channels Palette

Okay, you've been briefly introduced to the channels family. You know their names (color, spot, and alpha), and you know, in the most general sense, what they're intended for. Before we look at them any more closely, let's take a moment to get familiar with their place of residence—the Channels palette.

If you've read Chapter 3, "Layers Primer" (I hope you did) and now you're sitting there staring at the Channels palette, you'll probably notice that channels look almost identical to layers. Well, Adobe did this for a good reason. They want you to get used to one style of palette. They assumed that if you became comfortable with one kind of palette, you would quickly adapt to other palettes that were similar in design and function. So the Layers, Channels, and Paths palettes look almost identical (**Figures 12.2 to 12.4**). Just a few of the icons at the bottom of each palette are different. And even with these they tried to be consistent. For instance, the icon you use to create a new layer looks the same as the one you use to create a new channel or path.

As with layers, the eyeballs in the Channels palette control what is being displayed within the main image window. Just click in the column that contains the eyeballs to toggle them on or off. The channels that are active for editing are the ones that are highlighted. Click the name of a channel to make it active; to activate more than one channel at a time, Shift-click their names (I wish I could do that with layers). To change the stacking order of the channels, drag the name of a channel up or down within the stack (you can't change the order of the color channels). To create a new empty channel, click on the icon that resembles a piece of paper with a folded corner. To change the name of a channel, double-click its name. Finally, to delete a channel, drag it to the Trash icon (**Figure 12.5**).

Okay, that's enough for now. We'll cover the rest of the palette as we go through the different types of channels. So put on your thinking cap and let's get started.

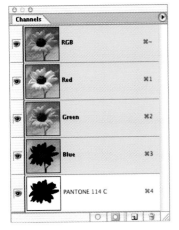

Figure 12.2 Channels palette.

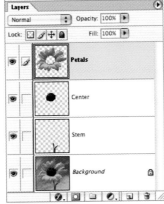

Figure 12.3 Layers palette.

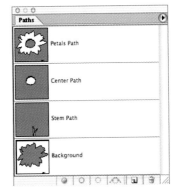

Figure 12.4 Paths palette.

Understanding Color Channels

Using color channels is like peeking behind the scenes and seeing how Photoshop is creating your image. You might think of color channels as the engine in your car: When you push the gas pedal, you are causing a whole chain reaction of events under the hood. In this case, while you are working in layers, the chain reaction is occurring in the color channels. They store up-to-the-minute information about RGB colors (red, green, and blue light), CMYK colors (cyan, magenta, yellow, and black ink), or any other color modes you are using. If you don't tamper with the channels, Photoshop will assume that whatever you're doing, you want it to affect all of the channels at the same time. But if you pop the hood and designate specific channels, you can do some very precise sculpting and manipulations that would be virtually impossible without using color channels.

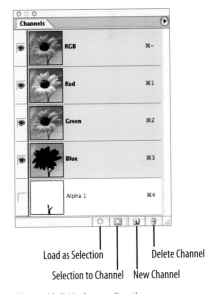

Load as Selection — Delete Channel
Selection to Channel — New Channel

Figure 12.5 Understanding the Channels palette.

You'll need to choose a color mode to work in, but before you do, you might want to know a little something about your options.

Choosing a Color Mode

Most non-PostScript printers (read: inexpensive printers, like inkjets) must convert CMYK files to RGB before they are sent to the printer driver, which means it's best to print to them from RGB mode. That's right—even though these printers have CMYK inks built in, it's best to print to the files from RGB mode and let the printer driver make the conversion, instead of feeding them CMYK files that the printer will convert twice (once to RGB, then again to CMYK in the printer driver). I know it sounds odd, but that's how it works.

In RGB mode, Photoshop constructs your image out of red, green, and blue light (**Figure 12.6**). This is the mode most images start in, because all scanners and digital cameras use RGB light to capture images, and all computer monitors use RGB light to display images. Some fancy (and very expensive) high-end scanners might deliver a CMYK result, but that conversion occurs in software after the RGB scan. RGB mode is ideal for images that will be displayed using light (including those that will be used onscreen for multimedia or the Internet and those that will be output to video). You'll also want to use RGB mode when outputting images to 35mm slides, because the output device (a film recorder) will use RGB light to expose the photographic film. And because you view all your images on an RGB monitor while you are editing them, RGB turns out to be an excellent "working mode." Once you have finished editing the image, you can convert it to any mode you desire.

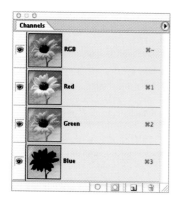

Figure 12.6 RGB channels.

CMYK mode creates your image out of cyan, magenta, yellow, and black ink, also known as process colors (**Figure 12.7**). This is the mode that your image should end up in if your final destination is a printing press. When you convert an image to CMYK, Photoshop compensates for many factors (dot gain, total ink limit, and the like) that are specific to the type of paper and press that will be used.

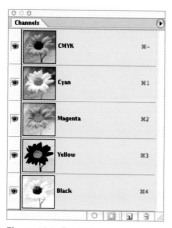

Figure 12.7 CMYK channels.

I recommend that you perform most editing and adjusting in RGB mode. This will allow you to adjust an image once and use it for multiple types of printing.

Lab mode is a different animal. It separates your image into lightness, which means how bright or dark the image is, and two channels called A and B (**Figure 12.8**). The A and B channels are weird because they don't contain just one color. The A channel contains colors that are between green and red, and the B channel contains colors that are between blue and yellow. This makes it the only mode that separates how bright your image is from the color information, and that's what makes it so useful. Lab mode safeguards the brightness of your image so you can adjust the colors without shifting its brightness, whereas with RGB and CMYK mode, if you tried to do the same adjustments, the brightness would probably change. Lab mode is usually a temporary stop on your way to one of the other modes. It's not usually your final destination.

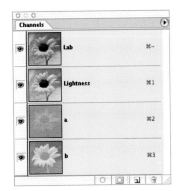

Figure 12.8 Lab channels.

Because of impurities in the CMYK inks, the CMYK mode cannot reproduce all the colors available in RGB mode. When choosing a color using the Color Picker, a small triangular Warning symbol (known as the gamut warning) will appear next to the color you have chosen if it is one of the colors that are not reproducible in CMYK mode. Clicking on the triangle will give you the closest reproducible color.

How Channels Relate to Layers

All of the information in the color channels is assembled from the elements in the Layers palette. If you view a single layer, the color channels display just that particular layer's content, as shown in **Figure 12.9**. If you view multiple layers, the color channels show the result of combining those layers, as shown in **Figure 12.10**. Because you can edit only one layer at a time, any changes made using the color channels will affect the currently active layer only.

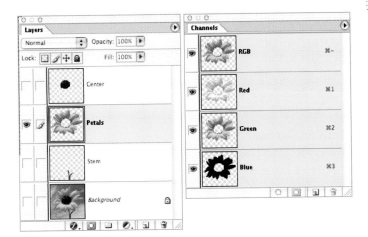

Figure 12.9 When a single layer is visible, the channels indicate what is contained in that layer.

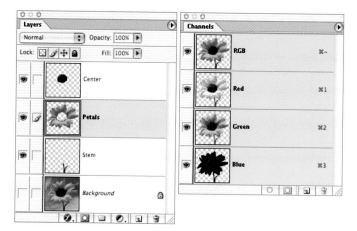

Figure 12.10 When multiple layers are visible, the channels reflect the combination of those layers.

The Composite Color Channel

If the image contains more than one color channel (RGB, CMYK, or Lab), then the topmost channel will be a special one known as the composite channel (**Figure 12.11**). This composite channel doesn't contain any information; it's just a shortcut to make all the color channels visible and active for editing, which is their default state if you haven't been editing the individual channels. So, in effect, this is how you get things back to normal after messing with the individual channels.

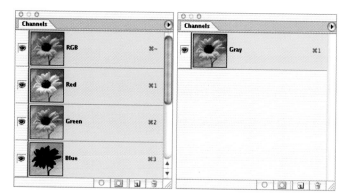

Figure 12.11 When multiple color channels are present, the topmost channel is known as the composite channel.

Viewing Channels in Color

When viewing a single-color channel (by clicking on its name in the Channels palette), the main image window will appear as a grayscale image. This was done on purpose to make it easy for you to see exactly what the channel contains. If you view more than one color channel at a time (by turning on more eyeballs in the palette), the main image window will show the channels in color.

Figure 12.12 The Display & Cursors Preferences dialog box.

You can force Photoshop to display individual channels in color (instead of grayscale) by choosing Photoshop > Preferences > Display & Cursors and turning on the Color Channels in Color check box (**Figure 12.12**). I don't find this all that useful because it becomes much harder to see exactly what is in each channel, especially when viewing the yellow channel of a CMYK image (it's just so light!). Go ahead and try it: Open an image, convert it to CMYK mode, and take a peek at the yellow channel; then turn the preference on and off (**Figures 12.13** and **12.14**). Then you'll understand why they chose grayscale as the best way to view a channel.

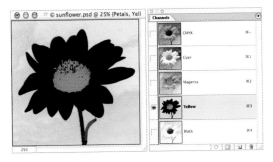

Figure 12.13 Color Channels in Color check box off. (©2003 PhotoSpin, www.photospin.com).

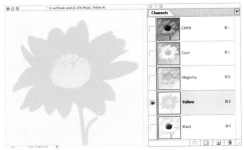

Figure 12.14 Color Channels in Color check box on.

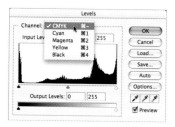

Figure 12.15 When applying Levels, you can adjust either a single color channel or all of them.

Editing Multiple Channels

When you are adjusting an image using Levels or Curves, you'll notice a pop-up menu at the top of the dialog box, such as the one in **Figure 12.15**. This little menu determines which color channels you are editing (you can edit either a single channel or all of them).

But by using the Channels palette, you can force Levels or Curves (or any control, for that matter) to affect more than one channel at a time (**Figure 12.16**). Just click on the first channel you would like to change, and then Shift-click on another channel. Finally, turn on the eyeball of the composite channel (the topmost one) to make the rest of the color channels visible without making them all active. This can be extremely useful when working on flesh tones, because they are mainly made from magenta and yellow ink.

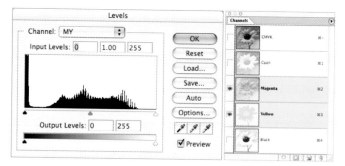

Figure 12.16 By messing with the Channels palette, you can get the Levels dialog box to affect the channels of your choice.

Applying a Filter to a Single Channel

Without using the Channels palette, it's impossible to get a filter to affect only one channel. When you don't use the Channels palette, a filter will always apply to all the color channels that are present in the document.

Images taken from digital cameras often appear noisy. If you blur the entire image to get rid of the noise, it usually looks terrible because you discard most of the important detail. But if you click through the channels, you might notice that the noise is most prominent in one channel (usually blue). By blurring just the offending channel, your image will look better without throwing away too much detail. To blur just the offending channel, click on its name in the Channels palette, and then apply the Blur filter (**Figures 12.17** and **12.18**). You might also try the Despeckle and Median filters. If you would like to see the image in full color, turn on the eyeball of the composite channel before applying the filter.

You can also improve the image by sharpening only those channels that don't contain a large amount of noise (usually the red and green channels), as shown in **Figures 12.19** and **12.20**.

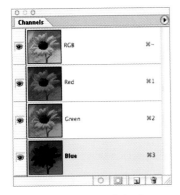

Figure 12.17 Viewing all the channels, but editing the blue channel only.

Figure 12.18 Applying the Gaussian Blur filter to remove noise.

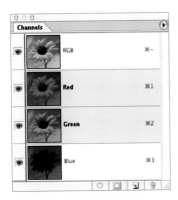

Figure 12.19 Viewing all the channels, but editing the red and green channels only.

Figure 12.20 Applying the Unsharp Mask filter to bring out detail.

Figure 12.21 Choosing Image > Adjustments > Desaturate produces a four-color grayscale image, which often appears brownish. (©2003 Stockbyte, www.stockbyte.com)

Figure 12.22 After pasting into the black channel and deleting the remaining information from the other channels, you should have an area that prints with only black ink.

Black-Only Grayscale Images

Even with color images, there will be times when you want to force a portion of an image to black and white—for example, to make a color image pop all the more in contrast to a drab background. The most common way to force a portion of an image to black and white is to select the area and choose Image > Adjust > Desaturate. On-screen, Desaturate will make it appear as if the image will be printed with black ink only. But if you open the Info palette and move your cursor over that now-black-and-white area, you'll notice that the image contains equal amounts of cyan, magenta, and yellow ink (**Figure 12.21**), which will look brown if you remember the basic concepts from Chapter 8, "Color Management," and Chapter 9, "Color Correction."

To get the image to print with only black ink, you'll need to use the Channels palette. To begin, select the area you want to print with black ink, choose Edit > Copy, and then click on the black channel and choose Edit > Paste. That doesn't just paste the black channel information, but instead converts everything you copied to grayscale and then pastes the result into the black channel. But because you chose Copy instead of Cut, there will still be information left in the other channels, so click on each of the color channels (except black), and with the selection still active, press the Delete (Mac) or Backspace (Windows) key to remove all information from those areas (**Figure 12.22**). Remember, only one layer can be active at a time, so pressing Delete or Backspace will delete the channel information from only the currently active layer.

You can get the same result by choosing Image > Adjustments > Channel Mixer and turning on the Monochrome check box. You can even create a Channel Mixer adjustment layer—then Photoshop will force all the layers in the selected area to print with only black ink. Try it; it literally does all the work for you!

There are many more uses for the color channels, and we'll get to some of them in later chapters.

Understanding Spot Channels

Remember when you got your first box of crayons? I'll bet you that it was the standard-issue eight-color box from Crayola. I remember mine vividly. I thought it was great—that is, until the rich kid across the street swaggered over and showed me his box. It was the gigantic 64-color model with the built-in sharpener. My box was limited to black, brown, blue, red, violet, orange, yellow, and green, which seemed adequate until I discovered Periwinkle, Prussian Blue, and Raw Sienna in his huge set. Well, you can think of spot channels as a way to get all those colors that don't come in the standard (CMYK) box.

It all comes down to this: If you are planning to print an image using inks other than (or in addition to) cyan, magenta, yellow, and black (such as fluorescent orange), you'll need to use one or more spot channels. These channels will allow you to paint with PANTONE colors (the most popular brand of spot color ink). Spot channels also allow your image to look correct onscreen and print correctly from both Photoshop and your page-layout program. But I should warn you before we get too far into this: If you are not actually purchasing a PANTONE ink, but would just like to simulate the look of PANTONE colors, then stay in RGB or CMYK mode and stay away from spot channels. Instead, just click on your foreground color and then click the Custom button to get to the PANTONE color picker. But beware that simulations are just that—the closest possible approximation—and they'll use a combination of the regular CMYK inks, which will cause those colors to look different from what they look like in a PANTONE swatchbook. But if you are really purchasing a PANTONE ink, then continue, and I'll show you how to get it set up.

No Layers Support

Just because Photoshop has direct support for spot colors doesn't mean it's easy to use them. The information you add to a spot channel will not appear on any layer—not even the background layer (**Figure 12.23**). It's as if the spot color information were sitting on an invisible overlay slapped on top of everything else. In fact, any information

NOTES

Because spot colors will not be reproduced using CMYK ink, you can completely ignore the gamut Warning icon when choosing colors for use with a spot channel. For more information about working with spot channels, see Chapter 11, "Color Manipulation."

you put on a layer will be in the same mode as the document you're working on (RGB, CMYK, grayscale, and so on). That means that you can use layers, but none of the information on the layers will print using a spot color. If you'd like to use strictly PANTONE colors, start with a grayscale image and then choose Image > Mode > Multichannel. Then you can change the grayscale channel into a spot channel by Option-double-clicking (Mac) or Alt-double-clicking (Windows) on its name.

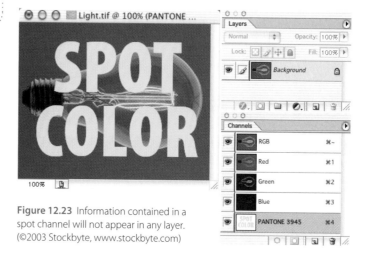

Figure 12.23 Information contained in a spot channel will not appear in any layer. (©2003 Stockbyte, www.stockbyte.com)

Figure 12.24 Spot Channel Options dialog box.

Creating Spot Channels

You'll need to create one spot channel for each PANTONE color you would like to use. To create one, choose New Spot Channel from the side menu of the Channels palette. A dialog box will appear, asking for the specific color you would like to use and its Solidity setting (**Figure 12.24**). To specify the color, click on the color swatch at the left of the dialog box. This will bring up a standard Color Picker dialog box. To get to PANTONE colors, click on the Custom button.

Unlike process colors, which are transparent, many PANTONE inks are almost completely opaque. Certain PANTONE colors (such as the metallic inks) will completely obstruct the view of colors that appear underneath them, whereas others will allow you to see a hint of the colors that are underneath. The Solidity setting controls how translucent these inks will appear onscreen (**Figures 12.25** and **12.26**). Unfortunately, Photoshop doesn't automatically supply a setting for you, and there is no resource I can think of that will give you great settings. I contacted both Adobe and PANTONE, and neither of them could supply recommended settings. So, this is a setting you have to guess at unless you have a lot of experience with the inks you are using or have the time and money needed to perform a press check.

After you have created some spot channels, you can view those channels at the same time as the normal color channels by turning on the Eyeball icon next to the composite channel as well as the ones next to each spot channel.

Painting with Spot Colors

To paint with a spot color, you must first click on the name of the color you would like to use from the Channels palette. Next, open the Color palette and, from the grayscale slider, choose the percentage of this ink you would like to use (**Figure 12.27**). Then paint away. Photoshop acts as if you are working on a separate grayscale image when you paint in one of the spot channels, so if you attempt to paint with a color chosen from the Color Picker, Photoshop will convert it to a shade of gray when you are painting.

When you paint in a spot channel, Photoshop leaves the normal color channels unchanged (also known as overprinting). That means if you don't want the spot color you are painting with to print on top of the CMYK image (that is, if you want it to knock out as opposed to overprint), you'll have to manually switch to the color channels and delete the areas you painted across with the spot color. This can take a tremendous amount of time and isn't always the easiest thing to accomplish.

You can also paste images into the spot channels, use the Type tool, or apply any filter or adjustment that is available to grayscale images.

Proofing on a Desktop Printer

Most desktop printers aren't capable of printing an image that contains spot colors. The information in spot channels

Figure 12.25 Solidity: 100%.

Figure 12.26 Solidity: 40%.

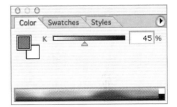

Figure 12.27 Color palette.

stays separate from the information in the RGB, CMYK, or grayscale channels, which are the ones your desktop printer uses to figure out what to print. That means you'll need to do a few things to get your image to print correctly on a desktop color printer (**Figure 12.28**). To start with, you don't want to mess up the document you've worked so hard to create, so save the image and then choose Image > Duplicate to work on a duplicate image. Next, choose Image > Mode > RGB Color, Shift-click on each of the spot channels to make them all active, and choose Merge Spot Channel from the side menu of the Channels palette (**Figure 12.29**). This will make your image printable on a desktop color printer by simulating the look of the spot colors using the normal RGB color channels. After the image has been printed, you can discard this file and go back to editing the original image.

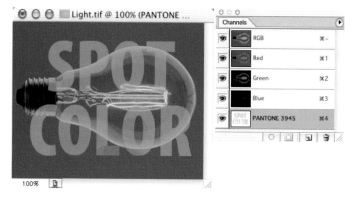

Figure 12.28 Information in the spot channels is difficult to print on desktop color printers.

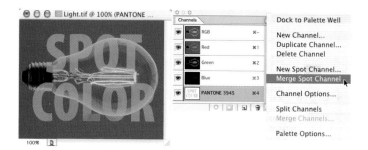

Figure 12.29 Merging the spot channels will simulate the look of spot colors in RGB mode.

Saving the Image

Only three file formats support spot channels: Photoshop, TIFF, and DCS 2.0 (DCS is short for Desktop Color Separations). Because most page-layout programs can't deal with spot color images in the TIFF or Photoshop file format, you'll have to use DCS 2.0. The DCS file format is really part of the EPS file format, which is supported by most page-layout programs. To be able to save your image in the DCS 2.0 format, the image must be in grayscale or CMYK mode. When saving a DCS 2.0 file, you will be offered a bunch of options; unfortunately, most of them aren't all that straightforward, so let's take a peek at them (**Figure 12.30**).

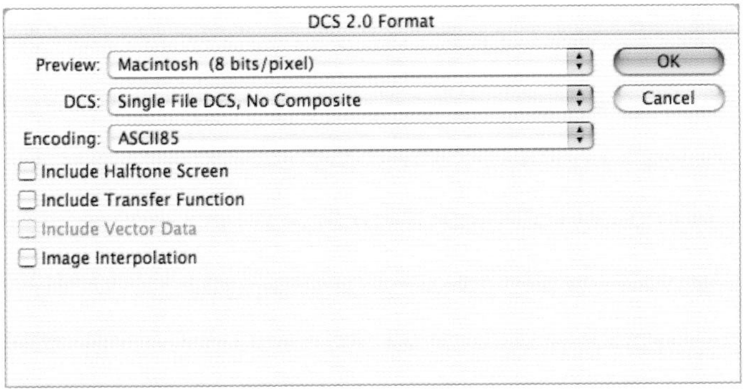

Figure 12.30 DCS 2.0 Save dialog box.

The Preview menu (which pops up when you save your file in the DCS 2.0 format) determines what will be seen onscreen in your page-layout program (**Figure 12.31**).

Why can't they use English!? Let's try to decipher these choices. Use the TIFF options when the image will be used on the Windows platform, and use the Macintosh options for a Mac (duh). The option "1 bit/pixel" means pure black and pure white (that looks terrible); "8 bits/pixel" means 256 colors (that looks okay); and "JPEG" means full color (that looks great) (**Figures 12.32** and **12.33**). These choices affect only the onscreen image that appears in other programs, not the printed version. No matter which option you choose, the printed version of the image will look great. So, what do I use? I always use the JPEG choice because it looks great and doesn't make the files overly large.

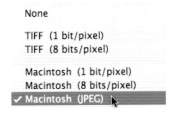

Figure 12.31 The DCS Preview choices. (I think JPEG usually produces the best onscreen previews.)

Figure 12.32 An 8-bit preview, as seen in a page-layout program. (©2003 PhotoDisc)

Figure 12.33 A JPEG preview, as seen in a page-layout program.

Figure 12.34 Single-file DCS documents are the easiest to keep track of.

Figure 12.35 Use Binary for Macs and ASCII for Windows.

Figure 12.36 Channels set up for CMYK conversion.

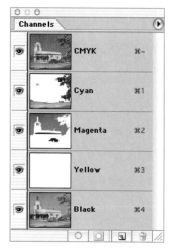

Figure 12.37 Result of CMYK conversion.

The DCS pop-up menu determines how many files you'll end up with (**Figure 12.34**). Unless you really know what you're doing and have a good reason to mess with this (some people can come up with one), leave it set to Single File with Color Composite. I haven't needed to use the other options for any of the files I've output.

The Encoding menu determines how the information that will be printed (as opposed to the onscreen preview) will be stored. Mac users should use the Binary option, and Windows users should use ASCII (**Figure 12.35**). Binary files are almost half the size of ASCII files, so if your printer can handle them, use them. Some really old Mac programs and printers cannot handle Binary files, so if you run into a problem, resave your image using ASCII encoding. The JPEG choices will degrade the quality of the printed image and deliver a dramatically smaller file. Use JPEG only if the image will not need to be resaved and if quality is not your first concern. (JPEG degrades the image more each time it is closed, reopened, and then saved.)

If you've added spot colors to a grayscale image and find that your printing company dislikes DCS files, you'll need to use CMYK mode in an unusual way. Start by choosing Image > Mode > Multichannel, and add empty channels until you have a total of four channels. Arrange the channels so that black is at the bottom and the other channels are organized by brightness (of the spot color, not the contents of the channel), darkest on top and lightest toward the bottom (**Figure 12.36**). If you're using a third ink, then put it right below the darkest spot channel. Finally, choose Image > Mode > CMYK Color and save your file (**Figure 12.37**). Now give that file to your printing company; tell them to only output the channels that contain information, and tell them which spot colors to substitute for the CMYK colors.

Understanding Alpha Channels

Alpha channels are like big storage bins for selections. Whenever you spend more than a few minutes creating a selection and there's the remotest chance that you might need it again, you should transform it into an alpha channel for safekeeping. That way it will be available for you to use again and again. And the great thing about alpha channels is that they're not limited to being just a storage device; the channels are also malleable, like modeling clay, so that you can sculpt and manipulate your selections in ways that are not possible with mere mortal selection tools. Mastering alpha channels is the mark of a true Photoshop virtuoso.

Loading and Saving Selections

If you make a selection, and then choose Select > Save Selection, Photoshop will store the selection at the bottom of the Channels palette (**Figure 12.38**). Go ahead and try it. Make sure the Channels palette is open, so you can see what's going on. An alpha channel is a saved selection—it's that simple (well, almost).

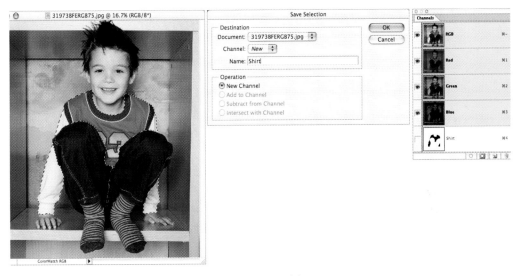

Figure 12.38 Choosing Select > Save Selection will produce a new alpha channel.

Now let's find out how to reload the selection you just saved. But first, choose Select > Deselect (or Command-D on the Mac, Ctrl-D in Windows) to get rid of the selection that is currently active. Good. Now, back to reloading: As long as you saved a selection, you should be able to get it back at any time by choosing Select > Load Selection, and choosing the proper name from the Channel pop-up menu (**Figure 12.39**). That will bring back the marching ants without changing the look of your image.

Figure 12.39 Choose Select > Load Selection to reload a saved selection.

Now let's try the same thing using the Channels palette. To save a selection, Option-click (Mac) or Alt-click (Windows) on the Save Selection icon at the bottom of the Channels palette (it's the second from the left). This accomplishes the same end result as choosing Select > Save Selection—a new channel (**Figure 12.40**). If you click on the Save Selection icon without holding down the Option or Alt key, Photoshop will assign the new channel a generic name such as "Alpha 1."

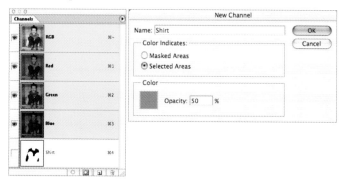

Figure 12.40 Option-clicking (Mac) or Alt-clicking (Windows) on the Save Selection icon is the same as choosing Select > Save Selection.

Figure 12.41 Dragging the name of a channel onto the Load Selection icon is the same as choosing Select > Load Selection.

You can also Command-click (Mac) or Ctrl-click (Windows) on the name of a channel in the Channels palette to load it as a selection.

To get the selection back, drag the name of the channel onto the far left icon at the bottom of the palette (**Figure 12.41**). That does the exact same thing as choosing Select > Load Selection. The advantage to using the Channels palette is that you get a visual preview of the shape of the selection.

Deleting Alpha Channels

There is no way to delete a saved selection (channel) when using the Select menu. Instead, you need to open the Channels palette and drag the name of a channel onto the rightmost icon (the one that looks like a little trash can).

Viewing Individual Channels

If you would like to see what a channel contains without loading it as a selection, you can simply click on the name of the channel in the Channels palette. This will display the channel in the main image window (**Figure 12.42**). White areas in the channel indicate areas that will be selected, and black areas indicate nonselected areas. After you're done looking at a channel, just click on the composite (topmost) channel to get back to editing all the color channels.

New Channels

So far, all we've been doing is saving and reloading selections that we've made with the normal selection tools. But you can also create a selection by creating a brand-new (empty) channel and editing the channel. Try this: Click on the second icon from the right at the bottom of the Channels palette (the one that looks like a sheet of paper with a folded corner). This action will create a new empty channel and display it in the image window. Now change your foreground color to white, choose the Paintbrush tool and a hard-edged brush, and sign your name in the channel. If you're using a mouse (instead of a graphics tablet), it might not look exactly like your signature, but that's okay. Once you're finished, click on the topmost channel to get back to the main image, drag the name of the channel you were messing with to the Load Selection icon, and bingo! The shape of your signature is selected. Photoshop can't tell the difference between a channel that was created by saving a selection and one that was created from scratch (**Figure 12.43**). That means that you're no longer limited to creating selections with the Marquee, Lasso, and Magic Wand tools.

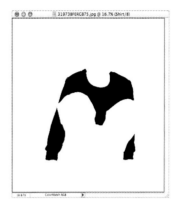

Figure 12.42 Click on the name of a channel to view it in the main image window.

Figure 12.43 Result of painting in a new channel and then loading the channel as a selection.

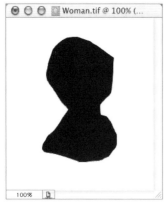

Figure 12.44 Normal.

Figure 12.45 Feathered.

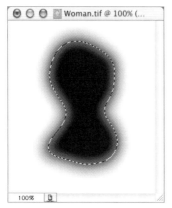

Figure 12.46 The marching ants show up where an area is at least 50% selected.

Feathered Selections

Let's see what a feathered selection looks like when saved as a channel. Make a selection using the Lasso tool, and then save it as a channel. Next, choose Select > Feather and use a setting of 10, and then, again, save the selection as a channel. Now click on the name of the first alpha channel and take a look at it; next, click on the name of the second one to see the difference (**Figures 12.44** and **12.45**). Feathered selections appear with blurry edges in the Channels palette. This happens because shades of gray in a channel indicate an area that is partially selected (50% gray means 50% selected). You can make the first alpha channel look identical to the second by making it active, choosing Filter > Blur > Gaussian Blur, and using the same setting that was used to feather the other selection (10, in this case).

But when you look at the marching ants that appear after the channel has been loaded as a selection, they show you only where the selection is at least 50% selected. That isn't a very accurate picture of what the selection really looks like (**Figure 12.46**). But if you save the same selection as a channel, you can see exactly what is happening on its edge. So if you want to create a feathered selection when editing a channel, just choose a soft-edged brush to paint with.

Shades of Gray

Try this out: Create a new channel. Paint in it with 20% gray (choose Window > Color to choose shades of gray), load that as a selection, and paint in the selected area with bright red. Now choose Select > Deselect, lower the opacity of the painting tool to 80%, and paint with bright red in an area where you haven't yet painted. They should look exactly the same. That's how Photoshop makes a selection fade out—by simply lowering the opacity of the tool you are using. The only problem is that the marching ants show up only where an image is at least 50% selected (that's 50% gray or brighter in a channel). So, try this one on for size. Create a new channel and paint in one area with 49% gray, and then paint in another area with 51% gray. Then load the channel as a selection and paint across the entire image. Only the areas that are less than 50%

gray in the channel show up, but the other areas are still selected (**Figure 12.47**). Try creating a channel and then paint with 55% gray. Now load that one, and you'll even get a warning message (**Figure 12.48**).

We really haven't done anything fancy with channels yet, so let's try something fun. To start with, you have to remember that when you are editing a channel, Photoshop treats it as if it is a grayscale image. That means you can use any tool that is available when working on grayscale images. So give this a try: Select an area using the Marquee tool, and save it in the Channels palette. View the channel, choose Select > Deselect, Filter > Distort > Ripple, and mess with the settings until you've created something that looks a little kooky (**Figure 12.49**). Finally, click on the composite (topmost) channel and load that channel as a selection. You can create infinite varieties of fascinating selections with this simple technique.

You can also "unfeather" a selection using the Channels palette (**Figure 12.50**). Remember, a feathered edge looks blurry when saved as a channel. Well, all you have to do to remove that blurry look is to save the selection as a channel, and then choose Image > Adjust > Threshold. This will give the channel a very crisp, and therefore unfeathered, edge.

Figure 12.47 When painting in a channel, only the areas that contain less than 50% gray will be visible when the channel is loaded as a selection.

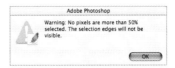

Figure 12.48 When you load a channel that does not contain any shades brighter than 50% gray, a Warning will appear.

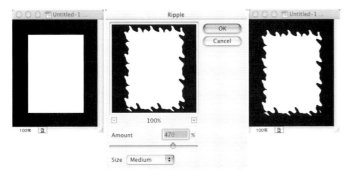

Figure 12.49 Applying the Ripple filter to a channel.

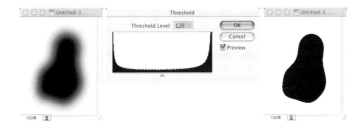

Figure 12.50 Unfeathering a selection using Threshold.

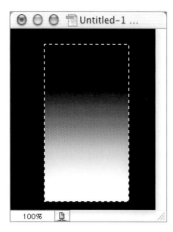

Figure 12.51 Using a selection within a channel to restrict which areas can be edited.

Viewing a channel at the same time as the main image is the same as using Quick Mask mode, which we talked about back in Chapter 2, "Selection Primer."

Selections Within Channels

You can even use a selection to isolate a particular area of a channel (**Figure 12.51**). A selection within a channel can help you create a selection that is distorted on only one side. To accomplish this, open any photograph, use the Marquee tool to make a selection, and then save it as a channel. Next, select half of the channel using the Marquee tool. Now, apply one of the filters that are found in the Filter > Distort menu. Once you're done, switch back to the main image (by clicking on the topmost channel) and load the channel you just created. To see exactly how this selection will affect the image, choose Image > Adjustments > Hue/Saturation and move the Saturation slider all the way to the left.

View with the Image

We've covered some ideal uses for alpha channels, but their usefulness is very limited if you can't see how the channels line up with the main image. At any time, you can overlay a channel onto the main image by simply turning on the Eyeball icon next to the composite (topmost) channel while you are editing an alpha channel (**Figure 12.52**). This enables you to see exactly which areas of the image will be selected. When you do this, the dark areas of the alpha channel will be overlaid onto the main image. Photoshop substitutes a color for the shades of gray in a channel to make them easier to see. You can change the color that is used by Option-double-clicking (Mac) or

Figure 12.52 Viewing a channel at the same time as the main image. (©2003 Stockbyte, www.stockbyte.com)

Alt-double-clicking (Windows) on the name of the alpha channel (**Figure 12.53**). This setup is ideal when you create a selection that is feathered in one area and crisp-edged in another. All you have to do is paint with a soft-edged brush for the feathered area, and then switch back to a crisp-edged brush for the rest.

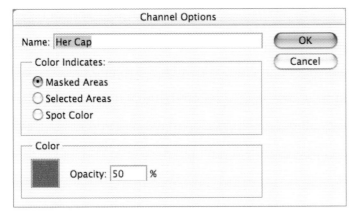

Figure 12.53 Channel Options settings used.

Photoshop also allows you to switch where the color shows up. You can specify whether you want the selected or unselected areas to appear. To change this setting, Option-double-click (Mac) or Alt-double-click (Windows) on the name of the alpha channel, and change the Color Indicates setting (**Figures 12.54** and **12.55**). Photoshop uses the term Masked Areas to describe areas that are not selected. Here's a way to help understand the reasoning of this. If you're painting a room in your house, what do you do to all the trim that you don't want to get paint on? You mask it off, right? Well, in Photoshop, you do the same—you select the areas you want to change, and the nonselected areas are the masked areas.

The Opacity setting determines how much you will be able to see through the overlaid channel. Viewing a channel at the same time as the main image is not a way to colorize your images. The channel that's being overlaid won't print that way; it's just a method for creating a selection, and nothing else. If you'd like to colorize an image, then check out Chapter 17, "Enhancement," to find methods that are much easier than anything we're doing here.

Keep an eye on the Channel Options dialog box (specifically, the Color Indicates setting). Because the dark areas of a channel are the only parts that show up when overlaying it onto the main image, this setting changes what black means in an alpha channel. When viewing a single channel, just substitute the words "black indicates" where it says "color indicates," and it should make a lot more sense.

Figure 12.54 The Color Indicates setting changes where the color overlay appears.

Figure 12.55 Channel Options settings used.

Figure 12.56 When viewing multiple channels, the channel or channels that are highlighted are the only ones being edited.

When you are viewing an alpha channel at the same time as the main image, you'll need to keep track of exactly what you are editing. The channel or channels that are highlighted in color are always the ones that you are currently editing (**Figure 12.56**). Other channels might be visible, but if they aren't highlighted, you won't be able to change them.

Saving Channels with Your Image

If you want to save your spot or alpha channels with your file, you'll have to use a file format that understands them. First of all, the Photoshop file format completely supports all kinds of channels, which makes it a great working file format. Unfortunately, most other programs can't understand images saved in the Photoshop format. The TIFF format also supports alpha channels, but it doesn't know the difference between spot and alpha channels, so it is not usually used for spot channels. The DCS 2.0 format supports spot channels and is compatible with the majority of publishing programs, so it is usually used for spot color work. Most of the formats do not support alpha or spot channels. When saving your image, keep an eye on the Alpha Channels and Spot Colors check boxes that show up near the bottom of the Save dialog box. A warning symbol will appear next to those check boxes when you choose a file format that doesn't support extra channels. Anytime those check boxes are turned off, all your alpha and spot channels will automatically be discarded.

Closing Thoughts

I truly hope that after going through this chapter you've come to terms with channels. They don't really deserve the mind-boggling reputation that seems to follow them. I like to think of them as three friendly little dogs: Spot, Color, and Alpha. They will be loyal to you throughout your lifetime as a Photoshopper, and will take care of all sorts of special needs, especially when you're working with color or with complex selections (or, for that matter, any selection that you'd like to save for later). So if for any reason you're still one of those people who want to throw their hands up in the air when the subject of channels comes up, think twice. It's worth the pain, and believe me when I tell you that the pain will turn into pure pleasure once you've realized what a gem the Channels palette is.

Ben's Techno-Babble Decoder Ring

Alpha channel: Alpha channels are basically saved selections. They do not affect how your image will be printed.

Bits: In Photoshop, 256 shades of gray is known as 8 bits, while 32,767 shades is known as 16-bits. This describes how much memory Photoshop uses to keep track of all those shades. So if you find a setting in your scanning software that is called "8-bit grayscale," it just means a normal 256-shade grayscale scan. If you hear someone say, "I have a 24-bit color image," that means they have an image that is in RGB mode (RGB has three channels, and each channel is 8 bits: 8 + 8 + 8 = 24). Or, if you hear about a 32-bit image, that just means the image contains four channels; they are either talking about an image that is in CMYK mode (four channels) or an RGB image plus one alpha channel (for a total of four channels).

Color channel: When you edit an image in Photoshop, you are really editing the color channels. These channels break your image into one or more color components. The mode of the document will determine how many color channels will be present: RGB mode will have three channels (red, green, and blue); CMYK mode will have four channels (cyan, magenta, yellow, and black); and grayscale will contain only one channel (called gray).

Composite channel: The composite channel does not contain any information; in fact, it is simply a shortcut to view and edit all the color channels at the same time. This is often used to return the Channels palette back to its "normal" state after isolating a single channel for editing.

DCS: Desktop Color Separation (DCS) is a special version of the EPS file format that comes in two versions, DCS 1.0 and DCS 2.0. You can think of DCS 1.0 as the old version of this file format, because prior to Photoshop 5 it was the only version available in Photoshop, and it used to be integrated into the normal EPS save dialog box. DCS 1.0 files allow you to save a CMYK image and get five files total—one for each channel in the image, and one preview image. DCS 2.0 is special because it is the only file format (other than Photoshop's own format) that allows you to save spot channels in addition to the CMYK channels.

EPS: Encapsulated PostScript (EPS) is a file format used to transfer PostScript-language page descriptions between programs and output devices. EPS files should be used only with PostScript-aware printers; otherwise, the resulting images will appear with a low-resolution "jaggy" appearance because they print only the onscreen preview.

Gamut: A term used to describe the entire range of colors that is reproducible using a certain set of inks, dyes, or light (as defined by a profile). The gamut warning in Photoshop warns you that the currently chosen color is not reproducible using CMYK inks.

Mask: Anytime you view a selection as a grayscale image (as opposed to a "marching ants" selection), it is also called a mask. That means it's okay to call a channel a mask if you'd like. And when you see features like Quick Mask and Layer Masks mentioned in Photoshop, those are things that will also be stored in the Channels palette.

PANTONE: A brand of ink commonly used when printing with fewer than four inks, or when colors are needed that cannot be reproduced using CMYK inks (metallic colors, fluorescent colors, deep blues, and bright greens cannot be accurately simulated using CMYK inks). PANTONE inks are commonly referred to as spot color inks.

Spot channel: Spot channels are a special variety of color channel that allow you to construct your image out of inks other than, or in addition to, cyan, magenta, yellow, and black. Spot channels are typically used when printing with PANTONE inks.

Keyboard Shortcuts

Function	Macintosh	Windows
View Composite	Command-~	Ctrl-~
View Channel	Command-Channel #	Ctrl-Channel #
Load Channel as a Selection	Option-Command-Channel #	Alt-Ctrl-Channel #

PART III

Creative Explorations

13

Advanced Masking

©2003 Richard Tuschman, www.richardtuschman.com

Society is a masked ball, where every one hides his real character, and reveals it by hiding.

— Ralph Waldo Emerson

Advanced Masking

This is a brand new chapter that did not appear in previous versions of this book, so make sure not to skip this one.

As I trot around the planet spreading the Photoshop gospel, I am besieged by users who really struggle when they try to isolate a complex object from its background. In almost every case, the problem is caused by using the wrong tool for the particular task, or by not knowing how to properly use the right tool. Imagine giving a brain surgeon a pair of schoolroom safety scissors for his next operation. He would fling them on the floor in disdain and banish you from the operating room. Well, using advanced masking tools is like throwing away your school scissors (the basic selection tools), and trading them in for some finely tuned instruments that allow you to precisely isolate a complex object from its background and place that object on a different background.

This chapter will take you far beyond the basic selection tools I describe in Chapter 2, "Selection Primer," and will help you develop the advanced masking skills you need to tackle those less than simple images. You know the ones I'm talking about; they make most people wail in protest when they think about having to extract them from their backgrounds: people with frizzy semi-transparent hair, trees with a thousand leaves, objects in motion, or something that is so similar to its background you can barely see where one ends and the other begins. By the end of this chapter, you should no longer be wailing. Instead, you should be able to easily evaluate the situation, quickly pick out the best tools for the job, and like a finely trained surgeon, understand how to go about executing the extraction in the most efficient, refined way possible. If you are someone who regularly faces this particular challenge (folks who do catalog, magazine, or newspaper work immediately come to mind), this chapter is a must read. But even if you don't get paid to use Photoshop, and just want to torture your girlfriend by placing her head on the body of a sumo wrestler, then this chapter has something for you, too.

The Key Is to Choose the Right Tool

In Photoshop, there is almost always more than one way of getting the job done. In the area of masking, however, certain tools were designed for specific types of images, and it's all too common to find someone becoming frustrated with a tool because it's the only one they know, and they're trying to force it to do something it's not really meant for. The key to getting good at masking is to be familiar with as many masking tools as possible and to have a good grasp of what each tool was designed for so you can choose the right tool for the job at hand. Let's take a brief look at what's available, and then we'll dig deeper and explore each feature in depth:

▶ **The Background Eraser:** This tool is best for crisp-edged objects that have a noticeable difference in color or brightness from the background that surrounds them. With this tool, you have to manually paint around the edges of objects to tell Photoshop which areas should be deleted, and Photoshop will try to figure out what should be kept or deleted.

▶ **The Extract command:** This command is best for images that have soft or fuzzy edges, like hair or objects in motion. With this command, you need to define three areas on your image: areas that should be left alone, areas that should be deleted, and areas that have a mix of both. Then, by comparing the first two areas, Photoshop figures out what to do with the third.

▶ **The Blending sliders:** These are a quick and dirty way to isolate objects that are radically different in brightness from what surrounds them. The most obvious uses for these would be things like fireworks, lightning, and text on paper.

▶ **Channels:** These are the old-fashioned way to remove the background on images. They used to be essential before the more sophisticated masking tools (Background Eraser and the Extract command) came along, but they are still useful when using those other tools would be too time-consuming. Channels are useful in a multitude of situations, but I most often use them on simple images.

▶ **The Pen tool:** This tool is best with crisp-edged objects that have mainly straight lines and very smooth curves. That means that it's ideal for images that are in-focus and contain man-made objects like cars and computers. I would never think of using the Pen tool on overly complex images like trees or hair.

▶ **Layer Masks:** These are mainly used to refine the results you get from the other masking tools. Used all by themselves, they are no different than manually erasing the background with the standard Eraser tool; combined with other tools, however, they become a powerhouse that can often make the difference between a mediocre result and one that you'd be proud of.

Now that you have a general idea of what differentiates the various masking tools, let's jump in and explore each one in depth.

The Background Eraser

Hiding under the normal Eraser tool is a special version known as the Background Eraser. Click and hold on the Eraser tool until you see a drop-down menu—the Background Eraser is the middle tool shown in that menu (**Figure 13.1**). When you move your cursor over an image, you'll notice that the Background Eraser gives you a round brush with a crosshair in the middle (**Figure 13.2**). When you click and drag on an image, Photoshop keeps a constant eye on what color is under the crosshair and deletes everything within the circle that is similar to that color (**Figure 13.3**). Your job is to trace around the edge of the object you want to keep. It's OK to have the circular part of your cursor overlap the subject. Just never let the crosshair hit the subject; otherwise, it will start to delete that area as well (**Figure 13.4**). The settings in the options bar at the top of your screen determine what should be kept or thrown away (**Figure 13.5**).

Figure 13.1 The Background Eraser tool is positioned in the same slot as the Eraser tool in Photoshop's tool palette.

Figure 13.2 The Background Eraser presents you with a circle and a crosshair cursor. (©2003 Stockbyte, www.stockbyte.com)

Figure 13.3 Clicking will delete the color that's under the crosshair from within the circle.

Figure 13.4 Be careful not to let the crosshair hit the subject of the photo; otherwise, it will be deleted.

Figure 13.5 The options bar settings for the Background Eraser tool.

Tolerance

Getting the right Tolerance setting is essential to using the Background Eraser tool successfully. This setting determines how much Photoshop will be able to stray from the color under the crosshair (**Figure 13.6**). If the background you are attempting to remove is very similar to the subject in brightness or color, then you'll need to use a low Tolerance setting. Or, if the background is quite different from the subject, try a much higher Tolerance setting so that you can quickly remove the background without being overly careful about what you're dragging over.

I don't have any hard and fast guidelines to give you because this setting really depends on the image you're working with. I suggest that you start with the default setting of 50%, and then if you notice that some of the subject of the photo is being deleted along with the background, try a lower setting. If, on the other hand, not enough of the background is being deleted, you'll need to ramp up the Tolerance to allow Photoshop to delete a wider range of colors. You can change the Tolerance using the number keys on your keyboard (1 = 10%, 3 = 30%, 23 = 23%, and so on), and you can change the setting each time you

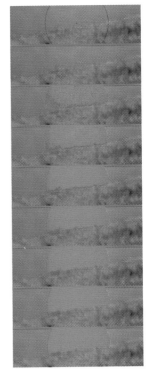

Figure 13.6 Tolerance settings used, from top to bottom: Original image, 1%, 5%, 10%, 20%, 30%, 40%, 50%, 60%.

409

The Background Eraser tool uses the Brush Presets palette that appears in the options bar. You can quickly change the size of your brush (eraser) using the bracket keys on your keyboard ( ][ ). To change how hard the edge of the brush is, use Shift in conjunction with those same bracket keys.

release the mouse button. I usually work in sections using different tolerance settings as the background changes. If you mess up, just press Command-Z (Mac) or Ctrl-Z (Windows) to undo the last step and then try again.

Protect Foreground Color

On occasion, you'll find that the Tolerance setting alone isn't enough to isolate the subject from the background (**Figure 13.7**). That's when you'll want to start using the Protect Foreground Color check box. With that check box turned on, Photoshop will start thinking about two colors: the one under the crosshair, which will tell it what to delete, and the foreground color, which will tell it what to save (**Figure 13.8**). While the Background Eraser tool is active, you can hold Option (Mac) or Alt (Windows) and click on the part of your image you want to save—that will change your foreground color and therefore prevent the color you click on from being deleted. The only problem is that you might forget that you're protecting your foreground color, which can mess you up once you start working on a different part of the image where the color you are protecting is similar to the background you are attempting to delete. So make sure to keep one eye on this check box, and turn it off and on as you think necessary.

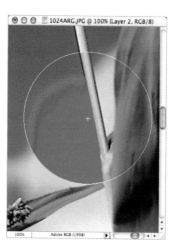

Figure 13.7 The green area was too similar to the background for the Background Eraser to successfully isolate it.

Figure 13.8 Result of sampling a color from the brightest area of the green area and turning on the Protect Foreground Color check box.

Sampling

If you find yourself getting frustrated because Photoshop is forcing you to be overly precise with your mousing, and you can see yourself going gray and toothless before you're done, then you'll want to mess with the choices found under the Sampling pop-up menu. With this menu set to Continuous, Photoshop will constantly keep an eye on the color that appears under the crosshair as you're moving your mouse (**Figures 13.9** and **13.10**). That's the default setting, and it works great with images that have multi-colored backgrounds. If you have a background that doesn't vary in color much, however, you might want to try using the Once setting. With that setting, Photoshop will pay attention to only the color under the crosshair at the exact moment that you click the mouse button. It won't stray from that color. That allows you to click on the background and then paint back and forth across your image without having to constantly pay attention to what's under the crosshair (**Figure 13.11**). Just make sure that you don't drag across any areas of the subject that are very similar to the background color. I mainly use this option on simple images that have a pretty big difference between the subject and background (like a dark tree against an almost solid blue sky). The last option in the Sampling menu is Background Swatch, which is useful on those rare occasions when you can't find an easily clickable area of background color. I often use that option after I've attempted to remove the background on an image using other tools, and then I notice a slight halo around the edge of my object (**Figure 13.12**). The halo is often too thin to target with this tool. Instead, you can click on the background color in the Color Picker, choose a color that is visually similar to the halo you are trying to remove, and then experiment with the Tolerance setting until you're able to remove it.

Figure 13.9 Original image. (©2003 Stockbyte, www.stockbyte.com)

Figure 13.10 Result of using the Continuous option.

Figure 13.11 Result of using the Once option.

411

Figure 13.12 This image is divided into two halves. The left side shows what the image looked like after attempting to remove the background; the right side shows what it looked like after using the Background Swatch setting with a cyanish-blue background color.

Limits

With default settings, the Background Eraser tool will delete only those areas that actually touch the crosshair. It won't be able to jump across one area that shouldn't be deleted to find another area similar to the one being deleted. That can cause problems when you're working with images of trees, fences, or other objects that break the background into multiple disconnected regions (**Figure 13.13**). You can change that behavior by changing the Limits menu from Contiguous (meaning only touching the crosshair) to Discontiguous, which will allow it to delete the color that's under the crosshair from the entire circle, even if something like a tree branch isolates an area so it doesn't touch the crosshair (**Figure 13.14**).

Figure 13.13 Result of using the Contiguous option. (©2003 Stockbyte, www.stockbyte.com)

Figure 13.14 Result of using the Discontiguous option.

You'll also find an option in the Limits menu called Find Edges, which works similarly to the Contiguous setting but tries to prevent the subject from fading out into the background and becoming semi-transparent. So, if you ever notice that part of the subject is becoming semi-transparent (**Figure 13.15**), choose Undo and try working on that area a second time using the Find Edges setting (**Figure 13.16**).

Figure 13.15 Result of using the Contiguous option. (©2003 Stockbyte, www.stockbyte.com)

Figure 13.16 Result of using the Find Edges option.

Tips and Tweaks

Now that you've seen all the options that go along with the Background Eraser, let's look at a few things that can help you get better results. When I first started to use this tool, I was very impressed with the results; later, however, I discovered that I wasn't really seeing the whole story. You see, the checkerboard that shows up under your image to indicate an area has been deleted makes it difficult to find the more finely detailed problem areas—it just makes the overall result look good (**Figure 13.17**).

To really see what you're getting, Command-click (Mac) or Ctrl-click (Windows) on the New Layer icon at the bottom of the Layers palette to create a new layer below the currently active layer. Next, change your foreground color to something that contrasts with your image (like a vivid orange color), and then press Option-Delete (Mac) or Alt-Backspace (Windows) to fill the active layer with your foreground color (**Figure 13.18**). After doing that, you should be able to see any residue that the Background Eraser tool left behind (**Figure 13.19**). Just remember to click on the layer that contains the image you were working with so you don't start deleting this solid-colored layer when you get back to using the Background Eraser.

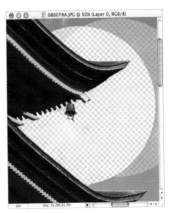

Figure 13.17 The checkerboard background disguises most problems. (© 2003 Stockbyte, www.stockbyte.com)

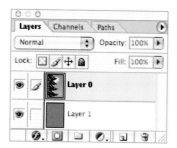

Figure 13.18 Fill a layer with a solid color and place it below your image to reveal any problem areas.

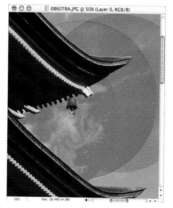

Figure 13.19 Adding a layer full of a solid color reveals problem areas.

Figure 13.22 A Wacom pressure-sensitive graphics tablet makes the Background Eraser tool much more versatile.

You'll want to stay away from hard-edged brushes when you're working with an object that has a slightly soft edge. Hard-edged brushes often produce a series of circles that can make the edge of your image resemble a pearl necklace (**Figure 13.20**). When you switch to a soft-edged brush, the edge of the area you are working on should be nice and smooth (**Figure 13.21**).

Figure 13.20 Using a hard-edged brush produces abrupt transitions in soft-edged objects. (©2003 Stockbyte, www.stockbyte.com)

Figure 13.21 Using a soft-edged brush produces an acceptable transition on soft-edged objects.

For the ultimate in control, consider getting a Wacom pressure-sensitive graphics tablet (**Figure 13.22**). When using a tablet, you can click on the brush preview that shows up in the options bar at the top of your screen and set the Size or Tolerance setting to Pen Pressure. That will vary either the size of your brush or the Tolerance setting based on how hard you press with the pen. I like to use the Tolerance setting because then I can press lightly where there is a slight difference between the subject and background and press harder where there is a more pronounced difference. That allows me to trace around the entire edge of an object in a single stroke, which can save quite a bit of time.

The Extract Filter

When you choose Filter > Extract, a huge dialog box will pretty much take over your screen (**Figure 13.23**). This is command central for removing the backgrounds on soft-edged objects and for objects in motion. Before we start working with the tools in the Extract dialog box, let me give you an overview of what's needed to successfully

Figure 13.23 The Extract dialog box offers a multitude of features designed for removing the background on complex images. (©2003 Stockbyte, www.stockbyte.com)

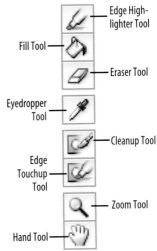

Figure 13.24 The Extract command's tools.

Edge Highlighter Tool
Fill Tool
Eraser Tool
Eyedropper Tool
Cleanup Tool
Edge Touchup Tool
Zoom Tool
Hand Tool

extract an image from its background. Extract needs three pieces of information: which areas should be thrown away, which areas should be kept, and which areas contain the transition between the first two areas (including semi-transparent areas).

The general idea is to use the Edge Highlighter tool (**Figure 13.24**) to define the boundary between subject and background (it shows up as a green overlay) (**Figure 13.25**), and then to click with the Fill tool (which looks like a paint bucket) to fill whichever side of that boundary you'd like to keep (it shows up as a blue overlay) (**Figure 13.26**). The only thing that prevents the Fill tool from filling the entire image is the green highlighting. That makes it important to create a continuous outline around the subject of the photo with no breaks in it. When you preview the extraction, Photoshop will throw away the areas that don't have any color on top of them and keep the areas that are covered with blue. It will also figure out what to do in the transition areas that are covered with green by comparing that area to the keep and throw-away areas (**Figure 13.27**).

Figure 13.25 The green highlighting defines the transition from subject to background.

Figure 13.26 The blue fill defines the area you'd like to keep.

Figure 13.27 Previewing the extraction shows you what Photoshop is planning on keeping and throwing away.

Figure 13.28 Try not to leave a gap between the highlighting and the subject, like I did on the top portion of this image. It's better to have a slight overlap on the subject of the photo, like I did at the bottom of this image.

Figure 13.29 The bottom portion of this image was highlighted using the Smart Highlighting option, whereas the top portion was not.

Start with the Highlighter

Go ahead and grab an image of someone with flyaway hair; if you don't have one, you're welcome to grab the image I'm working on from the CD at the back of the book. You'll find it in the folder called Practice Images. Just go to the Chapter 13 folder and look for a file called Flyaway Hair.tif. Now with your image open, choose Filter > Extract. Next, take a glance at the tools in the upper left of the dialog box; the Highlighter tool is active by default, and that's where we need to start.

Before you start tracing around the edge of your image, you should know that any areas that you cover with the Highlighter have the potential of being deleted. All other areas will either be kept or thrown away. This means that your highlighting needs to overlap both the subject and the background; otherwise, you won't get a good transition. It also means that if you're going to be sloppy, it's best to overspray onto the background because that area will be deleted anyway. In fact, it's good to have a little overspray on the subject; otherwise, you'll end up leaving a tiny one-pixel rim of the background between your highlighting and the subject of the image (**Figure 13.28**). That tiny rim will confuse the Extract command, making it think that things similar to that rim should be kept instead of deleted.

Change the size of your brush based on how far the edge of the subject fades. Areas that gradually fade out (like blurry edges) will need a wider highlight than crisp-edged areas. If you run across an area that has a very crisp edge with no fuzzy or partially transparent areas, then you'll want to turn on the Smart Highlighting check box. With that option turned on, Photoshop will attempt to find the edge within your cursor and put minimal highlighting on it (**Figure 13.29**). That will prevent the area from having a soft edge. Just be sure that option is turned off when working on areas that have very soft or complex edges. So, go forth and highlight the entire edge of the subject to show Photoshop which areas of the image contain a combination of background and subject.

After you've defined the boundary between subject and background, you'll need to check for parts of the subject that extend beyond the edge of the highlighted area. Anything beyond the edge of the highlighting will be deleted, so if you find any of the subject (like wisps of hair) out there, go cover it up with highlighting (**Figure 13.30**). Then you'll need to make one last highlighting pass, this time looking on the other side of the highlighting for any hint of the background (**Figure 13.31**). Because that side will eventually be filled (defining it as an area that should be kept), hints of the background in that area will cause remnants of the background to remain after the extraction. Remember: The highlighting should overlap the subject of the photo—you just don't want huge amounts of highlighting on the areas you want to keep.

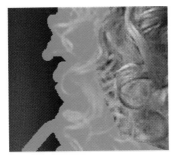

Figure 13.30 These wisps of hair need to be covered with highlighting; otherwise, they will be deleted and might confuse Photoshop as to what should be deleted in the rest of the image.

Figure 13.31 The small black areas within the hair are actually parts of the background, so they should be covered by highlighting; otherwise, they will be kept.

When you're painting with the highlighter, you can change the Brush Size setting by pressing the bracket keys (] [). If it's taking you too long to highlight the entire edge of the object, try holding the Shift key and clicking in multiple areas (don't drag). Photoshop will connect the "dots" with straight lines, which can really speed things up. You can also hold the Option key (Mac) or Alt key (Windows) to temporarily transform the Highlighter into an eraser so you can remove overspray from your image. Also, if you're working on a green object and you find that the green highlighting is too hard to see, you can choose a different color from the Highlight pop-up menu in the upper right of your screen.

Fill with the Paint Bucket Tool

Once you've finished highlighting the edge of the image (**Figure 13.32**), choose the Fill tool and click in the middle of the subject of your photo. When you do that, the Fill tool will completely ignore the photograph you are working on and instead use the highlighting to determine which area should be filled (**Figure 13.33**). If, after clicking once with the Fill tool, the entire subject is not covered in blue, click on additional areas of the subject that aren't yet covered. If you find that the entire image (minus the highlighting) is covered with blue, that means that your highlighting didn't make it all the way around the subject of the photograph, so go touch up the highlighting and then try to fill the subject again.

Figure 13.32 Make sure your highlighting makes a continuous line around the edge of the subject with no breaks.

Keeping in mind that all areas that are covered with the blue fill will not be deleted, take a quick look to make sure no part of the background you are looking to delete is covered in blue. If you've messed up, then fine-tune your highlighting and refill the subject. If you find the blue fill is too difficult to see, you are welcome to choose another color from the Fill pop-up menu in the upper right of the dialog box. If you think that you have everything set up correctly, then click the Preview button to see what your extraction will look like.

Figure 13.33 Click on the area of the image you'd like to keep with the Fill tool.

If the subject of the photo is quite similar to the background, but they differ in texture, then try turning on the Textured Image check box. With that option turned on, Photoshop will look for differences in both color and texture between the subject and background areas, which can produce a much better result (**Figures 13.34** to **13.36**).

Figure 13.34 The original image. (© 2003 Stockbyte, www.stockbyte.com)

Figure 13.35 The result of extracting an image with the Textured Image check box turned off.

Figure 13.36 The Textured Image check box can help to differentiate between textured and nontextured areas.

Most of the time, the preview will look rather promising, but that can be deceptive because the checkerboard behind your image can hide a lot of problems. I find it much more effective to replace the checkerboard with a solid color that contrasts with the subject. You can do this by choosing Other from the Display pop-up menu in the lower right of the dialog box.

Zoom In and Fine Tune

Now it's time to use the Zoom tool to check things up close. Just remember that any area that's covered with the blue fill will not be deleted. So, scroll around your image and look for remnants of the old background (**Figure 13.37**). If you find any, then turn on the Show Fill check box and see if they become covered with blue. If they are, grab the Highlighter tool and cover up those areas.

If the area is not covered with blue fill, then you most likely have an area with way too much highlighting (**Figure 13.38**). When that happens, Photoshop gets confused because it doesn't have enough information about what should be kept or thrown away. You're simply giving it too large of an area to do a good job with. When that's the case, grab the Eraser tool and use a tiny brush to poke holes in the highlighting in areas where you see hints of the background (**Figures 13.39 and 13.40**). Anytime you use the Highlighter tool, the fill will disappear, so you'll need to use the Fill tool to refill the subject area and then repreview the extraction.

Figure 13.37 Replacing the checkerboard with a solid color will often reveal problem areas.

Figure 13.38 This area has way too much highlighting for Photoshop to know the difference between the hair and the bright area of the background.

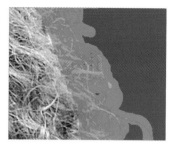

Figure 13.39 Use the Eraser tool and a small brush to poke holes in the highlighting to uncover parts of the background.

Figure 13.40 After modifying the highlighting, Photoshop is able to do a much better job of isolating the subject, but we'll need to refine the result later.

After you've made sure that none of the background is visible, then switch gears and look for areas of the subject that might have been unintentionally deleted. You can do that by toggling back and forth between the Extracted and Original choices in the Show pop-up menu. If it looks like areas of the subject were deleted, choose Original from the Show pop-up menu. Turn on the Show Highlight and Show Fill check boxes, and then search around your image for areas that contain the hints of the subject that aren't covered with highlight or fill. Remember: Areas that do not have any color on them (either highlight or fill) will be deleted. So grab the Highlighter tool and cover up all those areas of the subject that don't have color on top of them. Now you'll need to refill the subject and repreview the image.

If just a tiny bit of the background is visible after previewing, and most of the subject is intact, start experimenting with the Smooth setting. As you raise the Smooth setting, the transition between the subject and the area that's been extracted should become softer (**Figures 13.41** and **13.42**). To see the effect of changing the Smooth setting, you'll need to repreview the image.

Figure 13.41 This image was extracted using a Smooth setting of 0.

Figure 13.42 This image was extracted using a Smooth setting of 100. The difference is subtle and more noticeable on-screen.

Clean It Up

At this point, you can still refine the result, but let's get away from the Highlighter and Fill tools and take a look at the Cleanup and Edge Touchup tools. You can drag across your image using the Cleanup tool to slowly lower the opacity of an area. This can be useful when attempting to rid your image of specks that don't quite touch the subject of the photograph. Or, if you hold down the Option key (Mac) or Alt key (Windows), the Cleanup tool will increase the opacity of an area, which will allow you to bring back areas that should not have been deleted (**Figures 13.43** and **13.44**). Then, to make the edge crisper, use the Edge Touchup tool. If you hold the Command key (Mac) or Ctrl key (Windows), a crosshair will appear in the center of your cursor. Move the crosshair to the place where the subject of the photo should end, and Photoshop will create a crisp edge in that position. That can be useful when Photoshop leaves too much leftover information near the edge of your image.

WARNING

When you're playing with the highlight and fill, you might be tempted to click OK to see how the image would look with the rest of the layers in your image—don't do it! If you click OK and then try to return to the Extract dialog box, you'll have to start over from scratch because the feature will not remember where your highlight was. So, make sure the edge of the object looks right before clicking OK.

Figure 13.43 Areas of the hair have been deleted.

Figure 13.44 Areas were brought back by painting across the image with the Cleanup tool while the Option or Alt key was held.

Use Force Foreground for Intricate Images

If the subject of your photo is too small or intricate to trace around and leave space for the fill in the middle (**Figure 13.45**), then cover the entire subject with the Highlighter tool (**Figure 13.46**). When it comes time to define the fill, turn on the Force Foreground check box and click on the color of the subject using the Eyedropper tool. (The Fill tool will become grayed out.) That will make Photoshop look through the entire highlight area and attempt to keep things that are similar to the color you clicked on with the Eyedropper (**Figure 13.47**).

I like to use the Force Foreground option to remove the background from translucent objects like glass or plastic bottles (**Figure 13.48**). The main thing that makes a bottle show up is its highlights. So, to remove the background from a bottle, cover the translucent areas of the bottle with the Highlighter tool (**Figure 13.49**), turn on the Force Foreground check box, and then use the Eyedropper tool to click on the brightest highlight on the bottle. That will get Photoshop to look for the brightest areas within the highlighted area, which should deliver the bottle without the background (**Figure 13.50**).

Figure 13.45 Thin objects are too small to leave room for a fill. (©2003 Stockbyte, www.stockbyte.com)

Figure 13.46 Cover the entire subject with the Highlighter tool.

Figure 13.47 Result of using the Force Foreground check box after clicking on the darkest area of the highlighted area with the Eyedropper tool.

Figure 13.48 A translucent object is mainly defined by its highlights. (©2003 Stockbyte, www.stockbyte.com)

Figure 13.49 Cover the entire subject with highlighting. In this case, I also covered the lid of the jar because it was the same color as the subject, which can confuse Photoshop about what should be kept and deleted.

Figure 13.50 Result of extracting the jar using the Force Foreground setting.

Once you click OK and exit the Extract dialog box, Photo-shop will truly delete the background—as opposed to just selecting it—and will clean up any hint of the old background from the edge.

Using Extract to Make a Selection

If you'd rather get a selection out of the Extract command, then Command-click (Mac) or Ctrl-click (Windows) on the layer (after extracting it from its background), and choose Select > Save Selection. Next, choose Select > Deselect, and then View > History, and click in the indent to the left of the step listed before the Extract command (**Figure 13.51**). Finally, choose Edit > Fill and choose History from the Use pop-up menu. Now you should have the original image back, as well as a saved selection that you can retrieve at any time by choosing Select > Load Selection.

Figure 13.51 Click to the left of the step listed before the Extract command.

The Blending Sliders

Don't let this ho-hum name fool you. When it comes to advanced masking, this feature is like the sleepy-eyed pitcher with the secret curve ball that can win the game. You'll definitely want to give this baby a test drive. The Blending sliders are found by choosing Layer > Layer Style > Blending Options, or by double-clicking in the empty area on a layer in the Layers palette to the right of its name. We'll talk about these sliders in more detail in Chapter 16, "Collage," so for now we're going to limit our discussion to the top set of sliders, the ones labeled "This Layer" (**Figure 13.52**). These sliders allow you to show or hide part of a layer based on its brightness. I find them to be very useful when the subject of a photograph is radically brighter (such as lightning or fireworks) or darker (such as text) than the background. The Blending sliders are available on any layer other than the background image. If you need to apply them to the background, double-click on the background and change its name first.

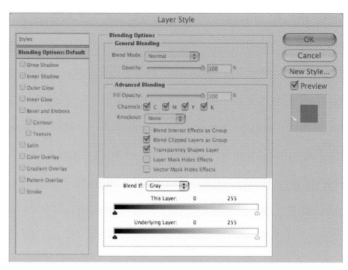

Figure 13.52 The Blending sliders are found at the bottom of the Blending Options dialog box.

Figure 13.53 The subject of this photo is much brighter than the background, which makes it an ideal candidate for the Blending sliders. (©2003 Stockbyte, www.stockbyte.com)

Figure 13.54 Hiding the dark areas has caused the background to disappear.

If you have a subject that is brighter than the background (**Figure 13.53**), then you'll want to slide the upper-left slider toward the middle until every hint of the background disappears from view (**Figure 13.54**). Then, to control the edge quality (how soft or hard it is), hold the Option key (Mac) or Alt key (Windows) and pull on the left edge of the slider you adjusted a minute ago (**Figure 13.55**). That will cause the brightness levels that are just a little darker than the subject to start to show up as partially transparent areas, which should produce a softer edge (**Figure 13.56**). If the subject is darker than the background, then you'll want to move the upper-right slider toward the middle to hide the background. Then Option-drag (Mac) or Alt-drag (Windows) the right edge of the slider to control the transition from visible areas to hidden areas.

If you have an image in which the background or subject happens to be predominantly a single color that is not found in the surrounding area (**Figure 13.57**), then you might be able to use the Blending If pop-up menu to help isolate it from its surroundings. You'll first need to open the Channels palette (Window > Channels), and then click through all the channels (they show up as grayscale images) to find which one shows the most contrast between the subject and background (**Figure 13.58**). Once you've found the right channel, take note of it, and then click on the top-most channel to get back to your full-color image. Now go to the Blending sliders, choose the name of that channel from the Blend If pop-up menu, and pull in the left or right slider (depending on if the background in that channel was dark or bright) until the background disappears (**Figures 13.59** and **13.60**).

Figure 13.55 Option/Alt-drag the edge of a slider to split it into two halves and create a more gradual transition between visible and hidden areas.

Figure 13.56 This is the end result of splitting the sliders. You'll have to look very closely, but you should notice more partially transparent areas.

Figure 13.57 The Blending sliders can be very useful when the subject of a photo is a color that is not contained in the rest of the image. (©2003 Stockbyte, www.stockbyte.com)

Figure 13.58 Click through the channels to figure out which choice to make in the Blending Options dialog box.

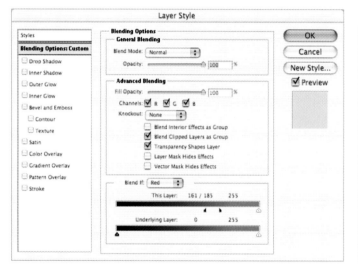

Figure 13.59 Choose the name of the channel that had the most contrast between subject and background from the Blend If pop-up menu.

Figure 13.60 The end result of applying the sliders shown in Figure 13.59.

Unlike the Extract command and the Background Eraser, which truly delete the background of your image, the Blending sliders temporarily hide areas. You can go back to the sliders and move them to their default locations to bring back the areas that were being hidden by the sliders. To permanently delete the hidden areas, do the following: Command-click (Mac) or Ctrl-click (Windows) the New Layer icon at the bottom of the Layers palette to create a new layer below the one that has the sliders applied. Click on the layer above the one you just created to make the slider-applied layer active. Finally, choose Layer > Merge Down, and the slider-applied layer will combine with the empty layer. Because the underlying layer didn't have the sliders applied, Photoshop will be forced to retain the look of the slider-applied layer without actually using the sliders.

Channels

In the ancient days of Photoshop (that would be five or six years ago), you were almost forced to use channels to isolate complex images from their backgrounds. These days, I mainly use them with simpler images, especially when I'm working with an illustration instead of a photographic image. When that's the case, I often convert the image into spot colors so that each color in the image prints with a different color of ink (instead of printing with standard CMYK inks). We covered much of this back in the Channels palette, but in this chapter, because we're learning how to isolate objects, it's useful to look at channels from a different angle and see how to use the Channels palette to isolate each color within an image. This might seem cumbersome at first, but stick with me and I think you'll see the value of this approach. If you want to follow along with my example (**Figure 13.61**), grab the image called potato Chips.tif from the CD at the back of the book. You'll find it in Chapter 13 of the folder called Practice Images.

Let's say you have a logo or graphic that you'd like to reproduce on a commercial printing press using red, blue, and yellow ink. I'd look at the original and decide which areas will use each ink and if any areas need a combination of more than one ink. In the example we're using here, it's rather obvious which areas should use red and blue ink, but I'd like to use a combination of yellow and red to make up the potato chips. Then, to determine which channels we'll need to work with, click through all the channels in the Channels palette and look for good contrast between the color we're attempting to isolate and whatever surrounds it (**Figure 13.62**). In our example, we'll use the red channel to isolate the blue areas, the blue channel to isolate the red areas, and a combination of the red and blue channels for the potato chips.

Figure 13.61 I'll be working with this image of a bag of potato chips. (© 2003 PhotoSpin, www.photospin.com)

WARNING

If you followed the techniques we talked about in Chapter 9, "Color Correction," then the eyedroppers will need to be reset to their default settings. To do that, double-click on the white eyedropper and change the RGB numbers to 255, 255, 255. Then double-click on the black eyedropper and change the RGB numbers to 0, 0, 0.

Figure 13.62 From left to right: the red channel, the green channel, the blue channel.

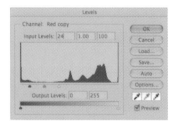

Figure 13.63 Use the eyedroppers that show up in the lower right of the Levels dialog box.

To isolate the blues in this image, drag the red channel to the New Channel icon at the bottom of the Channels palette. (It looks like a sheet of paper with the corner folded over.) Then, isolate the area that should print with blue ink by making it black, while the surrounding areas should end up white to indicate that no blue ink should be used. To accomplish that, choose Image > Adjustments > Levels, and then work with the eyedroppers that show up in the lower right of the dialog box (**Figure 13.63**).

Now click on the black eyedropper, and then click on the darkest area that should print with blue ink. That will force the area you click on to black. Then, before you click OK in the Levels dialog box, click on the white eyedropper and then click on the darkest area of the image that should not print with blue ink to force it to white (**Figure 13.64**). That should do most of the work needed to isolate the blues in the image. If you find any residue left over, just use the Eraser tool to clean it up. Set up this channel to print with blue ink by double-clicking just to the right of the channel's name in the Channels palette (which will bring up the Channel Options dialog box). Click Spot Color and choose the color you'd like to use (**Figure 13.65**), just like I detailed in Chapter 12, "Channels." (I used PMS 2748, which is 8R, 32G, 120B.)

Figure 13.64 Result of forcing areas to white.

Duplicate the blue channel and use the Levels dialog box once again to isolate the reds in the image. This will force the areas that should print with red ink to black and the areas that shouldn't be red to become white (**Figure 13.66**). You don't have to get every non-red area to become white; just get as much of those areas to be white as you can without sacrificing how dark the red areas look. In this case, you might need to manually select a few areas and fill them with white to get rid of the potato chips in the image (**Figure 13.67**). Once you have all the red areas isolated, double-click on the channel and choose the spot color you'd like to use in that area. (I used PMS 1805, which is 151R, 40G, 46B.)

The potato chips blend in with the surrounding image in each channel (no good isolation possible), so you'll have to manually select those areas with the Lasso tool. Then, to get that information into a channel that prints with yellow ink, duplicate the blue channel, choose Select > Inverse, and then press Delete (Mac) or Backspace (Windows) (assuming your background color is white) (**Figure 13.68**). Double-click on the channel, set it to Spot Color, and choose a yellow color. (I used PMS 141, which is 228R, 199G, 109B.) Because you'll need to use a lot of yellow ink in the chips, you might need to choose Select > Deselect, and then Image > Adjustments > Levels, and bring in the upper-left slider until a good portion of the chips becomes black (**Figure 13.69**). Now you can view your red, blue, and yellow ink image by turning on the eyeballs next to those three channels and turning off the eyeball on the top-most (RGB) channel.

Figure 13.65 Double-click to the right of the channel name to change its options.

Figure 13.66 Result of forcing areas to white.

Figure 13.67 Result of cleaning up the remaining areas.

Figure 13.68 Result of duplicating the blue channel and removing everything but the potato chips.

Figure 13.69 Result of adjusting the chips area with levels.

You can fine-tune the image some more by reselecting the chips (by choosing Select > Reselect from the menu), clicking on the cyan channel, choosing Edit > Copy, pasting the chips into the red channel, and then adjusting the result with levels (**Figure 13.70**). That will put a hint of red in the chips, giving them a warmer feeling. You could also select the white parts of the bag and paste them into the blue ink channel to add some shading to the bag (**Figures 13.71 and 13.72**).

Figure 13.70 Result of adding the chips to the red channel.

Figure 13.71 Result of adding the white and gray areas of the bag to the blue channel.

Figure 13.72 Completed image.

The Pen Tool

The Pen tool, which can be found on the toolbar and looks like the tip of an old-fashioned ink pen, gives you a result that more closely resembles the work of a pair of scissors than anything else we've covered in this chapter. If you're sloppy with it, the result will look very crude. If you take enough time with it, you can end up with a nice, crisp result, but you definitely wouldn't want to use this tool with an object that has a soft or blurry edge.

Figure 13.73 A path is made from many points and directional handles.

The Pen tool can be a bit tricky to learn because it doesn't work like anything else in Photoshop. Instead of creating shapes out of a grid of solid-colored squares (pixels), the Pen tool creates shapes from a collection of points and directional handles (**Figure 13.73**). If you've used Adobe

Illustrator, then you might be familiar with paths, but just in case you're not, let's take a look at how they work. Before we get started creating paths, take a look in the options bar at the top of your screen (**Figure 13.74**) and make sure the Paths icon is active so you end up making a path instead of a shape layer. The Paths icon is the second from the left of the icons that appear just to the right of the Pen tool icon.

Figure 13.74 The options bar for the Pen tool.

First off, you'll need to think of the shape that you'd like to create as being made of a series of curves and straight lines that connect to one another. Visualize tracing around the shape and looking for transitions where one curve connects with another. That might be in an area where a very tight curve starts to become more gradual, like on some coffee cup handles (**Figure 13.75**). At each of these transitions, you'll want to click with the Pen tool to add a point.

When adding a point, you'll need to click and drag if you are looking to create a smooth curve. If you don't drag, you'll end up with a sharp corner instead of a curve. When you click and drag, you'll add a point and pull a set of directional handles out of that point. The angle of the directional handles determines what direction the path will go in when it leaves that handle, so make sure it points in the direction you want the curve to go in (**Figure 13.76**). Think of it as if you were walking around the edge of the shape using baby steps. What direction would you take for your first step? That's the same direction the directional handle should point in when entering and exiting a point. When you first pull out a set of handles, they will both move at the same time and act a bit like a seesaw in that their angles will create a straight line that goes all the way through the point.

The lengths of the directional handles determine the overall shape of the curve (**Figure 13.77**). Getting the length of the handles to be just right is difficult because the curve won't show up until the next handle is made, and its handles will also influence the shape of the curve—so for now, keep your handles short.

Figure 13.75 The curve of the handle changes from a tight curve to a more gradual one right where a point would be needed. (©2003 Stockbyte, www.stockbyte.com)

431

Figure 13.76 Click and drag to create a smooth curve.

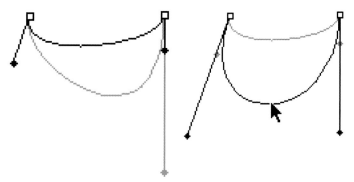

Figure 13.77 The length of the directional handles determines the overall shape of the curve.

Figure 13.78 Hold Command or Ctrl and drag the curve to adjust the length of the directional handles.

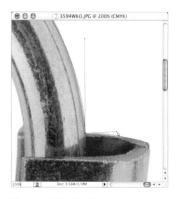

Figure 13.79 Hold Option or Alt to change the angle of one directional handle without affecting the other handle connected to that point. (©2003 Stockbyte, www.stockbyte.com)

Once you've added the next point and have gotten the angle of the handle that points toward the last point positioned correctly, it'll be time to adjust the length of the handles. I find it easiest to adjust the handle lengths by holding the Command key (Mac) or Ctrl key (Windows) and dragging the middle of the curve that appears between the two points you just created (**Figure 13.78**). It's a little troublesome at first, but by pulling on the middle of the curve, you should be able to get the curve to fit the shape you were attempting to create. If you find that you just can't get it to the shape you want, then one of the directional handles must be pointing in the wrong direction. If you continue to hold down the Command key (Mac) or Ctrl key (Windows), then you will be able to reposition the directional handles as well.

On occasion, you'll find that you need one curve to abruptly change direction instead of smoothly flowing into another curve. When that happens, remember that the directional handles determine which direction your path will go in when it leaves a point. That means you'll need the two handles that come out of a point to be at radically different angles. You can accomplish that by holding the Option key (Mac) or Alt key (Windows) and dragging one of the handles that protrude from the point you just created (**Figure 13.79**).

Sometimes you will need to have a curve end at an abrupt corner, where the next portion of the shape will be a straight line. In that case, you'll need a handle on the side of the point that points toward the curve, and no handle on the side of the straight line. To accomplish that, right after adding the point and pulling out the handles, Option-click (Mac) or Alt-click (Windows) the point, and Photoshop will retract the handle on the open end of the path (**Figure 13.80**).

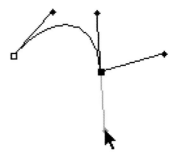

By combining these ideas, you should be able to create just about any smooth shape you can think of. But because it's not an overly natural process, it might take you a while to master using the Pen tool. Once you've got a path, you can drag it to the selection icon (third icon from the left) at the bottom of the Paths palette (Window > Paths) to turn it into a selection.

Figure 13.80 A curve ending in an abrupt corner.

Layer Masks

Now that you've seen how Photoshop's masking features work, let's take a look at how we can refine the results using a Layer Mask. A Layer Mask will hide areas of the image instead of permanently deleting them. That will allow us to fix areas that didn't quite look right and to modify the edge quality of the image. But before we can play with a Layer Mask, we'll need to convert the results we got with the masking tools into a Layer Mask so that the areas that have been deleted will instead be hidden in such a way that you can easily bring them back into view.

So, with the image that you've already isolated using one of the other masking tools, you'll first need to Command-click (Mac) or Ctrl-click (Windows) in the Layers palette on the layer you removed the background from. That will give you a selection of the visible areas of the layer (**Figure 13.81**). To use that selection as the basis for a Layer Mask, click the Layer Mask icon at the bottom of the Layers palette. (It's the second from the left icon.) Now take a look at the currently active layer in the Layers palette (**Figure 13.82**). You should see two thumbnail preview images for that layer: one of the actual layer contents and a second that's full of black wherever the layer is transparent, and white where the layer contains information. That second layer is the Layer thumbnail. Black hides layers in a Layer Mask, whereas white lets an area show up.

NOTES

Now that you know how to use the Pen tool, be sure to read Chapter 16, "Collage," to find out how to turn a path into a Vector mask.

If you used the Blending sliders to hide the background, be sure to convert the result into a permanent deletion (as described in that section of this chapter) *before* attempting to convert it into a Layer Mask.

If you'd like to know more about the general concept of working with Layer Masks, be sure to check out Chapter 16.

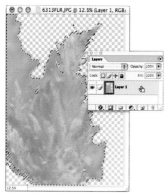

Figure 13.81 Command- or Ctrl-click on the layer to get a selection based on its contents.

Figure 13.82 After adding a Layer Mask, you'll find two thumbnail preview images for that layer.

Figure 13.83 Option- or Alt-click on the Layer Mask thumbnail preview image in the Layers palette to view the mask within the document window.

Now all we have to do is bring back the areas of the image that have been deleted, and then the Layer Mask will be the only thing preventing those areas from being visible. In the Layers palette, click the left thumbnail preview icon to make the image active instead of the Layer Mask (a double border indicates what's active), and then choose Edit > Fill. In the Fill dialog box, set the Use pop-up menu to History, set the Opacity to 100% and the Mode menu to Normal, and then click OK. Now, to double-check that everything worked as planned, hold down the Shift key and click in the middle of the Layer Mask thumbnail preview image in the Layers palette. That should cause the background of your image to become visible again. If that's the case, then Shift-click it again; if the background doesn't become visible, choose Window > History, click in the empty space to the left of the step just above the one that references the masking technique you used to remove the background, and then try using Edit > Fill again. Bear in mind that the "history" feature works only while you are in the same session of Photoshop. If you close out your file and reopen it, the history (that is, the old background) will no longer be available.

Now that the Layer Mask is the only thing causing the background to be hidden, we can refine the result in a multitude of ways. But before we start, be sure to click in the middle of the Layer Mask thumbnail preview image in the Layers palette to make it active. (A double border should appear around it in the Layers palette.) If you'd like to hide additional parts of your image, choose the Paintbrush tool and paint with black. To bring areas back into view, paint with white instead.

You can Option-click (Mac) or Alt-click (Windows) the Layer Mask preview thumbnail image in the Layers palette to view the Layer Mask on the main screen (**Figure 13.83**). Look for black areas that contain specks of white or gray (**Figure 13.84**). That's where the image hasn't been completely hidden. You might need to paint over those areas with black to force those parts of the image to become hidden. If you see a bunch of gray areas that shouldn't be visible, try choosing Image > Adjustments > Levels, and move in the upper-left slider until those gray areas turn solid black (**Figure 13.85**). Or, if you see a bunch of tiny white specks, choose Filter > Noise > Despeckle. If that doesn't get rid of them, then try Filter > Noise > Median, and use the lowest setting that rids your image of the specks. After cleaning up the obvious problem areas, Option-click (Mac) or Alt-click (Windows) on the Layer Mask preview thumbnail image in the Layers palette to hide the Layer Mask and show the image.

Figure 13.84 The background of this image is full of gray specks.

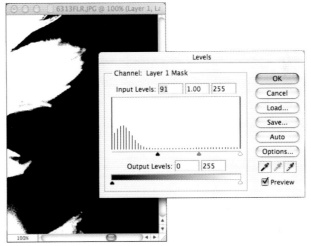

Figure 13.85 After adjusting the layer mask with Levels, the gray specks are gone.

Next, look at areas that have soft edges and make sure that they don't look too noisy (**Figure 13.86**). You can smooth out a noisy transition by painting across an area with the Blur tool. (It looks like a drop of water in the tool palette (**Figure 13.87**.) You can also use the Blur tool if you notice a crisp edge that looks a little jaggy. The Blur tool will soften that edge without making the image itself blurry.

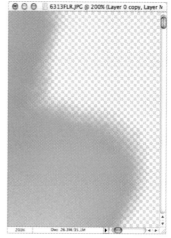

Figure 13.86 This soft-edged transition looks rather noisy.

Figure 13.87 After blurring the Layer Mask, the transition looks much smoother.

If you find a tiny halo of the old background showing up around the edge of an object (**Figure 13.88**), make a general selection that includes that area and then choose Filter > Other > Minimum (**Figure 13.89**). You can also use the Filter > Other > Maximum selection to cause more of the image to show up. (It's the opposite of the Minimum filter.)

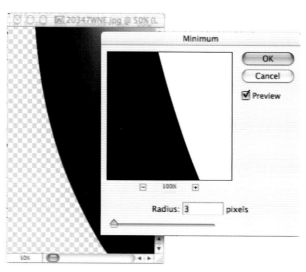

Figure 13.88 If you look closely at the edge of this object, you should be able to see a rim of the old background showing up. (© 2003 Stockbyte, www.stockbyte.com)

Figure 13.89 Applying the Minimum filter can eliminate the rim.

Once you think the image looks good, make one last check by Shift-clicking on the Layer Mask thumbnail preview image in the Layers palette to view the entire image, and then press the \ key to view the mask as a color overlay (**Figure 13.90**). That will allow you to zoom in on the image and look for areas where the color overlay doesn't quite match the edge of the original image. That's when I'd paint or blur the Layer Mask until it matches the edge of the original image. To get back to normal, press \ again to turn off the color overlay, and then Shift-click the Layer Mask preview again to hide the background of the image.

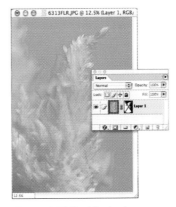

Figure 13.90 Double-check your work by disabling the Layer Mask, and then view it as a red overlay by pressing \.

I also occasionally copy and paste areas of a Layer Mask to fill in other areas that need the right texture. I'll even resort to using Photoshop's funky brushes to produce the right transition on images where none of the masking tools were able to produce the correct edge—like where a white goat's hair was blown out against a backdrop of the sun. (I'd just use the brush that produces something similar to grass.)

If you ever want to permanently delete the background, just drag the Layer Mask thumbnail to the Trash icon at the bottom of the Layers palette. When prompted, choose Apply and you will have permanently deleted the background on the image. To remove the empty space around your image, you can choose Image > Trim and use the Transparent Pixels option. If you later notice a tiny halo around the edge of objects (and don't feel like going back to edit the Layer Mask to remove it), choose Layer > Matting > Defringe, and use a setting of 1, which should remove the halo.

Closing Thoughts

When trying to mask out the background of an image, try to make the process as easy as possible by thinking about the following concepts. Consider making a general selection of the background area and pressing Delete or Backspace before using any of the masking tools. That way you won't waste your time using the finer, surgical tools to delete the big obvious areas that don't require that kind of precision. Then you can let the masking tools concentrate on the difficult edge areas between the subject and background.

Perform color correction on your image before attempting to isolate the subject from the background. Any unwanted colorcasts in the image will cause the subject and background to be more similar in color and contrast, making it more difficult to remove the background.

If the subject and background are rather similar, consider using a temporary adjustment layer to exaggerate the difference between subject and background before attempting to remove the background.

Don't limit yourself to a single technique when removing a background. Instead, think about the strengths of each technique and use it wherever it's appropriate (Extract on hair, Pen on crisp curves, and so on).

If you have any control over the photography, be sure to use a simple background that contrasts with the subject of the photo so it's easy to extract.

Finally, no tool is perfect, and sometimes you have to fall back on manual techniques like painting on Layer Masks or tracing objects with the Lasso tool. We all need to do that on occasion, but the more you know about Photoshop's masking tools, the less you'll have to rely on those cruder selection tools that usually produce less than elegant results.

Ben's Techno-Babble Decoder Ring

Color channel: A grayscale image that represents one of the primary colors an image is made out of (red, green, blue, or cyan, magenta, yellow, black).

Contiguous: An area that is uninterrupted by obstructions that would divide a color or brightness region into multiple independent regions.

Mask: A grayscale image that represents a selection (also known as an alpha channel). White areas indicate selected areas, black areas indicate nonselected areas, and gray areas indicate partially selected areas. A mask can be attached to a layer (then known as a Layer Mask); white areas will cause the layer to be visible, black areas will hide the layer, and gray areas will cause areas to become partially transparent.

Vector data: Any data that is created by the Pen tool or similar tools that create shapes from points, handles, and line segments instead of pixels.

Keyboard Shortcuts

Function	Macintosh	Windows
Cycle through Eraser tools	Shift-E	Shift-E
Extract	Option-Command-X	Alt-Ctrl-X
Pen Tool	P	P
Make Layer Mask Active	Command-\	Ctrl-\
Make Image Active	Command-~	Ctrl-~
While in the Extract Dialog Box:		
Highlighter Tool	B	B
Fill tool	G	G
Eraser tool	E	E
Eyedropper tool	I	I
Cleanup tool	C	C
Edge Cleanup tool	T	T
Zoom tool	Z	Z
Hand tool	H	H

14

Sharpening

Obviously, you failed to detect the subtle diamond pattern in my tie.

—Niles from *Frasier*

Sharpening

This chapter is about those very subtle details that can make the difference between a so-so image and one that pops off the page. Almost all digital images start life looking slightly soft. It's just a fact of life that all of our capture devices (digital cameras, scanners, and so on) can't deliver as much detail as the original image contained. (High-end drum scans are the one exception because they get sharpened during the scanning process.) Only images that are created from scratch in Photoshop or another program (like a 3D rendering application) will be 100% sharp to begin with. And even those images can become soft if you attempt to make the image larger or smaller in Photoshop (known as interpolating the image). Finally, when you output your image to an inkjet printer, printing press, or other output device, you will lose additional detail because most output devices simply are not capable of reproducing the amount of detail you see on-screen. By exaggerating the differences between areas (sharpening), we can attempt to compensate for all the factors that can make an image look soft.

After you learn to properly sharpen your images, you'll find that they look much more crisp when you print them and that they are an obvious improvement over unsharpened scans (**Figures 14.1** and **14.2**). But no matter how much sharpening we apply to an image, it won't compensate for an out-of-focus original, so try to stick with images that aren't overly blurry.

Figure 14.1 A properly sharpened image. (©2003 Ben Willmore)

Figure 14.2 A raw scan looks rather dull compared to one that's been sharpened.

Figure 14.3 Original, unsharpened image. (© 2003 Stockbyte, www.stockbyte.com)

When to Sharpen an Image

Before we get into the process of sharpening, we should talk about a few workflow issues. Sharpening works by exaggerating the differences between objects in your image. It does that by finding the pixels that make up the edge of an object, comparing them, and darkening the darker pixels while lightening the lighter ones (**Figures 14.3** and **14.4**). That makes it easier to see the detail that was already in your image and effectively sharpens the image.

Sharpening can do wonderful things for your image, but it is critical that you apply it at the right stage of your workflow, or it could end up degrading your image instead of improving it. Sharpening introduces tiny halos around the edge of objects, so make sure you apply sharpening in your image *after* it's been scaled to the size at which it will be used for final output. If you were to sharpen the image first and then scale the image up, it would exaggerate the sharpening, whereas scaling the image down would lessen or completely remove the effect of sharpening. If you're working with layers, you should know that the filters we'll be using to sharpen our images work on

Figure 14.4 After sharpening the image, the edges of objects are exaggerated.

Figure 14.5 This original image contains a lot of film grain. (©2003 Stockbyte, www.stockbyte.com)

Figure 14.6 Sharpening the image exaggerates the film grain.

one layer at a time. Because of that, sharpening is usually performed after the layers in the image have been flattened. And if you're working with multiple output devices (inkjet, newspaper, and so on), you should know that each output device is capable of reproducing a unique amount of detail. When that's the case, multiple files should be prepared and each one sharpened with a particular output device in mind. Because of all these factors, I prefer to save and archive a full-size layered image in Photoshop file format (.psd) before scaling or sharpening the image. Then I'll flatten the image, scale it to the proper size and resolution for the output device I have in mind, sharpen it, and save it in a file format appropriate for that particular output device.

Sharpening an image will exaggerate almost all the detail in the image, so any film grain or noise will also get exaggerated when you sharpen an image (**Figures 14.5** and **14.6**). That's fine if you want an image with pronounced grain, but if you'd rather have a smoother look, then you might want to check out my techniques for removing grain/noise from your images.

Removing Film Grain and Scanner/Camera Noise

Four main filters are used to remove noise from your images: Gaussian Blur, Despeckle, Median, and Dust & Scratches. (As I discuss this topic, I'll call film grain *noise* just to simplify matters.) Let's look at these filters one at a time, starting with the least sophisticated and moving to the most advanced. With each filter I describe, I'll show you the results on two images: a simple image that contains different sized black dots that represent noise (**Figure 14.7**) and a normal image (**Figure 14.8**) to show how much the filter trashes the real detail in the image. That way you'll be able to see how effective each filter is at removing noise, while at the same time seeing how much of the detail in your images you'll lose in the process. (You might have to look very closely to see if the fine detail is being lost.)

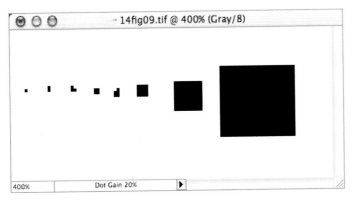

Figure 14.7 This image contains black dots that vary from one pixel in size to over 25 pixels wide.

Figure 14.8 This image represents a normal photo that has slight noise. (©2003 Stockbyte, www.stockbyte.com)

Gaussian Blur

This filter will do the opposite of what we are trying to accomplish when we sharpen an image—it makes the transitions in the image less distinct and therefore renders the image less sharp (**Figures 14.9** and **14.10**). This is a common method used to remove noise; however, just because it's common doesn't mean that I'm going to recommend it. There are much more sophisticated methods that won't trash the general detail in your image.

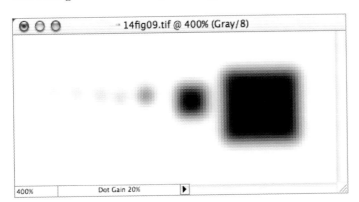

Figure 14.9 A setting of 2.0 Pixels was necessary to blend the smallest dots into the surrounding image.

Figure 14.10 After blurring the image, it looks nowhere near as sharp as the original.

Despeckle

The next few filters we'll explore are found under the Filter > Noise menu. The first choice in that menu is Add Noise, which is designed for adding specks to your image; the rest of the filters listed in that menu are designed for getting rid of noise. The Despeckle filter will blend the tiniest specks into the surrounding image while leaving the major detail in your image untouched (**Figures 14.11** and **14.12**). The only problem with this filter is that it isn't always strong enough to completely remove noise from your image. So, if you get an image with minimal noise, then you might want to give this filter a try; but when the noise in your image is considerable, then try the other options found in the Filter > Noise menu.

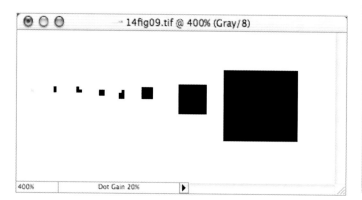

Figure 14.11 After applying the Despeckle filter, the single-pixel speck has changed to a light gray speck. (I doubt you can see it here.)

Figure 14.12 After applying the Despeckle filter to this image, the film grain has started to blend into the surrounding image.

Median

The Median filter uses an interesting approach to rid your image of unwanted noise—it rounds the corners of things, which causes tiny specks to literally implode. As you increase the Amount setting, the filter will round the corners to a larger degree, which will make larger specks in the image blend into the surrounding image (**Figures 14.13** and **14.14**). What's really nice about this filter is that it doesn't make anything look blurry. I don't usually need to use settings above 2 when applying this filter.

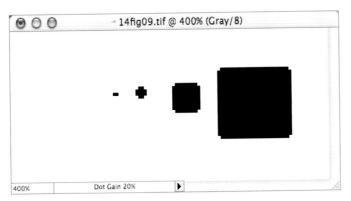

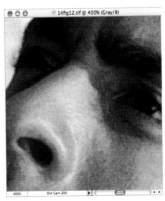

Figure 14.13 Using the Median filter with a Radius of 1 (its lowest setting) effectively removed the small specks.

Figure 14.14 Applying Median to this image caused it to lose some detail, but it didn't get blurry.

Dust & Scratches

The Dust & Scratches filter uses the same technology as the Median filter, but it adds a Threshold setting to determine which shades in your image should be affected by the filter. A setting of zero will allow the filter to apply to the entire image, and will therefore work exactly like the Median filter. Raising the Threshold setting will limit the changes to areas that are similar in brightness. The general idea here is to start with a Threshold of zero so you work on the whole image, and then adjust the Radius setting until the noise in the image is gone. Then, to make sure you lose the absolute minimal amount of true detail, change the Threshold setting to 255 and then use the down arrow key to slowly change that setting until you find the highest number that will rid your image of unwanted noise (**Figures 14.15** and **14.16**).

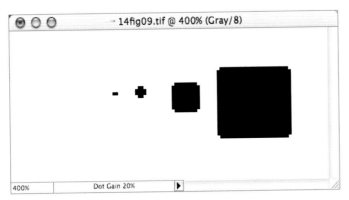

Figure 14.15 Using the Dust & Scratches filter with a Radius of 1 and a Threshold of 16 produced the same result on our specks.

Figure 14.16 Applying the Dust & Scratches filter helped to remove the noise while maintaining more detail than using the Median filter.

Figure 14.17 Click just to the left of the History State that is directly above the one that lists a noise reduction filter.

Reclaiming Detail with the History Brush

You might find that after applying one of the noise reduction filters, the important detail in your image, such as eyes or freckles, has been lost. When that's the case, you can use the History brush right after a noise reduction filter to paint back the desired detail, effectively removing the effect of the filter from the areas you paint across. If the History brush presents you with a "no" symbol (circle with a diagonal line across it), then it means that you've either changed the dimensions of your image or changed the color mode of your image since you've opened it. When that's the case, choose Window > History and click just to the left of the History State that is directly above the one that lists the noise reduction filter you just applied (**Figure 14.17**). Once you've done that, the History brush should work on your image. Just paint across the areas that have lost important detail, and you should see them come back.

Working on a Per-Channel Basis

If your image has very fine detail or considerable noise, then you'll need to take additional steps to make sure that you don't trash too much detail in the image when you're attempting to remove noise. Color images are made out of three (RGB) or four (CMYK) color components, which are known as color channels. It's rather common to find more noise in one of those channels than the others (**Figures 14.18** to **14.20**). When that's the case, you might want to apply the noise removal filters to the individual channels; otherwise, you might end up trashing the detail in most of the channels just to rid one pesky channel of noise (usually the blue or yellow channel). So the next time you're having to be heavy-handed with the Median or Dust & Scratches filter, try clicking through the RGB or CMYK channels to see if the noise shows up more in one channel than another. Treat each channel individually (**Figures 14.21** to **14.24**) and you should end up with a better result than applying the filters to the entire image (**Figures 14.25** to **14.28**). If you're not familiar with channels, I suggest you read Chapter 12, "Channels," before attempting this approach.

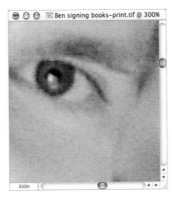

Figure 14.18 The red channel.

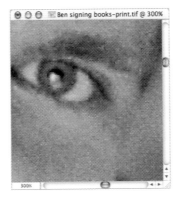

Figure 14.19 The green channel.

Figure 14.20 The blue channel.

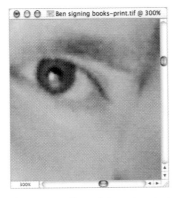

Figure 14.21 The red channel treated separately.

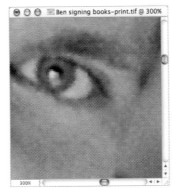

Figure 14.22 The green channel treated separately.

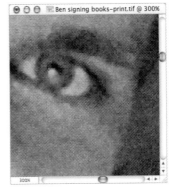

Figure 14.23 The blue channel treated separately.

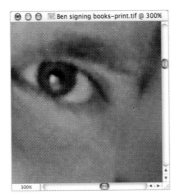

Figure 14.24 The full-color image after each channel is treated separately.

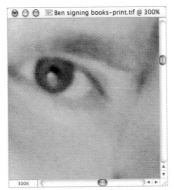

Figure 14.25 The red channel after adjusting all channels at once.

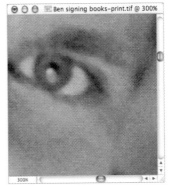

Figure 14.26 The green channel after adjusting all channels at once.

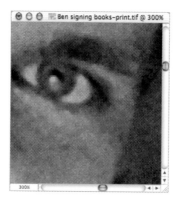

Figure 14.27 The blue channel after adjusting all channels at once.

Figure 14.28 The full-color image after adjusting all channels at once.

Rainbow Noise

You might notice that certain images contain noise that is very colorful, producing specks in an assortment of colors (**Figure 14.29**). When that's the case, apply any of the noise removal filters (even Gaussian Blur will work) with settings high enough to blend the colored specks into the surrounding image. Don't worry if you end up trashing most of the image's detail in the process (**Figure 14.30**). Then immediately after you apply one of those filters, choose Edit > Fade and set the Mode pop-up menu to Color. That will cause the filter you just applied to affect only the *colors* in the image, and therefore not tamper with the brightness of the image. The brightness values are where most of the detail resides, so blurring the color information is often not a very noticeable change to the image, but it's usually enough to change the colorful specks so that they are the same color as the surrounding image, and therefore less noticeable (**Figure 14.31**).

Now that we've figured out how to rid our images of unwanted noise and film grain, let's look at how sharpening is able to exaggerate detail, and then we'll explore the exact steps needed to sharpen any image.

Figure 14.29 The original image contains specks of various colors. (©2003 Ben Willmore)

Figure 14.30 Result of applying the Gaussian Blur filter to blend the color specks into the image.

Figure 14.31 After fading the filter in Color mode, the specks are no longer odd colors.

How Sharpening Works

To sharpen an image, choose Filter > Sharpen. Photoshop will present you with a submenu of choices. The top three might sound friendly (Sharpen, Sharpen More, Sharpen Edges), but ignore those and go straight for the bottom one (Unsharp Mask). It's the only one that allows you to control exactly how much the image will be sharpened. You can think of the other choices as being simple presets that just enter different numbers into the Unsharp Mask filter.

The reason Unsharp Mask has its confusing name is because way back before people used desktop computers, they sharpened images in a photographic darkroom. They would have to go through a process that involved a blurry (unsharp) version of the image. This would take well over an hour (don't worry—in Photoshop it takes only seconds) and would not be much fun. The process they'd go through in the darkroom was known as making an unsharp mask, so Adobe just borrowed that term.

The Unsharp Mask filter increases the contrast where two colors (or shades of gray) touch in the image, making their edges more prominent and therefore easier to see. To easily view the effect of the Unsharp Mask filter (**Figure 14.32**), I'll demonstrate using two documents: one that contains only three shades of gray (20%, 30%, and 50%), and one that is a normal photographic image. With both examples, I'll show a normal-sized image as well as a portion of each image that has been magnified by 800% (**Figures 14.33** and **14.34**). When you choose Unsharp Mask, you'll be presented with three sliders: Amount, Radius, and Threshold.

Figure 14.32 The Unsharp Mask dialog box.

Figure 14.33 This simple document contains only three shades of gray.

Figure 14.34 This will be our photographic reference image. (©2003 Andy Katz)

- ▶ **Amount:** Determines how much contrast will be added to the edges of objects and, therefore, how obvious the sharpening will be (**Figure 14.35**).

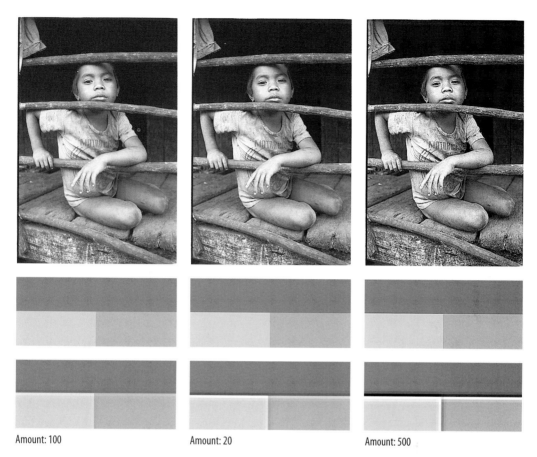

Amount: 100   Amount: 20   Amount: 500

Figure 14.35 The effect of the Amount setting.

▶ **Radius:** Determines how much space will be used for the contrast boost that the Amount setting creates. No matter which settings you use, sharpening will produce a bright halo on one side of the edge of an object and a dark halo on the opposite side of that same edge. If you use too much, you'll be adding a very noticeable glow around the edges of objects instead of a barely noticeable halo (**Figure 14.36**).

Radius: 1   Radius: 2   Radius: 5

Figure 14.36 The effect of the Radius setting.

▶ **Threshold:** Determines how different two touching colors have to be for sharpening to kick in. With Threshold set at 0, everything will get sharpened. As you increase this setting, only the areas that are drastically different will be sharpened (**Figure 14.37**). If the setting is too low, then unwanted artifacts like noise and film grain will be exaggerated and relatively smooth areas might start to show texture. If the setting is too high, then the sharpening will apply to very few areas in the image, which will look too obvious because those areas will not fit in with their surroundings (which didn't get sharpened).

Now that we've explored all the options that are available with the Unsharp Mask filter, let's get down to business and find out how to apply them to an image. But before you start applying the Unsharp Mask filter, double-click on the Zoom tool to view your image at 100% view; otherwise, you won't be able to see the full effect of the sharpening you apply to the image.

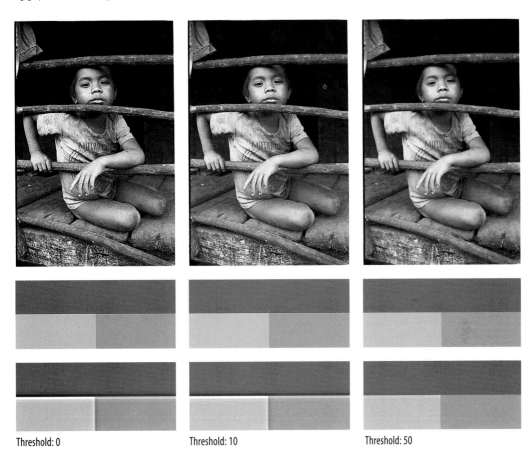

Threshold: 0   Threshold: 10   Threshold: 50

Figure 14.37 The effect of the Threshold setting.

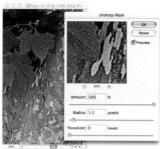

Figure 14.38 Start with the generic settings of 500, 1, and 0. (©2003 Andy Katz)

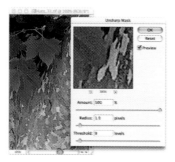

Figure 14.39 Adjust the Threshold setting until smooth areas look smooth.

Sharpening an Image

To sharpen an image, choose Filter > Sharpen > Unsharp Mask and type in the generic numbers of Amount = **500**, Radius = **1**, and Threshold = **0**, just to make sure you can easily see the effect of sharpening the image (**Figure 14.38**). Now, adjust the Threshold setting. With it set to 0, everything in the image will be sharpened. That can cause areas that used to have fine detail (like a brick wall) or areas that used to look relatively smooth (like a skin tone or a shadow) to suddenly have overly exaggerated detail. That will make those bricks look noisy and will add years to anyone's face because you've exaggerated every imperfection. To avoid that, slowly increase the Threshold setting until those areas smooth out (**Figure 14.39**). You'll usually end up using settings in the single digits. Next, experiment with the Radius setting and try to find the highest setting that makes the image look like it's been sharpened without making it look like everything is glowing (**Figures 14.40 and 14.41**) (usually in the range of .5 to 2). Images with very fine detail will look best with lower Radius settings, whereas images that contain little detail or that will be printed large and viewed from a distance will look best with higher Radius settings. Then adjust the Amount setting until the image looks naturally sharp instead of artificial (**Figure 14.42**) (usually in the range of 15 to 200, depending on the Radius setting you used). Let your eyes be your guide. There are two common indicators that the Amount setting is too high.

Figure 14.40 Too high of a Radius setting makes everything look as if it's glowing.

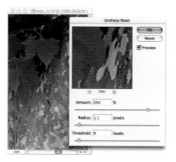

Figure 14.41 Try to find the highest Radius setting that doesn't make objects look like they're glowing.

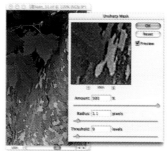

Figure 14.42 Finally, adjust the Amount setting until the image looks realistically sharp.

▶ Obvious bright halos appear around the edge of objects. (There will always be halos; you just want to make sure they aren't very noticeable.)

▶ Very fine detail (like hair, or texture in bricks) will become overly contrasty—almost pure black and pure white.

Figure 14.43 This is a grainy image. (©2003 Andy Katz)

That's how I approach sharpening most images, but sometimes you'll need to take a different approach. The Radius setting can have a radical effect on sharpening. You'll need to achieve a balance between Amount and Radius. High Amount settings (90–250ish) will require low Radius settings (.5–1.5), and low Amount settings (10–30) will require higher Radius settings (5–20). High Amount settings work for most images, and that's why we took the initial approach I just talked about. But if you have a grainy image and you want to maintain but not exaggerate the grain (**Figure 14.43**), you'll need to take a slightly different approach. A grainy image will start to look unusual when you get an Amount setting anywhere near 100 (**Figure 14.44**); you might even need to bring the Amount setting down to near 20 before the grain stops being exaggerated too much. At that point, you'll barely be able to tell that the image has been sharpened (**Figure 14.45**), so to compensate for that, you'll need to get the Radius setting up until the image starts to look sharp (**Figure 14.46**) (maybe up to 15 or so) (**Figures 14.47** and **14.48**). But on most images, you'll find that you'll be able to get away with much higher Amount settings without causing grain problems. In that case, you might end up with an Amount setting around 120, and then you'll need to experiment with the Radius setting to see what looks best (probably between .5 and 1.5).

Figure 14.44 With the Amount setting at 150, the grain is becoming too obvious. (Look very closely to see the difference.)

Figure 14.45 With the Amount setting at 20, you can barely tell the image has been sharpened.

Figure 14.46 Bringing the Radius setting up to 20 makes the sharpening more prominent.

Figure 14.47 This image was sharpened using settings of 150, 1.2, and 3.

Figure 14.48 This image was sharpened using settings of 20, 20, and 3.

The process of sharpening an image is more of an art than a science, so it will take a good bit of practice before you start feeling confident in this area. Everyone has a different idea of how sharp an image should look, and most output devices aren't capable of reproducing the amount of detail you see on-screen. So, if you sharpen the image so it looks great on-screen, then when you print the image, it might still look rather soft. The following are some general thoughts on how to approach sharpening for different types of output:

▶ **Web/Multimedia:** When the final image will be displayed on-screen, you can completely trust your screen when sharpening the image. Most of the time you'll end up with Radius settings between .5 and 1 and Amount settings below 100%. Just be aware that sharpening will increase the file size of JPEG file format images (**Figures 14.49** to **14.51**). So, if you're planning on saving your image as a JPEG file, use the absolute minimum amount of sharpening that makes the image not look soft.

▶ **Photographic output devices:** These devices include film recorders, LightJets, and other devices that use photographic film or paper to reproduce an image. They can reproduce the majority of the detail you see onscreen. With these devices, you have to be very careful to make sure the Radius setting you use is quite low (.25 to .7 for most images) so that the halos that come from sharpening aren't obvious on the end result.

Figure 14.49 Original unsharpened image (File Size: 25.51Kbytes). (©2003 Andy Katz)

Figure 14.50 Sharpened with settings of 70, .5, and 4 (File Size: 28.63Kbytes).

Figure 14.51 Sharpened with settings of 175, .7, and 4 (File Size: 37.51Kbytes).

▶ **Desktop printer:** This would include inkjet and laser printers as well as any other printer that you have immediate access to. I like to experiment with an image that is representative of the type of image you use the most. With your experimental image open, choose File > Automate > Picture Package (**Figure 14.52**). Set the Page Size pop-up menu to the choice that is closest to the size of paper you typically use, and set the resolution to what is best for your particular printer. (See Chapter 4, "Resolution Solutions," if you're not sure which resolution is best for your device.) Now choose a Layout setting that gives you at least four images, and click OK. That will produce a document that contains multiple copies of your experimental image.

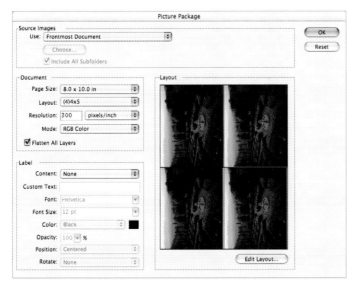

Figure 14.52 Use Picture Package to create multiple copies of an image on a single page.

Select one of the images with the Marquee tool and sharpen it until it looks great on-screen, and make note of the settings you used. Then move to the second image and be a little more aggressive with the Amount or Radius setting. Continue experimenting with more aggressive settings until you've sharpened each image a different amount, and write down the setting you used for each. Now print that image at 100% scale and compare the resulting print to what you see on-screen at 100% view. Look over the printed images and find the one that has the most realistic looking sharpness, and then look at that same image on-screen to see how much you'll need to exaggerate your sharpening in order to achieve that amount of sharpening in the print.

▶ **Commercial printing press:** Start by sharpening your images until they look very sharp on-screen, and then analyze the printed result when you get a job back from the printing company. If the printed result doesn't look too sharp, then slowly ratchet up the Amount and Radius settings on subsequent images until you find that the printed images look very sharp, but still natural. Each time compare the printed result to the original digital file, viewing the image at 100% magnification. As you work on more and more jobs, you'll start to get a feeling for how much you need to overdo the sharpening on-screen to get a nice sharp end result. You'll find that different types of printing will reproduce differing amounts of detail. (Newspaper images need to be sharpened much more than images that will be printed in a glossy brochure.)

If thinking about all the different settings needed for different output devices drives you crazy, then you might want to think about adding a commercial plug-in filter to Photoshop. Nik multimedia (www.nikmultimedia.com) makes a set of plug-in filters known as Nik Sharpener Pro (**Figure 14.53**), which takes a lot of the guesswork out of sharpening your images. The package comes with separate filters for different types of output (including Ink Jet, Color Laser, Offset Printing, and Internet) and compensates for different viewing distances and image sizes, all without having to think about Amount, Radius, and Threshold settings. I find that the results are just a little bit too aggressive, so I choose Edit > Fade right after applying the filter and lower the Opacity setting a bit. It's a personal preference as to what you consider to be a naturally sharp result, so the Opacity setting you'll end up using will be unique to you.

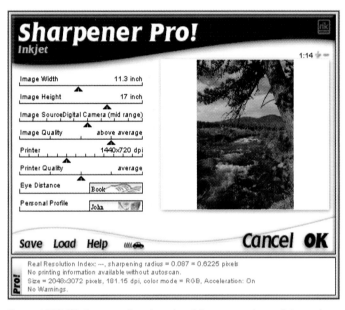

Figure 14.53 Nik Sharpener Pro takes a lot of the guesswork out of sharpening.

If you plan on using an image for more than one purpose, then it would be ideal if you were to create a unique image for each use. You can choose Image > Duplicate to create an exact copy of an image. Then, be sure to choose Image > Image Size (**Figure 14.54**) to set the size and resolution that is proper for the output device for which this particular image is destined. Finally, sharpen the image based on your experience with that particular device and repeat the process, always going back to the full-sized master image and repeating those steps for each device you plan on using. Or, if you simply can't deal with one image for each device, then work with a single image and do the following: Set the resolution to what's needed for your most demanding output device (needing the highest resolution image) and sharpen it for the device that looks the closest to your screen (the one that needs the least radical sharpening).

Then use that one image for all output devices. That's kind of like buying one size of shoe for an entire basketball team. As long as it's large enough for the biggest person, then everyone should be able to fit in it, but it will be ideal for only one individual.

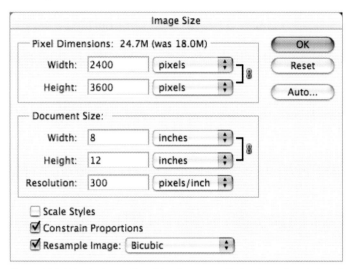

Figure 14.54 Use the Image Size dialog box to specify the size and resolution of your image.

Tricks of the Trade

Now that we've talked about the general process of sharpening an image, let's start to explore some more advanced ideas that will allow you to get more control over your sharpening.

Sharpen Luminosity

If you look closely at a color image after it's been sharpened, you might notice bright-colored halos around objects that were not all that colorful in the original photo (**Figure 14.55**) (like a red halo around a pink dress). To prevent that type of unwanted sharpening artifact, choose Edit > Fade immediately after sharpening an image. When the Fade dialog box appears, set the Mode pop-up menu to Luminosity and then click the OK button (**Figure 14.56**). That will force the sharpening you just applied to affect only the brightness of the image and will prevent it from shifting or intensifying the colors in your image (**Figure 14.57**). If you read a lot of books and magazine articles about Photoshop, you might discover that many people attempt to get the same result by converting their image to LAB mode and then sharpening the image. The only problem with that approach is that any time you change the mode of your image, you lose a little quality. So, I only switch modes when I have a good reason to do so. Fade gives us the same benefits as converting to LAB mode, so I prefer to leave my image in the mode it started in when I sharpen it.

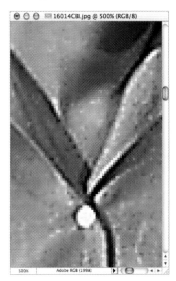

Figure 14.55 After sharpening this image, the color became more intense in the transition areas. (©2003 Stockbyte, www.stockbyte.com)

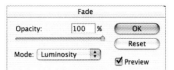

Figure 14.56 Choose Edit > Fade and set the Mode pop-up menu to Luminosity.

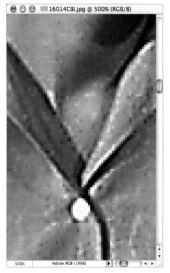

Figure 14.57 After fading with Luminosity, the color went back to normal. This might be hard to see in printed form; look closely at the edge of the collar where it touches her skin.

Sharpen the Black Channel

If your image is destined for CMYK mode, then be sure to make an extra sharpening pass on the black channel. Just open the Channels palette (Window > Channels), click on the Black channel, and sharpen away. Because black ink is mainly used in the darker areas of the image, you can get away with some rather aggressive settings. (Try these: Amount = 350, Radius = 1, Threshold = 2.) Perform this sharpening pass after you've already sharpened the full color image (**Figures 14.58** to **14.60**).

Figure 14.58 Original unsharpened image. (©2003 Stockbyte, www.stockbyte.com)

Figure 14.59 Result of sharpening the image while in RGB mode.

Figure 14.60 Result of converting the sharpened RGB image to CMYK and sharpening the black channel. Look in the darkest part of the image to see the subtle difference.

Sharpen Channels Separately

Certain images don't look all that good after being sharpened. For instance, when you sharpen a face, it sometimes seems to just fall apart, making the person look years older. Another example would be scanned images where color noise is exaggerated. In those cases, you should consider clicking through the channels that appear in the Channels palette and sharpen only the channels that would help the image. When it comes to skin, that would be the channel that is the lightest (red in RGB mode or cyan in CMYK mode) (**Figure 14.61**). For noisy images, you should avoid sharpening the channel that contains the most noise (usually blue in RGB mode or yellow in CMYK mode) (**Figure 14.62**). I don't use this technique every time I'm sharpening, but I'll think about it when sharpening the full color image makes it look worse than the original.

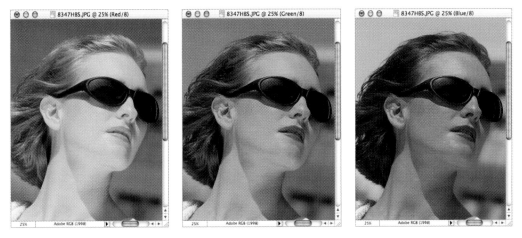

Figure 14.61 From left to right: red channel, green channel, blue channel. (©2003 Stockbyte, www.stockbyte.com)

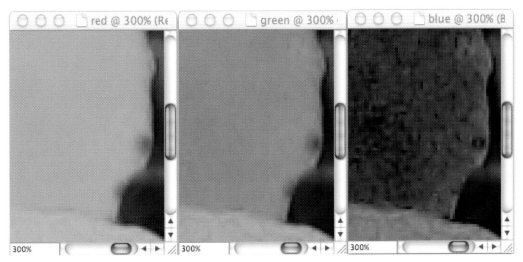

Figure 14.62 From left to right: red channel, green channel, blue channel.

Control Highlight and Shadow Separately

When you sharpen an image, Photoshop will add a dark halo on one side of an edge and a bright halo on the opposite side of the edge. When you're working with dark backgrounds (like a deep blue sky), the bright halos can be rather easy to see (**Figure 14.63**). That's when you might want to try controlling the bright and dark halos separately so that you can minimize the bright halo while maintaining the dark one. You can accomplish that by making two duplicates of the layer you want to sharpen. Then, click on each of those duplicate layers and set the Blending mode at the top of the Layers palette to Lighten for one and Darken for the other (**Figure 14.64**). Now you can sharpen the two layers separately; the setting you apply to the layer that is set to Lighten will control the bright halos, while the setting used on the layer set to Darken will control the dark halo (**Figure 14.65**).

Figure 14.63 The bright halos in this image are getting to be obvious. (©2003 Ben Willmore)

Figure 14.64 Duplicate the layer twice and set one layer to Lighten mode and the other to Darken mode.

Figure 14.65 When you separate the dark and bright halos, you have more control.

Closing Thoughts

If you read this chapter and felt like you were drowning in details, try a few of the techniques, then come back and read it again, and things will start to gel. It may take you a while to become truly comfortable with sharpening your images, but it's well worth the time because you can transform your flat and lifeless images into ones that are lively and ready to pop off the page. I'll leave you with one very important piece of sharpening advice: Oversharpened images never look good, so if you are ever unsure of how much sharpening to apply, always err on the side of conservatism.

Ben's Techno-Babble Decoder Ring

Interpolation: The processes of adding or removing pixels to an image to either change the image's dimensions or to change how large the pixels will be when the image is printed. When interpolation is done, the cropping of the image will not change.

Threshold: A setting that determines how many shades of gray or color (measured with numbers from 0 to 255) will be affected in an image. A Threshold of 4 means that Photoshop will either apply something to only four shades of gray in the image or it will ignore those four shades and work on the rest of the image.

Unsharp Mask: A term used to describe the traditional process of sharpening an image by combining a blurry (unsharp) version of the image with a normal version. The idea behind Unsharp Mask is to increase contrast, and therefore detail.

Keyboard Shortcuts

Function	Macintosh	Windows
Fade	Shift-Command-F	Shift-Ctrl-F
100% View	Option-Command-0	Alt-Ctrl-0
View Individual Channels	Command-1, 2, 3, 4	Ctrl-1, 2, 3, 4
View All Color Channels	Command-~	Ctrl-~

15
Shadows

Between the idea
And the reality
Between the motion
And the act
Falls the Shadow.

—T.S. Eliot, *The Hollow Men*, V

Shadows

Go figure. You spend hours creating a great shadow. You sweat over the minutiae. You listen to an entire CD while you fuss over the tiniest details. And when you're done, nobody notices it. Good! You've got the right shadow.

Shadows can make or break an image. Even though we don't notice them, shadows help create a sense of solidness, of physical existence. Just try this: Close your eyes and think about all the shadows that were present within your field of vision. You probably can't remember a single one. The presence of subtle shadows brings the illusion of substance to your digital images as well; remove the shadows and you remove the realism of the image. Shadowless images seem to float in thin air. On the occasion when anyone does happen to notice a shadow in your image, it's almost surely because it is too dark.

How to Think About Shadows

Lay your hand on top of the desk at which you are sitting (assuming you're not lounging on the sofa). Notice how dark the shadow below your hand appears. Now, slowly lift your hand above the surface and see what happens to the shadow. It should become lighter, and the edge should become softer. You might also notice that the shadow became larger—it's not always easy to see that happening, but it does. If there is more than one light source above your hand, you will most likely see multiple shadows. If you were to draw a line from one of the light sources to the middle of your hand, and then continue the line through your

If you combine two images that have radically different light sources, it will be difficult to recreate realistic shadows. The dissimilar lighting of the subjects will not relate in a natural way to the new shadows you're creating, and your mind will know something is not right about the image.

hand until it hit the desk, the line should be smack dab in the middle of the shadow.

But finding the light source in the real world is much easier than finding the light source in an image. If you can't see the light source in a photo (say there's no lamp or fiery sun), you can instead look at the part of the image that is darker than the rest. This will indicate from which direction the light was coming. Being aware of the source will really help you create natural-looking shadows.

Four Shadow Types

Ideally, when you want a shadowed image, you'd simply remove the background of the image and leave its shadow. This is possible if you happen to have a solid-colored background. But if the background is complicated, you'll have to resort to reconstructing a shadow that resembles the original. The farther you get from the original shadow, the less realistic the image will appear.

There are many techniques for creating great shadows; the complexity of the image will determine which technique you should use. The following four shadow types will cover most of the shadow situations you might encounter:

▶ **Drop shadow:** Keeps, as a simple offset shadow, the same shape as the object casting it.

▶ **Cast shadow:** Exaggerates the height of an object. A cast shadow is based on the shape of the object that's doing the casting.

▶ **Reconstructed shadow:** Replaces the original shadow with a new one so you can remove a complex background and still retain the basic shape of the original shadow.

▶ **Natural shadow:** Transforms an existing shadow into one that can be overlaid onto another image. Also removes any grays from beyond the edge of the shadow.

Let's start with the easiest technique, drop shadows, and then we'll progress to more advanced techniques later in the chapter.

NOTES

You can adjust the position of the shadow by clicking on the main image window and dragging the shadow while the Drop Shadow dialog box is still open.

You can also add a drop shadow by choosing that option from the Layer Style pop-up menu at the bottom of the Layers palette (it's the left-most icon).

Drop Shadows

If you have a simple subject like a playing card, coin, or other relatively flat object, you can choose Layer > Layer Style > Drop Shadow to quickly add a drop shadow, as shown in **Figures 15.1** and **15.2**.

Figure 15.1 Original image. (©2003 Stockbyte, www.stockbyte.com)

Figure 15.2 After a drop shadow has been applied.

First you must get the subject of the photo onto its own layer so you can create and edit shadows without changing the subject. Do this by selecting the subject with any selection tool and choosing Layer > New > Layer Via Copy. The result is shown in **Figure 15.3**. Now choose Layer > Layer Style > Drop Shadow and adjust the controls until the shadow looks appropriate (**Figure 15.4**).

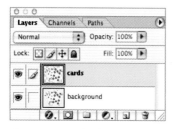

Figure 15.3 Result of choosing Layer > New > Layer Via Copy to isolate the subject onto its own layer.

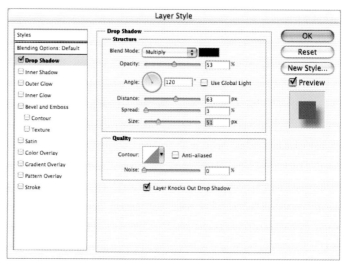

Figure 15.4 Apply a Layer Style to add a drop shadow.

Sometimes you might need to isolate the shadow onto its own layer so you can distort it using filters or place a layer between the subject and its shadow. You can do that by choosing Layer > Layer Style > Create Layer. After placing the shadow onto an independent layer, I often distort it using the Ripple filter that's found in the Filter > Distort menu.

Cast Shadows

To exaggerate the height of an object, you can create a shadow that falls at an angle away from the subject, also known as a cast shadow. The longer the shadow, the taller the object will appear. This will also make it appear as if the light source that's hitting the subject is coming from a specific direction (**Figures 15.5** and **15.6**).

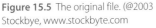

Figure 15.5 The original file. (@2003 Stockbye, www.stockbyte.com

Figure 15.6 Cast Shadow added.

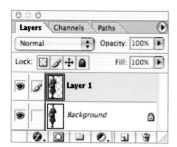

Figure 15.7 Isolate the subject onto its own layer.

If you're working from the sample image on the CD, you can Command-click (Mac) or Ctrl-click (Windows) on the path that appears in the Window > Paths palette to select the subject of the photo.

Isolating the Subject

To create a cast shadow, you'll first need to get the subject of the photo onto its own layer (**Figure 15.7**) so you can create a shadow without damaging the subject. Do this by selecting the subject with any selection tool, and then choosing Layer > New > Layer Via Copy.

Filling with a Gradient

Cast shadows are usually based on a blatant copy of the shape of the subject. To create such a shadow, Command-click (Mac) or Ctrl-click (Windows) on the layer in the Layers palette that contains the subject (not the background). This should give you a selection based on the information in that layer (**Figures 15.8** and **15.9**). Now, create a new layer, press D to reset your foreground color to black, click on the Gradient tool, and in the Options bar at the top of your screen, click on the triangle next to the gradient preview to get your drop-down presets palette. Choose Small List from the side menu of that drop-down palette. Now choose the preset that's called Foreground to Transparent (**Figure 15.10**). To fill the selection with a gradient, click on the bottom of the subject, drag to just above the top of the subject, and then release the mouse button. Then get rid of the selection by choosing Select > Deselect.

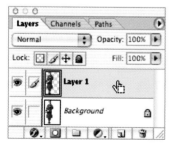

Figure 15.8 Command-click (Mac) or Ctrl-click (Windows) the subject layer.

Figure 15.9 The result of Command-clicking (Mac) or Ctrl-clicking (Windows) on the subject layer.

Figure 15.10 Choose Foreground to Transparent from the gradient drop-down menu in the Options bar.

Distorting the Shadow Layer

You want the shadow to appear beneath the subject, so drag the shadow layer until it is below the subject layer in the Layers palette. To make the shadow fall at an angle, choose Edit > Transform > Distort; the transform bounding box will appear. Move the squares (or handles) on the upper corners of that box around until you have the desired angle, as in **Figure 15.11**.

Blurring the Shadow

Now that we've applied a gradient and skewed the shadow layer, our shadow is fading out pretty nicely, but it still has a crisp edge. In the real world, shadows become more blurry as they get farther from the subject of the photograph (or, in my case, the woman's feet). To get a natural-looking fade-out, choose the Marquee tool, then click and drag the selection from the upper-left corner of the image until the bottom of the marching ants slightly overlaps the topmost part of the shadow.

Next, choose Filter > Blur > Gaussian Blur and use a setting just high enough to slightly blur the shadow (**Figure 15.12**). Click on OK. Now move the selection down by pressing Shift–down arrow a few times, and then blur the shadow again, using the same setting (**Figure 15.13**). Repeat this process until the selection is all the way at the bottom of the shadow.

> If you can't locate the Foreground to Transparent preset, then choose Reset Gradients from the side menu of the drop-down palette.

Figure 15.11 Distorting the shadow by using Edit > Transform > Distort.

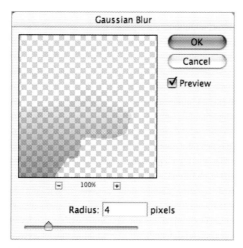

Figure 15.12 Gaussian Blur filter.

Figure 15.13 The placement for the first blur. Move the selection down for each subsequent blur.

NOTES

Instead of going up and choosing Blur each time, you can press Command-F (Mac) or Ctrl-F (Windows) to reapply the last filter you used with identical settings. Add Option (Mac) or Alt (Windows) to the above keyboard shortcut if you'd rather not use the same settings as the last time you applied the filter.

To create a more natural, less refined edge, choose Filter > Stylize > Diffuse and use the default settings. The Diffuse filter will add noise to the edge of the shadow, making it appear less artificial.

Achieving Proper Brightness

To brighten the shadow, adjust the Opacity setting of the shadow layer in the Layers palette (**Figures 15.14** and **15.15**). Make the shadow a little lighter than you think it should be; otherwise, people might notice it.

Figure 15.14 Shadow is too dark.

Figure 15.15 Shadow after lowering Opacity setting to 30%.

Reconstructed Shadows

If the background of an image is complex, then I'd completely remove the background on the image and attempt to re-create new shadows that resemble the originals (**Figures 15.16** to **15.18**).

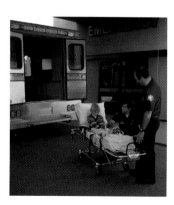

Figure 15.16 Original image. (©2003 PhotoSpin, www.photospin.com)

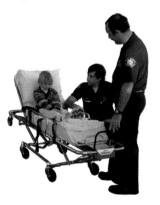

Figure 15.17 Background removed.

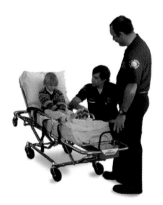

Figure 15.18 Shadows added.

Isolating the Subject

As with cast shadows, the first thing you need to do is to get the subject of the photo onto its own layer, so you can create and edit shadows without changing the subject. Do this by selecting the subject with any selection tool and then choosing Layer > New > Layer Via Copy (**Figure 15.19**).

Tracing Shadow Edges

Before removing the layer that contains the shadows, it will be helpful if you trace the shape of the original shadows. That way, any new shadows you create can have the same shape and position. Use the Freeform Pen tool to trace around the edges of each shadow that appears in the image (**Figures 15.20** and **15.21**). Most images contain more than one shadow—maybe a hard-edged shadow on one object and a softer-edged shadow on another. You want to create a new path for each shadow (or small group of shadows) in the image. After you've done that, make a mental note about how soft the edges are and how dark the shadow is. Now you can finally delete the layer that contains the shadows.

Rebuilding the Shadows

To re-create the shadows, first create a new layer below the subject of the image. Now set your foreground color to black and drag the first path in the Paths palette to the first icon in the Paths palette. This should fill the shape of the path with your foreground color, which is black (**Figure 15.22**, where I've added a white background to make it easier to see what the end result will look like). The black shape should appear on the layer you just created. This shape represents one of the shadows. To lighten the shadow, just lower the Opacity setting in the Layers palette (**Figure 15.23**). To make it look more realistic, choose Filter > Blur > Gaussian Blur and move the slider until the edge is as soft as the original, as shown in **Figure 15.24**. Repeat this process for each shadow in the image. It's a good idea to make a new layer for each shadow, so you can control each one separately.

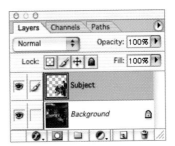

Figure 15.19 Isolate the subject onto its own layer.

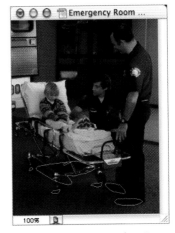

Figure 15.20 Use the Freeform Pen tool to trace the shadows.

Figure 15.21 Each shadow has its own path.

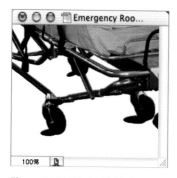

Figure 15.22 Filled with black.

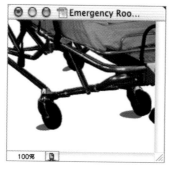

Figure 15.23 Opacity lowered.

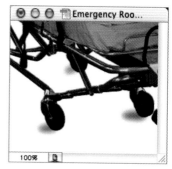

Figure 15.24 Gaussian Blur applied.

NOTES

You can also use a gradient layer mask to control the direction and intensity of the shadows. Fill your shadow selection with solid black, and then create a new layer mask for that layer. Drag across your shadow with a white-to-black linear or radial gradient, in the direction light is falling. Drag as many times as you like to experiment with different directions and intensities.

To quickly change the opacity of a layer, switch to the Move tool and press the number keys on your keyboard (1 = 10%, 3 = 30%, 35 = 35%, and so on).

To make the shadow fade out in a particular direction, drag the name of a path to the selection icon at the bottom of the Paths palette (it looks like a dotted circle). Choose Select > Feather to soften the edge, and then use the Linear Gradient tool (set to Foreground to Transparent) and drag across the selected area (**Figures 15.25** and **15.26**). Or, if you've already filled that area, you can make it fade out by choosing Filter > Blur > Motion Blur.

Once all your shadows look appropriate, link all the shadow layers together and then choose Layer > Merge Linked. This will create a single shadow layer.

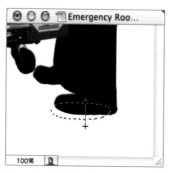

Figure 15.25 Selection.

Figure 15.26 After gradient is applied.

Natural Shadows

Let's finish with my favorite technique. We'll simply (well, not quite simply) slip the background out from beneath the original shadow, leaving just the shadow intact. That way you could feature it on a large poster and you wouldn't be able to tell the difference between the background of the image and the white paper the poster is printed on (**Figure 15.27**). After we've done that, we'll make this original shadow transparent so we can overlay it on any other image within Photoshop. This technique works when your image has a simple, low-contrast background; a white or gray background will give you the best results (**Figure 15.28**).

Figure 15.27 The bottom half of this image is the original; the top half has been adjusted to blend with the white background. (©2003 Stockbyte, www.stockbyte.com)

Figure 15.28 Here the shadow under the butterfly image was made transparent so it could be overlaid onto a new background. (background image ©2003 PhotoSpin, www.photospin.com)

Isolating the Subject

The first thing you need to do is to get the subject of the photo (a butterfly, in this case) onto its own layer (**Figure 15.29**). (These steps should be starting to sound very familiar by now!) That way you can isolate the shadow from its background without affecting the subject of the image. Do this by selecting the subject with any selection tool and then choosing Layer > New > Layer Via Copy. Or, if you have a complicated object, you can duplicate the layer and then use the Background Eraser or Extract command. This will leave you with two layers: one that contains the butterfly and one that contains the butterfly

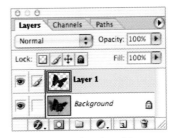

Figure 15.29 Isolate the subject onto its own layer.

It is important to choose Layer Via Copy instead of Layer Via Cut to avoid getting a bright halo around your image. Halos are caused by replacing the underlying image with white, which happens when you cut the subject from its original layer. If you're curious, go ahead and try using Layer > New > Layer Via Cut and then look closely at the edge of the subject.

and its shadow. To avoid confusion, whenever I mention the subject of the photo, I'm referring to the top layer (the one that contains only the butterfly); whenever I talk about the shadow layer, I mean the one that is under the subject (which contains both the butterfly and its shadow).

Now click on the shadow layer (the "Background" layer in this example). This will allow you to modify the shadow layer of the image without messing up the subject of the image. If the background on your image is not white or gray, then you'll need to choose Image > Adjustments > Desaturate before continuing; otherwise, the next step might not work as designed.

Finding Edge of Shadow

Next, you'll want to locate the exact edge of the shadow and then force the rest of the background to white, leaving just the shadow visible (**Figure 15.30**). To do this, choose Layer > New Adjustment Layer > Threshold and move the slider all the way to the right (**Figure 15.31**). A good portion of your screen should now appear black, because the Threshold adjustment is exposing all areas that are darker than white. Now, click on the shadow layer (**Figure 15.32**), choose Image > Adjustments > Levels, and move the upper-right slider around until the shadow (which will appear as solid black) is as large as possible without bumping into the edge of the document (**Figures 15.33** and **15.34**). The black mass will indicate where the shadow ends and the background begins. After you've moved the slider a little, you can use the up arrow and down arrow keys on the keyboard to move the slider in small increments. It's much too difficult to find the edge of a shadow with the naked eye, so you'll always want to use Threshold to help you.

Figure 15.30 The entire background is black, indicating that the shadow is bumping into the edge of the document.

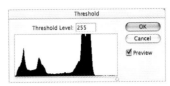

Figure 15.31 Move the Threshold slider all the way to the right.

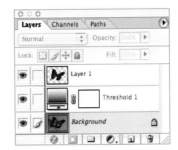

Figure 15.32 Make sure you are working on the shadow layer before applying Levels.

Figure 15.33 Shadow is as large as possible without bumping into the edge of the document.

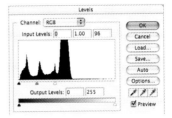

Figure 15.34 Move the upper-right slider to change where the shadow stops fading out.

Figure 15.35 Use the Eraser tool to clean up any stray specks.

Figure 15.36 Original shadow brightness.

Figure 15.37 Lightened by using Levels.

Cleaning Up Unwanted Grays

After getting the proper Levels settings, you may still have some unwanted shades of gray near the edge of the document (they would look like tiny black specks). Not all images will have the extra grays. To remove any specks, click on the shadow layer in the Layers palette and use the Eraser tool to brush over the "dirty" areas (you can see them in **Figures 15.33** and **15.35**). After you've gotten rid of all the extra grays, drag the Threshold adjustment layer to the trash icon at the bottom of the Layers palette.

Refining the Result

If you open the Levels dialog box a second time, you'll be able to control many aspects of the shadow's appearance. If you move the lower-left slider, you will lighten the shadow (compare **Figures 15.36** and **15.37**). Remember to make your shadows a little lighter than you think they should be; otherwise, people might notice them, which would ruin the realism of the image. Also, if the image will be printed on a printing press, the image will often appear darker than it does onscreen.

You can also control how the shadow fades out by moving the upper-middle slider. If the shadow isn't dark enough, you can move the upper-left slider over until it touches the beginning of the histogram.

Controlling the Shadow's Color

If you started with a white or gray background, then you might notice some color in the shadow after you're done applying Levels. Most of the time, the color will make the shadow appear more realistic, but sometimes the color is too intense. To adjust it, choose Image > Adjustments > Hue/Saturation and move the Saturation slider (**Figure 15.38**). If you move the slider all the way to the left, there will be no hint of color in the shadow.

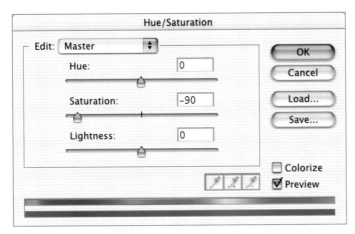

Figure 15.38 Lower the Saturation setting to reduce the amount of color that appears in the shadow.

If you can't tell if the shadow has color in it, just choose Image > Adjustments > Desaturate to re-move all the color from the shadow. Then choose Edit > Undo to see exactly how much color was in the shadow. If you want the shadow to have no hint of color, just don't choose Edit > Undo.

If the edge of the shadow is not soft enough, choose Filter > Blur > Gaussian Blur and use a very low setting, such as 1 or 2.

On the other hand, if you would like to add color to the shadow, turn on the Colorize check box in the Hue/Saturation dialog box, move the Hue slider to pick the basic color, and adjust the Saturation slider to change how intense it appears. This can be useful when you have a shiny object that should reflect some of its color into the shadow area.

Overprinting the Shadow

Using the butterfly and the textured paper background as an example, we'll overlay the butterfly's shadow onto the new background and then make that shadow print on top of the new background as if it were made out of ink. When you place the final image (in this case, the butterfly) on top of another image, you might want its shadow to appear transparent so that the two images look like they belong together. To accomplish this integration, open the image upon which you want to cast the shadow (here, the textured paper background). Now, switch back to the im-age that contains the shadow (the butterfly) and link the layer that contains the subject to the layer that contains its shadow by clicking to the left of the layer in the Layers palette. A link symbol should appear, as shown in **Figure 15.39**. Now use the Move tool to drag the butterfly onto the second document. This should copy both layers into that document, as **Figure 15.40** depicts.

To make the shadow transparent, first be sure you are working on the shadow layer. Then, in the Layers palette, set its blending mode menu to Multiply, and bingo!—transparent shadow (**Figure 15.41**).

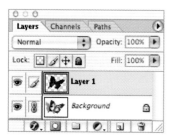

Figure 15.39 Link the layers by clicking to the left of the layer preview icon.

Figure 15.40 Using the Move tool, drag the image on top of another document.

Figure 15.41 Use the Multiply blending mode to make the shadow transparent.

Creating a Truly Transparent Shadow

Using the Multiply blending mode to print the shadow on top of another image works great when you end up combining your shadow with an underlying image in Photoshop, as we did earlier. But what if you need to export your image and slide something under it in another program? I wouldn't suggest this for images destined for a printing press (the file formats we are forced to use don't support transparency), but sometimes you might need to do just that when working with multimedia applications—for instance, when creating a video. Let's rewind our technique back to the point where we were about to drag the butterfly on top of the textured paper background.

To get true transparency out of our shadow, it must be the only thing visible. That means you'll have to Option-click (Mac) or Alt-click (Windows) on the eyeball icon for the shadow layer (that's a shortcut for hiding all the other layers). First I'm going to tell you to do a few steps without explaining what's going on behind the scenes. Then, after we get everything to look right, I'll clue you in on what you just did.

Now that you only have one layer visible, press Option-Command-~ on the Mac or Alt-Ctrl-~ in Windows, which should give you an unusual-looking selection (**Figure 15.42**). (Use the tilde (~) key, just to the left of the number 1 key.) Choose Select > Inverse, create a new layer, and then fill that selection with black by pressing D and then Option-Delete (Mac) or Alt-Backspace (Windows). Now, to finish the effect, throw away the old shadow layer, click on the butterfly layer, and choose Layer > Merge Down (**Figure 15.43**). You're done!

Now that you have this wonderful-looking transparent shadow, you might want to know how we accomplished that effect. The effect was possible because of the keyboard command we used (Option-Command~ on the Mac, Alt-Ctrl~ in Windows). Remember what was on your screen at the time you pressed that command? Weren't you just looking at the shadow layer? Well, that command takes what's visible and selects all the areas that are pure white. It also partially selects shades of gray. For example, if there is an area that is 10% gray, it will become 90% selected. After we got that selection, we chose Select > Inverse, which gave us what we really needed—areas that used to be 10% gray became 10% selected; areas that were 40% gray became 40% selected, and so on. Then we created a new layer and filled our selection with black. That effectively took areas that used to be 10% gray and made them black with an opacity setting of 10%. This can be a difficult concept to grasp if you've never attempted it before, but actually the concept is simple—you are just translating brightness levels into opacity levels.

Figure 15.42 Option-Command-~ (Mac) or Alt-Ctrl-~ (Windows) will give you an unusual-looking selection.

Figure 15.43 When you're done, you'll have a truly transparent shadow.

RGB Versus CMYK

I usually create all my shadows while I'm in RGB mode, even if the end result will need to be in CMYK mode. Here are a few reasons why I prefer to work in RGB mode:

▶ The natural shadow technique described earlier in this chapter will produce shadows that appear slightly brown if applied while in CMYK mode.

▶ The Multiply blending mode can cause problems with too much ink in an area if used in CMYK mode.

▶ File sizes remain smaller with RGB.

▶ All the filters work in RGB mode.

When you convert an image that contains layers to CMYK mode, a dialog box always appears asking if you would like to flatten the image. I usually choose to flatten it when converting; otherwise, I might run into problems with too much ink coverage (because I used the Multiply blending mode). The only time I don't flatten the image is when I'll be creating black-only shadows; there are no problems using the Multiply blending mode on these.

Closing Thoughts

If you feel funny taking so much time to perfect something that will never be noticed, you have two good reasons not to fret. First, shadows are every bit as important as light, but—strangely—the very best shadows are the ones that go undetected. Second, as with everything else in Photoshop, after you've test-driven them a few times, the techniques you learned in this chapter should take only a few minutes to perform. Isn't it worth a few minutes to get those subtle, flawless, ethereal shadows that no one will ever notice?

Keyboard Shortcuts

Function	Macintosh	Windows
New Layer Via Cut	Shift-Command-J	Shift-Ctrl-J
New Layer Via Copy	Command-J	Ctrl-J
Hue/Saturation	Command-U	Ctrl-U
Desaturate	Shift-Command-U	Shift-Ctrl-U
Levels	Command-L	Ctrl-L
Feather	Option-Command-D	Alt-Ctrl-D
Fill Dialog	Shift-Delete	Shift-Backspace
Fill with Foreground Color	Option-Delete	Alt-Backspace

©2003 Bert Monroy, www.bertmonroy.com

©2003 Bert Monroy, www.bertmonroy.com

16
Collage

What you see on these screens up here is a fantasy, a computer-enhanced hallucination!

—Stephen Falken in *WarGames*

Collage

NEW IN CS

The techniques used for creating collages haven't changed much in Adobe Photoshop CS. You'll find coverage of the new Photo Merge feature as well as a bunch of new examples.

No matter how many times I see them, I'm always in awe of the amazing special effects you see in big-budget Hollywood flicks. I know it's all man-made digital voodoo, but I still get a thrill when the effects are done so well. Consider *Jurassic Park*, where they blended the computer-generated dinos with actors and live-action backgrounds— so incredibly lifelike that you wouldn't be surprised to find yourself standing behind a Velociraptor in the popcorn line.

In Photoshop, you can create your own kind of movie magic by blending diverse visual elements into one big picture. (The only difference is the picture doesn't move.) Some people call this compositing or image blending. This is where Photoshop really gets to strut its stuff, and where you can put your creative agility to the test. The possibilities with compositing are truly boundless. Where else could you create a passionate embrace between an ugly, smelly, wrinkly bulldog and his archrival, a prim and proper kitty-cat? (Robert Bowen did it, and the piece won the Golden Lion Award in Cannes! See **Figure 16.1**.) With Photoshop, all you need is your imagination and a bag full of good collage techniques.

Four Ways to Blend

In this chapter, we'll explore the features that allow you to blend multiple images into one seamless composite. We'll cover Clipping Masks, Blending sliders, Layer Masks, and Vector Masks. Once you've mastered all four, you'll be able to blend your images together like magic. But before we start to create collages, let's take an introductory look at how these features work.

See Chapter 13, "Advanced Masking," for ideas on how to isolate objects from their backgrounds.

Figure 16.1 Robert Bowen, working with Howard Berman, created this image for Sony using Photoshop and won a Golden Lion Award. (Courtesy of Robert Bowen Studio, Sony Electronics, Inc., and Lowe & Partners/SMS. Photography by Howard Berman. Art Director: Maria Kostyk-Petro)

Clipping Masks

When you create a Clipping Mask, the layer you're working on will show up only in those places where there is information on the layer directly below it. This can be useful for simple effects like controlling where shadows fall or placing a photo inside of some text.

Sample Use: You've spent hours creating a big "retro" headline that could have come from the movie poster of *Creature from the Black Lagoon*. Your client—not exactly the king of good taste—calls and says he wants you to put flames inside the headline. You put aside your better judgment and agree to the flames, but only because he pays on time. Then he calls back; he's got some unresolved issues. He doesn't know whether he wants flames or hot lava inside the text, and he's also thinking about changing the headline altogether. He wonders out loud if it will take long or cost much more to do this. "Well," you say, "I think I could wrap this up in about three hours." Greatly relieved, he tells you you're a miracle worker and hangs up. Then you

Creating a Clipping Mask in Photoshop CS is the same as choosing Group with Previous in earlier versions of Photoshop. Only the name has changed. The feature still works identically to how it did in previous versions of Photoshop. Adobe changed the name to make the terminology more consistent with Adobe Illustrator, and because they added a new feature in ImageReady that they decided to call Grouped Layers.

pop open the Layers palette, where you've used a clipping mask to get the flames to show up in inside the shape of the headline, and faster than you can say hocus pocus you've tweaked the text and swapped out some lava for the flames and are off to the beach for a three-hour (paid) vacation.

Blending Sliders

The Blending sliders allow you to make certain areas of a layer disappear or show up based on how bright or dark they are. For example, it's very easy to make all of the dark parts of an object disappear.

Sample Use: A "big fish" prospect that you've been trying to snag for months finally throws you a bone. She's desperate because the super-swanky design studio she usually uses can't meet her deadline. You know she's just using you, but what the hey, it's a shot at a new client. She's given you some images that you've loaded into Photoshop. One is a photograph of some big, fat, billowy clouds; the other is of a bunch of whales. She wants you to make it look like the whales are swimming around in the clouds. In some places, she wants the whales to replace the sky that is behind the clouds, but in other places, she wants the whales to actually blend in with the clouds. Very surreal. She impatiently bites her nails and wants to know how many hours it will take to get the effect. You know you can nail this job in a jiffy with the Blending sliders, so while your hands are busy with the mouse, you give her a fearless look and reply, "I'll do it while you wait." She frowns, "I can't just sit around here for hours!" You smile, "No problem it's already done." The look on her face delivers the good news—you've got a client for life.

Layer Masks

I consider Layer Masks to be the most powerful feature for creating collages in Photoshop. With Layer Masks, you can make any part of a layer disappear, and you can control exactly how much you'd like its edge to fade out. What you can do with Layer Masks is infinite.

Sample Use: You're waiting for your biggest client, a 20-year-old creative genius with a ring in his nose. Although this is just a planning meeting, you know from experience that The Genius will want to see some action. Armed with your fastest computer and with Photoshop at the ready, you're not fazed when the kid comes in and starts throwing around madcap ideas like they're going out of style. Blending seems to be the theme of the day. First he wants something that looks like a skyscraper growing out of a pencil. Then he changes his mind and decides he wants to fuse together a hippopotamus and a ballerina. But then he gets a funny look on his face and says, "I know! Let's put Godzilla in an Elvis suit!" Ahhh, you think, a perfect day for Layer Masks. Without batting an eyelash, you go about the business of giving 'Zilla his new look. Six months later, you almost choke on your coffee when you find out that your Elvis-Zilla ad got an award.

Vector Masks

Vector Masks allow you to attach a crisp-edged path to a layer; anything outside of the path will be hidden both on-screen and when printed. This feature is special because the edge will remain smooth when printed to a PostScript printer, even if the pixels in the image are so large that the rest of the image appears jaggy.

Sample Use: You're doing a freebie brochure for your non-profit client, Defenders of the Naked Mole Rat. They want the rat to be the most noticeable image on the cover, so you make their logo small and place it in the corner so it doesn't distract from the lovely rat. But at the last minute (of course!), your penniless client does an about-face and wants you to enlarge the logo to make it almost fill the page. You're tired of doing things for free and fed up with her endless requests, so you tell the client that scaling up the logo that large is a big request when it comes to Photoshop. You even demonstrate your point by scaling one of the photographic elements of the brochure up to a huge size, and of course it looks terrible—very blurry and jaggy. She squeezes out a few tears and gives you her song and dance about the plight of this dear little creature, and how crucial it is to have this brochure just right. You tell her that you'll work on it through the night, and send her on her way. The minute she's out the door, you scale up the logo in a millisecond, and because you used a Vector Mask, the edge remains perfectly crisp and will print that way as well. The job is done. The Naked Mole Rat lives on; unfortunately, since you're so good, the client will never go away.

Now that you have a feeling for the blending options that are available, let's get into the specifics of how this all works.

Clipping Masks

This feature is not new; it was known as Grouping in earlier versions of Photoshop. (You chose Layer > Group with Previous to access it.) All Adobe has done is rename the menu choice from Group with Previous to Create Clipping Mask. But because they've done away with the concept of grouping, it makes it a bit more difficult to describe. So, if you've used this feature in previous versions of Photoshop, you should know that Adobe hasn't changed anything but its name.

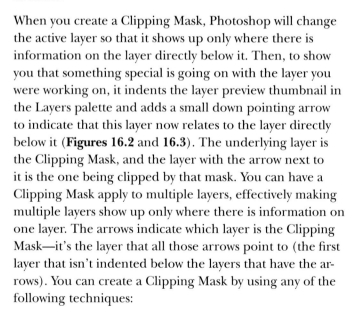

When you create a Clipping Mask, Photoshop will change the active layer so that it shows up only where there is information on the layer directly below it. Then, to show you that something special is going on with the layer you were working on, it indents the layer preview thumbnail in the Layers palette and adds a small down pointing arrow to indicate that this layer now relates to the layer directly below it (**Figures 16.2** and **16.3**). The underlying layer is the Clipping Mask, and the layer with the arrow next to it is the one being clipped by that mask. You can have a Clipping Mask apply to multiple layers, effectively making multiple layers show up only where there is information on one layer. The arrows indicate which layer is the Clipping Mask—it's the layer that all those arrows point to (the first layer that isn't indented below the layers that have the arrows). You can create a Clipping Mask by using any of the following techniques:

Figure 16.2 Result of creating a Clipping Mask to clip the photo so that it shows up only within the text. (©2003 Stockbyte, www.stockbyte.com)

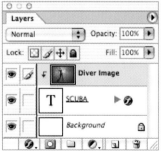

Figure 16.3 Layers palette view.

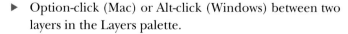

▶ Option-click (Mac) or Alt-click (Windows) between two layers in the Layers palette.

▶ Choose Layer > Create Clipping Mask.

▶ Press Command-G (Mac) or Ctrl-G (Windows).

Changing the Stacking Order

Changing the stacking order of the layers may accidentally deactivate the Clipping Mask on some layers, so you'll want to be careful. If you have a bunch of layers with a Clipping Mask applied, and you move one of them above a layer that doesn't have a Clipping Mask applied, then you'll be deactivating the Clipping Mask on that layer. Or if you move a layer with no Clipping Mask between two layers that do have Clipping Masks, then it will suddenly have the same Clipping Mask applied to it. If you move the Clipping Mask layer (the one that's not indented and has all those arrows pointing to it) above or below a layer that isn't part of that Clipping Mask, then all the layers that are affected by the Clipping Mask will move with it.

Now that you know how to use Clipping Masks, let's take a look at a few of the things you can accomplish by doing so.

Adjustment Layers

Clipping Masks can also be helpful when you're using adjustment layers. An adjustment layer allows you to apply an adjustment (like levels, Curves, and so on) as a layer that affects all the layers that are below it. That's nice, because the change is not permanent—you can always trash that layer and the adjustment is no longer applied. But, by creating a Clipping Mask between the adjustment layer and the underlying layer, you can force it to affect only the layer that is directly below it. This can be extremely helpful when you want to brighten or darken a single layer and you don't want to make the change permanent (**Figures 16.4** to **16.7**).

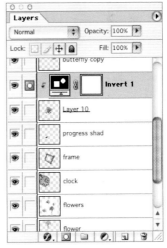

Figure 16.4 Layers palette view.

Figure 16.5 Original image. (courtesy of Chris Klimek)

Figure 16.6 Adding an adjustment layer at the top of the layers stack affects the entire image.

Figure 16.7 Creating a Clipping Mask between the adjustment layer and the underlying layer makes it apply only to the layers within the group.

Figure 16.8 Original image. (©2003 Stockbyte, www.stockbyte.com)

Figure 16.9 Creating a Clipping Mask between the shadow and the dustpan layer.

Figure 16.10 Layers palette view.

Figure 16.11 Remove the background of the magnifying glass and place it on top of the image.

Limiting Shadows

I use Clipping Masks all the time when I'm creating shadows. Let's say you have a flower, and underneath the flower is a dustpan, and you want the flower to cast a shadow on the dustpan. Once you create a layer that contains a shadow, all you need to do is create a Clipping Mask (make sure the flower layer is directly below it), and then the shadow will show up only where the dustpan is (**Figures 16.8** to **16.10**).

If you've created your shadow using a Layer Style, choose Layer > Layer Style > Create Layer to isolate the shadow onto its own layer. Then you can mask it with any layer you'd like.

The Magnifying Glass Trick

I travel all over the country presenting seminars and speaking at conferences, and I know I can always get people to ask questions by showing them my magnifying glass trick. I start by opening what looks like a simple image of an ampersand (&). Then, as I move my cursor, a magnifying glass passes over the ampersand and it appears as if it's really magnifying the image! That's not really possible in Photoshop, of course, but I can still trick people into thinking that it's happening for a few seconds. Let's see how the magnifying glass trick works.

Start off by opening any image you'd like to work with. I use a simple one of a black ampersand on a white background. Next, you'll need an image of a magnifying glass or loupe that you can place on a layer above the ampersand. (I've included two on the CD at the back of this book.) Now select the background and the glass portion of the magnifying glass and press Delete (Mac) or Backspace (Windows) to remove those areas (**Figure 16.11**).

The magnifying glass trick images shown here are a little special. The glass area is partially transparent instead of being completely removed. If you're feeling a little adventuresome and want to work with a similar image, then you'll need to follow a quick but complex series of steps that are related to what we discussed back in Chapter 15, "Shadows." I don't want to take too big of a side trip here, so it's going to feel like rapid-fire keyboard commands. If you want to know a little more about how this technique works, then refer back to the Shadows chapter. Here are the steps you should follow instead of deleting the glass area.

Start by selecting the glass portion of the magnifying glass and then press Shift-Command-J (Mac) or Shift-Ctrl-J (Windows) to move it to its own layer. Next Option-click (Mac) or Alt-click (Windows) on the Eyeball icon next to the layer that was just created (the one that contains the glass area) to hide all the other layers. Now comes the weird part: With only that one layer visible, press Option-Command-~ (Mac) or Alt-Ctrl-~ (Windows), which should produce a selection, then type Shift-Command-I (Mac) or Shift-Ctrl-I (Windows) to invert the selection. With that selection still active, press Shift-Command-N (Mac) or Shift-Ctrl-N (Windows) to create a new layer, press D to reset the foreground/background colors, press Option-Delete (Mac) or Alt-Backspace (Windows) to fill the selection with black, and then press Command-D (Mac) or Ctrl-D (Windows) to get rid of the selection. Then to finish the effect, drag the layer that is directly below the active one (which should contain the nontransparent version of the glass) to the trash, click on the layer that contains that transparent glass, and then press Command-E (Mac) or Ctrl-E (Windows) to merge it into the main magnifying glass image. If you followed those keyboard shortcuts to the letter, then you should end up with a magnifying glass image that contains a partially transparent glass area. Now, with that little detour out of the way, let's continue on with the steps needed to make the magnifying glass trick work.

Next, drag the name of the image you are using (not the magnifying glass) to the New Layer icon to duplicate it. Use a simple filter like Mosaic (choose Filter > Pixelate > Mosaic) to make an obvious change to the duplicate image (**Figure 16.12**).

Figure 16.12 Make a drastic change to the duplicate layer using a filter.

NOTES

To quickly group multiple layers, link the layers by clicking and dragging in the column just to the left of their preview icons in the Layers palette, and then choose Layer > Create Clipping Mask from Linked. After you have done that, you can drag across the link symbols to turn them off.

When using the Marquee tool, you can press the spacebar to reposition the selection (but don't release the mouse button).

If you're going to remove the background on the magnifying glass before dragging on top of another image, you should be aware that you can't remove a background layer. So, if that's what you have, double-click it to change its name and make it a normal layer.

Now let's get that modified image to show up only within the glass area of the magnifying glass. Grab the Elliptical Marquee tool and make a selection where the glass should be in the magnifying glass image. Make sure it lines up perfectly on all sides. Next, create a new empty layer, press Option-Delete (Mac) or Alt-Delete (Windows) to fill that area with your foreground color (it doesn't matter which color you use), and then choose Select > Deselect. Move the layer you just created so that it's positioned directly between the original image and the filtered version in the stacking order of the Layers palette (**Figure 16.13**).

Now, let's get the whole trick to work. Click on the layer directly above the one that contains the circle you just made, and then choose Layer > Create Clipping Mask. Now click on the magnifying glass layer and link it to the circle layer by clicking just to the left of the circle layer's thumbnail image in the Layers palette. That'll make both layers move at the same time (**Figure 16.14**). To see if the trick is working, use the Move tool to drag around your screen. That should make it so the filtered image shows up only in the "magnified" area (**Figure 16.15**).

The concept of Clipping Masks is rather simple—they make one layer show up only when there is information on the layer directly below it. But when you incorporate them into a complex image (like the magnifying glass trick), they can become the centerpiece of a mind-bending technique. Clipping Masks aren't the only way to make multiple layers interact, so let's move on and explore the Blending sliders.

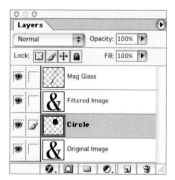

Figure 16.13 The new layer should be placed between the two image layers.

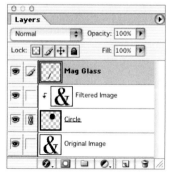

Figure 16.14 The final setup in the Layers palette.

Figure 16.15 The magnifying glass trick in action.

Blending Sliders

The Blending sliders allow you to quickly make areas of a layer transparent, based on how bright or dark the image appears. You'll find the Blending sliders by double-clicking in the empty space to the right of the name of a layer. (This will open the Layer Style dialog box.) The Blending sliders are at the bottom of the Layer Style dialog box (**Figure 16.16**). The first thing you'll notice is that there are two sets of sliders. One is labeled "This Layer" and the other is labeled "Underlying Layer." The slider called This Layer will make areas of the active layer disappear. The slider labeled Underlying Layer deals with all the layers underneath the layer that was double-clicked. This slider will make parts of the underlying image show up as if a hole has been punched through the active layer.

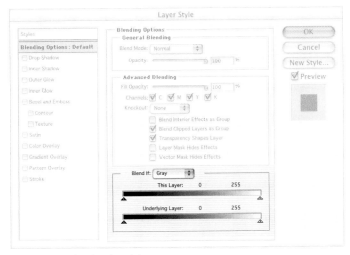

Figure 16.16 The Blending sliders.

"This Layer" Sliders

First, let's take a look at the topmost sliders. If you move the left slider toward the middle, the dark areas of the image (that is, all the shades that are to the left of the slider) will start to disappear. This slider can be a great help when you're trying to remove the background from fireworks or lightning. The only problem is, once you get the background to disappear, the edges of the lightning will have hard, jagged edges (**Figures 16.17** to **16.19**).

Figure 16.17 Original unblended image. (© 2003 Stockbyte, www.stockbyte.com)

Figure 16.19 Moving the upper-left slider makes the dark areas of the current layer disappear.

Figure 16.18 Removing the dark sky from the lightning image.

To remedy this situation, all you have to do is split the slider into two pieces by Option-dragging (Mac) or Alt-dragging (Windows) on its right edge. When this slider is split into two parts, the shades of gray that are between the halves will become partially transparent and blend into the underlying image (**Figures 16.20** and **16.21**). The shades close to the left half of the slider will be almost completely transparent, and the shades near the right half will be almost completely opaque.

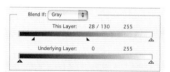

Figure 16.21 Splitting a triangle into halves allows the image to smoothly blend into the underlying image.

Figure 16.20 The edges of the lightning blend into the underlying image.

When you move the right slider, you will be making the bright areas of the image (all the shades of gray to the right of the slider) disappear. This slider can be useful when you come across a multi-colored logo that needs to be removed from its white background. Just like with the upper-left slider, you can split this slider into two halves by Option-dragging (Mac) or Alt-dragging (Windows) its left edge (**Figures 16.22** to **16.24**).

Figure 16.22 Original image. (©2003 Stockbyte, www.stockbyte.com)

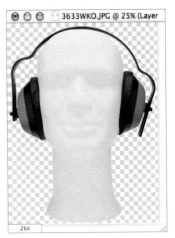

Figure 16.23 Result of removing all white areas by using the Blending sliders.

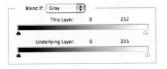

Figure 16.24 Moving the upper-right sliders makes the bright areas of this layer disappear.

"Underlying" Sliders

By moving the two sliders on the Underlying bar, you'll be able to make areas of the underlying image show up as if they were creating a hole in the layer you Option (Mac) or Alt (Windows) double-clicked. These sliders are useful when you don't want a layer to completely obstruct the view of the underlying image. I might use this to reveal some of the texture in the underlying image. And, just like the top sliders, you can Option-click (Mac) or Alt-click (Windows) to separate the sliders into two parts (**Figures 16.25** to **16.27**).

Figure 16.25 Original image.

Figure 16.26 Result of blending in the dark parts of the underlying image.

Figure 16.27 Moving the lower-left slider makes the dark areas of the underlying image show up as if they are poking a hole in the active layer.

Understanding the Numbers

The numbers that appear above the sliders indicate the exact location of each slider. If you haven't split any of the sliders, then you should see a total of four numbers (one for each slider). When you split one of the sliders into two parts, you'll see one number for each half of the slider. These numbers use the same numbering system as the Levels dialog box. (See Chapter 6, "Optimizing Grayscale Images," for a percentage to 0–255 conversion table.)

If you move the upper-left slider until its number changes to 166, for example, you'll have made all the shades darker than 35% gray on that layer disappear. It would be much easier if Adobe would allow us to switch between percentages and the 0–255 numbering system like you can when using the Curves dialog box.

Using Color Channels

Figure 16.28 The Blend If pop-up menu in the Layer Style dialog box determines which channels will be analyzed.

If you leave the pop-up menu at the top of the Blending slider area set to gray, then Photoshop will ignore the colors in your document and just analyze the brightness of the image (as if the image were in Grayscale mode). By changing this menu, you will be telling Photoshop to look at the information in the individual color channels to determine which areas should be visible (**Figure 16.28**). For example, if you have a document that is in CMYK mode and you change the pop-up menu to cyan and move the upper-right slider to 26, you'll make all areas of the layer that contain 10% or less cyan disappear. This can be useful when you want to remove a background that contains one dominant color.

Choosing the best channel from this pop-up menu usually involves a lot of trial and error. I'll show you how I usually figure out which color would be most effective for different images.

First of all, if the color you would like to work with matches one of the components of your image (red, green, or blue in RGB mode), then the choice is pretty straightforward. For example, to work on someone's blue eyes, just work on the blue channel. But what if you want to work on an area that is yellow and your image is in RGB mode? Well, to find out what to do, I usually hold down the Command key (Mac) or Ctrl key (Windows) and press the number keys on my keyboard (1–3 for RGB mode, 1–4 for CMYK mode, ~ to return to the full-color image); this will display the different color channels. You'll want to look for the channel that separates the area you're interested in from the areas surrounding it (**Figures 16.29** to **16.31**). When you find the one that looks best, choose its name from the Blend If pop-up menu in the Layer Style dialog box. Once you've found the best channel, glance up at the top of your document and you'll see the name of the channel you are viewing right next to the name of the document.

Now that you have a general feeling for how the Blending sliders work, let's take a look at some of the things we can do with them.

NOTES

If you've chosen a color from the pop-up menu before applying the Blending sliders, be sure to flatten your image when converting it to another color mode (RGB to CMYK, for example). The appearance of unflattened layers will change because the blending settings will no longer affect the same color channels. If you apply the sliders to the red channel (first choice in the menu) and then convert the image to CMYK mode, the same slider settings will now be applied to the cyan channel (because it's the first choice in the menu). The image will not look the same because the cyan channel doesn't contain the same information that was in the red channel.

Figure 16.29 Red channel. (©2003 Stockbyte, www.stockbyte.com)

Figure 16.30 Green channel.

Figure 16.31 Blue channel.

Enhancing Clouds

When you choose Filter > Render > Clouds, you'll get great-looking clouds, but there is one problem—you can't see through them. You'll probably want to see through the dark parts of the clouds, so double-click in the empty area to the right of the name of the layer your clouds are on. By moving the upper-left slider in, you're going to make the dark parts of the clouds disappear so you can see the underlying image. To make the edges of the clouds blend into the underlying image, hold down the Option key (Mac) or Alt key (Windows) and split the upper-left slider into two parts. Now by experimenting with the halves of the slider, you'll be able to create the look of fog, faint clouds, or dense clouds (**Figures 16.32** to **16.35**). This technique also works great with photos of real clouds. You can even transform Photoshop's Clouds filter into a hurricane by applying the Twirl filter to it (Filter > Distort > Twirl).

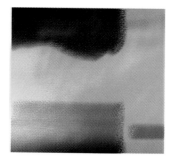

Figure 16.32 Original image.

Figure 16.33 After creating a new layer and applying the Clouds and Twirl filters.

Figure 16.34 Result of discarding the dark area of the clouds by using the Blending sliders.

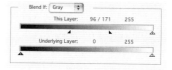

Figure 16.35 Settings used on the preceding image.

Homemade Lightning

If you want to play Zeus and create your own lightning, you'll need to start with some clouds; so create a new layer, and then reset your foreground and background colors to their default colors. (Just press **D**.) Next, choose Filter > Render > Clouds. This will give you clouds, but it won't look anything like lightning, as **Figure 16.36** reveals.

To get closer to something that resembles lightning, after applying the normal Clouds filter, choose Filter > Render > Difference Clouds. Then go to the Image menu and choose Adjust > Invert. This should get you a little bit closer to lightning (**Figure 16.37**), but we still have a few steps before it looks electric.

If you remove all the dark information from this image, it might resemble lightning. So double-click in the empty area to the right of the layer name, and then pull in the upper-left slider. You'll want to hold down the Option key (Mac) or Alt key (Windows) to split the slider into two pieces. Move the right half of the slider all the way to the right edge, as far as you can move it. Then grab the left edge of the slider and start moving it to the right until the lightning looks appropriate for the image (**Figure 16.38**). You'll have to move the slider almost all the way across.

> The "Homemade 'Lightning'" technique works best on low-resolution images. If you use a high-resolution document for this technique, you probably won't be happy with the results. For a more customizable version of lightning, read Chapter 17, "Enhancement."

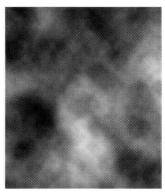

Figure 16.36 The Clouds filter is the starting point for creating artificial lightning.

Figure 16.37 Result of applying Difference Clouds and then inverting.

Figure 16.38 Result of removing all the dark information.

Making the Changes Permanent

The problem with the Blending sliders is that they are just settings attached to a layer, and Photoshop doesn't provide an obvious way to permanently apply their effects. Well, if you've used only the top sliders, there is an easy way to get Photoshop to permanently delete the hidden areas. To do this, create a brand-new empty layer, and then move that empty layer underneath the layer that is using the Blending sliders. All you have to do is merge those two layers. To do that, click on the layer that is using the Blending sliders, go to the side menu on the Layers palette, and choose Merge Down. Photoshop will then permanently delete the

Figure 16.39 To permanently apply Blending slider settings, merge the layer with an empty one.

Figure 16.40 The result.

Figure 16.41 This image is divided into thirds. The middle is what the image looked like before it was adjusted, the left is what I got after tweaking the image with Curves, and the right is the result of limiting the changes so they don't affect the areas that contain a lot of blue light (the sky). (©2003 Ben Willmore)

areas that were transparent. This can be nice if your client requested the layered file, but you don't want them to know how you did it (**Figures 16.39** and **16.40**)!

Adjustment Layers

Using the Blending sliders to cause areas of a layer to become hidden or visible is just the beginning of using this awesome feature. I find that they are immensely useful in combination with adjustment layers.

In particular, I like to use Blending sliders when darkening or adding contrast to part of an image using a Levels or Curves adjustment layer. I often find that certain areas of the image change too much as I attempt to adjust the image. But by simply letting parts of the underlying image show through (using the Blending sliders), the adjustment doesn't affect the whole image (**Figure 16.41**).

I also use them when colorizing an image. I create a Hue/Saturation adjustment layer, and turn on the Colorize check box to add some color. Then, I double-click just to the right of the adjustment layer's name and allow the darkest areas of the underlying image to show through (lower-left slider). I make sure I split the sliders rather wide to ensure a very smooth transition. This is what usually separates realistic-looking images from the fake ones, because not much color shows up in the darkest areas of most color photographs (**Figures 16.42** to **16.44**).

When working with adjustment layers, the This Layer sliders act as if the adjustment layer contains the underlying image as it would look after the adjustment has been applied.

We've only scratched the surface of what you can do with Blending sliders. Use them anytime you want to make something show up or disappear based on how bright it is. Now let's move on to my favorite method for creating collages—Layer Masks.

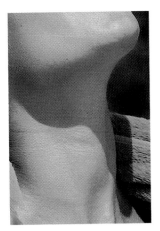

Figure 16.42 The original full-color image. (©2003 Stockbyte, www.stockbyte.com)

Figure 16.43 Result of converting to grayscale and then adding false color.

Figure 16.44 Result of using the Blending sliders to limit how much color is applied to the darkest areas of the image.

Layer Masks

By adding a Layer Mask to a layer, you can control exactly where that layer is transparent and where it's opaque. You'll find that Layer Masks are used to create most high-end images—this feature really separates the beginners from the pros. But there's no reason why you can't be as adept at Layer Masks as the most seasoned veteran. It just takes a little time and sweat.

Creating a Layer Mask

You can add a Layer Mask to the active layer by clicking on the icon second from the left at the bottom of the Layers palette. (It looks like a rectangle with a circle inside it.) Once you click this icon, you'll notice that the layer you're working on contains two thumbnail images in the palette. The one on the left is its normal preview thumbnail; the one on the right is the Layer Mask thumbnail. The Layer Mask is not empty (empty looks like a checkerboard); instead, it's full of white. After adding a Layer Mask, you can edit it by painting across the image window with any painting tool. Even though this would usually change the image, you're really just editing the Layer Mask; it just isn't visible on the main screen. The color you paint with

NOTES

When you click the New Layer icon at the bottom of the Layers palette, the new layer will appear above the layer that was active at the time you clicked that icon. You can Command-click (Mac) or Ctrl-click (Windows) on the New Layer icon to create an empty layer below the active one.

(which is really a shade of gray) determines what happens to the image. Painting with black will make areas disappear, and painting with white will bring back the areas again. And remember, because you are using a painting tool, you can choose a hard- or soft-edged brush to control what the edge looks like (**Figures 16.45** and **16.46**).

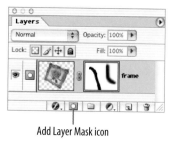

Add Layer Mask icon

Figure 16.45 Layers palette view.

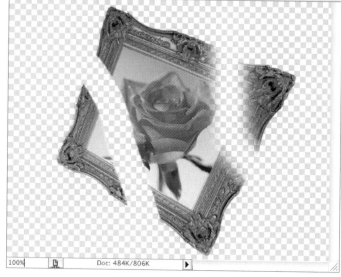

Figure 16.46 The softness of your brush determines how soft the edge of the image will appear. (©2003 Stockbyte, www.stockbyte.com)

What's nice about a Layer Mask is that it doesn't permanently delete areas; it just makes them temporarily disappear. If you paint with white, you'll be able to bring back areas that are transparent. This can be helpful if you're doing a very quick job for a client who wants to see a general concept. You can do just a very crude job of getting rid of the backgrounds of images, and then later on go back in and refine that Layer Mask to get it to look just right.

Switching Between the Layer Mask and the Image

Now that you have two thumbnails attached to a layer, you have to be able to determine if you are working on the Layer Mask or the main image. If you look at the Layer Mask thumbnail right after you've created one, you'll notice an extra outline around its edge (**Figures 16.47** and **16.48**). That border indicates what you're working on. If you want to work on the main image instead of the Layer Mask, click the image thumbnail in the Layers palette. The outline will appear around the image thumbnail, indicating that you are editing the main image instead of the Layer Mask. To work on the Layer Mask again, just click its thumbnail and the outline will move.

There is another way to get a visual indication of whether you're working on the main image or the Layer Mask. If you look just to the left of the image thumbnail, you'll see a Paintbrush icon if you are working on the main image, or the Add Layer Mask icon if you're working on a Layer Mask.

Hiding Selected Areas

If a selection is present when adding a Layer Mask, Photoshop will automatically fill the nonselected areas of the Layer Mask with black so the image is visible in the selected area only (**Figures 16.49** and **16.50**). Or, if you'd like to hide the selected area and show the rest of the image, hold the Option key (Mac) or Alt key (Windows) when you click the Layer Mask icon. You can see exactly what Photoshop has done by glancing at the Layer Mask thumbnail in the Layers palette (**Figure 16.51**).

To quickly switch between editing the Layer Mask and editing the main image, use the following keyboard commands: Command-~ (Mac) or Ctrl-~ (Windows) to work on the image, or Command-\ (Mac) or Ctrl-\ (Windows) to work on the Layer Mask.

Figure 16.47 Editing the main image.

Figure 16.48 Editing the Layer Mask.

Figure 16.49 Make a selection before adding a Layer Mask. (©2003 Stockbyte, www.stockbyte.com)

Figure 16.50 Result of adding a Layer Mask.

Figure 16.51 Layers palette view.

When a selection is present, you can Option-click (Mac) or Alt-click (Windows) the Layer Mask icon in the Layers palette to add a Layer Mask and hide the selected areas. If no selection is present, Option-click (Mac) or Alt-click (Windows) the icon to hide the entire image.

When you drag a large image into a smaller document, you'll need to scale down the image by pressing Command-T (Mac) or Ctrl-T (Windows). But because the image you are scaling is much larger than the document it is now residing in, you won't be able to see the corner handles that you need to drag to resize the image. When that happens, just press Command-0 (Mac) or Ctrl-0 (Windows), and Photoshop will zoom out on the document until you can see the handles on each corner of the image. (That's a zero, not an "oh," by the way.)

If you choose Add Layer Mask from the Layer menu instead of just using the icon in the palette, you will be offered some choices:

▶ **Reveal Selection:** Hides the nonselected areas, giving you the same result as using the Layer Mask icon in the Layers palette.

▶ **Hide Selection:** Hides only the areas that are currently selected, leaving the nonselected areas visible.

▶ **Reveal All:** Does not hide any areas of the layer.

▶ **Hide All:** Hides the entire layer.

Paste Into

If there is a selection present when you're pasting an image into your document, you can choose Edit > Paste Into (instead of Edit > Paste) to automatically create a Layer Mask. This Layer Mask will make the image show up only in the area that was selected. You can also hold down the Option key (Mac) or Alt key (Windows) and choose Edit > Paste Into to hide the selected areas. If you choose Select > All before choosing Paste Into, Photoshop will create a Layer Mask and reveal the entire image. You can also hold down the Option key (Mac) or Alt key (Windows) and choose Paste Into to hide the entire image.

Disabling a Layer Mask

After you've created a Layer Mask, you can temporarily disable it by Shift-clicking its thumbnail in the Layers palette (**Figures 16.52** to **16.54**). With each click, you will toggle the Layer Mask on or off. This is a great help when you want to see what the layer would look like if you didn't have a Layer Mask restricting where it shows up.

Figure 16.52 Layer Mask active.

Figure 16.53 Layer Mask disabled.

Figure 16.54 Layers palette view.

Viewing a Layer Mask

The thumbnails that show up in the Layers palette are just miniature versions of the images that show up in the main document window. That's true for not only the Layer thumbnail image, but also the Layer Mask thumbnail. You can view the Layer Mask in the main image window by holding down the Option key (Mac) or Alt key (Windows) and clicking on the Layer Mask thumbnail (**Figure 16.55**). You'll see it looks just like a grayscale image, and you can actually paint right on this image. I use this a lot when I get someone else's document, or when I open an old document I worked on months ago and can't remember exactly what I did in the Layer Mask. To stop viewing the Layer Mask, just Option-click (Mac) or Alt-click (Windows) its thumbnail a second time.

Shades of Gray

Photoshop treats a Layer Mask as if it were a grayscale document. That means that you can use any editing tool that is available to a grayscale image. Areas that are full of pure black will become transparent, pure white areas will become completely opaque, and areas that contain shades of gray will become partially transparent. Painting with 20% gray in a Layer Mask will hide 20% of the layer's opacity, leaving 80% of the layer visible. So using a painting tool with an Opacity setting of 80% will produce the same result

Figure 16.55 Viewing the Layer Mask in the main image window.

You can view a Layer Mask as a color overlay (just like Quick Mask mode) by Shift-Option-clicking (Mac) or Shift-Alt-clicking (Windows) on the Layer Mask icon, or by just pressing \ (blackslash).

Figure 16.56 Image before adding a Layer Mask (©2003 Stockbyte, www.stockbyte.com)

Figure 16.57 Result of applying a gradient to each Layer Mask.

Figure 16.58 Layers palette view.

as painting with 100% opacity and then adding a Layer Mask that is full of 20% gray.

Filling Areas

Because Photoshop treats Layer Masks as if they are gray-scale documents, you can create selections and fill those areas with black or white to hide or show the contents of a layer. To fill a selected area with the current foreground color (which is black by default), press Option-Delete (Mac) or Alt-Backspace (Windows). To fill a selected area with the current background color (white by default), press Command-Delete (Mac) or Ctrl-Backspace (Windows). This is nice because it frees you from having to use the painting tools.

Using Gradients

The most common way to make one image fade into another is to add a Layer Mask and then use the Gradient tool. In a Layer Mask, areas that are pure black become completely transparent, and areas that are pure white become completely opaque. Shades of gray in a Layer Mask will make the image become partially transparent. So, if you would like one image to fade into another, apply a gradient to a Layer Mask with the Gradient tool set to Black, White (**Figures 16.56** to **16.58**).

If you try to apply the gradient a second time, you might run into a few problems. If you apply the gradient from right to left one time, and then immediately after that you apply a second gradient in the other direction, the second gradient will completely obstruct the first one. To combine two gradients, set the Gradient tool to Foreground to Transparent, and make sure the foreground color is set to black. Then you should be able to apply the Gradient tool as many times as you want within a Layer Mask, and it simply adds to what was already in the Layer Mask (**Figures 16.59** to **16.62**).

Figure 16.59 First gradient.

Figure 16.60 Second gradient using Foreground to Background setting.

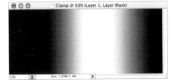

Figure 16.61 Second gradient using Foreground to Transparent setting.

Figure 16.62 Both ends of the ruler image blend into the underlying image (the C-clamp) because two gradients were used.

Applying Filters

After painting in a Layer Mask, you can enhance the result by applying filters to it (**Figures 16.63** to **16.66**). Choose Filter > Distort, and then select something like Ripple. Then, instead of having a really smooth transition, there will be some texture in it.

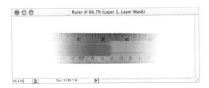

Figure 16.63 Original image.

Figure 16.64 Original Layer Mask.

Figure 16.65 Result of applying the Ripple filter to the Layer Mask.

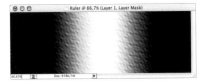

Figure 16.66 Modified Layer Mask.

If you want the edge of an image to fade out slowly, you can choose Filter > Blur > Gaussian Blur. You can blur a Layer Mask as many times as you'd like; each time you blur it, the edge will become softer (**Figures 16.67** to **16.69**).

Figure 16.67 Dartboard image contains a pure black and pure white Layer Mask. (©2003 Stockbyte, www.stockbyte.com)

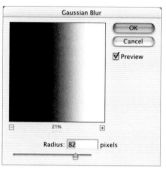

Figure 16.68 Apply the Gaussian Blur filter to a Layer Mask to give it softer edges.

Figure 16.69 Result of blurring the Layer Mask.

You can also expand or contract the areas that are transparent by choosing Minimum or Maximum from the Filter > Other menu (**Figures 16.70** to **16.72**). The Minimum filter will make more areas transparent, whereas the Maximum filter will make fewer areas transparent.

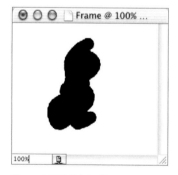

Figure 16.70 Original image.

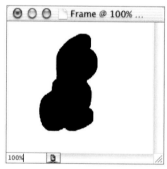

Figure 16.71 Result of applying the Minimum filter.

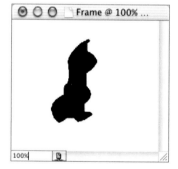

Figure 16.72 Result of applying the Maximum filter.

Interesting Edges

To create a rippled-edge effect on your mask, try this out: Open the photograph you want to apply the effect to, and make a selection with the Marquee tool. Make sure your selection is a little inside the edge of the photograph (so there's room for our effect). To get the photograph to show up only where the rectangular selection is, click the Layer Mask icon at the bottom of the Layers palette.

Now you can distort the edge of the photo by using any filter you'd like (**Figures 16.73** to **16.75**). For now, just use one of the filters under the Filter > Distort menu, such as Ripple, Twirl, or Polar Coordinates.

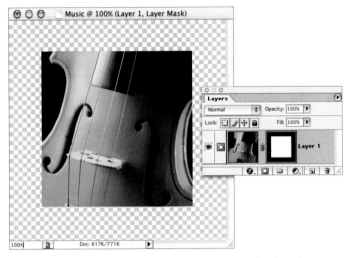

Figure 16.73 Result of adding a Layer Mask to limit where the photo shows up. (©2003 Stockbyte, www.stockbyte.com)

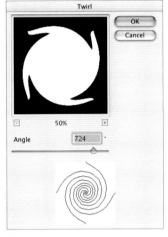

Figure 16.74 First apply the Twirl filter.

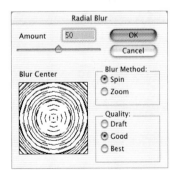

Figure 16.75 Then apply the Radial Blur filter.

Once you're happy with how the edge looks, you might want to add some other effects, such as a black border around our shape. There's a trick for that, too. Choose Layer > Layer Style > Inner Glow (**Figures 17.76** and **17.77**). Now click on the color swatch to pick the color you would like to use and set the Mode pop-up menu to Normal. To get the color to appear around the edge of the image only, be sure Edge is chosen at the bottom of the dialog box. Now you can experiment with the Opacity, Size, and Choke settings to fine-tune the result. If you are having trouble getting the edge to completely show up, try increasing the Opacity and Choke settings. You don't have to restrict yourself to the Inner Glow effect, so experiment with the other Layer Styles until you find your favorite.

Figure 16.76 Result of adding an Inner Glow layer effect.

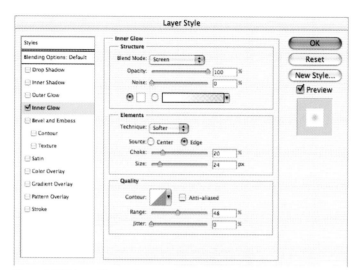

Figure 16.77 Inner Glow settings used to create the border.

Adjusting with Levels

You can also adjust the appearance of a Layer Mask (as long as it contains shades of gray) by choosing Image > Adjust > Levels. The sliders in the Levels dialog box (**Figure 16.78**) will do the following to your image:

▶ **Upper-left slider:** Forces the darkest shades of gray to black, which will make more areas transparent.

▶ **Upper-right slider:** Forces the brightest shades of gray to white, which will make more areas opaque.

▶ **Middle slider:** Changes the transition from black to white and therefore changes the transition from opaque to transparent.

▶ **Lower-left slider:** Lightens the dark shades of gray, which will make transparent areas appear more opaque.

▶ **Lower-right slider:** Darkens the bright shades of gray, which will make opaque areas appear more transparent.

Image as Layer Mask

You can achieve interesting transition effects by pasting scanned images into a Layer Mask (**Figures 16.79** and **16.80**). I like to run off to the art supply store, purchase interesting handmade papers, and spatter a bunch of ink

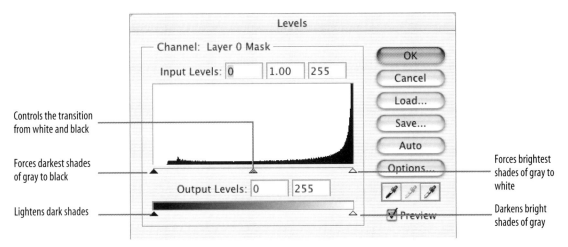

Controls the transition from white and black

Forces darkest shades of gray to black

Lightens dark shades

Forces brightest shades of gray to white

Darkens bright shades of gray

Figure 16.78 The Levels dialog box.

on them using paintbrushes. Then, to get the image into a Layer Mask, I scan the paper, select the entire image by choosing Select > Select All, and then copy the image by choosing Edit > Copy. After I've done that, I close the scanned image and switch over to the image I would like to use it in. Next, I click on the layer I would like to work on and add a Layer Mask. In order to paste something into a Layer Mask, you must be viewing the Layer Mask. That means you must Option-click (Mac) or Alt-click (Windows) the Layer Mask before pasting something into it. To stop viewing the Layer Mask, just Option-click (Mac) or Alt-click (Windows) its thumbnail again.

To quickly paste something into a Layer Mask, press the \ key to view the Layer Mask, press Command-V (Mac) or Ctrl-V (Windows) to paste the image, and finally press \ again to stop viewing the Layer Mask. This technique does not view the Layer Mask as it would normally appear; it shows up as a color overlay.

Figure 16.79 Scanned image to be used as a Layer Mask.

Figure 16.80 Two images blended together using the scanned image as a Layer Mask. (©2003 Stockbyte, www.stockbyte.com)

Using the Move Tool

After you have created the perfect Layer Mask, you might want to start rearranging your document by using the Move tool. You have three choices: You can move just the layer, just the layer mask, or both at the same time. The link symbol between the Layer Mask and image thumbnails determines what the Move tool will actually move. If the link symbol is present (that's the default), the layer and Layer Mask will move together (**Figures 16.81** to **16.83**).

Figure 16.81 Original image. (©2003 Stockbyte, www.stockbyte.com)

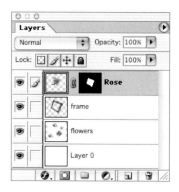

Figure 16.82 Layer and Layer Mask thumbnails linked together.

Figure 16.83 Rose layer and Layer Mask moved together.

If you turn off the link symbol (by clicking it), then you'll only be moving whatever has the extra-outline border around it. That means if the Layer Mask has it, you'll just be moving that around the screen. If the main image has it, you'll move just the main image around the screen, leaving the Layer Mask in its original position (**Figures 16.84** and **16.85**). If part of the Layer Mask lines up with another part of the image, you'll want to move just the layer and not the Layer Mask (**Figures 16.86** and **16.87**).

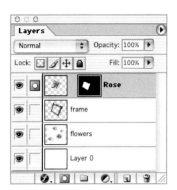

Figure 16.85 When the link symbol is missing, the outlined border (Layer Mask) determines what will get moved.

Figure 16.84 Moving just the Layer Mask, leaving the main image stationary.

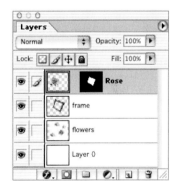

Figure 16.87 When the link symbol is missing, the outlined border (layer) determines what will get moved.

Figure 16.86 Moving the main image, leaving the Layer Mask stationary.

NOTES

On occasion, it can be useful to have two Layer Masks masking a single layer. To accomplish that, add the first Layer Mask directly to the layer, then place that layer into a layer set (which looks like a folder), and add a Layer Mask to the set. That way you can remove the background on the image using the Layer Mask that is attached directly to the layer, and further mask using the Layer Mask that is attached to the set. That allows you to experiment with the Layer Mask that is attached to the set without any chance of screwing up the mask that is applied directly to the layer.

Copying to Another Layer

If you'd like to copy a Layer Mask from one layer and apply it to another, then you'll need to be very precise in doing the following: Click on the layer that you'd like to copy the mask to, which will make it active. (Make sure that layer doesn't have a Layer Mask to begin with.) Next, click on the Layer Mask you'd like to copy (but be very careful not to release the mouse button just yet). Now drag it to the Layer Mask icon at the bottom of the Layers palette and release the mouse button. That will copy the mask from the layer you dragged it from and apply it to the layer that was active at the time (**Figures 16.88** and **16.89**).

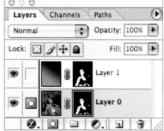

Figure 16.88 With the layer you'd like to apply it to active, drag a Layer Mask to the Layer Mask icon at the bottom of the Layers palette.

Figure 16.89 The result of copying a Layer Mask from one layer to another.

Load as Selection

Once you have perfected a Layer Mask, you might need to select the areas that are visible in order to add a border or perform another effect. You can do this in many ways. The fastest method is to Command-click (Mac) or Ctrl-click (Windows) the Layer Mask thumbnail (**Figures 16.90** and **16.91**). If there is already a selection present, you can Shift-Command-click (Mac) or Shift-Ctrl-click (Windows) to add to the selection; Option-Command-click (Mac) or Alt-Ctrl-click (Windows) to subtract from it; or Shift-Option-Command-click (Mac) or Shift-Alt-Ctrl-click (Windows) to intersect the selection. Or, if you are not very good at remembering a bunch of keyboard commands, you can Control-click (Mac) or right-click (Windows) the Layer Mask thumbnail to get a menu of options.

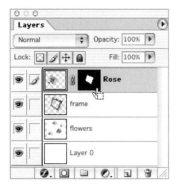

Figure 16.90 Command-click (Mac) or Ctrl-click (Windows) the Layer Mask thumbnail to select the areas that are visible.

Figure 16.91 Result of Command-clicking (Mac) or Ctrl-clicking (Windows) on the "x" layer's Layer Mask thumbnail.

Masking Layer Styles

If you have a Layer Style (like Bevel and Emboss) applied to a layer that contains a Layer Mask, you'll find that the mask changes where the style shows up (**Figures 16.92** and **16.93**). If you'd rather have the Layer Mask hide the style instead of changing where it shows up, then hold Option (Mac) or Alt (Windows) and double-click on the layer to access the Layer Style dialog box. Turning on the Layer Mask Hides Effects check box will cause the Layer Mask to hide the original style position instead of changing where it shows up (**Figures 16.94** and **16.95**).

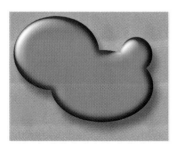

Figure 16.92 The original image included a Layer Style.

Figure 16.93 Applying a Layer Mask changes where the style appears.

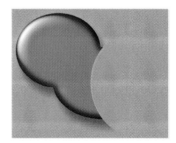

Figure 16.94 Using the Layer Mask Hides Effects check box causes the Layer Mask to hide the Layer Style.

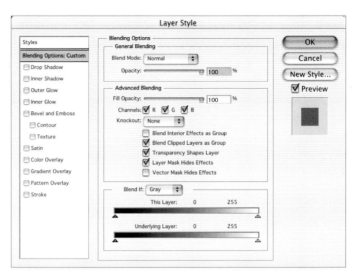

Figure 16.95 The Layer Style dialog box.

Figure 16.96 Result of typing Option-Command-E (Mac) or Alt-Ctrl-E (Windows) with an empty layer.

Figure 16.97 Layer Mask added after Command-clicking (Mac) or Ctrl-clicking (Windows) the merged layer.

Converting the Blending Sliders into a Layer Mask

Earlier in this chapter, we talked about making areas of a layer transparent using the Blending sliders in the Layer Style dialog box. Occasionally, you might need to turn off the sliders and create a Layer Mask that produces the same result. (Why? Well, you might want to be able to edit the Layer Mask using painting tools and filters instead of just the Blending sliders.) To accomplish this, you'll need to go through a multi-step process.

First, create a new empty layer below the layer that is using the Blending sliders. Next, click the layer above it (the one that uses the Blending sliders) and press Option-Command-E (Mac) or Alt-Ctrl-E (Windows). This deposits information into the layer that does not use the Blending sliders, but produces the same results (permanently deleting the transparent areas).

Now you can double-click to the right of the name of the layer that uses the Blending sliders, and then set all the sliders back to their default positions so they are no longer affecting the layer. Then, to add a Layer Mask that produces the same result, Command-click (Mac) or Ctrl-click (Windows) the layer directly below the one that was using the sliders (to select the nontransparent areas of the layer). Finally, click the Layer Mask icon on the layer that used the sliders to add a Layer Mask based on that selection, and then trash the middle layer (**Figures 16.96** and **16.97**).

Removing a Layer Mask

If you know you will no longer need to edit a Layer Mask and would like to permanently delete the areas that are transparent, you can choose one of the options from the Layer > Remove Layer Mask menu (**Figures 16.98** and **16.99**). When you do this, you will be presented with two choices:

A quick way to remove a Layer Mask is to drag its thumbnail to the Trash Can icon that is located at the bottom of the Layers palette.

▶ **Apply:** Removes the Layer Mask and deletes all transparent areas.

▶ **Discard:** Removes the Layer Mask and brings the image back into full view.

Now that we've covered the mechanics of using Layer Masks, let's take a look at how Photoshop can help automate the process of combining multiple images into one seamless panoramic image.

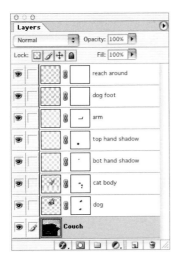

Figure 16.98 Layers view of a simplified version of the "Dog & Cat" image shown at the beginning of this chapter. I removed over a dozen adjustment layers, all of which had Layer Masks attached to them.

Figure 16.99 Final "Dog & Cat" image. (original image courtesy of Robert Bowen Studio, Sony Electronics, Inc., and Lowe & Partners/SMS. Photography by Howard Berman)

Figure 16.100 The initial Photo merge dialog box allows you to specify which images you'd like to merge into a panoramic.

Figure 16.101 The main Photomerge dialog box. (©2003 Ben Willmore)

Figure 16.102 Any images that Photomerge couldn't automatically line up will be shown at the top of the dialog box.

Creating a Panoramic Image with Photomerge

The new Photomerge feature in Photoshop CS attempts to automate the process of combining images into a seamless panoramic. To start creating your own panoramic images, open the images in Photoshop and then choose File > Automate > Photomerge. The initial Photomerge dialog box will prompt you to specify which images you'd like to use to create a panoramic (**Figure 16.100**). Because you've already opened the images you want to use, just set the Use pop-up menu to Open Files. Next, turn on the Attempt to Automatically Arrange Source Images check box so that Photomerge will try to line up each image automatically. Once you click the OK button in the initial Photomerge dialog box, Photoshop will chug for quite a while, and then you will be sent to the main Photomerge interface (**Figure 16.101**).

I find that the vast majority of the time, Photomerge will not be able to line up all the images automatically. When that's the case, you'll find a few images at the top of the Photomerge dialog box. Those are the images that it couldn't line up with the rest of the image. To add them to your overall composition, just grab the Arrow tool in the upper left of the dialog box and drag each image into the main composition area (**Figure 16.102**). When you drag an image over the main composition, you will be able to see through it to see how it lines up with the underlying image. When you release the mouse button, Photoshop will attempt to nudge that piece of the image into the proper position based on where it was relative to the other images in the composition. If Photoshop doesn't do a good job of nudging it into position, then turn off the Snap to Image check box in the lower right of the dialog box, and Photoshop will leave the images exactly where you place them. You can also use the Rotate tool to change the angle of an element to make it match the overall composition.

Once you have all the pieces in place and lined up properly, you'll want to experiment with the options that are available on the right side of the dialog box. When you turn on the Perspective option, Photomerge will assume that the images on the outer edges of the image should be larger because they might have been closer to the camera lens when the photos were taken (**Figure 16.103**). That feature works fine if you have a simple image of three or four pieces, but I find that the vast majority of the time, it simply can't do its job properly (**Figure 16.104**). When that's the case, just switch back to the Normal setting and wait for the image to update again.

If you find that it's too easy to see the transitions between the individual images that make up your panoramic image, then turn on the Advanced Blending check box and click the Preview button to allow Photomerge to spend more time blending the transitions between images (**Figure 16.105**). That option helps tremendously on some images and looks terrible on others, so just try it and see if it does an OK job on your image. If it isn't successful, then click the Exit Preview button and then turn the Advanced Blending check box back off.

Figure 16.103 The result of applying perspective correction.

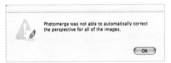

Figure 16.104 If Photomerge is not able to figure out how to correct the perspective on your panoramic, then you'll get this warning.

Figure 16.105 The Advanced Blending feature will attempt to blend your images with more precision.

Once you're done improving your image in Photomerge, click the Save Composition button and give this arrangement of images a name. That way you can always come back to Photomerge and reload your composition instead of having to start from scratch. Finally, you have two choices for what type of end result you'd like to get from Photomerge—a layered image or a flat file. You'd think that a layered file would be the most versatile, but anytime you ask for layers (via the Keep as Layers check box), Photomerge will make no attempt at all to blend the edges and colors of the image (**Figure 16.106**). That means that you'll have to do all that work manually (by adding Layer Masks to each layer and filling them with gradients to blend the images together) (**Figure 16.107**). I use this option only when Photomerge wasn't successful in blending the images (**Figure 16.108**). But if everything looks fine in Photomerge, then I'd prefer to turn off the Keep as Layers check box so that I end up with an image that looks just like what I saw in Photomerge (**Figure 16.109**). Then I can always use the Healing Brush tool to touch up any tiny imperfections in the blending (**Figure 16.110**).

Figure 16.106 When the Keep as Layers check box is turned on, Photo merge will not blend the edges of the images.

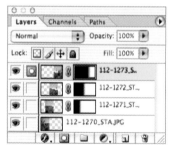

Figure 16.107 Each layer has a Layer Mask attached that contains a gradient.

Figure 16.108 The result of manually blending the images using Layer Masks.

Figure 16.109 The panoramic as Photomerge created it.

Figure 16.110 The result of cleaning up the transitions and background with the Healing Brush tool and cropping the image.

If you find that you need to tweak your images too much when using Photomerge, then consider getting a point and shoot digital camera that has a panoramic shooting mode. (Many Canon cameras have this feature.) When using panoramic shooting mode, the camera will help you to line up each shot, and then you can use special software that comes with the camera to have them automatically stitched together. The results are often much better than anything you could get out of Photoshop's Photomerge because the special software knows exactly how much overlap there was between images and can also correct for lens distortion because the camera recorded all the settings used when shooting the image.

Now let's move on to the last method for creating collages—Vector Masks. I use this method the least out of all the techniques we've covered in this chapter, but still find them to be useful.

Vector Masks

Vector Masks allow you to control which area of a layer will be visible, by using an easily editable, smooth-shaped, crisp-edged path. This capability was first added in Photoshop 6.0 and it represented a rather radical shift from what was possible in the past. Before 6.0, everything created in Photoshop was made out of pixels, and the resolution of the file determined how large the pixels would be when printed. If those pixels were large enough, then the image would appear jaggy when printed. But with Vector Masks, you can create a very low resolution (read: jaggy) image and still get a smooth-shaped, crisp-edged transition between the content of a layer and the underlying image.

Adding a Vector Mask

The simplest way to add a Vector Mask is to choose Layer > Add Vector Mask > Reveal All. After you choose that option, the layer that is active will have two thumbnail images in the Layers palette (**Figure 16.111**). It should look like you just added a Layer Mask, but there will be a vertical line just to the right of the layer thumbnail image

Figure 16.111 After adding a Vector Mask, you will see two thumbnail images in the Layers palette.

to indicate that it's a Vector Mask instead of a Layer Mask. The only difference is that with a Layer Mask, you paint with shades of gray to control which areas of a layer will be hidden or visible, whereas with a Vector Mask, you define the area that will be visible using a path.

The easiest way to define where the image should be visible is to use one of the shape tools. Before you start creating shapes, be sure to take a peek at the settings in the options bar. You should find four options available on the left side of the options bar when a layer that contains a Vector Mask is active. The leftmost choice allows you to create a shape to define where the image should be visible (**Figure 16.112**). The second choice will allow you to define a shape where the image should be hidden (**Figure 16.113**). The third choice will limit the areas that are already visible, so they show up only within the shape you draw (**Figure 16.114**). The last choice will invert the visibility of the area inside the shape you draw, making visible areas hidden and hidden areas visible (**Figure 16.115**).

You can also use any of the Pen tools to create and modify a Vector Mask. If you're not already familiar with the Pen tools, then start out with the Freeform Pen tool because it allows you to create a path by drawing a freeform shape, much like the Lasso tool allows you to create a selection. If you'd like to learn how to use the Pen tool, check out Chapter 13, "Advanced Masking."

Figure 16.112 This shape defines where the image is visible.

Figure 16.113 The shape that was added is being used to hide part of the image.

Figure 16.114 The shape that was added is being used to limit where the image is visible.

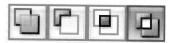

Figure 16.115 The shape that was added is being used to invert the visibility of the image.

If you already have a path saved in your file (it will show up in the Paths palette), you can use it as a Vector Mask. Just make sure the layer you'd like to apply it to is active (you can't add one to the background layer), click on the name of the path in the Paths palette, and then choose Layer > Add Vector Mask > Current Path. That will allow you to use any paths that are included with stock photos you have purchased.

Disabling the Vector Mask

After you have created a Vector Mask, you can temporarily disable it by Shift-clicking its thumbnail in the Layers palette (**Figures 16.116** and **16.117**). With each click, you will toggle the Vector Mask on and off. This is a great help when you want to see what a layer would look like if you didn't have a Vector Mask restricting where it shows up.

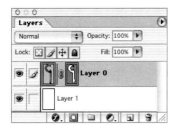
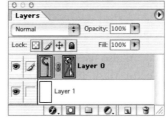

Figure 16.116 Vector Mask active.

Figure 16.117 Vector Mask disabled.

Using the Move Tool

When you use the Move tool to reposition a layer, you'll notice that the layer and the Vector Mask move together (**Figures 16.118** to **16.120**). If you turn off the link symbol (by clicking it), you'll leave the Vector Mask alone and just move the image (**Figure 16.121**).

If you'd like to move the Vector Mask and leave the image stationary, use the Solid Arrow tool that appears directly above the Pen tools (**Figure 16.122**).

Figure 16.118 Layer and Vector Mask linked together.

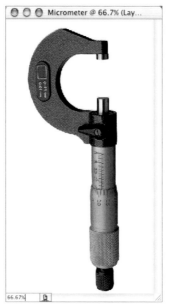

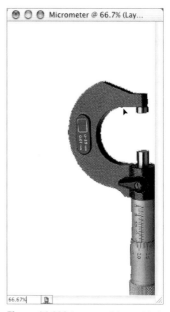

Figure 16.119 Original image.
(©2003 Stockbyte, www.stockbyte.com)

Figure 16.120 Layer and Vector Mask
moved together.

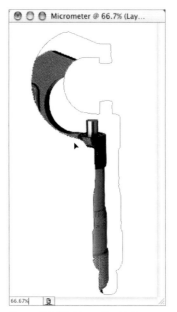

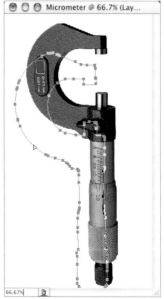

Figure 16.121 Vector Mask left stationary while the layer is repositioned.

Figure 16.122 Use the Solid Arrow
tool to reposition a Vector Mask.

Transforming the Vector Mask

The Edit > Transform commands are very useful when working on a Vector Mask. Because the path is made from a collection of points and directional handles (instead of pixels), scaling, rotating, and other transformations will not degrade the quality of the shape. All you have to do is make sure the path is visible before you choose Transform Path from the Edit menu. You can toggle the visibility of a Vector Mask by clicking its thumbnail in the Layers palette.

Using Vector Masks with Layer Masks

You can have both a Layer Mask and a Vector Mask attached to a single layer. (Just click the Layer Mask icon twice.) When that's the case, you'll end up with your image visible only where both the Layer Mask and Vector Mask allow things to be visible (**Figure 16.123**). If you have multiple layers that have Layer Masks applied to them, then you can mask the cumulative effect of those layers with a Vector Mask by doing the following: Link the layers you'd like to apply a Vector Mask to by clicking in the empty space to the right of the Eyeball icon on each layer (**Figure 16.124**). Next, choose New Set From Linked from the side menu of the Layers palette, which will place all of those layers in a folder (known as a layer set) (**Figure 16.125**). Click on the layer set to make it active, and then add a Vector Mask. Any shapes that you add to the Vector Mask will limit where all the layers that are contained in that set show up (**Figure 16.126**). That's how I'd create the feather images you see in the new Photoshop CS packaging (**Figure 16.127**).

Removing the Vector Mask

If you find that you'd like to remove the Vector Mask from your image, just choose Layer > Delete Vector Mask, or drag its thumbnail to the trash can that appears at the bottom of the Layers palette. You can also convert a Vector Mask into a Layer Mask by choosing Layer > Rasterize > Vector Mask. But be aware that you'll lose the crisp-edged, smooth look of the path, and any transformations applied to the Layer Mask will cause it to appear blurry.

Figure 16.123 You can have both a Layer Mask and a Vector Mask attached to the same layer.

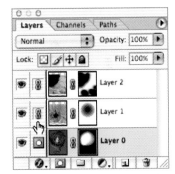

Figure 16.124 Link the layers you'd like to have in a set.

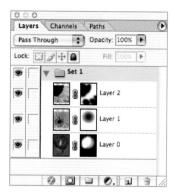

Figure 16.125 After choosing New Set From Linked, the layers will appear inside a folder in the Layers palette.

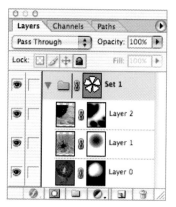

Figure 16.126 Add a Vector Mask to the set to limit where all the layers within the set show up.

Figure 16.127 The result is something that resembles Adobe's new product identity campaign. (©2003 Stockbyte, www.stockbyte.com)

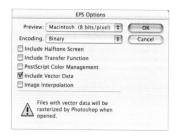

Figure 16.128 Turn on the Include Vector Data check box when saving an image for print-based publishing.

Saving Vector Data

If you plan on saving your image and using it in a page layout program (instead of using it for a web site), then you'll need to be careful about how you save it; otherwise, the crisp edge of your path may be lost. Remember when I said that a path is different from pixels in that it's made out of points and directional handles? Well, technically, that's known as vector information, whereas images made from pixels are known as raster information. In order to maintain the crisp edges of your paths, you'll need to save your image in the EPS or PDF file formats (which support vector data). Not only that, but you'll have to turn on the Include Vector Data check box (**Figure 16.128**) when saving your file. (This option shows up only after you click the Save button.) There's one last thing: Your paths will only print with crisp edges if you print to a PostScript output device like a $500+ laser printer. Most inkjet printers don't understand PostScript, so your image has the potential of appearing jaggy on those.

Clipping Paths

You can also assign a path to a document, as opposed to a single layer. A clipping path will limit which areas of an image will show up and print in a page layout program (**Figures 16.129** and **16.130**). To create one, use the Pen or a shape tool to create a path, and then choose Window

> Paths to open the Paths palette. Next, double-click the name of the path and assign it a name. Then choose Clipping Path from the side menu of the Paths palette (**Figure 16.131**). When prompted, be sure to enter a Flatness setting. When the image is printed, it will be converted into a polygon made out of straight lines of identical length. The Flatness setting will determine the length of those lines. Low settings produce short lines, which require more memory and processing time to output. If you use too low of a setting, then your printer might run out of memory when attempting to output your image. The more complex your path is (lots of points and directional handles), the higher the Flatness setting needs to be to avoid printing problems. In general, I use a setting between 3 and 10, depending on the complexity of the path I'm using. After you've assigned a clipping path to an image, you'll need to save it in the TIFF or EPS file format in order for it to be understood by a page layout program.

NOTES

You can print an image that contains vector data on a non-PostScript printer and maintain the crisp edges by saving it as a PDF file and printing it from Adobe Acrobat.

Figure 16.129 Image imported into a page layout program without a clipping path. (©2003 Stockbyte, www.stockbyte.com)

Figure 16.130 Image imported into a page layout program with a clipping path.

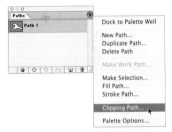

Figure 16.131 Choose Clipping Path from the side menu of the Paths palette.

Closing Thoughts

I hope that you get as much of a kick out of creating collages as I do. It's one of those things that never gets old; I can always count on another surprise waiting for me around the corner. If you want to create truly realistic-looking collages, then you should keep the following ideas in mind:

▶ When creating a collage out of images that were shot under different lighting conditions, be sure to color correct the images individually before turning them into a collage; otherwise, each one will have a different colorcast.

▶ If you're basing a collage on an image that has a desirable colorcast (such as candlelight, fireplace, sunrise, sunset), then use the techniques mentioned in Chapter 11, "Color Manipulation," (Auto Color and Match Color) to infuse all the images with the same desirable colorcast.

▶ When combining images, make sure that the direction the light is coming from in each image is consistent; otherwise, your viewers' eyes will pick up on the fact that the image is a fake, but they might not be able to pinpoint exactly why they think that.

▶ The direction the light is coming from in your image should also dictate the direction in which shadows fall. Shadows should fall directly opposite of where the light is coming from.

▶ When placing objects in a scene, think about where each object appears in 3D space and make sure it has the appropriate focus compared to the objects that surround it.

▶ The film grain that shows up in an image is usually consistent across the image, so either use the noise removal techniques covered in the Sharpening chapter on each image, or apply the Filter > Noise > Add Noise filter to images to make sure each one has the same amount of grain.

If you keep these ideas in mind, then with a little practice and a lot of perspiration, you should be able to create collages that fool even a trained eye.

Keyboard Shortcuts

Function	Macintosh	Windows
Activate layer instead of mask	Command-~	Ctrl-~
Activate Layer Mask instead of image	Command-\	Ctrl-\
Create Clipping Mask	Command-G	Ctrl-G

©2003 Richard Tuschman, www.richardtuschman.com

©2003 Richard Tuschman, www.richardtuschman.com

Enhancement

Digital Artist: Robert Bowen; Photographer: Howard Berman

I'm trying to free your mind, Neo. But I can only show you the door. You're the one that has to walk through it.

—Morpheus, from *The Matrix*

Enhancement

NEW IN CS

Not much has changed in this area of Adobe Photoshop CS. However, we will cover the new Hard Mix blending mode.

In this chapter we're going to explore a tantalizing variety of enhancement techniques. The truth is that you can't put a measuring stick on the many ways there are to enhance your image. The possibilities in Photoshop are beyond the horizon, and limited only by your willingness to experiment. But I think I can get you off to a good start so that you can feel comfortable tackling most jobs.

In an effort to impose some order on this somewhat random collection of techniques, I've structured this chapter around Photoshop's blending modes. They are what you find at the top of the Layers palette and in many other areas. Blending modes comprise one of the most powerful features in Photoshop—and one of my personal favorites.

The Battalion of Blending Modes

The Blending Modes menu draws the map for this chapter, so let's just start at the top and work our way down the list. We'll take a detour or two on our way, but at least we'll know where we're headed. Let's start by taking a look at how the modes are organized; then we can jump in and start using them. The blending modes are divided into six categories (**Figure 17.1**).

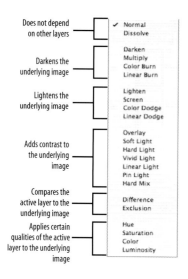

Figure 17.1 The Blending Modes menu is organized into six sections.

Dissolve Mode

The first blending mode is called Dissolve, and although it might be useful to some people, it's the one that I use the least out of the whole collection. It only affects areas that are partially transparent. All it does is take areas that are partially transparent and transform them into a scattered spray of solid pixels. As a result, those areas end up looking noisy (**Figures 17.2** and **17.3**). I do see the Dissolve blending mode used on occasion for product packaging, usually to create a noisy-looking shadow or glow around some text. You can accomplish this quite easily by adding a Drop Shadow or an Outer Glow layer style to a layer and setting its blending mode (in the Layer Style dialog box) to Dissolve (**Figure 17.4**). It's not very often that I need this kind of a look, so let's move on and see what the other blending modes can do.

Figure 17.2 A drop shadow created in Photoshop's default blending mode.

Figure 17.3 The same drop shadow created in Dissolve mode.

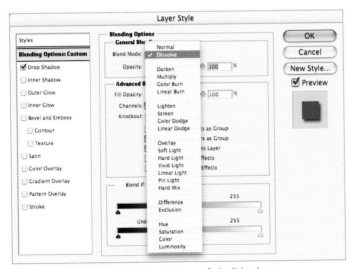

Figure 17.4 Choosing Dissolve from the Layer Style dialog box.

Behind Mode

Most of the blending modes available in Photoshop show up in the pop-up menu at the top of the Layers palette, but the Behind blending mode shows up in only a few areas of Photoshop (painting tools and the Edit > Fill dialog box). Behind mode limits the changes you make to a layer so that they only affect the transparent areas of the active layer. Using Behind mode is similar to working on a layer directly below the one that is active. Painting on a layer in Behind mode gives the impression that you're painting underneath the active layer (**Figures 17.5** to **17.7**).

I mainly use this mode with the Edit > Fill dialog box as a quick-and-dirty way to fill the empty parts of a layer. I use it when I'm creating a slide show and don't want to see the checkerboard background anywhere. Choosing Edit > Fill, setting the Use pop-up menu to White, and changing the Mode pop-up menu to Behind, for example, fills all transparent pixels with white.

If you find that the Behind mode isn't working as you expected, then glance at the top of the Layers palette to see if the Lock Transparency icon is turned on. When that icon is turned on, you can't change the transparent areas of the active layer, which makes the Behind mode useless.

Figure 17.5 A layer that contains transparent areas. (©2003 Photospin, www.photospin.com)

Figure 17.6 Painting in Behind mode.

Figure 17.7 The brush strokes appear to be underneath the active layer.

Clear Mode

This is another blending mode that shows up only in certain areas of Photoshop (like in the painting tools and Edit > Fill command). Clear mode is basically the same as using the Eraser tool, or selecting an area and then pressing Delete (Mac) or Backspace (Windows).

I generally use this mode to lower the opacity of a large area. Choosing Edit > Fill in Clear mode at 40% opacity, for example, reduces the opacity of the layer by 40%, leaving it 60% opaque (**Figures 17.8** and **17.9**).

When you use Clear mode, Photoshop will completely ignore the color you are attempting to fill or paint with. It only pays attention to the Opacity setting and uses the paint or selection that is active to determine which areas should be deleted.

You'll find Clear mode in only a few areas of Photoshop, including the Line tool (using the Fill setting on the far left of the options bar), the Paint Bucket tool, the Brush tool, the Pencil tool, the Fill command, and the Stroke command.

NOTES

If you'd rather not permanently lower the opacity of an area, then you might want to think about using a Layer Mask instead (see the previous chapter for general info on Layer Masks). Clear mode is like putting gray in a Layer Mask. Filling with 40% opacity in Clear mode is the same as filling part of a Layer Mask with 40% gray.

The Lock Transparency icon at the top of the Layers palette prevents you from changing how transparent an area is. When that check box is turned on, the Behind and Clear modes will be grayed out.

Figure 17.8 The original foreground image with a white background.

Figure 17.9 The foreground image filled using Clear mode, at 50% opacity.

Darken Blending Modes

The blending modes on the second section of the menu are grouped together because they can only darken the underlying image. In all of these modes, white simply disappears, and in most of them, anything darker than white will darken the underlying image. Each mode has its own personality, so let's look at them one at a time.

Darken Mode

Darken compares the active layer to the underlying image and allows only those areas that are darker than that image to show up (**Figures 17.10** to **17.12**). It's that simple when you're working on grayscale images, but if you try the same mode out on a color image, you might be surprised by the result.

Figure 17.10 The top layer. (©2003 PhotoSpin, www.photospin.com)

Figure 17.11 The bottom layer. (© 2003 Stockbyte, www.stockbyte.com)

Figure 17.12 Result of using Darken mode on the top layer.

Color images are usually made up of three components: red, green, and blue. Darken mode compares two layers by looking at red, green, and blue individually. So, let's say you have a layer with some red in it that's made out of 230 Red, 50 Green, and 30 Blue, and you have a layer above it that contains a blue color made from 50 Red, 55 Green, and 200 Blue. The blue in the top layer would usually completely cover up the color below (**Figure 17.13**), but when you set the top layer to Darken mode, Photoshop will compare the red, green, and blue components of each layer and use the darkest of each. In this case, it would see that the red information on the top layer is darker (50 versus 230; lower numbers mean less light). When comparing the green components, it would see that the bottom layer is darker, and it would see that the blue component is darkest on the bottom layer. So, once it picked the darkest of each, it would end up with 50 Red, 50 Green, and 30 Blue, which would result in a dark yellow color (**Figure 17.14**). I don't usually think about the red, green, and blue components of each layer when I'm using Darken mode, but I occasionally blame them when I don't get the result I am looking for.

Figure 17.13 In Normal mode, the top layer obstructs your view of the underlying image.

Figure 17.14 In Darken mode, Photoshop uses the darkest of the red, green, and blue components.

I mainly use Darken mode when I'm retouching an image, which we'll talk about in the next chapter, but for now, let's see how we might use it with Photoshop's filters. Let's say you've chosen Filter > Pixelate > Pointillize, but you don't like all the white areas that show up (**Figure 17.15**). If that's the case, you can choose Edit > Fade Pointillize immediately after applying the filter, and then you can tell Photoshop how to apply that filter to the original. If you choose Darken, Photoshop will compare the filtered result with the original and only allow the filter to darken the original, which should in effect get rid of the white areas (unless the original contained white) (**Figure 17.16**). I often use this technique after applying the Sharpen filter, because the bright halos it produces are often distracting. By using Darken mode, I can limit that filter so that it will create only dark halos.

Figure 17.15 Result of applying the Pointillize filter. (©2003 Stockbyte, www.stockbyte.com)

Figure 17.16 Result of fading the Pointillize filter in Darken mode.

Multiply Mode

Of all the Darken blending modes, the one I use the most is Multiply. Multiply acts just like ink. To see what I mean, just imagine taking **Figure 17.17** and printing it on an inkjet printer. Then, imagine sending the sheet back through the printer and printing a second image on top of the first (**Figure 17.18**). All the second printing can do is darken the first because all an inkjet printer can do is add ink to the page (**Figure 17.19**). Or, if you're a photographer, think about what happens when you sandwich two 35mm slides together. The second can only darken the first, right? Well, it's the same concept. In this mode, white simply disappears. After all, how do you print white with an inkjet printer? You don't. Instead you just leave the paper alone. It's the same way in Multiply mode; white simply disappears. But anything darker than white will darken the underlying image.

Figure 17.17 The first image to be printed. (©2003 Stockbyte, www.stockbyte.com)

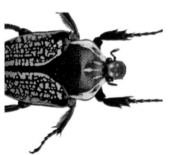

Figure 17.18 Image to be printed on the second pass. (©2003 Stockbyte, www.stockbyte.com)

Figure 17.19 Result of combining the two images.

This is a simple way to make text or graphics "overprint" on the underlying image instead of just covering it up (**Figures 17.20** and **17.21**). In essence, using Multiply mode causes one layer to act like a Magic Marker on the layer below. I find this mode to be extremely useful when working with images that contain natural shadows. Back in Chapter 15, "Shadows," we used this mode to make an existing shadow print on top of a new image (**Figures 17.22** to **17.24**). You can also use it anytime you have scanned text or other graphics that you'd like to print on something else. The main problem you'll have to look out for is areas that are not completely white. Any area that is darker than white will darken the underlying image. This means that you'll occasionally need to choose Image > Adjustments > Levels and move the upper-right slider to make sure the background is pure white. As an example, let's say that I'd like to take the tattoo from **Figure 17.25** and make it look as if it were on **Figure 17.26** instead. I'd go about that by placing the tattoo on a layer above the second image, setting the blending mode of that layer to Multiply (**Figure 17.27**), choosing Image > Adjustments > Desaturate, and then adjusting the image using Levels until only the tattoo appeared and the background surrounding it disappeared (**Figure 17.28**). If there ended up being a few areas that simply didn't disappear, I'd switch to the Eraser tool to eradicate those trouble areas.

Figure 17.20 Top layer set to Normal mode. (©2003 Stockbyte, www.stockbyte.com)

Figure 17.21 Top layer set to Multiply mode.

Figure 17.22 Image that contains two layers: subject and shadow. (©2003 PhotoSpin, www.photospin.com)

Figure 17.23 Image to overlay the shadow onto. (©2003 Stockbyte, www.stockbyte.com)

Figure 17.24 Result of combining two images and setting the shadow layer to Multiply.

Figure 17.25 Tattoo to be transplanted to another image. (©2003 Stockbyte, www.stockbyte.com)

Figure 17.26 Image that the tattoo will be applied to. (©2003 Stockbyte, www.stockbyte.com)

Figure 17.27 Result of setting the tattoo layer to Multiply mode.

Figure 17.28 Result of desaturating and then adjusting the image with Levels.

During my seminars, I usually end up talking about how both your screen and printer simulate a wide range of colors using just red, green, and blue light, or cyan, magenta, and yellow ink. To demonstrate this, I usually create an image that contains three circles, one per layer: one cyan, one magenta, and the third yellow. The problem is that they don't act like ink when they overlap (**Figure 17.29**). So I simply set the blending mode for each layer to Multiply, and then everything works the way I want it to (**Figure 17.30**).

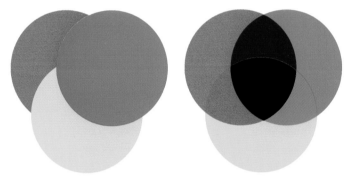

Figure 17.29 In Normal mode, the three circles don't interact with each other.

Figure 17.30 Result of setting each layer to Multiply mode.

Now let's see how we might be able to use Multiply in a project where you need to create a contour drawing out of a photograph (**Figure 17.31**). To start out, open any image. (Faces work rather well.) Because we're going to end up with black lines and no color information, let's choose Image > Mode > Grayscale. Now let's start playing with Photoshop's filters to get our contours. Choose Filter > Stylize > Trace Contour, and move the slider around a bit just to see what happens (**Figure 17.32**). You'll see that Trace Contour puts a black line around the edge of a particular shade of gray. There are just two problems: First, the contours aren't usually smooth, and second, there's only one contour for the entire image. To fix the first problem, just smooth out your image by applying either the Gaussian Blur or the Median filter. The latter will require a little more effort, and that's where we can start putting the

Figure 17.31 Left: The original image. Right: Result of conversion to a contour drawing. (©2003 Stockbyte, www.stockbyte.com)

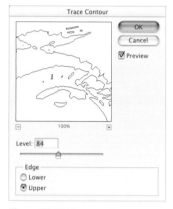

Figure 17.32 The Trace Contour dialog box.

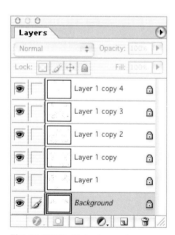

Figure 17.33 All the layers that are needed to create the drawing.

Multiply blending mode to work. Duplicate the layer enough times so that you have one layer for each contour that you'd like to end up with. (I want to end up with six, so I'll press Command-J [Mac] or Ctrl-J [Windows] five times to end up with six layers total.) Then apply the Trace Contour filter to each layer, using a different level setting each time. The level setting can be found in the Trace Contour dialog box. You'll end up with six layers, each containing a different contour (**Figure 17.33**). Now to combine those images into one, set the blending mode of each layer to Multiply so they print on top of each other, which will make the white areas disappear (**Figure 17.34**).

Here's another way of using blending modes with filters. Let's say you've opened an image and then chosen Filter > Stylize > Find Edges. After doing that, you'd end up with a bunch of black lines that represent the edges of all the objects that were in your photo (**Figure 17.35**). But what if you wanted those black lines to print on top of the original image? Well, immediately after applying the filter, you could choose Edit > Fade Fine Edges and set the Blending Mode menu to Multiply. Photoshop would then apply the filtered image to the original as if you had printed on top of it (**Figure 17.36**).

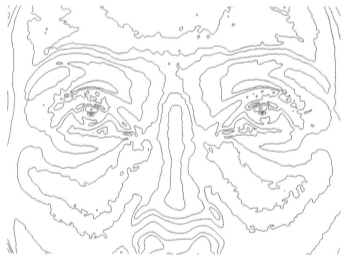

Figure 17.34 Result of combining all the layers in Multiply mode.

Figure 17.35 Result of applying the Find Edges filter. (original image © 2003 Stockbyte, www.stockbyte.com)

Figure 17.36 Result of fading the edges in Multiply mode.

You'll find that Multiply mode is used quite a bit in Photoshop's Layer Styles. This occasionally messes me up when I'm trying to do something unusual. Here's an example. Let's say I have some black text on a red background, and I'd like to add a drop shadow. So, with the text layer active, I choose Layer > Layer Style > Drop Shadow. But a black drop shadow with black text makes the text hard to see (**Figure 17.37**), so I decide to change the shadow color to white. When I do this, however, the shadow simply disappears! That's because its mode is automatically set to Multiply (in the Layer Style dialog box), and white disappears in Multiply mode. To get things to work the way I want them to, I simply change the mode from Multiply to Normal, and everything works fine (**Figure 17.38**).

Figure 17.37 The black drop shadow does not contribute to the legibility of the text.

Figure 17.38 A white shadow isn't possible in Multiply mode, so the mode has been changed to Normal.

Color Burn Mode

This mode is not easy to describe or understand, but can be very useful nonetheless. Just as with all the Darken blending modes, white doesn't do anything in Color Burn mode. Black will leave any red, green, or blue numbers that are 255 alone and force all others to zero. When you paint with a primary color (pure red, green, or blue), you'll end up with the amount of that primary color that was in the underlying image and nothing else. When you paint with a color that's made out of two primaries, Photoshop will strip the third primary color out of the underlying image. Here's where the goodies come in. Paint with shades of gray to darken and intensify the colors that are in the underlying image. This can work wonders for darkening bland-looking skies, making them more colorful while at the same time maintaining the bright white clouds (**Figures 17.39** and **17.40**). I sometimes like the way shadows look when I use Color Burn. If a shadow is falling on a textured background, then more of the texture will come through because it will maintain more of the highlights (**Figures 17.41** and **17.42**). I also use this mode to colorize grayscale images. If you're going to try it, just make sure to change the mode of your image from grayscale to RGB or CMYK. You'll most likely want to lower the opacity of the painting tool you use; otherwise, you'll end up with a rather dark result. I'll talk more about using the mode for colorizing once we've had a chance to cover some of the other modes that are also used for that purpose.

Figure 17.39 The original image.
(© 2003 Stockbyte, www.stockbyte.com)

Figure 17.40 Result of painting with gray across the sky in Color Burn mode.

Linear Burn Mode

This mode acts much like Multiply mode, but has a greater tendency to make areas pure black. It also seems to maintain more of the color from the underlying image. Use it anytime you'd think about using Multiply mode, but would like a higher-contrast result. If you ever find that standard shadows (which usually use Multiply mode) look a little too gray, then try Linear Burn; you might like the result better (**Figures 17.43** and **17.44**), although you will need to lower the Opacity setting to avoid getting an overly dark result. So, anytime you'd normally use Multiply mode, be sure to also try Linear Burn mode—especially if you're looking for a darker, more saturated result (**Figures 17.45** and **17.46**).

Figure 17.41 Shadow applied in the default blending mode: Multiply mode.

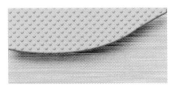

Figure 17.42 Shadow applied in Color Burn mode.

Figure 17.43 Shadow applied in Multiply mode.

Figure 17.44 Shadow applied in Linear Burn mode.

Figure 17.45 Two images combined in Multiply mode.

Figure 17.46 Two images combined in Linear Burn mode.

Lighten Blending Modes

For each of the darken blending modes (Darken, Multiply, Color Burn, and Linear Burn), there is an equally useful opposite mode. With all the lighten blending modes, black simply disappears, and anything brighter than black has the potential to brighten the underlying image.

Lighten Mode

This mode compares the active layer to the underlying image, and allows the areas of the active layer to show up that are brighter than the underlying image. But again, it looks at the red, green, and blue components of the image separately, which makes for some unpredictable results. Lighten mode was a lifesaver the last time I visited my brother in New York. He's an artist who has no sense for normal sleeping hours. Right when I was getting ready to call it a night, my brother decided to work on a computer project. The problem was that his computer was in the guest room, so I knew he was going to keep me up until he finished his project. Knowing that, I took a keen interest in the project. It turned out that he was attempting to create a photo-realistic 3D rendering of a lamp that he was thinking of making. The only problem was that he could either get the glass part of the bulb to show up or the glowing filament, but he couldn't get both (**Figures 17.47** and **17.48**). It looked as if it was going to take him hours to figure it out, so in the interest of a good night's sleep, I volunteered to help. After looking at the two images he had created, I thought that if Photoshop could only compare them and let one image lighten the other, then I could get to sleep. So I loaded both images into Photoshop, one atop the other, and set the blending mode of the top layer to Lighten and—bingo, I could call it a night (**Figure 17.49**).

Figure 17.47 Image with bulbs visible. (courtesy Nik Willmore, www.e-dot.com)

Figure 17.48 Image with filament visible.

Figure 17.49 Result of combining two images in Lighten mode.

I use Lighten mode a lot when I'm experimenting with filters. For instance, choosing Filter > Stylize > Glowing Edges will create bright lines where the edges of an object were in your image (**Figure 17.50**). I sometimes use this filter to add extra interest to an image by choosing Edit > Fade Glowing Edges, and then setting the Blending Mode menu to Lighten immediately after applying the filter (**Figure 17.51**). That way I can get the bright edge effect while maintaining the overall look of the original image. The same concept works great when you're using the Lighting Effects filter, which usually brightens or darkens an image. In Lighten mode, you can force that filter to only brighten the image (**Figures 17.52** to **17.54**). I like to use it after applying the Blur filter to add a soft-focus look (**Figure 17.55**). It can also be wonderful when sharpening an image. You can duplicate the layer twice, set the top layer to Lighten and the middle layer to Darken, and then sharpen the top two layers. Then you can control the dark and bright halos separately by lowering the opacity of each of those two layers. (This mode will be helpful in the next chapter when we talk about retouching.)

Figure 17.50 The colors shift when the Glowing Edges filter is applied. (original image ©2003 Stockbyte, www.stockbyte.com)

Figure 17.51 More of the original image is visible after Lighten mode is used.

Figure 17.52 The original image. (© 2003 Stockbyte, www.stockbyte.com)

Figure 17.53 The Lighting Effects filter both brightens and darkens the image.

Figure 17.54 Result of fading the Lighting Effects filter in Lighten mode.

Figure 17.55 Top: The original image. Bottom: A soft-focus look. (©2003 Stockbyte, www.stockbyte.com)

Screen Mode

If Multiply mode acts like ink, then Screen mode is its opposite, acting like light instead. In this mode, black simply disappears, while anything brighter than black will brighten the underlying image. Screen mode is useful when you have an image with a black background, with anything that resembles light. I like to use it with things like sparklers and lightning. I just put the sparkler on a layer above another image, set the layer mode to Screen, and then choose Image > Adjust > Levels and pull the upper-left slider in until the background of the sparkler disappears (**Figures 17.56** and **17.57**).

Figure 17.56 Result of using Screen mode to combine images. (©2003 Stockbyte, www.stockbyte.com)

Figure 17.57 Result of applying Levels to darken the background of the sparkler to black.

Screen mode is used in many of Photoshop's Layer Styles. Let's say you have some text and you add a glow around it by choosing Layer > Layer Style > Outer Glow. That will work fine as long as you choose a color that is bright like white or yellow, but it won't look so good if you use a dark color like navy blue (**Figure 17.58**). This is because Photoshop uses Screen mode as the default method for applying the glow to the underlying image, and shining a dark blue light at something isn't going to change it much. To remedy the situation, just change the blending mode (in the Layer Style dialog box) to either Normal or Multiply (**Figure 17.59**).

In my Photoshop seminars, I usually talk about how red, green, and blue light interact to create all the colors that a computer monitor can display. To demonstrate this, I start with a document that has a black background layer. Then I create three layers: one with a red circle, one with a blue one, and the third using green. But when I move these circles so they overlap, they don't interact like they would if they were made by shining a flashlight at a wall (**Figure 17.60**). By setting each of the layers to Screen mode, I can get the circles to interact with each other as if they were circles of light (**Figure 17.61**).

Color Dodge Mode

This mode will usually brighten the underlying image while at the same time making the colors more saturated. It's very useful because it doesn't change the darkest part of your image much, which allows you to brighten an area while still maintaining good contrast. I usually just use the

Figure 17.58 A deep blue outer glow created in the default blending mode: Screen mode.

Figure 17.59 Result of switching from Screen mode to Normal mode.

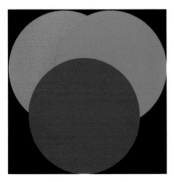

Figure 17.60 In Normal mode, the three circles don't interact with each other.

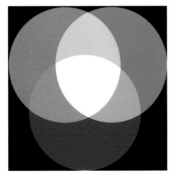

Figure 17.61 Result of switching each layer to Screen mode.

Paintbrush tool and paint with a dark shade of gray on a layer set to Color Dodge mode (**Figures 17.62** and **17.63**). It's sometimes useful for adding more interest to otherwise dull-looking hair. (Photographers often use a separate light source just to add highlights to hair.) I often use Color Dodge mode as a replacement for Screen mode when I'm adding an outer glow Layer Style to text (see **Figures 17.64** and **17.65**).

Figure 17.62 The original image. (©2003 Stockbyte, www.stockbyte.com)

Figure 17.64 Yellow glow created in Screen mode. (original image ©2003 Stockbyte, www.stockbyte.com)

Figure 17.63 The water was brightened with gray paint in Color Dodge mode.

Figure 17.65 The same yellow glow created in Color Dodge mode.

Linear Dodge

This mode works much like Screen mode but it has a greater tendency to make areas pure white. Use it any time you're considering Screen mode but would like a higher-contrast result (**Figures 17.66** and **17.67**).

Figure 17.66 A simple glow created in Screen mode. (original image ©2003 Stockbyte, www.stockbyte.com)

Figure 17.67 The same glow created in Linear Dodge mode.

Contrast Blending Modes

The majority of blending modes available on the next section of the menu combine the ideas we've used in the Darken and Lighten blending modes. In all of these modes, 50% gray simply disappears, and anything darker than 50% has the potential of darkening the underlying image, while areas brighter than 50% have the potential to brighten the underlying image. In essence, these modes increase the contrast of the underlying image by brightening one area while darkening another.

Figure 17.68 The original image. (©2003 Stockbyte, www.stockbyte.com)

Overlay Mode

In Overlay mode, the information on the underlying image is used to brighten or darken the active layer. Any areas that are darker than 50% gray will act like ink (or Multiply mode), while any areas brighter than 50% gray will act like light (or Screen mode). Overlay mode is useful when you want to add color to the underlying image while maintaining its highlights and shadows (**Figures 17.68** and **17.69**). I also use this mode a lot when I'm working with Layer

Figure 17.69 Result of placing solid red on a layer set to Overlay mode.

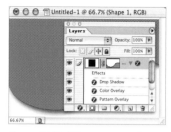

Figure 17.70 When you use color overlay and a pattern fill, the color obstructs your view of the pattern.

Figure 17.71 Applying the color overlay in Overlay mode allows it to combine with the underlying pattern.

Styles. If I use both a pattern fill and a color overlay, then the color overlay always completely covers up the pattern that is underneath it. But if I apply the color using the Overlay blending mode (in the Layer Style dialog box), it allows the highlights and shadows from the texture to brighten and darken the color that I'm applying (**Figures 17.70** and **17.71**). This allows me to create many grayscale patterns and then colorize them with the Color Overlay layer style.

Soft Light Mode

As with the other modes in this category, Soft Light mode makes 50% gray disappear while making brighter areas brighten and darker areas darken the underlying image. It usually does this with more subtle results than those you get in either Overlay or Hard Light mode. I primarily use this mode for applying textures to photographs. I cover a bunch of texture techniques in Chapter 19, "Type and Background Effects," but for now let's create just one. Open any photographic image and create a new, empty layer above that image. Next, type **D** to reset your foreground and background colors, and then choose Filter > Render Clouds. Now choose Filter > Stylize > Find Edges, and then Filter > Stylize > Emboss. Set the angle to 45°, the height to 1, and the amount as high as it can go. If you've done everything right, you should end up with a texture that resembles most refrigerators. To apply that texture to the underlying image, set its blending mode to Soft Light at the top of the Layers palette (**Figure 17.72**).

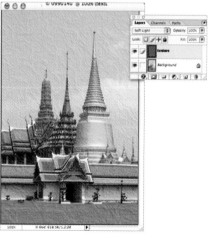

Figure 17.72 A texture applied in Soft Light mode. (©2003 PhotoSpin, www.photospin.com)

Soft Light mode is also useful when you're attempting to add a reflection to a metallic image. Just place the image you want to reflect on a layer above the metallic object, and set its blending mode to Soft Light (**Figures 17.73** and **17.74**).

Figure 17.73 Two layers, both set to Normal mode. (©2003 Stockbyte, www.stockbyte.com)

Figure 17.74 Result of switching the top layer to Soft Light mode.

Hard Light Mode

This has got to be one of my absolute favorite blending modes. In essence, it's a combination of Multiply mode (which acts like ink) and Screen mode (which acts like light). In Hard Light mode, any areas that are 50% gray will disappear, areas darker than 50% will darken the underlying image, and areas brighter than 50% will brighten the underlying image. You'll find me using this mode anytime I use the Emboss filter. When I choose Filter > Stylize > Emboss, I end up with a gray image that has almost no hint of the colors from the original image (**Figures 17.75** and **17.76**). But the gray gunk I do end up with happens to be exactly 50% gray (in RGB mode), which means that I can choose Edit > Fade Emboss and set the mode to Hard Light, and bingo…the gray is gone (**Figure 17.77**)! So Hard Light mode allows me to emboss an image while maintaining its color qualities. You can go one better by duplicating the layer before you emboss it. Then, choose Image > Adjustments > Desaturate to ensure there won't be any color shifts (**Figures 17.78** and **17.79**). Next, set the duplicate layer to Hard Light mode, and then apply the Emboss filter. This way you'll get a real-time preview instead of staring at a bunch of gray stuff while you're applying the filter.

Figure 17.75 The original image. (©2003 Andy Katz)

Figure 17.76 The Emboss filter delivers a gray result.

Figure 17.77 Result of applying the Emboss filter in Hard Light mode.

Figure 17.78 Embossing a color image produces color residue.

Figure 17.79 Desaturating the image prevents color residue.

Vivid Light

This mode is a combination of Color Dodge and Color Burn. In Vivid Light mode, areas darker than 50% darken and the colors become more saturated; areas brighter than 50% brighten and the colors become more saturated. This mode is great when an image really needs some kick. Just duplicate the layer and set it to Vivid Light mode. You'll most likely need to turn down the Opacity setting in order to get an acceptable result (**Figures 17.80** and **17.81**). I also use Vivid Light when I want to apply a texture to an image and I'm concerned that Overlay, Soft Light, or Hard Light mode will make the colors look a little too dull. For example, you can create a new layer above the image you want to texturize. Next, choose Filter > Render > Clouds, then apply Filter > Sharpen > Unsharp Mask with settings of 500, 1.5, and 0, and finish by applying Filter > Stylize > Emboss with settings of 145, 1, and 500. Now if you set the texture layer to Vivid Light mode, you'll be adding texture and enhancing the colors in the image (**Figures 17.82** and **17.83**).

Figure 17.80 The original image could use a little contrast and saturation. (©2003 PhotoSpin, www.photospin.com)

Figure 17.81 Result of duplicating the layer and setting it to Vivid Light mode.

Figure 17.82 The original image. (©2003 Stockbyte, www.stockbyte.com)

Figure 17.83 Texture applied in Vivid Light mode.

Linear Light

This mode is a combination of Linear Dodge and Linear Burn. I try this mode anytime I'm considering using Hard Light mode. It produces a higher-contrast result where more areas will become pure black and pure white. This is another mode that is great with textures. I mainly use it when I want the highlights and shadow areas of a texture to become pure white and pure black, which usually makes the texture look extra crisp. If you'd like to give it a try, just create a new layer above the image you want to enhance, then fill that layer with white. Now, to make the texture, choose Filter > Artistic > Sponge, and use settings of 2, 12, and 5 to pull out some contrast; then choose Image > Adjustments > Auto Levels and finish it off with Filter > Stylize > Emboss with settings of 135, 1, and 65. Once you set the blending mode to Linear Light, you should see what I'm talking about (**Figures 17.84** and **17.85**). If you find that the colors become too vivid, then duplicate the original image, place it on top of the layers stack, and set its blending mode to Color (**Figures 17.86** and **17.87**). (We'll talk about Color mode in a bit.) I often use this technique to create a high-contrast, soft-focus look. I'll end up with three versions of the original image, the bottom one being normal, the middle one being blurred and set to Linear Light mode, and the top one being set to Color mode and not blurred (**Figures 17.88** to **17.90**).

Figure 17.84 The texture that will be applied to a photo.

Figure 17.85 Applying the texture in Linear Light mode produces more saturated colors. (©2003 Andy Katz)

Figure 17.86 Place a duplicate of the original image on top, and set the mode to Color.

Figure 17.87 Result of applying a duplicate of the original in Color mode.

Figure 17.88 The original image.
(©2003 Stockbyte, www.stockbyte.com)

Figure 17.89 Blurring a duplicate layer set to Linear Light mode produces saturated colors.

Figure 17.90 Result of applying the original image in Color mode.

Pin Light

This mode is a combination of Lighten and Darken modes. I find that I use this mode mainly when I'm experimenting with filters. I'll end up trying all the contrast modes, and on occasion Pin Light will be the most effective. But it's not very often that I think of a technique that is created specifically with Pin Light in mind. Here's an example of a situation where I ended up liking what Pin Light gave me. I duplicated the original layer, set the top layer to Pin Light, and left the bottom layer set to Normal. Then, with the top layer active, I chose Filter > Sketch > Note Paper and used settings of 25, 5, and 2. That created 3D highlights, but too much of the gray background was showing up (**Figure 17.91**). To finish it off, I chose Image > Adjustments > Levels and moved the middle slider until the background disappeared (**Figure 17.92**).

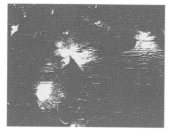

Figure 17.91 The Note Paper filter delivers a result that contains large areas of gray.

Figure 17.92 Applying the filter in Pin Light mode and adjusting the image with Levels. (©2003 Stockbyte, www.stockbyte.com)

Hard Mix

The Hard Mix blend mode is new to Photoshop CS. This mode will posterize the underlying layers based on the Fill Opacity setting of the layer that is using the Hard Mix blending mode. A high Fill Opacity will deliver extreme posterization, whereas lower Fill Opacity settings will deliver a smoother-looking image (**Figures 17.93** to **17.95**).

If the brightness of the layer is near 50% gray, then the brightness of the underlying image will not change. Anything brighter than 50% gray will brighten the underlying image, whereas anything darker will darken it (**Figures 17.96** to **17.99**). A layer filled with 50% gray (RGB = 128, 128, 128) will neither brighten nor darken the underlying image, although varying the Fill Opacity will still control its posterization.

Figure 17.93 The original image.

Figure 17.94 Result of duplicating the layer and setting the blending mode to Hard Mix.

Figure 17.95 Result of lowering the Fill Opacity of the duplicate layer to 70%.

Figure 17.96 The original image.

Figure 17.97 Using 50% gray will leave the brightness of the underlying image unchanged.

Figure 17.98 Using a shade brighter than 50% gray will brighten the underlying image.

Figure 17.99 Using a shade darker than 50% gray will darken the underlying image.

I like to use Hard Mix to create a "clipping display" just like what you'd get when you Option-drag (Mac) or Alt-drag (Windows) one of the sliders in Image > Adjustments > Levels or the Camera Raw dialog box. All you have to do is choose Layer > New Fill Layer > Solid Color, set the Mode pop-up menu to Hard Mix, and then work with a shade of gray. Using black will show you all the areas that are being blown out to white, whereas using white will show you all the areas that are plugged up to black. I just create two layers at the top of the Layers palette and turn them on whenever I need to check to see if I've lost detail in the highlights or shadows. This technique will be useful to you only if you're knowledgeable about clipping displays, so be sure to read Chapter 10, "Using Camera Raw," if you need a refresher.

Using Hard Mix mode with a 50% Fill Opacity often looks identical to the results you get using the Vivid Light blending mode at 100% Fill Opacity. For that reason, I try Hard Mix and experiment with the Fill Opacity setting anytime I'm experimenting with the Vivid Light blending mode.

How to Tell Them Apart

Here's my general thinking when using the contrast blending modes. Overlay mode will make the underlying image more prominent than the active layer. Hard Light mode does the opposite, making the active layer more prominent. Soft Light mode usually makes both layers equally prominent. Vivid Light acts a lot like Hard Light, but will increase the saturation of the colors while preserving more of the highlights and shadows from the underlying image. Linear Light is also like Hard Light, but it has a greater tendency to make areas pure black and pure white. Finally, Pinlight and Hard Mix are the loners in this group. Hard Mix mode will increase the saturation of the colors and posterize the image, while lightening the underlying image in the highlight areas of the active layer and darkening the underlying image in the shadow areas. Pin Light compares the two layers, brightens the underlying image in the highlight areas of the active layer, and darkens the underlying image where there are shadows in the active layer (in a rather unpredictable way).

Comparative Blending Modes

The next two modes are very similar to each other. In general, they compare the active layer to the underlying image, looking for areas that are identical in both. Those areas appear as black, while all nonmatching areas show up as shades of gray or color. The closer the nonmatching areas are to being black in the end result, the more similar the areas are to the underlying image. In these modes, white on the active layer will invert whatever appears on the underlying image, but black on the active layer will not change the underlying image.

Difference Mode

This mode works exactly as just described. Let's use it to create some homemade lightning. Start with a new document that contains a white background. Next, create a new layer, and reset your foreground and background colors by typing **D**; then choose Filter > Render Clouds, and set the layer containing the clouds to Difference mode. Now choose a large, soft-edged brush, and paint with black on the bottom layer. You should end up with a cloudy-looking image that has black areas around the edges of the area where you've painted (**Figure 17.100**). Now it's time to transform those black areas into lightning. We'll start the process by inverting the image to make black areas white. Do this by clicking on the topmost layer and then choosing Layer > New Adjustment Layer > Invert (**Figure 17.101**). Finally, choose Layer > New Adjustment Layer > Levels and move the upper-left slider until all you can see is the white "lightning" (**Figure 17.102**). Now you can continue painting on the bottommost layer to create more and more lightning. When you're all done, choose Layer > Merge Visible to combine the layers. You can apply the lightning to another image at any time by placing your lightning on a layer above and then setting the blending mode of the layer to Screen, so it acts like light. There are a number of other neat things to do with the Difference mode, which we'll explore again in Chapter 19, "Type and Background Effects."

Figure 17.100 Painting on a layer below some clouds that are set to Difference mode.

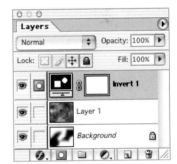

Figure 17.101 Adding an Invert adjustment layer above the clouds.

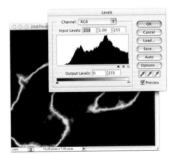

Figure 17.102 Pulling in the upper-left slider in Levels isolates the "lightning."

Figure 17.103 Result of applying the Clouds filter.

Figure 17.104 Smoothing out the clouds by using the Median filter.

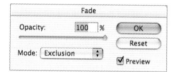

Figure 17.105 Fading the Chrome filter in Exclusion mode.

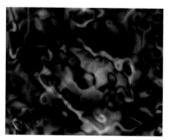

Figure 17.106 The end result after application of a gradient map.

Exclusion Mode

I'm sorry to say that this mode, along with Diffuse mode, usually just sits around collecting dust. It's just not very often that I have an image that will benefit from Exclusion mode, unless I'm going for a psychedelic, tripped-out '60s look. Let's see what I came up with when randomly experimenting with filters. I started by typing **D** to reset my foreground and background colors; then I chose Filter > Render Clouds (**Figure 17.103**). Next, I chose Filter > Noise > Median and used a setting somewhere around 10 (**Figure 17.104**). Then, to spice things up, I chose Filter > Sketch > Chrome with settings of 4 and 7. I chose Edit > Fade Chrome and tried both Difference and Exclusion modes (**Figure 17.105**). I preferred the look of Exclusion mode, so I clicked OK. I then chose Layer > New Adjustment Layer > Gradient Map and used the Color Burn blending mode. I created a gradient that went from orange to yellow, experimenting until I liked what I ended up with (**Figure 17.106**).

Hue/Saturation/Brightness Blending Modes

The next set of modes divides the colors of your image into three components: hue, saturation, and brightness. Photoshop applies only one or two of these qualities to the underlying image. These are wonderfully helpful modes, and the ones that I feel have the most practical and obvious uses.

Hue Mode

This mode looks at the basic colors contained on the active layer and applies them to the brightness and saturation information on the underlying layers. You can think of hue as the pure form of a color. In order to get to the pure form of a color, you have to ignore how dark the color is and how vivid it is, so you can concentrate just on its basic color. It's kind of like when you were a kid and only knew about a dozen words to describe color. Back then, you might have thought of a maroon car, or a pink dress, as being red.

That's because you were limited to describing things by their hue. This mode is great for changing the colors of objects that are already in color. All you have to do is create a new layer above the image, set it to Hue mode, and then paint away (**Figure 17.107**). I like to use the Gradient tool to create a two-tone look (**Figure 17.108**). You can even set the Gradient tool to Foreground to Transparent in order to shift one area and have it slowly fade out to the original color of the image (**Figures 17.109** and **17.110**). And then, after painting on the layer, you can really refine things by using the Eraser tool to bring areas back to normal (**Figure 17.111**). Be careful, though, because there are a few things that might mess you up when you're using Hue mode. First off, this mode cannot introduce color into an area that does not already contain color. (In order to do this, it would need to change the saturation of the area.) Secondly, it will not change the saturation of the underlying image. This means that if an area has just a hint of color in it, it will still have just as much color when you're done, because you will have only shifted that color to a different hue. It also can't change how bright areas are. This means that painting across a white area will not change the image, because there is no way to introduce color into a white area without darkening it. You should use this mode when you need to shift the color of something that already contains color.

Figure 17.107 Changing the color of an image in Hue mode. (©2003 Stockbyte, www.stockbyte.com)

Figure 17.108 A car with two-tone coloring created by applying the Gradient tool in Hue mode. (©2003 PhotoSpin, www.photospin.com)

Figure 17.109 Adding a gradient set to Foreground to Transparent.

Figure 17.110 Result of applying the gradient in Hue mode.

Figure 17.111 Final result after the Eraser tool was used to remove the color change from a few spots.

Saturation Mode

As a seminar speaker, I often find myself in a room filled with Photoshop users, and I'm fond of getting them to think in new ways that will help them understand what's really going on with their pixels. When I talk about Saturation mode, I usually ask the participants to close their eyes and visualize what fluorescent…gray looks like! That usually sends them for a spin, because there is no such thing as fluorescent gray. However, the attempt to visualize it forces their brains to think completely about saturation and nothing else. Saturation determines how much color shows up in your image. If there is no saturation, then there is no color at all, which just leaves brightness (grays). As things become more saturated, the color in that area becomes more vivid. When you get everything completely saturated, you end up with almost fluorescent colors. Now, with that in mind, let's see how Photoshop's Saturation mode works. First off, it completely ignores what colors (red, green, yellow, orange, etc.) are on a layer. It also ignores how bright those colors are and just concentrates on how vivid they are. Then it changes the colors in the underlying image until they become just as saturated as those on the active layer. If you paint with the most vivid green you can find, the colors in the underlying image will become just as vivid—*but* bear in mind that the only areas that will end up as green will be those areas that were green to begin with (**Figures 17.112** and **17.113**). Saturation mode simply can't shift any of the basic colors; reds stay red, blues stay blue, and so on. They just become more or less vivid to match the quality of the active layer.

Figure 17.112 The original image. (©2003 Stockbyte, www.stockbyte.com)

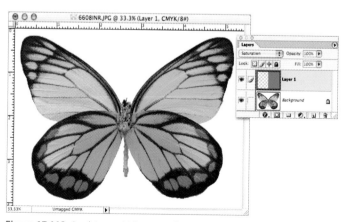

Figure 17.113 Applying a vivid green color to half the image in Saturation mode.

One of the most common uses for this mode is to force areas of an image to appear in black and white. All you have to do is create a new layer, set its blending mode to Saturation, and then paint with any shade of gray. Because grays don't contain any color (they are pure brightness information), they will change the underlying image to grayscale (**Figure 17.114**). If you don't want to take the image all the way to grayscale, then just lower the Opacity setting of the painting tool you are using (**Figures 17.115** and **17.116**). You can even use the Gradient tool to make the transition fade out. Just set it to Foreground to Transparent, and drag across the layer that is set to Saturation mode (**Figure 17.117**).

Figure 17.114 Painting with black on a layer set to Saturation mode changes the painted areas to grayscale. (©2003 Stockbyte, www.stockbyte.com)

Figure 17.115 The original image. (©2003 Andy Katz)

Figure 17.116 The area surrounding the bottle was painted in Saturation mode with gray at a medium opacity setting.

Figure 17.117 Applying a gradient causes the color to slowly fade out. (©2003 Stockbyte, www.stockbyte.com)

Color Mode

This mode applies both the hue (basic color) and saturation (vividness) of the active layer to the underlying image, leaving its brightness intact. In essence, it applies the color of the active layer to the brightness information of the underlying image. It's almost the same as Hue mode, with the exception that it can change the saturation of an area and therefore introduce color into an area that did not have it to begin with.

The most common (and most fun) use for this mode is to colorize grayscale photographs. All you have to do is change the mode of the image from grayscale to RGB or CMYK, create a new layer, set it to Color, and then paint away (**Figure 17.118**). If you feel the color you're adding is just too vivid, then lower the opacity of your brush (**Figure 17.119**). Or, if you just can't get enough color into an area, then you might want to try using Color Burn mode instead (**Figure 17.120**). If the highlights and shadows of the underlying image don't quite look right, then try using Overlay mode (**Figure 17.121**).

Figure 17.118 Color applied in Color mode at 100% opacity. (©2003 Stockbyte, www.stockbyte.com)

Figure 17.119 Lowering the opacity reduces the amount of color applied.

Figure 17.120 Color applied in Color Burn mode with a medium opacity setting.

Figure 17.121 Color applied in Overlay mode.

Luminosity Mode

This mode applies the brightness information of the active layer to the color in the underlying image. It can't shift colors or change how saturated those colors are. All it can do is change how bright they are.

I'm connected at the hip to Luminosity mode, because it seems that no matter what I'm doing, this mode is equipped to help out. Here are a few examples: Immediately after sharpening an image, I choose Edit > Fade Unsharp Mask and set the mode to Luminosity. This prevents the sharpening from adding odd colors to the edges of objects (**Figures 17.122** and **17.123**). A lot of people sharpen their images after converting them to Lab mode, but you can achieve the same result using the technique I just mentioned. Any time I adjust the brightness or contrast of an image using levels, Curves, or anything else, I'll end up choosing Edit > Fade and setting the mode to Luminosity; otherwise, the colors might become too vivid (**Figure 17.124**). If you're using an adjustment layer instead of applying the adjustment directly to the image, just set the blending mode of the adjustment layer to Luminosity instead of using the fade feature. If you apply a filter and you notice it shifting the color of the image (**Figures 17.125** to **17.127**), then choose Edit > Fade, and then use Luminosity mode to limit the filter so that it changes only the brightness of the image.

Figure 17.122 The Unsharp Mask filter produces vividly colored halos. (original image ©2003 Stockbyte, www.stockbyte.com)

Figure 17.123 Fading the filter in Luminosity mode prevents the overly saturated halos.

Figure 17.124 Left: The original image. Middle: A Curves adjustment designed to darken the image. Right: Result of fading the Curves adjustment in Luminosity mode. (©2003 Ben Willmore)

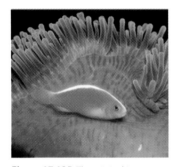

Figure 17.125 The original image. (©2003 Stockbyte, www.stockbyte.com)

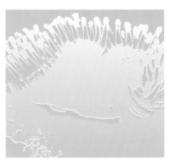

Figure 17.126 The Plaster filter.

Figure 17.127 Fading the filter in Luminosity mode prevents the filter from shifting colors.

Using Hue/Saturation as a Substitute

You can perform the same types of changes we made when we used the last set of modes by choosing Image > Adjustments > Hue/Saturation. The Hue/Saturation dialog box divides your image into three components (again, hue, saturation, and brightness), but it allows you to do some more interesting things.

To get a feeling for how the Hue/Saturation options work, open a colorful image and then choose Image > Adjustments > Hue/Saturation. Move the Hue slider around and see what happens to the image (**Figures 17.128 and 17.129**). You'll notice that all the colors in the image are shifting. Move the slider back to the middle, and this time concentrate on what happens to the two color bars at the bottom of the dialog box. The top bar shows all the hues you could possibly have in your image. The bottom bar indicates what they will shift to once you apply the adjustment (**Figure 17.130**). Because all the colors shift, you'll need to make a selection of the area that you want to change before you start adjusting the image.

Figure 17.128 The original image. (©2003 Stockbyte, www.stockbyte.com)

Figure 17.129 Moving the Hue slider shifts all the colors in the image.

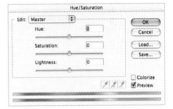

Figure 17.130 The color bars at the bottom of the Hue/Saturation dialog box indicate how the changes will affect the image.

You can also make areas black and white using this dialog box. All you have to do is select the area you want to change, choose Image > Adjustments > Hue/Saturation, and then move the Saturation slider all the way to the left. I usually don't move it all the way to the left because I like to keep a hint of color in every area of the image (**Figure 17.131**).

I use the Saturation slider on about 90% of the images that I scan. I find that raw scans just feel a little flat, and that even after color correction and contrast adjustments, they still need a bit more saturation. When this is the case, I choose Hue/Saturation and then bump up the colors by moving the Saturation slider toward the right (**Figures 17.132 and 17.133**).

Figure 17.131 Leaving a little saturation leaves a hint of color. (©2003 Stockbyte, www.stockbyte.com)

NOTES

Some saturated colors are difficult to reproduce on a commercial printing press. I suggest you choose View > Proof Colors to preview what your image will look like when it's converted to CMYK mode before increasing the Saturation setting.

Figure 17.132 The image after color correction has been performed. (©2003 Ben Willmore)

Figure 17.133 Result of boosting the saturation of the image.

It's not very often that I use the Lightness slider in the Hue/Saturation dialog box. That is, I don't use it all by itself because it's rather crude; I prefer to use more sophisticated tools such as levels and Curves. However, I do use it on occasion after I've shifted the color of an object if some color just seems too bright and vivid.

You can colorize black-and-white photographs using Hue/Saturation. All you need to do is convert from grayscale to RGB or CMYK mode and then choose Image > Adjustments > Hue/Saturation. You'll find that the Hue and Saturation sliders don't do anything on a grayscale image. In order to add color, you'll need to check the Colorize check box. I often make a selection and then create a new Hue/Saturation adjustment layer to colorize an area. Then I repeat the process until I've added color to the entire image (**Figures 17.134** and **17.135**).

Figure 17.134 The Colorize check box (found in Image > Adjustments > Hue/Saturation) will introduce color into a grayscale image that has been converted to RGB mode. (©2003 Andy Katz)

Figure 17.135 Result of creating a bunch of Hue/Saturation layers to colorize the image.

Figure 17.136 Choosing a color from the pop-up menu at the top of the dialog box causes sliders to appear between the color bars

Figure 17.137 Smashing the sliders together limits the range of colors that you can change.

Figure 17.138 Clicking on the image will center the sliders on the color you've selected. (original image ©2003 Stockbyte, www.stockbyte.com)

So far, the Hue/Saturation dialog box sounds like an easy shortcut to changing the color of your image, but as you toy with it, you'll realize that it's changing all of the colors of your image, and most times that's not what you'll want. Instead, you'll want to be able to control exactly where and how the color is changing. To do this you have to make some pretty surgical selections, which can be painstaking and time-consuming. But you'll be happy to know that you can avoid having to make those icky selections by practicing with Hue/Saturation until you can use it to isolate areas of your image based on color.

Let's see how it works: You can isolate a range of colors to work on by choosing a color from the Edit pop-up menu at the top of the Hue/Saturation dialog box. Once you've done that, you should see a few slider bars showing up between the two color bars at the bottom of the dialog box (**Figure 17.136**). These bars allow you to change only the colors that appear between them. The problem, however, is that the range of colors you'll be changing will be too wide for most uses. To remedy the situation, grab the small triangle that makes up one end of the slider and move it toward the others until they all smash together into a single mass (**Figure 17.137**). After you've done this, the sliders will probably no longer be below the color you were looking to change, so move the cursor onto your image and click on the area you'd like to change. This will precisely center the sliders on the color you've selected (**Figure 17.138**). Next, make a radical change to the hue or saturation of that area (I like to bring the Saturation setting down to –100) (**Figure 17.139**). Now hold down the Shift key and click on other areas until all of the areas you want to change shift in color (**Figure 17.140**). If you accidentally click on an area that shouldn't shift, then press down Option (Mac) or Alt (Windows) and click on that area again to remove it from the range of colors being changed. Once you've isolated the range of colors you want to change, experiment with the Hue and Saturation sliders until you get the effect you're looking for (**Figure 17.141**).

 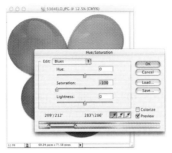 

Figure 17.139 Make a radical shift to the image so you can see which areas are changing.

Figure 17.140 Shift-click on additional areas to expand the range of colors that change.

Figure 17.141 Once you've isolated the range of colors you'd like to change, fine-tune the Hue and Saturation settings to get the color you desire.

You can use this technique to shift the colors of objects (using Hue) and to make areas black and white (using Saturation). I've also used it to pull all the color out of all but one color in an image. I usually do this by manually moving the sliders so they are under all the colors except for the one that I want to keep; then I bring the Saturation setting all the way to the left (**Figures 17.142** and **17.143**).

Figure 17.142 The original image.
(© 2003 PhotoSpin, www.photospin.com)

Figure 17.143 Result of desaturating all colors except red.

Closing Thoughts

If someone were to actually publish all of the great enhancement techniques out there, you'd be wading through a book 10 times the size of *War and Peace*. With this chapter, I've tried to give you some nice, tasty samples that will inspire you to go forth and try some more on your own. I hope you've enjoyed it. This part of Photoshop is always a pure pleasure for me—I could do this stuff every day. (Wait a minute—I do!) The more you work with Photoshop, the more you'll be able to add to your own personal cookbook of enhancement recipes. The trick is to find the time to experiment. I used to stay at work until rush-hour traffic died down just so I could have more time to play with Photoshop. When I went to college, there weren't any Photoshop classes, so I'm self-taught, thanks to a lot of midnight jam sessions with the tunes cranked up and Photoshop glowing on my computer screen. And look at me...I got to write this book!

Keyboard Shortcuts

The following keyboard commands change the blending mode of the current tool (if it supports blending modes); otherwise, they will change the blending mode of the currently active layer.

FUNCTION	MACINTOSH	WINDOWS
Previous blending mode	Shift-– (minus sign)	Shift-– (minus sign)
Next blending mode	Shift-+ (plus sign)	Shift-+ (plus sign)
Normal	Shift-Option-N	Shift-Alt-N
Dissolve	Shift-Option-I	Shift-Alt-I
Clear	Shift-Option-R	Shift-Alt-R
Darken	Shift-Option-K	Shift-Alt-K
Multiply	Shift-Option-M	Shift-Alt-M
Color Burn	Shift-Option-B	Shift-Alt-B
Linear Burn	Shift-Option-A	Shift-Alt-A
Lighten	Shift-Option-G	Shift-Alt-G
Screen	Shift-Option-S	Shift-Alt-S
Color Dodge	Shift-Option-D	Shift-Alt-D
Linear Dodge	Shift-Option-W	Shift-Alt-W
Overlay	Shift-Option-O	Shift-Alt-O
Soft Light	Shift-Option-F	Shift-Alt-F
Hard Light	Shift-Option-H	Shift-Alt-H
Vivid Light	Shift-Option-V	Shift-Alt-V
Linear Light	Shift-Option-J	Shift-Alt-J
Pin Light	Shift-Option-Z	Shift-Alt-Z
Hard Mix	Shift-Option-L	Shift-Alt-L
Color Dodge	Shift-Option-D	Shift-Alt-D
Difference	Shift-Option-E	Shift-Alt-E
Exclusion	Shift-Option-X	Shift-Alt-X
Hue	Shift-Option-U	Shift-Alt-U
Saturation	Shift-Option-T	Shift-Alt-T
Color	Shift-Option-C	Shift-Alt-C
Luminosity	Shift-Option-Y	Shift-Alt-Y

Courtesy of Gregg Lauer, www.gregglauer.com

Courtesy of Gregg Lauer, www.gregglauer.com

18
Retouching

*A doctor can bury his mistakes, but an architect can
only advise his clients to plant vines.*

— Frank Lloyd Wright

Retouching

NEW IN CS

Photoshop CS hasn't introduced
any new retouching tools, but I've
made considerable changes to this
chapter since the last edition of
this book, and I think you'll find it a
worthwhile read.

The doctoring of photographs didn't begin with the advent of computers in magazine production departments. One of history's most notorious photograph "doctors" was Joseph Stalin, who used photo retouching as a way to manipulate the masses. People who vanished in real life, whether banished to the farthest reaches of the Soviet Union or eliminated by the secret police, vanished from photos as well, and even from paintings. In many cases, they were airbrushed out completely; in others, their faces were clumsily blacked out with ink.

And then there were the Hollywood photo doctors. They didn't want to get rid of anyone; they just wanted to make them look better. I think they actually coined the term "too good to be true." Think about it—have you ever seen a photograph of a starlet with a blemish, or a wart, or bags under her eyes, or even the slightest indication that her skin actually had pores? Of course not!

If you look at it from these two extremes, you can appreciate why the subject of retouching is something of a, well, touchy subject. If you're brave enough to bring it up at a photographer's convention, you're likely to spark a pretty lively debate. A purist might tell you that every aspect of a photograph (including the flaws) is a perfect reflection of reality and should never be tampered with. Then again, a graphic artist, who makes a living from altering images, might tell you that an original photograph is just the foundation of an image, and that the so-called tampering is, in fact, a means of enhancing and improving upon it. Either way you look at it, you can't deny the fact that retouching photographs has become an everyday necessity for almost anyone who deals with graphic images. And when it comes to retouching, hands down, nothing does it better than Photoshop.

Photoshop packs an awesome arsenal of retouching tools. These include the Patch tool, Healing Brush tool, Clone Stamp tool, Dodge and Burn tools, and Blur and Sharpen tools, among others. We'll get to play with all of them, and for each one I'll also give you a little bag of tricks. You'll learn how to do all sorts of neat things, including retouching old ripped photos, getting rid of those shiny spots on foreheads, and adjusting the saturation of small areas. Or, you can put yourself in the doctor's seat and give someone instant plastic surgery. Remove a few wrinkles, perform an eye lift, reduce those dark rings around the eyes, and poof!—you've taken off 10 years. So let's look at these tools one at a time, starting with what I consider to be the most important one.

Patch Tool

The Patch tool (which is hidden under the Healing Brush, and looks like a Band-Aid in the Tools palette) is one of the most innovative yet simple tools I've ever seen Adobe come up with. The general concept is simple. You select an area of your image that needs to be touched up (maybe a blemish on skin) (**Figure 18.1**), and then you click in the middle of the selection and drag it to an area of your image that has similar texture but with no blemishes. As you move your mouse, Photoshop will preview the area you're going to copy from in the area you initially selected (**Figure 18.2**). Then, when you release the mouse button, Photoshop does an amazing job of blending the second area into the first (**Figure 18.3**). It makes sure that the brightness and color is consistent with what was on the edge of the original selection, and it blends the texture from the second area with that color. You simply have to try it to see what I mean.

You can even sample from an area that is radically different in brightness and color (**Figure 18.4**), because the Patch tool will pick up only the texture from the area that is sampled (**Figure 18.5**). The main thing you should look for is an area that has the proper texture for the area you are attempting to retouch.

Figure 18.1 Original image. (©2003 Stockbyte, www.stockbyte.com)

Figure 18.2 Drag the selection to an area of clean texture.

Figure 18.3 The result of using the Patch tool.

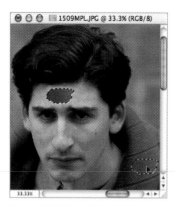

Figure 18.4 Drag the selection to an area that contains radically different colors and brightness. (©2003 Stockbyte, www.stockbyte.com)

Figure 18.5 Only the texture gets copied from the area you drag the selection to.

Just because this tool is rather sophisticated in the way it blends with the image, that doesn't mean you shouldn't be careful when making the selection. I always try to make the smallest selection that will completely encompass the defect I'm trying to retouch (**Figure 18.6**). The larger the area being patched, the less likely it will look good (**Figure 18.7**).

Figure 18.6 A small selection produces a nice blend. (©2003 Stockbyte, www.stockbyte.com)

Figure 18.7 A large selection makes the image look artificial.

This tool doesn't have many options to deal with (**Figure 18.8**). The main choice is whether to patch the source or the destination. With the Patch option set to Source (which I use 95% of the time), Photoshop will replace the area that was originally selected with a combination of the brightness and color values from its edge, along with the texture from the area you drag the selection to (**Figures 18.9** and **18.10**). Using the Destination setting does the opposite, letting you pick from a clean area of the original and then dragging it over the area that needs to be patched (**Figures 18.11** and **18.12**).

Figure 18.8 The options bar for the Patch tool.

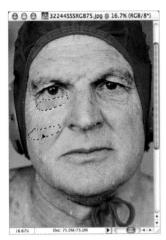

The Patch tool will have limited options available when editing an image that is in 16-bit mode. It will always use the Source settings, and most of the options found in the options bar at the top of your screen will be grayed out.

Figure 18.9 Using the source setting while dragging an area under the eye to an area of clean texture. (©2003 Stockbyte, www.stockbyte.com)

Figure 18.10 After releasing the mouse button, the clean texture is copied to the area under the eye and blended in automatically.

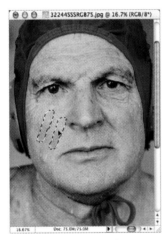

Figure 18.11 Using the destination setting while dragging a clean area of the skin to an area that needs retouching.

Figure 18.12 After releasing the mouse button, the area that was moved gets blended into the surrounding image.

If you can't find a clean area from which to steal texture, then you can select a pattern by clicking on the down-pointing arrow in the options bar (**Figure 18.13**) and then clicking the Use Pattern button. You'll find that patching with a pattern isn't all that effective unless you've created a custom pattern for this specific purpose. Be sure to check out Chapter 19, "Type and Background Effects," for details on how to create your own patterns.

Figure 18.13 Choosing a texture.

I find that the Patch tool is best for those situations where you have scratches, blemishes, or other defects in an area that should otherwise be relatively consistent in color (such as skin). It can even maintain some of the three-dimensionality of the surface with its blending capabilities (**Figures 18.14** and **18.15**). But you'll find that it's not very useful when you have an area that has multiple colors bordering it that shouldn't blend together. That's because Photoshop will attempt to blend the patched area into all the surrounding colors. In that case, you should switch to the Clone Stamp tool.

Figure 18.14 The original image. (©2003 Stockbyte, www.stockbyte.com)

Figure 18.15 Result of using the Patch tool (three passes were used to cover such a large area).

If you use the Patch tool to remove all wrinkles and blemishes from someone's face, then you might find that the person is no longer recognizable. When I retouch facial features, I like to choose Edit > Fade immediately after applying a patch (**Figure 18.16**). That allows me to change how the patch applies to the original image. I like to move the Opacity slider all the way to the left and then slowly move it toward the right until I find the lowest Opacity setting that will lessen the look of the undesirable feature without completely removing it (**Figures 18.17** to **18.19**). This technique is essential when working with shiny skin. If you use the Patch tool at full strength, you'll lose the dimensionality of the forehead, but fading it back will make the area look less shiny, without completely evening out the lighting on the person's skin.

I find that the Patch tool is most useful when working on large areas. It's just too cumbersome when you have to retouch dozens of small blemishes. When that's the case, I usually switch to the Healing Brush, which can make those small retouching jobs a breeze.

Figure 18.16 The Fade dialog box.

Figure 18.17 The original image. (©2003 Stockbyte, www.stockbyte.com)

Figure 18.18 Result of using the Patch tool at full strength to reduce shiny skin on chin.

Figure 18.19 Result of fading each application of the Patch tool to approximately 50% opacity.

Healing Brush Tool

The Healing Brush works using the same general concepts as the Patch tool. It attempts to patch a defect in your image using the texture from another area while blending all the edges with the surrounding colors. The main difference is that the Patch tool works by moving a selection, whereas the Healing Brush allows you to paint over the area that needs to be repaired. To use it, you'll first have to Option-click (Mac) or Alt-click (Windows) on the area you would like to use to fix an area (**Figure 18.20**), and then click and drag across the area that needs fixing (**Figure 18.21**). When you do that, be sure to cover the entire area without releasing the mouse button. Once you let go, Photoshop will check out the edges of the area you covered to make sure your "patch" blends with the color and brightness that is in the surrounding area (**Figure 18.22**). You might need to use a soft-edged brush to get a good blend (**Figures 18.23** and **18.24**). Just make sure that you choose your brush from the Brush drop-down menu in the options bar. This tool will ignore the stand-alone Brushes palette because it doesn't use the advanced settings available in that palette. I prefer to use a brush with a Hardness setting between 50% and 75%.

Figure 18.20 Option- or Alt-clicking on the original image to choose the area to sample from. (©2003 Stockbyte, www.stockbyte.com)

Figure 18.21 Painting across the area that needs to be retouched. Look closely at her chin.

Figure 18.22 When you release the mouse button, Photoshop blends the retouched area into the surrounding image.

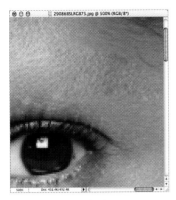

Figure 18.23 Result of using a hard-edged brush. (©2003 Stockbyte, www.stockbyte.com)

Figure 18.24 The difference is very subtle, but a soft-edged brush blends with the surrounding image more than the hard-edged version.

Layers

If you are using layers in your document, the Healing Brush tool will work on one layer at a time, unless you turn on the Use All Layers check box located on the options bar. With this option turned on, Photoshop will act as if your document has no layers at all. In other words, it will be able to take from any layer that is below your cursor, as if they were all combined. However, it will apply, or deposit, the information you are healing only onto the currently active layer. That way, you can create a new empty layer, turn on the Use All Layers check box, and retouch your image (**Figure 18.25**). Don't worry if you mess up, because the information is sitting on its own layer, with the unretouched image directly below it (**Figures 18.26** and **18.27**). This allows you to switch over to the Eraser tool and erase small areas of that layer, or do other things such as lower the opacity of the layer.

A few blending modes, such as Multiply, are available in the options bar, but you'll find that they work a little differently from what you might be used to. Most tools would apply their general effect, and then once everything is done, they would apply the blending mode. But in this tool, the blending mode is applied before Photoshop does the work needed to blend the patched area with the surrounding image (**Figures 18.28** and **18.29**).

NOTES

When healing with the Use All Layers check box, you'll need to be careful how your retouched layers interact with adjustment layers. If your document contains adjustment layers, then click the Eyeball icon for each adjustment layer before using the Healing Brush; otherwise, the retouched areas will be adjusted twice and will no longer match the overall look of the image.

When you've reached the point where you think you're done working on an image, zoom in to 100% magnification (by double-clicking the Zoom tool) and look for any tiny defects in the image (such as dust, scratches, or pin holes), and fix them with the Healing Brush. To make sure that you inspect the entire image, press the Home key (available on most extended keyboards) to get to the upper-left corner of the image. Then use the Page Up and Page Down keys to move one full screen up or down (add Shift to move less than one full screen). Adding Command (Mac) or Ctrl (Windows) to the Page Up and Page Down keys will move you one full screen to the right or left.

Figure 18.25 You can place your retouching on a new layer so it is isolated from the underlying image.

Figure 18.26 The underlying image will be untouched under the retouching layer. (©2003 Stockbyte, www.stockbyte.com)

Figure 18.27 When the layers are viewed at the same time, you can see the final retouched image.

Figure 18.28 How Multiply mode would usually look. (©2003 Stockbyte, www.stockbyte.com)

Figure 18.29 How Multiply mode looks when using the Healing Brush.

The Patch tool and Healing Brush are useful only when the area that needs to be retouched should match the color and brightness of the areas that surround it. When you run across an area that shouldn't blend into its surroundings, then you'll have to switch over to the trusty old standby—the Clone Stamp tool (**Figures 18.30** and **18.31**).

Figure 18.30 The areas that need to be retouched out of this image shouldn't simply blend in with the colors that surround them. (©2003 Andy Katz)

Figure 18.31 The Clone Stamp tool was used to retouch this image.

Clone Stamp Tool

The Clone Stamp tool copies information from one area of your image and applies it somewhere else. Before applying the Clone Stamp tool, there is one thing you should know: All retouching tools use the Brush Presets palette, shown in **Figure 18.32**. The brush that you use with the Healing Brush isn't all that important because it will end up blending your retouching into the surrounding image, but the brush you choose is critical when using the Clone Stamp tool because it doesn't have those blending capabilities. So you have to decide if you want what you're about to apply to fade into the image or to have a distinct edge. For most applications it helps to have a soft edge on your brush so you can't see the exact edge of where you've stopped.

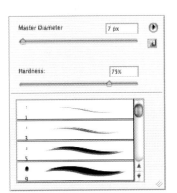

Figure 18.32 The brush that you choose determines how much your retouching work will blend into the underlying image.

NOTES

If you really need to use a soft-edged brush (0% hardness brush), then consider using the Healing Brush with its blending mode set to Replace. That will make it act just like the Clone Stamp tool, but it will not produce blurry results with soft-edged brushes.

If you've messed with the settings in the Preferences > Displays & Cursors area, the second cursor might also look like a crosshair. When that's the case, you can set the Painting Cursors setting to Brush Size to get it back to the default setting.

If you find that you're still getting a crosshair cursor after changing your preferences, then make sure your Caps Lock key is not turned on. When it's turned on, your painting cursors turn into a crosshair.

I find that the default soft-edged brushes are often too soft, which can cause the area you retouch to look blurry compared with the rest of the image. To prevent that from happening, hold Shift and press the right bracket key (]) while you keep an eye on the brush preview in the options bar. Each time you press that key combination you'll be changing your brush's hardness setting in increments of 25%. The default brushes have a hardness of either 100% (for hard-edged brushes) or 0% (for soft ones). I find that 25% and 50% are better for retouching with soft-edged brushes.

Cloning Around

After you've chosen your brush, you'll need to tell Photoshop exactly where you'd like to copy from. Do this by holding down the Option key (Mac) or Alt key (Windows) and clicking the mouse button (**Figure 18.33**). Then move to a different part of the image and click and drag the mouse. When you do, you'll notice two cursors (**Figure 18.34**). The first one is in the shape of a crosshair; it shows you the source of Photoshop's cloning. When you apply the Clone Stamp tool, there will be a second cursor—a circle showing you exactly where it's being applied. When you move your mouse around you'll notice both of the cursors moving in the same direction. As you drag, Photoshop is constantly copying from the crosshair and pasting into the circle.

Figure 18.33 Option- or Alt-click to define the spot you'd like to start cloning from. (©2003 Stockbyte, www.stockbyte.com)

Figure 18.34 The Clone Stamp tool copies from under the crosshair and pastes into the circle.

Clone Aligned

The Clone Stamp tool operates in two different modes: Aligned and Non-aligned (it's just a simple check box in the options bar). In Aligned mode, when you apply the Clone Stamp tool, it doesn't matter if you let go of the mouse button and click again. Each time you let go and click again, the pieces that you're applying line up (**Figure 18.35**). It's as if you're putting together a puzzle: Once you have all of the pieces together, it looks like a complete image (**Figure 18.36**).

Figure 18.35 You can release the mouse button as many times as you want with the Aligned check box turned on because the pieces of the cloned image will line up like puzzle pieces. (©2003 Stockbyte, www.stockbyte.com)

Figure 18.36 Once you put all the pieces together, you'll end up with a complete image.

Clone Non-Aligned

If you turn off the Aligned check box, it's a different story. Apply the tool and let go of the mouse button. The next time you click the mouse button it will reset itself, starting back at the original point from where it was cloning (**Figure 18.37**). If you click in the middle of someone's nose, go up to the forehead, and click and drag, you'll be planting a nose in the middle of the forehead. Then if you let go, move over a little bit, and click again, you'll add a second nose. But this will happen only if you have the Aligned check box off. For most retouching, leave the check box on. That way you don't have to be careful with letting go of the mouse button. Assume you'll need to have it turned on to follow the techniques I cover here, unless I specifically tell you to turn it off.

Figure 18.37 When the Aligned check box is turned off, the Clone Stamp tool resets itself to the original starting point each time you release the mouse button. (©2003 Stockbyte, www.stockbyte.com)

Figure 18.38 You might want to play down some recognizable feature. (©2003 Stockbyte, www.stockbyte.com)

Figure 18.39 By lowering the opacity of the Clone Stamp tool, you can reduce the impact of undesirable features.

Opacity Settings

Sometimes you don't want to completely cover something up; you may just want to lessen its impact (**Figure 18.38**). For example, you might not want to completely wipe out a recognizable feature (such as Gorbachev's birthmark) for fear that it'll be obvious the image was enhanced. To do this, lower the opacity on the Clone Stamp tool (**Figure 18.39**). You can also press the number keys on your keyboard; pressing 1 will give you 10%, 2 will give you 20%, and so on. To get it all the way up to 100%, just press 0 (zero). This will allow you to paint over an area and partially replace it, so that the area you're applying blends with what used to be in that area.

Straight Lines

Have you ever seen a carpenter "snap a chalk line" to get a straight line over an area? There are occasions when I've been grateful to know how to do something similar in Photoshop. Let's say you have an image of a woman that you need to remove from a background that contains a straight line (a wall in my case). That means that you're going to have to replace the woman with a new section of wall. For that to look realistic, the section of wall you use to replace the woman will have to perfectly line up with the sections of wall on either side of her head. When you get into this kind of situation, try this: Move your cursor until it's touching the original line (or edge of the wall, in this case). When it's perfectly touching it, Option-click (Mac) or Alt-click (Windows), as shown in **Figure 18.40**. Then go to the area where you want the new piece of wall to appear and click where you think it would naturally line up with the other part of the wall. Then when you drag, your two cursors will line up just right, making the line look continuous and straight, as in **Figure 18.41**. You can even Shift-click in two spots, and Photoshop will trace a straight line with the Clone Stamp between those two areas. Other examples of when to use this tool would be for stairs, a lamppost, or any object with straight lines that has been obstructed by another object.

Figure 18.40 When retouching straight lines, Option-click or Alt-click when your cursor touches the line; then click in another area that also touches the line. (©2003 Stockbyte, www.stockbyte.com)

Figure 18.41 If the cursors align, lines will remain nice and straight.

Patchwork

Sampling from one area and applying it all over the place will make it look pretty obvious that you've cloned something. You'll start seeing repeated shapes. For instance, if there happens to be a little dark area in the image you were cloning from, you will see that same dark area in the image you've applied it to. And if you look at it closely enough, you will see the shape repeat itself, which can start to look like a pattern. (You've just been busted cloning!) Sometimes, though, you might want to do this just to fill in an area, but then go back and fix up the places that appear patterned. You can do this by Option-clicking (Mac) or Alt-clicking (Windows) a random area around the place you've retouched, and then applying it on top of one of the patterned areas. But watch out—Photoshop's round brushes can be a dead giveaway, because you can easily pick out the areas that you're trying to disguise. This is a great time to use one of the odd-shaped brushes that appear at the bottom of the Brushes palette (**Figure 18.42**). These will provide better cover for areas that look obviously cloned.

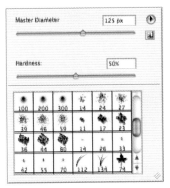

Figure 18.42 To eliminate repeated patterns, use the unusual brushes found at the bottom of the Brushes palette.

Figure 18.43 Original image.

Figure 18.44 Scratch retouched by using the Clone Stamp tool set to Darken.

Another trick is to apply some noise to the entire image, which will make any retouching you've performed blend right into the image. To accomplish that, choose Filter > Noise > Add Noise, use an amount somewhere around 3, set the Distribution to Uniform, and turn off the Monochromatic check box.

Lighten/Darken

Anyone who does retouching will invariably find themselves needing to retouch the wrinkles that show up under people's eyes. In most cases, the Healing brush does an excellent job because it will automatically blend into the surrounding image, but it does have one weakness: It sometimes tries to blend into the eyelashes, which causes the area under the eyes to become too dark. When that's the case, you can use the Clone Stamp tool and sample the area directly below the wrinkles to clone over the wrinkles. But before you start retouching that area, I suggest that you mess with the blending mode settings from the options bar. (We talked about blending modes in Chapter 17, "Enhancement," so here we'll just look at what we need for the Clone Stamp tool.) The blending mode pop-up menu in the options bar is labeled Mode. The Lighten and Darken options are both very useful when retouching. If you set that menu to Darken, it will compare what you're about to apply to what the image looks like underneath, and it will only allow you to darken things. So let's say you had a light-colored scratch in the background of your image (**Figure 18.43**). You could clone from an area directly around it that is the correct brightness. But before you apply the cloned material to the scratch, you might want to set the blending mode to Darken (**Figure 18.44**). In Darken, all Photoshop can do is darken your picture. Under no circumstances will it be able to lighten it. When working with the wrinkles under eyes, I use the Lighten blending mode and lower the Opacity setting of the Clone Stamp tool to somewhere around 40%.

Automatic Sharpening

The automatic sharpening function that's built into some scanners makes retouching much more difficult. If possible, turn off any sharpening settings in your scanning software (**Figures 18.45** and **14.46**).

Cloning Between Documents

With the Clone Stamp tool, you're not limited to cloning from what's in the active document. You can open a second image and clone from that image as well (**Figure 18.47**). All you have to do is move your cursor outside the current image window and on top of another open document. Now you can Option-click (Mac) or Alt-click (Windows) anywhere in that second document and apply your selection within the document you are working on. It will copy from one document and paste into another.

Unlike with the Patch tool and Healing Brush, the Clone Stamp tool forces you to take full control over how your retouched image matches the surrounding image. You have to think about how the brightness, color, and texture of the cloned area will affect the area you plan on retouching as well as how the softness of the brush you choose will cause that information to blend into the surrounding image. That makes the Clone Stamp tool essential in those instances when the area you are retouching shouldn't completely blend into the surrounding areas. Now that we've had some fun with the Clone Stamp tool, let's take a look at the Dodge and Burn tools.

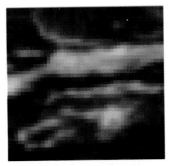

Figure 18.45 Unsharpened image.

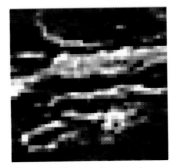

Figure 18.46 Image sharpened during a scan.

To clone between two documents, both documents need to be in the same color mode. If one of the documents is in RGB and the other is in CMYK, Photoshop won't allow you to cross-clone.

Figure 18.47 Cloning between two documents. (©2003 Stockbyte, www.stockbyte.com)

The Dodge and Burn Tools

The words *dodge* and *burn* are taken from a traditional photographic darkroom. In a darkroom, an enlarger projects an image onto a sheet of photographic paper. While the image is being projected, you could put something in the way of the light source, which would obstruct the light in such a way that it would hit certain areas more than others—a technique known as dodging. Or you could intensify the light by cupping your hands together, creating just a small hole in between them, and allowing the light to concentrate on a certain area more than others—a technique known as burning. Using a combination of these two methods, you can brighten or darken your image. Photoshop reproduces these techniques with two tools: Dodge and Burn. If you look at the icons for these tools, you'll see that one of them looks like a hand; that would be for burning, allowing the light to go through the opening of your hand. The other one looks like (at least I think it looks like) a lollipop, which you can use for obstructing, or dodging, the light.

The Dodge Tool

Let's take a closer look at the Dodge tool. Because it can lighten your image, the Dodge tool comes in handy when you are working on people with dark shadows under their eyes. But before we get into cosmetic surgery, I'll introduce you to a very important pop-up menu, called the Range menu, which is associated with this tool. You'll find it in the options bar at the top of your screen (**Figure 18.48**). The pop-up menu has three choices: Shadows, Midtones, and Highlights. This menu tells Photoshop which shades of gray it should concentrate on when you pan across your image.

Figure 18.48 Dodge tool options bar.

If you use the Shadows setting, you will change mainly the dark part of your image. As you paint across your image, your brush will brighten the areas it touches. But as you get into the midtones of the image, it will apply less and less paint. And if you paint over the light parts of the image, it won't change them much, if at all. The second choice is Midtones. If you use this setting, you will affect mainly the middle shades of gray in your image, or those areas that are about 25% to 75% gray. It shouldn't change the shadows or highlights very much. They may change a little bit, but only so they can blend into those areas. The third choice is Highlights. Highlights will mainly affect the lightest parts of your image and slowly blend into the middle tones of your image. You can see the effects of all of these settings in **Figure 18.49**.

Figure 18.49 Top: Shadows. Middle: Midtones. Bottom: Highlights.

Obviously, you'll need to decide exactly which setting would work best for your situation. If you don't do this before using the Dodge tool, you might cause yourself some grief. Let's say you're trying to fix dark areas around someone's eyes, but the Dodge tool doesn't seem to be doing the job (**Figure 18.50**). Then, after dozens of tries, you finally realize that the Range pop-up menu is set to Highlights instead of Midtones (look at the eyes in **Figures 18.51** and **18.52**).

You also have an Exposure setting on the options bar that controls how much brighter the image will become. You can use the number keys on your keyboard to change this setting.

Figure 18.50 Original image. (©2003 Stockbyte, www.stockbyte.com)

Figure 18.51 Dodge tool set to Highlights.

Figure 18.52 Dodge tool set to Midtones.

Color Images

The Dodge tool works exceptionally well on grayscale images. All you have to do is choose which part of the image you want to work on—Shadows, Midtones, or Highlights—and paint across an area. Unfortunately, it's not as slick with color images. If you use the Dodge tool on color, you'll find that it tends to wash out some of the colors, and in some cases even change them (**Figures 18.53** and **18.54**).

One good solution is to duplicate the layer you're working on and set the blending mode of the duplicate to Luminosity before using the Dodge tool. That should maintain the original colors and limit your changes to the brightness of the image. Or, you can forgo the Dodge tool and just use the Paintbrush tool. You can set your Paintbrush tool's blending mode to Color Dodge and choose a bright shade of gray to paint with. But just going ahead and painting across an image will look rather ridiculous, because all it's doing is blowing out the detail (**Figure 18.55**).

To get the Color Dodge technique to work correctly, just choose a medium to light shade of gray to paint with (**Figure 18.56**). This will allow you to create highlights or to brighten areas. Sometimes this works a little bit better than the Dodge tool.

Figure 18.53 Original image. (©2003 Andy Katz)

Figure 18.54 Large area lightened by using the Dodge tool.

Figure 18.55 Painting with a light shade of gray by using the Color Dodge mode.

Figure 18.56 Area lightened by painting with a medium shade of gray by using the Color Dodge blending mode.

The Burn Tool

The Burn tool is designed for darkening areas of an image. Like the Dodge tool, it has Range options in its palette for Highlights, Midtones, and Shadows, as well as an Exposure setting. It, too, works great with grayscale images. So if you are ever dealing with a shiny spot on someone's forehead or nose because the light is reflecting off it, you can go ahead and try to fix it with the Burn tool (compare **Figures 18.57** and **18.58**).

Color Fixes

Just as with the Dodge tool, you'll start having problems when you use the Burn tool with a color image (**Figures 18.59** and **18.60**). When that happens, you're welcome to try painting with a shade of gray (with the Paintbrush tool) and setting the blending mode to Color Burn, which will darken the image, making the colors more vivid while leaving the highlights largely untouched (**Figure 18.61**).

Another technique is to Option-click (Mac) or Alt-click (Windows) the New Layer icon at the bottom of the Layers palette. When you get the New Layer dialog box, change the Mode menu from Normal to Overlay, turn on the Fill with Overlay-Neutral Color check box, and then click OK (**Figure 18.62**). Now, with that new layer active, use the Dodge and Burn tools with the Range setting in the options bar set to Midtones (**Figures 18.63** and **18.64**). That will allow you to perform your dodging and burning on a separate layer and will give you fewer color problems.

Figure 18.57 The original image. (©2003 Stockbyte, www.stockbyte.com)

Figure 18.58 Forehead darkened (subtly) by using the Burn tool.

Figure 18.59 Original image. (©2003 Stockbyte, www.stockbyte.com)

Figure 18.60 Image darkened using the Burn tool.

Figure 18.61 Image darkened by painting with a shade of gray in Color Burn mode.

Figure 18.62 Creating a new layer in Overlay mode.

Figure 18.63 Original image. (©2003 Andy Katz)

Figure 18.64 Dodge and Burn used on a layer set to Overlay mode.

When I'm using this technique, I prefer to hold the Option key (Mac) or Alt key (Windows) to temporarily switch between the Dodge and Burn tools. That way I don't have to go back to the Tools palette each time I want to switch from brightening to darkening my photo.

Now that you've learned how to brighten and darken your images with the Dodge and Burn tools, it's time to move on and learn how to adjust how colorful your images are with the Sponge tool.

The Sponge Tool

Hiding in with the Dodge and Burn tools is the Sponge tool. It works as if you have a sponge full of bleach, allowing you to paint across your image and soak up the color. Or you can do the opposite and intensify the colors—it's all determined by what you choose from the Mode menu in the options bar.

Figure 18.65 Front and rear apples were desaturated to make the central one stand out. (©2003 Stockbyte, www.stockbyte.com)

If you choose Desaturate, the Sponge tool will tone down the colors in the area you are painting. The more you paint across an area, the closer it will become to being grayscale. This can be useful when you'd like to make a product stand out from an otherwise distracting background (**Figure 18.65**). I also use it (with a very low Pressure setting) to minimize the yellow/orange colorcast that usually shows up in the teeth of people who smoke or drink coffee a lot.

The Saturate setting will intensify the colors as you paint over them, which is great for giving people rosy cheeks (**Figure 18.66**). This can also be great for adding a bit more color to people's lips.

The Blur and Sharpen Tools

When you need to blur or sharpen an area, you have two choices: Select an area and apply a filter, or use the Blur and Sharpen tools. Using filters to blur and sharpen your image has a few advantages over using the tools, including getting a preview of the image before you commit to the settings being used and having the ability to apply the filter effect evenly to the area you are changing. But occasionally the Blur and Sharpen tools can really help when working on small areas, so let's take a look at how they work and when to use them.

The Blur Tool

The Blur tool is pretty straightforward. You can paint across any part of your image and blur everything that your cursor passes over. In the Blur tool options bar, you will find a Pressure setting that determines how much you will blur the image; higher settings blur the image more. This can be useful if there are little, itty-bitty areas of detail obstructing your image. I generally prefer to use the Gaussian Blur filter instead of this Blur tool because it does a better job of evenly blurring an area.

I like to use the Blur tool for reducing—not removing—wrinkles (**Figure 18.67**). If you turn the pressure way up on this tool and paint across a wrinkle a few times, you'll see it begin to disappear. But you'll also notice that it doesn't look very realistic. It might look as if you had smeared some Vaseline on the face. To really do a wrinkle justice, you have to take a closer look. Wrinkles are made out of two parts, a highlight and a shadow (light part and dark part). If you paint across that with the Blur tool, the darker part of the wrinkle will be lightened, while the lightest part will be darkened, so that they become more similar in shade (**Figure 18.68**).

Figure 18.66 The cheek on the right was enhanced using the Sponge tool set to Saturate. (©2003 Stockbyte, www.stockbyte.com)

WARNING

Don't go over the image with the Blur tool set to Lighten and then switch over to Darken and go over it again. That would be the same as leaving it set to Normal, and you would be back to Vaseline face. So use it just once, with it set to either Lighten or Darken. Just think about what is most prominent in a wrinkle. Is it the light area of the wrinkle, or the dark area? That will indicate which setting you should use.

To reduce the impact of a wrinkle without completely getting rid of it (if I wanted to get rid of it, I would use the Healing Brush tool), turn the Pressure setting all the way up. Then change the blending mode to either Darken or Lighten. If the part that makes that wrinkle most prominent is the dark area, then set the blending mode menu to Lighten (**Figure 18.69**). Then when you paint across the area, the only thing it will be able to do is lighten that wrinkle. But because you are using the Blur tool, it's not going to completely lighten it and make it disappear. Instead, it will reduce the impact of it. You really have to try this to see how it looks.

Figure 18.67 Original image. (©2003 Stockbyte, www.stockbyte.com)

Figure 18.68 Wrinkles around her right eye have been blurred.

Figure 18.69 Wrinkles around eye lessened by using the Blur tool with a blending mode of Lighten.

Layers

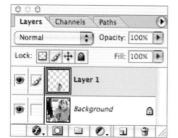

Figure 18.70 By creating a new layer before using the Blur tool, you can isolate the unretouched image.

When I'm retouching wrinkles, I usually create a brand-new, empty layer (**Figure 18.70**). Then, in order to be able to use the Blur tool, I have to turn on the Use All Layers check box in the options bar (**Figure 18.71**). Otherwise, Photoshop can look at only one layer at a time, and it won't have any information to blur. By doing all these steps, Photoshop will copy the information from the underlying layers, blur it, and then paste it onto the layer you just created, leaving the underlying layers untouched. By using this technique, I can easily delete areas or redo them without having to worry about permanently changing the original image. If you're attempting the wrinkle technique

I mentioned earlier, then you'll need to set the blending mode of the layer to Lighten, and you might need to lower the Pressure setting of the Blur tool.

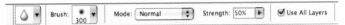

Figure 18.71 The Blur tool will not be able to use information on other layers unless you turn on the Use All Layers check box.

The Lens Blur Filter

If you'd like to make a large area of your image blurry, then you should try out Photoshop CS's new Lens Blur filter. Unlike the standard blur filters (Blur, Blur More, and Gaussian Blur), which blur your entire image the same amount, the Lens Blur filter will vary the amount of blurring that occurs (**Figures 18.72** and **18.73**), based on the contents of a grayscale image (**Figure 18.74**) (which you can create by using the Paintbrush tool). You can specify which shade of gray should represent an area that you want to keep in focus. Photoshop will then make all the other areas of the image progressively out of focus based on how different the surrounding shades of gray are compared to the one you specified as the in-focus shade. But it's really much easier to see it in action than to try to understand the concept. So, here's what you need to do:

Start by creating a new empty layer on top of the image you'd like to blur. Next, type **D** to reset your foreground color to black, and then use the Paintbrush tool to paint across the areas you'd like to keep in focus (**Figure 18.75**). The softness of your brush will determine how quickly the focus falls off, so use a really soft-edged brush if you want a smooth transition from the in-focus areas to the ones that should be blurred. You can also choose Filter > Blur > Gaussian Blur after you paint to create a much softer edge (**Figure 18.76**). Once you're done painting, choose Edit > Fill, set the Use pop-up menu to White, set the Mode pop-up menu to Behind, and then click the OK button (**Figure 18.77**). That should fill the empty areas of the active layer with white. Now we need to get the contents of the active layer to show up in an alpha channel. To accomplish that, open the Channels palette (Window > Channels), Command-click (Mac) or Ctrl-click (Windows) on the

Figure 18.72 Original image. (©2003 PhotoSpin, www.photospin.com)

Figure 18.73 Result of applying the Lens Blur filter using the grayscale image shown in Figure 18.74.

Figure 18.74 Grayscale image used to blur Figure 18.73.

top-most channel (it will be called Gray, RGB, or CMYK depending on which mode your image is in) to get a selection, and then click the second icon from the left at the bottom of the Channels palette. To get back to working on the original image, switch back to the Layers palette (Window > Layers), drag the layer you painted onto the trash, choose Select > Deselect, click on the layer you'd like to blur, and then choose Filter > Blur > Lens Blur.

Figure 18.75 Paint with black on a new layer to define the areas that should remain in focus.

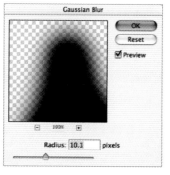

Figure 18.76 The Gaussian Blur filter.

Figure 18.77 Use the Fill dialog box to fill the empty parts of the layer with white.

When the Lens Blur filter dialog box appears (**Figure 18.78**), turn on the Preview check box and choose Faster for the Preview method. (I find that the More Accurate setting is just too darn slow.) Next, choose the name of the alpha channel you created from the Source pop-up menu (it will usually be called Alpha 1, unless you renamed it), and then move your mouse over the preview image and click on the area you wanted to keep in focus. Clicking on your image will set the Blur Focal Distance setting, which determines which shade of gray in the alpha channel will be used to represent an area that should be in focus (0 = black). If you'd rather have that area become blurry instead, turn on the Invert check box. If you'd like to compare the blurred version of the image to the original, toggle the Preview check box off and on again.

Figure 18.78 The Lens Blur dialog box.

Now that you have the filter thinking about the proper information, it's time to figure out what you'd like the blurry areas of the image to look like. The Radius slider determines just how blurry areas should become. When you purposefully throw an area out of focus using a camera (by using a low aperture setting), you will often see the shape of the aperture in the highlights of the image (**Figure 18.79**). The Shape, Blade Curvature, and Rotation settings attempt to simulate the shape of an aperture in the brightest areas of the image.

When you blur an image, the brightest areas of the image will often start to look a bit dull (**Figures 18.80** and **18.81**). That happens because blurring blends those bright areas

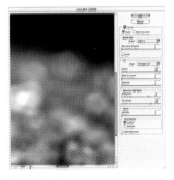

Figure 18.79 The shape of the camera aperture often shows up in the brightest areas of the image.

into their surroundings, which makes them become darker. To compensate for that, you can increase the Brightness setting until the highlights in your image become bright again (**Figure 18.82**). The Threshold setting will determine which shades will be brightened. Moving the slider toward the left will cause Photoshop to brighten more shades, while moving it toward the right will make Photoshop brighten only the brightest shades in the image.

Figure 18.80 Original image.

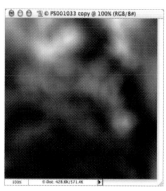

Figure 18.81 The highlights look dull after blurring the image.

Figure 18.82 Adjusting the Brightness and Threshold settings brings back the brightness in the highlights.

Blurring an image will usually remove any grain or noise that was in the image (**Figure 18.83**). Because the Lens Blur filter doesn't blur the entire image, you might end up with a lot of grain in the in-focus areas of the image and no grain in the areas you have blurred. That will make the image look very unnatural because the original image contained consistent grain across the entire image. To add grain into the areas you've blurred, experiment with the Noise setting found at the bottom of the Lens Blur dialog box. Just move the Amount slider up until the blurry areas have as much grain as the in-focus areas (**Figure 18.84**); then switch between the Uniform and Gaussian options until you determine which one delivers the best match to the grain of the original photo. Turn on the monochromatic check box if the blurred areas look too colorful compared to the areas that haven't been blurred.

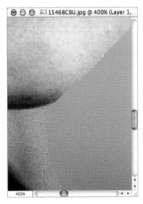

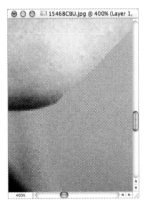

Figure 18.83 All the grain was removed when the right side of this image was blurred. (©2003 Stockbyte, www.stockbyte.com)

Figure 18.84 Adjusting the Noise settings added grain back into the blurred area.

The Sharpen Tool

The Sharpen tool works in a fashion similar to that of its relative, the Sharpen filter. But with this tool you have to adjust the Pressure setting in the options bar to determine how much you want to sharpen the image. And you have to be careful: If you turn the Pressure setting up too high or paint across an area too many times, you're going to get some really weird effects (**Figures 18.85** to **18.87**).

Figure 18.85 Original image. (©2003 Stockbyte, www.stockbyte.com)

Figure 18.86 Sharpened using the Sharpen tool with a medium Pressure setting.

Figure 18.87 Sharpened using the Sharpen tool with a high Pressure setting.

Reflected Highlights

When you run across an image that contains glass, metal, or other shiny objects, it usually contains extremely bright highlights (known as specular highlights). This usually happens when light reflects directly off one of those very shiny areas, such as the edge of a glass. These extra-bright highlights often look rather flat and lifeless after being adjusted (**Figure 18.88**). This happens because whenever we adjust an image to perform color correction, or prepare it for printing or multimedia, the brightest areas of the image usually become 3%, or 4% gray (instead of white). But if you sharpen those areas, you're going to brighten them and make them pure white. This will make them stand out and look more realistic. So any time you have jewelry, glassware, or reflected light in people's eyes, you'll want to use the Sharpen tool, bring down the Strength to about 30%, and go over those areas once (**Figures 18.89** and **18.90**). That will make them almost pure white; when you print them, they will almost jump off the page, as they should (**Figure 18.91**).

Figure 18.88 Metallic highlights often look a bit dull after performing color correction. (©2003 Stockbyte, www.stockbyte.com)

Figure 18.89 The areas covered in red were sharpened to make them pop.

Figure 18.91 Metallic highlights sharpened.

Figure 18.90 The Sharpen tool setting to use on reflections.

I use the Blur and Sharpen tools to make subtle changes to my images. When I want a bit more radical of a change, I often use the Blur and Sharpen filters instead. The Lens Blur filter will give you the most control over blurring your image, but at the same time it's usually the slowest method for blurring your image. Now let's move on to Photoshop's Liquify filter, where we'll be able to make radical or subtle changes to our images in seconds.

The Liquify Filter

The Liquify filter will allow you to pull and push on your image as if it were printed on Silly Putty. The results you will get out of this filter will either be overly obvious (looking like a reflection in a fun house mirror), or not noticeable to the untrained eye. It all depends on your intentions. When you choose Filter > Liquify, you'll see a dialog box that dominates your screen (**Figure 18.92**). Let's run down the tools that appear in the upper left of the dialog box. We'll start out by making radical changes to an image just so you can see what each tool does; once you're familiar with each one, we'll explore some real-world applications of these tools where the results are much more subtle.

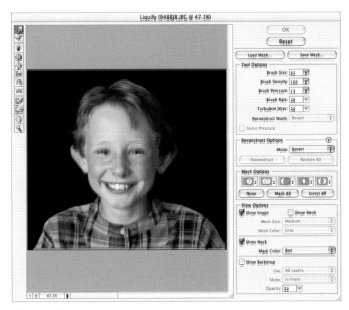

Figure 18.92 The Liquify dialog box. (©2003 Stockbyte, www.stockbyte.com)

The first tool you'll find in the upper left of the Liquify dialog box is the Forward Warp tool. With that tool active, you can paint on your image to push the image in the direction that you're dragging (**Figure 18.93**). Once you're done manipulating your image, you might find that you've gone a little too far in a few areas. If that's the case, grab the Reconstruct tool (second from the top tool) and paint across the area that you'd like to take back to normal (**Figure 18.94**). The more you paint across an area, the closer it will become to what the image looked like before you applied the Liquify command. Next is the Twirl Clockwise tool, which will slowly rotate the area inside your cursor clockwise (hold Option or Alt to rotate areas counterclockwise) (**Figure 18.95**). Under that you'll find the Pucker tool, which allows you to pull the image in toward the center of your brush (**Figure 18.96**). Or, you can do the opposite of that by using the Bloat tool (**Figure 18.97**). (Hold Option on the Mac or Alt in Windows to temporarily switch between the Pucker and Bloat tools.) Below the Bloat tool is the Push Left tool, which acts as though the line you draw is a bulldozer, and pushes the image away from it on the left side (**Figure 18.98**). (Press down Option on the Mac or Alt in Windows to move the image on the right side instead.) After that you'll find the Mirror tool, which will flip a portion of the image horizontally or vertically, depending on the direction you drag. If you drag downward, then you'll be reflecting the area to the left of the cursor. Drag up and you'll reflect what's to the right (**Figure 18.99**). Drag right and you'll reflect the area below the cursor, and drag left to reflect the area above. Finally, the last general tool is the Turbulence tool, which allows you to push and pull on your image, much like the Warp tool, but it will add more of a wavy look, which can be useful when you're attempting to create water ripples and smoke (**Figure 18.100**).

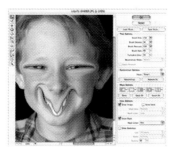

Figure 18.93 Result of using the Warp tool.

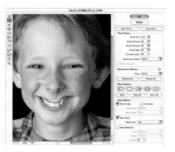

Figure 18.94 Result of using the Reconstruct tool.

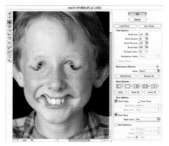

Figure 18.95 Result of using the Rotate tool.

Figure 18.96 Result of using the Pucker tool.

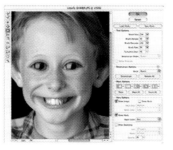

Figure 18.97 Result of using the Bloat tool.

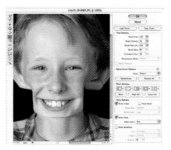

Figure 18.98 Result of using the Push Left tool.

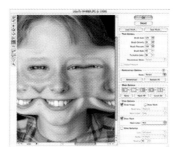

Figure 18.99 Result of using the Reflect tool.

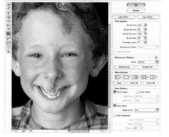

Figure 18.100 Result of using the Turbulence tool (mainly on the hair).

Now that you have an idea of what each tool does, let's explore the options that show up in the upper right of the Liquify dialog box.

▶ **Brush Size:** There is no Brushes palette available to change the size of your brush in the Liquify dialog box. The size of the brush is determined by the number entered in the Brush Size field in the upper right of the dialog box. You can use the bracket keys (] [) to change this setting in small increments, or press Shift with them to change the size in larger increments.

▶ **Brush Density:** This setting determines how thick the center of your brush is before it starts to fade out and affect your image less. Just imagine you're warping the image with your finger. You could think of that setting as how pointy of a finger are you using to warp your image (**Figures 18.101** to **18.103**). Low settings cause a radical change in a small area and then fade out to the edge of your brush, while higher settings spread the radical change into a wider area before it fades out to the edge of your brush.

Figure 18.101 Original image. (©2003 Stockbyte, www.stockbyte.com)

Figure 18.102 Image warped using a low Brush Density setting.

Figure 18.103 Image warped using a high Brush Density setting.

▶ **Brush Pressure:** For all of these tools, the Brush Pressure setting will determine how radical a change you'll make when you paint across the image. You can think of the Brush Pressure setting as determining how hard you'd be pushing with your finger. The harder you push, the more of the image you'll move with each paint stroke (**Figures 18.104** to **18.106**). If you have a pressure-sensitive graphics tablet, then you can turn on the Stylus Pressure check box to make Photoshop pay attention to how much pressure you're using with the pen. With this option turned on, the Brush Pressure setting will be determined by how hard you press down on your graphics tablet.

Figure 18.104 Original image.
(© 2003 Stockbyte, www.stockbyte.com)

Figure 18.105 Warped using a medium Brush Pressure setting.

Figure 18.106 Warped using a high Brush Pressure setting.

▶ **Brush Rate:** This setting is available only with the Reconstruct, Twirl, Pucker, Bloat, and Turbulence tools. It determines how much of a change you'll make when you are stationary with the mouse button held down. The higher the setting, the more quickly the image will change when you pause on top of an area (**Figures 18.107** to **18.109**). This setting has no affect on what happens when the mouse is in motion.

Figure 18.107 Original image.
(© 2003 Stockbyte, www.stockbyte.com)

Figure 18.108 Bloated for three seconds using a low Brush Rate setting.

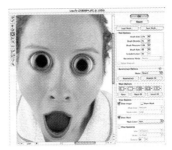

Figure 18.109 Bloated for three seconds using a high Brush Rate setting.

▶ **Turbulent Jitter:** This setting determines how smooth of a result you'll get with the Turbulence tool (it doesn't affect the other tools). Low settings produce a smoother distortion, while higher settings produce a more random distortion (**Figures 18.110** and **18.111**).

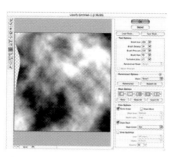

Figure 18.110 Turbulence tool applied (left side) for 10 seconds with a low Turbulent Jitter setting.

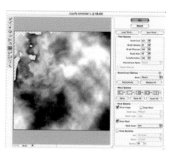

Figure 18.111 Turbulence tool applied (left side) for 10 seconds with a high Turbulent Jitter setting.

Figure 18.112 When creating an image like this one, I often experiment with the Reconstruction modes. (©2003 Andy Katz)

▶ **Reconstruction Mode:** This pop-up menu determines how the Reconstruct tool will attempt to bring the image back to its original state. You'll get radically different results depending on which setting you choose. The vast majority of the time I use the Revert setting; I generally only change the setting when I'm looking to create a creative image (**Figure 18.112**).

Before we move on, I want to make sure you know how to navigate around your image and how to undo changes. You can use standard keyboard shortcuts to zoom in or out on your image: Command-+ or Command- – (Mac), or Ctrl-+, Ctrl- – (Windows), or use the Zoom tool at the bottom of the tool list. To scroll around your image either choose the Hand tool or hold the Spacebar while you're in any other tool to temporarily access the Hand tool. You can perform multiple undo's by pressing Command-Z (Mac) or Ctrl-Z (Windows) multiple times (add Shift to redo what you've just undone). Now that you know how to get around your image, let's look at how you can limit which areas of the image you can change.

If you find that you end up changing too much of the image, you can mask an area (known as freezing in previous versions of Photoshop) to prevent it from changing. The Freeze Mask tool (found along with the distortion tools on the left side of the dialog box) will apply a red overlay on your image to indicate which areas have been masked (**Figure 18.113**). The Freeze Mask tool also uses the Brush Density and Brush Pressure settings, which means that you can partially mask an area to make it change less than the nonmasked areas. (For example, 50% masked areas will change half as much as unmasked areas when they're painted over.) Areas that are partially masked will appear with a more transparent red overlay. If you'd rather not see the overlay, click to uncheck the Show Mask check box. If you'd like to unmask an area, use the Thaw Mask tool to remove some of the red overlay, or click the None check box in the Mask Options area to unmask the entire image. The Freeze Mask and Thaw Mask options are great when used with the Backdrop setting, which allows you to see through the transparent areas of a layer to the underlying layers. This way you can see exactly how your image lines up with the rest of the document (**Figure 18.114**).

After you play around in this dialog box, it's often difficult to determine the exact areas in your image that have changed. You can see a different view of the changes you've made by checking the Show Mesh check box (**Figure 18.115**). You might also want to uncheck the Show Image check box so you can get a clear view of the mesh (**Figure 18.116**). You can also control the size and color of the mesh, which can help make the changes more noticeable when viewed at the same time as the image. You can still use all the Liquify tools while the mesh is visible.

Figure 18.113 The red overlay indicates an area that has been masked. (©2003 Stockbyte, www.stockbyte.com)

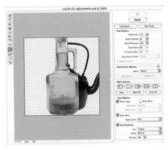

Figure 18.114 The left side indicates what you see when the Backdrop check box is unchecked. The right side shows what you see when an underlying layer is visible. (©2003 Stockbyte, www.stockbyte.com)

Figure 18.115 An image with the mesh visible. (©2003 Stockbyte, www.stockbyte.com)

Figure 18.116 Viewing the mesh with the image hidden.

Real-World Retouching with Liquify

Now that you know how to think about these tools, let's explore how you might use them when retouching an image. When you're trying each of these techniques be extra careful not to go too far with your distortions; otherwise, the changes will become overly obvious. The idea is to change the image so that it looks better than the original, without changing it so much that anyone would notice that it's been tampered with.

Retouching Eyes

In the world of fashion, it is not unusual to enlarge a model's eyes so that your attention is drawn to that part of his or her face (**Figures 18.117** and **18.118**). Even if you're not a fashion photographer and you want to give it a whirl, here's what you need to do. (If you want to work on the same image I'm using, open the retouching eyes.jpg image in the Practice Images > Retouching folder on the CD.) First, use the Freeze Mask tool to mask off the surrounding areas of the eye that would probably not look right if they were distorted. That usually includes the eyebrows, nose, and sometimes the sides of the head (**Figure 18.119**). Next, switch to the Bloat tool, move your mouse over one of the eyes, placing the crosshair that shows up in the middle of the cursor in the pupil of the eye, and then adjust the Brush Size setting (by pressing the] or [keys) until your brush is just larger than the perimeter of the eye (**Figure 18.120**). You'll need to set the Brush Density setting to 100; otherwise, you'll end up enlarging the center of the eye more than the rest of the eye. While you're at it, you might as well change the Brush Rate setting to a low setting like 20 so that you don't have to be overly careful thinking about how long to hold down the mouse button to get the proper change in the image. Now that you have everything set up properly, center your cursor on the blacks of the eye, and then press the mouse button until the eyes look slightly larger (about a second should do it) (**Figure 18.121**). Then repeat the process on the second eye, making sure that you hold the mouse button for the same amount of time; otherwise, you'll have one eye larger than the other, and we want to avoid anything that would make our subject look like the Bride of Frankenstein.

Figure 18.117 Original image. (©2003 Stockbyte, www.stockbyte.com)

Figure 18.118 The eyes have been enlarged slightly.

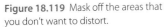

Figure 18.119 Mask off the areas that you don't want to distort.

Figure 18.120 Use a brush slightly wider than the eye.

Figure 18.121 His right eye has been enlarged, but the left one hasn't.

You can also use Liquify to open eyes that are partially shut (**Figure 18.122**). Liquify isn't my personal preference for this kind of work, however; I'd much rather have multiple photos to work with so that I can copy an open eye from one photo, paste it onto a closed eye in another image, and use the Healing Brush to blend in the edges. But for those times when you have only one shot to work with, you'll want to use the Bloat and Warp tools to help pry an eye open (**Figure 18.123**). Start by choosing the Bloat tool. Set the Brush Size setting so that your brush is about 3/4 of the width of the eye; set the Brush Density to a low setting (somewhere around 20 should work) so that you mainly scale the center of the eye; and set the Brush Rate to 20. Now, click on the center of the eye four or five times so that it starts to enlarge (**Figure 18.124**). Then, to get the rest of the eye to look natural, make a few single clicks just to the right and left of the center of the eye (**Figure 18.125**). Finally, switch to the Warp tool, bring up the Brush Density setting to around 50, and set the Brush Pressure to around 60. Place the crosshair in the center of the brush onto the eyelid and drag up or down to reshape it (**Figure 18.126**). Keep tweaking the image until each eye has the proper shape. If you mess up and create a ghoulish rendition of an eye, then switch to the Reconstruct tool, bring down the Brush Pressure and Brush Rate settings to around 20, and then click or paint across the eye to see if you can smooth it out.

Figure 18.122 Original image. (©2003 Ben Willmore)

Figure 18.123 First try at opening an eye.

Figure 18.124 Click in the center of the eye a few times to pry it open.

Figure 18.125 Click on the sides to even out the eye.

Figure 18.126 Reshape the eyelid with the Warp tool if necessary.

Retouching Mouths

Remember Jack Nicholson when he played the Joker in the Batman movie? How he always had that maniacal smile frozen on his face? Well, we're not going to go that far, but we are going to use the Warp tool to transform a straight mouth into a smiling one. (**Figures 18.127** and **18.128**). Start by choosing the Warp tool. Change the Brush Size setting until you get a brush about half the width of the mouth, set the Brush Density to 75, and set the Brush Pressure to 50. Next, move your mouse so that the crosshair is just below the right edge of the mouth, and drag upward and to the side slightly to move the corner of the mouth up and out (**Figure 18.129**). Repeat this process on the left side of the mouth. Then, change the Brush Size setting to get a brush just smaller than the width of the mouth and change the Brush Density setting to 100. Now place the crosshair on the top edge of the lips centered horizontally and drag down a small distance (**Figure 18.130**). If your mouth is looking too much like the Joker or it's just plain weird, don't worry, it just takes some practice to get an acceptable result. If you mess up then either paint across the area with the Reconstruct tool to get it closer to the original or click the Restore All button to start over.

Figure 18.127 Original image. (©2003 Stockbyte, www.stockbyte.com)

Figure 18.128 Result of forcing a smile with Liquify.

Figure 18.129 Use the Warp tool to push the side up and out.

Figure 18.130 Pull the middle of the lip down slightly.

Digital Liposuction

Forget the plastic surgeon! Forget handing over your life savings to some personal trainer to help you get rid of a few lousy pounds of cellulite. You've got Photoshop! If you need to nip or tuck some bulging flesh then you can do it by mastering the Warp, Pucker, and Push Left tools. When working on waistlines, you can use the Warp tool with a largish brush, a medium Brush Density setting (50ish), and a high Brush Pressure (80ish), and drag the background toward the waist (**Figures 18.131** and **18.132**). If you need to move a large area, then you might want to consider using the Push tool. You'll want to choose a large brush, set the Brush Density to 100, and use a very low Brush Pressure (around 10). Then move your cursor so that the crosshair just touches the edge you need to move, and drag to push the flesh in one direction (**Figures 18.133** and **18.134**). Drag straight down if you need to push the skin toward the right of your cursor; hold Option (Mac) or Alt (Windows) if you need to move the skin in the opposite direction. But after doing that, you might find that the background gets distorted too much. When that happens, click OK in the Liquify dialog box and use the Clone Stamp tool to replace the distorted background with something that looks more appropriate.

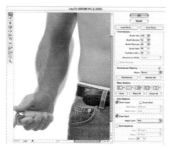

Figure 18.131 The original image with the arm masked so it won't shift. (©2003 Stockbyte, www.stockbyte.com)

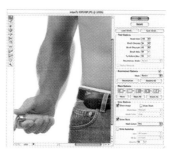

Figure 18.132 Result of warping the waist with a large brush.

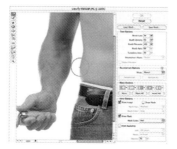

Figure 18.133 There is no need to mask when using the Push Left tool; just use a downward stroke with the crosshair on the edge you want to push.

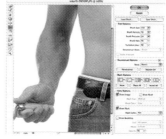

Figure 18.134 Result of pushing quite a bit of flesh using the Push Left tool.

Retouching and Restoring Real-World Photos

Now let's combine the ideas we've covered in this chapter with some of the features from other chapters to retouch and restore some real-world examples.

Fixing a Faded Image

The following image was submitted to my Image Ambulance service (at www.digitalmastery.com/problems) (**Figure 18.135**). It's an image that was exposed to sunlight while it was framed and hung on the wall. To restore it, we're going to use some color correction techniques from Chapter 9, "Color Correction"; some color manipulation ideas from Chapter 11, "Color Manipulation"; and a few tricks we talked about in this chapter. You're welcome to follow along by opening the wedding.jpg image in the Practice Images > Retouching folder on the CD.

Let's start by fixing the faded area in the center of the image. To isolate that area, choose the Elliptical Marquee tool and click and drag across the center area. If you need to reposition the selection before you release the mouse button, then hold the Spacebar and drag around your image. If you need to continue changing the size of the selection, then release the spacebar, but keep the mouse button pressed. Only release the mouse button when your selection closely matches the boundary of the faded area (**Figure 18.136**). Once you have that area isolated, choose Curves from the Adjustment Layer icon at the bottom of the Layers palette (third from the right). Now click the Options button to access the Auto Color dialog box and use the settings shown in **Figure 18.137**. Then click OK in both the Auto Color and Curves dialog boxes. That should transform the faded center of the image into a much better looking image (**Figure 18.138**), but the adjustment doesn't yet blend into the surrounding image. With the newly created adjustment layer active, choose Filter > Blur > Gaussian Blur, and experiment with the Amount setting until the adjustment blends with the surrounding image (I used 4) (**Figure 18.139**).

Now that the center of the image has more contrast, the outer area is looking a little faded in comparison. To target that area, hold the Command key (Mac) or Ctrl key (Windows) and click on the Layer Mask that is attached to the adjustment layer created a few minutes ago (**Figure 18.140**). That should produce a selection of the central area of the image. To get the outer area, choose Select > Inverse. Now create another Curves adjustment layer, click the Auto button to apply the same Auto Color settings that we used on the middle of the image, and then click OK.

Figure 18.135 The original image was faded from exposure to the sun. (©2003 Conner Huff, www.conman.net)

Figure 18.136 Select the center faded area with the Elliptical Marquee tool.

Figure 18.137 Apply the Auto Color settings shown here.

Figure 18.140 Command- or Ctrl-click on the Layer Mask that's attached to the adjustment layer.

Figure 18.138 After applying Auto Color, the center of the image should no longer be faded.

Figure 18.139 Blur the Layer Mask attached to the adjustment layer to blend in the adjustment blend.

That should add a bit of contrast to the outer area of the image (**Figure 18.141**).

Now I notice that the color in the wood wall behind the newlyweds doesn't quite match the surrounding image. To remedy the situation, create a new empty layer and place it at the top of the layers stack. Change the Blending Mode pop-up menu at the top of the Layers palette to Hue so that any paint that we apply to this layer will change the basic color of what's underneath without changing its brightness (**Figure 18.142**). Next, choose the Paintbrush tool and Option-click (Mac) or Alt-click (Windows) on the wood area where you think the color looks appropriate (**Figure 18.143**). Then release the Option/Alt key and paint over the areas that have discolored wood (**Figure 18.144**). You might also need to sample a color in his suit and paint across the lower-right corner to get consistent color there.

Now that the contrast and color look about right, I think the lower-right of the suit needs to be fixed so you no longer see the shape of the oval frame (**Figure 18.145**). I think the Healing Brush will be great for this. But before we start playing with it, create a new layer at the top of the layers stack, choose the Healing Brush, and turn on the Use All Layers check box in the options bar at the top of your screen. Then, to fix that transition, choose a brush wide enough to cover the transition we're attempting to fix and Option-click (Mac) or Alt-click (Windows) in the dark area just below the transition we need to fix. Now center your cursor on the transition just above the area you clicked on and drag across a small area of that transition. When you release the mouse button, Photoshop should blend that transition into the image (**Figure 18.146**). You'll need to work on small areas and make sure you don't hit too much of the pocket or fabric edges; otherwise, they will end up being blended into the surrounding image.

Figure 18.141 After applying Auto Color to the surrounding image, the contrast on both sides should be similar.

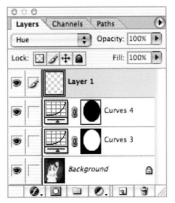

Figure 18.142 Add an empty layer to the top of the layers stack and set its Blending Mode to Hue.

Figure 18.143 Option- or Alt-click on an area where the color looks good.

Figure 18.144 After painting over the wood areas, the colors look much better.

Figure 18.145 The outline of the old frame is still visible in the dark areas of his suit.

Figure 18.146 After healing, the transition where the old frame used to be is no longer visible.

Once you get used to the techniques we used to fix this image, you'll be able to tackle similar images in about five minutes. The following section provides an example of when I prefer to distort an image using multiple layers instead of visiting the Liquify command. This technique will distort the image without giving it the overly soft or stretched look that often comes from using the Liquify command.

Plastic Surgery

Now let's combine the ideas from Chapter 16, "Collage," with the Healing Brush to perform some surgery on yours truly (**Figure 18.147**). We'll attempt to transform my every-man nose into a Hollywood masterpiece, worthy of the best Beverly Hills doctor that money can buy (**Figure 18.148**). The general concept for performing plastic surgery is to isolate areas, rotate/transform them into a new position, and then blend in the seams so that nobody can tell that we messed with the image. Here's the play by play:

Figure 18.147 The author, awaiting a nose job. (©2003 Gary Isaacs)

Figure 18.148 After a little surgery, my nose is much slimmer.

If you'd like to follow along, then open the Ben.jpg image in the Practice Images > Retouching folder on the CD (no heckling from you readers allowed in this section). Start by making a generic selection around my nose using the Lasso tool (**Figure 18.149**). To make sure the edge blends into its surroundings, choose Select > Feather, and use a medium setting (it will depend on the size and resolution of your image—I used 5 for this image). Now let's copy that area onto its own layer so that we can work on it independently from the rest of the image. Do that by either choosing Layer > New > Layer Via Copy or typing Command-J (Mac) or Ctrl-J (Windows). With that new layer active, choose Image > Transform > Distort, and then move the bottom two corners until my nose starts to look a bit slimmer (**Figure 18.150**).

Figure 18.149 Make a generic selection around the nose.

Figure 18.150 Slim down my nose by adjusting the four corners.

We'll need to transform a few other areas in order to cover up my old nose, which is peeking out from behind my new slim nose. So, click on the bottom layer in the image and then make a loose selection of the crease that runs between one side of my nose and the edge of my mouth/goatee (**Figure 18.151**). Then feather the selection and copy it to another layer, just like we did with my nose. Once it's on its own layer, move that layer up in the Layers palette so it appears above the slim version of my nose. To transform that area, type Command-T (Mac) or Ctrl-T

(Windows), and then move your mouse just outside the upper-right corner and drag to rotate the crease so that it matches up with the new slimmer nose (use the arrow keys if you need to reposition the transformed layer) (**Figure 18.152**). Don't worry if the edges don't blend in; we'll fix that later. Before we move on, repeat the steps that we did with the crease and apply them to the crease that appears on the other side of my nose/mouth (**Figure 18.153**).

Figure 18.151 Select one of the creases to the side of my nose.

Figure 18.152 Transform the crease so it matches up with my new nose.

Figure 18.153 Transform the other side as well.

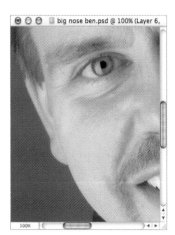

Figure 18.154 Use the Healing Brush to fix any transition areas.

Now that we have all the proper pieces transformed into new positions, we need to blend in all the transitions. That's where the Healing Brush comes in. Create a new layer and place it at the top of the Layers palette. Switch to the Healing Brush and turn on the Use All Layers check box in the options bar at the top of your screen. Now, Option-click (Mac) or Alt-click (Windows) in the general cheek area just outside one of the creases that we transformed. Then, with a brush big enough to cover the transition between the crease and the cheek, paint across the entire transition to blend it into the surrounding image (do it as one paint stroke so it blends properly) (**Figure 18.154**). If you're not comfortable using the Healing Brush, then make sure you review the beginning of this chapter and practice on a few images first.

If you'd like to compare the original image to the re-touched version, just Option-click (Mac) or Alt-click (Windows) on the Eyeball icon for the bottom layer in the Layers palette. That should toggle the visibility of all the layers we just created, effectively showing you before (new layers hidden) and after (new layers visible).

This jump-to-a-new-layer, transform, heal technique is a great way to resculpt faces. A perfect model is hard to find (and expensive), but a 10-minute visit to Photoshop can easily transform a less-than-perfect face into one that looks like a million bucks.

Closing Thoughts

We've covered all the tools you'll need to become a bona fide "photo doctor." Bear in mind that you don't need to limit yourself to just photographs; the tools and techniques we've covered in this chapter can be used for nonphotographic images as well. And, as with everything else in Photoshop, once you've gone around the block with these tools a few times, you'll probably think of a dozen other things you can do with them.

So, whether you're giving someone a face-lift, removing your former boy- or girlfriend from a photograph, or clear-cutting telephone poles from an otherwise perfect Kodak moment, just promise me that you won't do anything underhanded for some ethically challenged dictator.

Ben's Techno-Babble Decoder Ring

Specular highlight: An area that shines light directly into the camera lens, usually caused by a light source reflecting off the reflective surface of glass, metal, or other shiny objects. Specular highlights do not contain any detail and should be reproduced as solid white to maintain realism.

Keyboard Shortcuts

Function	Macintosh	Windows
Enlarge Brush	Right Bracket	Right Bracket
Reduce Brush	Left Bracket	Left Bracket
Harder Brush	Shift-Right Bracket	Shift-Right Bracket
Softer Brush	Shift-Left Bracket	Shift-Left Bracket
Tool Opacity	0 through 9	0 through 9
Dodge/Burn/Sponge tools	O	O
Cycle through Dodge/Burn/Sponge tools	Shift-O	Shift-O
Blur/Sharpen tools	R	R
Switch between Blur and Sharpen	Shift-R	Shift-R
Use Shadows	Shift-Option-S	Shift-Alt-S
Use Midtones	Shift-Option-M	Shift-Alt-M
Use Highlights	Shift-Option-H	Shift-Alt-H

19

Type and Background Effects

Courtesy of Alicia Buelow, www.aliciabuelow.com

When ideas fail, words come in very handy.

—Goethe

Type and Background Effects

For me, coming up with the ideal text and background to complement an image is a thoroughly enjoyable process. It's like putting the icing on the cake and then being able to stand back and admire the final creation. I can't help you with your design, but I can help you master the tools you'll need to create some awesome type and background effects.

No More Jaggy Text

Jaggy text is an unsightly blemish that we've all experienced and wished we could make go away. The unwanted jaggies appear when the pixels in an image are big enough that you can easily see them when printed (**Figure 19.1**). They show up as rough, jagged edges on your printouts, and they are the cause of much hair-pulling and sudden bursts of profanity in the graphic arts industry.

Pixel-based text is great for the web, but was less than ideal when you had to save the text in a file, use it in a page layout program, and send it off to the printer. Invariably you would get some degree of jagginess, which is why so many professional designers would bypass Photoshop (pre-6.0, that is) and create text in their page layout program, or in Adobe Illustrator, where it would be object-based (also known as vector-based).

Stick with me on this. In the graphic arts industry, the distinction between object-based and pixel-based is an extremely important one, and understanding it will serve you well. Object-based simply means that text is no longer made up of pixels; it's a single element that can be scaled up or down without losing the integrity of its shape. For example, if you import a photograph of a circular object into

Figure 19.1 Photoshop 5.5's text was pixel-based, which could cause it to appear jaggy.

your page layout program and then try to scale it up, it doesn't make more pixels to accommodate the larger size. Instead, it simply makes each pixel larger to fill the space. Thus the jaggy look. Not so with object-based shapes! If you created that same circle in Adobe Illustrator (which creates strictly object-based images), you could do anything you want to that circle (make it bigger, smaller, oval, or the like), and it will always retain its smooth edge. That's why most logos are created in Illustrator. But with Photoshop 6.0 and above, we can have object-based text (**Figure 19.2**).

But not everything is roses and chocolate. The one stipulation about the new object-based text is that it must be printed on a PostScript printer. Otherwise it will revert to being plain old pixel-based text again, and the jaggies you love to hate will be back staring you in the face. So if you have a $200 inkjet printer, you're really no further ahead when it comes to the jaggies, unless your printer happens to have a PostScript RIP, which is usually a software accessory you can add to a low-end inkjet printer.

Entering Text

This is going to be a short section, because all you have to do to lay down some text is click with the Type tool and start typing directly on your image. Photoshop will automatically create a new Type layer. If you want Photoshop to act like an old Smith Corona typewriter—that is, where you have to press Return (Mac) or Enter (Windows) to create a new line—just click the mouse button without dragging, and begin typing. This is known as point text, and is useful for creating headlines that you don't want to wrap onto multiple lines. But if you'd rather have Photoshop automatically wrap your text into a multiline paragraph, then click and drag to create a rectangular box that will contain your text. Then you can enter your text and press Return (Mac) or Enter (Windows) whenever you need to create a new paragraph. Photoshop will do the rest, wrapping your text onto multiple lines based on the column width you define. While you are in the Type tool, you can always change the column width by dragging one of the side handles, causing the text to reflow.

NOTES

You can achieve crisp text on a non-PostScript printer by saving your image as a PDF file and printing it from Adobe Acrobat.

Figure 19.2 In Photoshop 6.0, text became object-based, which allows it to stay crisp as long as it is printed on a PostScript printer.

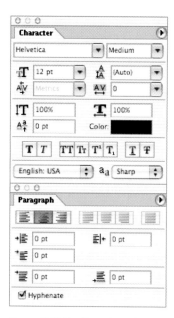

Figure 19.3 The Character and Paragraph palettes.

You can double-click to select a word, triple-click to select a line, quadruple-click to select a paragraph, and quintuple-click to select all.

You can type Command-H (Macintosh) or Ctrl-H (Windows) to hide the highlighting that indicates a range of text is selected. If you type that shortcut a second time, the highlighting will become visible again.

Editing Text

The Character and Paragraph palettes offer a wide range of choices for editing text (**Figure 19.3**). But before you start messing with these settings, you'll need to highlight the text you would like to edit. You can do this by dragging across a range of text or by typing Command-A (Mac) or Ctrl-A (Windows) to select all the text. The Character palette will work exclusively on the text that is highlighted, whereas the Paragraph palette will work on entire paragraphs regardless of whether all the text is selected.

Some of you Photoshoppers may not have been steeped in desktop publishing, so here's a basic rundown of the typographical controls you're going to know and love:

▶ **Font:** I like to click on the Font field and then use the up and down arrow keys to cycle through all the choices that appear in the list. You can also click on the Font field and start typing a font name, and Photoshop will move you to the first font that starts with those letters. Or, if you want to do it the traditional way, just click on the arrow to the right of the Font field, and you'll be presented with a full font menu. If you have more than one version of the same font installed, then Photoshop will add (T1) next to the PostScript Type 1 version of the font, (TT) next to the TrueType version, or (OT) for an OpenType font.

▶ **Style:** Once you've chosen the font family you'd like to use, you can find out which styles (bold, italic, and so on) are available by clicking on the Style menu. If you find that the font you want to use doesn't contain a bold or italic style, you can experiment with the Faux Bold and Faux Italic icons near the bottom of the Character palette to have Photoshop thicken or slant the typeface.

▶ **Size:** You can specify the measurement system that will be used to determine the size of your type by choosing Edit > Preferences > Units & Rulers. There are three ways to measure your text: in pixels, in millimeters, or in points. The pixels option is resolution-independent, meaning that the height of the text in pixels will be the same regardless of the resolution of your image. The only time I use the pixels option is when I need to match the height of some existing text that has already been measured in pixels. More often than not, I prefer to measure text in points because I can use the same setting in multiple documents and know that the text will appear the same size when printed regardless of the resolution of the file it is used in. It's also a system that's consistent with most publishing programs. I have never used the millimeters option because I don't know of any other program that uses that system to measure type.

To be honest, it isn't very often that I pay attention to the actual type-size settings. Instead, I eyeball it and compare the size of my text to the rest of the image. To quickly adjust the size of the text in increments of two, highlight the text and type Shift-Command-> or Shift-Command-< (Mac) or Shift-Ctrl-> or Shift-Ctrl-< (Windows). To change the size in increments of 10, just add the Option key (Mac) or the Alt key (Windows) to these keyboard commands. Also, you can scale text up or down using the Edit > Transform > Scale option; it won't harm your text.

▶ **Leading:** To change the vertical space between lines of text, you'll need to change the Leading setting. If you leave it set to (Auto), Photoshop will automatically calculate its own setting and keep it hidden from you (**Figure 19.4**). It does this by multiplying the size of the text by the percentage specified in the Justification dialog box that appears in the side menu of the Paragraph palette; the default setting is 120%. So 100-point text, for example, would have an automatic leading setting of 120. The Auto setting is useful if you know you'll be changing the size of the text later on, because the Leading setting will change as you change the size of the text. If you don't like the Auto setting, you can type in your own setting (**Figure 19.5**). To quickly change the leading in increments of two, highlight the text, then type Option-up arrow and Option-down arrow (Mac) or Alt-up arrow and Alt-down arrow (Windows).

Graphic Savage

Figure 19.4 Leading setting determined by Photoshop (Auto).

Graphic Savage

Figure 19.5 Leading setting adjusted manually.

To set the leading to Auto, either type (Auto) into the Leading field or type Shift-Option-Command-A (Mac) or Shift-Alt-Ctrl-A (Windows).

▶ **Kerning:** If you need to tighten up or loosen the space between two letters, click between the letters, and then change the Kerning setting to increase (positive numbers) or decrease (negative numbers) the amount of space between those letters (**Figures 19.6** and **19.7**). Kerning is essential when working with numbers, because they are designed to line up in a spreadsheet program, which means the number 1 will always have a bunch of space around it to force it to take up as much space as the other numbers. To quickly change the Kerning setting in increments of 20, type Option-right arrow and Option-left arrow (Mac) or Alt-right arrow and Alt-left arrow (Windows). You can also add the Command key (Mac) or the Ctrl key (Windows) to these keyboard commands to increase the Kerning setting in increments of 100. If you use the Metrics setting, Photoshop will use the kerning settings that are built into the typeface.

DAVE DAVE

Figure 19.6 Text entered with the Metrics kerning setting selected.

Figure 19.7 The space between each letter has been manually kerned.

▶ **Tracking:** To add or remove space between all the letters in a range of text, highlight the text, and then change the Tracking setting (compare **Figures 19.8** and **19.9**). Or type Option-right arrow and Option-left arrow (Mac) or Alt-right arrow and Alt-left arrow (Windows) to change the Tracking in increments of 20. To change the Tracking setting in increments of 100, just add the Command key (Mac) or Ctrl key (Windows) to these keyboard commands. To set the tracking to zero, just leave the Tracking field empty, or type Shift-Command-Q (Mac) or Shift-Ctrl-Q (Windows). I often use a negative Tracking setting for headlines where I like the text to be nice and tight. I use positive tracking any time I have all caps text because it seems to make it easier to read.

SPIFFY

Figure 19.8 Tracking: 0.

SPIFFY

Figure 19.9 Tracking: 260.

▶ **Vertical Scale:** This setting allows you to stretch your text vertically without changing its width. I often do this when I want to create a raised capital at the beginning of a paragraph. I just set both the vertical and horizontal scale settings to an equal number, and then, when I change the size of the text, the raised cap will change along with it, as long as all the text is selected (**Figure 19.10**). To set the Vertical Scale to 100%, type Shift-Option-Command-X (Mac) or Shift-Alt-Ctrl-X (Windows).

▶ **Horizontal Scale:** This setting allows you to stretch or compress your text horizontally without changing its height. I often lower this setting a small amount (like by 1%) to make a line of text take up less space and prevent it from overflowing the space I have allotted. The alternative would be to use tracking, which leaves the shape of the characters intact, and simply removes an equal amount of space between each letter. To set the Horizontal Scale to 100%, type Shift-Command-X (Mac) or Shift-Ctrl-X (Windows).

▶ **Baseline Shift:** To shift one or more letters up or down, highlight the letters, and then change the Baseline Shift setting (**Figures 19.11** and **19.12**). This is very useful when working with symbols, where a parenthesis might appear to be too low compared to the text, or an equals sign needs to be shifted to make it look better. To change this setting in increments of two, type Shift-Option-up arrow and Shift-Option-down arrow (Mac) or Shift-Alt-up arrow and Shift-Alt-down arrow (Windows).

▶ **Color:** To change the color of the text, click on the color swatch to bring up the standard Color Picker. To use your foreground color, type Option-Delete (Mac) or Alt-Backspace (Windows). To use your background color, type Command-Delete (Mac) or Ctrl-Backspace (Windows).

▶ **Anti-aliased:** You'll find five options in this pop-up menu: None, Sharp, Crisp, Strong, and Smooth (**Figure 19.13**). Using anything other than None will cause the pixels on the edge of the text to blend into the image

A solid foundation of knowledge is essential before attempting to understand Photoshop's more advanced features.

Figure 19.10 The initial capital in this paragraph was created by setting the Vertical and Horizontal Scale settings to 200%.

Figure 19.11 No baseline shift.

Figure 19.12 Equals sign and small 2 baseline shifted.

and create a smooth edge. Sharp will make the edges appear the sharpest, while Crisp will come in a close second in sharpness. Strong will make the text look a little bolder, and Smooth will make the edges appear softer. These options are great when creating small text that will be used on the Web. I suggest experimenting with each setting until you think the text looks its best. You can also use the Strong setting when creating text that will be printed, because it can help disguise the jaggies that appear on non-PostScript printers.

Figure 19.13 Anti-aliased settings from top to bottom: None, Sharp, Crisp, Strong, Smooth.

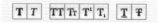

Figure 19.14 From left to right; Faux Bold, Faux Italic, All Caps, Small Caps, Superscript, Subscript, Underline, and Strikethrough.

Next, let's take a look at what the tiny icons are for near the bottom of the Characters palette (**Figure 19.14**).

▶ **All Caps:** Changes your text to all capital letters. This can be useful if, for example, you decide to make a few subheads uppercase after the text has been entered. (Remember that all-capped text is more difficult to read, so you may want to add some tracking, which can make reading a bit easier.) Type Shift-Command-K (Mac) or Shift-Ctrl-K (Windows) to specify All Caps type.

▶ **Small Caps:** Changes all lowercase letters into smaller capital letters, while the capital letters you entered remain full size. This is useful for headings (**Figure 19.15**), but is not as good as using a typeface that is specifically designed as a small caps font (the smaller letters don't have the same thickness when using this feature). Type Shift-Command-H (Mac) or Shift-Ctrl-H (Windows) to specify Small Caps type.

The Small Caps style will convert your text into all capital letters, where the characters that were created using the shift key will be larger than the characters that were previously lowercase.

THE SMALL CAPS STYLE WILL CONVERT YOUR TEXT INTO ALL CAPITAL LETTERS, WHERE THE CHARACTERS THAT WERE CREATED USING THE SHIFT KEY WILL BE LARGER THAN THE CHARACTERS THAT WERE PREVI-OUSLY LOWERCASE.

Figure 19.15 Top: Type entered without formatting. Bottom: Small Caps style applied.

▶ **Superscript:** This will reduce the size of the selected text and move the characters above the baseline of the rest of the text. I use this all the time when I'm typesetting prices—I remove the decimal and then use this option for the dollar sign and cents (**Figure 19.16**). Type Shift-Command-+ (Mac) or Shift-Ctrl-+ (Windows) to specify Superscript type.

▶ **Subscript:** This option will also make your text smaller, but will shift things downward. It's useful when entering scientific and chemical formulas (**Figure 19.17**). Type Shift-Option-Command-+ (Mac) or Shift-Alt-Ctrl-+ (Windows) to specify Subscript type.

▶ **Underline:** This option will place a line under each letter of your text in the same color as the type. (You cannot control the placement or thickness of the underline.) This feature can be useful when you want to make a selection of text stand out, like a link on a Web page or the cents in a price (**Figure 19.18**). Type Shift-Command-U (Mac) or Shift-Ctrl-U (Windows) to specify Underlined type.

20^{00}

Figure 19.16 The dollar sign and last two numbers were set using the Superscript style.

H_2O

Figure 19.17 The 2 was set using the Subscript style.

$371^{\underline{50}}$

Figure 19.18 The last two digits were set with both the Superscript and Underline styles.

On a Macintosh, type Option-8 to create a bullet; in Windows, type Alt-0149 on your numeric keypad.

Photoshop has keyboard shortcuts for just about everything. The key is to remember and use what's important to your particular workflow.

Photoshop has keyboard shortcuts for just about everything. The key is to remember and use what's important to your particular workflow.

Photoshop has keyboard shortcuts for just about everything. The key is to remember and use what's important to your particular workflow.

Photoshop has keyboard shortcuts for just about everything. The key is to remember and use what's important to your particular workflow.

Figure 19.19 Paragraph alignment settings from top to bottom: Centered, Flush Left, Flush Right, Justified.

▶ **Strikethrough:** This option will place a line through the center of the text using the same color as the type. (You cannot control the size or placement of the line.) This can be useful when advertising prices; you can cross out the old price and place the new one right next to it. Type Shift-Command-/ (Mac) or Shift-Ctrl-/ (Windows) to specify Strikethrough type. I find that the Underline and Strikethrough options are usually too thin and often appear as semi-transparent lines on small text.

Now let's move on to the Paragraph palette and see what's in store for us.

▶ **Alignment:** The Alignment choices determine the method used to align multiple lines of text (**Figure 19.19**). Most of the time I use the flush left option because it seems to be the easiest to read. Type Shift-Command-L (Mac) or Shift-Ctrl-L (Windows) to specify flush left text. Centered is good for headlines; type Shift-Command-C (Mac) or Shift-Ctrl-C (Windows) to specify centered text. Flush right is often useful for numbers, because it will line up the decimal points. Type Shift-Command-R (Mac) or Shift-Ctrl-R (Windows) to specify flush right text. I only use the justified option when I'm using a rather long column width; otherwise, it causes huge spaces between words. Type Shift-Command-J (Mac) or Shift-Ctrl-J (Windows) to specify justified text.

▶ **Indent Left Margin:** This setting is useful when you have a bulleted list that you want to set off from the main flow of text (**Figure 19.20**).

With a little practice, even the most complicated topics can be mastered including:
- Line Art Scanning
- Grayscale Adjustment
- Color Correction
- Understanding Levels and Curves

Figure 19.20 Bulleted list set using a left indent of 12 pts.

► **Indent Right Margin:** I often use this setting along with the left indent setting to make a long quotation stand out from the rest of the text (**Figure 19.21**). You can also make the quotation marks extend beyond the margins by choosing Hanging Roman Punctuation from the side menu of the Paragraph palette.

It can be more pleasing when the flow of text is interrupted by other elements such as quotes and bullet points.

> "This is a mighty fine example of a spiffy looking quote that is set off from the rest of the text"

Figure 19.21 Quote was set using a left indent of 24 pts and a right indent of 30 pts.

Did you know that the proper quote characters used by typography professionals are the curly ones, and not the straight ones (which are really inch and feet marks)? Photoshop will create quotes like a pro as long as the Use Smart Quotes option is turned on in the General Preferences dialog box.

Unfortunately, the Hanging Roman Punctuation option did not recognize proper curly quotes in previous versions of Photoshop.

► **Indent First Line:** This function indents the first line of each paragraph as if you pressed the Tab key on your keyboard. I also find this useful when I have a list of bulleted items that have more than one line each. I'll end up changing the Left Indent setting to something like 20 pts and the First Line Indent setting to –20 pts. That will force all the lines after the bulleted line to be indented (you may need to put some spaces after the bullet on the first line to make the text there line up with the lines below). Compare **Figures 19.22** and **19.23**. This technique is also useful when you want the first letter of a paragraph to extend into the margin.

Bulleted lists can pose many problems unless you are thoughtful when using Photoshop's settings.

- Some bulleted lists might extend to more than a single line, which can make them less than ideal for a simple left indent.
- That's when you might want to consider

Figure 19.22 Bulleted list set using a left indent of 12 pts.

Bulleted lists can pose many problems unless you are thoughtful when using Photoshop's settings.

- Some bulleted lists might extend to more than a single line, which can make them less than ideal for a simple left indent.
- That's when you might want to consider using a negative first line indent setting along with a simple left indent to control the rest of the lines.

Figure 19.23 Bulleted list set with a left indent of 32 pts and a first line indent of −20 pts.

▶ **Space Before Paragraph and Space After Paragraph:** These settings are exactly what their names indicate. They control the space before and after (above and below) your paragraph. I use Space Before as a substitute for indenting the first line of every paragraph (like all the paragraphs in this book). It is also useful when you have a bulleted list that contains more than one line per bullet point. I use Space After to add a bit of extra space below the last line of a bulleted list so it doesn't look like it has melded with the paragraphs below it.

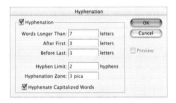

Figure 19.24 The Hyphenation dialog box.

▶ **Hyphenate:** This setting will use the settings in the Hyphenation dialog box (from the side menu of the Paragraph palette) to determine which words should break onto the next line of the text (**Figure 19.24**). Type Shift-Option-Command-H (Mac) or Shift-Alt-Ctrl-H (Windows) to toggle Hyphenation on and off. If you want to prevent a word from breaking, select the letters you'd like to keep together and then choose No Break from the side menu of the Character palette. The No Break feature is useful when you have initials, web addresses, or company names that don't read well when broken onto multiple lines.

You'll also find other useful options in the side menu of the Character and Paragraph palettes. Let's take a look at the choices in these side menus that we haven't covered already. First we'll look at the Character palette.

- ► **Standard Vertical Roman Alignment:** This option is available only for vertical type. When selected, it changes the orientation of the individual characters, standing them upright one atop the other, and aligning their horizontal centers (**Figure 19.25**).

- ► **Fractional Widths:** When this option is turned off, it forces Photoshop to use full pixels for spacing between words. This is useful for web graphics where your text can be extra small and you want to prevent your text from smashing together (**Figure 19.26**).

1111111   1111111

Figure 19.26 Left: Fractional Widths turned on. Right: Fractional Widths turned off.

- ► **Reset Character:** This option will reset all the Character palette settings to their defaults. This can be useful when you've just finished messing with a bunch of options and need to get back to setting some normal type.

The rest of the choices available in this menu are available only with OpenType fonts, and not all OpenType fonts contain the information needed to use these features.

- ► **Old Style:** This option tells Photoshop to use an alternative set of numerals that are smaller than the standard ones (**Figure 19.27**).

- ► **Ordinals:** This option makes the two letters that are next to a number (like in 1st, 2nd, 3rd, and so on) appear smaller and raised. Listing a series in that fashion is known as using ordinal numbers (**Figure 19.28**).

2929 2929   2nd

Figure 19.27 Left: Text entered with no formatting applied. Right: Text with Old Style applied (it affects only the numerals).

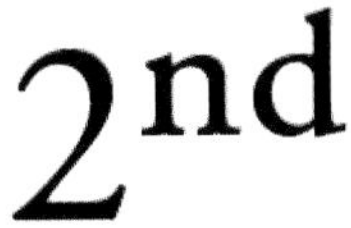

Figure 19.28 OpenType text with Ordinals turned on. Type is formatted with superscripts.

ROMAN VERTICAL

VERTICAL

Figure 19.25 Left: Vertical text entered with no formatting applied. Right: Text with Standard Vertical Roman Alignment applied.

▶ **Swash:** This option replaces some characters with more calligraphic versions of the letters (**Figure 19.29**).

Design Panache   *Design Panache*

Figure 19.29 Left: Text as entered with no formatting applied. Right: Text with Swash applied.

▶ **Titling:** This option replaces characters with a new set of characters, usually all uppercase, specially designed to be used at large sizes for titles and headlines (**Figure 19.30**).

Photoshop CS   PHOTOSHOP CS

Figure 19.30 Left: Text as entered with no formatting applied. Right: Text with Titling applied.

▶ **Contextual Alternates:** Contextual Alternates are similar to ligatures (and are sometimes called connection forms). When selected, this replaces certain default characters with alternate forms that better join together. This feature is most common in script-style fonts.

▶ **Stylistic Alternate:** Formats stylized characters that create a purely aesthetic effect (**Figure 19.31**).

Joseph Wurner   Joſeph Wurner

Figure 19.31 Left: Text as entered with no formatting applied. Right: Text with Stylistic Alternates applied.

Figure 19.32 These ornaments are hiding within the Silentium Pro font.

▶ **Ornaments:** Ornaments are wing dings that can serve as borders and decoration (**Figure 19.32**).

▶ **Ligatures:** This option allows Photoshop to automatically replace certain combinations of characters (like "fi" and "fl") with a specially designed character that is a combination of those two, which makes them look more aesthetically pleasing (**Figure 19.33**).

fitness flex fitness flex

Figure 19.33 Left: Text as entered with no formatting applied. Right: Text with ligatures applied.

▶ **Discretionary Ligatures:** Like the Ligature option, this allows Photoshop to replace certain combinations of characters (like "ct" and "st") with specially designed characters that are a combination of the two. These are less commonly used than the standard ligatures (**Figure 19.34**).

Just in time! Just in time!

Figure 19.34 Left: Text as entered with no formatting applied. Right: Text with Discretionary Ligatures applied.

▶ **Fractions:** When selected, this setting converts fractions written as a slash, like 1/3, into proper fractions (**Figure 19.35**).

Now let's move on to the choices that appear in the side menu of the Paragraph palette.

1/3

Figure 19.35 OpenType text with Fractions turned on. Now 1/3 is formatted as a true fraction.

▶ **Adobe Single-Line Composer:** This option is best when you want to "massage" type by hand and want to precisely control character and word spacing by manually kerning and tracking the characters.

▶ **Adobe Every-Line Composer:** This option will evaluate an entire paragraph to determine where each line of text should break. That means that the upper lines in a paragraph might suddenly change as you continue to add text to the bottom of a paragraph. This option usually gives you the best-looking text, but makes it a bit more difficult to manually tweak everything. Type Shift-Option-Command-T (Mac) or Shift-Alt-Ctrl-T (Windows) to toggle between the Single-Line and Every-Line Composer settings.

▶ **Reset Paragraph:** This option will reset all the Paragraph palette settings back to their defaults. But be careful using it, because it will also reset all the settings in the Hyphenation and Justification dialog boxes.

The options bar at the top of your screen contains the most commonly used choices from the Character and Paragraph palettes, along with a few options that can't be found in the other palettes. Let's take a look at the options that are exclusive to this palette (**Figure 19.36**).

Figure 19.36 Photoshop options bar for typographical controls.

C
O
O
L

Figure 19.37 Text set using the Vertical Type option.

Now we're on to the choices that are available under the edit menu, which is where you'll find the Spell Checker and the Find and Replace Text option.

▶ **Warp:** This option is simply a shortcut for choosing Layer > Type > Warp Text. Either one will bring up the Type Warp dialog box, which we will cover later in this chapter.

▶ **Palettes:** The Palettes icon button will open the Character and Paragraph palettes. This allows you to close those two palettes (which I usually have stacked together, as shown in Chapter 1) to avoid screen clutter, and then quickly make them available with a single click.

If you click and hold on the Type tool, you'll notice a few extra choices. Let's see what these can do; then we'll see if there's anything unique in the options bar.

▶ **Type Mask:** This option will deliver a selection shaped like text, instead of an actual Type layer. While you are entering your text, you will see a colored overlay that represents the bounds of the text. Once you finalize the text, it will create a selection. Just be aware that you will not be able to edit the text after it has become a selection. If you're worried that you might find a typo later, then use the normal Type tool, and once you're done editing the text, Command-click (Mac) or Ctrl-click (Windows) on the name of the layer to get a selection.

▶ **Vertical Type:** This option will allow your text to run vertically, with each letter appearing below the previous one. This can be useful when setting type for the spine of a book, or when using Asian typefaces (**Figure 19.37**).

▶ **Spell Checker:** The spell checker is pretty easy to use (**Figure 19.38**). It will indicate any words that it thinks are misspelled and then display a list of suggested alternatives at the bottom. Double-clicking on one of the alternatives will substitute that word and move on to the next questionable word. If Photoshop isn't able to come up with the correct alternative, then you can enter your own in the Change To field, and then click the Change button. I just wish it could spell check the words that you manually enter. Clicking the Add button will add the highlighted word to Photoshop's dictionary so that it won't flag that word as a misspelling in the future. That's useful for company names and other unusual words that aren't in Photoshop's default dictionary. The Check All Layers check box will force Photoshop to spell check every Type layer that is available in the currently open document.

Figure 19.38 The Check Spelling dialog box.

▶ **Find and Replace Text:** This allows you to search all the Type layers in the active document and replace the specified string of characters (**Figure 19.39**). If you've clicked within the text of a Type layer, then Photoshop will start searching from that point. This is useful when you find out that you've been misspelling someone's name for the entire length of a project, or when someone suddenly decides to change the name of a product.

Figure 19.39 The Find and Replace Text dialog box.

Type Layers

After you add text to your image, the text will appear on a Type layer (indicated by a T where there would usually be a preview thumbnail in the Layers palette). This layer is special because you can edit the text at any time by using the Type tool and clicking within the text. If a yellow warning triangle appears along with the T that designates a Type layer, that's an indication that the typeface you've chosen is not currently installed in your operating system (**Figure 19.40**). When a font is missing, you will not be able to edit the text without having Photoshop substitute a different typeface. You might also run into a gray warning triangle on a Type layer. That's an indication that the text will be reflowed if it is edited; that might change the way the paragraph breaks into multiple lines. You'll get that symbol any time you open an image that was created in a version of Photoshop prior to 6.0.

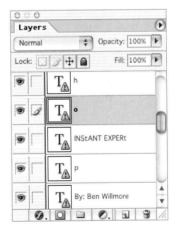

Figure 19.40 The Type layer's warning triangles.

If you double-click the T that appears in the Layers palette for a Type layer, Photoshop will switch you to the Type tool and select the full range of text.

A Type layer is also special because when you print your image on a PostScript printer, your text will appear crisp, even if the pixels in your image are large enough to make the rest of the image appear jaggy. That's because the text is object-based, instead of being made out of pixels. Photoshop will not convert the text to pixels unless you choose Layer > Rasterize > Type or merge a Type layer with another layer. Not only that, but Photoshop allows you to do a whole bunch of stuff to the Type layers without having to permanently convert them to pixels. Let's take a quick look at your choices. You can:

▶ Apply any of the choices in the Layer > Type > Warp Text dialog box.

▶ Apply most of the Edit > Transform functions.

▶ Add layer styles.

▶ Add a layer mask.

Before you can apply a filter or perform adjustments to the text, you have to convert the Type layer into a normal layer by choosing Layer > Rasterize > Type. That will convert the text from being object-based to being pixel-based. Once you've done that, you'll no longer be able to edit the text (Photoshop will treat it as a scanned image instead) and the text will no longer print with an absolutely crisp edge. If you don't rasterize, and you attempt to apply a filter to your text, Photoshop will warn you and then offer to rasterize the text for you.

Sometimes Photoshop insists on putting your text *on* a path when you actually wanted it *near* the path. If you're having trouble, hold the Shift key while clicking with the Text tool to force Photoshop to create a new text layer.

Now that you've seen the options that are available when creating text, let's get into the juicy stuff and start creating type effects.

Type on a Path

If you are one of those Adobe Illustrator–phobics who longs for that elegantly curved and swooping text but finds Illustrator way too scary, then you are in for a whopping treat. Photoshop CS has added the ability to place type on a path (**Figure 19.41**). Your text can swoop up and down in lines, curves, and even circles. To place text on a path, you must first create a path. Grab the Freeform Pen tool (found by clicking and holding on the regular Pen tool in

Figure 19.41 The type follows the curve wherever it goes.

the Tool palette) and sketch a curve with Paths selected in the options bar (review Chapter 13, "Advanced Masking," for more information about creating paths). Now choose the Horizontal Type tool. When you bring the Type cursor close to the path, it changes into the new Type on a Path cursor—the standard I-beam intersected with a line (**Figure 19.42**). Click and start typing. Your text will follow the path, no matter where it curves.

Figure 19.42 The Type on a Path cursor.

Once your text is entered, you can slide it back and forth along the path. Choose either the Path Selection tool or the Direct Selection tool and position it over the beginning of the text. It changes to an I-beam with an arrow (**Figure 19.43**). Click and drag along the path, and the text will slide to follow (**Figure 19.44**). If you drag this cursor across the path, from the top to the bottom or from the bottom to the top, it will pull your text to the other side of the path (**Figure 19.45**).

Figure 19.43 Position the Path Selection or Direct Selection tool over type on a path and it changes to an I-beam with an arrow.

Figure 19.44 The type follows the curve wherever it goes.

Sometimes type will get a bit "pinched" when trying to follow a sharp bend in a path. You may have to select a few characters and adjust their tracking in the Character dialog box, or click between characters and adjust their kerning, to spread things out a bit and restore the text's legibility (**Figure 19.46**).

Figure 19.45 You can use the Path Selection tool to drag your type to the other side of the path.

Type on a Path places a small x on the path at the start point of the text, and a small circle on the path at the end point of the text (**Figure 19.47**). Click and drag on the end-point circle with the Path Selection or Direct Selection tool to hide words at the end of the text (**Figure 19.48**).

Figure 19.46 If type becomes pinched at a sharp turn, you can adjust the tracking for selected letters to restore legibility.

Figure 19.47 When you create type on a path, Photoshop marks the beginning and end points of the text with a small x and o. If the text is center aligned, Photoshop will also mark the center point.

Figure 19.48 Click and drag with the Path Selection or Direct Selection tool on the circle at the end of the type on a path to truncate the visibility of words at the end of the text.

Figure 19.49 Text placed around a closed path created with the shape tool.

If you find that the Warp option is grayed out, then you most likely have used the Faux Bold style from the side menu of the Character palette. Unfortunately, warping doesn't work when that style is applied.

Figure 19.52 The Warp Text dialog box, and the styles available on its drop-down menu.

You can also place text along the inside or outside of a closed path, such as one created with Photoshop's Shape tool (**Figure 19.49**).

Type in a Shape

With Photoshop CS you can also effortlessly flow your text in just about any shape you can dream up: squiggly snakes, hearts, flowers, diamonds, hourglasses, elephants, and coffee cups! Anything you can turn into a path (including anything created with the Pen tool and Shape tools), you can use to guide the contour of your text.

If you hold the Text tool within a closed path, it changes to an I-beam with a pair of dotted arcs around it (**Figure 19.50**). Click now, and any text you type will be constrained within the boundaries of the path (**Figure 19.51**).

Figure 19.50 Position the Type tool within a closed path and it changes to an I-beam with dotted arcs.

Figure 19.51 Text placed within a closed path created with the Shape tool.

Text placed on or within a path is completely editable; you can add or remove characters, add layer effects such as drop shadow, change the font and color, and so forth.

Type Warping

Placing type on a path changes the characters' orientation, but it does not change their shape. To actually change the *shape* of the letters, begin by choosing Layer > Type > Warp Text. You'll find 15 different warping effects you can use to contort your text into numerous shapes (**Figure 19.52**). Remember, this is a layer-based feature, so you can't warp only a part of a layer, or just a few words on a layer.

The Bend setting determines how dramatically your text will change (**Figure 19.53**). The Horizontal and Vertical Distortion settings can make it look as if your text is being viewed from different 3D angles (**Figure 19.54**).

After you've warped your type, you'll notice that a curve has been added below the T in the Layers palette. That signifies that the layer is a Type layer with warping applied, but you can still edit the text by using the Type tool and clicking within the text. The Warp function is also great for creating animations in ImageReady, which we'll explore in a later chapter.

Can you warp text that's been placed on a path? Yes you can. Simply place your text along the path and then apply the warp effect of your choice (**Figure 19.55**). There's a catch, though: Warping destroys the text path in the warping process. Once the text has been warped, you can't alter the shape of the path, or drag the text back and forth along it; the path is no longer editable.

Layer Styles

Okay, you've got your text formatted just the way you want it—you've typed and kerned and aligned and warped into wildness. Now you can rub your hands together and get ready for a thrill, because it's time to explore the Layer Style dialog box (which is ground zero for creating type effects). Why the excitement? Because you'll be able to add a multitude of effects and still be able to edit your text! And because the effects are made by using layer styles, they won't require much memory (they are just simple settings applied to a layer) and should not increase the file size of your image too much. That means you can go crazy creating some great effects such as edge embossing, extruded or

Figure 19.53 Bend settings from top to bottom: -50%, -25%, 0, +25, +50 (with the Arc effect).

Figure 19.54 Top: Horizontal and Vertical Distortion set to zero. Bottom: Horizontal Distortion of 85% and Vertical Distortion of 50%.

Figure 19.55 Left: Text on a path. Right: The same text warped with the Twist option.

indented type, shadows, and beveled type, and you don't have to worry about bloating your file size. There are four ways to access the Layer Style dialog box:

- ▶ Option-Double-click (Mac) or Alt-Double-click (Windows) any layer name in the Layers palette.

- ▶ Choose one of the options from the Layer > Layer Style menu.

- ▶ Choose one of the options from the Layer Style menu at the bottom of the Layers palette (it's the black circle with the "f" inside).

- ▶ Choose Blending Options from the side menu of the Layers palette.

Once you've made it into the Layer Style dialog box, you can click on the name of any style listed on the left side of the dialog box to turn on that style and view its options. If you just click the check box next to a style's name, you will toggle that style on or off, but you will not view its settings—you have to click its name for that.

Layer styles determine their shape based on the contents of the layer that they are applied to. Typically, the entire content of a layer is fully visible, and an effect adds dimension on top of, or a shadow underneath, that content. It doesn't have to be that way. Sometimes you might want just the effect to be in the shape of a letter or word, but you don't want the original solid text to be visible. In that case, you have the option of tricking Photoshop into hiding the solid text that's in the Type layer. That will allow you to use just the shape of the text to figure out where to apply the layer style. To accomplish that, either change the Fill setting at the top of the Layers palette to zero, or click on the Blending Options choice in the upper left of the Layer Style dialog box, and then set the Fill Opacity (in the Advanced Blending section) to zero (**Figure 19.56**). That should make the contents of the layer disappear, but will not affect any of the layer styles applied to the layer.

NOTES

In order to add a layer style to the Background image, you must first change its name (by double-clicking on it) to convert it into a normal layer.

Figure 19.56 Top: Fill Opacity 100%. Bottom: Fill Opacity 0%. (background ©2002 Stockbyte, www.stockbyte.com)

Beveled Edge Type

Now let's make our text disappear and then add some effects around its edge. Start by changing the Fill setting to 0 at the top of the Layers palette. That should make the text completely disappear. Now let's get its outline to show up by adding a 10-pixel stroke on the outside of the text. Then, to add a little more interest to that edge, add a Bevel and Emboss with the Style set to Stroke Emboss, the Technique set to Chisel Hard, and the Size set to 10. Add a Contour to the Bevel and Emboss, click on the Contour preview, and experiment with different shapes until you like the result (mine looked a little like a shark's fin). The final touch would be to add both a drop shadow and an inner shadow (**Figure 19.57**).

Figure 19.57 Result of applying a stroke, stroke emboss, and both a drop and inner shadow. (background©2003 Stockbyte, www.stockbyte.com)

Textured Type

Let's make a type effect that has some texture to it and an interesting beveled edge. Start by adding a Pattern Overlay with the fourth preset pattern (it looks a little like brown cloth). Next, add a Bevel and Emboss, set the Style to Inner Bevel, the Technique to Chisel Hard, and the Size to 10, and experiment with the other settings until you like the general look. To add a little more interesting texture, click the Texture choice just below the Bevel and Emboss choice on the left side of the Layer Style dialog box. Use the same pattern we used for the Pattern Overlay and experiment with the Depth setting until you get some good dimension to your text. Then to finish it off, add a nice drop shadow (**Figure 19.58**).

Figure 19.58 Result of applying pattern overlay, bevel and emboss (using texture), and drop shadow. (background ©2003 Stockbyte, www.stockbyte.com)

Jelly Type

Now let's create something a bit more complex. Let's make the style that Apple made famous that is often called Aqua, but just in case they copyrighted that name, we'll call it Jelly Type. Start by setting the Fill setting at the top of the Layers palette to 0, and then add a Color Overlay with a color made from H: 200°, S: 70%, and B: 80%, and an Opacity of 80%. Now add a Bevel and Emboss, setting the Style to Inner Bevel, the Technique to Smooth, the Size to 10 pixels, the Altitude to 70, and both Opacity settings to 100%. While you're at it, set the Shadow mode to Color Burn.

Well, that's a start, but we still have a lot to do if we really want this to look good. Add an Inner Glow with the Blend mode set to Multiply, the Opacity to 75%, the color to H: 225°, S: 70%, B: 60%, the Choke to 35%, and the Size to 7 pixels. That should add a nice dark blue edge to the text. Now let's add a drop shadow with a color made from H: 200°, S: 50%, B: 60%, set the Opacity to 70%, the Distance to 7 and the Size to 5. Then to really make it look like light can pass through the text, let's add an Outer Glow using an Opacity of 30%, a color made from H: 200°, S: 60%, B: 50%, and a Size of 10 pixels.

One more thing to finish it off: Add an Inner Shadow using H: 200°, S: 50%, B: 60%, an Opacity of 50%, a Distance of 5 pixels, a 5-pixel Choke, and a Size of 10 pixels (**Figure 19.59**). After doing all that work, you might find that the beveled edge is either too large or small. If that's the case, then choose Layer > Layer Style > Scale Effects and move the slider around until the effect looks appropriate for your type size.

Figure 19.59 Result of creating Jelly Type. (background ©2003 Stockbyte, www.stockbyte.com)

Figure 19.60 An example of what can be accomplished by combining many layer styles. (background ©2003 Stockbyte, www.stockbyte.com)

Wild Type

We've created some pretty cool effects, but we've really only scratched the surface of what's possible. What's exciting is that you can combine as many of these layer styles as you'd like to create some truly eye-popping effects. In **Figure 19.60**, I've used the following styles: Pattern Overlay, Gradient Overlay (set to Hard Light), Stroke (with the Gradient setting), Bevel and Emboss (using the Stroke Emboss option), Inner Shadow, Drop Shadow, and an Inner Glow!

The Styles Palette

If it feels like it took too darn much time to create these effects, then you can take comfort in knowing that Photoshop's Styles palette allows you to store a collection of layer styles so they can be applied over and over again.

To save a style, just make sure the layer with the style(s) applied is active, and then click the New Style icon at the bottom of the Styles palette (**Figure 19.61**). Your style should appear at the bottom of the palette. To apply that style to another layer, just make that layer active and then click on the style you created in the Styles palette. (Or you can choose Layer > Layer Style > Copy Style, click on the layer you'd like to apply it to, and then choose Paste Style from the same menu.) That's all there is to it! You can also remove all the styles applied to a layer by clicking on the No Style icon at the bottom of the Styles palette. The styles that appear in this palette will stay there (available in any document) until you decide to change them.

Figure 19.61 The Layer Styles palette (with a lot of my own styles added).

Now this is significant, so please pay close attention. With all the effects we just created, you have the freedom to edit the text and the effects will update. That's a giant stride toward creative freedom. But not all effects out there in Photoshop allow you to edit the text. With the next technique we'll be converting our text into a shape; after you've done that, you'll no longer be able to edit it as text.

Intertwined Type

All of the effects we've just tried out can be a little more interesting if you make the letters of your type interact with each other. To do that, right after entering your text, choose Layer > Type > Convert To Shape. Next, grab the Solid Arrow tool that appears directly above the Pen tool, and drag the individual letters around your screen. (You can drag a box around multiple adjacent letters to move them as a group.) To create holes where the letters overlap, click on the rightmost of the four icons that appear in the options bar (**Figure 19.62**). You'll need to do that to each letter in order to get all of them to work that way. I used this technique to create the art that appears in **Figure 19.63**.

Figure 19.62 Solid Arrow options.

Figure 19.63 Image created using the rightmost solid arrow option.

Backgrounds and Textures

Backgrounds and textures might not be something that you'd think you want to spend a lot of time learning about. But if you look around at what's considered "high art" in the world of print, and especially on the web, you'll notice that a skilled hand with backgrounds and textures can make the difference between elegance and clunkiness. In this section I'll show you how to create some background effects that I find interesting, and in the making you should be able to gain the skills you need to create your own elegant inventions. The first ones will be simple black and white textures that can be applied to photographs or colorized using the techniques described in Chapter 17, "Enhancement."

In general, we'll be starting with some raw material, and then we'll enhance it to turn it into a texture. Most of Photoshop's filters require a detailed image in order to produce a noticeable result, but there is a select group of filters that can create something out of nothing.

Filters That Can Create Something Out of Nothing

The following filters are capable of creating detail where none existed before. Some of the filters will work on an empty layer, whereas others don't work on empty layers, but work just fine with any layer that is full of something as simple as a solid color.

- ▶ Artistic > Sponge
- ▶ Noise > Add Noise
- ▶ Pixelate > Mezzotint
- ▶ Pixelate > Pointillize
- ▶ Render > Clouds
- ▶ Sketch > Halftone Pattern
- ▶ Sketch > Note Paper
- ▶ Sketch > Reticulation
- ▶ Stylize > Extrude
- ▶ Stylize > Tiles
- ▶ All filters in the Texturize submenu

We'll walk through a few of these raw-material filters to give you some ideas. Then you'll be free to go off and play with your new filter toys and come up with your own uniquely wonderful backgrounds.

A Simple Texture

Let's start with an easy texture. Start by typing **D** to reset your foreground/background colors, and then choosing Filter > Render > Clouds. Next, choose Filter > Artistic > Dry Brush, and move all three sliders all the way to the right. Apply that filter a total of three times in a row, and then choose Filter > Stylize > Emboss, set the Angle to 135°, the Height to 2 pixels, and the Amount to 100% (**Figure 19.64**).

Not all of the raw material filters are capable of working on an empty layer. If you get an error message while attempting to apply one of these filters, then fill the active layer with white and try again.

Figure 19.64 The simple texture.

Figure 19.65 The moon texture.

Moon Texture

We'll start this one the same as the last by applying the Clouds filter. Then choose Filter > Artistic Paint Daubs, set the Brush Size to 15, set the Sharpness to 7, and use a Brush Type of Simple. To finish things off, choose Filter > Stylize > Emboss, set the Angle to 135°, the Height to 2 pixels, and the Amount to 500% (**Figure 19.65**).

Figure 19.66 The stucco wall texture.

Stucco Wall

Our base texture will be clouds again, so go ahead and apply it. Then follow that with three applications of the Difference Clouds filter. Then, to shake things up a bit, choose Filter > Stylize > Find Edges, and then immediately choose Edit > Fade > Find Edges and set the Mode to Linear Burn. Then, as usual, the last step is to choose Filter > Stylize > Emboss. This time set the Angle to 135°, the Height to 1 pixel, and the Amount to 500% (**Figure 19.66**).

Figure 19.67 The painterly wall texture.

Painterly Wall

I'm sure you'll get sick of this, but, we're going to start this one with the Clouds filter—again. Follow that with three passes of the Artistic > Dry Brush filter using a Brush Size of 3, Brush Detail of 9, and Texture of 2. Next, choose Filter > Stylize > Find Edges, then choose Image > Adjustments > Auto Levels. Finally, choose Filter > Other > High Pass, use a Radius of 3.3, and then apply the Emboss filter with whatever settings you'd like (you've used that one enough already) (**Figure 19.67**).

Figure 19.68 The sponged stuff texture.

Sponged Stuff

Okay, I think we've used the Clouds filter enough for a base, so let's try something else now. Start by choosing Filter > Artistic > Sponge, and use settings of 2, 12, and 5. To get a little more contrast, choose Image > Adjustments > Auto Levels. Next, choose Filter > Stylize > Solorize, and then finish it off with the usual—Emboss (**Figure 19.68**).

Artificial Map

This time we're going to make a map of some fake countries. Start by applying the Clouds filter, and then get good contrast with Auto Levels. To get your countries, choose Filter > Sketch > Plaster and use settings of 38, 7, and Top Left (**Figure 19.69**).

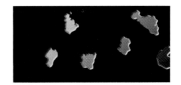

Figure 19.69 The artificial map texture.

Patchy Paint

So far, we've used Clouds and Sponge, so now let's see what we get with the Noise > Add Noise filter. Apply that with an Amount of 330, using uniform distribution, and turn on the Monochrome check box. Next, choose Filter > Noise > Median, use a setting of 21, and then apply Auto Levels. Choose Filter > Brush Strokes > Spatter, set the Spray Radius to 25 and the Smoothness to 15, and then emboss it using settings of 45°, 1 pixel, and 146%. Finally, choose Edit > Fade Emboss and set the Mode to Hardlight. If you'd like to add some color, then either go back to the Enhancement chapter (Chapter 17) and read away, or paint with your brush set to Overlay mode (**Figure 19.70**).

Figure 19.70 The patchy paint texture.

All the textures we've created so far have been grayscale. That makes them ideal as raw material to texturize photographs. All you have to do is place the texture above a photograph, and then try any one of the contrast blending modes that we talked about in the Enhancement chapter.

Brown Reeds

Okay, it's time to get fancy. No more grayscale textures. This one will be photo-realistic. We'll start by choosing Filter > Sketch > Halftone Pattern and use a Size of 7, a Contrast of 23, and a Dot Pattern Type. Now choose Filter > Distort > Ripple, and use an Amount of 110% and a Size of Medium. Next, Choose Filter > Sketch > Chrome, set the Detail to 2 and the Smoothness to 7, and then Choose Edit > Fade and set the Mode to Difference. Now it's time to choose Filter > Blur > Motion Blur, set the angle to 0, and use a Distance of 14. Now to add some color (it's about time we got to color, huh?), choose Layer > New Adjustment Layer > Gradient Map, and set the Mode to Overlay. When the Gradient Map dialog box appears, click the

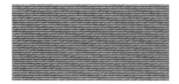

Figure 19.71 The brown reeds texture.

gradient preview and then double-click on the leftmost color and choose a nice orange, then change the right color to yellow and click OK. Finally, choose Layer > Merge Down, and we're done (**Figure 19.71**)!

Repeating Patterns

Try this out: Choose Edit > Fill and set the Use pop-up menu to Pattern. Then take a look at the preset custom patterns. These patterns are actually tiny images repeated over and over (like tiles on a bathroom wall). If you stood back, they would appear to be one large image instead of what they were—a bunch of small repeating images with their edges lined up with each other. These default patterns are alright for adding interest to simple shapes; but this is Photoshop, which means we're not stuck using plain old vanilla defaults. We can create our own exquisitely unique patterns! They can be used in many situations, especially when it comes to producing graphics for the web. So, let's dive in and see what we can come up with.

There are two general methods I use to create a seamless pattern. The first one involves using filters that produce tileable results. Then, after using a combination of filters, we'll find the smallest tileable area and turn that into a pattern. The second method is to take an image that is not tileable and to retouch the areas that would appear as seams.

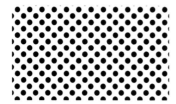

Figure 19.72 Result of applying the Color Halftone filter.

Using Tileable Filters

Let's start with a pattern that is tileable from the beginning. We can use that small image to fill a larger area without it looking like the simple repeating image that it really is. First, create a new document in Grayscale mode. Next, choose a light shade of gray and then type Option-Delete (Mac) or Alt-Backspace (Windows) to fill the image with that color. Now, choose Filter > Pixelate > Color Halftone, set the Max Radius to 14, and set all the angles to 45. That should produce a bunch of circles on a grid (**Figure 19.72**). Next, let's add some dimension by choosing Filter > Stylize > Emboss; set the Angle to 135, the Height to 1, and the Amount to 75 (**Figure 19.73**).

Figure 19.73 Result of applying the Emboss filter.

Now that we've got something that is seamless, let's find the smallest area that can be tiled. That way, the pattern won't take up memory and our file size can stay small when we apply the pattern using layer styles and pattern layers. Use the Marquee tool to select a relatively small but wide selection near the top of the image. Next, choose View > Show Rulers, click on the top ruler, and drag down a guide until it snaps to the top of the selection you just made (**Figure 19.74**).

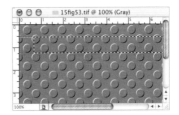

Figure 19.74 Drag a guide down until it snaps to the edge of your selection.

Now you want to find out whether the information you just selected is used elsewhere in the image, and if so, where. We use an odd little technique to do that. Choose Layer > New > Layer Via Copy to place a copy of the currently selected area onto a brand-spankin'-new layer. Next, change the Blending mode of that layer (at the top of the Layers palette) to Difference. That mode will compare the layer that is active to the one below it, and will show you where the two layers are different. Because both layers are identical in that area, it should appear black. Now change to the Move tool and use the down-arrow key to nudge the layer one pixel at a time. As you move it down, the black area should change to indicate that the information no longer lines up with what's underneath it. You'll want to continue to nudge it down until that area becomes black again. Once that happens, drag out another guide and let it snap to the top edge of that layer (**Figure 19.75**).

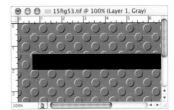

Figure 19.75 When the layer turns black again, add a guide that lines up with the top of that layer.

Now you'll want to trash the layer you've been working with and repeat the exact same process using a vertical selection. So, make a tall, skinny selection, pull out a guide, and snap it to the left side of the marching ants. Then choose Layer > New > Layer Via Copy, set the Blending mode to Difference, and then nudge that layer horizontally (using the Move tool) until it becomes black again. Finally, pull out another guide, snap it to the left edge of that layer, and then trash the layer (**Figure 19.76**).

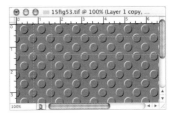

Figure 19.76 Repeat the process using a vertical selection.

You should end up with a total of four guides that define the smallest tileable area of the image. To turn that area into a pattern, use the Marquee tool to select the area defined by the guides, and then choose Edit > Define Pattern. Finally, test your pattern by creating a new

I've found that the Healing Brush and Patch tools work great for patching the seams on organic textures (like the ones we created earlier in this chapter).

Figure 19.77 Cropping the image down to the area you'd like to use.

Figure 19.78 The Offset filter will expose the seams in your pattern as a pattern.

document, choosing Edit > Fill, and selecting Pattern from the Use pop-up menu. You should find your pattern listed at the bottom of the pattern pop-up list.

The process of finding the smallest tileable area can be difficult if you are working on a very low-contrast pattern. If that's the case, choose Layer > Duplicate Layer and then choose Image > Adjust > Auto Levels to exaggerate the contrast in that new layer. Then go through the exact steps mentioned earlier for finding the smallest tileable area. Once you have all four guides placed, just trash the high-contrast layer so you'll end up with your original image and the four guides you need to create a pattern.

Creating Your Own Pattern

Now that you've seen how to create a tileable pattern from scratch, let's see how we can produce one from an existing image (like a photograph or one of the textures we created earlier). We are striving for "seamless," so we will first expose the seams of our image, and then retouch them to make them disappear. For this example, let's create a brushed-metal effect and transform it into a seamless tile. To create the metal look, create a new grayscale image and then choose Filter > Noise > Add Noise (I used Amount = 400%, Distribution = Uniform, and I turned on Monochromatic). Now choose Filter > Blur > Motion Blur (I used Angle = 0 and Distance = 60). You can see the resulting brushed-metal look in **Figure 19.77**. Once you have the texture made (or you have the photo you'd like to work with) choose Select > All, and then Edit > Copy (though you won't be pasting for a while). Use the Crop tool to select the area you'd like to use for your pattern and then press Return or Enter to crop it. Now let's expose the seams that would show up if we used that image as a pattern. To accomplish that, choose Filter > Other > Offset and set the Vertical and Horizontal Offset settings to approximately half the width of your image (**Figure 19.78**).

Now that we can see the seams that prevent our image from being a seamless tile, all we have to do is retouch them to make them disappear. If you are working with a photographic image, you'll most likely want to use the Clone Stamp tool, but since we copied our full-size original to start with, we can take advantage of a different approach. Choose Edit > Paste to create a new layer, and fill it with part of the original image. Next, choose Layer > Add Layer Mask > Hide All. Now you should notice two thumbnail images for the currently active layer (**Figure 19.79**). Next, choose the Paintbrush tool, choose white to paint with, and choose a very large, soft-edged brush (one that's about 1/3 of the width of your image). Use that large brush to cover up the seam by painting over it vertically. That should make the pasted image show up over the seam and blend into the rest of the image, resulting in a seamless pattern. To define your pattern, choose Layer > Merge Down, then Select > All, and then Edit > Define Pattern. Now you should be able to create a new, large document and choose Edit > Fill to apply your pattern (**Figure 19.80**).

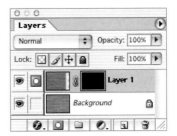

Figure 19.79 After adding a layer mask, the layer should contain two thumbnail images.

Figure 19.80 The pattern applied to a large area.

Using the Pattern Maker Filter

The Pattern Maker filter is designed for creating seamless patterns. It's no substitute for using the manual tiling techniques we just discussed, but it can do a decent job of generating textures that tile.

The general concept is to find an image in which you like the colors and overall texture, and then choose Filter > Pattern Maker. Once the dialog box appears (**Figure 19.81**), you make a selection of the area you'd like to use to create a pattern, and then click the Generate button multiple times until you like the result you are presented with (**Figure 19.82**). If you find that the seams in the repeating pattern are too obvious, try increasing the Smoothness setting, which will lower the contrast of the next pattern you generate. If Pattern Maker chops up a photo's objects beyond recognition, then bring the Sample Detail setting up a bit and regenerate the pattern. I've found that the Pattern Maker works best on images with a lot of sharp-edged detail, because it seems to literally rip your image to shreds and then reassemble the pieces in a random way. Once you've achieved the look you desire, click the Disk icon that appears in the lower-right area to save the pattern. Saved patterns can be used with the layer styles that we talked about earlier in this chapter.

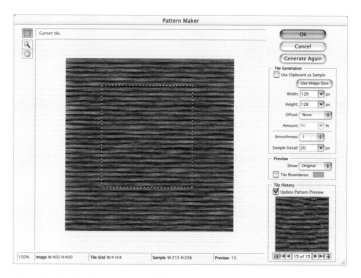

Figure 19.81 The Pattern Maker dialog box before generating a pattern.

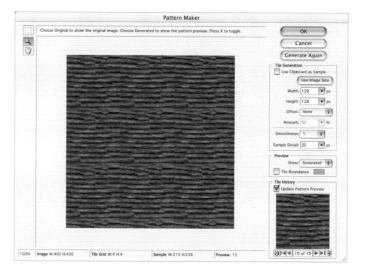

Figure 19.82 A seamless pattern created from the image shown in Figure 19.81.

Closing Thoughts

With almost 100 filters and the awesome new type on a shape feature, plus the idea that you can throw them all together in any combination, it's probably safe to say that you will be well into retirement before you could exhaust the supply of unique text and background effects that can be produced in Photoshop. That makes your job both challenging and exhilarating. Never stop testing the limits; never stop playing. And if you run out of ideas, do what I do—read through your favorite magazines for interesting-looking text and backgrounds, rip out the pages with the best ones, and then try to reproduce them on your own.

Ben's Techno-Babble Decoder Ring

Baseline: The invisible rule that a line of text sits on. Letters that drop below the baseline (such as lowercase j, g, q, and y) are known as descenders.

Leading: The line spacing of a paragraph of text measured from one baseline to the next. It's named after the strips of lead that were used to increase line spacing in hot metal typography. In order to make sure the lines of text don't overlap, you'll usually want to use a leading setting larger than the point size of the text.

Kerning: The art (lost art, really) of removing space between letters to create consistent letter spacing. In Photoshop, the kerning increases (positive setting) or decreases (negative setting) the space between two letters.

Point: A unit of measurement, used in the publishing industry, that is 1/72 of an inch (there are 12 points to a pica, and 6 picas per inch). Most programs measure text in point sizes because it is much more friendly than using fractions of an inch. But there is very little consistency in the size of text. For example, 12-point Times is taller than 12-point Helvetica, so you can think of the point size as a general (not exact) measure of the size of your text.

Tracking: The act of increasing or reducing the space between all the letters in a range of text. Often used with uppercase text to increase readability.

Courtesy of Alicia Buelow, www.aliciabuelow.com

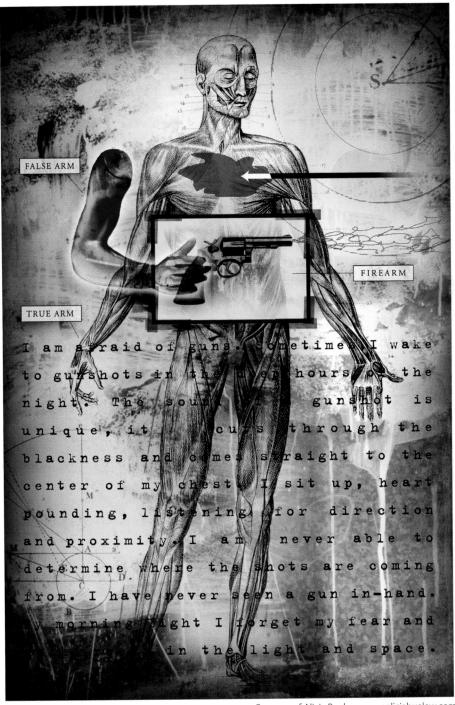

Courtesy of Alicia Buelow, www.aliciabuelow.com

Courtesy of Alicia Buelow, www.aliciabuelow.com

Index

Q-R

perfection

stockbyte®
Premium Royalty Free
www.stockbyte.com
Free research 1 800 660 9262

Licensing Agreement

By opening this package, you are agreeing to be bound by the following:

This software product is copyrighted, and all rights are reserved by the publisher and author(s). You are licensed to use this software on a single computer. You may copy and/or modify this software as needed to facilitate your use of it on a single computer. Making copies of this software for any other purpose is a violation of the United States copyright laws.

Please remember that existing artwork or images that you may want to include in your project may be protected under copyright law. The unauthorized incorporation of such material into your new work could be a violation of the rights of the copyright owner. Please be sure to obtain any permission required from the copyright owner.

This software is sold as is without warranty of any kind, either expressed or implied, including but not limited to the implied warranties of merchantability and fitness for a particular purpose. Neither the publisher nor its dealers or distributors assumes any liability for any alleged or actual damages arising from the use of this program. (Some states do not allow for the exclusion of implied warranties, so the exclusion may not apply to you.)

WARNING! The Stockbyte low resolution (comping) images contained on the accompanying CD may not be used for any item which will be printed or published in any medium. Please carefully read the full text of your License Agreement, contained in the CD folder titled "Image Use Restrictions." By using the images you are consenting to the full terms of the license.